A World Bank Group Flagship Report

JANUARY 2020

Global Economic Prospects

Slow Growth, Policy Challenges

WORLD BANK GROUP

ISSN: 1014-8906
ISBN (paper): 978-1-4648-1468-6
ISBN (electronic): 978-1-4648-1469-3
DOI: 10.1596/ 978-1-4648-1468-6

Cover design: Bill Pragluski (Critical Stages).

The cutoff date for the data used in this report was December 20, 2019.

Summary of Contents

Table of Contents

Foreword

Following a year during which weak trade and investment dragged the world economy to its feeblest performance since the global financial crisis, economic growth is poised for a modest rebound this year. However, for even that modest uptick to occur, many things have to go right.

Global growth is set to rise by 2.5 percent this year, a small rise from an estimated 2.4 percent in 2019, as trade and investment gradually recover.

Emerging market and developing economies are anticipated to see growth accelerate to 4.1 percent from 3.5 percent last year. However, that acceleration will not be broad-based: the pickup is anticipated to come largely from a handful of large emerging economies stabilizing after deep recessions or sharp slowdowns.

Even this tepid global rally could be disrupted by any number of threats. Trade tensions could re-escalate. A sharper-than-expected growth slow-down in major economies would reverberate widely. A resurgence of financial stress in large emerging markets, an escalation of geopolitical tensions, or a series of extreme weather events could all have adverse effects on economic activity.

This edition of *Global Economic Prospects* analyzes several topical themes underlying the fragile outlook.

One is the largest, fastest, and most broad-based wave of debt accumulation in advanced economies as well as in emerging and developing economies in the last 50 years. Public borrowing can be beneficial and spur economic development, if used to finance growth-enhancing investments. However, although currently low interest rates mitigate risks, the three previous waves of debt accumulation in debt have ended badly.

A second is the widespread slowdown in productivity growth over the last ten years. Growth in productivity—output per worker—is essential to raising living standards. However, weaker investment and efficiency gains, dwindling gains

from the reallocation of resources to more productive sectors, and slowing improvements in the key drivers of productivity have sapped momentum in this key driver of lasting growth.

Additional key themes explored in this edition include price controls—which, despite good intentions, can dampen investment and growth, worsen poverty outcomes, and lead to heavier fiscal burdens—and the drivers of the long recent period of low inflation among low-income countries and necessary policies to maintain low and stable inflation.

These messages have serious implications for the goals of eradicating poverty and sharing prosperity. Even if the recovery in emerging and developing economy growth were to take place as expected, per capita growth would advance at a pace too slow to meet development goals.

Yet policymakers have it in their capacity to ensure the recovery not only stays on track, but even surprises to the upside. Recent policy actions—particularly those that have mitigated trade tensions—could augur a sustained reduction in policy uncertainty. Countries could pursue decisive reforms to bolster governance and business climate, improve tax policy, promote trade integration, and rekindle productivity growth, all while protecting vulnerable groups. Building resilient monetary and fiscal frameworks, instituting robust supervisory and regulatory regimes, and following transparent debt management practices could reduce the risk of shocks, or soften their impact, and strengthen resilience against them.

As a philosopher once said, one swallow does not a summer make. There are signs that global growth skirted a rough patch and is recovering; it is up to policy makers to make sure it thrives.

Ceyla Pazarbasioglu
Vice President
Equitable Growth, Finance, and Institutions
World Bank Group

Acknowledgments

This World Bank Group Flagship Report is a product of the Prospects Group in the Equitable Growth, Finance and Institutions (EFI) Vice Presidency. The project was managed by M. Ayhan Kose and Franziska Ohnsorge, under the general guidance of Ceyla Pazarbasioglu.

Global and regional surveillance work was coordinated by Carlos Arteta. The primary authors of this report were Alistair Dieppe, Justin-Damien Guénette, Jongrim Ha, Gene Kindberg-Hanlon, Patrick Kirby, Peter Nagle, Rudi Steinbach, Naotaka Sugawara, Temel Taskin, Ekaterine Vashakmadze, Dana Vorisek, Collette M. Wheeler, and Lei Sandy Ye.

Other contributors included John Baffes, Csilla Lakatos, Alain Kabundi, Sergiy Kasyanenko, Atsushi Kawamoto, Sinem Kilic Celik, Wee Chian Koh, Hideaki Matsuoka, Yoki Okawa, Cedric Okou, Franz Ulrich Ruch, and Shu Yu.

Research assistance was provided by Vanessa Arellano Banoni, Yushu Chen, Zhuo Chen, Khamal Antonio Clayton, Aygul Evdokimova, Awais Khuhro, Yi Li, Shihui Liu, Maria Hazel Macadangdang, Julia R. R. Norfleet, Vasiliki Papagianni, Jankeesh Sandhu, Shijie Shi, Xinyue Wang, Jinxin Wu, Heqing Zhao, and Juncheng Zhou. Modeling and data work were provided by Rajesh Kumar Danda, Julia R. R. Norfleet, and Shijie Shi.

The online publication was produced by Paul Blake, Graeme Littler, Venkat Ganeshan Gopalakrishnan, and Torie Smith. Mark Felsenthal and Alejandra Viveros managed media relations and dissemination. Graeme Littler provided editorial support, with contributions from Adriana Maximiliano.

Regional projections and write-ups were produced in coordination with country teams, country directors, and the offices of the regional chief economists.

The print publication was produced by Maria Hazel Macadangdang, Adriana Maximiliano, and Quinn Sutton, in collaboration with Luiz H. Almeida, Andrew Charles Berghauser, Aziz Gökdemir, Michael Harrup, and Jewel McFadden.

Many reviewers provided extensive advice and comments. The analysis also benefited from comments and suggestions by staff members from World Bank Group country teams and other World Bank Group Vice Presidencies as well as Executive Directors in their discussion of the report on December 17, 2019. However, both forecasts and analysis are those of the World Bank Group staff and should not be attributed to Executive Directors or their national authorities.

Executive Summary

Global growth is projected to reach 2.5 percent in 2020, slightly faster than the post-crisis low registered last year. While growth could be stronger if reduced trade tensions lead to a sustained reduction in uncertainty, the balance of risks to the outlook is to the downside. Growth in emerging market and developing economies (EMDEs) is also expected to remain subdued, continuing a decade of disappointing outcomes. A steep and widespread productivity growth slowdown has been underway in EMDEs since the global financial crisis, despite the largest, fastest, and most broad-based accumulation of debt since the 1970s. In addition, many EMDEs, including low-income countries, face the challenge of phasing out price controls that impose heavy fiscal burdens and dampen investment. These circumstances add urgency to the need to implement measures to rebuild macroeconomic policy space and to undertake reforms to rekindle productivity growth. These efforts need to be supplemented by policies to promote inclusive long-term growth and accelerate poverty alleviation.

Global Outlook: Fragile, Handle with Care. Global growth is expected to recover to 2.5 percent in 2020—up slightly from the post-crisis low of 2.4 percent registered last year amid weakening trade and investment—and edge up further over the forecast horizon. This projected recovery could be stronger if recent policy actions—particularly those that have mitigated trade tensions—lead to a sustained reduction in policy uncertainty. Nevertheless, downside risks predominate, including the possibility of a re-escalation of global trade tensions, sharp downturns in major economies, and financial disruptions in emerging market and developing economies (EMDEs). The materialization of these risks would test the ability of policymakers to respond effectively to negative events. Associated policy challenges are compounded by high debt levels and subdued productivity growth. Many EMDEs need to rebuild macroeconomic policy space to enhance resilience to possible adverse developments. They also need to pursue decisive reforms to bolster governance and business climates, improve tax policy, promote trade integration, and rekindle productivity growth, while protecting vulnerable groups. These policy actions would help foster inclusive and sustainable long-term growth and poverty alleviation.

Regional Prospects. Growth in almost all EMDE regions has been weaker than expected, reflecting downgrades to almost half of EMDEs. Activity in most regions is expected to pick up in 2020-21,

but the recovery will largely depend on a rebound in a small number of large EMDEs, some of which are emerging from deep recessions or sharp slowdowns.

This edition of *Global Economic Prospects* also includes chapters on the productivity growth slowdown in EMDEs since the global financial crisis and on the rapid debt buildup in these economies over the same period, and special focus pieces on the implications of price controls in EMDEs and on the challenges of maintaining low inflation in low-income economies (LICs).

Fading Promise: How to Rekindle Productivity Growth. A broad-based slowdown in labor productivity growth has been underway since the global financial crisis. In EMDEs, the slowdown has reflected weakness in investment and moderating efficiency gains as well as dwindling resource reallocation between sectors. The pace of improvements in key drivers of labor productivity—including education, urbanization, and institutions—has slowed or stagnated since the global financial crisis and is expected to remain subdued. To rekindle productivity growth, a comprehensive approach is necessary: facilitating investment in physical, intangible, and human capital; encouraging reallocation of resources towards more productive sectors; fostering firm capabilities to reinvigorate technology adoption and innovation; and promoting a growth-friendly macroeconomic and institutional environment. Specific policy priorities will depend on individual country circumstances.

The Fourth Wave: Rapid Debt Buildup. The global economy has experienced four waves of debt accumulation over the past fifty years. The first three ended with financial crises in many EMDEs. During the current wave, which started in 2010, the increase in debt in these economies has already been larger, faster, and more broad-based than in any of the previous three waves. Current low interest rates—which markets expect to be sustained into the medium term—appear to mitigate some of the risks associated with high debt. However, EMDEs are also confronted by weak growth prospects, mounting vulnerabilities, and elevated global risks. A menu of policy options is available to reduce the likelihood of the current debt wave ending in crises and, if crises were to take place, to alleviate their impact.

Price Controls: Good Intentions, Bad Outcomes. The use of price controls is widespread across EMDEs, including for food and key imported and exported commodities. While sometimes used as a tool for social policy, price controls can dampen investment and growth, worsen poverty outcomes, cause countries to incur heavy fiscal burdens, and complicate the effective conduct of monetary policy. Replacing price controls with expanded and better-targeted social safety nets, coupled with reforms to encourage competition and a sound regulatory environment, can be both pro-poor and pro-growth. Such reforms need to be carefully communicated and sequenced to ensure political and social acceptance. Where they exist, price control regimes should be transparent and supported by well-capitalized stabilization funds or national hedging strategies to ensure fiscal sustainability.

Low for How Much Longer? Inflation in Low-Income Countries. Inflation in LICs has declined sharply to a median of 3 percent in mid-2019 from a peak of 25 percent in 1994. The drop has been supported by the move to more flexible exchange rate regimes, greater central bank independence, and a generally more benign external environment since the 1990s. However, low LIC inflation cannot be taken for granted amid mounting fiscal pressures and the risk of exchange rate shocks. To maintain low and stable inflation, monetary and fiscal policy frameworks need to be strengthened and supported by efforts to replace price controls with more efficient policies.

Abbreviations

ACP	African, Caribbean and Pacific Group of States
AE	advanced economy
CDS	credit default swap
CPTPP	Comprehensive and Progressive Agreement for Trans-Pacific Partnership
DR-CAFTA	Central America-Dominican Republic Free Trade Agreement
EAP	East Asia and Pacific
ECA	Europe and Central Asia
ECB	European Central Bank
ECI	Economic Complexity Index
EMBI	Emerging Market Bond Index
EMDE	emerging market and developing economies
ERPTR	exchange rate pass-through ratio
EU	European Union
FAVAR	Bayesian factor-augmented vector autoregression
FCV	fragility, conflict, and violence
FDI	foreign direct investment
GCC	Gulf Cooperation Council
GDP	gross domestic product
GEP	*Global Economic Prospects*
GMM	generalized methods of moments
GNFS	goods and nonfactor services
GNI	gross national income
GST	goods and services tax
GVCs	global value chains
HIPC	Heavily Indebted Poor Countries
ICE	Intercontinental Exchange
ICRG	International Country Risk Guide
IMF	International Monetary Fund
IT	inflation targeting
LAC	Latin America and the Caribbean
LFPR	labor force participation rate
LIC	low-income country
LSAP	Large-Scale Asset Purchase
MDRI	Multilateral Debt Relief Initiative
MENA	Middle East and North Africa
MEP	Maturity Extension Program
MIC	middle-income country

NEER	nominal effective exchange rate
NPL	nonperforming loan
ONI	Oceanic Niño Index
OPEC	Organization of the Petroleum Exporting Countries
PMI	Purchasing Managers' Index
PPP	purchasing power parity
REER	real effective exchange rate
RHS	right-hand side (in figures)
RMB	renminbi
SAR	South Asia Region
SSA	Sub-Saharan Africa
SSE	Shanghai Stock Exchange
TFP	total factor productivity
TiVA	trade in value added
USMCA	United States-Mexico-Canada Agreement
VAT	value-added tax
WAEMU	West African Economic and Monetary Union
WGI	World Governance Indicators
WTO	World Trade Organization

CHAPTER 1

GLOBAL OUTLOOK

Fragile, Handle with Care

Global growth is expected to recover to 2.5 percent in 2020—up slightly from the post-crisis low of 2.4 percent registered last year amid weakening trade and investment—and edge up further over the forecast horizon. This projected recovery could be stronger if recent policy actions—particularly those that have mitigated trade tensions—lead to a sustained reduction in policy uncertainty. Nevertheless, downside risks predominate, including the possibility of a re-escalation of global trade tensions, sharp downturns in major economies, and financial disruptions in emerging market and developing economies (EMDEs). The materialization of these risks would test the ability of policymakers to respond effectively to negative events. Associated policy challenges are compounded by high debt levels and subdued productivity growth. Many EMDEs need to rebuild macroeconomic policy space to enhance resilience to possible adverse developments. They also need to pursue decisive reforms to bolster governance and business climates, improve tax policy, promote trade integration, and rekindle productivity growth, while protecting vulnerable groups. These policy actions would help foster inclusive and sustainable long-term growth and poverty alleviation.

Summary

Global growth decelerated markedly in 2019, with continued weakness in global trade and investment (Figures 1.1.A and 1.1.B). This weakness was widespread, affecting both advanced economies—particularly the Euro Area—and emerging market and developing economies (EMDEs). Various key indicators of economic activity declined in parallel, approaching their lowest levels since the global financial crisis (Figure 1.1.C). In particular, global trade in goods was in contraction for a significant part of 2019, and manufacturing activity slowed markedly over the course of the year; recent high-frequency readings suggest some tentative stabilization of manufacturing output at weak levels. To a lesser extent, services activity also moderated. A broad range of economies have experienced feeble growth, with close to 90 percent of advanced economies and 60 percent of EMDEs going through varying degrees of deceleration last year.

Bilateral negotiations between the United States and China since mid-October resulted in a Phase One agreement—including a planned partial rollback of tariffs—that has de-escalated trade tensions. This comes after a prolonged period of rising trade disputes between the two countries,

which has heightened policy uncertainty and weighed on international trade, confidence, and investment. As a result of the increase of tariffs between the two countries over the past couple of years, a substantially higher share of world trade has become subject to protectionist measures (Figure 1.1.D).

Financial market sentiment improved appreciably toward the end of last year along with the alleviation of trade tensions. That said, it had been fragile for most of 2019. Concerns about growth prospects triggered widespread monetary policy easing by major central banks last year, as well as flight to safety flows into advanced-economy bond markets. In a context of subdued inflation, this pushed global yields down—in some advanced economies, further into negative territory—for most of 2019. Heightened risk aversion contributed to subdued EMDE capital inflows in the second half of last year, as a number of EMDEs faced renewed currency and equity price pressures. The subdued outlook led to declines in most commodity prices, which are expected to remain near current levels over the forecast period.

Against this international context, global growth weakened to an estimated 2.4 percent last year—the lowest rate of expansion since the global financial crisis. With some recent data pointing to an incipient stabilization of economic conditions, global growth is projected to edge up to 2.5 percent in 2020, 0.2 percentage point below previous forecasts, as investment and trade gradually recover. In particular, global trade growth—which is estimated to have slowed sharply from 4 percent in 2018 to 1.4 percent in

_____

Note: This chapter was prepared by Carlos Arteta and Patrick Kirby, with contributions from Collette M. Wheeler, Justin-Damien Guénette, Csilla Lakatos, Rudi Steinbach, and Ekaterine Vashakmadze. Additional inputs were provided by John Baffes, Sergiy Kasyanenko, Peter Nagle, and Franz Ulrich Ruch. Research assistance was provided by Yushu Chen, Shihui Liu, Julia Norfleet, Vasiliki Papagianni, Shijie Shi, and Jinxin Wu.

TABLE 1.1 Real GDP[1]

(Percent change from previous year)

Percentage point differences
from June 2019 projections

	2017	2018	2019e	2020f	2021f	2022f	2019e	2020f	2021f
World	**3.2**	**3.0**	**2.4**	**2.5**	**2.6**	**2.7**	**-0.2**	**-0.2**	**-0.2**
Advanced economies	**2.4**	**2.2**	**1.6**	**1.4**	**1.5**	**1.5**	**-0.1**	**-0.1**	**0.0**
United States	2.4	2.9	2.3	1.8	1.7	1.7	-0.2	0.1	0.1
Euro Area	2.5	1.9	1.1	1.0	1.3	1.3	-0.1	-0.4	0.0
Japan	1.9	0.8	1.1	0.7	0.6	0.4	0.3	0.0	0.0
Emerging market and developing economies	**4.5**	**4.3**	**3.5**	**4.1**	**4.3**	**4.4**	**-0.5**	**-0.5**	**-0.3**
Commodity-exporting EMDEs	2.2	2.0	1.5	2.6	2.9	3.0	-0.6	-0.5	-0.1
Other EMDEs	6.2	5.8	4.8	5.1	5.2	5.2	-0.4	-0.4	-0.3
Other EMDEs excluding China	5.4	5.0	3.3	4.0	4.4	4.5	-0.9	-0.8	-0.6
East Asia and Pacific	6.5	6.3	5.8	5.7	5.6	5.6	-0.1	-0.2	-0.2
China	6.8	6.6	6.1	5.9	5.8	5.7	-0.1	-0.2	-0.2
Indonesia	5.1	5.2	5.0	5.1	5.2	5.2	-0.2	-0.2	-0.1
Thailand	4.0	4.1	2.5	2.7	2.8	2.9	-1.0	-0.9	-0.9
Europe and Central Asia	4.1	3.2	2.0	2.6	2.9	2.9	0.4	-0.1	0.0
Russia	1.6	2.3	1.2	1.6	1.8	1.8	0.0	-0.2	0.0
Turkey	7.5	2.8	0.0	3.0	4.0	4.0	1.0	0.0	0.0
Poland	4.9	5.1	4.3	3.6	3.3	3.1	0.3	0.0	0.0
Latin America and the Caribbean	1.9	1.7	0.8	1.8	2.4	2.6	-0.9	-0.8	-0.3
Brazil	1.3	1.3	1.1	2.0	2.5	2.4	-0.4	-0.5	0.2
Mexico	2.1	2.1	0.0	1.2	1.8	2.3	-1.7	-0.8	-0.6
Argentina	2.7	-2.5	-3.1	-1.3	1.4	2.3	-1.9	-3.5	-1.8
Middle East and North Africa	1.1	0.8	0.1	2.4	2.7	2.8	-1.2	-0.8	0.0
Saudi Arabia	-0.7	2.4	0.4	1.9	2.2	2.4	-1.3	-1.2	-0.1
Iran	3.8	-4.9	-8.7	0.0	1.0	1.0	-4.2	-0.9	0.0
Egypt[2]	4.2	5.3	5.6	5.8	6.0	6.0	0.1	0.0	0.0
South Asia	6.7	7.1	4.9	5.5	5.9	6.0	-2.0	-1.5	-1.2
India[3]	7.2	6.8	5.0	5.8	6.1	6.1	-2.5	-1.7	-1.4
Pakistan[2]	5.2	5.5	3.3	2.4	3.0	3.9	-0.1	-0.3	-1.0
Bangladesh[2]	7.3	7.9	8.1	7.2	7.3	7.3	0.8	-0.2	0.0
Sub-Saharan Africa	2.7	2.6	2.4	2.9	3.1	3.3	-0.5	-0.4	-0.4
Nigeria	0.8	1.9	2.0	2.1	2.1	2.1	-0.1	-0.1	-0.3
South Africa	1.4	0.8	0.4	0.9	1.3	1.5	-0.7	-0.6	-0.4
Angola	-0.1	-1.2	-0.7	1.5	2.4	3.0	-1.7	-1.4	-0.4
Memorandum items:									
Real GDP[1]									
High-income countries	2.4	2.2	1.7	1.5	1.5	1.6	-0.1	-0.1	-0.1
Developing countries	4.8	4.4	3.7	4.3	4.5	4.5	-0.4	-0.4	-0.3
Low-income countries	5.5	5.8	5.4	5.4	5.5	5.8	-0.3	-0.6	-0.6
BRICS	5.3	5.4	4.6	4.9	4.9	5.0	-0.5	-0.4	-0.4
World (2010 PPP weights)	3.9	3.7	2.9	3.2	3.3	3.4	-0.4	-0.3	-0.3
World trade volume[4]	**5.9**	**4.0**	**1.4**	**1.9**	**2.5**	**2.8**	**-1.2**	**-1.3**	**-0.7**
Commodity prices[5]									
Oil price	23.3	29.4	-10.3	-5.4	1.9	1.9	-6.9	-3.9	1.2
Non-energy commodity price index	5.5	1.7	-4.7	0.1	1.7	1.7	-2.6	0.2	0.3

Source: World Bank.

Note: PPP = purchasing power parity; e = estimate; f = forecast. World Bank forecasts are frequently updated based on new information. Consequently, projections presented here may differ from those contained in other World Bank documents, even if basic assessments of countries' prospects do not differ at any given moment in time. Country classifications and lists of emerging market and developing economies (EMDEs) are presented in Table 1.2. BRICS include: Brazil, Russia, India, China, and South Africa. The World Bank has ceased producing a growth forecast for Venezuela and has removed Venezuela from all growth aggregates in which it was previously included.

1. Headline aggregate growth rates calculated using GDP weights at 2010 prices and market exchange rates. World growth rates based on purchasing power parity (PPP) weights attribute a greater portion of global GDP to EMDEs relative to market exchange rates due to the PPP methodology, which uses an exchange rate that is calculated from the difference in the price levels of a basket of goods and services between economies.

2. GDP growth values are on a fiscal year basis. Aggregates that include these countries are calculated using data compiled on a calendar year basis. Pakistan's growth rates are based on GDP at factor cost. The column labeled 2019 refers to FY2018/19.

3. The column labeled 2018 refers to FY2018/19.

4. World trade volume of goods and non-factor services.

5. Oil is the simple average of Brent, Dubai, and West Texas Intermediate. The non-energy index is comprised of the weighted average of 39 commodities (7 metals, 5 fertilizers, 27 agricultural commodities). For additional details, please see http://www.worldbank.org/en/research/commodity-markets.

To download the data in this table, please visit www.worldbank.org/gep.

2019, by far the weakest pace since the global financial crisis—is projected to firm throughout 2020 and reach 1.9 percent, assuming trade tensions do not re-escalate. In the near term, monetary policy across the world is generally expected to remain accommodative; however, fiscal policy support is likely to fade (Figure 1.1.E).

Near-term projections for global growth mask different contours in advanced economies and EMDEs. Growth in advanced economies is projected to slow to 1.4 percent this year—below previous projections, in part reflecting lingering weakness in manufacturing—and improve slightly over the rest of the forecast horizon.

In contrast, after decelerating to an estimated weaker-than-expected 3.5 percent last year, growth in EMDEs is projected to increase to 4.1 percent in 2020—0.5 percentage point below previous forecasts, reflecting downgrades to half of EMDEs due in part to downward revisions to trade and investment growth. Nonetheless, the recovery in aggregate EMDE growth this year—which assumes continued monetary policy support in many economies, no major swings in commodity prices, and generally benign borrowing costs—is not envisioned to be broad-based: About a third of EMDEs are expected to decelerate. Instead, it is largely predicated on a rebound in a small number of large EMDEs, most of which are emerging from deep recessions or sharp slowdowns but remain fragile. Excluding this group of countries, there would be almost no acceleration in EMDE growth this year—and, with advanced economies slowing, global growth would actually decelerate.

Going forward, EMDE growth is projected to stabilize at an average of 4.4 percent in 2021-22, as trade and investment firm. In low-income countries, growth is expected to remain little changed at 5.4 percent in 2020 and edge up to an average of 5.7 percent later in the forecast horizon, boosted by increased investment in infrastructure and rebuilding efforts in some countries following extreme weather-related devastation.

Even if the recovery in EMDE growth proceeds as expected, per capita growth will remain well below long-term averages and far from sufficient to meet

FIGURE 1.1 Global growth prospects

Global growth decelerated last year to 2.4 percent—its slowest pace since the global financial crisis—amid weakening trade and investment. Key indicators deteriorated in parallel, in part reflecting heightened trade protectionism. While monetary accommodation has increased, fiscal support is expected to wane. Global growth is projected to recover to 2.5 percent in 2020 and edge further up thereafter as trade and investment firm and EMDE activity rebounds; however, per capita growth in EMDEs will remain insufficient to meet poverty alleviation goals.

A. Global growth

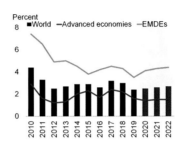

B. Global trade, investment, and consumption growth

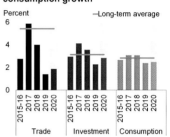

C. Global indicators of activity in 2019

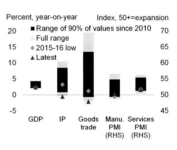

D. Global trade subject to new protectionist measures

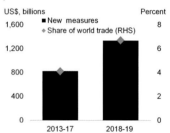

E. Stance of global fiscal and monetary policy

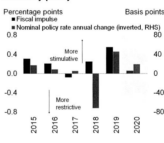

F. Per capita income growth

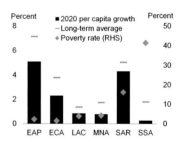

Source: Bank for International Settlements; Consensus Economics; CPB Netherlands Bureau for Economic Policy Analysis; Haver Analytics; International Monetary Fund; World Bank; World Trade Organization.
Note: AEs = advanced economies; EMDEs = emerging market and developing economies.
A.B.E. Shaded areas indicate forecasts. Data for 2019 are estimates.
B.C. Trade measured as the average of export and import volumes.
A. Aggregate growth rates calculated using GDP weights at 2010 prices and market exchange rates.
B. Data for 2015-16 are simple averages. Green lines indicate average over period 1990-2018.
C. Manu. = manufacturing. PMI = Purchasing Managers' Index. PMI readings above 50 indicate expansion in economic activity; readings below 50 indicate contraction. Last observation is 2019Q3 for GDP, October 2019 for industrial production and goods trade, and November 2019 for PMI.
D. Figure includes new import-restrictive measures, including tariff and non-tariff trade barriers. Annual data are mid-October to mid-October.
E. Aggregates calculated using nominal U.S. dollar GDP weights. Fiscal impulse is the negative change in general government cyclically adjusted primary balance. Policy rates are the December to December change. Sample includes 35 AEs and 77 EMDEs for fiscal impulse and 16 AEs and 21 EMDEs for policy rates. Policy rates for 2020 use the December 2019 *Consensus Forecasts* report for central bank policy rates. When these are unavailable, the change in short-term yields is used.
F. EAP = East Asia and Pacific, ECA = Europe and Central Asia, LAC = Latin America and the Caribbean, MNA = Middle East and North Africa, SAR = South Asia, SSA = Sub-Saharan Africa. Long-term average is calculated over the period 2000-19. Poverty rates represent latest data.

FIGURE 1.2 Global risks and policy challenges

Current projections represent a benign but fragile outlook given ongoing global headwinds. Downside risks predominate and increase the likelihood of much weaker-than-expected global growth. However, recent policy actions that have reduced trade tensions could lead to a sustained mitigation of policy uncertainty and bolster investment. In advanced economies, the room for monetary accommodation is limited. In EMDEs, fiscal space is constrained by weak tax capacity and high debt levels, which also hinders the ability to fund basic public services. Boosting EMDE productivity, which has been on a downward trend in recent years, is essential to foster long-term growth and poverty reduction.

A. Average share of EMDEs with annual growth accelerating by more than 0.1 percentage point, 1962-2019

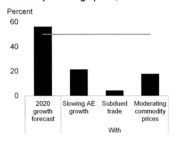

B. Probability of global growth being 1 percentage point below baseline

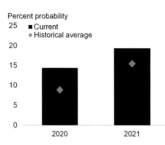

C. Impact of a 10-percent decrease in U.S. policy uncertainty on investment growth

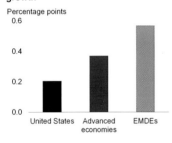

D. Monetary policy rate increases during current and previous expansions

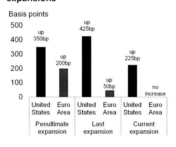

E. Share of EMDEs with limited tax revenues to fund basic public services

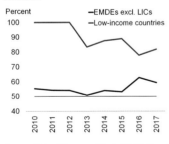

F. Productivity growth

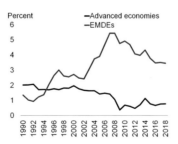

Source: Baker, Bloom, and Davis (2016); Bloomberg; Haver Analytics; International Monetary Fund; National Bureau of Economic Research; Penn World Table; The Conference Board; World Bank.
A.F. Aggregates calculated using GDP weights at 2010 prices and market exchange rates.
A. AE = advanced economies. "Subdued trade" refers to growth below 2.5 percent. "Moderating commodity prices" refers to a year-on-year contraction in the non-energy commodity index.
B. Probabilities computed from the forecast distributions of 12- and 24-month-ahead oil price futures; S&P 500 futures, and term spread forecasts. Risk factor weights are derived from the model described in Ohnsorge, Stocker, and Some (2016). Last observation is December 19, 2019.
C. Figure shows median impact. See Annex SF.1B of World Bank (2017a) for methodology.
D. U.S. expansions: 1991-2001, 2001-07, 2009-present. Euro Area expansions: 1999-2008, 2009-11, 2013-present. Calculations based on trough and peak of policy rates of each period. Last observation is November 2019 for the United States and 2019Q3 for the Euro Area.
E. Revenue threshold needed to provide basic public services is 15 percent of GDP, per Gaspar, Jaramillo, and Wingender (2016). Unbalanced sample includes 70 EMDEs, of which 11 are LICs.
F. Figure shows 5-year moving averages. Productivity is defined as output per worker. Sample includes 74 EMDEs and 29 advanced economies. Refer to Chapter 3 for details.

poverty alleviation goals. More specifically, income growth will be slowest in Sub-Saharan Africa—the region where most low-income countries are clustered and most of the world's poor live (Figure 1.1.F).

The near-term forecast for a pickup in EMDE growth represents a benign, but fragile, scenario given ongoing global headwinds such as slowing advanced-economy growth, subdued global trade, and moderating commodity prices (Figure 1.2.A). More generally, a deeper global downturn could result if global trade tensions re-emerge, policy uncertainty persists and becomes entrenched, or activity in major economies deteriorates significantly. Other risks include financial stress in large EMDEs, heightened geopolitical tensions, or a higher incidence of extreme weather events. Amid these downside risks, the probability that global growth in 2020 will be below baseline projections is above its historical average (Figure 1.2.B). That said, the projected recovery could be stronger than expected if recent policy actions—particularly those that have alleviated U.S.-China trade tensions—lead to a sustained reduction in policy uncertainty and bolster confidence, trade, and investment (Figure 1.2.C).

Against the backdrop of a fragile outlook, the policy challenges confronting the global economy are compounded by subdued productivity growth and high levels of debt (Chapters 3 and 4). In advanced economies, the weakness of the current expansion has made it difficult for central banks to create room for additional easing (Figure 1.2.D). Low global interest rates and the associated reduction in debt service burdens may provide some countries with additional flexibility for the implementation of structural reforms, such as investments in public infrastructure or the adoption of other growth-friendly policies. In addition, governments can create further fiscal space through better tax compliance and enforcement.

Most EMDEs are not well positioned to confront negative shocks, since policy buffers generally remain inadequate. While moderating inflation has allowed many EMDEs to cut policy rates to support growth, underlying price pressures are building in some cases, and policy space would be further eroded in the event of renewed financial market pressures. Many EMDEs, including LICs, face the additional challenge of phasing out price controls and their associated distortions amid moderate inflation (Special Focus 1 and Special Focus 2).

Although fiscal accommodation in some EMDEs may be warranted in response to adverse developments, record-high debt levels and fragile public finance positions limit the ability to implement countercyclical policy—indeed, a large share of EMDEs, particularly LICs, do not even have the capacity to adequately fund basic public services (Figure 1.2.E; Chapter 4). If faced with negative shocks, authorities would need to ensure that any fiscal support prioritizes growth-enhancing spending and domestic revenue mobilization to avoid further erosion of public debt sustainability. Tax policy reforms that broaden the revenue base are needed to fund investment, which could be complemented by measures that help reduce inequality.

EMDE policymakers also need to pursue decisive structural reforms, while protecting vulnerable groups, to promote inclusive long-term growth. Policy actions that improve EMDE governance frameworks and business climates, and facilitate integration in existing supply chains or spur the creation of new ones, could help counter the adverse effects of weak global growth and subdued international trade (World Bank 2019a). Measures to improve connectivity, lower trade costs, and ensure a stable and predictable legal environment could facilitate this integration. A strong and stable multilateral trading system remains an important foundation for robust growth in EMDEs.

The downward trend in EMDE productivity growth in recent years complicates these policy challenges (Figure 1.2.F; Chapter 3). Measures to boost EMDE productivity growth are essential to foster potential growth and ensure continued progress in improving living standards and alleviating poverty. To rekindle productivity growth, a comprehensive approach needs to be employed involving policies that facilitate investment in physical and human capital,

encourage the reallocation of resources toward more productive sectors, reinvigorate technology adoption and innovation among firms, and promote a growth-friendly macroeconomic and institutional environment. Within this four-pronged approach, specific policy priorities will depend on country circumstances. In addition, investments in green infrastructure can also help achieve development goals and improve resilience to climate change.

Major economies: Recent developments and outlook

In major economies, activity has slowed more markedly than previously expected. Very weak manufacturing activity has dampened growth in advanced economies, and policy uncertainty associated with trade tensions has also weighed on activity in the United States and China.

The growth forecast for advanced economies has again been revised down as a consequence of weaker-than-expected trade and manufacturing activity (Figure 1.3.A). Recent data show particular weakness in investment and exports, particularly in the Euro Area. This, along with below-target inflation in many economies, has prompted a broad shift toward monetary policy easing (Figure 1.3.B). Labor markets and the services sector generally remain more resilient, but the latter has shown signs of moderation (Figure 1.3.C). Aggregate activity is expected to edge down in 2020, with continued softness in investment and trade (Figure 1.3.D).

United States

Growth has decelerated amid slowing investment and exports (Figure 1.4.A). Notwithstanding the recent trade deal with China, rising tariffs have increased trade costs, while policy uncertainty has weighed on investment and confidence (Baker, Bloom, and Davis 2016; Fajgelbaum et al. 2019). As in many other advanced economies, the U.S. manufacturing sector has been very weak. Support from tax cuts and changes in government spending is expected to fade this year and become a drag on growth thereafter (Figure 1.4.B; IMF 2019a).

FIGURE 1.3 Advanced economies

The growth forecast for advanced economies has been steadily revised down, prompting a general shift toward monetary policy easing. Services activity has so far been more resilient than investment and trade, but it has also moderated. Activity is expected to edge down in 2020, with continued softness in investment and trade.

A. Evolution of the growth forecast for advanced economies

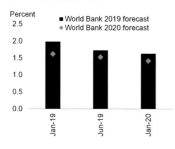

B. Monetary policy in advanced economies

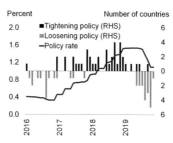

C. Services sector expectations

D. Advanced-economy trade, investment, and consumption growth

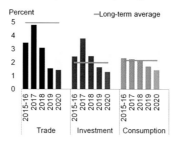

Source: Bank for International Settlements; Haver Analytics; World Bank.
A. Aggregate growth rates calculated using GDP weights at 2010 prices and market exchange rates. Blue bars and orange diamonds denote forecasts in the January 2019, June 2019, and January 2020 editions of the *Global Economic Prospects* report.
B. Aggregate nominal policy rates calculated using moving real GDP weights at 2010 prices and market exchange rates. Sample includes 15 advanced economies. Last observation is November 2019.
C. Figure shows 3-month moving averages of PMI service business expectations for the year ahead. PMI readings above 50 indicate expansion in economic activity; readings below 50 indicate contraction. Last observation is November 2019.
D. Trade is the average of import and export volumes. Data for 2015-16 are simple averages. Long-term average calculated over the period from 1990-2018. Shaded area indicates forecasts.

Despite these headwinds, the labor market remains robust and has benefited from a rising participation rate. Unemployment is near a five-decade low and wage growth has been solid, fueling resilient consumption. Concerns about the global outlook and persistent below-target inflation have resulted in the Federal Reserve cutting its policy rates by 75 basis points since mid-2019.

Growth is expected to slow over the course of the forecast period, from 2.3 percent in 2019 to 1.8 percent in 2020 and 1.7 percent in 2021-22. In the near term, the slowdown reflects the negative

impacts of lingering uncertainty and a waning contribution from tax cuts and government spending, which are only partly offset by accommodative monetary policy. The forecast is predicated on tariffs staying at planned levels, fiscal policy progressing as currently legislated, and the heightened degree of policy uncertainty gradually dissipating. Additional progress in U.S.-China trade negotiations that leads to a further reduction in trade policy uncertainty could result in higher-than-expected U.S. growth.

Euro Area

Economic activity in the Euro Area has deteriorated significantly. Several economies were on the verge of recession at some point last year, with particular weakness in the German industrial sector as it struggled with falling demand from Asia and disruptions to car production (Figures 1.5.A and 1.5.B). Uncertainty concerning Brexit also weighed on growth.

The ECB has provided monetary stimulus by pushing its policy rate deeper into negative territory, restarting quantitative easing, and providing inexpensive credit to banks. The overall fiscal position of the Euro Area is expected to be roughly balanced over the forecast period, providing little additional support to activity despite existing space in some economies.

Growth is expected to slow to 1 percent in 2020, 0.4 percentage point down from previous projections due to worse-than-expected incoming data, especially industrial production. Growth is forecast to recover modestly to an average of 1.3 percent in 2021-22, assuming that policy support gains traction, the Brexit process unfolds with minimal disruption, and there is no further escalation in trade restrictions.

Japan

Activity in Japan declined sharply following the impact of Typhoon Hagibis and the increase in the value-added tax (VAT) in October last year. The economy is also suffering from acute weakness in manufacturing and exports, particularly those to China, alongside declining consumer confidence. In response, the government is providing significant support. Despite recent weakness in activity, the unemployment rate remains near multidecade lows, labor force participation continues to climb, and per capita income growth remains healthy.

Growth is expected to slow from 1.1 percent in 2019 to 0.7 percent in 2020, as anticipatory purchases prior to the VAT increase in October 2019 are unwound. Growth in 2021-22 is expected to average about 0.5 percent.

China

Growth has decelerated more than previously expected amid cooling domestic demand and heightened trade tensions. Trade policy uncertainty and higher tariffs on trade with the United States weighed on investor sentiment for most of 2019. Industrial production growth has reached multiyear lows (Figure 1.6.A).

Trade flows have weakened substantially. Imports, especially those of intermediate goods, have declined, falling more than exports, partly reflecting a deceleration in domestic demand. The contraction in exports to the United States has deepened, although shipments to the rest of the world have been somewhat more resilient.

In response to the deceleration in activity, monetary policy has become more accommodative, but regulatory tightening to reduce non-bank lending has continued. The government has also stepped up some fiscal measures, including tax cuts and support for local governments for public investment spending (Figure 1.6.B; World Bank 2019b). Total debt has surpassed 260 percent of GDP, but the share of non-bank lending has continued to decline (World Bank 2019c).

After decelerating to an estimated 6.1 percent in 2019, growth is expected to moderate to 5.9 percent in 2020 and 5.8 percent in 2021—0.2 percentage point below previous projections in both years. This is the first time China will register a pace of expansion below 6 percent since 1990, amid a slowdown in labor productivity growth and continued external headwinds (Chapter 3; World Bank 2018a). A permanent and lasting

FIGURE 1.4 **United States**

Growth has decelerated, reflecting slowing investment and exports. While the labor market remains robust, manufacturing activity has been contracting, higher tariffs have increased trade costs, and policy uncertainty has continued to weigh on investment. Support from tax cuts and government spending is expected to fade.

A. Selected activity indicators

B. Change in the general government cyclically-adjusted primary deficit

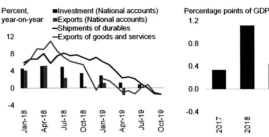

Source: Haver Analytics; International Monetary Fund; World Bank.
A. Last observation is October 2019 for shipments of durables and exports of goods and services, and 2019Q3 for national accounts data.
B. Shaded area indicates forecasts.

FIGURE 1.5 **Euro Area**

Many economies in the region were on the verge of recession during most of 2019. The German industrial sector remains particularly weak.

A. Contributions to Euro Area growth

B. Industrial production in the Euro Area and Germany

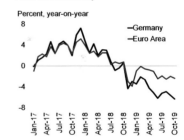

Source: Haver Analytics; World Bank.
A. "Other countries" includes Euro Area economies not listed. Data for 2019 are for 2019Q1-Q3 and are seasonally-adjusted annualized quarter-on-quarter growth rates.
B. Industrial production excludes construction. Last observation is October 2019.

resolution of trade disputes with the United States that builds upon recent progress could bolster China's growth prospects and reduce reliance on policy support.

Global trends

International trade and investment have weakened further, impeded by slowing global demand, as well as heightened policy uncertainty and an overall increase in the level of tariffs despite recent de-

FIGURE 1.6 China

Growth has continued to decelerate amid weakening industrial activity. Imports have experienced a sharp decline. The government has also stepped up fiscal support, including tax cuts and support to local governments for public investment spending.

A. Import volume and industrial production growth

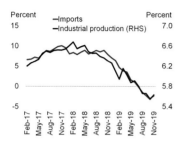

B. General government gross debt and decomposition of fiscal support measures

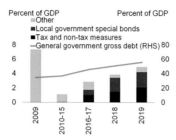

Source: Haver Analytics; International Monetary Fund; World Bank.
A. Figure shows 12-month moving averages. Import data include only goods. Import volumes are calculated as import values deflated by import price deflators. Import price deflators for October and November are estimates. Last observation is November 2019.
B. Gross debt consists of all liabilities that require payment or payments of interest and/or principal by the debtor to the creditor at a date or dates in the future. This includes debt liabilities in the form of SDRs, currency and deposits, debt securities, loans, insurance, pensions and standardized guarantee schemes, and other accounts payable. "Other" includes other net expenditures (including social security and State-Owned Enterprise funds). Fiscal support measures are World Bank staff estimates. General government gross debt in 2019 are estimates.

escalation. Major central banks have loosened policy in response, with interest rates in many advanced economies reaching unprecedented lows last year. Financial conditions in EMDEs have generally improved in parallel, except in economies perceived as higher risk. Weak demand has pushed most commodity prices down, which has been partially offset in some cases by supply restrictions.

Global trade

The sharp slowdown in the trade-intensive manufacturing sector has continued to weigh on global trade. Global goods trade spent a significant part of 2019 in contraction, with especially pronounced weakness in advanced economies and EMDEs such as China and the rest of East Asia (Figure 1.7.A). The severe decline in the production of capital and intermediate goods in G20 countries seen last year is consistent with continuing weakness in trade and investment (Figure 1.7.B). Manufacturing export orders have been contracting since late 2018 and services export orders, while more resilient, have also decelerated (Figure 1.7.C). The softness in services trade has so far been concentrated in global

financial transactions, construction, and travel services, which together account for more than one-third of world services trade (WTO 2019a).

The slowdown in trade and manufacturing stems from a variety of factors. Weakening demand in Europe and Asia, in particular for trade-intensive automobiles and technology products, and the slowdown in investment growth have been important drags. Protectionist measures implemented by G20 countries since 2018 have affected over $1 trillion worth of trade flows, or nearly 7 percent of global goods trade (Figure 1.7.D; WTO 2019b). The number of regulatory restrictions affecting foreign direct investment flows has also been on the rise, increasing by more than a third in 2018 (UNCTAD 2019a). Additionally, despite recent moderation, global trade policy uncertainty remains near historic highs (Ahir, Bloom, and Furceri 2018; Baker, Bloom, and Davis 2019).

Trade tensions between the United States and China escalated throughout most of 2019, and new tariffs were implemented on the majority of their bilateral trade. These tensions, and the ensuing increase in policy uncertainty, have resulted in sizable aggregate losses for world trade; while they have also had a positive impact on some EMDEs through trade diversion, this impact has been relatively small. Trade frictions have also risen elsewhere, including between the United States and some of its other trading partners such as the European Union (EU), as well as between Japan and the Republic of Korea.

Nevertheless, negotiations between the United States and China since mid-October resulted in a Phase One agreement between the two countries, including plans to partially roll back a subset of U.S. tariffs in exchange for Chinese commitments to make additional purchases of U.S. products, strengthen intellectual property protection, and pursue financial services liberalization. The recent agreement, coupled with continued negotiations and recent unilateral tariff reductions by China, signals a notable de-escalation of trade tensions. Moreover, protectionist measures implemented since 2016 have been partially offset by various liberalizing measures that affected 5 percent of global goods trade in 2019. The U.S.-China Phase One agreement, as well as other positive developments—such as progress in the ratification or implementation of the Africa Continental Free Trade Agreement, the U.S-Japan trade agreement, and the United States-Mexico-Canada Agreement—could give a much-needed boost to trade growth.

In sum, growth in global goods and services trade slowed sharply from 4 percent in 2018 to an estimated 1.4 percent last year, by far the weakest pace since the global financial crisis, and is projected to firm throughout 2020 and reach 1.9 percent. Critically, these projections assume no further escalation or reduction of trade restrictions going forward. An additional decline in trade tensions and the associated policy uncertainty—if, for instance, ongoing U.S.-China negotiations were to result in further reductions in tariffs— could lead to a stronger-than-expected pickup in global trade growth.

Financial markets

Global financing conditions eased considerably in 2019 (Figure 1.8.A). Bond yields in advanced economies fell to unprecedented lows, notwithstanding a pickup toward the end of the year amid improvement in market sentiment. Close to $12 trillion of outstanding global debt— nearly a quarter of the total stock, and almost entirely from Western Europe and Japan—is trading at negative interest rates. Major central banks, most notably the U.S. Federal Reserve and the ECB, eased monetary policy last year in the face of softening global economic prospects, heightened downside risks, and persistently low inflation. Despite weak global investment, corporate debt has been rising in many countries, with particularly rapid growth in some riskier categories, such as lending to highly leveraged firms in the United States and the Euro Area (FSB 2019a).

In general, EMDE borrowing costs have fallen and debt issuances have increased. Not all countries benefited equally, however—EMDEs that already had low spreads experienced further declines, while economies with low sovereign credit ratings

FIGURE 1.7 Global trade

The slowdown in global goods trade has been broad-based, with particularly pronounced weakness in EMDEs in the East Asia and Pacific region. The marked decline in global capital and intermediate goods production last year highlights the weakness in trade and investment. Manufacturing export orders have continued to contract, and services export orders have decelerated. Despite a recent de-escalation of trade tensions, the incidence of protectionist measures affecting global goods trade has risen.

A. EMDE goods trade growth, by region

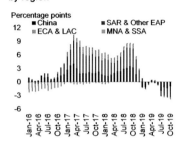

B. Global production of capital and intermediate goods

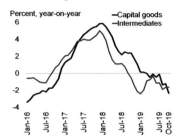

C. Manufacturing and services export orders

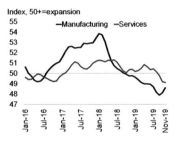

D. Global trade subject to new protectionist measures

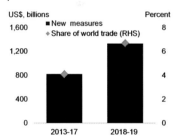

Source: CPB Netherlands Bureau for Economic Policy Analysis; Haver Analytics; World Trade Organization; World Bank.
A. Other EAP = East Asia and Pacific excl. China, ECA = Europe and Central Asia, LAC = Latin America and the Caribbean, MNA = Middle East and North Africa, SAR = South Asia, SSA = Sub-Saharan Africa. Figure shows 3-month moving averages. Trade is the average of export and import volumes. Last observation is October 2019.
B. Aggregate growth rates calculated using GDP weights at 2010 prices and market exchange rates. Sample includes the G20 countries for which capital goods and intermediates goods data are available. Last observation is October 2019.
C. Figure shows 3-month moving average. PMI readings above 50 indicate expansion in economic activity, readings below 50 indicate contraction. Last observation is November 2019.
D. Figure includes new import-restrictive measures, including tariff and non-tariff trade barriers. Annual data are mid-October to mid-October.

suffered from a flight to safety (Figure 1.8.B). Investors were particularly cautious about equity markets in riskier EMDEs, which experienced significant portfolio outflows during the period of heightened trade tensions and global growth concerns starting around August of last year, before recovering more recently (Figure 1.8.C). While equity and bond market developments in EMDEs have diverged considerably according to risk perception, many EMDE currencies have

FIGURE 1.8 Global finance

Global financing conditions have eased considerably, as major central banks have provided accommodation in response to softening economic prospects. However, EMDEs with low credit ratings have not benefitted from the global decline in borrowing costs. Prior to their recent recovery, EMDE equity markets had been suffering significant outflows. A rising share of EMDE currencies are at their lowest level against the U.S. dollar in a decade.

A. Global financing conditions

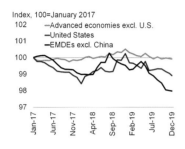

B. Change in EMDE bond spreads, by credit rating

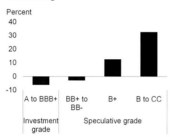

C. EMDE portfolio flows

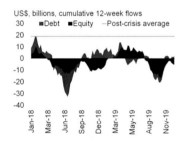

D. Share of EMDE currencies at their lowest level against the U.S. dollar since 2009

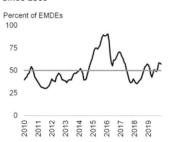

Source: Bloomberg; Haver Analytics; Institute of International Finance; International Monetary Fund; J.P. Morgan; World Bank.
A. Based on Goldman Sachs Financial Conditions Index for the United States, United Kingdom, Japan, Euro Area, India, Indonesia, Brazil, Mexico, Russia, and Turkey. Aggregates are calculated using GDP weights at 2010 prices and market exchange rates. Last observation is December 2019, which includes data through December 17, 2019.
B. Figure shows change in unweighted annual averages of daily data from 2018 to 2019. Sample includes 42 EMDEs. Countries are grouped based on Fitch long-term sovereign rating. S&P ratings are used for countries not rated by Fitch (Belize, Senegal). Fitch and S&P use similar rating grades. Bond spread shows percentage improvement in EMBI spreads versus a year ago. Last observation is December 16, 2019.
C. Equity flows include Brazil, India, Indonesia, Pakistan, Philippines, Sri Lanka, South Africa, Thailand, Turkey, and Vietnam. Debt flows include Hungary, India, Indonesia, Mexico, Poland, South Africa, Thailand, and Turkey. Post-crisis average over January 1, 2010 to December 29, 2017. Last observation is December 16, 2019.
D. Figure shows 3-month moving average. To avoid excessive volatility, figure shows share of countries whose monthly average exchange rate against the U.S. dollar is within 5 percent of their most depreciated level. Sample includes 32 EMDEs. Last observation is December 2019, which includes data through December 17, 2019.

depreciated, and a growing share have fallen to their lowest exchange rate with the U.S. dollar in a decade (Figure 1.8.D).

Foreign direct investment (FDI) has continued its downward trend, with some of the recent weakness attributable to global policy uncertainty. FDI weakened across all EMDE regions in the

first half of 2019, with the decline being particularly pronounced in EMDEs that had earlier experienced financial pressures (UNCTAD 2019b). By contrast, remittances to EMDEs continued to grow and recently surpassed FDI (World Bank 2019d).

Commodity markets

The prices of most commodities fell in 2019, mainly reflecting the deterioration in the growth outlook—especially that of EMDEs, which tend to have a larger income elasticity of demand for commodities (Figure 1.9.A; Baffes, Kabundi, and Nagle forthcoming). Forecasts have been revised down for most commodities in 2020 (Figure 1.9.B).

Oil prices averaged $61/bbl in 2019, a 10 percent fall from 2018 and $5/bbl below previous projections. Prices were supported by production cuts by OPEC and its partners, including the December 2019 decision to remove 0.5 mb/d of production on top of previous reductions of 1.2 mb/d implemented since January 2019. Production has also been constrained in the Islamic Republic of Iran and the República Bolivariana de Venezuela by a variety of geopolitical and domestic factors. However, these pressures were offset by weakening oil demand, as exemplified by downward revisions to demand projections (Figure 1.9.C; IEA 2019).

Oil prices are forecast to decline slightly to an average of $59/bbl in 2020 and 2021. U.S. supply is expected to continue to increase in 2020 as new pipeline capacity comes onstream. The greatest downside risk to the forecast is a further deterioration in growth. Current expectations are for oil consumption growth to pick up to just over 1 percent in 2020, which is comparable to the pace of global oil demand seen during previous global downturns (Figure 1.9.D). A critical upside risk to the forecast is the possibility of a further significant reduction in trade tensions between the United States and China, which could boost oil demand prospects.

Prices for most base metals weakened in the second half of 2019, primarily reflecting weaker global growth and trade tensions. Metals prices are expected to decline further in 2020, reflecting subdued industrial commodity demand. As with oil, a significant continued mitigation of U.S.-China trade tensions presents a key upside risk to metals price projections. Agricultural prices declined in the second half of 2019 on improved weather conditions that ensured elevated stock levels for grains. Agricultural prices are expected to stabilize in 2020, with risks to the forecast broadly balanced.

Emerging market and developing economies

The outlook for EMDEs has weakened significantly. As trade and investment firm, EMDE growth is projected to pick up to 4.1 in 2020—0.5 percentage point below previous forecasts—and stabilize at 4.4 percent in 2021-22, with the pace of the recovery restrained by soft global demand and structural constraints, including subdued productivity growth. The near-term rebound in EMDE growth will be mainly driven by a projected pickup in a small number of large countries. Per capita income growth will remain well below long-term averages, making progress toward poverty alleviation and development goals more challenging.

Recent developments

EMDEs have continued to experience substantial weakness, with industrial production, trade flows, and investment decelerating sharply last year (Figures 1.10.A to 1.10.C). While services activity has been appreciably more resilient than manufacturing, it has also moderated (Figure 1.10.D). Growth has been particularly anemic in EMDEs that have experienced the lingering effects of varying degrees of financial pressures or other idiosyncratic factors in the past couple of years.[1] This weakness has also spread to other economies

---

[1] These EMDEs include: (1) countries that have had an increase in their J.P. Morgan EMBI credit spread of at least one standard deviation above the 2010-19 average at any time since April 2018 (Argentina, Brazil, Egypt, Gabon, Jordan, Lebanon, Mexico, Nigeria, South Africa, Sri Lanka, Tunisia, Turkey); or (2) countries that have been subject to sanctions (Iran, Russia). Additional details about this classification can be found in World Bank 2019e.

FIGURE 1.9 **Commodity markets**

Most commodity prices fell in 2019, and forecasts for 2020 have been revised down. Despite oil supply disruptions, deteriorating expectations for demand growth have put downward pressure on oil prices. A further softening in growth prospects is the key downside risk to oil demand and price forecasts, while a sustained reduction of trade tensions represents a major upside risk.

A. Commodity price indexes

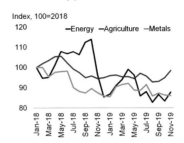

B. Commodity price forecast revisions

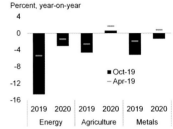

C. Change in oil demand forecasts

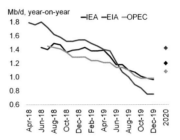

D. Oil demand and price growth around periods of economic downturn

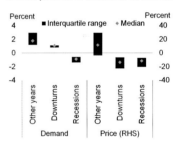

Source: Energy Information Administration (EIA); International Energy Agency (IEA); Kose and Terrones (2015); Organization of Petroleum Exporting Countries (OPEC); World Bank.
A. Last observation is November 2019.
C. Figure shows evolution of oil demand forecasts for 2019 by source. Diamonds show forecasts for oil demand in 2020.
D. Figure shows oil demand by component of global business cycle from 1971 to 2018. Over the time period, there have been four global recessions, defined as a contraction in growth, in 1975, 1982, 1991, and 2009, and three global slowdowns, defined by very low output growth, in 1998, 2001, and 2012 (Kose and Terrones 2015).

that had previously shown resilience. In all, growth in about 60 percent of EMDEs is estimated to have slowed last year. In many economies, subdued economic activity has been somewhat cushioned by still-resilient consumption and a shift toward more supportive monetary policy.

Growth in EMDEs that experienced recent financial or country-specific stresses remains feeble (Kose and Ohnsorge 2019). To different degrees, these economies continue to face heightened policy uncertainty and various domestic challenges. With notable exceptions, activity has started to firm somewhat; however, the recovery in

FIGURE 1.10 **EMDE recent developments**

EMDEs have continued to experience substantial weakness, which has spread to countries that, until recently, had shown resilience. Industrial production, trade flows, and investment have decelerated sharply. While services activity has been appreciably more resilient than manufacturing, it has also moderated.

A. Industrial production growth

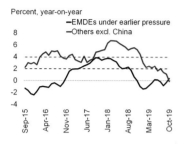

B. Export and import volume growth

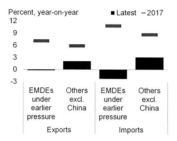

C. Investment growth

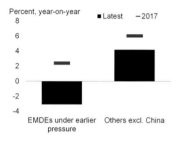

D. Manufacturing and services PMIs

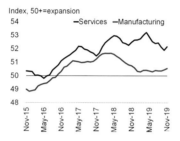

Source: Haver Analytics; J.P. Morgan; World Bank.
A.-C. EMDEs under earlier pressure include: a) countries that have had an increase in their J.P. Morgan EMBI credit spread of at least one standard deviation above the 2010-19 average at any time since April 2018 (Argentina, Brazil, Egypt, Gabon, Jordan, Lebanon, Mexico, Nigeria, South Africa, Sri Lanka, Tunisia, Turkey), or b) countries that have been subject to sanctions (Iran, Russia).
A. Figure shows 3-month moving averages. Dashed horizontal lines indicate the March 2006 to October 2019 averages. Industrial production growth for EMDEs under earlier pressure includes those countries in the group for which data are available. Last observation is October 2019, which is estimated for Tunisia.
B. Import and export data are volumes of goods and non-factor services. Aggregate growth rates calculated using GDP weights at 2010 prices and market exchange rates. "Latest" indicates 2019 full year estimate.
C. Investment is defined as gross fixed capital formation. EMDEs under earlier pressure includes those countries in the group for which data are available. "Latest" indicates 2019Q1-Q3 simple average. Last observation is 2019Q3.
D. Figure shows 6-month moving averages. Manufacturing and services output are measured by Purchasing Managers' Index (PMI). PMI readings above 50 indicate expansion in economic activity; readings below 50 indicate contraction. Horizontal line indicates expansionary threshold. Last observation is November 2019.

most of these economies is proceeding at a markedly slower pace than previously envisioned. Some easing of lending conditions, as well as progress on the reform agenda, are beginning to support a modest pickup in Brazil. In the Russian Federation, monetary policy easing and public infrastructure projects from the National Projects program are buoying activity. In Turkey, activity is rebounding from earlier financial turmoil at a faster-than-expected pace as domestic demand improves; however, the pickup remains fragile amid subdued confidence and investment. In

Mexico, easing monetary policy is providing some support to growth. In contrast, activity in Argentina has been contracting amid high policy uncertainty in the aftermath of severe financial stress in mid-2019. In Iran, sanctions have been weighing significantly on growth.

Growth in other EMDEs has generally softened owing to global and domestic headwinds. Economies that are deeply integrated into global and regional production and trade networks—most notably in Asia and Europe—particularly suffered from global trade tensions and decelerating trade flows last year (Philippines, Thailand; World Bank 2019f, 2019g, 2019h). Tighter credit conditions in the non-banking sector are contributing to a substantial weakening of domestic demand in India, while activity in Pakistan has decelerated in response to contractionary monetary policy intended to restore domestic and external balances. In some countries, capacity constraints are also limiting growth (Poland, Romania). Other economies have experienced temporary setbacks to construction and infrastructure projects (Costa Rica, Panama), the effects of natural disasters (Guatemala, Papua New Guinea), and the negative impact of social unrest (Bolivia, Chile).

Commodity exporters

Growth in commodity exporters slowed from 2 percent in 2018 to an estimated 1.5 percent in 2019, 0.6 percentage point below earlier forecasts, reflecting softer-than-projected commodity prices, oil production cuts, decelerating investment in extractive sectors, and weakness in the largest countries that earlier experienced financial pressures or other country-specific stresses—particularly Argentina, Brazil, Iran, and Russia (Figure 1.11.A). Weakening global demand and ongoing domestic challenges—including large macroeconomic imbalances and domestic policy uncertainty—continue to discourage investment and delay recovery in many commodity exporters (Nigeria, South Africa; World Bank 2019h).

Despite supportive fiscal policy and stable non-oil activity, difficulties in the oil sector and heightened geopolitical tensions are weighing on activity in oil exporters in the MENA region

(Algeria, Iran, Saudi Arabia; World Bank 2019i). In other commodity exporters with more policy space, countercyclical policy measures have been partly offsetting the drag from weakening global demand and lower commodity prices, resulting in stable or moderately slower growth (Indonesia, Peru).

Commodity importers

Growth in commodity importers excluding China eased from 5 percent in 2018 to an estimated 3.3 percent in 2019—0.9 percentage point below previous projections and the slowest rate since the global financial crisis (Figure 1.11.B). This slowdown in part reflected a marked deceleration in Turkey due to earlier financial stress, in Mexico due to heightened policy uncertainty, and in India due to a tightening of domestic non-bank credit conditions. Policy adjustments to address macroeconomic imbalances in Pakistan also weighed on aggregate growth in this group.

For many commodity importers, momentum last year was weaker than expected, reflecting declining exports and investment, only partly offset by more accommodative monetary policy stances and fiscal support measures (Philippines, Thailand; World Bank 2019j). Nonetheless, growth in many commodity importers remains solid due to robust private consumption and supportive policies in a context of subdued inflation and resilient capital flows (Bangladesh, Cambodia, Vietnam). Moreover, decelerating activity in some commodity importers also reflected a narrowing of positive output gaps (Poland, Romania).

Low-income countries

The recovery in low-income countries (LICs) has faltered amid softening external demand, weaker commodity prices, political instability, and devastation from extreme weather events (Box 1.1; Steinbach 2019; World Bank 2019e). Growth among fragile LICs, in particular, has slowed markedly. In the Democratic Republic of Congo, falling metals prices stifled mining activity, while the Ebola outbreak in the conflict-affected northeastern region has persisted. Subdued growth in Mozambique reflected widespread damage

FIGURE 1.11 EMDE commodity exporters and importers

Growth in both commodity exporters and importers decelerated last year. In both groups, growth remains particularly subdued in the largest EMDEs that earlier experienced varying degrees of financial or country-specific stresses.

A. Growth in commodity exporters

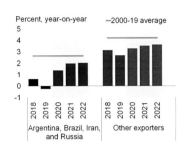

B. Growth in commodity importers, excluding China

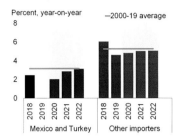

Source: World Bank.
A.B. Data for 2019 are estimates. Aggregate growth rates calculated using GDP weights at 2010 prices and market exchange rates. Shaded areas indicate forecasts. Green lines indicate 2000-19 simple averages.

caused by two tropical cyclones and weaker-than-expected coal production.

Activity in other LICs, however, has been somewhat more robust, reflecting improved harvests (Malawi, Nepal), as well as continued services sector strength and solid public and private investment growth (Guinea-Bissau, Uganda). Nonetheless, softer external demand and lower agricultural prices have dampened export revenues and slowed growth in some countries (Madagascar, Rwanda).

Outlook

Growth outlook

EMDE growth is expected to experience a moderate cyclical recovery from an estimated 3.5 percent last year to 4.1 percent in 2020—0.5 percentage point lower than previously projected (Figure 1.12.A). Forecasts for almost all regions and half of EMDEs have been downgraded for this year, largely reflecting weaker-than-expected exports and investment (Box 1.2; Chapter 2). EMDE growth is projected to stabilize at an average rate of 4.4 percent in 2021-22, as trade and investment firm. These baseline projections are predicated on resilient consumption, a diminishing drag from earlier pressures in some

BOX 1.1 Recent developments and outlook for low-income countries

Growth in low-income countries (LICs) has faltered in 2019, falling to 5.4 percent. The slowdown partly reflects global factors (softening external demand and weaker commodity prices), and idiosyncratic factors (political instability and devastation from extreme weather events). Growth is expected to firm over the forecast horizon, reaching an average of 5.7 percent in 2021-22. This pickup assumes improved stability, recovery from extreme weather events, continued investment in infrastructure, and the implementation of structural reforms and measures to strengthen business environments. Nonetheless, projected growth will be insufficient to markedly reduce poverty, particularly in LICs affected by fragility, conflict, and violence. Risks to the outlook include slower-than-expected growth in major trading partners, rising debt vulnerabilities, and growing insecurity.

Recent developments

Economic activity. The recovery in low-income countries (LICs) stalled in 2019 as global and idiosyncratic factors dampened activity. The global backdrop reflected softening external demand and weaker commodity prices, while activity in some countries was weighed down further by political instability and extreme weather events. Growth in LICs fell to an estimated 5.4 percent, 0.3 percentage point lower than previous forecasts (Figure 1.1.1.A).

The weaker-than-expected performance reflected a marked slowdown in activity among fragile LICs.[1] Growth in the Democratic Republic of Congo decelerated as weakening external demand and lower metal prices weighed on exports. The conflict-affected northeastern region of the country is grappling with the second-largest Ebola outbreak on record, which began in the middle of 2018. In Haiti, growth is estimated to have contracted in 2019 amid severe political instability, rapid exchange rate depreciation, elevated inflation, and rising food insecurity exacerbated by drought. Similarly, in Liberia, the estimated contraction in activity last year reflected the erosion of incomes from elevated inflation, weak harvests, and moderating mining production due to lower commodity prices. In Mozambique—which has been on a reduced growth path since 2016—slowing growth in 2019 was largely due to the devastation caused by last year's cyclones alongside moderating coal production. In addition to their heavy human toll, the cyclones have likely reversed recent gains in poverty reduction in affected economies (Malawi, Mozambique; Baez, Caruso and Niu 2019; World Bank 2019k).

Activity also slowed among other LICs (Benin, Burkina Faso, Madagascar, Rwanda, The Gambia, Tajikistan). In Rwanda—one of the fastest growing economies in the world—growth edged down as weakening external

demand and lower commodity prices constrained export revenues; however, sustained public investment helped offset some of this weakness. Nonetheless, activity remained resilient, or strengthened, among some LICs. Improved harvests supported rising agricultural production (Malawi, Nepal), and services sector activity continued to accelerate (Guinea-Bissau, Uganda). In Malawi, agricultural production strengthened despite the impact of Cyclone Idai, reflecting improved tobacco and maize harvests in unaffected districts. In Ethiopia—the largest LIC economy—agricultural production slowed while constrained hydroelectric power generation due to low dam levels dampened industrial activity; however, these weaknesses were more than offset by continued robust services sector activity, particularly in travel, banking, and telecommunications. On the demand side, activity was supported by robust private consumption helped by strong harvests (Malawi, Nepal), and solid investment growth—both public and private (Guinea-Bissau, Uganda). Despite a sharp fall in aluminum prices, growth edged up in Guinea, partly due to continued infrastructure investment in mining-related activities. In Sierra Leone, the resumption of iron ore production helped boost activity.

External positions. Current account balances widened among more than half of LICs. In some countries, larger deficits reflected weaker exports related to softening external demand and lower international commodity prices (Guinea-Bissau, Rwanda, Togo). Elsewhere, deficits widened primarily due to imports of capital goods related to large infrastructure investment projects (Mozambique, Togo, Uganda). Imports associated with cyclone-related reconstruction added to existing deficits (Malawi, Mozambique). In Ethiopia, however, the current account deficit narrowed amid improved services exports—largely transport services with Addis Ababa increasingly becoming a key regional hub—and as fiscal consolidation contributed to slower import growth. By the second half of 2019, capital flows into LICs appear to have weakened noticeably, as growing concerns over global growth prospects and heightened trade tensions weighed on investor sentiment. As a result, international reserves in the median LIC have weakened somewhat and remain below the three-months-of-imports benchmark in about one-

---

Note: This box was prepared by Rudi Steinbach. Research assistance was provided by Hazel Macadangdang.

[1] Fragile LICs are those affected by fragility, conflict, and violence, according to the World Bank's Harmonized List of Fragile Situations.

BOX 1.1 Recent developments and outlook for low-income countries (*continued*)

FIGURE 1.1.1 Recent developments in low-income countries

Growth in low-income countries (LICs) has fallen to 5.4 percent in 2019 amid rising domestic and external headwinds. Growth is, however, expected to firm to an average of 5.7 percent in 2021-22, reflecting improved stability, recovery from extreme weather events, and continued investment in infrastructure. Fiscal deficits deteriorated sharply among LICs affected by fragility, conflict, and violence. Subdued inflation has allowed some central banks to easy policy rates.

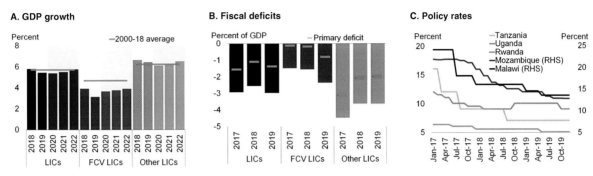

Source: Haver Analytics; *World Economic Outlook*, International Monetary Fund; Reserve Bank of Malawi; World Bank.
Note: LICs = low-income countries. FCV LICs are LICs affected by fragility, conflict, and violence.
A. Aggregate growth rates calculated using GDP weights at 2010 prices and market exchange rates.
B. Unweighted averages. Sample includes 27 LICs.
C. Reflects data up to December 19th, 2019. Prior to April 2017, data for Mozambique reflects the money market rate.

quarter of countries—leaving these countries more vulnerable to negative shocks.

Fiscal positions. LIC fiscal balances deteriorated, on average, in 2019 with the average deficit widening to an estimated 3 percent, from 2.6 percent in 2018 (Figure 1.1.1.B). Fiscal deficits mostly widened among fragile LICs, partly reflecting low domestic revenue mobilization while public spending remained elevated. In the Democratic Republic of Congo, efforts to contain spending were not sufficient to offset the decline in fiscal revenues resulting from the weaker mining sector performance. In contrast, increased fiscal consolidation supported by greater revenue mobilization, as well as broad-ranging tax administration reforms have helped deficits improve in several LICs (Burkina Faso, Ethiopia, Malawi, Mali).

Outlook for 2020-22

Economic growth. Growth in LICs is projected to remain unchanged at 5.4 percent in 2020, before firming to an average of 5.7 percent in 2021-22. Forecasts for this year and next are 0.6 percentage point lower than previous projections, reflecting weaker external demand, lower commodity prices, and policy tightening among some large LICs. The expected pickup is predicated on no further deceleration in external demand and a stabilization of commodity prices, albeit at lower levels.

Among fragile LICs, growth is forecast to rise to 3.7 percent in 2020, from 3.2 percent in 2019, in part due to improved political stability in some countries, strengthening business environments, and as the lingering effects of extreme weather events wane. In Afghanistan, greater political stability following elections in late 2019 is expected to help support activity. Notable business environment reforms in Togo will continue to bolster growth (World Bank 2020). In Chad and Mozambique, investment in new production capacity should spur growth and boost exports, more than offsetting softer commodity prices and weaker external demand. In the Democratic Republic of Congo, however, growth is projected to moderate further as lower metal prices—particularly for cobalt—continue to suppress mining production.

In other LICs, economic activity is expected to remain resilient, with growth above 6 percent over the forecast horizon. In countries such as Benin and Rwanda, the expansion will be supported by public investment in infrastructure, strong agricultural growth, and increased private sector activity as reforms continue to bolster the business environment. Accommodative monetary policy stances amid relatively subdued inflation will further support activity in some countries (Malawi, Tanzania; Special Focus 2; Figure 1.1.1.C). In Uganda, growth will be boosted by public and private infrastructure investments, as well as in energy projects, as the country

BOX 1.1 Recent developments and outlook for low-income countries (*continued*)

FIGURE 1.1.2 Outlook for per capita GDP and risks

Growth in per capita incomes is expected to firm to an average of 2.9 percent in 2021-22; however, it will be markedly weaker among LICs affected by fragility, conflict, and violence. For these countries, per capita growth will be insufficient to make significant progress in poverty alleviation. Productivity in LICs is a mere 2 percent of the advanced-economy average, reflecting low productivity in comparatively larger agricultural sectors. Labor shifting to more productive sectors has been an important source of productivity growth in LICs. Debt sustainability concerns remain elevated, with a rising number of countries in debt distress. Insecurity, conflicts, and insurgencies, are leading to an increase in displaced populations.

A. Per capita GDP growth

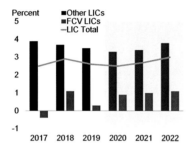

B. Changes in LIC extreme poverty rates between 2015 and 2020

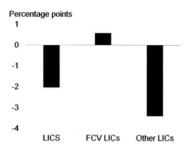

C. LIC productivity and agriculture value added

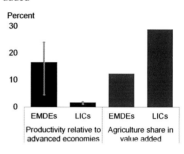

D. Contribution to aggregate productivity growth

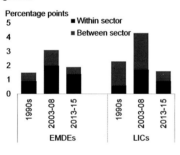

E. LICs in debt distress

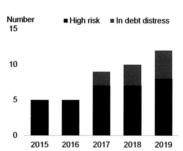

F. Internally displaced populations in LICs

Source: APO productivity database; Easterly and Fischer (1994); Expanded African Sector, Groningen Growth Development Center; Haver Analytics; ILOSTAT; International Monetary Fund; Penn World Table; United Nations High Commissioner for Refugees (UNHCR); *World Development Indicators*, World Bank.
Note: Shaded area indicates forecasts. LICs = low-income countries. FCV = fragility, conflict, and violence.
A. Aggregate per capita growth rates calculated by dividing the total GDP at 2010 prices and market exchange rates for each subgroup by its total population. Sample includes 25 LICs, 12 "FCV LICs", and 13 "Other LICs".
B. The number of people living on or below the international poverty line of $1.90 per day as a share of the total population. Data for 2020 are estimates and calculated using data from World Bank. "FCV LICs" and "Other LICs" samples each include 12 and 13 countries, respectively.
C. Productivity data based on 74 emerging market and developing economies (EMDEs), including 11 low-income countries (LICs). Blue bars show unweighted average output per worker during 2013-18 relative to the advanced-economy average. Whiskers indicate interquartile range relative to the advanced-economy average. Agriculture value added reflects 2018 data and is based on 132 EMDEs, including 23 LICs. Red bars show unweighted average share of agriculture in value added.
D. Growth "within sector" shows the contribution to aggregate productivity growth of each sector holding employment shares fixed. The 'between sector' effect shows the contribution arising from changes in sectoral employment shares. Sample includes 46 EMDEs of which 8 are LICs.
E. Number of LICs eligible to access the IMF's concessional lending facilities that are either at high risk of, or in, debt distress according to the joint World Bank-IMF Debt Sustainability Framework for Low-Income Countries. The sample includes 28 LICs.
F. MNA = Middle East and North Africa, SAR = South Asia, SSA = Sub-Saharan Africa. Internally Displaced Populations (IDPs) are persons or groups of persons who have been forced or obliged to flee or to leave their homes or places of habitual residence, in particular as a result of or in order to avoid the effects of armed conflict, situations of generalized violence, violations of human rights or natural or human-made disasters, and who have not crossed an internationally recognized state border. Data reflects only internally displaced populations (IDPs) who are protected or assisted by UNHCR, and country totals are not necessarily representative of the entire IDP population in that country. Sample includes 15 countries, of which 2 are in the Middle East and North Africa, 1 is in South Asia, and 12 are in Sub-Saharan Africa.

prepares to export oil by 2023. Similarly, higher growth in Niger in 2022 reflects a sharp pickup in crude oil exports as oil production is expected to quadruple from current levels. Activity in Guinea will benefit from investments in new mining production capacity. In Ethiopia, however,

growth is expected to slow due to tighter fiscal and monetary policy stances aimed at containing inflation.

Prospects for per capita income convergence and poverty alleviation. Per capita GDP growth in LICs is expected to

BOX 1.1 Recent developments and outlook for low-income countries (*continued*)

TABLE 1.1.1 Low-income country forecasts[a]
(Real GDP growth at market prices in percent, unless indicated otherwise)

Percentage point differences from June 2019 projections[d]

	2017	2018	2019e	2020f	2021f	2022f	2019e	2020f	2021f
Low-Income Country, GDP[b]	**5.5**	**5.8**	**5.4**	**5.4**	**5.5**	**5.8**	**-0.3**	**-0.6**	**-0.6**
Afghanistan	2.7	1.8	2.5	3.0	3.5	3.5	0.1	-0.2	-0.1
Benin	5.8	6.7	6.4	6.7	6.7	6.7	-0.1	0.2	0.2
Burkina Faso	6.3	6.8	6.0	6.0	6.0	6.0	0.0	0.0	0.0
Burundi	0.5	1.6	1.8	2.0	2.1	2.2	0.0	-0.1	0.1
Chad	-3.0	2.6	3.0	5.5	4.8	4.8	-0.4	-0.1	0.0
Congo, Dem. Rep.	3.7	5.8	4.3	3.9	3.4	3.6	-1.6	-2.6	-3.4
Ethiopia[c]	10.0	7.9	9.0	6.3	6.4	7.1	1.1	-1.9	-1.8
Gambia, The	4.8	6.6	6.0	6.3	5.8	5.5	0.6	1.1	0.8
Guinea	10.0	5.8	5.9	6.0	6.0	6.0	0.0	0.0	0.0
Guinea-Bissau	5.9	3.8	4.6	4.9	5.0	5.0	0.3	0.1	-0.5
Haiti[c]	1.2	1.5	-0.9	-1.4	-0.5	1.4	-1.3	-3.0	-1.8
Liberia	2.5	1.2	-1.4	1.4	3.4	4.2	-1.8	-0.2	2.1
Madagascar	4.3	5.1	4.7	5.3	4.4	5.0	-0.5	0.0	-0.7
Malawi	4.0	3.5	4.4	4.8	5.2	5.3	-0.1	0.1	0.1
Mali	5.3	4.7	5.0	5.0	4.9	4.9	0.0	0.1	0.1
Mozambique	3.7	3.4	2.0	3.7	4.2	4.4	0.0	0.2	0.0
Nepal[c]	8.2	6.7	7.1	6.4	6.5	6.6	0.0	0.0	0.0
Niger	4.9	6.5	6.3	6.0	5.6	11.9	-0.2	0.0	0.0
Rwanda	6.1	8.6	8.5	8.1	8.0	8.0	0.7	0.1	0.5
Sierra Leone	3.8	3.5	4.8	4.9	4.9	5.0	-0.6	-0.5	-0.3
Tajikistan	7.1	7.3	6.2	5.5	5.0	5.0	0.2	-0.5	-1.0
Tanzania	6.8	5.4	5.6	5.8	6.1	6.2	0.2	0.1	0.0
Togo	4.4	4.9	5.3	5.5	5.5	5.5	0.3	0.3	0.4
Uganda[c]	3.9	5.9	6.1	6.5	5.9	6.0	0.0	0.0	0.1

Source: World Bank.
Note: World Bank forecasts are frequently updated based on new information and changing (global) circumstances. Consequently, projections presented here may differ from those contained in other Bank documents, even if basic assessments of countries' prospects do not significantly differ at any given moment in time.
a. Central African Republic, the Democratic People's Republic of Korea, Somalia, Syria, and Yemen are not forecast because of to data limitations.
b. Aggregate growth rate calculated using GDP weights at 2010 prices and market exchange rates.
c. GDP growth based on fiscal year data. For Nepal, the year 2019 refers to FY2018/19.
d. Due to changes in the official list of countries classified as low income by the World Bank, the sample of LICs in this table is not comparable to June 2019. However, an identical sample is used for the comparison of the aggregate LIC GDP projection.
To download the data in this table, please visit www.worldbank.org/gep.

remain broadly unchanged at 2.5 percent in 2020, before firming to an average of 2.9 percent in 2021-22. This pace is insufficient to yield substantial progress in poverty reduction as growth in LICs is often not inclusive and the conversion of growth into poverty reduction is therefore low (Christiaensen, Chuhan-Pole, and Sanoh 2013; Christiaensen and Hill 2018; Figure 1.1.2.A). Among

fragile LICs—where the incidence of extreme poverty is even higher—per capita GDP is expected to grow by a mere 1 percent in 2020-22, after having contracted in 40 percent of cases last year. As a result, the number of people in LICs living below the international poverty line of $1.90 per day will remain elevated, while continuing to rise among fragile LICs (Figure 1.1.2.B).

BOX 1.1 Recent developments and outlook for low-income countries (*continued*)

To raise LIC growth over the medium term requires sustained improvements in labor productivity (Chapter 3). Labor productivity—average output per worker—in LICs is a mere 2 percent of that in the average advanced economy and one-tenth of the productivity level in the average emerging market and developing economy (EMDE), and LIC productivity growth has been persistently below that of EMDEs (Figure 1.1.2.C). This partly reflects LICs' heavy reliance on agricultural sectors, including widespread subsistence farming, as well as the misallocation of resources—often caused by distortionary price controls (Special Focus 1). Raising LIC aggregate productivity will face several challenges. The reallocation of labor from mostly agriculture to higher-productivity sectors such as mining and construction has been an important driver of LIC productivity in the pre-crisis period; however, this engine of productivity growth has largely stalled following the collapse in global industrial commodity prices (Figure 1.1.2.D). Moreover, longer-term prospects for commodity demand are weakening as growth in China—the largest source of commodity demand—slows and shifts towards less resource-intensive sectors (World Bank 2018b). Climate change will pose increasing challenges to efforts to raise productivity in the agricultural sector, with large falls in crop yields expected as global temperatures rise (Fuglie et al. 2019).

Risks. Risks to the outlook are firmly to the downside. A faster-than-expected deceleration in growth of major world economies and key trading partners—such as the United States, the Euro Area, or China—would adversely affect export demand and investment in several LICs. Together, these three economies account for four-tenths of both LIC goods exports and foreign direct investment, and about one-quarter of remittance inflows. Countries that depend on extractive industries—specifically metals producers—would be hard-hit by a sharp slowdown in China, as it accounts for more than half of global metals demand (World Bank 2018b).

LIC government debt reached 55 percent of GDP, on average, in 2019—a 19 percentage point rise since 2013—keeping debt sustainability concerns elevated (World Bank 2019l). By November 2019, 12 out of 28 LICs were regarded as being in debt distress, or at high risk thereof, under the IMF-World Bank debt sustainability framework—two more than at the end of 2018 (Figure 1.1.2.C). The ratio of interest payments to GDP has doubled since 2013, in part reflecting the rising share of non-concessional debt as commercial creditors have become an important source of credit (Essl et al. 2019;

World Bank 2019m; World Bank and IMF 2018). Non–Paris Club creditors have also become a more important source of financing over the past decade, especially in Sub-Saharan Africa (World Bank 2015). Increased access to market-based debt may also be increasing governments' exposure to interest rate and refinancing risks. Sharp increases in debt-servicing costs would undermine much-needed fiscal consolidation efforts and absorb revenues that could otherwise be used for productivity-enhancing investments in health care, education, and infrastructure.

LICs' weakening reserve buffers mean that renewed episodes of financial stress, accompanied by an unexpected tightening of international financial conditions, could disrupt capital inflows, fuel disorderly exchange rate depreciations, and raise financing costs. LICs with weaker macroeconomic fundamentals, higher foreign-currency-denominated debt, or greater political risks would be most vulnerable.

Insecurity, conflicts, and insurgencies—particularly in the Sahel and conflict-affected economies in the Middle East and North Africa—may further weigh on economic activity as well as food security in many countries if they were to intensify (Burkina Faso, Central African Republic, Chad, the Democratic Republic of Congo, Ethiopia, Mali, Niger, Republic of Yemen, Somalia, South Sudan, Syrian Arab Republic; FAO 2019). Moreover, the large populations that are forcibly displaced by these conflicts cluster in areas that often become a source of further instability, with poverty rates being worse than in their places of origin (Figure 1.1.2.D; Beegle and Christiaensen 2019).

Natural disasters related to growing climate extremes, such as flooding or severe and prolonged drought episodes, remain an important risk for many LICs, as agricultural output often accounts for a high share of domestic value added, and infrastructure is generally less resilient than in more developed economies (World Bank 2019e).

Health crises are a continuous concern. Although the pace of new Ebola infections in the Democratic Republic of Congo has slowed in the second half of 2019, efforts to contain the second-largest outbreak in history have been complicated by conflict (Wannier et al. 2019). As evidenced by the West African Ebola outbreak of 2014-16, the current outbreak poses a significant risk to economic activity, particularly if it were to spread to major urban centers, or to neighboring countries (De la Fuente, Jacoby, and Lawin 2019).

large economies, reduced policy uncertainty, varying degrees of monetary policy support, generally benign borrowing costs, no major swings in commodity prices, no further deterioration in global activity, and no new adverse shocks. They therefore represent a benign but fragile scenario, given the ongoing global headwinds of slowing advanced-economy growth, subdued global trade, and declining commodity prices (Figure 1.12.B).

The expected pickup in aggregate EMDE growth is not broad-based: A third of EMDEs are projected to decelerate this year. Instead, it is largely predicated on a rebound in a small group of large EMDEs, most of which are emerging from deep recessions or sharp slowdowns caused by earlier financial pressures or other idiosyncratic factors. Indeed, about 90 percent of the pickup in EMDE growth in 2020 is accounted for by just eight countries—Argentina, Brazil, India, Iran, Mexico, Russia, Saudi Arabia, and Turkey—even though they represent just a third of EMDE GDP (Figure 1.12.C). Excluding these eight countries, aggregate EMDE growth would experience almost no acceleration. More generally, aggregate economic slack in EMDEs will persist in the near term, and actual EMDE growth this year will remain below potential (Figure 1.12.D).

Projections for Argentina have been downgraded following the severe financial market turmoil last year; the impact of this event is assumed to gradually diminish over the forecast horizon. In Brazil, Russia, and South Africa, elevated policy uncertainty is expected to moderate; however, recovery in these countries is projected to be fragile due to continued challenges associated with the implementation of reforms, sanctions, or infrastructure bottlenecks. Growth in some other large economies (Egypt, India, Thailand) is expected to pick up, supported by policy easing and gradually improving business confidence in response to recent reforms.

Growth in LICs is projected to remain little changed at 5.4 percent in 2020 and edge up to an average of 5.7 percent in 2021-22. Forecasts for this year and next are 0.6 percentage point lower than previous projections, reflecting weaker external demand, lower commodity prices, and

FIGURE 1.12 **EMDE outlook**

EMDE growth is expected to recover moderately, reaching 4.1 percent in 2020 and stabilizing at an average of 4.4 percent in 2021-22. This is a benign but fragile scenario given ongoing global headwinds. The recovery will not be broad-based and will instead mainly be driven by a projected pickup in a small number of large economies. Aggregate economic slack in EMDEs will persist in the near term, with actual EMDE growth expected to remain below potential.

A. Growth outlook

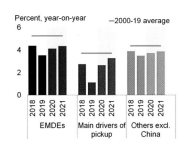

B. Average share of EMDEs with annual growth accelerating by more than 0.1 percentage point, 1962-2019

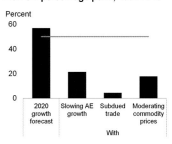

C. Contributions to the change in EMDE annual growth

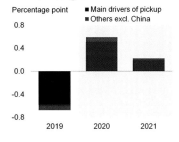

D. EMDE growth

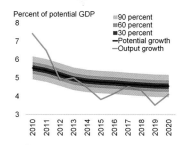

Source: J.P. Morgan; World Bank.
A.C. Data for 2019 are estimates. "Main drivers of pickup" includes the eight largest EMDEs that account for 90 percent of the acceleration in EMDE growth between 2019 and 2020 (Argentina, Brazil, India, Iran, Mexico, the Russian Federation, Saudi Arabia, and Turkey). Aggregate growth rates calculated using GDP weights at 2010 prices and market exchange rates. Shaded areas indicate forecasts.
A. Green lines indicate 2000-19 simple averages.
B. AE = advanced economies. "Subdued trade" refers to growth below 2.5 percent. "Moderating commodity prices" refers to a year-on-year contraction in the non-energy commodity index.
D. Estimates of potential growth are from a multivariate filter model of World Bank (2018a). Aggregate growth rates are calculated using GDP weights at 2010 prices and market exchange rates. Sample includes 57 EMDEs. Data for 2020 are forecasts.

policy tightening among some large LICs (Box 1.1). The expected pickup later in the forecast horizon assumes that activity among fragile LICs recovers as political stability improves (Afghanistan, Guinea-Bissau), investments in new capacity offset weaker external demand (Chad, Mozambique), and as rebuilding efforts following last year's cyclones boost activity (Malawi, Mozambique; World Bank 2019h). Among other LICs, activity is expected to remain generally

FIGURE 1.13 EMDE per capita income growth and poverty

Despite significant gains in poverty alleviation over the last three decades, meeting the Sustainable Development Goals by 2030 appears out of reach for many EMDEs, partly because of the recent loss of momentum in per capita income growth. In Sub-Saharan Africa, per capita growth is expected to remain below 1 percent, exacerbating the concentration of extreme poverty.

A. Sustainable Development Goals

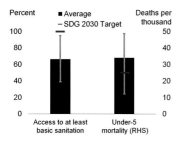

B. Per capita growth in EMDEs

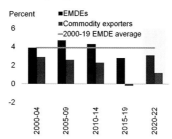

C. Cumulative per capita income gains and losses relative to 1990-2014 trend

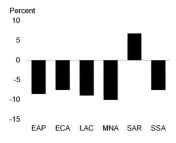

D. Global extreme poverty

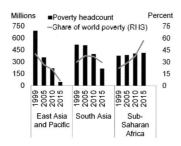

Source: United Nations; World Bank.
A. Sample includes 155 EMDEs. Orange lines indicate interquartile ranges. "Access to at least basic sanitation" and "Under-5 mortality" data reflect 2017 and 2018, respectively.
B. Data for 2019 are estimates. Aggregate growth rates calculated using GDP weights at 2010 prices and market exchange rates. EMDE sample includes 144 countries, with 83 commodity exporters.
C. EAP = East Asia and Pacific, ECA = Europe and Central Asia, LAC = Latin America and the Caribbean, MNA = Middle East and North Africa, SAR = South Asia, SSA = Sub-Saharan Africa. Negative bars represent the cumulative shortfalls in regional per capita income growth from 2015 to 2019 relative to the 1990-2014 average growth rate. For ECA, the average uses data for 1995-2014 to exclude the immediate aftermath of the collapse of the Soviet Union.
D. Data for South Asia in 2015 are estimates.

resilient spurred by sustained public investment in infrastructure along with greater private sector activity (Benin, Rwanda, Uganda). In some countries, more accommodative monetary policy amid relatively subdued inflation will support growth (Special Focus 2; Malawi, Tanzania). However, in Ethiopia—the largest LIC—growth is expected to slow due to tighter fiscal and monetary policy stances aimed at containing inflation.

Longer-term growth prospects for EMDEs are also challenging (Ruch 2019a). In particular, the post-crisis weakness in several fundamental drivers of

EMDE productivity growth is expected to persist or deepen (Chapter 3; World Bank 2018a). Going forward, EMDE potential growth is likely to be dampened by the lingering effects of past weak investment and subdued investment prospects, diminishing demographic dividends, and more limited avenues for technological diffusion, especially in the face of rising protectionism (World Bank 2019e).

Per capita income growth and poverty

The number of people living in extreme poverty—below $1.90 per day—has fallen by more than 1 billion over the past three decades, and remarkable progress has been made on several development indicators. Yet, meeting the Sustainable Development Goals (SDGs) by 2030 appears out of reach for many EMDEs (Figure 1.13.A). Extreme poverty rates are estimated to exceed 30 percent of the population in one-quarter of economies. Around 830 million people still live without electricity. Approximately 2 billion people do not have access to at least basic sanitation services. In LICs, child mortality rates are around triple their SDG target, while access to essential health services remains deficient.

To meet the infrastructure-related SDGs alone will require annual investment equivalent to 4.5 percent to 8.2 percent of low- and middle-income countries' GDP between 2015 and 2030 (Rozenberg and Fay 2019; Vorisek and Yu, forthcoming). The severity of this challenge has been amplified by the loss of momentum in EMDE per capita income growth during recent years (Figures 1.13.B and 1.13.C). Given sustained headwinds to activity, per capita income growth in EMDEs is expected to stabilize around 3.2 percent over the near term—well below long-term averages. Lower income growth will also adversely affect poverty reduction efforts, and there is already evidence that poverty reduction has started to slow (Ruch 2019a; World Bank 2018c).

In about one-quarter of EMDEs—mostly commodity exporters—per capita growth will be inadequate to prevent income gaps from widening relative to advanced economies. In Sub-Saharan Africa—home to 24 of the 31 LICs and almost 60 percent of the world's extreme poor—per capita

BOX 1.2 Regional perspectives: Recent developments and outlook

Growth in almost all EMDE regions was weaker than expected in 2019, reflecting downgrades to more than half of EMDEs. Activity in most regions is expected to pick up in 2020-21, but the recovery will largely depend on a rebound in a small number of large EMDEs, some of which are emerging from deep recessions or sharp slowdowns.

East Asia and Pacific. Growth in the region is projected to slow from an estimated 5.8 percent in 2019 to 5.7 percent in 2020 and moderate further to 5.6 percent in 2021-22. Easier financing conditions and fiscal policy support will partly mitigate the lingering impact of trade tensions amid domestic challenges. In China, growth is expected to slow gradually, from an estimated 6.1 percent in 2019, to 5.9 percent in 2020, and to 5.7 percent by 2022. In the rest of the region, growth is expected to recover slightly to 4.9 percent in 2020 and firm further to 5 percent in 2021-22. The balance of risks has improved, but risks to the outlook are still tilted to the downside. They include a sharp slowdown in global trade due to renewed escalation of trade tensions amid a fragile global outlook; a sharper-than-expected slowdown in major economies; and a sudden reversal of capital flows due to an abrupt deterioration in financing conditions, investor sentiment, or geopolitical relations. An upside risk to the forecast is related to stronger-than-expected recovery of regional investment and trade amid a sustained de-escalation of trade tensions between China and the United States.

Europe and Central Asia. Growth in the region decelerated to an estimated 2 percent in 2019, reflecting a sharp slowdown in Turkey as a result of acute financial market stress in 2018, as well as in the Russian Federation amid weak demand and cuts in oil production. Regional growth is projected to strengthen in 2020, to 2.6 percent, as activity recovers in Turkey and Russia, and to stabilize to 2.9 percent in 2021-22. Key external risks to the regional growth outlook include spillovers from weaker-than-expected activity in the Euro Area and escalation of global policy uncertainty. The region also remains vulnerable to disorderly commodity and financial market developments.

Latin America and the Caribbean. Growth in the region slowed markedly in 2019, to an estimated 0.8 percent, held back by idiosyncratic factors in large economies, headwinds from slowing global trade, and social unrest in several countries. As activity in Brazil gathers pace amid improving investment conditions, policy uncertainty in

Mexico fades, and the recession in Argentina eases after bouts of severe market stress, regional growth is projected to rise to 1.8 percent in 2020 and about 2.4 percent in 2021. This recovery will not be sufficient to reverse the growing per capita income gap with advanced economies in some LAC economies. Moreover, the regional outlook is subject to significant downside risks, including from market volatility and adverse market responses to weak fiscal conditions; deeper-than-expected spillovers from slowdowns in Argentina, China, and the United States; heightened social unrest; and disruptions from natural disasters and severe weather.

Middle East and North Africa. Regional growth decelerated to an estimated 0.1 percent in 2019. Geopolitical and policy constraints on oil sector production slowed growth in oil-exporting economies, despite support from public spending. Growth in oil importers remained stable, as reform progress and resilient tourism activity were offset by structural and external headwinds. Regional growth is projected to pick up to 2.4 percent in 2020 and to about 2.8 percent in 2021-22, as infrastructure investment and business climate reforms proceed. Risks are tilted firmly to the downside—geopolitical tensions, escalation of armed conflicts, slower-than-expected pace of reforms, or weaker-than-expected growth in key trading partners could heavily constrain activity.

South Asia. Growth in the region is estimated to have decelerated to 4.9 percent in 2019, reflecting a sharper-than-expected and broad-based weakening in domestic demand. In India, activity was constrained by insufficient credit availability, as well as by subdued private consumption. Regional growth is expected to pick up gradually, to 6 percent in 2022, on the assumption of a modest rebound in domestic demand. While growth in Bangladesh is projected to remain above 7 percent through the forecast horizon, growth in Pakistan is projected to languish at 3 percent or less through 2020 as macroeconomic stabilization efforts weigh on activity. Growth in India is projected to decelerate to 5 percent in FY2019/20 amid enduring financial sector issues. Key risks to the outlook include a sharper-than-expected slowdown in major economies, a reescalation of regional geopolitical tensions, and a setback in reforms to address impaired balance sheets in the financial and corporate sectors.

Note: This box was prepared by Patrick Kirby with contributions from Rudi Steinbach, Temel Taskin, Ekaterine Vashakmadze, Dana Vorisek, Collette Wheeler, and Lei Ye. Research assistance was provided by Hazel Macadangdang.

BOX 1.2 Regional perspectives: Recent developments and outlook (*continued*)

FIGURE 1.2.1 Regional growth

Growth in almost all EMDE regions was weaker than expected in 2019, reflecting downgrades to more than half of EMDEs. Activity in most regions is expected to pick up in 2020-21, but the recovery will largely depend on a rebound in a small number of large EMDEs, some of which are emerging from deep recessions or sharp slowdowns.

A. Regional growth, weighted average

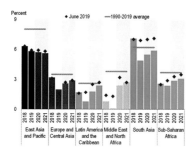

B. Regional growth, unweighted average

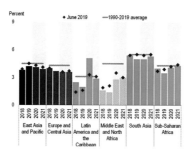

C. Regional investment, weighted average

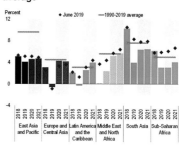

D. Regional exports, weighted average

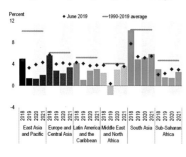

E. GDP growth in ECA, weighted average

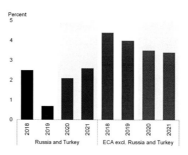

F. GDP growth in LAC, weighted average

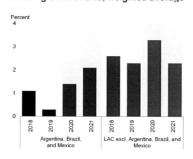

Source: World Bank.

A.-D. Bars denote latest forecast; diamonds correspond to January 2020 forecasts in the *Global Economic Prospects* report. Average for 1990-2019 is constructed depending on data availability. For Europe and Central Asia, the long-term average uses data for 1995-2019 to exclude the immediate aftermath of the collapse of the Soviet Union.

A.C.D.E.F. Aggregate growth rates calculated using GDP weights at 2010 prices and market exchange rates. Since the largest economies account for about 50 percent of GDP in some regions, weighted averages predominantly reflect the developments in the largest economies in each region. Shaded areas indicate forecasts.

B. Unweighted average regional growth is used to ensure broad reflection of regional trends across all countries in the region.

Sub-Saharan Africa. Growth in the region moderated to a slower-than-expected 2.4 percent in 2019. Activity was dampened by softening external demand, heightened global policy uncertainty, and falling commodity prices. Domestic fragilities in several countries further constrained activity. Growth is projected to firm to 2.9 percent in 2020 and strengthen to 3.2 percent in 2021-22—notably weaker than previous projections. The growth pickup is predicated on improving investor confidence in some large economies, a strengthening cyclical recovery among industrial commodity exporters along with a pickup in oil production, and robust growth among several exporters of agricultural commodities. Nonetheless, these growth rates will be insufficient to make significant progress in reducing poverty in many countries in Sub-Saharan Africa, highlighting the need for lasting improvements in labor productivity to bolster growth over the medium term. Downside risks to the outlook include a sharper-than-expected deceleration in major trading partners; increased investor risk aversion and capital outflows triggered by elevated debt burdens; and growing insecurity.

income growth over the forecast horizon is expected to remain below 1 percent. In contrast, per capita incomes are forecast to rise close to 5 percent per year in East Asia and Pacific and South Asia. As a result, the rapid declines in the number of extreme poor living in these two fast-growing regions are likely to continue over the near term. Absent major policy efforts to lift per capita growth, global extreme poverty will become increasingly concentrated in Sub-Saharan Africa (Figure 1.13.D; Beegle and Christiaensen 2019; World Bank 2018c).

Risks to the outlook

Global growth, which weakened to an estimated 2.4 percent in 2019, is projected to edge up to 2.5 percent this year, following an expected recovery of trade and investment. Despite a recent notable reduction in the threat of protectionism, risks to the global outlook remain on the downside. A re-escalation of global trade tensions could further weigh on world activity. Amid financial sector vulnerabilities, major economies could slow more than expected. EMDEs remain at risk of financial stress, especially those with elevated debt, while some EMDE regions could be affected by geopolitical tensions, social unrest, large swings in commodity prices, or increasingly volatile weather patterns. On the upside, further de-escalation of trade tensions between the United States and China could continue to mitigate global policy uncertainty and bolster activity.

Summary of global outlook and risks

In light of softening trade and manufacturing, global growth weakened to an estimated 2.4 percent last year. This was the slowest pace of expansion since the global financial crisis—below that registered in 2012, when the Euro Area suffered a serious debt crisis, and in 2015-16, when many EMDE commodity exporters were facing large declines in commodity prices and concerns about China's economy were widespread. As international trade and investment recover, global growth is projected to edge up to 2.5 percent in 2020—0.2 percentage point below previous forecasts—and gradually firm over the forecast horizon, reaching 2.7 percent by 2022.

Near-term projections for global growth mask diverging contours for the forecasts for advanced economies and EMDEs. Aggregate growth in advanced economies is expected to slow from 1.6 percent in 2019 to 1.4 percent in 2020, primarily reflecting a deceleration in the United States and anemic activity elsewhere. In contrast, EMDE growth is envisioned to pick up from 3.5 percent in 2019 to 4.1 percent this year, mostly as a result of a pickup in a small number of large economies, some of which are emerging from deep recessions or sharp slowdowns and whose outlooks are therefore fragile. Absent this group of countries, EMDE growth would be essentially stagnant and, with advanced economies decelerating, global growth would actually slow. This indicates that weaker-than-expected activity in this small set of EMDEs could derail the expected recovery in EMDE—and global—growth.

The contribution of EMDEs to the projected pickup in global growth also hinges on the weighting methodology. Using market exchange rates, as is done in these baseline projections, yields the aforementioned tepid recovery of global growth. Using purchasing power parity (PPP), however, places greater weight on EMDEs—which are forecast to grow faster than advanced economies—and thus results in a somewhat more pronounced global pickup.

As a result of the greater emphasis on the contribution of EMDEs—especially large, fast-growing ones—to global activity, global growth is projected at 3.2 percent in 2020 using PPP weights, compared to 2.5 percent using market exchange rates (Table 1.1). This is because EMDEs are expected to account for 40 percent of this year's global output using market exchange rates but 60 percent using PPP weights. In particular, China's share of global GDP in 2020 is expected to be around 15 percent using market exchange rates but 20 percent using PPP weights. In fact, of the 0.7 percentage point difference in 2020 global growth projections between the two weighting methods, China accounts for over 50 percent, with the three next largest contributors to the difference in global growth accounting for the vast majority of the remainder.

FIGURE 1.14 Balance of risks

Amid heightened uncertainty about the economic outlook, risks to global growth remain tilted to the downside. The probability of 2020 global growth being a full 1 percentage point or more below baseline forecasts is almost 20 percent and above historical averages.

A. Probability distribution around global growth forecasts

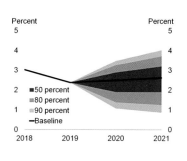

B. Probability of global growth being 1 percentage point below current baseline

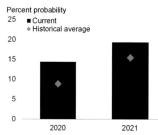

Source: Bloomberg; World Bank.
A.B. The fan chart shows the forecast distribution of global growth using time-varying estimates of the standard deviation and skewness extracted from the forecast distribution of three underlying risk factors: Oil price futures, S&P 500 equity price futures, and term spread forecasts. Each of the risk factor's weight is derived from the model described in Ohnsorge, Stocker, and Some (2016). Values for 2020 are computed from the forecast distribution of 12-month-ahead oil price futures, S&P 500 equity price futures, and term spread forecasts. Values for 2021 are based on 24-month-ahead forecast distributions. Last observation is December 19, 2019.

Regardless of the weighting scheme, baseline projections for global growth represent a scenario based on numerous benign assumptions. They include no re-escalation of global trade tensions, a mitigation in global policy uncertainty, no sharp slowdown in major economies, no financial stress in large EMDEs, stability in commodity prices, and—critically—the avoidance of policy missteps. Accordingly, there is substantial uncertainty surrounding these baseline projections (Figure 1.14.A).

On balance, risks to the outlook are on the downside (Ruch 2019a). The trade conflict between the United States and China could re-escalate, and trade tensions involving other major economies could emerge. Policy uncertainty could rise significantly and persistently. Some EMDEs could suffer full-fledged financial crises. Commodity markets could see disruptive swings. The United States or the Euro Area could suffer deepening slowdowns, or China could slow sharply—and the potentially large associated spillovers could substantially erode the EMDE outlook. Importantly, many of these risks are intertwined.

The materialization of one or more of these risks could lead to a more severe global downturn—a situation many economies are not adequately prepared to confront (Ruch 2019b). Reflecting a preponderance of downside risks, the probability that global growth in 2020 will be at least one percentage point below baseline projections is almost 20 percent, above historical averages. (Figure 1.14.B).

Although downside risks predominate, there is also the possibility that major headwinds dissipate and the expected recovery is stronger than expected. In particular, recent policy developments—particularly those that have mitigated U.S.-China trade tensions—could lead to a sustained reduction in policy uncertainty and bolster confidence, trade, and investment, which is an important upside risk to the outlook.

Rising trade barriers and protracted policy uncertainty

After decades of trade liberalization, protectionist measures have been implemented on a growing share of global trade (WTO 2019b). At the same time, the number of trade agreements coming into effect has fallen sharply. Progress on the ratification of important trade agreements such as EU-MERCOSUR has stalled. The WTO dispute settlement system became deadlocked in December, threatening a key pillar of the global rules-based trading system. Without a well-established arbitration system, countries may use damaging unilateral or retaliatory trade policies to resolve the increasing number of trade disputes (Figure 1.15.A). The rising number of trade restrictions and the associated uncertainty around them have contributed to the recent contraction in global trade and the slowdown in global growth. The ratio of global trade-to-GDP growth has fallen below 1, far exceeding the slowdown that would be expected from the ongoing maturation of global value chains (Figure 1.15.B).

Additional tariffs have been imposed on the majority of bilateral trade between the United States and China over the past year. Despite the announcement of the Phase One trade agreement that resulted in the cancellation of planned tariff increases, re-escalation remains possible—many commitments, including items related to the expansion of bilateral trade, intellectual property, and technology transfer, may be difficult to enforce.

The United States and China together account for nearly 40 percent of global GDP, nearly a quarter of global trade, and an even larger share of capital goods trade (Figure 1.15.C). Accordingly, renewed disruption to U.S.-China economic ties could result in damage not only to these two economies but to the rest of the world, as its effects would propagate through trade, financial, and commodity linkages. There is also the risk that trade tensions could extend to a broader set of countries. The imposition of U.S. tariffs on automobiles and parts imports would impact a globally important sector that is already struggling, likely resulting in retaliation. The global multilateral trading system could be put at risk by a continuous rise in trade barriers stemming from many countries.

In the longer run, protectionism would have serious negative consequences for the global economy, including by contributing to a further decline in the trade intensity of global growth, reducing productivity growth, and lowering real incomes (Barattieri, Cacciatore, and Ghironi 2018). The fragmentation of global value chains would cause efficiency losses for producers and higher prices for consumers. Exporting firms, which tend to be more productive than exclusively domestic firms, may need to redesign their supply chains using costlier inputs and bearing the cost of writing off stranded assets (Atkin, Khandelwal, and Osman 2017; Bernard and Jensen 2004).

Despite recent progress in the resolution of trade conflicts, the impact of rising protectionism on global growth has been magnified by protracted policy uncertainty and a decline in confidence (Figure 1.15.D). A further increase in trade policy uncertainty could continue to be a material contributor to the softening of global growth (Caldara et al. 2019). Companies that are uncertain about the framework for doing business in the future are reluctant to invest, often preferring to delay major, irreversible decisions until the uncertainty has been resolved (Handley and Limão 2015; Stokey 2016). If, in contrast to

FIGURE 1.15 Rising trade barriers and protracted policy uncertainty

After decades of trade liberalization, there has been a marked increase in protectionist measures and trade disputes, contributing to a slowdown in global trade growth. A re-escalation of U.S.-China trade tensions, or a deterioration in trade relations involving a broader set of countries, could substantially heighten policy uncertainty and further damage business confidence and activity.

A. Trade disputes

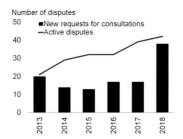

B. Ratio of global trade to GDP growth

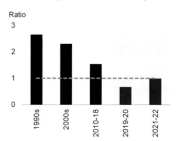

C. U.S. and China share of global indicators, in 2018

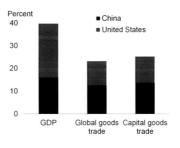

D. Global trade policy uncertainty and business confidence

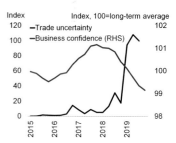

Source: Ahir, Bloom, and Furceri (2018); Haver Analytics; International Monetary Fund; Organisation for Economic Co-operation and Development; World Bank; World Trade Organization.
A. Figure shows monthly average of active disputes.
B. Shaded area indicates forecasts. Trade measured as the average of import and export volumes.
C. Trade measured as the average of goods exports and imports. Capital goods trade includes capital goods and transport equipment.
D. Trade policy-related uncertainty is an index presented in Ahir, Bloom, and Furceri (2018) for 143 countries on a quarterly basis. Business confidence data are end of period and include 7 advanced economies and 5 EMDEs. Aggregate business confidence calculated using GDP weights at 2010 prices and market exchange rates. Last observation is 2019Q3 for trade policy uncertainty. Business confidence data for 2019Q4 use October 2019.

baseline assumptions, policy uncertainty was to rise further, the resulting impact on investment would have critical consequences for activity in both the short and long term.

A deepening slowdown in major economies

The United States, the Euro Area, and China are the world's largest economies. All three suffered a marked deceleration of activity in 2019 and face downside risks (Figure 1.16.A). A deepening slowdown in any of these economies would worsen economic prospects in countries around

FIGURE 1.16 A deepening slowdown in major economies

Activity decelerated substantially in major economies in 2019. The U.S. corporate sector and the Euro Area banking sector exhibit vulnerabilities that could contribute to a deeper slowdown, which would have sizable spillovers and increase the probability of a global downturn. In China, private debt as a share of GDP is well above levels observed prior to slowdowns in other EMDEs. Stress in the financial system could lead to either a crisis or an extended period of slow growth as deleveraging drags on activity.

A. Growth in the United States, Euro Area, and China

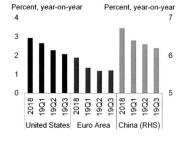

B. U.S. financial vulnerability indicators

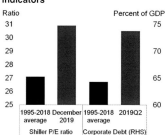

C. Measures of health for Euro Area banks

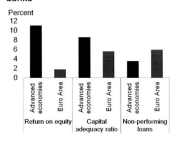

D. Probability of global downturn given U.S. or Euro Area recession

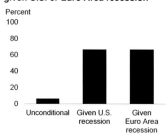

E. Private sector debt in China compared with peaks in other EMDEs

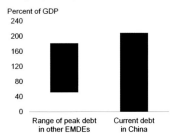

F. Share of EMDEs slowing after reaching debt peaks

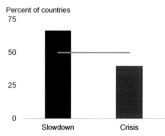

Source: Bank for International Settlements; Center for Economic Policy and Research; Economic Cycle Research Institute; European Central Bank; Haver Analytics; Institute of International Finance; International Monetary Fund; Kose and Terrones (2015); Laeven and Valencia (2018); National Bureau of Economic Research; Shiller (2015); World Bank.
A. Data are seasonally adjusted for the United States and the Euro Area, and not for China.
B. Last observation is December 2019 for Shiller Price-to-Earnings (P/E) ratio and 2019Q2 for debt.
C. Return on equity is calculated using the average of 2008 to 2018. Euro Area aggregates calculated using nominal U.S. dollar GDP weights of France, Germany, Italy, and Spain, as available. Capital adequacy ratio and non-performing loans are calculated using the average of 2009 to 2017. Advanced economy aggregates calculated using available data for 37 advanced economies.
D. Figure shows the probability of a global downturn occurring given a U.S. or Euro Area recession. Probabilities are based on annual data—the number of years with events divided by the total number of years. U.S. recessions dated by National Bureau of Economic Research. Euro Area recessions dated by the Center for Economic and Policy Research. German recessions are used prior to the formation of the Euro Area. From 1958 to 2018, there have been four global recessions, in 1975, 1982, 1991, and 2009, and three global slowdowns, in 1998, 2001, and 2012.
E. Debt peaks defined as the highest value of private non-financial credit to GDP over the period 1960Q1 to 2019Q2. Sample includes 15 EMDEs. For China, the last observation is 2019Q2.
F. Economies must have experienced a currency, systemic banking, or sovereign debt crisis within two years after reaching the peak debt-to-GDP ratio. A slowdown is defined as a 1 percentage point or more drop in GDP growth between the two years before and the two years after peak debt-to-GDP ratio. Sample includes 15 EMDEs from 1960Q1 to 2019Q1.

the world through direct trade linkages and commodity prices, as well as through financial and confidence channels. This could derail the anticipated recovery in EMDE growth (World Bank 2016a). The Latin America and the Caribbean region would be particularly impacted by a sharp deceleration in the United States, while economies in Europe and Central Asia would be disproportionately affected by deepening weakness in the Euro Area. Spillovers from a slowdown in China would have sizable effects on the country's trading partners and in commodity producers (Ahmed et al. 2019; Stocker et al. 2018; World Bank 2016a).

United States

In the United States, growth is expected to decelerate as earlier tariff increases, lingering uncertainty, and fiscal policy all exert a drag on activity. High corporate debt and elevated equity valuations increase the economy's susceptibility to a more severe downturn (Figure 1.16.B). In the current environment of low rates, some high-yield borrowers have benefited from investors' search for yield. For example, leveraged loan issuance has increased rapidly, with borrowers benefitting from low spreads and loose lending standards. This increase has been facilitated by financial institutions bundling many lower-rated loans into more highly rated securities known as collateralized loan obligations (Federal Reserve Board 2019). A sudden decline in the perceived creditworthiness of borrowers could lead to a rapid fall in asset valuations and a localized credit crunch (Bank of England 2019). More generally, rising interest rates could slow activity across the entire corporate sector. Consumption has been the sole pillar supporting economic growth in recent quarters, but this would be undermined if tightening credit conditions and declining business confidence—for example, triggered by further increases in policy uncertainty—slowed hiring and wage growth.

Euro Area

The Euro Area economy has already weakened considerably. Vulnerabilities in the banking system could lead to a further slowdown, given that banks are the region's primary source of credit and—despite some recent improvement—continue to suffer from low profitability and elevated levels of non-performing loans (Figure 1.16.C). Negative interest rates in the region could further undermine bank profitability and erode financial stability, possibly impacting sovereign borrowing costs through the "sovereign-bank" nexus (Arteta et al. 2016; Feyen and Zuccardi 2019; Molyneux, Reghezza, and Xie forthcoming). An unexpected bank failure—generated, for example, by exposure to Germany's struggling industrial sector or sharp movements in asset prices following Brexit—could trigger broader financial stress and an associated loss of confidence. As with the United States, a severe slowdown in the Euro Area would substantially increase the probability of a more severe global downturn (Figure 1.16.D).

China

China's primary vulnerability is its high and rising stock of private debt in its increasingly complex and interconnected financial system (Arteta and Kasyanenko 2019; IMF and World Bank 2017). Credit to non-financial corporates and households as a share of GDP nearly doubled in the last decade, reaching about 210 percent in the first quarter of 2019, well above the share observed prior to previous growth slowdowns and financial crises in other EMDEs (Figure 1.16.E). The effectiveness of credit in stimulating growth appears to be declining, which implies that the benefits of any further increase in credit would diminish while risks would rise (Chen and Kang 2018). Rising defaults in local banks or in the shadow banking system, a collapse in property prices, or large capital outflows alongside a sharp adjustment in asset prices could all ripple through the highly leveraged financial system. This risk is only partly mitigated by the country's low reliance on external financing and ample capacity for fiscal and monetary support.

Alternatively, while a crisis could be avoided with policy support given China's sizable policy buffers, the transition toward consumer-led and less credit-driven growth may lead to an extended period of subdued growth in the absence of deep structural reforms. Moreover, private deleveraging may act as a persistent drag on activity, as is commonly the

case following periods of rapid debt accumulation (Figure 1.16.F; Kose, Sugawara, and Terrones 2019).

Financial stress in EMDEs

EMDE debt burdens for both public and private borrowers have grown considerably in recent years as part of the most recent global wave of debt (Figure 1.17.A; Chapter 4). Generally benign global financial conditions have reduced debt-service burdens for many EMDEs, but they may also be encouraging further debt accumulation, with prospect of persistently low advanced-economy interest rates pushing some foreign lenders to look for higher returns in EMDEs. In some areas, debt is increasingly flowing to riskier borrowers. Elevated debt can make economies vulnerable to large depreciations, capital outflows, financial stress, and abrupt policy tightening, particularly when it is financed from abroad. In addition, solvency risks in the non-bank financial sector are mounting in some large EMDEs (Arteta and Kasyanenko 2019).

Recent credit booms in EMDEs have largely been used to fund consumption rather than investment (Figure 1.17.B; Chapter 4; Arteta and Kasyanenko 2019). This carries the risk that rising debt will not be matched by rising growth, increasing the likelihood and impact of a loss of investor confidence. When such a loss is combined with an elevated proportion of debt denominated in foreign currency, capital flight and depreciation would add to existing debt sustainability concerns and magnify the negative feedback loop (Bruno and Shin 2018).

In the past, EMDEs have been vulnerable to a broad-based strengthening of the U.S. dollar (Figure 1.17.C). Amid rapidly increasing non-financial-sector debt, sharp dollar appreciation due to interest rate differentials or generalized flight to safety can expose currency and maturity mismatches and trigger widespread corporate insolvencies (Caballero, Fernández, and Park 2019; Chui, Kuruc, and Turner 2016). Large depreciations are associated with higher borrowing costs, and monetary authorities are often required to tighten to stabilize currencies or resist the passthrough of higher import costs to domestic

FIGURE 1.17 Financial stress in EMDEs

EMDE debt burdens have grown considerably in recent years for both public and private borrowers; however, recent credit booms have generally not been accompanied by rising investment. A loss in investor confidence could lead to an increase in bond spreads, as could a sharp U.S. dollar appreciation arising from flight to safety or other factors.

A. EMDE debt levels

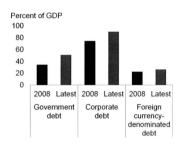

B. Investment surges during recent credit booms

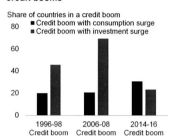

C. Bond spreads and exchange rates

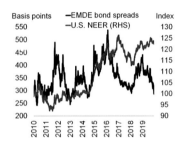

D. Bond spreads in previous episodes of stress

Source: Bank for International Settlements; Haver Analytics; International Monetary Fund; J.P. Morgan; Kose et al. (2017); World Bank.

A. Aggregate for foreign-currency-denominated debt is calculated using moving GDP weights at 2010 prices and market exchange rates, excluding 2002-05 due to missing data. "Latest" indicates 2019Q2 for government debt and corporate debt, and 2018 for foreign-currency-denominated debt.

B. A credit boom is defined as an episode during which the cyclical component of the nonfinancial private sector credit-to-GDP ratio (using a Hodrick-Prescott filter) is larger than 1.65 times its standard deviation in at least one year. The episode starts when the cyclical component first exceeds one standard deviation and ends in a peak year ("0") when the nonfinancial private sector credit-to-GDP ratio declines in the following year. Consumption and investment surges are defined as periods when the cyclical component of the consumption-to-GDP/investment-to-GDP ratio is at least one standard deviation above the HP-filtered trend. See Chapter 4 for more details.

C. NEER = nominal effective exchange rate. Bond spreads are represented by J.P. Morgan's Emerging Market Bond Index (EMBI). Last observation is December 18, 2019.

D. "t=0" indicates May 2013, June 2015, and March 2018. Bond spreads are represented by J.P. Morgan's Emerging Market Bond Index (EMBI).

inflation (Figure 1.17.D). Similarly, large swings in commodity prices can potentially lead to disruptive currency movements and balance of payments difficulties for vulnerable EMDEs.

The risk of contagion of country-specific financial distress across markets may be growing. Foreign portfolio investors and global mutual funds are becoming more active in local bond markets, accounting for an increasing share of local-currency-denominated sovereign bonds. As a result, EMDE financial markets are now more

tightly integrated into the global financial system. While this has benefits, it also facilitates the contagion of global financial shocks both to foreign-currency and, to a lesser extent, local-currency debt markets (Agur et al. 2018; Arteta and Kasyanenko 2019; Cerutti, Claessens, and Puy 2019). The risk of contagion is further amplified by constrained policy room for crisis response and weaker buffers against external shocks.

Geopolitical and region-specific downside risks

Downside risks to the global outlook are compounded by various geopolitical and region-specific concerns. Geopolitical risks remain acute globally and in several regions (Ruch 2019a). The disruption in Saudi oil production in mid-September highlights the potential for renewed tensions in the Middle East. In addition, if skirmishes in Eastern Europe and in South Asia escalate, there could be important consequences for growth in the associated regions.

Amid geopolitical concerns, a sustained disruption in oil production may increase energy prices, to the detriment of affected suppliers and commodity importers. While commodity producers left unaffected by the disruption could potentially benefit from higher prices, these benefits can be undone if the price increase is accompanied by heightened volatility (van Eyden et al. 2019).

Alternatively, regions with a large presence of oil producers, particularly MENA, would be adversely affected by a sharp fall in oil prices resulting from weaker-than-expected demand amid subdued global growth. A sudden increase in supply—reflecting, for instance, increased production in the United States—could also lead to a more meaningful decline in prices. Such a decline could lead to substantial fiscal tightening, as was the case in 2014-16 (Figure 1.18.A; Stocker et al. 2018). Falls in metals or agricultural prices could follow a similar pattern and would also have a serious impact on economies in regions such as Sub-Saharan Africa, Latin America and the Caribbean, or Europe and Central Asia. While regions with large numbers of commodity importers would face a positive terms-of-trade shock, these gains would likely be diffused across many economies, only partially offsetting the relatively larger losses faced by commodity exporters.

Social unrest has been on the rise in a growing number of countries in various regions, motivated by discontent about some combination of inequality, slow growth, governance, and economic policy. Unrest has the potential to disrupt activity and damage infrastructure. It may also make fiscal consolidation efforts more challenging for governments trying to ease tensions.

Climate change is increasing the frequency of severe weather events and lowering agricultural productivity in some regions (IPCC 2018). As such, its impact is more detrimental for regions that have large numbers of countries with less resilient infrastructure and a larger share of agricultural production. These countries tend to be poor and can ill-afford the lost infrastructure and income that accompanies extreme weather and poor harvests. Similarly, regions with large coastal populations are at risk, not only from extreme weather, but also from rising sea levels. Climate change also presents risks to the financial system in some EMDEs, as the need to incorporate climate risks into asset valuations and insurance coverage calculations increases the risk of mispricing (Figure 1.18.B). Rapid repricing is possible, for example, as more information becomes available about what assets are most at risk from rising sea levels or less habitable weather conditions (NGFS 2018).

Upside risks

Although downside risks predominate, there is also the possibility that the global recovery is stronger than expected. Existing headwinds to growth—including those related to policy uncertainty—could further dissipate, or additional macroeconomic policy support could be deployed in response.

Heightened policy uncertainty exerted a notable drag on activity throughout 2019, much of it related to concerns about rising trade barriers. The

FIGURE 1.18 Other downside risks

A sustained decline in the price of oil or other commodities could lead to substantial fiscal tightening in commodity exporters, as was the case in 2014-16. Climate change is increasing the frequency of severe weather events and the volatility of agricultural conditions. Rising losses from severe weather events related to climate change increase the risk of financial instability.

A. Change in overall fiscal balance in oil-exporting EMDE sub-groups, from 2014-16

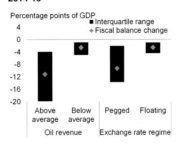

B. Rising frequency and costs from natural disasters

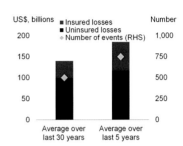

Source: International Monetary Fund; Munich Reinsurance Company; World Bank.
A. Exchange rate classification is based on the IMF's Annual Report on Exchange Arrangements and Exchange Restrictions database, in which countries are ranked 0 (no separate legal tender) to 10 (free float). "Pegged" denotes countries ranked 1 to 6. "Floating" denotes countries ranked 7 to 10. Sample includes 27 oil-exporting EMDEs, based on data availability. Change in overall fiscal balance is measured from 2014-16. Above average and below average oil revenue groups are defined by countries above or below the sample average of oil revenues as a share of GDP based on 2014 data.
B. Global natural disasters and economic losses statistics from Munich Reinsurance Company including loss estimation based on Property Claim Services (PCS). The 30-year average represents 1988-2017. 5-year average represents 2014-2018. Losses adjusted to inflation based on local CPI.

recent trade agreement between the United States and China that reverses some tariff increases could be the beginning of a constructive process leading to a sustained reduction in policy uncertainty and trade barriers. This could significantly improve confidence and unlock pent-up demand for investment, bolstering growth (Figure 1.19.A). Similarly, rapid progress on the post-Brexit trade negotiations between the United Kingdom and the European Union could lift a cloud on Europe's outlook.

Central banks provided significant accommodation over the course of 2019, which is expected to contribute to the pickup in activity over the near term. On a global level, falling policy rates have coincided with declining inflation, suggesting that there is scope for further monetary easing, mainly for some EMDEs (Figure 1.19.B). In addition to the potential boost to growth from monetary policy, some major advanced economies with sufficient space could choose to provide additional fiscal support.

FIGURE 1.19 **Upside risks**

Sustained progress in the resolution of U.S.-China trade tensions would reduce policy uncertainty, which could unlock pent-up demand for investment. A continued decline in global inflation could open the door to further monetary stimulus.

A. Impact of a 10-percent decrease in U.S. policy uncertainty on investment growth

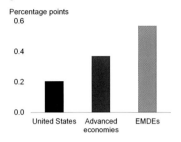

B. Change in global inflation and interest rates over the last year

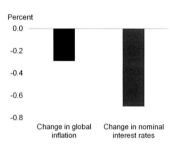

Source: Baker, Bloom, and Davis (2016); Bank for International Settlements; Bloomberg; Haver Analytics; World Bank.
A. Figure shows median growth impact of 10 percent fall in U.S. economic policy uncertainty (EPU). See Annex SF.1B of World Bank (2017a) for details on the methodology.
B. Calculations based on change in year-on-year global inflation and nominal interest rate between November 2018 and November 2019. Aggregate nominal interest rate calculated using GDP weights at 2010 prices and market exchange rates. Unbalanced samples include 35 advanced economies and 77 EMDEs, including 39 low-income countries, for nominal interest rates and include 36 advanced economies and 112 EMDEs for inflation. Last observation is November 2019.

FIGURE 1.20 **Monetary and financial policies in advanced economies**

Weak growth and low inflation have prevented major central banks from removing policy accommodation in the post-crisis period. As a result, policy rates are at or close to their effective lower bounds in many economies. Longer-term yields have also fallen, limiting the remaining room for other policy tools, such as forward guidance and quantitative easing.

A. Monetary policy rate increases during current and previous expansions

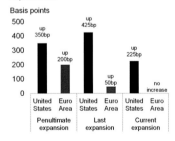

B. Policy rates and 10-year sovereign yields

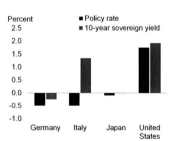

Source: Bank of Japan; Bloomberg; European Central Bank; Federal Reserve System; Haver Analytics; National Bureau of Economic Research; World Bank.
A. U.S. expansions: 1991-2001, 2001-07, 2009-present. Euro Area expansions: 1999-2008, 2009-11, 2013-present. Calculations based on trough and peak of policy rates of each period. Last observation is November 2019 for the United States and 2019Q3 for the Euro Area.
B. Figure shows data as of December 18, 2019.

Policy challenges

Challenges in advanced economies

Very low interest rates highlight the limited room that advanced-economy central banks have to provide additional accommodation. If persistent, they may also erode the health of financial institutions. However, low borrowing costs have loosened some of the constraints on fiscal policy allowing for increased public investment or other support in countries with fiscal space, if needed. Fiscal positions could also be improved through better tax compliance and enforcement. Productivity growth in advanced economies has declined due to weak investment growth and aging populations. Reducing policy uncertainty would buttress capital formation.

Monetary and financial policies

The combination of feeble growth and stubbornly subdued inflation in the post-crisis period has made it difficult for major central banks to remove policy accommodation (Figure 1.20.A). Policy rates remain very low in most countries, and close to their effective lower bound, greatly limiting the ability to further cut rates. Other policy tools, such as policy guidance or quantitative easing, have been used to help lower long-term interest rates as short-term rates approached their lower-bound (Woodford 2012). However, the limits of these tools may also have been reached, with long-term yields in many economies, including Germany and Japan, now below zero (Figure 1.20.B). The downward trend in interest rates, and the associated challenges for monetary policy, appears to be a persistent phenomenon, driven in part by a fundamental weaknesses in investment demand across advanced economies (Rachel and Summers 2019; Williams 2016).

A number of ideas have been put forward to improve the traction of monetary policy, including targeting price levels or nominal GDP rather than inflation, stimulating activity through direct transfers to households, and eliminating the lower bound by subordinating paper money to central-bank electronic money (Agarwal and Kimball 2019; Buiter 2014; Mertens and Williams 2019). These come with their own risks and tradeoffs, including the difficulty of transitioning from one framework to another while maintaining the credibility and public understanding that is essential for the effective operation of monetary policy.

Aside from the constraints it places on monetary policy, an extended period of low or negative interest rates may also be detrimental to the health of financial institutions, as their interest rate margins become squeezed (Arteta et al. 2016; Brunnermeier and Koby 2019). For banks, low interest rates can reduce profitability—and therefore resilience in the face of negative shocks—and encourage greater risk taking. Non-bank financial institutions, which account for an increasing share of credit issuance, are also affected. Pension funds and insurance companies often have fixed future liabilities and may be compelled to invest in riskier and less liquid assets in order to meet their nominal return targets. Increased lending to over-leveraged borrowers may be sowing the seeds for future financial stress, especially given uncertainty about non-bank behavior and its impact on the financial system during a downturn (IMF 2019b). Regulatory reforms have made the global financial system more resilient since the global financial crisis; however, prudential authorities need to remain vigilant to risks originating from the growing importance of non-bank financial institutions, and be wary of vulnerabilities being masked by technological innovations and complex financial products (FSB 2019b).

Fiscal policy

In many advanced economies, households are deleveraging and corporate investment is weak, leaving aggregate demand unusually dependent on government borrowing (Figure 1.21.A). Further fiscal support may become necessary given the combination of slowing activity, elevated downside risks, and limited room for monetary policy accommodation. Many countries are carrying persistent deficits, however, despite the budgetary benefits of the global decline in interest rates.

One growth-friendly approach that advanced economies can take to improve their fiscal

FIGURE 1.21 Fiscal policy in advanced economies

In many advanced economies, households are deleveraging and corporate investment is weak, leaving aggregate demand unusually dependent on government borrowing. Public investment can bolster growth in both the short and long term, and increase the stock of public capital, which has fallen in a number of economies.

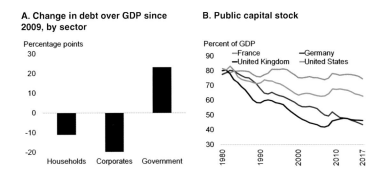

Source: Institute of International Finance; International Monetary Fund; World Bank.
A. Figure shows the change in the debt-to-GDP ratio since 2009. Sector aggregates are calculated using GDP weights at 2010 prices and market exchange rates. Sample includes 23 advanced economies. Last observation is 2019Q2.
B. Lines represent the ratio of general public capital stock to GDP, in billions of constant 2011 international dollars. Last observation is 2017.

positions is through better tax compliance and enforcement (OECD 2019a). Preventing corporate tax avoidance through profit shifting is one way to broaden the revenue base, especially with respect to companies that provide digital services in a given jurisdiction without any physical presence (World Bank 2018d). Providing tax agencies with more resources to bring down tax non-compliance could increase revenues while helping reduce inequality (Sarin and Summers 2019).

Should governments choose to provide fiscal support, the focus should be on spending that has a high multiplier. This could include transfers to low-income individuals, as well as to regional governments, whose spending tends to be more credit constrained and procyclical (Whalen and Reichling 2015). These multipliers may be particularly large when interest rates are constrained by their effective lower bound, and can benefit other countries through spillovers, especially if action is taken in an internationally coordinated fashion (Auerbach and Gorodnichenko 2013; Wieland 2010; Woodford 2011). By contrast, multipliers tend to be low when debt levels are elevated (Huidrom et al. 2019).

FIGURE 1.22 Structural policies in advanced economies

Productivity has slowed in advanced economies, primarily due to the decline in capital deepening, slowing gains in education and gender equality, and lower levels of innovation associated with a shrinking working -age population. Policymakers can help reverse this trend by fostering innovation and human capital, as well as avoiding policy choices that hinder investment.

A. Contributions to labor productivity

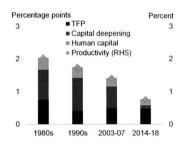

B. Share of advanced economies with a slowdown in productivity drivers in 2008-17 relative to 1998-2007

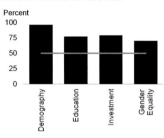

Source: Barro and Lee (2015); Penn World Table; The Conference Board, United Nations; World Bank.
A.B. Productivity defined as output per worker. Refer to Chapter 3 for details. Unbalanced sample includes 29 advanced economies.
A. Aggregate growth rates calculated using GDP weights at 2010 prices and market exchange rates
B. Share of AEs where improvements in each driver of productivity were lower during 2008-2017 than in the pre-crisis period 1998-2007 or improvements were negative. Variables corresponding to each concept are: Investment = investment-to-GDP ratio, Education = years of schooling, Demography = share of working-age population, Gender equality = female average years of education minus male average years.

Public investment may be an especially effective form of fiscal support in many advanced economies, as it can bolster growth in the short term by crowding in private capital, and in the long term by increasing productivity growth and mitigating climate change (Bouakez, Guillard, and Roulleau-Pasdeloup 2017; Dreger and Reimers 2016; World Bank 2019j). The falling stock of public capital as a share of GDP in some advanced economies suggests the need to fill infrastructure needs (Figure 1.21.B; Heintz 2010). To the extent that it boosts demand and potential output, borrowing to finance public investment may ultimately have a limited impact on public debt ratios (Abiad, Furceri, and Topalova 2015).

Structural policies

Potential growth has been slowing in advanced economies due to a combination of demographic trends and decelerating productivity growth. The latter primarily reflects the appreciably diminished role of capital deepening as a contributor to growth since the global financial crisis (Figure 1.22.A). There are a variety of tools policymakers

can use to help reverse this trend. Pursuing growth-enhancing public investment, fostering innovation, and increasing human capital can all be effective means of boosting productivity (Chapter 3).

The simplest option, however, is to avoid policy choices that actively hinder investment. The rise of trade protectionism and the associated uncertainty has made companies more reluctant to invest until the framework for global trade is normalized (Handley and Limão 2015; World Bank 2017a). A stable, predictable system based on a multilateral consensus about the rules governing global trade would foster investment and, thereby, strengthen potential output.

Alongside weak investment, the other main drags on productivity in advanced economies are related to slowing gains in education and gender equality (Figure 1.22.B). In addition, the working-age share of the population continues to shrink, which can slow productivity growth as younger generations tend to adopt new technology more rapidly (Chapter 3). This trend is expected to continue in coming decades, but could be partially mitigated by allowing new migrants, who tend to be prime-aged, in an orderly fashion and as appropriate to country-specific circumstances.

Challenges in emerging market and developing economies

While subdued inflation has allowed many EMDEs to cut policy rates, a deterioration in investor sentiment could require policy tightening. With the space for fiscal support constrained by record-high debt, tax policy reforms are needed to broaden the tax base to fund growth-enhancing and climate-friendly investment. Measures to improve governance and business climates and phase out price controls can make institutional environments more conducive to growth. Encouraging EMDE integration in supply chains could counterweigh the effects of weak global trade. Bolstering productivity growth by encouraging diversification and upgrading to high-value added, technology-intensive industries will be critical to shore up long-term growth. China's key policy challenge is to address lingering disruptions associated with trade tensions while shifting to more balanced and sustainable growth.

Policy challenges in China

China's authorities have provided monetary and fiscal support to mitigate the impact of higher tariffs on bilateral trade with the United States and weakening global demand. The central bank has eased policy mainly by cutting bank reserve requirements. On the fiscal front, authorities have focused on measures to accelerate investment spending at the subnational level. A number of initiatives to improve market access for foreign investors and various reforms to improve the business climate have also been implemented (World Bank 2019c, 2020).

China's key policy challenge is to achieve a permanent and lasting resolution of trade tensions while continuing to shift to more balanced growth and gradually reducing excessive leverage. This would require enhancing productivity by boosting investment in human capital; further improving market access, competition, and financial discipline; strengthening intellectual property rights; reducing barriers to entry; continuing the gradual opening of China's financial system to international investors; and fostering innovation (Chapter 3; World Bank 2018e; World Bank and DRC 2019).

EMDE monetary and financial policies

Consistent with flagging global growth, negative output gaps, and moderating inflation in many EMDEs, including some LICs, nearly 75 percent of EMDEs have lower policy rates now than at the start of 2019, with more than half implementing multiple cuts (Figure 1.23.A). Many EMDEs have space to cut rates further as interest rates remain relatively high and inflation below target (Figures 1.23.B and 1.23.C). However, the effectiveness of monetary policy in EMDEs is likely more limited than in advanced economies, as the interest rate channel may be weaker and the impact of external financing conditions larger (Aoki, Benigno, and Kiyotaki 2018; Choi et al. 2017).

Although global financing conditions have generally eased, policy uncertainty and risk aversion have tightened financing conditions in some EMDEs. An abrupt change in market sentiment could reignite capital outflows and currency depreciation, as well as force policy interest rate hikes, exerting greater pressure on economies still suffering the lingering effects of previous financial market stress. EMDEs with large external imbalances tend to be the most vulnerable to financial stress, including those that rely on short-term capital inflows to finance current accounts, borrow heavily in foreign-denominated currencies and from external lenders, and lack adequate reserve coverage levels.

Many EMDEs lack buffers to confront financial shocks—in nearly half of EMDEs, international reserves are currently below levels that would be consistent with reserve adequacy (IMF 2011; Kose and Ohnsorge 2019). Among LICs, reserve coverage has fallen to a two-year low (Figure 1.23.D). Following the taper tantrum of 2013, depreciations were less severe in countries with larger reserves, highlighting the importance of restoring monetary buffers (BIS 2019). In anticipation of renewed episodes of market volatility, EMDE policymakers need to keep expectations of longer-term inflation moderate and stable. This includes demonstrating a credible commitment to inflation targets in economies that have implemented such a framework (World Bank 2019n).

Since the global financial crisis, more than two thirds of EMDEs have strengthened macro-prudential policies to rein in the growth of credit to non-financial corporations and households (Figure 1.23.E; Cerutti, Claessens, and Laeven 2017; Koh and Yu 2019; World Bank 2019o). Supervisory and regulatory frameworks need to be further strengthened to confront future shocks and shore up financial stability, especially in a context where cross-border lending has shifted from banks headquartered in advanced economies to EMDE-headquartered banks (Figure 1.23.F). Macro-prudential measures, such as countercyclical capital buffers and limits on foreign-currency borrowing, can help contain systemic risk in banking and corporate sectors. Additionally, carefully calibrated regulatory measures, such as reporting and licensing criteria, could help support confidence and resilience in new platforms that expand the access to credit through financial technology innovations (BIS 2017). However, EMDEs will need to strike a careful balance when

FIGURE 1.23 EMDE monetary and financial policy

Moderating inflation and relatively high interest rates allowed many EMDEs to cut policy interest rates to support growth—consistent with negative output gaps and below-target inflation. Reserve coverage sharply fell in 2019, particularly in LICs, leaving many economies unprepared to respond to financial market shocks. Strengthening regulatory frameworks in EMDEs is crucial, especially in a context where cross-border lending has shifted to EMDE-headquartered banks.

A. Output gaps and policy interest rate actions

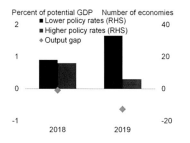

B. Real interest rates

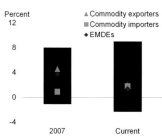

C. Inflation and inflation targeters, 2019

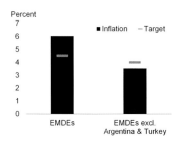

D. Reserve coverage

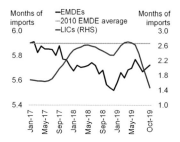

E. Macroprudential policies: Use of financial institution-targeted instruments

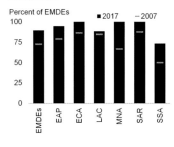

F. Sources of cross-border bank loans

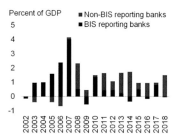

Source: Bank for International Settlements; Consensus Economics; Haver Analytics; International Monetary Fund; World Bank.
A. Output gaps aggregated using GDP weights at 2010 prices and market exchange rates and are estimated from a multivariate filter model of World Bank (2018a). Figure shows number of EMDEs with policy interest rates lower (higher) than start of the year. Sample includes 45 EMDEs. Countries with fixed exchange rates are excluded. Data as of December 19, 2019.
B. Real interest rates are nominal interest rates less expected inflation. Expected inflation is the one-year ahead forecast from Consensus Economics. Sample includes 17 EMDEs. Blue area shows minimum and maximum. Last observation is November 2019.
C. Sample includes the 34 EMDEs with inflation targets and is based on data availability. Figure shows the last observation, which is November 2019.
D. Figure shows number of months of reserve coverage. Data are 6-month moving averages of the sample median. Sample includes 66 EMDEs including 25 LICs. Last observation is October 2019. The Assessing Reserve Adequacy (ARA) metric is based on IMF (2011).
E. Each bar represents share of EMDEs using at least one macroprudential tool that is financial institution-targeted (for example, limits on foreign currency loans and leverage ratios).
F. Sample includes 115 EMDEs, excluding China. Due to data availability, 77 EMDEs are included in 2018. Lending by non-BIS banks is estimated as total bank loans and deposits from the IMF Balance of Payments Statistics (excluding central banks) minus cross-border lending by BIS reporting banks. This difference mostly accounts for the banking flows originating from non-BIS reporting countries.

considering the trade-offs between managing macroprudential risk and fostering financial development (Krishnamurti and Lee 2014).

EMDE fiscal policy

Many EMDEs face narrowing fiscal space and may struggle to quickly rebuild buffers, limiting their options to address a severe downturn (Figure 1.24.A; Ruch 2019b). Aggregate EMDE debt reached a historical high last year and is expected to rise further (Chapter 4). Fiscal sustainability remains a critical challenge in many EMDEs, reflecting increased spending in commodity exporters and reduced revenues in commodity importers (Figures 1.24.B and 1.24.C). Should a negative shock occur, the scope for fiscal accommodation may be constrained by the need to ensure long-term fiscal stability. The case for providing fiscal support would be strengthened where there are clear needs, such as infrastructure gaps, and a transparent public expenditure review process. In many cases, however, the expansion of credit over the past decade has not been channeled into investment, and was instead used to fund consumption (Chapter 4; Arteta and Kasyanenko 2019).

In particular, EMDE commodity exporters need to grapple with lower commodity prices, especially in those oil exporters where fiscal breakeven prices are higher than oil prices. In many commodity exporters, fiscal revenues are not well diversified, leaving revenues highly dependent on commodity production and exposed to global commodity price volatility (Gunter et al. 2019).

For fiscally constrained economies, building tax capacity is a crucial step towards mobilizing domestic resources, providing essential public services, pursuing appropriate redistributive policies to address inequality, and building fiscal buffers (Doumbia and Lauridsen 2019). This is particularly true in LICs, 80 percent of which lack the tax revenues to provide even basic services, let alone to meet the SDGs (Figure 1.24.D; Gaspar, Jaramillo, and Wingender 2016). Overall, policymakers need to ensure that public spending is cost effective and yields a positive growth dividend, while also protecting critical social safety nets and supporting climate-friendly measures.

Measures that help mitigate and adapt to climate change, such as environmental tax reforms, can reap a triple dividend by lowering pollution, raising welfare, and generating positive externalities (World Bank 2019p).

In many EMDEs, tax policy reform is a challenging process. To protect the most vulnerable, adjusting income tax brackets to rising inflation can ease the tax burden and prevent the erosion of real net incomes. Harmonizing tax rates across different savings instruments or a well-designed earned income tax credit can support labor participation and poverty reduction without distorting the incentive to work and save (OECD 2019a). When there is a clear rationale for tax cuts, negative revenue effects can be partly offset by measures that increase compliance—such as the introduction of a withholding mechanism or a simplification of the tax structure—or that spur innovation and investment—such as tax credits on vocational education and research and development (Clavey et al. 2019; Correa and Guceri 2013; World Bank et al. 2015). Additional measures that broaden the tax base, including those that eliminate costly loopholes, can be complemented with reforms that strengthen tax administration and collection to reduce avoidance, base erosion, and profit shifting (Awasthi and Bayraktar 2014; OECD 2017; Packard et al. 2019; Prichard et al. 2019; World Bank 2018d).

EMDEs with unsustainable fiscal positions can also prioritize rebuilding policy space by improving spending efficiency, by shifting spending toward growth-enhancing, climate-friendly investment from unproductive current spending, and by strengthening governance to contain and eliminate wasteful spending (World Bank 2017b). If public expenditure needs are high, rebalancing the tax structure can provide maneuvering room, particularly in economies with lower initial tax rates (Gunter et al. 2018, 2019). The realization of costly fiscal risks to public balance sheets, such as contingent liabilities, could be stemmed through use of macroprudential measures that help ensure the resilience of the banking sector. Building credible and transparent medium-term expenditure frameworks that align with the strategic goals of the government is also

FIGURE 1.24 EMDE fiscal policy

Fiscal deficits persist despite previous procyclical tightening in some EMDEs, as weaker-than-expected growth hindered revenue collection. Weak tax capacity has contributed to fragile fiscal positions, particularly in LICs, highlighting the urgency for fiscally constrained economies to better mobilize domestic resources or reform their tax structure to free up space to finance growth-enhancing spending.

A. Fiscal impulses and output gaps

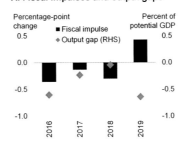

B. Fiscal sustainability gaps in EMDEs

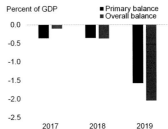

C. Contribution to change in fiscal balance, 2019

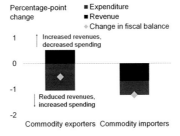

D. Share of EMDEs with limited tax revenues to fund basic public services

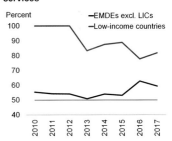

Source: International Monetary Fund; Kose et al. (2017); World Bank.
A. Output gaps are estimates from a multivariate filter model of World Bank (2018a). Average of quarterly output gap data. Fiscal impulse is defined as the change in the structural fiscal deficit from the previous year. A decline in structural deficit (a negative fiscal impulse) is a fiscal consolidation—countercyclical if implemented while output gaps are positive—while an increase in the structural deficit (positive fiscal impulse) is a fiscal stimulus—countercyclical if implemented while output gaps are negative.
B. Fiscal sustainability gaps are measured as the difference between the primary (overall) balance and the debt-stabilizing primary (overall) balance. A negative bar indicates government debt is rising along an accelerated trajectory.
C. Sample includes 152 EMDEs.
D. Figure shows the share of EMDEs with tax revenue-to-GDP ratios that are below 15 percent, the threshold needed to provide basic public services, as identified in Gaspar, Jaramillo, and Wingender (2016). Basic services include road infrastructure, health care, and public safety. Sample varies due to data limitations. In 2017, the sample includes 70 EMDEs, of which 11 are LICs.

crucial (Koh and Yu 2019; Munoz and Olaberria 2019).

EMDE structural policies

Over the long run, EMDE policymakers need to undertake the necessary structural reforms to buttress potential growth. Inadequate governance and business climates need to be improved to foster an institutional environment that is more conducive to growth. In a context of subdued trade growth, further integration of EMDEs into global value chains needs to be promoted. Critically, amid slowing capital deepening, productivity growth—an essential driver of long-term growth and poverty reduction—needs to be rekindled. Many EMDEs, including LICs, face the added challenge of phasing out distortionary price control policies that impede growth and development. In tackling these challenges, care should be taken to protect vulnerable populations by improving social safety nets.

Moreover, investment in green infrastructure and its integration with traditional infrastructure can lower costs, help achieve development goals, and contribute to improving infrastructure systems' resilience to climate change (Browder et al. 2019). Private sector financing to meet large infrastructure investment needs and foster capital formation and the leveraging of digital technologies to promote the inclusion, efficiency, and innovation of firms in EMDEs are all crucial in boosting potential growth (World Bank 2016b).

Implementing governance and business climate reforms

Governance reforms in EMDEs have stalled, and renewed momentum is needed (World Bank 2018a). The number of countries whose ranking for rule of law and control of corruption have significantly worsened in the last two decades outnumber those whose rankings have improved (Figure 1.25.A). Strikingly, very few large EMDEs had significant gains in any of the worldwide governance indicators, nor did LICs as a group. Strengthening institutional quality and governance to protect property rights would encourage the shift from informal to more productive formal activities (World Bank 2017c). Measures that improve public sector efficiency through the provision of high-quality and cost-effective public goods also need to be considered as they can help raise firm productivity (Giordano et al. 2015).

Since 2009, only about a third of EMDEs increased their doing business score significantly, with notable regional variations (Figure 1.25.B). Reforms should aim to accelerate improvements in the business climate by tackling burdensome regulations and enhancing the ease of doing business, in order to pave the way for more jobs,

higher incomes, and reduced poverty (World Bank 2020).

Phasing out distortionary price controls

While introduced with the best social intentions, price control policies, often coupled with onerous subsidies, pose important obstacles to growth and development in many EMDEs, including LICs (Special Focus 1). The removal of these costly controls can reduce misallocation of capital and labor, spur investment, and increase competition in sectors subject to these policies. Moreover, when paired with targeted social safety nets, their removal can help reduce poverty and inequality (Verme and Araar 2017). Some of the fiscal savings from the reforms can be used to fund growth-enhancing education and infrastructure spending.

Promoting integration into global value chains

The rise in the incidence of protectionist measures over the past couple of years not only weighs on global trade growth but could lead to the fragmentation of global supply chains and deprive EMDEs of a key source of growth and poverty reduction. Policy measures that help facilitate trade in EMDEs by boosting their integration in existing supply chains and spurring the creation of new ones could provide a counterweight to the global slowdown in growth and trade (World Bank 2019a). A 10-percent increase in GVC participation is estimated to boost per capita income growth by more than 10 percent, about twice as much as standard trade (Figure 1.25.C). Firms integrated in GVCs tend to be more productive and capital intensive; they represent only about 15 percent of all trading firms, yet account for almost 80 percent of total trade. GVC participation is positively associated with foreign direct investment in EMDEs, as well as technology and knowledge transfers (Martínez-Galán and Fontoura 2019; World Bank et al. 2017).

Reducing distortions to international trade can contribute to boosting EMDE participation in GVCs (Figure 1.25.D; OECD 2019b). The liberalization of barriers (both tariff and non-tariff) affecting imported intermediate inputs could expand sources of supply available to EMDEs and their ability to specialize. A one-standard-deviation decrease in a country's average manufacturing tariffs—8 percentage points—is associated with an increase in the country's backward GVC participation (captured by the foreign value-added content of exports) of about 0.2 standard deviations (Fernandes, Kee, and Winkler 2019). Liberalizing barriers to services trade, which are significantly higher than those for goods trade, is also important in promoting GVC growth.

Trade facilitation policies that improve connectivity by enhancing trade and transport logistics and lower trade costs can help EMDEs better integrate into GVCs. For many goods traded in GVCs, a day's delay has costs equivalent to a tariff of 1 percent or more. Improving customs and border procedures, promoting competition in transport services, and improving port structure and governance are all strategies that can help reduce trade costs related to time and uncertainty (Pathikonda and Farole 2016).

Because GVCs thrive on the flexible formation of networks of firms, a stable and predictable legal environment and contract enforcement are crucial (Ignatenko, Raei, and Micheva 2019). Better contract enforcement supports the supply of business services, which encourages the development of GVCs. The ability to enforce contracts relating to intellectual property is also important for more innovative and complex value chains.

Complementary policies are also needed to ensure that the gains from participation in GVCs are evenly distributed. These include labor market policies to help workers who may be hurt by structural change; mechanisms to ensure compliance with labor regulations; appropriate tax policies to attract GVCs without undermining tax revenues; and environmental protection measures (Taglioni and Winkler 2016).

Fostering productivity growth

EMDE productivity growth has been in a broad-based downward trend in recent years (Figure 1.26.A; Chapter 3). This deceleration has coincided with a slowdown in improvements in many correlates of strong productivity growth (Figure 1.26.B) The structural tailwinds that

FIGURE 1.25 EMDE structural policies—Governance, business climate, and GVC participation

The number of EMDEs whose rankings for some key governance indicators have significantly worsened in the last two decades outnumber those whose rankings have improved. Since 2009, only about a third of EMDEs increased their Doing Business score significantly. This highlights a critical need to foster institutional environments more conducive to growth. Trade liberalization can help boost EMDEs' participation in global value chains and contribute to rising per capita incomes.

A. Change in *Worldwide Governance Indicators*, 1996 to 2018

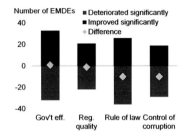

B. Change in *Doing Business* scores, 2009 to 2019

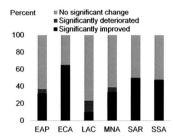

C. Impact of 1 percent increase in GVC participation on GDP per capita

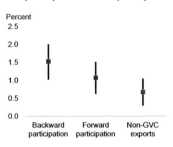

D. Impact of input tariffs on GVC participation

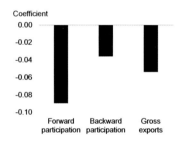

Source: World Bank.

A.B. A country significantly improved (deteriorated) if its rating increased (decreased) by two standard errors over the indicated periods. For *Worldwide Governance Indicators*, standard errors are the average between the two periods. For *Doing Business*, standard errors are the cross-country standard deviation of changes in scores.

A. Based on indicators from the *Worldwide Governance Indicators* (WGI) measuring aspects of governance. The four indicators are government effectiveness, regulatory quality, rule of law, and control of corruption.

B. EAP = East Asia and Pacific, ECA = Europe and Central Asia, LAC = Latin America and the Caribbean, MNA = Middle East and North Africa, SAR = South Asia, SSA = Sub-Saharan Africa.

C.D. Backward participation is defined as the share of foreign inputs in domestic value added. Forward participation is the share of domestic value added in exports.

C. GDP per capita increase as a result of 1 percent increase in x-axis indicators. Blue vertical lines indicate 95 percent confidence interval and red squares indicate point estimates. Estimates obtained from a panel of standard Solow growth models augmented with measures of GVC using System Generalized Method of Moments (World Bank 2019a). Panel includes 100 countries across income groups for the period of 1990-2015. Non-GVC exports is defined as exports that neither include foreign value-added nor are exports of domestic value added that are re-exported in other countries' exports.

D. Figure shows standardized beta coefficients for each variable from each of the three separate regressions listed. Results obtained from regressions using three-year lag of each determinant in addition to country-year fixed effects and sectoral fixed effects.

boosted EMDE productivity growth prior to 2008 are fading. Output per worker in EMDEs is, on average, less than one fifth than that of advanced economies, and at current rates of productivity growth the average EMDE would take over 100 years to close half of the productivity gap with

FIGURE 1.26 EMDE structural policies—Productivity

EMDE productivity growth has been in a broad-based downward trend in recent years. This deceleration has coincided with a slowdown in improvements in many correlates of strong productivity growth. A reform package that combines filling investment needs, boosting human capital, and improving the adoption of new technologies could lift productivity significantly. Fostering productivity is key to alleviate poverty.

A. EMDE productivity growth

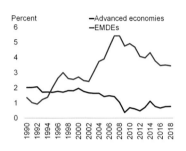

B. Share of EMDEs with a slowdown in productivity drivers in 2008-17 relative to 1998-2007

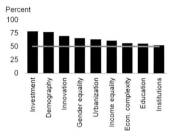

C. EMDE productivity reform scenario

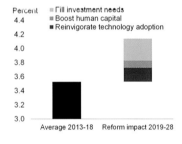

D. Productivity growth and global poverty

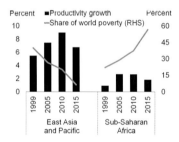

Source: Barro and Lee (2015); Observatory of Economic Complexity; Penn World Table; Rozenberg and Fay (2019); The Conference Board; United Nations; World Bank.
Note: Productivity is defined as output per worker. Sample includes 29 advanced economies and 74 EMDEs. Refer to Chapter 3 for details. Aggregate growth rates calculated using GDP weights at 2010 prices and market exchange rates.
A. Figure shows 5-year moving averages.
B. Econ. complexity = economic complexity. Post-crisis slowdown defined as the share of economies where improvements in each underlying driver of productivity during 2008-2018 was less than zero or the pace of improvement during the pre-crisis period 1998-2007. Unbalanced sample of 74 economies. Variables corresponding to each concept are (sample in parentheses): Demography =share of working-age population, Investment =investment to GDP ratio, Innovation =patents per capita, Gender equality = ratio of female labor market participation rate to male, Urbanization = urban population (% total), Institutions = WGI Rule of Law, Income equality = (-1)*Gini coefficient, Education = years of schooling, ECI defined as Economic Complexity Index of Hidalgo and Hausmann (2009). Orange line indicates 50 percent.
C. The reform scenario assumes: (1) Fill investment needs: the investment share of GDP increases by 4.5 percentage points as in the Rozenberg and Fay (2019) "preferred" infrastructure scenario. The increase is phased in linearly over 10 years; (2) Boost human capital: average years of education increases in each EMDE at its fastest cumulative 10-year pace during 2000-08; (3) Reinvigorate technology adoption: economic complexity (Hidalgo & Hausmann 2009) increases at the same pace as its fastest 10-year rate of increase during 2000-08.
D. Poverty is defined as the extreme poor living at or below $1.90 per day, in 2011 PPP terms.

advanced economies. In addition, cyclical headwinds, rising protectionist measures, and elevated policy uncertainty highlight the importance of productivity-enhancing policies, such as those that improve institutions, encourage investment, and promote diversification.

Policies to boost sectoral diversification are crucial, particularly for commodity exporters that have historically experienced low productivity growth—total factor productivity in commodity exporters has contracted by around 0.8 percent per year over the past four decades. Sectoral diversification may encourage productivity gains in sectors that are less dependent on volatile commodity prices (Bahar and Santos 2018; Frankel 2010). Removing bottlenecks and barriers to investment in high value-added services sectors provides opportunities for rapid catch-up in productivity growth.

Policymakers could significantly contribute to raising productivity in EMDEs by encouraging firms to upgrade to more high-value-added and technology-intensive subsectors (Cusolito and Maloney 2018; Syverson 2011). In addition, improving the business environment fostering capital market development, and encouraging FDI could contribute to reducing cross-country sectoral productivity dispersion. Action is also needed to help reduce the vulnerability to adverse productivity shocks, such as financial crises, disasters, and conflict (Cerra and Saxena 2008, 2017; Ray and Esteban 2017).

Social safety nets play a key role in mitigating the adverse effects of new technologies that may initially be disruptive to employment. Policies that improve social insurance for unemployment are needed in the formal and informal sectors. Policies that incentivize adult learning, particularly for high-order cognitive skills that complement new technologies, could help reintegrate displaced workers into the labor force (Andrews, Avitabile, and Gatti 2019; World Bank 2018d). Measures that help close the gender gap and improve female labor force participation would also contribute to raising growth and productivity (Ianchovichina and Leipziger 2019). Overall, a reform package that combines filling investment needs, boosting human capital, and improving the adoption of new technologies could lift productivity growth by just over half of a percentage point over 10 years (Figure 1.26.C). By bolstering productivity, these policies will support poverty alleviation (Figure 1.26.D).

TABLE 1.2 Emerging market and developing economies[1]

Commodity exporters[2]		Commodity importers[3]	
Albania*	Lao PDR	Afghanistan	Pakistan
Algeria*	Liberia	Antigua and Barbuda	Palau
Angola*	Madagascar	Bahamas, The	Panama
Argentina	Malawi	Bangladesh	Philippines
Armenia	Malaysia*	Barbados	Poland
Azerbaijan*	Mali	Belarus	Romania
Bahrain*	Mauritania	Bhutan	Samoa
Belize	Mongolia	Bosnia and Herzegovina	Serbia
Benin	Morocco	Bulgaria	Seychelles
Bolivia*	Mozambique	Cabo Verde	Solomon Islands
Botswana	Myanmar*	Cambodia	Sri Lanka
Brazil	Namibia	China	St. Kitts and Nevis
Burkina Faso	Nicaragua	Comoros	St. Lucia
Burundi	Niger	Croatia	St. Vincent and the Grenadines
Cameroon*	Nigeria*	Djibouti	Thailand
Chad*	Oman*	Dominica	Tonga
Chile	Papua New Guinea	Dominican Republic	Tunisia
Colombia*	Paraguay	Egypt	Turkey
Congo, Dem. Rep.	Peru	El Salvador	Tuvalu
Congo, Rep.*	Qatar*	Eritrea	Vanuatu
Costa Rica	Russia*	Eswatini	Vietnam
Côte d'Ivoire	Rwanda	Fiji	
Ecuador*	Saudi Arabia*	Georgia	
Equatorial Guinea*	Senegal	Grenada	
Ethiopia	Sierra Leone	Haiti	
Gabon*	South Africa	Hungary	
Gambia, The	Sudan*	India	
Ghana*	Suriname	Jamaica	
Guatemala	Tajikistan	Jordan	
Guinea	Tanzania	Kiribati	
Guinea-Bissau	Timor-Leste*	Lebanon	
Guyana	Togo	Lesotho	
Honduras	Turkmenistan*	Maldives	
Indonesia*	Uganda	Marshall Islands	
Iran*	Ukraine	Mauritius	
Iraq*	United Arab Emirates*	Mexico	
Kazakhstan*	Uruguay	Micronesia, Fed. Sts.	
Kenya	Uzbekistan	Moldova, Rep.	
Kosovo	West Bank and Gaza	Montenegro	
Kuwait*	Zambia	Nepal	
Kyrgyz Republic	Zimbabwe	North Macedonia	

* Energy exporters.

1. Emerging market and developing economies (EMDEs) include all those that are not classified as advanced economies and for which a forecast is published for this report. Dependent territories are excluded. Advanced economies include Australia; Austria; Belgium; Canada; Cyprus; the Czech Republic; Denmark; Estonia; Finland; France; Germany; Greece; Hong Kong SAR, China; Iceland; Ireland; Israel; Italy; Japan; the Republic of Korea; Latvia; Lithuania; Luxembourg; Malta; Netherlands; New Zealand; Norway; Portugal; Singapore; the Slovak Republic; Slovenia; Spain; Sweden; Switzerland; the United Kingdom; and the United States.

2. An economy is defined as commodity exporter when, on average in 2012-14, either (i) total commodities exports accounted for 30 percent or more of total goods exports or (ii) exports of any single commodity accounted for 20 percent or more of total goods exports. Economies for which these thresholds were met as a result of re-exports were excluded. When data were not available, judgment was used. This taxonomy results in the classification of some well-diversified economies as importers, even if they are exporters of certain commodities (e.g., Mexico).

3. Commodity importers are all EMDEs that are not classified as commodity exporters.

References

Abiad, A., D. Furceri, and P. Topalova. 2015. "The Macroeconomic Effects of Public Investment: Evidence from Advanced Economies." IMF Working Paper 15/95, International Monetary Fund, Washington, DC.

Agarwal, R., and M. Kimball. 2019. "Enabling Deep Negative Rates to Fight Recessions: A Guide." IMF Working Paper 19/84, International Monetary Fund, Washington, DC.

Agur, I., M. Chan, M. Goswami, and S. Sharma. 2018. "On International Integration of Emerging Sovereign Bond Markets." IMF Working Paper 18/18, International Monetary Fund, Washington, DC.

Ahir, H., N. Bloom, and D. Furceri. 2018. "The World Uncertainty Index." Available at https://papers.ssrn.com/sol3/papers.cfm?abstract_id=3275033.

Ahmed, S., R. Correa, D.A Dias, N. Gornemann, J. Hoek, A. Jain, E. Liu, and A. Wong. 2019. "Global Spillovers of a China Hard Landing". International Finance Discussion Papers 1260. Board of Governors of the Federal Reserve System, Washington, DC.

Andrews, K. G., C. Avitabile, and R. V. Gatti. 2019. "Domestic Government Spending on Human Capital: A Cross-Country Analysis of Recent Trends." Policy Research Working Paper 9033, World Bank, Washington, DC.

Aoki K., G. Benigno, and N. Kiyotaki. 2018. "Monetary and Financial Policies in Emerging Markets." Unpublished manuscript.

Arteta, C., and S. Kasyanenko. 2019. "Financial Market Developments." In *A Decade after the Global Recession: Lessons and Challenges for Emerging and Developing Economies*, edited by M. A. Kose and F. Ohnsorge. Washington, DC: World Bank.

Arteta, C., M. A. Kose, M. Stocker, and T. Taskin. 2016. "Negative Interest Rate Policies: Sources and Implications." Policy Research Working Paper 7791, World Bank, Washington, DC.

Atkin, D., A. K. Khandelwal, and A. Osman. 2017. "Exporting and firm performance: Evidence from a Randomized Experiment." *The Quarterly Journal of Economics* 132 (2): 551-615.

Auerbach, A. J., and Y. Gorodnichenko. 2013. "Output Spillovers from Fiscal Policy." *American Economic Review* 103 (3): 141-46.

Awasthi, R., and N. Bayraktar. 2014. "Can Tax Simplification Help Lower Tax Corruption?" Policy Research Working Paper 6988, World Bank, Washington, DC.

Baez, J. E., G. Caruso, and C. Niu. 2019. "Extreme Weather and Poverty Risk: Evidence from Multiple Shocks in Mozambique." Poverty and Equity Notes 11. World Bank, Washington, DC.

Baffes, J., A. Kabundi, and P. Nagle. Forthcoming. "The Role of Income and Substitution in Global Commodity Demand." World Bank Working Paper, World Bank, Washington, DC.

Bahar, D., and M. A. Santos. 2018. "One More Resource Curse: Dutch Disease and Export Concentration." *Journal of Development Economics* 132 (1): 102–14.

Baker, S. R., N. Bloom, and S. J. Davis. 2016. "Measuring Economic Policy Uncertainty". *The Quarterly Journal of Economics* 131 (4): 1593–1636.

———. 2019. "The Extraordinary Rise in Trade Policy Uncertainty." Vox CEPR Policy Portal, September 17. Available at https://voxeu.org/article/extraordinary-rise-trade-policy-uncertainty.

Bank of England. 2019. *Financial Stability Report.* July. Bank of England, London.

Barattieri, A., M. Cacciatore, and F. Ghironi. 2018. "Protectionism and the Business Cycle." NBER Working Paper 24353, National Bureau of Economic Research, Cambridge, MA.

Barro, R., and J. Lee. 2015. *Education Matters: Global Schooling Gains from the 19th to the 21st Century.* New York, NY: Oxford University Press.

Beegle, K., and L. Christiaensen. 2019. *Accelerating Poverty Reduction in Africa.* Washington, DC: World Bank.

Bernard, A. B., and J. B. Jensen. 2004. "Exporting and Productivity in the USA." *Oxford Review of Economic Policy* 20 (3): 343-357.

BIS (Bank for International Settlements). 2017. "FinTech Credit: Market Structure, Business Models and Financial Stability Implications." Committee on the Global Financial System and the Financial Stability Board Report, Bank for International Settlements, Basel.

———. 2019. *Annual Economic Report.* June. Basel: Bank for International Settlements.

Bouakez, H., M. Guillard, and J. Roulleau- Pasdeloup. 2017. "Public Investment, Time to Build, and the Zero Lower Bound." *Review of Economic Dynamics* 23 (January): 60-79. Available at https://www.science direct.com/science/article/pii/S109420251630026.

Browder, G. J., S. Ozment, I. Rehberger Bescos, T. Gartner, and G. M. Lange. 2019. "Integrating Green and Gray: Creating Next Generation Infrastructure." Washington, DC: World Bank

Brunnermeier, M. K., and Y. Koby. 2019. "The Reversal Interest Rate." Princeton University, Princeton, NJ.

Bruno, V., and H. Shin. 2018. "Currency Depreciation and Emerging Market Corporate Distress." BIS Working Paper 753, Bank for International Settlements, Basel.

Buiter, W. H. 2014. "The Simple Analytics of Helicopter Money: Why it Works – Always." *Economics* 8 (28). Available at https://papers.ssrn.com/sol3/papers.cfm?abstract_id=2484853.

Caballero, J., A. Fernández, and J. Park. 2019. "On Corporate Borrowing, Credit Spreads and Economic Activity in Emerging Economies: An Empirical Investigation." *Journal of International Economics* 118 (C): 160-178.

Caldara, D., M. Iacoviello, P. Molligo, A. Prestipino, and A. Raffo. 2019. "The Economic Effects of Trade Policy Uncertainty." International Finance Discussion Papers 1256, Board of Governors of the Federal Reserve System, Washington, DC.

Cerra, V., and S. C. Saxena. 2008. "Growth Dynamics: The Myth of Economic Recovery." *American Economic Review* 98 (1): 439–57.

_____. 2017. "Booms, Crises, and Recoveries: A New Paradigm of the Business Cycle and Its Policy Implications." IMF Working Paper 17/250, International Monetary Fund, Washington, DC.

Cerutti, E., S. Claessens, and L. Laeven. 2017. "The Use and Effectiveness of Macroprudential Policies: New Evidence." *Journal of Financial Stability* 28 (February): 203-224.

Cerutti, E., S. Claessens, and D. Puy. 2019. "Push Factors and Capital Flows to Emerging Markets: Why Knowing Your Lender Matters More Than Fundamentals." *Journal of International Economics* 119 (C): 133-149.

Chen, S., and J. S. Kang. 2018. "Credit Booms—Is China Different?" IMF Working Paper 18/2, International Monetary Fund, Washington, DC.

Choi, W. G., T. Kang, G.Y. Kim, and B. Lee. 2017. "Divergent Emerging Market Economy Responses to Global and Domestic Monetary Policy Shocks." ADB economics working paper series 532, Asian Development Bank, Manila, Philippines.

Christiaensen, L., P. Chuhan-Pole, and A. Sanoh. 2013. Africa's Growth, Poverty and Inequality Nexus–Fostering Shared Prosperity. Washington, DC: World Bank.

Christiaensen, L., and R. Hill. 2018. "Africa Is Not Poorer than Other Equally Poor Countries in Reducing Poverty." Background note prepared for Accelerating Poverty Reduction in Africa, World Bank, Washington, DC.

Chui, M., E. Kuruc, and P. Turner. 2016. "A New Dimension to Currency Mismatches in The Emerging Markets: Nonfinancial Companies." BIS Working Paper 550, Bank for International Settlements, Basel.

Clavey, C., J. L. Pemberton, J. Loeprick, and M. Verhoeven. 2019. "International Tax Reform, Digitalization, and Developing Economies." MTI Discussion Paper 16, World Bank, Washington, DC.

Correa, P. G., and I. Guceri. 2013. "Tax Incentives for Research and Development." Innovation, Technology and Entrepreneurship Policy Note No. 4, World Bank, Washington, DC.

Cusolito, A. P., and W. F. Maloney. 2018. *Productivity Revisited - Shifting Paradigms in Analysis and Policy.* Washington, DC: World Bank.

De la Fuente, A., H. G. Jacoby, and K. G. Lawin. 2019. "Impact of the West African Ebola Epidemic on Agricultural Production and Rural Welfare Evidence from Liberia." Policy Research Working Paper 8880, World Bank, Washington, DC.

Doumbia, D., and M. L. Lauridsen. 2019. "Closing the SDG Financing Gap—Trends and Data." World Bank IFC EM Compass Note 73, World Bank, Washington, DC.

Dreger C., and H. E. Reimers. 2016. "Does Public Investment Stimulate Private Investment? Evidence for the euro area." *Economic Modelling* 58 (November): 154-158.

Easterly, W., and S. Fischer. 1994. "The Soviet Economic Decline: Historical and Republican Data." NBER Working Paper 4735, National Bureau of Economic Research, Cambridge, MA.

Essl, S., S. K. Celik, P. Kirby, and A. Proite. 2019. "Debt in Low-Income Countries: Evolution, Implications, and Remedies." Policy Research Working Paper 8950, World Bank, Washington, DC.

Fajgelbaum, P. D., P. K. Goldberg, P. J. Kennedy, and A. K. Khandelwal. 2019. "The Return to Protectionism," NBER Working Paper 25638, National Bureau of Economic Research, Cambridge, MA.

FAO (Food and Agriculture Organization of the United Nations). 2019. *Crop Prospects and Food Situation.* July. Rome, Italy: FAO.

Federal Reserve Board. 2019. *Financial Stability Report. November.* Board of Governors of the Federal Reserve System, Washington, DC.

Fernandes, A., H. L. Kee, and D. Winkler. 2019. "Factors Affecting Global Value Chain Participation Across Countries." Unpublished working paper, World Bank, Washington, DC.

Feyen, E., and I. Zuccardi. 2019. "The Sovereign-Bank Nexus in EMDEs: What Is It, Is It Rising, and What Are the Policy Implications?" Policy Research Working Paper 8950, World Bank, Washington, DC.

FSB (Financial Stability Board). 2019a. "Vulnerabilities Associated with Leveraged Loans and Collateralised Loan Obligations." FSB, Basel.

———. 2019b. "Three Priorities for International Regulatory and Supervisory Cooperation." Speech by FSB Secretary General Dietrich Domanski at Eurofi, Helsinki, September 13.

Frankel, J. 2010. "The Natural Resource Curse: A Survey." NBER Working Paper 15836, National Bureau of Economic Research, Cambridge, MA.

Fuglie, K., M. Gautam, A. Goyal, and W. Maloney. 2019. *Harvesting Prosperity: Technology and Productivity Growth in Agriculture.* World Bank, Washington, DC.

Gaspar, V., L. Jaramillo, and P. Wingender. 2016. "Tax Capacity and Growth: Is There a Tipping Point?" IMF Working Paper 16/234, International Monetary Fund, Washington, DC.

Giordano, R., S. Lanau, P. Tommasino, and P. Topalova. 2015. "Does Public Sector Inefficiency Constrain Firm Productivity: Evidence from Italian Provinces." IMF Working Paper 15/168, International Monetary Fund, Washington, DC.

Gunter, S., D. Riera-Crichton, C. A. Vegh, and G. J. Vuletin. 2018. "Non-Linear Effects of Tax Changes on Output: The Role of the Initial Level of Taxation." Policy Research Working Paper 8668, World Bank, Washington, DC.

———. 2019. "Policy Implications of Non-linear Effects of Tax Changes on Output." Policy Research Working Paper 8720, World Bank, Washington, DC.

Handley, K., and N. Limão. 2015. "Trade and Investment Under Policy Uncertainty: Theory and Firm Evidence." *American Economic Journal: Economic Policy* 7(4): 189-222.

Heintz, J. 2010. "The Impact of Public Capital on the US Private Economy: New Evidence and Analysis." *International Review of Applied Economics,* 24 (5): 619-632.

Huidrom, R., M. A. Kose, J. J. Lim, and F. Ohnsorge. 2019. "Why Do Fiscal Multipliers Depend on Fiscal Positions?" *Journal of Monetary Economics.* Advance online publication. https://doi.org/10.1016/j.jmoneco.2019.03.004.

Ianchovichina, E., and D. Leipziger. 2019. "Combining Growth and Gender Diagnostics for the Benefit of Both." Policy Research Working Paper 8847, World Bank, Washington, DC.

IEA (International Energy Agency). 2019. *Oil Market Report.* September. Paris, France: IEA.

Ignatenko, A., F. Raei, and B. Mircheva. 2019. "Global Value Chains: What are the Benefits and Why Do Countries Participate?" IMF Working Paper 19/18, International Monetary Fund, Washington, DC.

IMF (International Monetary Fund). 2011. "Assessing Reserve Adequacy." International Monetary Fund, Washington, DC.

———. 2019a. *Fiscal Monitor: How to Mitigate Climate Change.* October. Washington, DC: International Monetary Fund.

———. 2019b. *Global Financial Stability Report: Lower for Longer.* October. Washington, DC: International Monetary Fund.

IMF and World Bank 2017. *China – Financial Sector Assessment.* Washington, DC: International Monetary Fund and World Bank.

IPCC (Intergovernmental Panel on Climate Change). 2018. *Global Warming of 1.5°C.*, edited by V. Masson-Delmotte, P. Zhai, H. O. Pörtner, D. Roberts, J. Skea, P. R. Shukla, A. Pirani, et al. Geneva: Intergovernmental Panel on Climate Change.

Koh, W. C., and S. Yu. 2019. "Macroeconomic and Financial Sector Policies." *In A Decade after the Global Recession: Lessons and Challenges for Emerging and*

Developing Economies, edited by M. A. Kose, and F. Ohnsorge. Washington, DC: World Bank.

Kose, M. A., S. Kurlat, F. Ohnsorge, and N. Sugawara. 2017. "A Cross-Country Database of Fiscal Space." Policy Research Working Paper 8157, World Bank, Washington, DC.

Kose, M. A., and F. Ohnsorge. 2019. *A Decade after the Global Recession: Lessons and Challenges for Emerging and Developing Economies*. Washington, DC: World Bank.

Kose, M. A., N. Sugawara, and M. E. Terrones. 2019. "What Happens During Global Recessions?" In *A Decade after the Global Recession: Lessons and Challenges for Emerging and Developing Economies*, edited by M. A. Kose, and F. Ohnsorge. Washington, DC: World Bank.

Kose, M. A., and M. E. Terrones. 2015. *Collapse and Revival: Understanding Global Recessions and Recoveries*. Washington, DC: International Monetary Fund.

Krishnamurti, D., and Y. C. Lee. 2014. *Macro-prudential Policy Framework: A Practice Guide*. Washington, DC: World Bank.

Laeven, L., and F. Valencia. 2018. "Systemic Banking Crises Revisited." IMF Working Paper 18/206, International Monetary Fund, Washington, DC.

Martínez-Galán, E., and M. P. Fontoura. 2019. "Global Value Chains and Inward Foreign Direct Investment in the 2000s." *The World Economy* 42 (1): 175-196.

Mertens, T. M., and J. C. Williams. 2019. "Monetary Policy Frameworks and the Effective Lower Bound on Interest Rates." Federal Reserve Bank of New York Staff Reports. https://www.newyorkfed.org/medialibrary/media/research/staff_reports/sr877.pdf.

Molyneux, P., A. Reghezza, and R. Xie. Forthcoming. "Bank Profits and Margins in a World of Negative Rates." *Journal of Banking and Finance*.

Munoz, E., and E. Olaberria. 2019. "Are Budget Rigidities a Source of Fiscal Distress and a Constraint for Fiscal Consolidation?" Policy Research Working Paper 8956, World Bank, Washington, DC.

NGFS (Network for Greening the Financial System). 2018. *NGFS First Progress Report*. October. Report coordinated by the NGFS Secretariat/Banque de France, Paris.

OECD (Organisation for Economic Co-operation and Development). 2017. *Tax Administration 2017:*

Comparative Information on OECD and Other Advanced and Emerging Economies. Paris: OECD Publishing.

———. 2019a. *Tax Policy Reforms 2019: OECD and Selected Partner Economies*. Paris: OECD Publishing.

———. 2019b. *The OECD Technical Report on Progress on Structural Reform under the G20 Enhanced Structural Reform Agenda (ESRA)*. Paris: OECD Publishing.

Ohnsorge, F., M. Stocker, and Y. M. Some. 2016. "Quantifying Uncertainties in Global Growth Forecasts." Policy Research Working Paper 7770, World Bank, Washington, DC.

Packard, T. G., U. Gentilini, M. E. Grosh, P. B. O'Keefe, R. J. Palacios, D. A. Robalino, and I. V. Santos. 2019. *Protecting All: Risk Sharing for a Diverse and Diversifying World of Work*. Washington, DC: World Bank.

Pathikonda, V., and T. Farole. 2016. "The Capabilities Driving Participation in Global Value Chains." Policy Research Paper 7804, World Bank, Washington, DC.

Prichard, W., A. L. Custers, R. Dom, S. R. Davenport, M. A. Roscitt. 2019. "Innovations in Tax Compliance: Conceptual Framework." Policy Research Working Paper 9032, World Bank, Washington, DC.

Rachel, L., and L. H. Summers. 2019. "On Secular Stagnation in the Industrialized World." Brookings Papers on Economic Activity (Spring).

Ray, D., and J. Esteban. 2017. "Conflict and Development." *Annual Review of Economics* 9 (1): 263–93.

Rozenberg, J., and M. Fay. 2019. *Beyond the Gap: How Countries Can Afford the Infrastructure They Need While Protecting the Planet*. Washington, DC: World Bank.

Ruch, F. 2019a. "Prospects, Risks, and Vulnerabilities." In *A Decade after the Global Recession: Lessons and Challenges for Emerging and Developing Economies*, edited by M. A. Kose, and F. Ohnsorge. Washington, DC: World Bank.

———. 2019b. "Policy Challenges." In *A Decade after the Global Recession: Lessons and Challenges for Emerging and Developing Economies*, edited by M. A. Kose, and F. Ohnsorge. Washington, DC: World Bank.

Sarin, N., and L. H. Summers. 2019. "Shrinking the Tax Gap: Approaches and Revenue Potential." NBER Working Paper 26475, National Bureau of Economic Research, Cambridge, MA.

Shiller, R. 2015. *Irrational Exuberance*. Princeton University Press, Princeton, NJ.

Steinbach, M. R. 2019. "Growth in Low-Income Countries: Evolution, Prospects, and Policies." World Bank Policy Research Paper 8949, World Bank, Washington, DC.

Stocker, M., J. Baffes, Y. Some, D. Vorisek, and C. M. Wheeler. 2018. "The 2014-16 Oil Price Collapse in Retrospect: Sources and Implications." Policy Research Working Paper 8419, World Bank, Washington, DC.

Stokey, N. L. 2016. "Wait-and-See: Investment Options Under Policy Uncertainty." *Review of Economic Dynamics* 21 (July): 246-265.

Syverson, C. 2011. "What Determines Productivity?" *Journal of Economic Literature* 49 (2): 326–65.

Taglioni, D., and D. Winkler. 2016. *Making Global Value Chains Work for Development.* Washington, DC: World Bank.

UNCTAD (United Nations Conference on Trade and Development). 2019a. *World Investment Report 2019: Special Economic Zones.* Geneva, Switzerland: UNCTAD.

———. 2019b. *Global Investment Trend Monitor No. 32. October.* Geneva, Switzerland: UNCTAD.

Van Eyden, R., M. Difeto, R. Gupta, and M. E. Wohar. 2019. "Oil Price Volatility and Economic Growth: Evidence from Advanced Economies using more than a Century's Data." *Applied Energy* 233-234 (January): 612-621.

Verme, P., and A. Araar. 2017. *The Quest for Subsidy Reforms in the Middle East and North Africa Region: A Microsimulation Approach to Policy Making.* Cham, Switzerland: Springer.

Vorisek, D., and S. Yu. Forthcoming. "Understanding the Cost of Achieving the Sustainable Development Goals: The World Bank Group's Contributions." Policy Research Working Paper, World Bank, Washington, DC.

Wannier, S.R., L. Worden, N.A Hoff, E. Amezcua, B. Selo, C. Sinai, M. Mossoko, et al. 2019. "Estimating the Impact of Violent Events on Transmission in Ebola Virus Disease Outbreak, Democratic Republic of the Congo, 2018–2019." *Epidemics* 28 (September): 1-9.

Whalen, C., and F. Reichling. 2015. "The Fiscal Multiplier and Economic Policy Analysis in the United States." Congressional Budget Office Working Paper Series. Congressional Budget Office, Washington, DC.

Wieland, J. 2010. "Fiscal Multipliers in the Liquidity Trap: International Theory and Evidence", 2010 Meeting Papers 717, Society for Economic Dynamics.

Williams, J. C. 2016. "Monetary Policy in a Low R-star World," FRBSF Economic Letter, Federal Reserve Bank of San Francisco.

Woodford, M. 2011. "Simple Analytics of the Government Expenditure Multiplier." *American Economic Journal: Macroeconomics* 3 (1): 1-35.

———. 2012. "Methods of Policy Accommodation at the Interest-Rate Lower Bound." Proceedings, Economic Policy Symposium, Jackson Hole, Federal Reserve Bank of Kansas City: 185-288.

World Bank. 2015. *Global Economic Prospects: The Global Economy in Transition.* June. Washington, DC: World Bank.

———. 2016a. *Global Economic Prospects: Spillovers amid Weak Growth.* January. Washington, DC: World Bank.

———. 2016b. *World Development Report 2016. Digital Dividends.* Washington, DC: World Bank.

———. 2017a. *Global Economic Prospects: Weak Investment in Uncertain Times.* January. Washington, DC: World Bank.

———. 2017b. *The Distributional Impact of Taxes and Transfers: Evidence from Eight Developing Countries.* Washington, DC: World Bank.

———. 2017c. *World Development Report 2017. Governance and the Law.* Washington, DC: World Bank.

———. 2018a. *Global Economic Prospects: Broad-Based Upturn, but for How Long?* January. Washington, DC: World Bank.

———. 2018b. *Global Economic Prospects: The Turning of the Tide?* June. Washington, DC: World Bank.

———. 2018c. *Poverty and Shared Prosperity Report 2018: Piecing Together the Poverty Puzzle.* Washington, DC: World Bank.

———. 2018d. *World Development Report 2019: The Changing Nature of Work.* Washington, DC: World Bank.

———. 2018e. *China—Systematic Country Diagnostic: Towards a More Inclusive and Sustainable Development.* Washington, DC: World Bank.

———. 2019a. *World Development Report 2020: Global Value Chains: Trading for Development in the*

Age of Global Value Chains. Washington, DC: World Bank.

―――. 2019b. *East Asia and Pacific Economic Update: Weathering Growing Risks. October.* Washington, DC: World Bank.

―――. 2019c. *China Economic Update: Cyclical Risks and Structural Imperatives.* December. Washington, DC: World Bank.

―――. 2019d. "Migration and Remittances: Recent Developments and Outlook." Migration and Development Brief 31. Washington, DC: World Bank.

―――. 2019e. *Global Economic Prospects: Heightened Tensions, Subdued Investment.* June. Washington, DC: World Bank.

―――. 2019f. *South Asia Economic Focus: Making (De)centralization Work.* Fall. Washington, DC: World Bank.

―――. 2019g. *Europe and Central Asia Economic Update: Migration and Brain Drain.* October. Washington, DC: World Bank.

―――. 2019h. *Africa's Pulse: An Analysis of Issues Shaping Africa's Economic Future.* October. Washington, DC: World Bank.

―――. 2019i. *Middle East and North Africa Economic Update.* October. Washington, DC: World Bank.

―――. 2019j. *Fiscal Policies for Development and Climate Action.* Washington, DC: World Bank.

―――. 2019k. *Malawi Economic Monitor: Charting a New Course.* June. Washington, DC: World Bank.

―――. 2019l. *International Debt Statistics 2020.* Washington, DC: World Bank.

―――. 2019m. *Global Economic Prospects: Darkening Skies.* January. Washington, DC: World Bank.

―――. 2019n. *Inflation in Emerging and Developing Economies: Evolutions, Drivers and Policies.* Washington, DC: World Bank.

―――. 2019o. *Global Financial Development Report 2019/2020: Bank Regulation and Supervision a Decade after the Global Financial Crisis.* Washington, DC: World Bank.

―――. 2019p. *Fiscal Policies for Development and Climate Action.* Washington, DC: World Bank.

―――. 2020. *Doing Business 2020: Comparing Business Regulation in 190 Economies.* Washington, DC: World Bank.

World Bank and DRC (Development Research Center of the State Council, the People's Republic of China). 2019. *Innovative China: New Drivers of Growth.* Washington, DC: World Bank.

World Bank and IMF (International Monetary Fund). 2018. *Debt Vulnerabilities in IDA Countries.* Washington, DC: World Bank and International Monetary Fund.

World Bank et al. 2015. *Options for Low Income Countries Effective and Efficient Use of Tax Incentives for Investment: A Report to the G-20 Development Working Group by the IMF, OECD, UN and World Bank.* Washington, DC: World Bank.

World Bank et al. 2017. *Global Value Chain Development Report: Measuring and Analyzing the Impact of GVCs on Economic Development.* A report by IDE-JETRO, OECD, UIBE, WTO, and World Bank. Washington, DC: World Bank.

World Trade Organization (WTO). 2019a. *Services Trade Barometer.* Geneva: World Trade Organization.

―――. 2019b. *Report of The TPRB From the Director-General on Trade-Related Developments.* Geneva: World Trade Organization.

SPECIAL FOCUS 1

Price Controls:
Good Intentions, Bad Outcomes

The use of price controls is widespread across emerging markets and developing economies (EMDEs), including for food and key imported and exported commodities. While sometimes used as a tool for social policy, price controls can dampen investment and growth, worsen poverty outcomes, cause countries to incur heavy fiscal burdens, and complicate the effective conduct of monetary policy. Replacing price controls with expanded and better-targeted social safety nets, coupled with reforms to encourage competition and a sound regulatory environment, can be both pro-poor and pro-growth. Such reforms need to be carefully communicated and sequenced to ensure political and social acceptance. Where they exist, price control regimes should be transparent and supported by well-capitalized stabilization funds or national hedging strategies to ensure fiscal sustainability.

Introduction

Price distortions are defined as instances "when prices and production are higher or lower than the level that would usually exist in a competitive market" (WTO 2019). One source of such distortions are price controls.[1] Price controls can be imposed in a variety of ways. They may involve price ceilings, or price floors, imposed on selected goods and services by the authorities.[2]

In emerging market and developing economies (EMDEs), price controls on goods are often imposed to serve social and economic objectives. They may be part of government efforts to protect vulnerable consumers, by addressing market failures or subsidizing the cost of essential goods. Or they may be intended to maintain the incomes of producers, as part of a price-support program. Alternatively, they can serve the purpose of price smoothing, especially for key commodities subject to high volatility in international markets. This can lower uncertainty about households' real incomes and firms' production costs.

This special focus seeks to answer two questions.

- How prevalent are price controls in EMDEs?

- What challenges do they impose for growth and development and government policies?

Contribution. The research adds to the literature on price controls in two ways. First, it presents findings from a new data set. Whereas earlier work is confined to advanced economies or selected emerging markets, this study covers an almost complete set of EMDEs.[3] Second, it reviews price controls on a wider range of goods.[4]

Use of price controls

Widespread price controls in EMDEs. Price controls are widely employed across advanced economies and EMDEs. They tend to be more pervasive in EMDEs than in advanced economies

---

Note: This Special Focus was prepared by Justin-Damien Guénette.

[1] Price controls have a long history with well documented examples stretching back to Revolutionary France (Morton 2001). In the 20th century, these policies were used extensively in several western countries during the Second World War, culminating with widespread controls in the United States and the United Kingdom in the 1970s (Coyne and Coyne 2015). Price controls were also ubiquitous in communist countries with planned economies, such as Poland (Tarr 1994). Generalized price controls fell out of favor in the 1980s, as inflation declined, and governments pursued deregulation. However, controlled pricing for certain goods and services, including rent and pharmaceuticals, remain in use to this day (Morton 2001).

[2] Government management of prices can also occur as a by-product of other policies. For instance, preferential exchange rates for certain goods and the imposition of non-tariff barriers can all push prices away from that which would prevail in a competitive market.

[3] The data set extracts the list of products subject to price controls from the latest available Trade Policy Reviews for each EMDE member country of the World Trade Organization. This list of products is compiled using existing legislation and additional material provided by country authorities. The data set provides a rough view of the prevalence of price control measures across countries, but does not include any information on the extent of these controls.

[4] The micro-founded theory of price controls was developed in part to examine the case of commodity producers in developing countries (Stiglitz and Newbery 1979; Newbery and Stiglitz 1982). More recently, for EMDEs, price controls for petroleum products have been studied extensively, while those on food products have received less attention (Verme and Araar 2017; Kojima 2013; Devarajan 2013; Murphy et al. 2019; Shi and Sun 2017; Clements, Jung and Gupta 2007; Ghosh and Whalley 2004). The World Bank's Energy Sector Management Assistant Program (ESMAP) has conducted in-depth studies of subsidy reforms for energy markets across EMDEs (ESMAP 2019; Ore et al. 2018). The use of price controls for pharmaceutical products, wages and rent has been widely studied in advanced economies (e.g., Coyne and Coyne 2015; Nguyen et al. 1994). Studies for individual EMDEs include China, Indonesia and several MENA countries (Shi and Sun 2017; Clements, Jung and Gupta 2007; Verme and Araar 2017). The OECD-WBG Product Market Regulation indicators provide summary statistics on price controls for a limited set of EMDEs.

(OECD and World Bank 2018). And among EMDEs, they are more prevalent in LICs (Figure SF1.1). In EMDEs that have become middle-income countries (MICs) since 2001, price controls are somewhat less common than in the average EMDE, especially in goods other than energy, food, and construction materials.[5]

- *Energy.* Virtually all EMDEs impose price controls on energy products, including electricity and petroleum products such as liquified petroleum gas and gasoline.

- *Food.* Price controls are frequently applied to basic foodstuffs. This practice is more widespread in LICs than in other EMDEs: virtually all LICs impose price controls on some food items, compared with three-quarters of other EMDEs. Products often subject to price controls include water, sugar, and rice.[6] Since food expenditures represent nearly 60 percent of the consumption basket in LICs, compared with 42 percent in other EMDEs, a larger portion of the LICs basket is typically subject to price controls (Laborde, Lakatos, and Martin 2019). Virtually all LICs and other EMDEs impose price controls on petroleum products.

- *Construction materials.* Nearly 20 percent of LICs impose price controls on construction materials. These include cement, reinforcing bars, and metal sheets. Beyond LICs, controls on construction materials are most common in the Middle East and North Africa (MNA) and Sub-Saharan Africa (SSA).

Price controls on traded goods. EMDEs, including LICs, apply price controls on export and import goods.[7] Governments often impose controls on the domestic prices of imports to maintain real incomes of domestic consumers, hold down costs to producers, or smooth domestic price volatility.

- *Energy imports.* In LICs, about 67 percent of energy imports—about 6 percentage points more than the average for other EMDEs—are potentially subject to domestic price controls (Figure SF1.2).[8]

- *Food imports.* In both LICs and other EMDEs, only a small share of food and beverages imports are potentially subject to controls.

- *Construction material imports.* The largest difference between LICs and other EMDEs lies in the share of construction-related imports that are potentially subject to price controls: in LICs, they amount to one-quarter of imported construction materials, compared with almost none in other EMDEs.

Commodity exports. LICs often impose price controls on exportable commodities. This may involve a monopoly marketing agency, which purchases from domestic producers at a fixed price, and resells to foreign purchasers at the world price. This arrangement implicitly taxes producers when the resale price exceeds the purchase price (Ghosh and Whalley 2004) or subsidizes producers when the resale price falls below the purchase price. About 25 percent of EMDEs that rely heavily (with more than 10 percent of goods exports) on a single export commodity group impose price controls on it. For example, Burundi imposes controls on the price of coffee while Benin imposes controls on cashew nuts.

---

[5] The set of LICs in 2001 that are now MICs includes Angola, Armenia, Azerbaijan, Bangladesh, Bhutan, Côte d'Ivoire, Cameroon, Republic of Congo, Comoros, Georgia, Ghana, Indonesia, India, Kenya, Kyrgyz Republic, Cambodia, People's Democratic Republic of Lao, Lesotho, Republic of Moldova, Myanmar, Mongolia, Mauritania, Nigeria, Nicaragua, Pakistan, Sudan, Senegal, Solomon Islands, São Tomé and Príncipe, Turkmenistan, Ukraine, Uzbekistan, Vietnam, Zambia, and Zimbabwe.

[6] Almost all LICs, including Ethiopia, Mali, Niger, Guinea, and Rwanda impose some form of price controls on petroleum products. As for food products, LICs such as Burkina Faso and the Democratic Republic of Congo impose price controls on sugar. Chad, Haiti, and Guinea-Bissau impose controls on rice, and Benin, Ethiopia, and Niger impose controls on bread. Burkina Faso imposes controls on cement, reinforcing bars and metal sheets. In addition to goods, price controls are also often imposed on public transportation services such as bus, train, and ship fares.

---

[7] Unregulated prices depend on the world price, transport costs, local monopoly power or other hurdles to the movement of goods, and harvest conditions (Aksoy and Ng 2010).

[8] Data on price controls on tradable goods combines the information on controlled prices from the World Trade Organization's Trade Policies Reviews with 4-digit HS trade values from the World Bank's World Integrated Trade Solutions database.

Price controls on financial services. While not covered in the price control data set, the financial sector is also often a target of price controls. Around 60 EMDEs have imposed ceilings on interest rates. These measures are often motivated by a desire to provide targeted support to strategic industries or to shield consumers from financial exploitation. For example, in the case of Zambia, controls were implemented from 2012 to 2015 to reduce the perceived risk of over indebtedness and broaden access to credit (Maimbo and Gallegos 2014).

Decline in price controls. Starting in the 1980s, several EMDEs reduced the scope of price controls, opting instead to strengthen their competition policies and regulation (WTO 2000-2019). In some cases, the liberalization of prices was supported and encouraged by policy lending programs and debt relief efforts in highly indebted poor countries (HIPC). The removal of controls often become more feasible following an easing of the conditions that led to their imposition. For example, after 2011, as food prices declined from cyclical highs, some countries eliminated controls. EMDEs such as Mexico, Rwanda, and Côte d'Ivoire took advantage of the sharp decline in oil prices in 2014-16 to reduce petroleum subsidies (Baffes et al. 2018; Stocker et al. 2015).

Reforms in MENA. Under pressure from social tensions during the Arab Spring, some countries in the region introduced or tightened food price controls in 2011 (Ianchovichina, Loening and Wood 2014). Conversely, however, high oil prices and fiscal pressures encouraged a few MENA countries, including the Arab Republic of Egypt, Morocco, and Tunisia, to reform price controls and related subsidies on energy between 2010 and 2014 (Verme and Araar 2017).[9] The reforms were associated with improvements in the ease of doing business. Within two years of the reform, enterprises in all three countries reported easier access to electricity (Figure SF1.2.D). The

---

[9] Djibouti, Egypt, Jordan, Libya, Morocco, Tunisia, and Yemen designed and implemented subsidy reform programs. These cases contrast with some other countries in the region, where social tensions during the Arab Spring, caused an increased use of food price controls in 2011 (Ianchovichina, Loening, and Wood 2014).

FIGURE SF1.1 Price controls

LICs use price controls more extensively than other EMDEs, especially for energy products such as petroleum and electricity, and basic foodstuffs such as cereal products and sugar. A large portion of the LICs consumption basket is subject to price controls given the elevated share of food in the consumption bundle. Across EMDEs more broadly, price controls are most prevalent in MENA and Sub-Saharan Africa and least prevalent in South Asia.

A. Economies with price controls

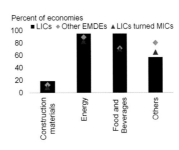

B. Goods most frequently subject to Price Controls in LICs

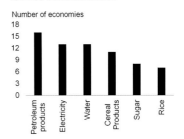

C. Share of food in total consumption expenditure

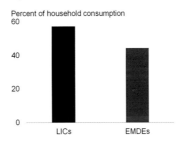

D. Economies with price controls by sub-region

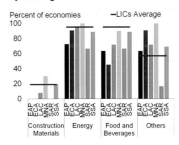

Source: World Bank; World Trade Organization.
Note: EMDEs = emerging markets and developing economies; LICs = low-income countries.
A. B. D. Listed price control policies are retrieved from the latest (2003-19) country Trade Policy Review publication.
A. C. D. Unweighted averages.
A. Sample includes 21 low-income countries, 23 LICs turned middle-income countries (MICs) since 2001, and 56 other EMDEs.
B. Sample includes 21 low-income countries.
C. Sample includes 23 low-income countries and 67 other EMDEs.
D. Sample includes 21 low-income countries and 79 other EMDEs. EAP = East Asia and Pacific, ECA = Europe and Central Asia, LAC = Latin America and the Caribbean, MNA = Middle East and North Africa, SAR = South Asia, SSA = Sub-Saharan Africa.

programs, however, differed substantially in their scope, and speed of implementation. They also varied with respect to compensatory transfers to disadvantaged population groups. Morocco reduced the fiscal burden of petroleum subsidies, while at the same time avoiding severe adverse consequences for poverty and inequality. Egypt, however, took a sequential, gradual, approach to reform especially for products such as liquified petroleum gas (LPG), which account for a disproportionately large expense for the poor.

FIGURE SF1.2 **Price controls on imported and exported goods**

The shares of imports and exports potentially covered by price controls are higher in LICs than in other EMDEs. Reforms of price controls on energy products in Egypt, Morocco and Tunisia were associated with improvements in an index of the ease of getting electricity within two years of energy price reforms.

A. Share of total imports subject to price controls

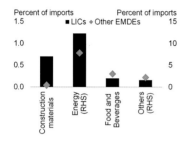

B. Share of 2-digit HS category imports subject to price controls

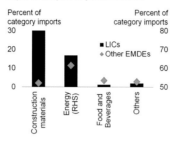

C. Share of countries with price controls on export goods

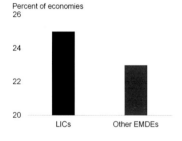

D. Ease of getting electricity

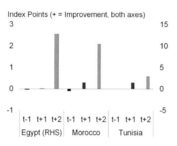

Source: World Bank; World Trade Organization.

Note: EMDEs = emerging markets and developing economies; LICs = low-income countries.

A.-C. 2017 data. Listed price control policies are retrieved from the latest (2003-19) country Trade Policy Review publication.

A. B. Sample includes 12 low-income countries and 63 other EMDEs.

B. Share of 4-digit Harmonized System (HS) category subject to controlled prices in high-level groupings of 2-digit HS categories. Construction materials aggregate includes HS68 and HS73, Energy aggregate includes HS27, Food and Beverage aggregate includes HS01 to HS22. Other aggregate includes all other imports.

C. Countries that rely heavily on a single export defined as a country in which exports of one or more 4-digit HS category represents 10 percent or more of its total exports in 2017. Chart shows the share of all LICs and other EMDEs that relying heavily on a single export whose price is subject to price controls. Sample includes 12 low-income countries and 61 other EMDEs.

D. Chart shows the World Bank's index for ease of getting electricity in year before (t-1) and the two years after (t+1, t+2) energy subsidy reform (World Bank 2019b). Time t=0 refers to 2014 for Egypt and Morocco and 2012 for Tunisia.

- *Egypt.* In July 2014, comprehensive reforms to fuel and electricity prices resulted in a significant rise in gasoline, natural gas, diesel, and electricity prices which contributed to a spurt of headline inflation. Initial price adjustments were followed by stepwise gradual increases to fully eliminate energy subsidies over a five-year period. While the initial price increases themselves are estimated to have raised the poverty rate and inequality, the government has put in place some mitigating measures for the poor, including expanding food subsidies (Verme and Araar 2017). Moreover, the government used a share of the proceeds from the reforms to increase expenditures on health care and education provision (ESMAP 2017a). However, attempts to communicate to the affected public that they might eventually benefit from the diversion of energy subsidies to more equitable uses failed, largely because the country does not have the social security net to implement an effective system of cash compensation (Verme and Araar 2017).

- *Morocco.* Starting in 2013, the government first transitioned to price indexation for petroleum products, and gradually moved to fully liberalize most energy products. In August 2014, prices of household utilities jumped as part of a multiyear effort to liberalize electricity prices. The reforms were implemented without triggering social unrest despite the absence of cash transfers to households. The fiscal savings from the reform were instead used to fund other reforms.

- *Tunisia.* The fiscal cost of Tunisia's energy subsidies had risen to unsustainable levels (7 percent of GDP in 2013), and in response the government gradually reduced them beginning in late 2012 in tandem with reforms to social benefits. Petroleum and electricity prices were increased over 2012-13 and an automatic price formula was introduced for gasoline in 2014. In 2016, the government agreed to further reduce subsidies as part of a reform program supported by IMF lending. Energy prices were increased several times since then, with the goal of fully eliminating energy subsidies by 2022. Over the years, measures were implemented to cushion the impact of reforms on vulnerable households, including expanded social housing and higher income tax deductions.

Reforms in other regions. In Ukraine in 2015-16, the government raised the price of natural gas, which had been heavily subsidized for decades. These reforms were coupled with a strong public communication campaign highlighting social assistance mechanisms targeted to cushion the impact on low-income households. The reforms were successful in allowing public utilities to achieve cost recovery, with the targeted support measures estimated to have reduced the poverty rate (ESMAP 2017b). In India starting in 2012, the government reformed its subsidy regime for liquified petroleum gas (LPG). LPG subsidies to households encouraged the formation of black markets where subsidized LPG distributed to households was diverted to the commercial sector. The government gradually increased the price of LPG for households while implementing a large-scale targeted cash transfer mechanism. The program successfully eliminated distortions in the LPG market, with limited adverse consequences for the poor, and the fiscal savings obtained from the reduction in subsidies fully offset the costs of the targeted cash transfer (ESMAP 2016).

Challenges of price controls

While they may be introduced with the best intentions to improve social outcomes, price controls often undermine growth and development, impose fiscal burdens and can weaken the effectiveness of monetary policy. At least in part, this is because price controls cause a shift in consumption towards the subsidized good, and away from other non-subsidized goods. Moreover, when there are trend increases in international prices, or when they interact with barriers to entry, price control measures frequently morph into distortive subsidy regimes. Important social, fiscal and environmental costs are likely to follow, as well as adverse consequences for investment and employment, and productivity growth.

Growth challenges. The use of price controls can have adverse consequences for growth for several reasons:

- *Stifled competition and reduced investment.* Price ceilings can depress producer margins and discourage domestic investment and entrepreneurial activity, as in Zimbabwe's transportation sector (Newfarmer and Pierola 2015). If margins depend on subsidies to local businesses to compensate for price controls,

they can discourage foreign investment in those sectors by increasing the country risk premium facing global firms (Sabal 2005). In the opposite case, where the controlled price is above that required for a competitive return to investment, its maintenance requires barriers to entry or costly government stockpiling of excess supply (a common occurrence with price support schemes in agriculture). Price-support controls can depress competition and sustain high producer margins (e.g., Rwanda's transportation sector; Teravaninthorn and Raballand 2009).

- *Lower productivity.* Price control regimes may tilt the allocation of resources towards the subsidized sector. In LICs, this is often most visible in the agricultural sector where output price controls have been complemented by input (especially fertilizer) subsidies. Yet, such policies can end up reducing productivity, and worsening income inequality (Goyal and Nash 2017). They may lead to inefficient use of subsidized inputs (Jayne, Mason, Burke and Ariga 2016). They can also adversely affect incentives to adopt productivity-raising new technologies. Empirical evidence suggests that market-oriented structural reforms, including the reduction of price controls and their related subsidies, are strongly associated with improved firm-level productivity in EMDEs (Kouame and Tapsoba 2018). Conversely, in the case of petroleum products in the Middle East and North Africa, high subsidies that underpin price controls appear to be associated with lower per capita output growth (Mundaca 2017).

- *Increased informality.* Price controls that distort consumption towards price-controlled goods, can cause chronic shortages of these goods, the formation of parallel markets with higher prices, and substitution towards lower-quality alternatives (Weitzman 1991; Patel and Villar 2016; Fengler 2012; Winkler 2015). Similarly, producers of price-controlled goods may turn to black markets which have elevated transaction costs and lack basic regulation (Murphy, Pierru and Smeers 2019). In addition, the situation encourages production to shift to firms in the informal sector, which avoid regulation (De Soto 2000; World Bank 2019a).

• *Distorted financial markets.* Price controls in the financial sector, such as ceilings on interest rates can distort financial markets (Maimbo and Gallegos 2014). These measures reduce the supply of credit to safer borrowers and small and medium-sized enterprises, increase the level of non-performing loans, reduce competition and innovation in lending markets, and increase informal lending. Moreover, they can exacerbate inequality by limiting the poor's access to lending.

• *Increased vulnerability to climate change.* Price controls and subsidies on energy products may heighten vulnerability to climate change and inhibit the transition to a climate-resilient, low-carbon economy.

Social policy and political economy challenges. The use of price controls combined with large subsidies is an inefficient tool for redistributing domestic income (Devarajan 2013; Coyne and Coyne 2015). These policies tend to be inequitable, as wealthier segments of the population, usually urban consumers, benefit disproportionately given their greater consumption of the price-controlled good compared to rural consumers and producers. For example, subsidies and below-market prices for gasoline and liquid natural gas have proven highly regressive, with only a small share of the subsidy benefiting the poorest segments of the population (Baffes et al. 2015; IEG 2008; Coady et al. 2006).

Fiscal challenges. Price controls impose an explicit or implicit set of taxes and subsidies that varies over time, and their enforcement may require additional regulations to constrain consumption and production. Typically, a system of price controls on goods ends up as a growing burden on either the fiscal budget and public debt or the profitability of producers (Alleyne 2013; World Bank 2014a). Potential or implicit fiscal costs from price controls can be particularly high in LICs due to their more widespread use of these policies. Even in EMDEs, subsidies for products

subject to price controls, such as petroleum, can be a large portion of government expenditures, in some cases exceeding 10 percent of GDP (Algeria, Iran; World Bank 2014b).

Monetary policy challenges. In all advanced economies, and in many EMDEs, monetary policy has played a major role in reducing inflation to a low, stable rate, often in the context of an explicit inflation-targeting regime. The key has been a transparent strategy aimed at the medium and longer term. This has largely stabilized longer-run expectations of inflation, in line with central bank objectives. In these circumstances, the one-off impact on the inflation rate of the removal of price controls can be handled with the help of careful communication from policymakers as to the strategy they will employ to get inflation back on track. In LICs, however, the monetary policy challenges go deeper. First, the wider use of price controls complicates the choice of inflation target by weakening the usefulness of the overall CPI as a measure of underlying inflation pressures (Patel and Villar 2016).[10] Second, it can raise inflation because the authorities tend to respond asymmetrically when faced with cost increases, as is often the case in response to food price shocks (De Mello 2008; Ianchovichina, Loening and Wood 2012). Third, it can increase the stickiness of the inflation process as changes in controlled prices often involve a lengthy regulatory process (Springer de Freitas and Bugarin 2007). Fourth, one-off changes in controlled prices can have persistent effects on inflation in LICs, where inflation expectations are less well anchored (Ha, Kose, and Ohnsorge 2019a; BIS 2003). Lastly, price controls in the financial sector, including ceilings on interest rates can reduce the ability of monetary policy to affect financial conditions.

Price controls in times of hyperinflation. The use of price controls has often coincided with historical episodes of hyperinflation. In Brazil in the 1980s, for example, the use of price controls

---

[10] In addition, volatility in headline CPI inflation is amplified by the high proportion of food in the LIC consumer basket. Food prices are liable to frequent large fluctuations from variations in local harvests, and in international supply and demand.

has proved ineffective at addressing hyperinflation in Brazil (Cardoso 1991). More recently, in the case of Zimbabwe, widespread shortages of goods in part due to excessively accommodative monetary policy were accompanied by extensive price controls (Munoz 2006; Coomer and Gstraunthaler 2011). Similarly, high inflation in República Bolivariana de Venezuela was accompanied by highly restrictive price controls (Vera 2017; Contreras and Guarata 2013).

Collateral damage from foreign price controls. LICs are also more vulnerable to the collateral damage from other countries' price controls on food and energy, because of the high share of food and energy in their consumption baskets and trade. Policies by individual countries to contain the effects of spikes in global commodity process in their local markets have been shown to have had the perverse effect of raising global prices (Laborde, Lakatos, and Martin 2019). Export restrictions in major commodity producers exacerbate global shortages, thus contributing to higher prices on the international market. In the case of the 2007-08 surge in food prices, a majority of EMDEs put in place policies to insulate domestic markets from the rise in international prices (World Bank 2009).

Policy implications

Price controls have been used to mitigate the impact of commodity price volatility on the most vulnerable members of society. For instance, the use of temporary stabilization funds, as introduced in Chile and Peru, or national hedging strategies, as introduced in Mexico, have been used to protect domestic consumers and firms from spikes in the prices of basic commodities on international markets (Kojima 2013; Ma and Valencia 2018). However, most governments have had difficulty designing frameworks that deliver lasting benefits. Over time, price stabilization policies often result in costly and distortionary subsidies, posing important challenges to growth, development, and macroeconomic policy suggesting that other policy instruments may be more effective in achieving social protection objectives.

Comprehensive reforms of price control policies and related subsidies. Replacing price controls with expanded and better-targeted social safety nets, coupled with structural reforms, can be both pro-poor and pro-growth. Indeed, policies to lower subsidies that underpin price controls appear to be associated with higher per capita output growth, in part because savings generated by lower subsidies can fund productivity-enhancing education and infrastructure (Mundaca 2017). The removal of price controls needs to be coupled with targeted support for those segments of the population that might be adversely affected (World Bank 2014a).[11] In India, for example, the removal of price controls was accompanied by targeted cash transfers and in Brazil by targeted assistance to low-income households for energy conservation (Deichmann and Zhang 2013). The different prongs of reforms, however, need to be carefully sequenced and communicated.

Enhanced competition. Improving the competitive environment can be a more effective means of lowering costs to consumers and producers than the use of price controls. Carefully-designed and properly enforced antitrust laws and consumer protection legislation, are essential components of institutional frameworks that support market mechanisms. A sound legal and regulatory framework favoring competitive markets provides a more effective response to many of the problems that price controls attempt to address (Kovasic 1995). For example, the removal of price controls and barriers to entry in the transportation sector significantly increased competition and lowered transportation costs in Rwanda (Teravaninthorn and Raballand 2009). Even in the case where incumbent firms maintained outsized market shares, the presence of competition, and the potential for new entrants, significantly lowered their markups (World Bank 2006).

---

[11] Despite the regressive nature of price controls and subsidies, poor households spend a higher share of their income on products subject to price controls and are liable to suffer distressful real income losses when price restrictions are lifted (World Bank 2014a).

References

Aaron, H. 1966. "Rent Controls and Urban Development: A Case Study of Mexico City." Social and Economic Studies 15 (4): 314-328.

Aksoy, A., and F. Ng. 2010. *Food Prices and Rural Poverty*. Washington, DC: World Bank.

Alleyne, T. 2013. *Energy Subsidy Reform in Sub-Saharan Africa: Experiences and Lessons*. Washington, DC: International Monetary Fund.

Baffes, J., M. A. Kose, F. Ohnsorge, and M. Stocker. 2015. "The Great Plunge in Oil Prices: Causes, Consequences, and Policy Responses." World Bank Policy Research Note 15(01).

Bank for International Settlements (BIS). 2003. *Fiscal Issues and Central Banking in Emerging Economics*. BIS Paper 20, Bank for International Settlements, Basel.

Cardoso, E. 1991. "Deficit Finance and Monetary Dynamics in Brazil and Mexico." *Journal of Development Economics* 37 (1-2): 173-197.

Clements, B., H.-S. Jung, and S. Gupta. 2007. "Real and Distributive Effects of Petroleum Price Liberalization: The Case of Indonesia." *The Developing Economies* XLV (2): 220-237.

Coady, D., M. El-Said, R. Gillingham, K. Kpodar, P. Medas, and D. Newhouse. 2006. "The Magnitude and Distribution of Fuel Subsidies: Evidence from Bolivia, Ghana, Jordan, Mali, and Sri Lanka." IMF Working Paper 06/247, International Monetary Fund, Washington, DC.

Contreras, J., and N. Guarata. 2013. "Inflacion y Variacion de Precios Relativos en Venezuela." *Economia* 38 (36) : 85-122.

Coomer, J., and T. Gstraunthaler. 2011. "The Hyperinflation in Zimbabwe." *The Quarterly Journal of Austrian Economics* 14(3): 311-346.

Coyne, C. and R. Coyne, eds. 2015. *Flaws and Ceilings Price Controls and the Damage They Cause*. London: Institute of Economic Affairs.

De Mello. L., ed. 2008. *Monetary Policies and Inflation Targeting in Emerging Economies*. Paris: Organisation for Economic Co-operation and Development.

Deichmann, U., and F. Zhang. 2013. *Growing Green the Economic Benefits of Climate Action*. Washington, DC: World Bank.

De Soto, H.. 2000. *The Mystery of Capital: Why Capitalism Triumphs in the West and Fails Everywhere Else*. New York: Basic Books.

Devarajan, S., and M. Giugale. 2013. "The Case for Direct Transfers of Resources Revenues in Africa". Working Paper 333, Center for Global Development, Washington, DC.

ESMAP (Energy Sector Management Assistance Program). 2017a. "Ukraine." Energy Subsidy Reform Facility Ukraine Country Brief, World Bank, Washington, DC.

———. 2017b. "Egypt." Energy Subsidy Reform Facility Ukraine Country Brief, World Bank, Washington, DC.

———. 2019. "Lifting the Burden of Electricity Subsidies, While Expanding Access." Energy Subsidy Reform Facility Rwanda Country Brief, World Bank, Washington, DC.

Fengler, W. 2012. "How Price Controls Can Lead to Higher Prices." World Bank Blogs, World Bank, Washington, DC.

Ghosh, M., and J. Whalley. 2004. "Are Price Controls Necessarily Bad? The Case of Rice in Vietnam." *Journal of Development Economics* 73(1): 215-232.

Goyal, A., and J. Nash. 2017. *Reaping Richer Returns: Public Spending Priorities for African Agriculture Productivity Growth*. Africa Development Forum. Washington, DC: World Bank.

Ha, J., M. A. Kose, and F. Ohnsorge, eds. 2019. *Inflation in Emerging and Developing Economies: Evolution, Drivers, and Policies*. Washington, DC: World Bank.

Ianchovichina, E., Loening, J. and Wood, C. 2012. "How Vulnerable are Arab Countries to Global Food Price Shocks?" Policy Research Working Paper 6018, World Bank, Washington, DC.

IEG (Independent Evaluation Group). 2008. "Climate Change and the World Bank Group. Phase 1—An Evaluation of World Bank Win-Win Energy Policy Reforms." World Bank, Washington, DC.

Jayne, T. S., N. M. Mason, W. J. Burke, and J. Ariga. 2016. "Agricultural Input Subsidy Programs in Africa: An Assessment of Recent Evidence." Working Paper 245892, Department of Agricultural, Food, and Resource Economics, Michigan State University.

Kojima, M. 2013. "Petroleum Product Pricing and Complementary Policies." World Bank Policy Research Working paper 6396, World Bank, Washington, DC.

Kouame, W., and S. J.-A. Tapsoba. "Structural Reforms and Firms' Productivity: Evidence from Developing Countries". Policy Research Working Paper 8308, World Bank, Washington, DC.

Kovasic, W. E. 1995. "Designing and Implementing Competition and Consumer Protection Reforms in Transitional Economies: Perspectives from Mongolia, Nepal, Ukraine and Zimbabwe." *DePaul Law Review* 44 (4): 1197-1224.

Laborde, D., C. Lakatos, and W. Martin. 2019. "Poverty Impact of Food Price Shocks and Policies." Policy Research Working Paper 8724. World Bank, Washington, DC.

Ma, C., and F. Valencia. 2018. "Welfare Gains from Market insurance: The Case of Mexican Oil Price Risk." IMF Working Paper 18/35, International Monetary Fund, Washington, DC.

Maimbo, S. M. and C. A. Henriquez Gallegos. 2014. "Interest Rate Caps around the World Still Popular, but a Blunt Instrument." Policy Research Working Paper 7070, World Bank, Washington, DC.

Morton, F. M. S. 2001. "The Problems of Price Controls." *Regulation* 24(1): 50-54.

Mpapalika, J., and C. Malikane. 2019. "The Determinants of Sovereign Risk Premium in African Countries." *Journal of Risk and Financial Management* 12 (1): 29-49.

Mundaca, G. 2017. "Energy Subsidies, Public Investment and Endogenous Growth." *Energy Policy* 110 (C): 693-709.

Munoz, S. 2006. "Suppressed Inflation and Money Demand in Zimbabwe." IMF Working Paper 06/15, International Monetary Fund, Washington, DC.

Murphy, F., A. Pierru, and Y. Smeers. 2019. "Measuring the Effects of Price Controls Using Mixed Complementarity Models." *European Journal of Operational Research* 275 (2): 666-676.

Newfarmer, R., and M. D. Pierola. 2015. *Trade in Zimbabwe Changing Incentives to Enhance Competitiveness*. Washington DC: World Bank.

Newbery, D. M. G., and J. E. Stiglitz. 1982. "Risk Aversion, Supply Response, and the Optimality of Random Prices: A Diagrammatic Analysis." The *Quarterly Journal of Economics* 97 (1): 1-26.

Nguyen, A. D. M., J. Dridi, F. Unsal, and O. H. Williams. 2017. "On the Drivers of Inflation in Sub-Saharan Africa." *International Economics* 151 (October): 71-84.

Ore, M. A. H., L. A. Sanchez, L. D. Sousa, and L. Tornarolli, eds. 2018. *Fiscal and Welfare Impacts of Electricity Subsidies in Central America*. Washington DC: World Bank.

OECD and World Bank. 2018. *Markets and Competition OECD-WBG PMR Indictors for Selected Non-OECD Countries (2013-2018)*. Washington, DC: World Bank.

Patel, N., and A. Villar. 2016. "Measuring Inflation." BIS Paper 89, Bank of International Settlements, Basel.

Pena Nelz, M. 2016. "LPG Subsidy Reform in India Put the Right Systems in Place First." Energy Sector Management Assistance Program, World Bank, Washington, DC.

Shi, X., and S. Sun. 2017. "Energy Price, Regulatory Price Distortion and Economic Growth: A Case Study of China." *Energy Economics* 63 (March): 261-271.

Silveira, R., and S. Malpezzi. 1991. "Welfare analysis of rent control in Brazil: the case of Rio de Janeiro." Discussion Paper INU 83, World Bank, Washington, DC.

Springer de Freitas, P., and M. Bugarin. 2007. "A Study on Administered Prices and Optimal Monetary Policy: The Brazilian Case." Centro de Estudios Monetarios Latinoamericanos, Mexico City.

Stiglitz, J. E., and D. M. G. Newbery. 1979. "The Theory of Commodity price Stabilization Rules: Welfare Impacts and Supply Responses." *The Economic Journal* 89 (December): 799-817.

Stocker, M., J. Baffes, Y. M. Some, D. Vorisek, and C. M. Wheeler. 2018. "The 2014-16 Oil Price Collapse in Retrospect." World Bank Policy Research Working Paper 8419, World Bank, Washington, DC.

Tarr, D. 1994. "The Welfare Costs of Price Controls for Cars and Color Televisions in Poland: Contrasting Estimates of Rent-Seeking from Recent Experience." World Bank Economic Review 8 (3): 415-443.

Teravaninthorn, S., and G. Raballand. 2009. *Transport Prices and Costs in Africa: A Review of the International Corridors*. Washington, DC: World Bank.

Vera, L. 2017. "In Search of Stabilization and Recovery: Macro Policy and Reforms in Venezuela." *Journal of Post Keynesian Economics* 40 (1): 9-26.

Verme, P., and A. Araar, eds. 2017. *The Quest for Subsidy Reforms in the Middle East and North Africa Region*. Washington DC: World Bank.

Weitzman, M. 1991. "Price Distortion and Shortage Deformation, or What Happened to the Soap?". *American Economic Review* 81 (3): 401-414.

Winkler, R. 2015. "Feast or Famine: The Welfare Impact of Food Price Controls in Nazi Germany." Discussion Papers in Economic and Social History 136, University of Oxford.

World Bank. 2006. *Review of Selected Railway Concessions in Sub-Saharan Africa*. Washington, DC: World Bank.

————. 2009. *Global Economic Prospects: Commodities at Crossroads*. January. Washington, DC: World Bank.

————. 2014a. "Transitional Policies to Assist the Poor While Phasing Out Inefficient Fossil Fuel Subsidies that Encourage Wasteful Consumption." Contribution by the World Bank to G20 Finance Ministers and Central Bank Governors. Washington, DC: World Bank (September).

————. 2014b. *MENA Economic Monitor: Corrosive Subsidies*. October. Washington, DC: World Bank.

————. 2018. *A New Economy for the Middle East and North Africa*. MENA Economic Monitor. Washington, DC: World Bank.

————. 2019. *Global Economic Prospects: Darkening Skies*. January. Washington, DC: World Bank.

————. 2019b. *Doing Business 2020: Sustaining the Pace of Reforms*. Washington DC: World Bank.

World Trade Organization. 2000-2019. *Trade Policy Review*. World Trade Organization, Switzerland.

————. 2019. "Distortion." WTO Glossary. Geneva, Switzerland: World Trade Organization, Geneva.

CHAPTER 2

REGIONAL OUTLOOKS

EAST ASIA and PACIFIC

Growth in the East Asia and Pacific (EAP) region is projected to slow from an estimated 5.8 percent in 2019 to 5.7 percent in 2020 and moderate further to 5.6 percent in 2021-22. Easier financing conditions and fiscal policy support will partly mitigate the lingering impact of trade tensions amid domestic challenges. Despite the recent slowdown, EAP remains the region with the fastest labor productivity growth. Nevertheless, productivity levels remain below the EMDE average in most EAP economies. In China, growth is expected to slow gradually, from an estimated 6.1 percent in 2019, to 5.9 percent in 2020, and to 5.7 percent by 2022. In the rest of the region, growth is expected to recover slightly to 4.9 percent in 2020 and firm further to 5 percent in 2021-22. The balance of risks to the outlook has improved, but is still tilted to the downside. Downside risks include a sharp slowdown in global trade due to a re-escalation of trade tensions; a sharper-than-expected slowdown in major economies; and a sudden reversal of capital flows due to an abrupt deterioration in financing conditions, investor sentiment, or geopolitical relations. An upside risk to the forecast is that the recent trade agreement between China and the United States leads to a sustained reduction in trade uncertainty, resulting in a stronger-than-expected recovery of regional investment and trade.

Recent developments

The East Asia and Pacific (EAP) region has been experiencing a continued cooling of domestic demand in China alongside sizable external headwinds (Figure 2.1.1). Global demand has weakened, and trade policy uncertainty related to trade disputes between China and the United States was elevated prior to the recent bilateral agreement. In addition, trade tensions between Japan and the Republic of Korea, a maturing electronics cycle, and disruptions caused by rapid shifts in technological and emission standards, have also weighed on regional manufacturing activity and trade (World Bank 2019a, 2019b).

The global trade slowdown and heightened trade policy uncertainty have affected regional growth through three main channels: weaker total exports; disruptions in cross-border supply chains; and declining private investment amid low business confidence (China, Indonesia, Malaysia, Thailand, the Philippines). Regional export growth has

decelerated sharply from its 2017-18 peak. Imports have also moderated, reflecting a drawdown of inventories and a slowdown in investment growth due to deteriorated business sentiment amid delays in certain major public infrastructure projects (China, Malaysia, Thailand, the Philippines).

In China, weakening exports have compounded the impact on GDP of the ongoing slowdown of domestic demand (Figure 2.1.2; World Bank 2019c). Regulatory tightening aimed at curbing non-bank lending has contributed to further cooling of domestic demand. Policy uncertainty and higher tariffs on exports to the United States, have dampened manufacturing activity, weighed on investor sentiment, and dented private investment. Despite this, net exports have been contributing to growth. Imports, especially intermediate goods imports, have contracted, partly reflecting high base effect, drawdown of inventories, disruptions in global and regional supply chains, an onshoring of foreign manufacturing operations, and a weaker renminbi. The negative shock to exports and output from trade tensions with the United States has been partly offset by currency depreciation, price

Note: This section was prepared by Ekaterine Vashakmadze. Research assistance was provided by Juncheng Zhou and Yushu Chen.

FIGURE 2.1.1 EAP: Recent developments

Growth continues to slow in China and has moderated in the rest of the region. Regional export growth has decelerated sharply from the 2017-18 peak. In the region excluding China, exports are showing incipient signs of recovery. Monetary policies have been eased across the region amid subdued inflation. Net capital outflows from China have resumed in 2019. In the rest of the region, capital flows have been essentially balanced. Bond spreads have generally declined.

A. Growth, 2019

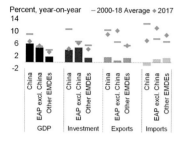

B. Export growth

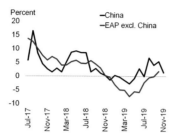

C. Consumer price inflation

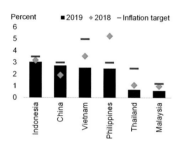

D. Nominal policy rates and change in inflation-adjusted policy rates

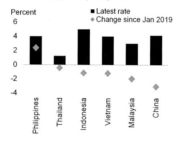

E. Net capital flows

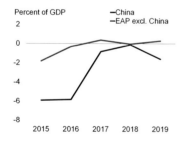

F. EMBI spreads

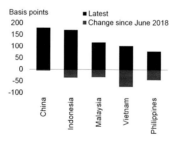

Source: Haver Analytics; World Bank.

A. Aggregate growth rates are calculated using GDP weights at 2010 prices and market exchange rates. Investment indicates fixed asset investment. Import and export data are volumes of goods and non-factor services. Investment, export, and import data for East Asia and Pacific region excl. China include Cambodia, Indonesia, Lao PDR, Malaysia, Mongolia, Philippines, Solomon Islands, Thailand, Vanuatu, and Vietnam. GDP data for East Asian and Pacific Countries excl. China include Cambodia, Fiji, Indonesia, Kiribati, Lao PDR, Malaysia, Marshall Islands, Micronesia Fed. Sets., Mongolia, Myanmar, Palau, Papua New Guinea, Philippines, Samoa, Solomon Islands, Thailand, Timor-Leste, Tonga, Tuvalu, Vanuatu, and Vietnam. Bars indicate 2019 which are estimates.

B. Export volumes. Data include only goods. 6-month moving average. Regional aggregate excludes Cambodia, Fiji, Lao PDR, Mongolia, Myanmar, Solomon Islands, Papua New Guinea, Timor-Leste, Vanuatu, and Vietnam due to data limitations. October-November export price deflators for China are estimates. Last observation is November 2019 for China and October 2019 for EAP excl. China.

C. Average year-on-year consumer price inflation. Mid-point of inflation target for Indonesia, Philippines, and Thailand. Inflation target for China and Vietnam. For Malaysia, the mid-point of Bank Negara's official forecast range of 0.7-1.7 percent in 2019. Last observation is November 2019.

D. Latest rate refers to Malaysia's overnight policy rate, Indonesia's 7-day reverse repo rate, China's loan prime rate, Thailand's one-day repurchase rate, Vietnam's discount rate and Philippines' overnight reverse repo rate. Change refers to the difference in real interest rate between November 2019 and January 2019. Last observation is November 2019.

E. Net capital flows are estimates. Net capital inflows include net capital and financial account balance, errors and omissions. Last observation is 2019Q3.

F. J.P. Moran Emerging Market Bond Index (EMBI) spread. Last observation is December 2019.

adjustments, some reshoring of production, and the redirection of exports to other countries. As a result, the current account surplus has widened.

In the rest of the region, some commodity importers operating at or above capacity have experienced a cyclical moderation of activity (Cambodia, the Philippines, Thailand, Vietnam). Weak export growth has added to the slowdown, especially in the economies that are deeply integrated into global and regional production networks (Thailand, the Philippines). Although Thailand and Vietnam have benefited somewhat from the diversion of U.S. demand away from China, the trade diversion only partially offset the decline in their exports to Asia arising from the overall negative impact of global trade tensions and cooling global demand, including in China, on the region.

In commodity exporters, which have only recently recovered from the effects of the earlier fall in commodity prices, the pace and composition of growth continues to reflect country-specific factors. In larger and more diversified economies, where past terms-of-trade shocks were less acute and macroeconomic fundamentals are solid, steady growth has continued at rates of around 4.5-5 percent per year (Indonesia, Malaysia). In Indonesia, growth has been supported by private consumption and a positive contribution from net exports amid import compression. In Malaysia, weak investment growth has been offset by robust consumption growth supported by tight labor markets.

The negative impact of slowing regional trade has so far been partly mitigated by monetary and fiscal policy support in major regional economies. Monetary policy in many countries has become more accommodative in response to slowing activity amid subdued inflation (Malaysia, the Philippines, Thailand, Vietnam). In China, the central bank has eased policy mainly by cutting bank reserve requirements, including the 0.5 percentage point cut implemented in early January 2020. In Indonesia, continued capital inflows, a stable exchange rate, and low inflation have provided the necessary space for Bank Indonesia to continue policy easing. Several countries have also provided fiscal support (China, Malaysia, Thailand). Thailand announced a broad range of stimulus measures, including a support package for farmers, SMEs, and low-income households (World Bank 2019a). China has introduced reductions in taxes and government fees, and a higher limit for local government on-budget borrowing. The consolidated fiscal and monetary policy support package implemented is, however, significantly smaller than the one adopted in the wake of the global financial crisis, and somewhat smaller than the one deployed in 2016.

Other factors—still-robust private consumption across much of the region and import compression—have dampened the impact of weakening manufacturing activity and exports on growth (Table 2.1.1). The recent de-escalation of China-U.S. trade tensions has buoyed asset prices and business confidence, and contributed to supportive external financing conditions. Bond spreads have narrowed, and net capital inflows have generally risen, despite sporadic episodes of market pressures.

Outlook

After moderating from an estimated 5.8 percent in 2019 to a projected 5.7 percent in 2020, regional growth is expected to ease further to 5.6 percent in 2021-22 (Tables 2.1.1 and 2.1.2). This mainly reflects a further moderate slowdown in China to 5.9 percent in 2020 amid continued domestic and external headwinds, including the lingering impact of trade tensions (Figure 2.1.3).

This outlook is predicated on no re-escalation of trade tensions between China and the United States going forward and a gradual stabilization in global trade. It also assumes that authorities in China continue to implement monetary and fiscal policies to offset the negative impact of weak exports. The baseline projections embody a weakened global outlook relative to June, partly reflecting a much weaker-than-expected outlook for global trade, manufacturing, and investment.

Despite recent de-escalation in China-U.S. bilateral trade tensions, heightened uncertainty surrounding the external environment is likely to

FIGURE 2.1.2 **Recent developments, China**

In China, growth has further decelerated amid continued cooling of domestic demand and heightened trade tensions. The negative shock to exports from higher tariffs on trade with the United States has been partly offset by currency depreciation. Imports from the United States have plummeted, while imports from other regions have also weakened. The current account surplus has widened. The government has stepped up its fiscal support measures, with a focus on tax- and non-tax-revenue cuts, and support for public investment spending through higher quotas for local government bonds. The stock of debt has stabilized, reflecting the decline of non-bank lending.

A. GDP growth

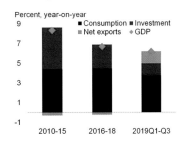

B. Export growth

C. Import growth

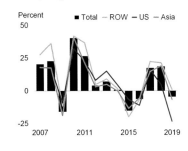

D. Balance of payments

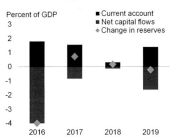

E. General government debt and fiscal balance

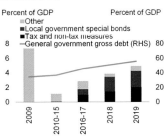

F. GDP growth and total debt

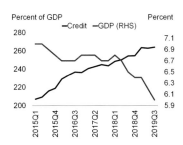

Source: Haver Analytics; International Monetary Fund; National Bureau of Statistics of China; World Bank.
A. Investment refers to gross capital formation, which includes change in inventories. Last observation is 2019Q3.
B.C. Data include only goods. Years cover January-November period. Last observation is November 2019. Asia includes both advanced and emerging Market and developing economies. ROW = all trading partners excluding the United States and Asia. Last observation for Asia and for ROW is October 2019. Export and import values. Data for total export growth in 2019 is -0.34 percent.
D. Net capital flows and change in reserves are estimates. Net capital inflows include net capital and financial account balance, errors and omissions. Last observation is 2019Q3.
E. Gross debt consists of all liabilities that require payment or payments of interest and/or principal by the debtor to the creditor at a date or dates in the future. Other includes other net expenditure (incl. social security and State-Owned Enterprise funds). Fiscal support measures are World Bank staff estimates. General government gross debt in 2019 are estimates.
F. Total debt is defined as a sum of domestic and external debt. Aggregate growth rates are calculated using GDP weights at 2010 prices and market exchange rates. Last observation for total credit and GDP growth is 2019Q3.

FIGURE 2.1.3 **EAP: Outlook and risks**

EAP growth is projected to gradually decline, mainly reflecting slower growth in China. Growth in the rest of the region is expected to stabilize by 2020, with notable cross-country heterogeneity reflecting country specific conditions. The long-term investment outlook is for broad-based deceleration. The region is characterized by deep global integration, which makes countries vulnerable to external trade or financial shocks.

A. GDP growth

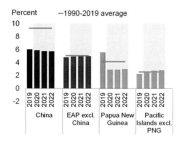

B. Output and potential growth

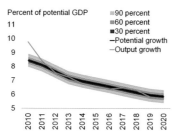

C. Contribution to productivity growth

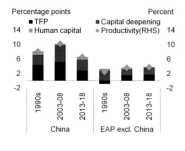

D. Ten-year ahead investment forecasts

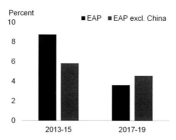

E. Export growth, 2013-18

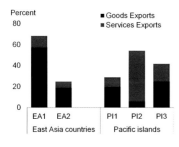

F. Growth impact of 1 percentage point slower growth in China, Japan, or other G7 countries

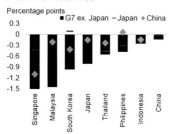

Source: International Monetary Fund; Penn World Tables; The Consensus Forecasts; World Bank.
A. EAP excl. China = Cambodia, Indonesia, Lao PDR, Malaysia, Mongolia, Myanmar, Philippines, Thailand, and Vietnam. Pacific Island excl. PNG includes Fiji, Kiribati, Marshall Islands, Micronesia, Palau, Samoa, Solomon Islands, Timor-Leste, Tonga, Tuvalu, and Vanuatu. 1990-2019 average for EAP excl. China excludes Myanmar and 1990-2019 for Pacific Island excl. PNG excludes Marshall Islands, Micronesia, Palau, Timor-Leste, and Tuvalu. Aggregate growth rates are calculated using GDP weights at 2010 prices and market exchange rates. Data in shaded areas are forecasts.
B. Potential growth estimates are from a multivariate filter model of WB (2018a). Aggregate growth rates are calculated using GDP weights at 2010 prices and market exchange rates. Includes China, Indonesia, Malaysia, Mongolia, the Philippines, and Thailand. Output growth in 2020 is a forecast.
C. Productivity defined as output per worker in 2010 U.S. dollars at 2010 prices and exchange rates.
D. 10-year-ahead forecasts surveyed in indicated year. Constant 2010 U.S. dollar investment-weighted averages. Sample includes China, Indonesia, Malaysia, the Philippines, and Thailand.
E. EA = East Asia. PI = Pacific Islands. EA1 = Brunei Darussalam, Cambodia, Malaysia, Mongolia, Thailand, and Vietnam; EA2 = Indonesia, Lao PDR, Myanmar and Philippines. PI1 = Kiribati, Marshall Islands, Micronesia, Timor-Leste, Tonga, and Tuvalu; PI2 = Palau and Vanuatu; PI3 comprises Fiji, Papua New Guinea, Samoa, and Solomon Islands.
F. Median cumulative responses after two years. Based on a Bayesian structural VAR model. Data coverage is 1998Q1-2018Q2 and is shorter for some countries. The endogenous variables include, in this Cholesky ordering: growth in G7 excluding Japan, EMBI, Japan's growth, China's growth, Korea's growth, and three variables for each shock-recipient country: real commodity price index, growth, and real effective exchange rates. Global spillovers refer to spillovers from growth shocks in the G7 excluding Japan. The model includes a dummy that captures the global financial crisis of 2008-09. Vertical lines represent the 33-66 percent confidence bands.

persist, amid a fragile global outlook, compounding the trade weakness over the near term.

Regional growth excluding China is projected to slightly recover to 4.9 percent in 2020 and firm further to 5 percent in 2021-22—toward its potential—assuming that weakness in manufacturing and export activity does not spill over to consumption and services. Domestic demand will continue to benefit from generally supportive financing conditions, amid low inflation and robust capital flows (Cambodia, the Philippines, Thailand, Vietnam). Some countries will benefit from large public infrastructure projects coming onstream (Thailand, the Philippines).

Growth in the economies that are deeply integrated into global and regional production networks is expected to moderate further in 2021-22, and to adjust a bit faster than expected toward potential, reflecting capacity constraints and subdued external demand. In particular, in Malaysia, growth is expected to inch down to 4.5 percent in 2020-21, with weak export growth partly offset by strong domestic demand, underpinned by favorable financing conditions, a rebound in investment, stable labor market conditions, and low inflation.

In Indonesia, which depends less on exports than other regional economies, growth is projected to fluctuate around 5 percent throughout the forecast horizon. This forecast is predicated on a continued support from private consumption, a pickup in investment, solid growth of the working-age population, and improving labor markets. In small commodity exporters, growth is expected to decelerate, but remain strong (Mongolia), or rebound in 2022 (Papua New Guinea), supported by investment in infrastructure and mining.

While growth in the region is projected to remain robust in the near term, underlying potential growth is likely to continue to decline over the long term (Chapter 3; World Bank 2018a, 2018b). The slowdown is expected to be broad-based, reflecting deteriorating demographic trends, especially in China, Thailand, and Vietnam, combined with a projected slowdown in capital accumulation and lower total factor productivity in China as credit growth is reined in (Box 2.1.1.; Chapter 3). Investment growth in the rest of the EAP region is also expected to be subdued and below historical averages, as the long-term prospects for investment growth in the region remain weak and have been persistently downgraded since 2010.

Risks

The balance of risks has improved, but remains tilted to the downside. Downside risks include a sharp slowdown in global trade due to a re-escalation of global trade tensions; a sharper-than-expected slowdown in major economies; and a sudden reversal of capital flows due to an abrupt deterioration in global financing conditions, investor sentiment, or geopolitical relations.

A renewed spike in trade policy uncertainty could cause a deterioration in confidence, investment, and trade (Caldara et al. 2019; Freund et al. 2018). Failure by China and the United States to reach a long-term, comprehensive, and durable agreement could lead to renewed trade tensions, with broad-ranging global and regional conse-quences.

An upside risk to the forecast is the possibility of a sustained de-escalation of trade tensions between China and the United States. The recent trade agreement that reverses some tariff increases could be the beginning of a constructive process leading to a sustained reduction in policy uncertainty and trade barriers. This could significantly improve confidence and unlock pent-up demand for investment, bolstering growth.

In the baseline scenario, the impact of slower global growth and external demand on the region is offset by more supportive financing conditions and stronger policy stimulus. However, a sharper-than-baseline deceleration of activity in large economies—the Euro Area, China, or the United States—could have adverse repercussions across the region through weaker demand for exports

and the disruption of global value chains, as well as through financial, investment, commodity, and confidence channels (Chapter 1; World Bank 2016a; World Bank 2019d).

Risks of a sharper-than-expected slowdown in China stem from domestic challenges, as well as from the difficult external environment. The total leverage of the economy—measured as the ratio of total credit (general government and non-financial private sector) to GDP—has surpassed 260 percent of GDP in 2019, although the share of non-bank lending continued to decline due to regulatory tightening. High corporate indebtedness in sectors with weak profitability is of concern (World Bank 2019e). A sizable portion of recent support measures has taken the form of expanding local government special bond quotas. The growing debt burden on local authorities may increase their vulnerability to shocks.

Most of the EAP region weathered the deterioration of external conditions in 2019 well, relying on exchange rate flexibility and monetary and fiscal stimulus. A further deterioration would test the resilience of the region's economies. Even though most large countries have generally sound economic fundamentals—track record of solid growth, fast labor productivity growth, large consumer bases, diversified economies, sound policy frameworks, and strong policy buffers—the region remains vulnerable to risks related to abrupt changes in global financial conditions.

Many countries have pockets of vulnerabilities. These include elevated debt (Lao People's Democratic Republic, Malaysia, Mongolia, Vietnam); sizable fiscal deficits (Lao PDR, Vietnam); or heavy reliance on volatile capital flows (Cambodia, Indonesia). Renewed episodes of financial market stress could have pronounced and widespread effects on countries with high indebtedness (Chapter 1). Vulnerabilities among some EAP countries could amplify the impact of external shocks, such as a sudden stop in capital flows or a rise in borrowing costs.

TABLE 2.1.1 East Asia and Pacific forecast summary

(Real GDP growth at market prices in percent, unless indicated otherwise)

Percentage point differences
from June 2019 projections

	2017	2018	2019e	2020f	2021f	2022f	2019e	2020f	2021f
EMDE EAP, GDP[1]	**6.5**	**6.3**	**5.8**	**5.7**	**5.6**	**5.6**	**-0.1**	**-0.2**	**-0.2**
(Average including countries with full national accounts and balance of payments data only)[2]									
EMDE EAP, GDP[2]	6.5	6.3	5.8	5.7	5.6	5.6	-0.1	-0.2	-0.2
GDP per capita (U.S. dollars)	5.8	5.6	5.2	5.1	5.1	5.1	-0.2	-0.2	-0.2
PPP GDP	6.4	6.3	5.8	5.7	5.6	5.6	-0.1	-0.2	-0.2
Private consumption	6.1	8.4	6.8	6.9	6.6	6.6	-0.2	-0.1	-0.4
Public consumption	8.9	8.7	7.7	7.6	7.5	7.5	0.1	0.1	0.1
Fixed investment	4.7	5.1	4.1	4.6	4.7	4.6	-1.0	-0.5	-0.2
Exports, GNFS[3]	9.5	5.0	1.4	1.3	2.0	2.4	-1.9	-2.6	-2.3
Imports, GNFS[3]	8.4	8.4	-0.3	2.0	2.5	2.9	-5.0	-3.0	-3.2
Net exports, contribution to growth	0.4	-0.9	0.5	-0.2	-0.1	-0.1	0.9	0.2	0.4
Memo items: GDP									
East Asia excluding China	5.4	5.2	4.8	4.9	5.0	5.0	-0.3	-0.3	-0.2
China	6.8	6.6	6.1	5.9	5.8	5.7	-0.1	-0.2	-0.2
Indonesia	5.1	5.2	5.0	5.1	5.2	5.2	-0.2	-0.2	-0.1
Thailand	4.0	4.1	2.5	2.7	2.8	2.9	-1.0	-0.9	-0.9

Source: World Bank.
Note: e = estimate; f = forecast. EMDE = emerging market and developing economies. World Bank forecasts are frequently updated based on new information and changing (global) circumstances. Consequently, projections presented here may differ from those contained in other Bank documents, even if basic assessments of countries' prospects do not differ at any given moment in time.
1. GDP and expenditure components are measured in 2010 prices and market exchange rates. Excludes Democratic People's Republic of Korea and dependent territories.
2. Sub-region aggregate excludes Democratic People's Republic of Korea, dependent territories, Fiji, Kiribati, the Marshall Islands, the Federated States of Micronesia, Myanmar, Nauru, Palau, Papua New Guinea, Samoa, Timor-Leste, Tonga, and Tuvalu, for which data limitations prevent the forecasting of GDP components.
3. Exports and imports of goods and non-factor services (GNFS).
To download the data in this table, please visit www.worldbank.org/gep.

TABLE 2.1.2 East Asia and Pacific country forecasts[1]

(Real GDP growth at market prices in percent, unless indicated otherwise)

Percentage point differences
from June 2019 projections

	2017	2018	2019e	2020f	2021f	2022f	2019e	2020f	2021f
Cambodia	7.0	7.5	7.0	6.8	6.8	6.8	0.0	-0.1	0.0
China	6.8	6.6	6.1	5.9	5.8	5.7	-0.1	-0.2	-0.2
Fiji	5.2	4.2	1.0	1.7	2.9	3.0	-2.4	-1.6	-0.4
Indonesia	5.1	5.2	5.0	5.1	5.2	5.2	-0.2	-0.2	-0.1
Lao PDR	6.9	6.3	5.2	5.8	5.7	5.6	-1.4	-0.9	-0.9
Malaysia	5.7	4.7	4.6	4.5	4.5	4.5	0.0	-0.1	-0.1
Mongolia	5.3	7.2	5.7	5.5	5.2	5.5	-1.5	-1.4	-1.0
Myanmar	6.8	6.5	6.6	6.7	6.8	6.8	0.1	0.1	0.0
Papua New Guinea	3.5	-0.8	5.6	2.9	2.9	3.0	0.0	-0.2	-0.6
Philippines	6.7	6.2	5.8	6.1	6.2	6.2	-0.6	-0.4	-0.3
Solomon Islands	3.0	3.5	2.9	2.8	2.8	2.7	0.0	0.0	0.1
Thailand	4.0	4.1	2.5	2.7	2.8	2.9	-1.0	-0.9	-0.9
Timor-Leste	-3.5	-1.1	4.2	4.6	4.9	5.0	0.3	0.0	-0.1
Vietnam	6.8	7.1	6.8	6.5	6.5	6.4	0.2	0.0	0.0

Source: World Bank.
Note: e = estimate; f = forecast. World Bank forecasts are frequently updated based on new information and changing (global) circumstances. Consequently, projections presented here may differ from those contained in other Bank documents, even if basic assessments of countries' prospects do not significantly differ at any given moment in time.
1. GDP and expenditure components are measured in 2010 prices and market exchange rates.
To download the data in this table, please visit www.worldbank.org/gep.

BOX 2.1.1 Labor productivity in East Asia and Pacific: Trends and drivers

East Asia and Pacific (EAP) remains the region with the fastest productivity growth, averaging 6.3 percent a year in 2013-18, notwithstanding the second-steepest post-crisis slowdown among emerging market and developing economy (EMDE) regions. Nevertheless, productivity levels remain below the EMDE average in most EAP economies. While factor reallocation toward more productive sectors, high investment, and trade integration with product upgrading have promoted above-average productivity growth, most of these drivers are expected to become less favorable in the future. A comprehensive set of reforms to liberalize services sectors, improve corporate management, level the playing field for private firms, enhance human capital, facilitate urban development, and foster innovation is needed to reverse the recent productivity growth slowdown.

Introduction

Growth of labor productivity, defined as output (GDP) per worker, averaged 6.3 percent a year in the East Asia and Pacific (EAP) region in 2013-18 (Figure 2.1.1.1).[1] While this pace remained the fastest among emerging market and developing economy (EMDE) regions, it was almost 3 percentage points below EAP's pre-crisis (2003-08) average after the second-steepest post-crisis decline in labor productivity growth among EMDE regions. The post-crisis slowdown in productivity growth has been broad-based, affecting 60 percent of EMDEs in EAP.

At 12 percent of the advanced-economy average in 2013-18, average productivity in EAP remains below the EMDE average.[2] Labor productivity *levels* in EAP are more homogeneous than in other EMDE regions. Similarly, productivity *growth* is more homogeneous across EAP than across other EMDE regions, possibly reflecting particularly close regional integration, including through regional supply chains.

This box builds on a considerable literature that examines productivity growth in EAP. Earlier studies have documented the recent productivity growth slowdown in EAP using country-level and firm-level data.[3] Others have identified education, innovation, market efficiency, institutions, and physical infrastructure as the main drivers of productivity improvements in EAP (Kim and Loayza 2019). Another set of studies has empirically documented

how product and labor market reforms have increased output and productivity.[4]

Against this backdrop and drawing on these studies, this box compares productivity developments in EAP with other EMDE regions. In particular, it discusses the following questions:

- How has productivity evolved in the region?

- What factors have been associated with productivity growth in the region?

- What policy options are available to boost regional productivity growth?

This box considers labor productivity, defined as real GDP per worker (at 2010 prices and market exchange rates). The data are available for sixteen countries: Cambodia, China, Fiji, Indonesia, Lao People's Democratic Republic, Malaysia, Mongolia, Myanmar, Papua New Guinea, the Philippines, Samoa, the Solomon Islands, Thailand, Tonga, Vanuatu, and Vietnam.

Evolution of regional productivity

Rapid productivity growth. Labor productivity growth in EAP averaged 6.4 percent a year between the early 1980s and 2018—the highest growth rate of all EMDE regions, mainly reflecting rapid growth in China. EAP labor productivity growth rose from 4.3 percent a year in the 1980s to 6.3 percent a year in the 1990s, and peaked at 8.9 percent a year in 2003-08 (Figure 2.1.1.2). Since the global financial crisis, EAP productivity growth has slowed to 6.3 percent a year on average during 2013-18. This post-crisis slowdown is also accounted for largely by China, in particular its policy-guided move towards more sustainable growth after a period of exceptionally rapid expansion of fixed investment and exports; in the region's

---

Note: This section was prepared by Ekaterine Vashakmadze, building upon analysis in Chapter 3. Research assistance was provided by Juncheng Zhou and Shijie Shi.

[1] Unless otherwise specified, productivity is defined as labor productivity, that is, output per worker.

[2] EAP averages are heavily influenced by China, which accounts for 80 percent of EAP output in 2013-18. That said, even the median productivity level in EAP is below that of the median EMDE region.

[3] For studies using country-level data, see APO (2018); IMF (2006), (2017); World Bank (2018a), and World Bank (2019a). For studies using firm-level data, see Di Mauro et al. (2018); de Nicola, Kehayova, and Nguyen (2018); OECD (2016); and World Bank and DRCSC (2019).

[4] See Adler et al. (2017); Bouis, Duval and Eugster (2016); Chen (2002); Nicoletti and Scarpetta (2005); Timmer and Szirmai (2000).

BOX 2.1.1 Labor productivity in East Asia and Pacific: Trends and drivers (*continued*)

FIGURE 2.1.1.1 Productivity in EAP compared with other country groups

EAP has remained the region with the fastest productivity growth, at 6.3 percent a year in 2013-18, notwithstanding the second-steepest post-crisis slowdown among EMDE regions. Nevertheless, productivity levels remain below the EMDE average in most EAP economies.

A. Average annual growth in EMDE regions

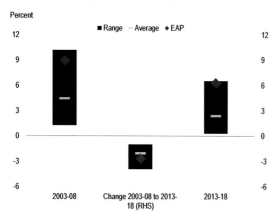

B. Productivity levels in 2013-18 and annual convergence rates in EMDE regions

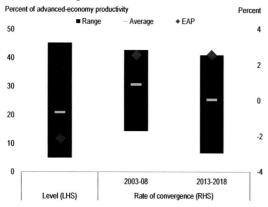

Source: Penn World Table; The Conference Board; World Bank (World Development Indicators).

Note: Unless otherwise specified, productivity refers to labor productivity, defined as output per worker. Sample comprises 35 advanced economies and 127 EMDEs, of which 16 are in East Asia and the Pacific (EAP), 21 are in Eastern Europe and Central Asia (ECA), 25 are in Latin America and the Caribbean (LAC), 14 are in Middle East and North Africa (MNA), 7 are in South Asia (SAR), and 44 are in Sub-Saharan Africa (SSA).

A. Blue bars denote range across GDP-weighted averages for 6 EMDE regions. Yellow lines denote simple average of the 6 EMDE regional averages. Red dots denote simple average of 16 EMDEs in EAP.

B. Rate of convergence calculated as the difference in productivity growth rates with the average advanced economy (AE) divided by the log difference in productivity levels with the average advanced economy. Regional rate of convergence is the GDP-weighted average of EMDE members of each region. "Level" of productivity refers to the GDP weighted average of regional productivity as a share of the average advanced economy during 2013-2018.

other major economies, productivity growth has been broadly stable. Around two-thirds of EAP economies in 2013-18 were still experiencing labor productivity growth above their long-run average.

Within-region heterogeneity. While productivity growth exceeded the EMDE average during 2013-18 in most EAP economies (the exceptions being some Pacific Islands), there was some cross-country heterogeneity. Productivity growth was particularly fast in China, followed by several large Association of Southeast Asian Nations (ASEAN) economies, including Vietnam. These countries were among the ten percent of EMDE economies with the fastest productivity growth in the period. They benefited from improvements in human capital, and trade openness, technology transfer and adaptation, high investment rates, and an industrial base that was rapidly becoming more sophisticated (Andrews et al. 2015). Productivity growth was slowest among EAP economies in some Pacific Islands, including Solomon Islands, partly reflecting political tensions.

Low productivity levels. Notwithstanding rapid productivity growth, average productivity levels in EAP (12 percent of the advanced-economy average in 2013-18), including China, remained below the EMDE average (which is close to 20 percent of the advanced-economy average; APO 2018; Di Mauro et al. 2018). Malaysia, the EAP economy with the highest productivity level (25 percent of the advanced-economy average), has benefited from several decades of sustained high growth rates reflecting its diversified production and export base and sound macroeconomic policies (Munoz et al. 2016).

Labor productivity convergence. Whereas convergence of productivity toward advanced-economy levels in most other EMDE regions has slowed since the financial crisis, it has remained robust in EAP reflecting macroeconomic stability, strong fundamentals, still high investment rates, and diversified and competitive production bases in the region's major economies (Chapter 3). Assuming recent productivity growth can be sustained, at least 50 percent of economies in the region are on course to halve their productivity gap relative to advanced-economy averages over the next 40 years. History shows how successful productivity convergence by such economies as Singapore and the Republic of Korea, which were reclassified as advanced economies in the 1990s, required high and sustained productivity growth differentials relative to established advanced economies over several decades (Chapter 3).

BOX 2.1.1 Labor productivity in East Asia and Pacific: Trends and drivers (*continued*)

FIGURE 2.1.1.2 Evolution of productivity in EAP

To a larger extent than in the average EMDE, the post-crisis slowdown in EAP's productivity growth has reflected slowing total factor productivity growth, especially in China. In EAP, slowing TFP growth accounted for two-thirds of the post-crisis slowdown in labor productivity growth, compared to about half in the average EMDE. Notwithstanding rapid productivity growth, average productivity levels in EAP—12 percent of the advanced-economy average—remain below the EMDE average.

A. Annual productivity growth in EAP

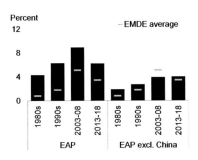

B. Share of economies with productivity growth in 2013-18 below long-run and pre-crisis averages

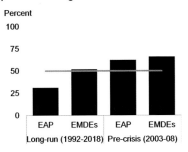

C. Contributions to annual productivity growth

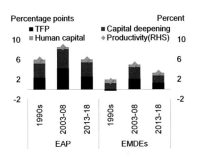

D. Contributions to annual productivity growth

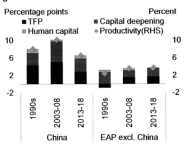

E. Productivity levels relative to advanced-economy average

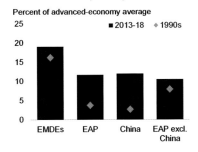

F. Annual labor force growth

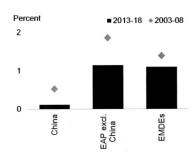

Source: Barro and Lee (2015); Haver Analytics; International Monetary Fund; Penn World Tables; United Nations; Wittgenstein Centre for Demography and Global Human Capital; World Bank (World Development Indicators).
Note. Unless otherwise specified, productivity refers to labor productivity, defined as output per worker in 2010 U.S. dollars at market exchange rates.
A. Average growth rates calculated using 2010 U.S. dollars at market exchange rates.
B. Share of countries for which productivity growth average over 2013-18 is lower compared to a long-run (1992-2018) and pre-crisis (2003-08) average. Yellow line denotes 50-percent line.
C.D. Aggregate growth rates calculated using GDP weights at 2010 prices and market exchange rates. Samples comprise 92 EMDEs and 16 EAP economies.
E. Aggregate growth rates calculated using GDP weights at 2010 prices and market exchange rates. Samples comprise 35 advanced economies, 127 EMDEs and 16 EAP economies.
F. Derived using data from International Labour Organization, ILOSTAT database and World Bank population estimates. Labor force data retrieved in September 2019.

Sources of productivity growth. Productivity growth can be decomposed into its sources: factor accumulation (human or physical capital) and increases in the efficiency of factor use (total factor productivity, or TFP). In EAP, slowing TFP growth accounted for two-thirds of the post-crisis slowdown in labor productivity growth, compared to about half in the average EMDE. This followed a decade of surging TFP growth in EAP, as China's World Trade Organization accession in 2001 was followed by rapid trade integration, large foreign direct investment (FDI) inflows into the region, and rapid technological adaptation

(Mason and Shetty 2019; Tuan, Ng, and Zhao 2009; Xu, Xinpeng and Sheng 2012). These reforms were accompanied by improvements in macroeconomic policies, strengthening institutions, and higher investment in infrastructure and human capital in several countries (China, Indonesia, Malaysia, the Philippines, Vietnam). The post-crisis slowdown in the region's TFP growth partly reflects a moderation in the pace of global integration (Ruta, Constantinescu, and Mattoo 2017). Weaker investment accounted for another one-third of the slowdown in labor productivity growth in EAP, as

BOX 2.1.1 Labor productivity in East Asia and Pacific: Trends and drivers (*continued*)

investment booms before the global financial crisis and in its immediate wake subsided, especially in response to policy guided moderation in China (Kose and Ohnsorge 2019).

Heterogeneity in productivity growth. EAP's high average productivity growth masks some divergence between China and the rest of EAP. Whereas TFP growth and capital deepening slowed in China between 2003-08 and 2013-18 amid a policy-guided investment slowdown, they accelerated in the rest of EAP and especially in some ASEAN countries (the Philippines and Vietnam) reflecting significant FDI inflows and high rates of investment spending. The decline in China's TFP growth has been attributed not only to the slowdown in investment growth, with its associated embodied technical progress, but also to fading gains from global trade integration and institutional reforms.[5]

Sources of productivity growth

Productivity growth through sectoral reallocation. Strong pre-crisis productivity growth in EAP was supported by policies that encouraged resource reallocation from low- to high-productivity sectors, as well as within-sector upgrades (IMF 2006). Following the crisis, however, and as in other EMDE regions, gains from factor reallocation toward more productive sectors slowed sharply, as the pace of urbanization slowed (in most cases well before reaching Organisation for Economic Co-operation and Development—average levels) and overcapacity in China weighed on the efficiency of investment. During 2013-15, sectoral reallocation is estimated to have accounted for under one-fifth of EAP productivity growth, less than half of its share during 2003-08 (two-fifths; Figure 2.1.1.3).

In East Asia, structural transformation, in the form of the movement of people and capital from agriculture to manufacturing and services, has been a key driver of productivity growth as countries have risen from low- to middle-income status. Once countries have reached middle-income levels, within-sector productivity gains have become a more important driver of productivity growth and cross-sectoral shifts less important (de Nicola, Kehayova and Nguyen, 2018; Mason and Shetty, 2019). However, there has been considerable heterogeneity across the region in this respect: thus in recent years sectoral reallocation has stalled in Thailand, proceeded slowly in Malaysia, and continued apace in Indonesia, Vietnam, and

the Philippines (World Bank 2018c). In Vietnam, intersectoral reallocation has continued to account for approximately half of labor productivity growth, with no sign of deceleration (World Bank and MPIV 2016).

Productivity growth in the manufacturing sector has been a major driving force behind overall productivity growth in most EAP countries (APO 2018; Figure 2.1.1.3). Since 2000s, the contribution of services to productivity growth has increased, albeit from a low base, as innovations in this sector took hold.[6] For example, e-commerce has accelerated sharply in China, with e-commerce firms having 30 percent higher productivity, as well as being more export-oriented than other firms (IMF 2019). Recent advances in information and communication technology have bolstered productivity growth in wholesale and retail trade, hotels, and restaurants; transport, storage, and communications; and finance, real estate, and business activities. It is likely that the growth in value-added generated by intangible services is underestimated to the extent they are incorporated in the production of manufactured goods (ADB 2019).

In contrast to most other EMDE regions, within-sector productivity growth accelerated in many EAP economies in the post-crisis period. China was an exception: there, within-sector productivity growth slowed amid increased overcapacity, declining firm dynamism, and increasing financial constraints, including as a result of rising leverage (IMF 2018a). This is notwithstanding considerable in-house research and development, and technology transfers both domestically and from abroad (Hu, Jefferson, and Jinchang 2005).

Drivers of productivity. Fundamental drivers of productivity have improved more rapidly in EAP than in the average EMDE (Figure 2.1.1.3). In general, productivity in economies with favorable initial conditions have grown by up to 0.8 percentage point per year faster than other economies (Chapter 3), which partly explains faster productivity growth in countries with strong human capital, including China, Malaysia, and Vietnam. Compared to many other EMDEs, productivity growth in EAP economies have benefited from high investment (IMF 2006; World Bank 2019b). Other factors contributing to relatively high productivity growth in the EAP region include trade integration, including through global supply chains; foreign investment, which supported rapid technology adoption from abroad; and progress

---

[5] See World Bank and DRCSC (2014); World Bank (2019a); Baldwin (2013), and Subramanian and Kessler (2013).

[6] See APO (2018); ADB (2019); Cirera and Maloney (2017); and Kinda (2019).

BOX 2.1.1 Labor productivity in East Asia and Pacific: Trends and drivers (*continued*)

FIGURE 2.1.1.3 Factors underlying productivity growth in EAP

Factor reallocation toward more productive sectors, high investment, trade integration with product upgrading, and rapid innovation have all contributed to above-EMDE-average productivity growth in EAP. Productivity growth in the manufacturing sector has been a major driving force behind overall productivity growth in most EAP countries. Fundamental drivers of productivity have improved more rapidly in EAP than in the average EMDE.

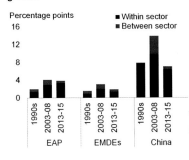

A. Contributions to annual productivity growth

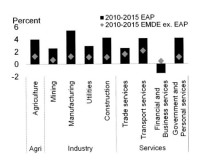

B. Annual sectoral productivity growth

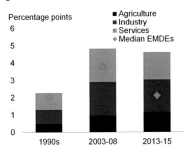

C. Contributions to annual productivity growth

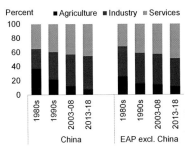

D. Composition of sectoral value-added

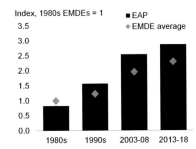

E. Drivers index

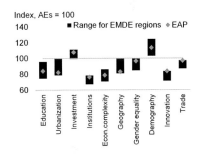

F. Level of drivers across regions, 2017

Source: APO productivity database; Expanded African Sector Database; Groningen Growth Development Center Database; Haver Analytics; ILOSTAT; OECD STAN; United Nations; World KLEMS.

A.B. Productivity refers to labor productivity, defined as output per worker. Medians of county-specific contributions. Sample comprises 9 EAP economies and 46 EMDEs.

A. Within-sector contribution shows the contribution to overall productivity growth of initial real value added-weighted sectoral productivity growth; between-sector contribution shows the contribution of intersectoral changes in employment shares.

C. Median of the country groups. Sample comprises 9 EAP economies.

D. Values are calculated using 2010 U.S. dollars at 2010 market exchange rates.

E. For each country, index is a weighted average—weighted by the normalized coefficients shown in Annex 3.5—of the normalized value of each driver of productivity. Drivers include the ICRG rule of law index, patents per capita, share of non-tropical area, investment in percent of GDP, ratio of female average years of education to male average years, share of population in urban area, Economic Complexity Index, years of schooling, and share of working-age population, and inflation. See Annex 3.5 for details. Regional and EMDE indexes are GDP-weighted averages. Samples comprise 7 economies in EAP.

F. Unweighted average levels of drivers, normalized as average of AEs as 100 and standard deviation of EMDEs as 10. Orange diamond represents average within EAP economies in 2017. Blue bar represents range of the average drivers for six regions in 2017. Variables corresponding to the concepts are follows: Education = years of education, Urbanization = share of population living in urban area, Investment = share of investment to GDP, Institution = Government Effectiveness, Econ. Complexity = Economic complexity index+, Geography = share of land area which are outside of tropical region, Gender Equality = Share of the year of schooling for female to male, Demography=share of population under 14, Innovation=Log patent per capita, Trade = Export + Import/GDP.

---

toward more complex products with higher value-added (World Bank 2019d).[7] Macroeconomic stability has

[7] EAP is characterized by an above-average share of larger and exporting firms (Chapter 3). In EAP, 35 percent of firms are large (compared with 25 percent in the average EMDE) and 16 percent of firms are exporters (compared with 12 percent in the average EMDE). More productive firms tend to self-select into exporting firms which have higher productivity, as they are exposed to frontier knowledge and best

encouraged investment, while trade and investment openness and above-EMDE-average research and development have supported innovation (Kim and Loayza 2019).

managerial practices that help them make better decisions regarding investment, input selection, and production process (Hallward-Driemeier, Iarossi, and Sokoloff 2002).

BOX 2.1.1 Labor productivity in East Asia and Pacific: Trends and drivers (*continued*)

FIGURE 2.1.1.4 Prospects for productivity growth in EAP

Being less able to rely on export growth than in the past, EAP countries need to unleash domestic sources of productivity growth. Priority areas include reforms to enhance human capital, address informality, foster innovation, and facilitate urban development. In addition, achieving long-term sustainable development calls for debt overhangs to be addressed and excessive leverage to be avoided.

A. Contribution of export growth to annual GDP growth

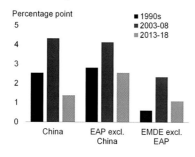

B. Human capital index and annual productivity growth

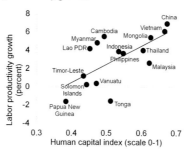

C. Informal economies

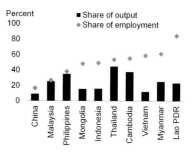

D. Research and development expenditure

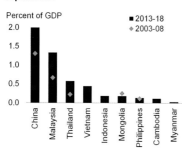

E. Urbanization

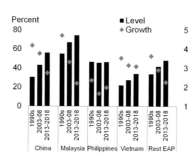

F. Debt and labor productivity

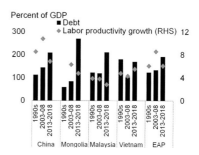

Source: Elgin et al. (forthcoming); Haver Analytics; World Bank (World Development Indicators).
A.B.F. Productivity refers to labor productivity, defined as output per worker.
A. Growth of volume of exports of goods and non-factor services.
B. The HCI calculates the contributions of health and education to worker productivity. The final index score ranges from zero to one and measures the productivity as a future worker of a child born today relative to the benchmark of a child with full health care and complete education. HCI data are for 2017. Labor productivity growth data are for 2018.
C. Blue bars show the share of informal output in total output based on the Dynamic General Equilibrium (DGE) model. The diamonds show the share of informal employment in total employment.
D. Data are not available for all featured economies.
E. Urbanization levels denote share of urban population in total population.
F. Total debt comprises bank credit to households, non-financial corporations, and general government debt (broad definition).

That said, the factors supporting post-crisis productivity growth have differed somewhat across EAP economies. Growth of the drivers most strongly associated with productivity growth, including labor force growth and investment, has slowed in EAP since 2008. Investment growth in many EAP economies has slowed, led by a policy-led moderation of investment rates to reduce credit expansion. In addition, earlier favorable demographic trends in China, Thailand, and Vietnam have waned as populations have started to age. Other factors that had

previously helped to spur EAP productivity growth have also deteriorated since the crisis. For example, the trend toward broadening production to a more diverse range of products at more upstream stages of the value chain slowed partly because of a stagnation in global value chains after 2008 (World Bank 2019b).

Prospects for productivity growth. Productivity gaps are still substantial between advanced economies and EAP countries, suggesting potential for further significant

BOX 2.1.1 Labor productivity in East Asia and Pacific: Trends and drivers (*continued*)

productivity gains. However, although EAP productivity growth remains solid relative to long-run historical rates, it is likely to soften further over the near future, as trends in a number of fundamental drivers of productivity become less favorable. Thus, trade and investment growth are expected to continue to ease in an environment of weakening global demand, heightened global policy uncertainty, and a continued policy-guided slowdown in investment growth in China (Figure 2.1.1.4). Slowing global trade growth may also lower incentives to innovate or upgrade products and processes (World Bank 2019b). Structural declines in working-age populations in major economies will also weaken growth momentum (World Bank 2016b, 2018a).

Policy implications

A comprehensive set of policy efforts can help countries in the region improve their investment and productivity growth and speed up their income convergence with the advanced economies. These policies fall into four broad categories: improving factors of production, including through human capital development; encouraging productivity at the firm level, including by leveling the playing field for private relative to state-owned firms and improving corporate governance; removing obstacles to between-sector reallocation, including through continued urban development; and fostering a productivity-friendly business environment. Specific policies within these four broad categories depend on country specific circumstances (World Bank 2018b; Kim and Loayza 2017; Munoz et al. 2016).

Improving factors of production

Slowing capital deepening has contributed to the post-crisis productivity growth slowdown in several EAP countries, while outside China the contribution of human capital gains to productivity growth has stalled. To boost productivity growth, policies are needed to improve public investment, lift private investment, and improve human capital.

Improve public investment. A wide range of policy efforts are needed to improve the investment outlook, especially in countries with particularly large investment needs (Cambodia, Indonesia, Lao PDR, Myanmar; World Bank 2018a). Access to adequate infrastructure in EAP remains fragmented, particularly in water and sanitation and transport, and in several lower-middle-income economies (World Bank 2018a). In these countries, strengthening the efficiency of public investment management and fiscal

transparency could boost productive public investment (World Bank 2018b).

Remove obstacles to private investment. Private investment could be spurred by higher FDI inflows that could offer knowledge and technology transfers, deeper regional trade integration and better institutional environments (World Bank 2018b, 2019b). In China, private investment could be lifted by improved market access, increased competition, policies that provide a more level playing field relative to state-owned enterprises (SOEs), greater financial discipline, stronger intellectual property rights, lower barriers to entry, and a gradual opening of China's financial system to international investors (World Bank 2018a, 2018d; World Bank and DRCSC 2019). Other major economies in the region, including Indonesia, Malaysia, Thailand, and Vietnam, could boost private investment by increasing private sector participation in major infrastructure projects and by changing their funding policies to provide more opportunities for international and domestic private investors.

Increase human capital. Children born in the EAP region today will, at age 18, be only 53 percent as productive as they could be if they benefited from best practices in education and health (World Bank 2019b). Several EAP economies have below-average educational attainment (Cambodia, Lao PDR). In general, reforms that augment human capital, through initiatives to strengthen the quality and flexibility of education systems and improve education outcomes, are critical to achieving and sustaining high productivity growth.

Boosting firm productivity

While within-sector productivity growth has been resilient in EAP, especially outside China, there is room for generating additional productivity gains. Factor misallocation, although it has declined, remains sizable (World Bank 2019b). In the current weak external environment that allows limited productivity gains through knowledge and technology spillovers from trade, this is likely to be a critical source of productivity gains for the region. Policy measures can include levelling the playing field for private and state-owned firms, improving firm capabilities, streamlining regulations to encourage informal enterprises to grow into more productive firms in the formal economy, and fostering innovation.

Reduce market distortions and level the playing field for private firms. A gradual transfer from public to private

BOX 2.1.1 Labor productivity in East Asia and Pacific: Trends and drivers (*continued*)

firm ownership in many cases, and greater involvement of international firms, as well as reforms to lower entry costs and encourage fair competition, including in trade and innovation, can help level the playing field for private firms and state owned enterprises. Curbing preferential lending agreements with state-owned enterprises and easing the access of private firms to long-term funding can improve the allocative efficiency of capital and raise productivity. Greater product market competition would spur innovation (Cusolito and Maloney 2018).

Encourage innovation. Effective policies to promote innovation begin with strengthening managerial and organizational practices (Cirera and Maloney 2017). In addition, strengthening the effectiveness of research and development (R&D) spending and measures to raise productivity in the services sectors are key (World Bank 2016c). Fiscal incentives for R&D are already in place in some EAP countries (China, Malaysia), but in many other cases R&D spending is small relative to GDP (Figure 2.1.1.4). Strengthening intellectual property rights regimes while avoiding undue limitations on competition could also encourage R&D, as could competition for research grants. These reforms could be complemented by efforts that facilitate moving up the value chain through innovation, especially in R&D-intensive sectors, and enabling new business processes, including through digitization, and higher energy efficiency.

Address informality. The share of informal output in the EAP region is below the EMDE average while the share of informal employment is above average (World Bank 2019f). Within the region, informality is higher in lower-income countries. However, even higher-income economies in EAP have urban informality (China, Malaysia, Thailand). To address challenges associated with informality higher-income countries can prioritize urban planning along with the provision of essential social protection to informal workers. Lower-income countries can focus on policies that encourage investment and reduce costs of regulatory compliance.

Encouraging sectoral reallocation

Productivity gains from sectoral reallocation have slowed in EAP. Policy measures to accelerate the process of reallocation again include reforms to allow the services sector to thrive and absorb labor and measures to sustain rapid urbanization.

Liberalize service markets and shift out of agriculture. A gradual liberalization of service sectors, including education, health care, the financial sector, communications, transport, and utilities, could encourage job creation in these sectors (Beverelli, Fiorini, and Hoekman 2017). It could also boost manufacturing productivity, as services sectors provide important inputs into manufacturing.

Encourage urbanization. The reallocation of factors, especially labor, from low-productivity agricultural activities to higher-productivity manufacturing and services can accelerate the convergence of EAP to the productivity frontier. Clarification of land ownership rights and transferable social benefits could encourage such labor movement (Fuglie et al 2019). Urban planning can encourage a reallocation of labor towards more productive sectors by improving access to jobs, affordable housing, public transportation, health care, education, and other services (World Bank 2015a). Road congestion, which is a major problem in many large cities may discourage job switching (World Bank 2018e, 2019f). Accelerated productivity growth will also require improved management of country and regional transportation, telecommunications, and utility infrastructure in metropolitan areas.

Creating a growth-friendly environment

Safeguard macroeconomic stability. Over the longer term, strong and sustained productivity gains require financial stability (Chapter 3; Box 3.4). Elevated corporate debt, especially in China, weighs on investment and productivity in exposed corporations. Policy measures to rein in financial risks are therefore critical.

EUROPE and CENTRAL ASIA

Growth in Europe and Central Asia decelerated to an estimated 2 percent in 2019, reflecting a sharp slowdown in Turkey as a result of acute financial market stress in 2018, as well as in the Russian Federation amid weak demand and cuts in oil production. Regional growth is projected to strengthen in 2020, to 2.6 percent, as activity recovers in Turkey and Russia, and to stabilize to 2.9 percent in 2021-22. Key external risks to the regional growth outlook include spillovers from weaker-than-expected activity in the Euro Area and escalation of global policy uncertainty. The region also remains vulnerable to disorderly commodity and financial market developments. A comprehensive reform agenda is needed to boost productivity, increase investment in physical and human capital, address continuing demographic pressures, and raise innovation.

Recent developments

Growth in Europe and Central Asia (ECA) is estimated to have decelerated markedly in 2019, to a three-year low of 2 percent (Table 2.2.1). The weak regional performance predominantly reflects slowdowns in the region's two largest economies, Russia and Turkey (Figure 2.2.1.A).

A sustained weakness in exports growth has continued amid slowing manufacturing activity and investment. Sluggish new export orders in recent months suggest that export growth will continue to be weak in the near term, especially in economies with deep trade and financial linkages to the Euro Area, such as those in Central Europe (Figure 2.2.1.B).

Headline inflation in ECA has eased, as the impact from the value-added tax (VAT) hike in Russia and earlier currency depreciation in Turkey faded. This, combined with weakening growth momentum, has allowed Russia and Turkey, as well as other ECA economies, to pause or reverse previous monetary policy tightening (Romania, Ukraine; Figure 2.2.1.C). Inflation remains above or near target, however, limiting the scope for

further policy rate cuts, with some economies tightening policy to rein in inflation (Georgia, Kazakhstan). Core inflation is also rising in some economies, especially those with increasing wages as a result of labor shortages and other capacity constraints (Poland, Romania; Figure 2.2.1.D).

In *Russia*, softer-than-expected investment and trade, together with a continuation of international economic sanctions, resulted in a growth slowdown to an estimated 1.2 percent. Industrial activity also softened, as oil production cuts agreed with OPEC took effect and pipeline-related disruptions occurred. Retail sales volumes weakened substantially following a VAT hike, while consumer confidence remained low. The central bank reversed a previous tightening stance, cutting the key policy rate five times since June.

In *Turkey*, industrial production and manufacturing data suggest that the economy began to stabilize in late 2019, following the disruptions from acute financial market pressures in the previous year. Still, growth slowed sharply for the year, falling 2.8 percentage points to near-nil. Elevated inflation and associated pressures on real incomes, as well as rising unemployment, dampened consumption. Investment contracted deeply, to rates comparable with the global financial crisis, partly reflecting lingering policy uncertainty (Figure 2.2.1.E). Although the

Note: This section was prepared by Collette M. Wheeler. Research assistance was provided by Vasiliki Papagianni and Julia Norfleet.

FIGURE 2.2.1 **ECA: Recent developments**

Europe and Central Asia faced substantial headwinds in 2019 amid a sharp slowdown in major economies, such as Turkey and Russia. Export growth weakened significantly, particularly in Central Europe, which is tightly connected to the Euro Area through value chains. Headline inflation moderated in the region's major economies, allowing for substantial policy rate cuts to support growth. Capacity constraints and a slowing Euro Area weighed on activity in Central Europe.

A. Contribution to regional GDP growth

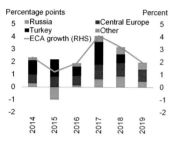

B. Export volume growth, by subregion

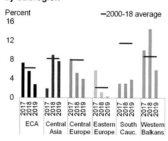

C. Real interest rates and bond spreads in ECA

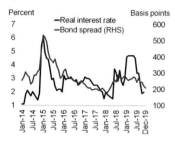

D. Core inflation and capacity utilization in Central Europe

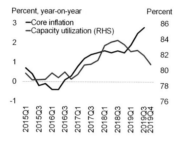

E. GDP and investment growth in Turkey

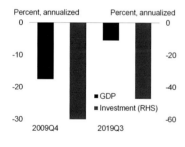

F. Industrial production and export volume growth in Central Europe

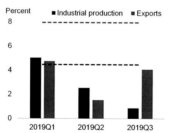

Source: Consensus Economics; Haver Analytics; J.P. Morgan; Organisation for Economic Co-operation and Development; World Bank.

A.B. ECA = Europe and Central Asia. Aggregate growth rates calculated using GDP weights at 2010 prices and market exchange rates. Data for 2019 are estimated. Refer to Table 2.2.1 for further details.

B. South Cauc. = South Caucasus.

C. Real interest rates calculated using the policy interest rate less the *Consensus Economics* forecast for inflation. Bond spreads are from the J.P. Morgan Emerging Market Bond Index (EMBI). Sample includes Hungary, Poland, Russia, Turkey, and Ukraine, due to data availability. Last observation is December 16, 2019 for the bond spread and November 2019 for the real interest rate.

D. Aggregates calculated using GDP weights at 2010 prices and market exchange rates. The sample includes Hungary, Poland, and Romania. Last observation is 2019Q4 for capacity utilization and 2019Q3 for core inflation.

E. Figure uses the annualized 4-quarter on 4-quarter average.

F. Dashed lines represent the 2000-18 average. Aggregate industrial production calculated using production weights at 2010 prices and market exchange rates; aggregate export volume growth calculated using GDP weights at 2010 prices and market exchange rates.

contribution of net exports to growth was positive, this was due in large part to import compression. In the second half of 2019, the central bank sharply reversed its policy stance by cutting the policy rate in half, to 12 percent, despite above-target inflation.

In *Central Europe*, the boost to private consumption in early 2019 from rising real wages and government transfers helped to sustain above-potential growth. This impact dissipated by the end of the year, however, contributing to a slowdown in growth to an estimated 4.2 percent, despite an investment-led construction sector pickup in some economies (Hungary, Romania). The slowdown in the Euro Area weighed on exports in some cases (Bulgaria, Romania; Figure 2.2.1.F).

In the *Western Balkans*, a deceleration in public investment (Kosovo), manufacturing (Serbia), and export growth (Albania, Serbia) contributed to a moderation in growth to an estimated 3.2 percent in 2019. Temporary factors related to weather and energy production dampened activity in Albania, while strong import demand for public investment projects led to negative contribution of net exports in Montenegro. In Eastern Europe, industrial production growth has softened, reflecting marked weakness in manufacturing amid slowing export growth, particularly in Belarus. Ukraine, however, benefited from a bumper crop harvest in the first half of 2019.

Firming growth in the *South Caucasus*, to an estimated 3.7 percent in 2019, was supported by private consumption, and on the supply side by strong manufacturing growth, as well as by a recovery in mining production in Armenia. Expanding natural gas production and steady growth in non-energy sectors supported Azerbaijan's economy in the first half of 2019. In Georgia, growth strengthened despite the imposition of travel restrictions by Russia. In Central Asia, the cyclical expansion moderated, yet growth was still robust at 4.5 percent in 2019. In Kazakhstan, the largest subregional economy, slowing exports from lower oil prices were offset by fiscal expansion.

Outlook

Regional growth is expected to firm over the forecast horizon, to 2.6 percent in 2020 and 2.9 percent in 2021-22, on the assumptions that key commodity prices and growth in the Euro Area stabilize, and that Turkey's economy recovers from earlier financial pressures and Russia firms on the back of policy support (Figure 2.2.2.A). Considerable variation across economies is expected to continue. Economies in Central Europe are anticipated to slow as fiscal policy support wanes and demographic pressures persist, while those in Central Asia are projected to continue growing at a robust pace, and more rapidly than previously envisaged, on the back of structural reform progress (World Bank 2019g).

The baseline projection for regional growth also assumes that trade tensions between the United States and China will not re-escalate; the United Kingdom's exit from the European Union will be orderly; and that fiscal and monetary policy avert further financial market turbulence in Turkey as the country moves past acute financial stress.

In *Russia*, growth is projected to firm moderately, to 1.8 percent by 2021 (Table 2.2.2). Despite OPEC and its partners recently announcing deeper cuts until March 2020, oil production is expected to remain stable in Russia due to an exemption on gas condensates (IEA 2019). National Projects—which are partly funded by the 2019 VAT hike and include investment in infrastructure and human capital—are expected to buoy growth over the forecast horizon. Nevertheless, private investment remains tepid in the projection, due to policy uncertainty and slowing potential growth over the longer term as demographic pressures increase, and as structural problems, such as the lack of competition, accumulate.

Growth is projected to recover in *Turkey*, to 3 percent in 2020, as investment recovers from a deep contraction in 2019. Gradual improvement in domestic demand is expected to support growth over the forecast horizon. This outlook assumes that fiscal and monetary policy remain steady, that

FIGURE 2.2.2 ECA: Outlook and risks

Growth in Europe and Central Asia is projected to firm to 2.6 percent in 2020, as activity recovers in Turkey and Russia, and to stabilize at 2.9 percent in 2021-22. Weaker-than-expected growth in the Euro Area or China could dent activity in tightly connected subregions. Heightened policy uncertainty in the broader region could impact portfolio flows to ECA, while the future of funding options in Central Europe remains uncertain. The ability to confront growth headwinds is reduced by limited fiscal space.

A. Growth

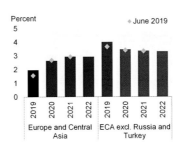

B. Share of exports by destination, 2017

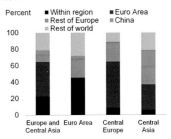

C. Turkey: Credit to firms and non-performing loan ratio

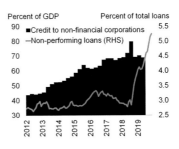

D. Gross portfolio outflows in ECA and Euro Area economic policy uncertainty

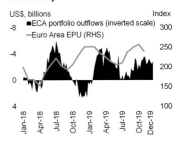

E. European Union structural fund payments to Central Europe, 2019

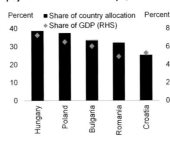

F. Gross government and external debt, by subregion

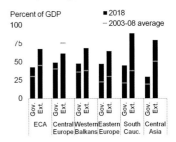

Source: Baker, Bloom, and Davis (2016); Bank for International Settlements; European Commission; Haver Analytics; Institute of International Finance; International Monetary Fund; World Bank.

A. Aggregate growth rates calculated using GDP weights at 2010 prices and market exchange rates. Shaded areas indicate forecasts. Data for 2019 are estimated. Yellow diamonds correspond to forecasts from the June 2019 *Global Economic Prospects* report.

B. The "Within region" data refer to within ECA for all stacked bars except the Euro Area, which refers to within the Euro Area. Shares are calculated from exports in millions of U.S. dollars.

C. Last observation is November 2019 for non-performing loans and 2019Q2 for credit to non-financial corporations.

D. EPU = economic policy uncertainty. The Euro Area economic policy uncertainty is calculated by Baker, Bloom, and Davis (2016), which is based on the frequency of words in domestic newspapers mentioning economic policy uncertainty. Figure shows the 3-month moving average. Sample for portfolio outflows includes Hungary, Poland, and Turkey, due to data availability. Last observation is December 20, 2019 for portfolio outflows and November 2019 for economic policy uncertainty.

E. Note: Figure shows the cumulated payments to EMDEs in Central Europe for the 2014-20 program period. Data on the "Share of country allocation" reflect the amount of EU structural fund allocations paid out to each economy as a share of its total EU structural fund allocation as of 2019Q2, due to data availability.

F. ECA = Europe and Central Asia, South Cauc. = South Caucasus, Gov. = government, Ext. = external. Aggregates calculated using the median. Sample includes 24 economies.

the currency does not come under pressure, and that corporate debt restructurings proceed smoothly.

Central Europe is forecast to sharply decelerate over the forecast horizon, to 3.4 percent GDP growth in 2020 and 3 percent by 2022. Fiscal support, and the resulting private consumption boost, will begin to fade in some of the subregion's largest economies by 2020-21, with limited fiscal space available to fully offset potential adverse spillovers from the Euro Area (Poland, Romania). Shrinking working-age populations, partly reflecting emigration to Western Europe in recent years, limits growth prospects. Progress on structural reforms is key to support private investment growth over the medium term. Growth in the subregion is highly dependent on the continued absorption of EU structural funds, with the current cycle expected to end in 2020.

Growth is projected to firm to 3.8 percent by 2021 in the *Western Balkans*, assuming political instability and policy uncertainty remain contained. Rising fiscal liabilities in the subregion, in some cases due to large public sector wage increases, social transfers, or higher-than-expected costs for infrastructure projects, could reduce space for future countercyclical fiscal stimulus and weaken the business climate (Kosovo, Montenegro, North Macedonia). Additionally, recent earthquakes in the Western Balkans—primarily affecting Albania—took a heavy toll on human life and physical infrastructure. The outlook for the subregion remains challenging as falling business confidence and heightened uncertainty coincide with a worsening external environment (World Bank 2019h).

The *South Caucasus* is estimated to grow 3.7 percent in 2019, and to decelerate to 3.1 percent over the remaining forecast horizon. In Azerbaijan, activity is expected to be dampened by the effects of subdued oil prices and lingering structural rigidities in the non-oil sector. Longer-term growth depends on continuation of domestic reforms to enhance private sector development and address fragilities emanating from the financial sector, as well as investment in human capital to boost the quality of education and reduce skills mismatches.

Growth is expected to firm over the forecast horizon in *Eastern Europe* and stabilize in *Central Asia*, but growth in both subregions is subject to considerable policy uncertainty. These subregions face a challenging external environment as growth remains tepid in key trading partners, including the Euro Area and Russia (for Eastern Europe) and China (for Central Asia). Ukraine, which is the largest economy in Eastern Europe, recently reached a preliminary agreement with the IMF for a $5.5 billion program, which should help advance structural reforms and foster growth over the forecast horizon. In Central Asia, growth is expected to slightly moderate this year following agreed-upon production cuts by a non-OPEC partner (Kazakhstan). Activity in Kazakhstan will likely be dampened by the waning effect of earlier fiscal stimulus, modest or slowing growth in key trading partners (Russia, China), and low productivity. In Eastern Europe and Central Asia, the pace of growth depends on the successful implementation of structural reforms to improve the business environment, achieve debt sustainability, and restructure state-owned enterprises to improve competition (EBRD 2017; Funke, Isakova, and Ivanyna 2017).

Risks

The regional outlook remains subject to significant downside risks, including slowing growth in major trading partners, geopolitical turbulence, heightened policy uncertainty, exposure to disorderly financial market developments, as well as weakening productivity growth over the long run (Box 2.2.1). A sharper-than-expected slowdown in the Euro Area, ECA's most important trading partner, could generate negative spillovers in economies with tightly linked trade and financial ties (Figure 2.2.2.B; Elekdag, Muir, and Wu 2015). Slowing growth in China could be propagated through trade and commodity price channels to Central Asia, as well as metals exporters in the ECA region, which are increasingly reliant on China as an export destination. The region's energy exporters—

Azerbaijan, Kazakhstan, and Russia—remain vulnerable to large swings in global commodity prices, particularly when accompanied by heightened volatility (van Eyden et al. 2019).

In many economies in Central Europe, the policy space to confront negative shocks is limited by persistent budget deficits. Fiscal support has contributed to these growing imbalances—increasing public sector wages, rising government transfers, and low tax capacity, have widened fiscal deficits, with the latter approaching or exceeding 3 percent of GDP—the upper limit of the EU threshold, particularly in Romania. Across ECA, public sector debt relative to GDP is higher than prior to the global financial crisis, with the largest increases observed in Eastern Europe and the South Caucasus. In Turkey, recent policies to support growth through credit expansion run the risk of worsened external imbalances (Figure 2.2.2.C).

Following military disagreements with the North Atlantic Treaty Organization, Turkey faces a new round of U.S. economic sanctions. Renewed involvement in conflicts in the Syrian Arab Republic or Ukraine, could trigger additional sanctions against large economies in the region.

More generally, a pervasive rise in policy uncertainty could undermine business and investor sentiment (Figure 2.2.2.D). The re-escalation of trade tensions, and a resulting slowdown in global demand, could weaken exports and commodity prices for the region, presenting challenges to growth and fiscal planning. Renewed trade tensions between the United States and Europe, particularly with respect to vehicle and auto part tariffs, could also sideswipe the ECA region, especially for economies in Central Europe that are tightly integrated into European value chains. Similarly, a triggering of trade tensions between the United States and China could adversely affect some

regional economies, particularly energy and metals exporters. Additional sanctions on Russia could have a negative impact on the region, particularly in economies where domestic demand relies on remittances (Central Asia, Eastern Europe, the South Caucasus).

Although policy uncertainty surrounding the United Kingdom's exit from the European Union has dissipated somewhat, the process remains vulnerable to disruption until the end of the transition period, currently scheduled for the end of the year (Bank of England 2018; H.M. Government 2018). The future program of EU structural funds after 2020 must also be determined, with the potential redirection of EU funds to advanced economies in Southern Europe limiting funding options for Central Europe. In several countries, structural fund payments represented 5 percent or more of GDP over the last program period from 2014-20 (Figure 2.2.2.E). Historically, when the absorption of EU funding was low, activity also decelerated substantially, as was the case in Poland in 2016.

An unexpected tightening of global financing conditions could generate financial market pressures in ECA, renewing capital outflows and currency volatility, particularly in economies with large external financing needs (Chapter 1; World Bank 2019f; EBRD 2019a). Many regional economies have relied on short-term capital inflows to finance large current account deficits. Low foreign-currency reserves leave these economies all the more vulnerable to capital flight and constrain the capacity of central banks to buffer the impact of negative external shocks. A fall in incomes in the region's largest economies would dent remittance inflows to Eastern Europe and Central Asia (World Bank 2016d). On the domestic front, increased public spending and low tax capacity have contributed to historically high public debt levels, which limit fiscal policy space (Figure 2.2.2.F).

TABLE 2.2.1 Europe and Central Asia forecast summary

(Real GDP growth at market prices in percent, unless indicated otherwise)

Percentage point differences
from June 2019 projections

	2017	2018	2019e	2020f	2021f	2022f	2019e	2020f	2021f
EMDE ECA, GDP[1]	4.1	3.2	2.0	2.6	2.9	2.9	0.4	-0.1	0.0
EMDE ECA, GDP excl. Turkey	3.0	3.3	2.6	2.5	2.6	2.6	0.2	-0.1	0.0
(Average including countries with full national accounts and balance of payments data only)[2]									
EMDE ECA, GDP[2]	4.1	3.1	1.8	2.5	2.8	2.8	0.4	-0.1	-0.1
GDP per capita (U.S. dollars)	3.6	2.7	1.5	2.3	2.6	2.7	0.4	-0.1	-0.1
PPP GDP	4.0	3.1	1.9	2.6	2.8	2.8	0.4	0.0	-0.1
Private consumption	5.0	2.6	1.5	2.6	2.6	2.6	0.2	0.0	-0.1
Public consumption	3.4	2.0	1.6	1.7	1.8	1.8	0.0	0.1	0.0
Fixed investment	6.7	3.1	-0.6	4.3	4.2	4.2	0.5	1.0	0.6
Exports, GNFS[3]	7.3	5.6	2.8	2.3	3.4	3.4	-1.2	-2.0	-0.6
Imports, GNFS[3]	11.5	3.2	1.3	4.1	4.9	5.0	-1.7	-1.4	-0.9
Net exports, contribution to growth	-0.8	1.0	0.6	-0.5	-0.3	-0.4	0.1	-0.4	0.1
Memo items: GDP									
Commodity exporters[4]	2.1	2.6	1.9	2.1	2.3	2.3	0.1	-0.1	0.0
Commodity importers[5]	6.1	3.7	2.1	3.1	3.5	3.4	0.7	0.0	0.0
Central Europe[6]	5.1	4.7	4.2	3.4	3.1	3.0	0.5	0.1	0.0
Western Balkans[7]	2.6	4.0	3.2	3.6	3.8	3.8	-0.3	-0.2	-0.1
Eastern Europe[8]	2.6	3.3	2.8	2.9	3.1	3.1	0.4	0.2	0.1
South Caucasus[9]	1.7	2.6	3.7	3.1	3.1	3.1	0.0	-0.8	-1.1
Central Asia[10]	4.6	4.7	4.5	4.4	4.6	4.5	0.3	0.4	0.5
Russia	1.6	2.3	1.2	1.6	1.8	1.8	0.0	-0.2	0.0
Turkey	7.5	2.8	0.0	3.0	4.0	4.0	1.0	0.0	0.0
Poland	4.9	5.1	4.3	3.6	3.3	3.1	0.3	0.0	0.0

Source: World Bank.

Note: e = estimate; f = forecast. EMDE = emerging market and developing economies. World Bank forecasts are frequently updated based on new information and changing (global) circumstances. Consequently, projections presented here may differ from those contained in other Bank documents, even if basic assessments of countries' prospects do not differ at any given moment in time.

1. GDP and expenditure components are measured in 2010 prices and market exchange rates.

2. Aggregates presented here exclude Bosnia and Herzegovina, Kazakhstan, Kosovo, Montenegro, Serbia, Tajikistan, and Turkmenistan, for which data limitations prevent the forecasting of GDP components.

3. Exports and imports of goods and non-factor services (GNFS).

4. Includes Albania, Armenia, Azerbaijan, Kazakhstan, the Kyrgyz Republic, Kosovo, Russia, Tajikistan, Turkmenistan, Ukraine, and Uzbekistan.

5. Includes Belarus, Bosnia and Herzegovina, Bulgaria, Croatia, Georgia, Hungary, Moldova, Montenegro, North Macedonia, Poland, Romania, Serbia, and Turkey.

6. Includes Bulgaria, Croatia, Hungary, Poland, and Romania.

7. Includes Albania, Bosnia and Herzegovina, Kosovo, Montenegro, North Macedonia, and Serbia.

8. Includes Belarus, Moldova, and Ukraine.

9. Includes Armenia, Azerbaijan, and Georgia.

10. Includes Kazakhstan, the Kyrgyz Republic, Tajikistan, Turkmenistan, and Uzbekistan.

To download the data in this table, please visit www.worldbank.org/gep.

TABLE 2.2.2 Europe and Central Asia country forecasts[1]

(Real GDP growth at market prices in percent, unless indicated otherwise)

Percentage point differences
from June 2019 projections

	2017	2018	2019e	2020f	2021f	2022f	2019e	2020f	2021f
Albania	3.8	4.1	2.9	3.4	3.6	3.5	-0.8	-0.3	-0.2
Armenia	7.5	5.2	6.9	5.1	5.2	5.2	2.7	0.2	0.0
Azerbaijan	-0.3	1.4	2.5	2.3	2.1	2.1	-0.8	-1.2	-1.6
Belarus	2.5	3.0	1.0	0.9	0.5	0.5	-0.8	-0.4	-0.7
Bosnia and Herzegovina[2]	3.2	3.6	3.1	3.4	3.9	3.9	-0.3	-0.5	-0.1
Bulgaria	3.5	3.1	3.6	3.0	3.1	3.1	0.6	0.2	0.3
Croatia	3.1	2.7	2.9	2.6	2.4	2.4	0.4	0.1	0.0
Georgia	4.8	4.8	5.2	4.3	4.5	4.5	0.6	-0.5	-0.5
Hungary	4.3	5.1	4.9	3.0	2.6	2.6	1.1	0.2	0.0
Kazakhstan	4.1	4.1	4.0	3.7	3.9	3.7	0.5	0.5	0.7
Kosovo	4.2	3.8	4.0	4.2	4.1	4.0	-0.4	-0.3	-0.4
Kyrgyz Republic	4.7	3.5	4.2	4.0	4.0	4.2	-0.1	0.0	-0.1
Moldova	4.7	4.0	3.6	3.6	3.8	3.8	0.2	0.0	0.0
Montenegro	4.7	5.1	3.0	3.1	2.8	3.2	0.1	0.7	0.5
North Macedonia	0.2	2.9	3.1	3.2	3.3	3.1	0.2	0.0	-0.3
Poland	4.9	5.1	4.3	3.6	3.3	3.1	0.3	0.0	0.0
Romania	7.1	4.0	3.9	3.4	3.1	3.1	0.3	0.1	0.0
Russia	1.6	2.3	1.2	1.6	1.8	1.8	0.0	-0.2	0.0
Serbia	2.0	4.4	3.3	3.9	4.0	4.0	-0.2	-0.1	0.0
Tajikistan	7.1	7.3	6.2	5.5	5.0	5.0	0.2	-0.5	-1.0
Turkey	7.5	2.8	0.0	3.0	4.0	4.0	1.0	0.0	0.0
Turkmenistan	6.5	6.2	5.0	5.2	5.5	5.5	-0.6	0.1	0.6
Ukraine	2.5	3.3	3.6	3.7	4.2	4.2	0.9	0.3	0.4
Uzbekistan	4.5	5.1	5.5	5.7	6.0	6.0	0.2	0.2	0.0

Source: World Bank.

Note: e = estimate; f = forecast. World Bank forecasts are frequently updated based on new information and changing (global) circumstances. Consequently, projections presented here may differ from those contained in other Bank documents, even if basic assessments of countries' prospects do not significantly differ at any given moment in time.

1. GDP and expenditure components are measured in 2010 prices and market exchange rates, unless indicated otherwise.

2. GDP growth rate at constant prices is based on production approach.

To download the data in this table, please visit www.worldbank.org/gep.

BOX 2.2.1 Labor productivity in Europe and Central Asia: Trends and drivers

Productivity growth in Europe and Central Asia (ECA) has fallen from an above-EMDE-average pre-crisis rate of 5.5 percent to a below-EMDE-average post-crisis rate of 1.6 percent—the steepest decline of any EMDE region. There has been wide heterogeneity within the region, however, with productivity growth near zero since 2013 in the Western Balkans and above 2.5 percent in Central Europe. In the Western Balkans and the Russian Federation, investment weakness has weighed on productivity growth. The productivity slowdown in ECA has predominantly reflected weaker within-sector productivity growth, with a particularly sharp decline in the growth of services productivity, and weaker total factor productivity growth in Eastern Europe, the South Caucasus, and the Western Balkans. Sectoral reallocation has also slowed in the post-crisis period, reflecting headwinds that have limited the ability of firms with higher productivity to continue to absorb additional labor from less productive sectors. A comprehensive reform agenda is needed to boost investment in physical and human capital, address continuing demographic pressures, and raise innovation. Such reforms are also needed to improve business climates and governance, reduce the role of the state in the economy, and promote the diversification of commodity-dependent economies.

Introduction

Productivity growth in the Europe and Central Asia (ECA) region has fallen from an above-EMDE-average pre-crisis (2003-08) rate of 5.5 percent to a below-average post-crisis (2013-18) rate of 1.6 percent—the steepest decline of any EMDE region (Figure 2.2.1.1). Productivity levels in ECA in 2018 were one-half above the EMDE average, but only 30 percent of the advanced-economy average. The sharp post-crisis slowdown in productivity growth has significantly reduced the pace of ECA's convergence with advanced economies.

Within the ECA region, there is wide heterogeneity across economies. Productivity growth in Central Europe has been solid in the post-crisis period, at 2.6 percent, while it has been near zero in Russia and the Western Balkans. The region's agricultural commodity exporters, most of which are in Central Asia (excluding Kazakhstan) and Eastern Europe, have ECA's lowest productivity levels, at 3 and 10 percent of the advanced-economy average, respectively. In contrast, Poland and Turkey have productivity levels over 35 percent of the advanced-economy average, reflecting their integration into global value chains and roles as regional financial centers. Central Europe, whose economies are members of the European Union (EU), is deeply embedded in Western European supply chains and has the highest productivity of the ECA subregions, at 34 percent of the advanced-economy average.

Against this backdrop, this box addresses the following questions.

- How has productivity growth evolved in the ECA region?

- What have been the factors associated with productivity growth in the region?

- What policy options are available to boost regional productivity growth?

For the purposes of this box, productivity, unless otherwise indicated, refers to labor productivity, defined as real GDP (at 2010 prices and market exchange rates) per worker. The data refer to a sample of 21 ECA economies: Kosovo, Turkmenistan, and Uzbekistan are excluded in some analysis due to limited data availability.[1]

Evolution of regional productivity

Sharp post-crisis productivity growth slowdown. In the steepest post-crisis decline of any EMDE region, average productivity growth in ECA fell to 1.6 percent in 2013-18, below the EMDE average, from the above-average rate of 5.5 percent in 2003-08. This slowdown was broad-based across the region, affecting nearly all economies, with post-crisis productivity growth below longer-term (1992-2018) averages in roughly two-thirds of the region's economies (Figure 2.2.1.2).

Within-region heterogeneity. There has been wide heterogeneity within the region. The productivity growth slowdown was particularly steep in the South Caucasus and Russia, as well as in the Western Balkans, the latter of which was hit by the Euro Area crisis of 2010-12 amid already elevated unemployment rates. In contrast, the deceleration was milder in Central Europe, which is better

---

Note: This box was prepared by Collette M. Wheeler, building upon analysis in Chapter 3. Research assistance was provided by Vasiliki Papagianni and Shijie Shi.

[1] Central Europe includes Bulgaria, Croatia, Hungary, Poland, and Romania. Western Balkans includes Albania, Bosnia and Herzegovina, Kosovo, Montenegro, North Macedonia, and Serbia. Eastern Europe includes Belarus, Moldova, and Ukraine. South Caucasus includes Armenia, Azerbaijan, and Georgia. Central Asia includes Kazakhstan, the Kyrgyz Republic, Tajikistan, Turkmenistan, and Uzbekistan.

BOX 2.2.1 Labor productivity in Europe and Central Asia: Trends and drivers (*continued*)

FIGURE 2.2.1.1 Productivity in ECA compared with other regions

Productivity growth in Europe and Central Asia (ECA) has fallen from an above-EMDE-average pre-crisis rate of 5.5 percent to a below-EMDE-average post-crisis rate of 1.6 percent—the steepest decline of any EMDE region. Convergence toward advanced economies slowed in the post-crisis period, after having been the fastest among EMDE regions in the pre-crisis period. Productivity levels in ECA, while above the EMDE average, are still one-third of those in advanced economies.

A. Average annual productivity growth in EMDE regions

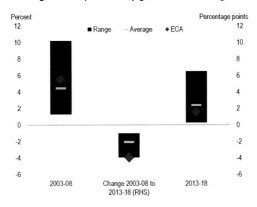

B. Productivity levels and convergence in EMDE regions

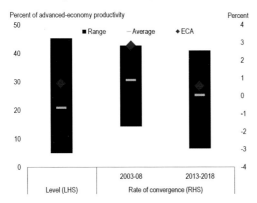

Source: Penn World Table; The Conference Board; *World Development Indicators*, World Bank.
Note: ECA = Europe and Central Asia, EMDE = emerging market and developing economies. Aggregate regional growth rates calculated using GDP weights at 2010 prices and market exchange rates. Unless otherwise specified, productivity refers to labor productivity, defined as output per worker. Sample includes 127 EMDEs, of which 21 are ECA economies.
A. Blue bars denote the range across six (GDP-weighted) averages for EMDE regions. Yellow bars denote the simple average of the six EMDE regional averages.
B. Rate of convergence calculated as the difference in productivity growth rates with the average advanced economy divided by the log difference in productivity levels with the average advanced economy. Regional rate of convergence is the GDP-weighted average of EMDE economies of each region. "Level" of productivity refers to the GDP-weighted average of regional productivity as a share of the average advanced economy during 2013-18. Advanced-economy sample includes 35 advanced economies.

integrated into global supply chains, and Central Asia, which has growing economic ties with China.

- *South Caucasus.* The post-crisis decline in productivity growth was most pronounced, at 14 percentage points, in the South Caucasus. After reaching double-digit annual productivity growth pre-crisis, the subregion suffered several post-crisis shocks, including conflict (Georgia), bouts of violence (Armenia), and a plunge in commodity prices (Armenia, Azerbaijan, Georgia).

- *Western Balkans.* Productivity growth also markedly declined in the Western Balkans (by 5.4 percentage points), where the Euro Area crisis disrupted financial intermediation, including foreign bank retrenchment, and progress on structural reforms stalled. Since 2013, productivity growth in this subregion has been near zero.

- *Russia.* Amid international sanctions and the 2014-16 oil price collapse, Russia's productivity growth was, on average, near zero in 2013-18—a sharp decline from 6.0 percent in 2003-08.

- *Turkey.* Productivity growth more than halved relative to its pre-crisis average, slowing to 2.1 percent in 2013-18, as the economy faced political and economic shocks.

- *Central Europe.* Annual productivity growth slowed by just over 1 percentage point, from 3.7 percent to 2.6 percent, in Central Europe in the post-crisis period, in tandem with the modest slowdown in the Euro Area. This partly reflects the close integration of this subregion with Western European supply chains. Notwithstanding anemic Euro Area growth since the global financial crisis, Central Europe achieved the second highest productivity growth of any ECA subregion in 2013-18, after only Central Asia. This, in part, reflected buoyed investment, which was supported by the absorption of EU structural funds.

- *Eastern Europe.* Annual productivity growth in Eastern Europe slowed by about 4.5 percentage points from pre-crisis rates, to 2.2 percent during 2013-18. Productivity growth averaged only 1.4 percent in 2013-16, which reflected the dual shocks of conflict in Ukraine and a commodity price plunge, but picked up in the next two years.

- *Central Asia.* Central Asia insulated itself somewhat from the impact of the oil price slump of 2014-16

BOX 2.2.1 Labor productivity in Europe and Central Asia: Trends and drivers (*continued*)

FIGURE 2.2.1.2 Evolution of productivity in ECA

The post-crisis slowdown in productivity growth has affected nearly all the economies in ECA. There is wide heterogeneity within the region, however, with productivity growth near-zero since 2013 in Russia and the Western Balkans but above 2.5 percent in Central Asia and Central Europe. The post-crisis productivity growth slowdown has reflected a sharp deceleration in total factor productivity growth in Eastern Europe, the South Caucasus, and the Western Balkans but investment weakness in Russia and Central Europe.

A. Productivity growth in ECA

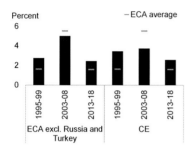

B. Productivity growth in Central Asia, South Caucasus, and Western Balkans

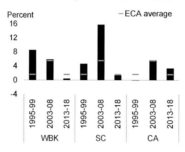

C. Productivity levels relative to advanced-economy average, 2018

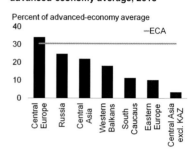

D. Share of economies with productivity growth below long-run and pre-crisis averages, 2013-18

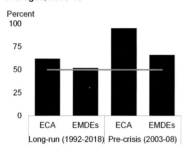

E. Contribution to productivity growth

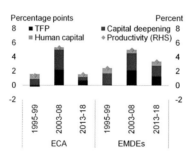

F. Contribution to productivity growth, by ECA subregion

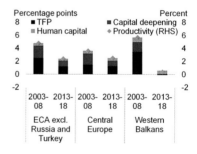

Source: Barro and Lee (2015); Haver Analytics; International Monetary Fund; Penn World Table; United Nations; Wittgenstein Centre for Demography and Global Human Capital; *World Development Indicators,* World Bank.

Note: CA=Central Asia, CE=Central Europe, KAZ=Kazakhstan, SC=South Caucasus, WBK=Western Balkans. Unless otherwise specified, productivity refers to labor productivity, defined as output per worker.

A.-F. Aggregate growth rates calculated using GDP weights at 2010 prices and market exchange rates.

C. Figure shows 2018 subregional productivity levels as a share of 2018 advanced-economy weighted average. Sample includes 35 advanced economies and 21 ECA economies.

D. Figure shows the share of economies for which average productivity growth in 2013-18 was lower than a long-run (1992-2018) and the pre-crisis (2003-08) average. Sample includes 127 EMDEs, of which 21 are ECA economies.

E.F. Productivity defined as output per worker in 2010 U.S. dollars. Samples are unbalanced due to data availability, and include up to 21 ECA economies and 92 EMDEs.

and recession in Russia during 2015-16 by pivoting its exports toward China. By 2018, China had become the second largest export market for Central Asia after the Euro Area, accounting for 20 percent of exports. As a result, the subregion's productivity growth slowed mildly in comparison to the rest of the region, by 2.3 percentage points to 3.4 percent in 2013-18—the fastest productivity growth in ECA in the period.

High productivity levels relative to EMDEs, but with wide range. Partly as a result of rapid productivity growth in 2003-08, the average productivity level in ECA in 2013-18 was 30 percent of the advanced-economy average—roughly one-half above the EMDE average. The ECA average, however, masks wide divergences across ECA subregions, from 3 and 10 percent of the advanced-economy average in predominantly agricultural commodity-exporting Central Asia (excluding Kazakhstan)

BOX 2.2.1 Labor productivity in Europe and Central Asia: Trends and drivers (*continued*)

and Eastern Europe, respectively, to 34 percent of the advanced-economy average in Central Europe, which is deeply embedded into Euro Area supply chains and which has benefited from the absorption of EU structural funds. Poland and Turkey had productivity levels above 35 percent of the advanced-economy average, partly reflecting their openness to trade and positions as regional financial centers (World Bank 2014; World Bank 2019i). Since the global financial crisis, the pace of convergence to advanced-economy productivity levels in the ECA region as a whole has slowed sharply, to average less than 1 percent per year over 2013-18—one-fifth of its rate in 2003-08.

Sources of productivity growth. Labor productivity growth can be decomposed into its sources: Factor accumulation (human or physical capital) and advances in the efficiency of factor use (total factor productivity, or TFP). Two-thirds of the post-crisis slowdown in productivity growth in ECA is estimated to have been due to slowing capital accumulation—partly reflecting weak investment amid lower foreign direct investment (FDI) inflows and declining commodity prices—and one-third to slowing TFP growth, compared with about equal contributions of these sources in the average EMDE.

In Russia and Central Europe, particularly Bulgaria and Romania, weakening capital services deepening accounted for most (three-quarters) of the slowdown in productivity growth in the post-crisis period. In Russia, international sanctions, combined with the 2014-16 oil price plunge, deterred investment, which was further dampened by the weak business environment (Russell 2018). Although EU structural funds have buoyed overall investment in Central Europe, they have not fully offset weakness in machinery and equipment investment, which has been due partly to reduced commercial credit supply (Gradzewicz et al. 2018; Levenko, Oja, and Staehr 2019).

In contrast, reduced TFP growth has been the main source (accounting for three-quarters) of the productivity growth slowdown in Eastern Europe, the Western Balkans, and the South Caucasus. This has partly reflected pockets of conflict and violence (Armenia, Georgia, Ukraine). However, private and public investment has also been weak in the post-crisis period, contributing to reduced TFP growth. As a result of weak investment, these subregions face large infrastructure gaps, particularly in transport and telecommunications networks, which limits the capacity to promote regional integration and, for energy exporters, diversification (IMF 2014). Obstacles to private sector development also constrain TFP in these subregions, with certain economies in the Western Balkans

facing notable challenges with corporate over-indebtedness and market concentration (EBRD 2018a). In both Turkey and Central Asia, the sources of the productivity deceleration were broad-based, reflecting a slowdown in physical capital deepening and human capital improvements, as well as in TFP growth, particularly in Kazakhstan. In Central Asia, Eastern Europe, and the Western Balkans, reform momentum has also slowed, with many of these economies falling short of completing the transition to competitive and inclusive markets.

Sources of regional productivity growth

Post-crisis slowdown across all sectors. Pre-crisis productivity growth in ECA was mostly driven by shifts of resources from agriculture and industry to higher-productivity services sectors, partly as a result of continued reforms to address resource misallocation inherited from central planning (World Bank 2008). The post-crisis period, however, was marked by weakness of growth across all sectors as a slowdown in manufacturing, exacerbated by dwindling global trade growth and a collapse in commodity prices, spilled over to services (Figure 2.2.1.3; Orlic, Hashi, and Hisarciklilar 2018). In contrast to the EMDE average, the contribution of services to productivity growth in 2013-15 was negative in ECA, likely reflecting, in part, spillovers from the Euro Area debt crisis and the continued migration of skilled labor to Western Europe.

Sectoral reallocation as a source of productivity growth in ECA. Resource reallocation toward more productive sectors accounted for almost half of ECA's productivity growth in the 1990s, as output of the region's services sectors increased by nearly 15 percentage points of GDP (World Bank 2008; Arnold, Javorcik, and Mattoo 2011; World Bank 2015b). In contrast, the surge in productivity growth of 2003-08 mostly reflected within-sector growth, as firms in Central Europe became integrated into Euro Area supply chains, technology transfer accelerated, and the services sectors became more liberalized.[2] After the global financial crisis, however, within-sector productivity

---

[2] As economies in Central Europe initiated the process to join the European Union, structural policies that boosted competition and facilitated integration with global value chains helped spur within-sector growth, particularly within services. Thus, liberalization of services sectors is likely to have increased the average productivity of incumbent firms and facilitated the entry of new and more innovative firms. Please refer to Bartelsman and Scarpetta (2007); Brown and Earle (2007); Georgiev, Nagy-Mohacsi, and Plekhanov (2017); Shepotylo and Vakhitov (2015); and World Bank (2008) for further detail.

BOX 2.2.1 Labor productivity in Europe and Central Asia: Trends and drivers (*continued*)

FIGURE 2.2.1.3 Factors supporting productivity growth in ECA

Within-sector productivity growth—the main driver of pre-crisis productivity growth in ECA—fell sharply in the post-crisis period, and productivity gains from sectoral reallocation halved as economies moved to services sectors with relatively low productivity levels. The deceleration of productivity reflected slower improvements in a broad range of its fundamental drivers.

A. Contribution to productivity growth

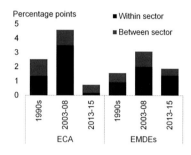

B. Sectoral productivity levels

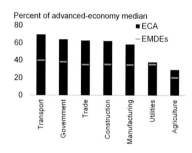

C. Sectoral contribution to productivity growth

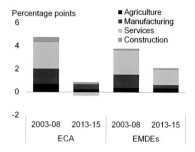

D. Sectoral composition of GDP

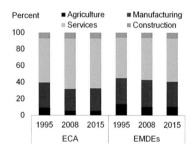

E. Share of EMDEs with a post-crisis slowdown in growth of underlying drivers of productivity

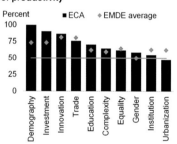

F. Drivers of productivity, 2017

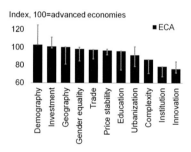

Source: APO productivity database; Expanded African Sector Database; Groningen Growth Development Center Database; Haver Analytics; International Country Risk Guide; ILOSTAT; Observatory of Economic Complexity; Organisation of Economic Co-operation and Development STAN; Penn World Table; United Nations; World Bank; World KLEMS.

Note: Unless otherwise specified, productivity refers to labor productivity, defined as output per worker.

A.-D. The sample includes 6 ECA economies and 46 EMDEs.

A.D. Aggregates calculated using GDP weights at 2010 prices and market exchange rates.

A. Growth "within sector" shows the contribution to aggregate productivity growth of each sector holding employment shares fixed. The "between sector" effect shows the contribution arising from changes in sectoral employment shares.

B. Figure shows the median of country groups.

C. Figure shows median values. "Manufacturing" includes manufacturing, mining and utilities; "Services" includes financial and business services, government and personal services, trade services, and transport services.

D. Figure shows the share of total value added within each sector. "Manufacturing" includes mining and utilities; "Finance" includes business services.

E. Post-crisis slowdown defined as a decline in the growth of each variable during 2008-17 compared to growth in the pre-crisis period, defined as 1998-2007. The blue bars represent share of 21 economies in Europe and Central Asia economies where improvements in each driver of productivity were lower during 2008-17 than in the pre-crisis period 1998-2007 or changes in 2008-17 were below zero. Orange diamond is the corresponding values for EMDE countries. Variables corresponding to each concept and their sample sizes are: Institutions=government effectiveness (20 ECAs; 126 EMDEs), Innovation=patents per capita (15 ECAs; 43 EMDEs), Investment=investment to GDP ratio (21 ECAs; 109 EMDEs), Income equality=(-1)*Gini (21 ECAs; 121 EMDEs), Urbanization=urban population percentage (21 ECAs; 127 EMDEs), Complexity = Hidalgo and Hausmann (2009)'s Economic Complexity Index (17 ECAs; 79 EMDEs), Education=years of schooling (17 ECAs; 103 EMDEs), Demography=share of working-age population (21 ECAs; 127 EMDEs), Gender equality= female average years of education divided by male average years (17 ECAs; 102 EMDEs). Green horizontal line indicates 50 percent.

F. Figure shows the unweighted average levels of drivers normalized as an average of AEs as 100 and standard deviation of 10. Blue bars represent average within Europe and Central Asia economies in 2017. Orange whiskers represent the range of the average drivers for six regions in 2017. Variables corresponding to the concepts are as follows: Education = years of education, Urbanization = share of population living in urban area, Investment = share of investment to GDP, Institution= rules of law, Complexity=Economic complexity index, Geography=share of land area which are not in tropical region, Gender equality= Share of the year of schooling for female to male, Demography=share of population under 14, Innovation=Log patent per capita, Trade=Export+Import/GDP, Price stability=(-1)*log inflation rate. Sample includes 21 ECA economies.

BOX 2.2.1 Labor productivity in Europe and Central Asia: Trends and drivers (*continued*)

growth collapsed, falling to near zero in 2013-15. This may have reflected falling investment in physical capital, particularly in commodity exporters amid the collapse of commodity prices, as well as stalling structural reforms to improve business environments (EBRD 2018b; Georgiev, Nagy-Mohacsi, and Plekhanov 2017).

Between-sector shifts in resources to productivity growth also declined in ECA after the crisis: In 2013-15 it was half its pre-crisis average. The fall may partly have reflected a shift out of agriculture into lower-productivity sectors post -crisis (trade services) than pre-crisis (manufacturing), such as was the case in Kazakhstan (World Bank 2019j). In Romania, reallocation towards more efficient firms was more important within the manufacturing sector, as other sectors, including services, were less exposed to foreign competition (Iootty, Pena, and De Rosa 2019). More broadly, spillovers from the Euro Area debt crisis, slowing global trade growth, and the oil price plunge dampened growth in sectors with higher levels of productivity—including in finance, manufacturing, and mining—limiting their ability to continue to absorb additional labor from other sectors with lower productivity (ILO 2017). Indeed, unemployment grew and labor participation fell in the region, particularly in the Western Balkans and South Caucasus.

Widely varying sectoral productivity levels across ECA. Although most sectors in ECA have productivity levels above EMDE averages, aggregate regional numbers mask significant variations. For example, although productivity has improved in most sectors, agricultural productivity has declined in the economies of Central Asia since their transition to market economies in the 1990s amid disruptions to markets and trade (Gharleghi and Popov 2018). While there are a few exceptions in Central Asia where productivity in the production of specific commodities has improved—mainly grains in Uzbekistan and oil seeds in Kazakhstan—reallocating labor and capital from less competitive agricultural subsectors to more productive sectors continues to have the potential to boost economy-wide productivity.

More broadly in ECA, cross-sectoral productivity differentials continue to imply scope for further overall productivity gains from resource reallocation. In sectors such as agriculture, mining and utilities, ECA's productivity lags about 50-70 percent behind advanced-economy averages, and in mining and utilities it lags behind even EMDE averages. On average in ECA, productivity in agriculture (which accounts for 18 percent of GDP) is about one-third of productivity in other low-skilled sectors such as construction or trade and less than one-sixth of productivity in high-skilled services such as finance, which accounts for 9 percent of GDP.

Reform momentum

Two waves of reform spurred pre-crisis productivity growth in ECA. In the first wave, in the 1990s, the region transitioned toward market from centrally planned economies. In the early 2000s, the second wave of reforms in ECA was associated with the initiation by countries in Central Europe and the Western Balkans of their EU accession process.

First wave. In the wake of the collapse of the Soviet Union in the early 1990s, productivity plunged as transition economies fell into deep recessions caused by the rupture of trade and financial links with the Soviet Union, the emigration of skilled labor, and armed conflict in parts of the region. Central planning was dismantled and replaced by more market-based approaches (Falcetti, Lysenko, and Sanfey 2006). ECA economies were opened up to international trade and capital markets, prices and interest rates were liberalized, and state-owned enterprises were privatized to a degree (Georgiev, Nagy-Mohacsi, and Plekhanov 2017). These reforms helped boost productivity growth in the mid-1990s, particularly in Central Asia and the South Caucasus (World Bank 2018f).

Second wave. In the early 2000s, accession to the EU by the countries of Central Europe accelerated their international economic integration, and drove institutional improvements, further privatization, and deepening of their capital markets (Bruszt and Campos 2016). FDI and private investment surged as reforms were anchored externally, with many ECA economies rapidly becoming integrated into global value chains with Western Europe, accelerating the adoption of new technologies and practices (Aiyar et al. 2013, EBRD 2014). The growing international integration of financial and banking systems helped deepen capital markets, particularly in Central Europe. It was subsequently accompanied by a credit boom (de Haas and van Lelyveld 2006).[3]

Post-crisis reform momentum. Post-crisis, ECA has faced multiple headwinds, including the legacy of the global

---

[3] The rise in foreign currency borrowing by households and firms, however, left sectors exposed to external vulnerabilities, such as capital flow reversals, and deepened the recession following the global financial crisis as economies faced a credit crunch and a period of deleveraging (Zettelmeyer et al. 2010; de Haas et al. 2015).

BOX 2.2.1 Labor productivity in Europe and Central Asia: Trends and drivers (*continued*)

financial crisis, the collapse of oil prices in 2014-16, heightened geopolitical tensions, and international sanctions on Russia. Meanwhile, reform momentum has slowed, with parts of the region witnessing reform reversals, leaving a need for substantial reform progress, especially in Central Asia and Eastern Europe—which are not anchored to an EU accession process—and the Western Balkans.[4] Many of the commodity exporters in the region also suffer from structural constraints, including a lack of export diversification, large state presence in firms, unfavorable business environments, and weak international competitiveness (Azerbaijan, Kazakhstan, Russia, Ukraine; EBRD 2017; Funke, Isakova, and Ivanyna 2017).

Post-crisis slowdown in drivers of productivity. There has been a broad-based slowdown in the growth of most key drivers of labor productivity in ECA in the post-crisis period. Demographic pressures have been intensifying, particularly in the past decade, in nearly all ECA economies. Growth in working-age populations in the region has long lagged the average for EMDEs as a result of significant migration to western European countries in the EU and to Russia and sharp declines in fertility rates. Additionally, more than three quarters of the economies in ECA have experienced post-crisis slowdowns in investment rates, reflecting adverse shifts in investor sentiment amid conflicts and financial pressures in the region, as well as weak external economic growth, including in the Euro Area, and adverse shocks to Russia. Low innovation rates—which partly stem from weak competitiveness, inadequate control of corruption, and a high presence of state-owned enterprises—also continue to dampen the business environment and hinder investment in the region, particularly in the absence of progress with other reforms (EBRD 2018a; EBRD 2019b).

Other factors affecting productivity in the region

Natural resource extraction. Standard productivity growth decompositions fold the extraction of natural capital into total factor productivity growth and, to a lesser extent, physical capital growth (Brandt, Schreyer, and Zipperer 2017; Calderón and Cantu 2019). An economy's natural capital consists of its natural resources such as oil, metals, and agricultural land, and is particularly relevant to ECA given the presence of large commodity exporters. During the pre-crisis commodity price boom and the accompanying boom in resource exploration and development, the increased extraction of natural capital lifted productivity growth in ECA (Khan et al. 2016). The rate of natural capital extraction declined in some economies following the boom and as commodity prices fell, dampening TFP growth.

Urbanization. Urbanization tends to be associated with productivity gains because it encourages more rapid dissemination of knowledge and technologies and facilitates the reallocation of resources from lower to higher-productivity sectors: such reallocation can be constrained by limited urban development, as has been the case in the Kyrgyz Republic (World Bank 2018g). The fact that ECA's population density is lower than in other EMDE regions with similar GDP per capita levels (such as Latin America and Caribbean) indicates scope for further productivity gains from urbanization. Yet, relative to the rest of the world, economies in ECA—particularly those in Central Europe, the Western Balkans, and Eastern Europe—have recently experienced declines in urban, as well as total, populations amid decades of below-replacement fertility and net emigration (World Bank 2017a).

Policy options

Across nearly all ECA economies, productivity growth has slowed since the financial crisis. To reinvigorate productivity growth, a four-pronged, comprehensive policy approach is needed to improve the provision and quality of factors of production, boost firm productivity, promote productivity-enhancing sectoral reallocation, and establish a more growth-friendly business environment. Some of these policies offer the prospect of relatively short-term productivity gains, such as changes in state-owned enterprise ownership and improvements in the investment climate, while others are more likely to lay the foundation for longer-term productivity gains, such as efforts to improve human capital or adjust migration policies. Within these broad categories, specific policy priorities need to be tailored to country-specific circumstances, especially given the region's wide heterogeneity.

Improving factors of production

In ECA, roughly two-thirds of the post-crisis slowdown in productivity growth has reflected slower physical capital

---

[4] A reversal of structural reforms remains a key risk in these regions, and the pace of growth will depend partly on the successful implementation of structural reforms to enhance the business environment, achieve debt sustainability, and restructure state-owned enterprises to improve competition. Please refer to EBRD (2013); Lehne, Mo, and Plekhanov (2014); Georgiev, Nagy-Mohacsi, and Plekhanov (2017); Rovo (2019); and World Bank (2019g) for further detail.

BOX 2.2.1 Labor productivity in Europe and Central Asia: Trends and drivers (*continued*)

FIGURE 2.2.1.4 Drivers of productivity growth in ECA

Investment growth across the region has fallen in the post-crisis period, reflecting external headwinds—including a commodity price plunge—and idiosyncratic factors—including conflict in pockets of the region and financial pressures in large economies. The workforce is continuing to age, and the working-age population share is declining. Learning gaps are sizable in parts of the region, the control of corruption indicator and business climates remain weak, and the role of the state has remained large.

A. Actual and *Consensus* forecasts for investment growth

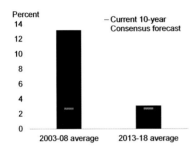

B. Learning gaps, 2017

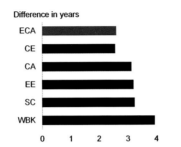

C. Share of regional GDP accounted for by economies with growing working-age populations

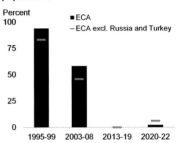

D. Doing Business indicators

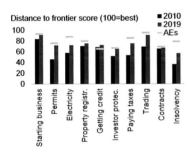

E. Assessment of transition to a competitive market economy, 2019

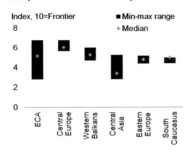

F. Control of corruption, 2017

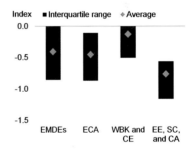

Source: Consensus Economics; European Bank for Reconstruction and Development; Kraay (2018); United Nations; World Bank.

Note: Unless otherwise specified, productivity refers to labor productivity, defined as output per worker.

A. Blue bars denote actual investment growth, where investment is measured as gross fixed capital formation. Actual growth aggregate calculated using GDP weights at 2010 prices and market exchange rates. *Consensus* forecasts aggregate calculated as a simple average of surveys for periods indicated based on data availability. Unbalanced sample includes 8 ECA economies, due to data availability.

B. CE = Central Europe, CA = Central Asia, EE = Eastern Europe, SC = South Caucasus, and WBK = Western Balkans. The learning gap is the difference between expected years of schooling and learning-adjusted years of schooling, as in Kraay (2018). The sample includes 21 ECA EMDEs.

C. The working-age population is defined as people aged 15-64. Unbalanced sample including 23 ECA economies.

D. AEs=advanced economies. Figure shows the median ECA value for 2010 and 2019, and the median advanced economy for 2019. The full names of the *Doing Business* reform areas given on the x-axis are: Making it easier to start a business, making it easier to deal with construction permits, making it easier to get electricity, making it easier to register property, making it easier to get credit, making it easier to protect minority investors, making it easier to pay taxes, making it easier to trade across borders, making it easier to enforce contracts, and making it easier to resolve insolvency. Sample includes 33 advanced economies and 22 ECA economies.

E. Figure shows the distance to the frontier for achieving a full transition to a competitive market economy, as measured by EBRD (2019b). Economies with higher index levels are closer to the frontier, where scores range from 1 to 10, with 10 denoting the synthetic frontier. The sample includes 24 ECA economies.

F. CE = Central Europe, CA = Central Asia, EE = Eastern Europe, SC = South Caucasus, and WBK = Western Balkans. The indicator reflects perceptions of the extent to which public power is exercised for private gain, including both petty and grand forms of corruption, as well as "capture" of the state by elites and private interests, as measured by the *World Governance Indicators*. Sample includes 23 ECA economies and 150 EMDEs.

accumulation, with investment weakness particularly notable in Central Europe, Russia, and, more recently, Turkey, which together account for over 85 percent of ECA's GDP. In some parts of the region, infrastructure investment gaps are sizable. There is thus need for a renewed push to close infrastructure gaps as well as to boost private investment. Meanwhile, human capital

accumulation has contributed less to productivity growth in ECA than in other EMDEs, suggesting there is also a need to improve this source of productivity growth.

Addressing investment and infrastructure gaps. Investment growth has fallen sharply in ECA in the post-crisis period, reflecting a commodity price plunge as well

BOX 2.2.1 Labor productivity in Europe and Central Asia: Trends and drivers (*continued*)

as weakening external economic growth and investor sentiment, amid conflict, international sanctions, and financial pressures (Figure 2.2.1.4). Across the region, reforms to boost private sector development, transition to competitive and inclusive markets, and regional integration are needed to attract private investment and capital flows, particularly to economies outside the EU that lack access to financing sources, such as EU structural funds (EBRD 2018a; World Bank 2019g).

In certain subregions, particularly Central Asia, removing key bottlenecks to private sector development, such as inadequate infrastructure, is especially important to support productivity growth. In some pockets of the region, improved connectivity could accelerate the absorption of technology and speed convergence with advanced economies (Gould 2018). Infrastructure needs remain large in ECA, particularly in transport and electricity. Unreliable electricity supply hinders activity in parts of the region: while the percentage of firms experiencing electrical outages is lower in ECA than in any other EMDE region, related losses for affected firms in Central Asia can exceed 9 percent of annual sales (Blimpo and Cosgrove-Davies 2019; IMF 2019a). In surveyed manufacturing firms in Uzbekistan, for instance, smaller firms report more interruptions of electricity, gas, and water supply, than larger firms, as well as a lack of territory or high lease rates on land as impediments to expanding output production (Trushin, E. 2018). Appropriate land use planning and urbanization policies can substantially reduce the cost of meeting transport needs while minimizing carbon footprints (ITF 2018; Rozenberg and Fay 2019).

Raising human capital. In a few economies in ECA, particularly in Central Asia, inadequate investment in human capital has left parts of the workforce poorly equipped with the skills required for the future, and unprepared for rapid technological change (Flabbi and Gatti 2018). Boosting human capital investment—including through education and health—could help remove bottlenecks to productivity growth. How education systems adapt to evolving skill needs will be a key determinant of the productivity and distributional effects of technological change (Barro and Lee 2015).

In several economies in ECA, educational attainment and the acquisition of needed skills have been lower than expected given the level of school enrollment and the average years of schooling (Altinok, Angrist, and Patrinos 2018). The learning gap (the difference between years spent in schools and educational assessment outcomes) is

wider than the global average in most Western Balkan economies—particularly in Kosovo and North Macedonia—as well as in a few economies in Eastern Europe (Moldova), Central Asia (the Kyrgyz Republic), and the South Caucasus (Georgia). While most economies in Central Europe have smaller gaps than ECA as a whole, Romania is an exception. Turkey also has a larger gap than ECA, in addition to low education attainment in the work force, large gender gaps in education, and an inadequacy of skills, which is often cited as a constraint for doing business and a bottleneck to innovation in the country (World Bank 2019d). Some economies in ECA with large learning gaps, including Georgia, have taken measures to reform the education sector and its funding (Kraay 2018).

Although ECA has the lowest rate of extreme poverty of all EMDE regions, the share of school-age children not enrolled in school is higher than in both East Asia and Pacific and Latin America and Caribbean (World Bank 2018h). Economies in the Western Balkans (Albania, Montenegro, Serbia), Eastern Europe (Moldova), Central Asia (the Kyrgyz Republic, Uzbekistan), and Turkey have elevated out-of-school rates relative to the ECA average for secondary education (UNICEF 2019). The diversity of situations in ECA—with human capital investment quite high in some economies but lagging in others (such as in Central Asia)—indicates a need for policies to be tailored to countries' specific needs (Kraay 2018). Education policy and training programs can also be redesigned to adapt the skills of aging populations to changing needs and new technologies (Hallward-Driemeier and Nayyar 2018; World Bank 2018a).

Counteracting unfavorable demographic trends. In ECA, the workforce is continuing to age, and the working-age population share is declining, with many young and skilled workers having emigrated. These developments are likely to weaken productivity growth and highlight the need for education to help workers adapt to new job requirements and technologies (Aiyar, Ebeke, and Shao 2016). Generating stronger productivity growth will require measures to mitigate the decline in skilled workforces. Implementing more flexible immigration policies could help relieve skilled labor shortages by attracting skilled foreign workers in an orderly way (Delogu, Docquier, and Machado 2014; World Bank 2019g).

Boosting firm productivity

Within-sector productivity gains stalled in ECA in 2013-15, consistent with slowing reallocation of resources between firms and slowing productivity growth within

BOX 2.2.1 Labor productivity in Europe and Central Asia: Trends and drivers (*continued*)

firms. This highlights the need to boost firm productivity in the region, including by completing the transition to competitive and inclusive markets, which could strengthen the environment for private investment and innovation (World Bank 2019a). Policy options include measures to level the playing field for private and state-owned firms and expanding access to finance to a wider range of firms.

Leveling the playing field. State-owned enterprises tend to be less efficient than those in the private sector (World Bank 1995). In Eastern Europe and Central Asia, and to some extent Russia, the state's presence in the economy remains large, with state ownership accounting for more than 10 percent of firms surveyed in some cases, and with ECA ranking second overall among EMDE regions, after Sub-Saharan Africa (World Bank 2019k). In Ukraine, firms with at least partial state presence account for roughly 20 percent of total turnover by firms and over 25 percent of firms' assets (Balabushko et al. 2018). State-owned enterprises also have a large presence in Moldova, accounting for one-third of GDP (World Bank 2019l). Restructuring or privatizing state-owned enterprises therefore still presents an opportunity to raise economy-wide productivity in several countries across the region, if it is accompanied by effective regulation and improvements in management, corporate governance, and the business environment (Brown, Earle, and Telegdy 2006; EBRD 2019b; Funke, Isakova, and Ivanyna 2017). Additionally, there are a number of economies, including in Eastern Europe, where price controls remain in place for particular goods, tending to constrain competition and lower productivity.

Financial market development and financial inclusion. Small and medium-sized enterprises (SMEs) have the largest potential for productivity catch-up with advanced economies. Their growth continues to be hindered by many factors, including insufficient access to finance and regulatory barriers (Ayyagari, Demirgüç-Kunt, and Maksimovic 2017; Cusolito, Safadi, and Taglioni 2017; Wang 2016). The largest gaps in financial inclusion for SMEs in ECA are in Central Asia and the South Caucasus (excluding Georgia), where access to financial services is nearly as limited as in the Middle East and North Africa, South Asia, and Sub-Saharan Africa (IMF 2019b).

Policies that promote more widespread adoption of digital technologies, including in the delivery of financial and public sector services, could bolster financial inclusion and boost productivity by helping spread innovation and improving private sector and government efficiency (Baldwin 2019). In economies with large informal sectors,

more widespread adoption of these technologies could also help expand tax bases through the fiscalization of informal sector transactions (World Bank 2019a). Increasing SMEs' access to finance could help these firms increase their average size and reduce their reliance on retained earnings to fund investment, which in turn would support job creation (Ayyagari, Demirgüç-Kunt, and Maksimovic 2017; Ayyagari et al. 2016).

Encouraging sectoral reallocation

Between-sector productivity gains from sectoral reallocation have slowed in ECA since the global financial crisis. Also, some ECA economies remain undiversified: renewed efforts to diversify commodity-based economies could generate new opportunities for labor to move toward more productive employment.

Diversifying economies. Energy-exporting economies, including those in ECA, are characterized by generally low levels of economic diversification, in terms of both exports and fiscal revenue (Grigoli, Herman, and Swiston 2017).[5] Energy sector production tends to be capital-intensive, with relatively high labor productivity (Aslam et al. 2016; Danforth, Medas, and Salins 2016; Stocker et al. 2018). Productivity growth, however, has been more tepid in ECA's energy-exporting countries than in the region overall, with post-crisis (2013-18) growth at 1.2 percent versus 1.6 percent, reflecting weaker TFP growth. Diversification therefore presents an opportunity to boost TFP and productivity growth, as well as macroeconomic stability (Brenton, Newfarmer, and Walkenhorst 2009; Papageorgiou and Spatafora 2012). Diversification of resource-based economies can be promoted by reforms that increase capital and skill accumulation, innovation, and reduce transaction costs.[6]

Enhancing a growth-friendly environment

Several ECA economies have severe institutional weaknesses that continue to erode incentives for innovation and investment. Addressing these weaknesses requires reforms to improve governance and business climates.

---

[5] On the budget front, Russia has made strides in anchoring fiscal policy by implementing a fiscal rule that targets a primary balance of zero at the benchmark oil price of $40 per barrel. Any excess fiscal reserves that are generated from higher oil prices are saved in the National Welfare Fund.

[6] Please refer to Beck (2018); Gylfason (2018); Lederman and Maloney (2007); Hesse (2008); and IMF (2016a) for further detail.

BOX 2.2.1 Labor productivity in Europe and Central Asia: Trends and drivers (*continued*)

Growth-friendly governance. Over the long term, institutional quality is one of the most important determinants of productivity growth (Chapter 3). In ECA, productivity catch-up to advanced economies was particularly pronounced in Central Europe during the pre-crisis period, reflecting the anchoring of structural and institutional reforms to the EU accession process (Rodríguez-Pose and Ketterer 2019). Overall, however, the region continues to face governance challenges with nearly 75 percent of ECA EMDEs falling below the global average for the control of corruption, including almost all of the economies of Central Europe, Eastern Europe, and the South Caucasus (Kaufmann, Kraay, and Mastruzzi 2010). Because progress in confronting perceived and actual corruption has been slow, continuing efforts have reinforced the perception that the control of corruption is higher than in other EMDEs (Transparency International 2019).

Structural reforms to improve governance can lead to sizable productivity gains, particularly in countries that are farthest from best practices (Chapter 3; Acemoglu, Johnson, and Robinson 2005; Cusolito and Maloney 2018). Major governance and business reforms in EMDEs have in the past been associated with higher growth rates in output, total factor productivity, and investment (Hodge et al. 2011; Divanbeigi and Ramalho 2015; World Bank 2018a). The detrimental effects of corruption on firm productivity can be exacerbated by excess or complex regulation (Amin and Ulku 2019). Anticorruption campaigns, as well as reductions in the number of regulations and tax complexity, have helped some economies tackle corruption (IMF 2019c).

Growth-friendly business climates. Lack of exposure to international competition—including from non-tariff barriers and complex trade rules—as well as restrictive product market and services regulation, remain structural bottlenecks in the region, hindering the ability to attract foreign direct investment and private investment in some economies (Kazakhstan, Russia, Ukraine; World Bank 2016b; Shepotylo and Vakhitov 2015). Over the past decade, several ECA economies made significant strides in improving their business environments. As a result, in several countries in Central Europe, the Western Balkans, and the South Caucasus, business environment indexes have recently approached the levels in advanced EU economies (World Bank 2018a).

Notwithstanding these improvements, business climates in Eastern Europe and Central Asia lag the ECA average, with the latter trailing the EMDE average in access to electricity and the ease of trading across borders (World Bank 2019j). For example, in Ukraine, the largest economy in Eastern Europe, the average worker takes one year to produce the same amount that the average worker in Germany produces in 17 days (World Bank 2019m). At current growth trends, Ukraine is unlikely to converge to Poland's per capita income, despite having had similar income levels in 1990; this partly reflects Ukraine's relatively low ratio of capital stock to GDP. Removing market distortions and improving resource allocation could triple manufacturing productivity and help improve prospects in Ukraine (Ryzhenkov 2016). The Western Balkans also struggle to attract FDI notwithstanding reforms to improve business climates and further integration into regional and global markets (Jirasavetakul and Rahman 2018; World Bank 2019h; World Bank 2019n). Although Turkey has high productivity levels, it lags well behind the ECA average for resolving insolvency, which could dampen overall productivity as less productive firms are more likely to remain in the market (World Bank 2019d). To address this, Turkey has recently introduced a more streamlined procedure that focuses on business continuation instead of liquidation.

LATIN AMERICA and THE CARIBBEAN

Growth in Latin American and the Caribbean slowed markedly in 2019, to an estimated 0.8 percent, held back by idiosyncratic factors in large economies, headwinds from slowing global trade, and social unrest in several countries. As activity in Brazil gathers pace amid improving investment conditions, policy uncertainty in Mexico fades, and the recession in Argentina eases after bouts of severe market stress, regional growth is projected to rise to 1.8 percent in 2020 and about 2.4 percent in 2021. This recovery will not be sufficient to reverse the growing per capita income gap with advanced economies in some LAC economies. Moreover, the regional outlook is subject to significant downside risks, including from market volatility and adverse market responses to weak fiscal conditions; deeper-than-expected spillovers from slowdowns in Argentina, China, and the United States; heightened social unrest; and disruptions from natural disasters and severe weather.

Recent developments

Growth in Latin America and the Caribbean (LAC) decelerated markedly in 2019, to an estimated 0.8 percent. The slowdown was broad-based across economies and sectors. All three of the largest economies in the region—Brazil, Mexico, and Argentina—grew significantly less than projected in June. Brazil experienced a larger-than-expected impact from a major mining accident, as well as slowing exports to China, and relatively sluggish improvements in labor market conditions. Growth in Mexico was hindered by an uncertain investment climate, tight monetary policy, and public spending cuts, while Argentina's economy was held back by the effects of renewed financial stress. In Colombia, however, growth accelerated as private consumption and investment picked in the context of accommodative monetary policy and fiscal incentives to support investment.

The regional growth slowdown was generally more acute in industrial sectors than in services (Figure 2.3.1.A). Industrial activity was stagnant or contracting in five of the region's six largest economies in the first half of 2019 (Argentina,

Brazil, Chile, Mexico, Peru), though conditions in most countries improved later in the year. Within the industrial sector, mining activity contracted sharply following an iron ore mining dam disaster in Brazil, continued oil production declines in Mexico, and temporary mining disruptions in Chile, while policy uncertainty contributed to a sharp contraction in mining and construction activity (Figure 2.3.1.B).

Sluggish investment and private consumption held back regional growth in 2019. Investment contracted as policy uncertainty lingered, investor sentiment worsened, and governments retrenched. In Mexico, the government cancelled public infrastructure projects. Several other countries cut public spending (Argentina, Ecuador, Haiti, Panama, Paraguay).

Regional export growth has slowed along with global trade activity. Yet export trends among the large regional economies are not uniform. Bilateral tariff hikes between China and the United States gave an initial boost to Brazil's soybean exports, which has since faded as demand slowed and the soybean price differential between Brazil and the rest of the world narrowed. Exports from Brazil, Chile, and Peru to China—the largest export destination of all three countries—plateaued or slowed in the second half of 2019 (Figure 2.3.1.C). However, exports from Mexico, 80

Note: This section was prepared by Dana Vorisek. Research assistance was provided by Vanessa Arellano Banoni. The regional aggregate statistics presented in this section do not include Venezuela.

FIGURE 2.3.1 LAC: Recent developments

Services sector growth has slowed in LAC, mirroring a much stronger slowdown in the industrial sector. Within the industrial sector, mining production contracted sharply in 2019. Economies highly reliant on China as a trade destination have seen their exports plateau or fall after tariff hikes between China and the United States, while Mexico's exports to the United States have continued to grow. A sharp recession in Argentina has impacted Bolivia, Brazil, and Paraguay through trade and remittance channels. With output gaps becoming more negative, and inflation at the low end of target ranges, monetary policy is easing in numerous countries.

A. Services and industrial sector growth

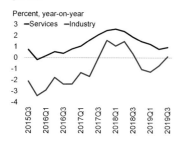

B. Industrial production growth, by subsector

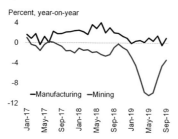

C. Exports to China and the United States

D. Exports to and remittances from Argentina

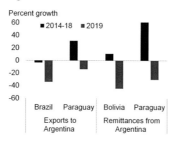

E. Regional output gap

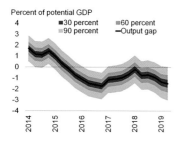

F. Inflation

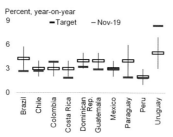

Source: Central Bank of Bolivia; Central Bank of Costa Rica; Central Bank of the Dominican Republic; Central Bank of Guatemala; Central Bank of Paraguay; Central Bank of Uruguay; Haver Analytics; International Monetary Fund (World Economic Outlook); World Bank.

A. Lines show GDP-weighted averages of Argentina, Brazil, Chile, Colombia, Mexico, and Peru (90 percent of regional GDP). Last observation is 2019Q3.

B. Lines show industrial production-weighted averages of Brazil, Chile, Colombia, Mexico, and Peru. Last observation is September 2019.

C. Index based on exports (in value) from Brazil, Chile and Peru to China, and from Mexico to the United States. Gray area begins when China and the United States began to increase bilateral tariffs, in July 2018. Last observation is October 2019.

D. Bars show average year-on-year growth of monthly flows during the indicated period. Bars for 2019 are constructed using monthly data through November (exports) and September (remittances).

E. Includes data for Argentina, Belize, Bolivia, Brazil, Chile, Colombia, Costa Rica, the Dominican Republic, Ecuador, El Salvador, Guatemala, Honduras, Mexico, Nicaragua, Panama, Paraguay, Peru, and Uruguay. Shaded areas around center line indicate confidence intervals. Last observation is 2019Q2.

F. Blue boxes show central inflation targets; vertical lines show target bands.

percent of which go to the United States, continued to grow. There is evidence that Mexico has benefitted from trade diversion to the United States as a result of the U.S.-China trade conflict (UNCTAD 2019; World Bank 2019o). In the first half of 2019, the electrical machinery, transport equipment, and agriculture and food sectors benefited the most, in value terms.

Late 2019 was marked by the emergence of social tensions in Bolivia, Chile, and Ecuador, related to economic policy decisions and elections. The events contributed to a downgrade of estimated growth in all of these countries. The recent developments follow similar events in Haiti and Nicaragua, which contributed to deteriorating economic conditions in both countries. Colombia, as well, experienced protests in late 2019.

Economic and social conditions in Venezuela continue to be dire. The population is experiencing frequent electricity outages and water shortages; widespread scarcity of basic goods; and a sharp rise in preventable diseases, malnutrition, and mortality rates. More than 4.7 million people have left. Several countries have imposed entry restrictions on Venezuelans as the provision of services to migrants becomes more fiscally burdensome and social tensions rise. However, these restrictions are not expected to halt outward migration from Venezuela, and migration may have growing policy implications elsewhere. In Colombia, for instance, the fiscal council has allowed additional spending related to migrants. In the medium to long term, host countries could benefit. The Colombian government estimates that the net impact of migration on growth, after accounting for the fiscal cost, will be 0.1-0.5 percentage point between 2018 and 2021 relative to a no-migration scenario, primarily via the consumption channel (Colombia Departamento Nacional de Planeación 2018).

In Argentina, following a sharp currency depreciation in the wake of the primary election results in August, the government implemented capital controls and imposed a maturity extension on part of its short-term debt. The bouts of financial stress in Argentina since early 2018 have affected neighboring countries through trade (lower exports to Argentina from Brazil and

Paraguay, in particular), remittances (sharply lower from Argentina to Bolivia and Paraguay), and tourism (downturn in spending and arrivals by Argentines in Uruguay; Figure 2.3.1.D).

With a small number of exceptions (Argentina, Ecuador, Venezuela), bond yields in the region have been broadly stable in recent months. Some currencies have depreciated against the U.S. dollar (Argentina, Brazil, Chile, Colombia, Paraguay, Uruguay). Capital inflows to the region, which come predominantly from the United States and the Euro Area, have slowed.

The output gap in nearly all economies has become steadily more negative, after the regional output gap nearly closed in late 2018 (Figure 2.3.1.E). With growth and inflation expectations broadly moderating and inflation at the low end of target ranges among most inflation-targeting countries, a growing number of central banks are easing monetary policy (Figure 2.3.1.F). Policy interest rates in Brazil, Chile, Costa Rica, the Dominican Republic, Jamaica, Mexico, Paraguay, and Peru were lowered in the second half of 2019, in most cases multiple times.

Several major policy developments have occurred in the region. Following revisions to the previously negotiated United-States-Mexico-Canada Agreement, among others on labor standard enforcement mechanisms, the agreement moved closer to ratification by the United States with the passage by the House of Representatives in December. Mexico has ratified the agreement. In Brazil, a long-awaited pension reform was passed by Congress in October. Policymakers have begun to work on tax reform, the next key item on the reform agenda. Mercosur (Argentina, Brazil, Paraguay, and Uruguay) reached a trade agreement with the European Union in June that was two decades in the making. The agreement will now need to be ratified and implemented at the country level.

Outlook

Although growth projections have been revised down since June, an expected easing of domestic constraints in the three largest economies, together with a continued growth acceleration in

Colombia, is still envisioned to boost the outlook for the region (Figure 2.3.2.A). Regional growth is forecast to increase to 1.8 percent in 2020, and to 2.4 percent in 2021 (Tables 2.3.1 and 2.3.2). Under this projection, growth is not expected to exceed the average during the past three decades. Moreover, the projected performance will not be sufficient to reverse the widening per capita income relative to advanced economies since 2014 in some countries in the region (Figure 2.3.2.B).

Metals and agriculture prices are projected to be flat due to weak global demand, providing little incremental support for exporters of these commodities. Likewise, lower global demand for oil, together with expanding production in the United States, will put downward pressure on oil prices in the short term.

Fiscal space is limited or absent in most of the region, leaving little capacity to pursue expansionary spending to support growth. One exception is Chile, which is planning a fiscal stimulus that will boost public investment and support small and medium enterprises. Policymakers in some other large economies (Brazil, Mexico) remain committed to spending restraint over the forecast horizon despite sluggish growth, in order to improve medium-term fiscal sustainability and retain investor confidence. In Argentina, continued fiscal consolidation will be a necessary component of the budget strategy.

In the baseline outlook, growth in the largest economies will pick up and domestic demand—in particular, investment—will strengthen. This outlook is also contingent on an acceleration of exports, after weakness in 2019 (Figure 2.3.2.C).

In Brazil, a boost to investor confidence following progress on major reforms, a moderate easing of lending conditions, and a gradual improvement in labor market conditions are slated to support a pickup in investment and private consumption, helping push growth to 2 percent in 2020 and 2.5 percent in 2021. Investment in Mexico is also expected to pick up as investor sentiment improves and the private sector is more involved in infrastructure projects, while easing monetary policy will provide modest support to private consumption. Growth is forecast to rise to a still

FIGURE 2.3.2 LAC: Outlook and risks

Growth in LAC is projected to firm during the forecast horizon, supported predominantly by an easing of domestic constraints in the three largest economies in the region. The recovery will be subdued, however, and will not be sufficient to offset a growing per capita income gap with advanced economies in some LAC economies. Faster regional growth is contingent on an upturn in investment, which has been repeatedly downgraded during the past year, and on a pickup in weak export growth. Weak fiscal positions are a risk for financial stability and growth in the region, while high levels of inequality could spark further social unrest and result in economic disruptions.

A. Growth

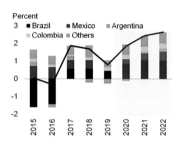

B. Per capita income in LAC relative to advanced economies

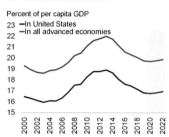

C. New export orders

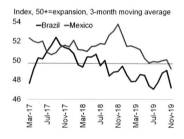

D. Investment growth forecast

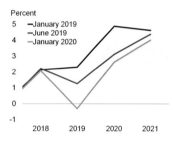

E. Fiscal balance and government debt

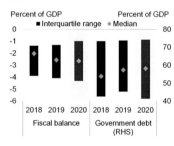

F. Income inequality

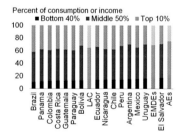

Source: Haver Analytics; International Monetary Fund (World Economic Outlook); World Bank. (PovcalNet).
B. Per capita GDP is calculated as the sum of GDP in the countries in the indicated groups divided by the sum of the population in the same country groups.
C. Last observation is November 2019.
D. Lines show GDP-weighted averages of all LAC economies (20 in total) for which expenditure components of GDP are available.
E. Sample includes 32 countries.
F. Bottom 40 percent refers to the bottom four deciles of consumption or income share, middle 50 percent to the middle five deciles, and top 10 percent to the top decile. Data are for latest available year from 2010 to 2017. EMDEs = emerging market and developing economies. AEs = advanced economies. LAC, EMDE, and AE bars show simple averages of 19, 111, and 31 countries, respectively.

subdued 1.2 percent in 2020 and 1.8 percent in 2021.

In the near-term projection, investment and consumption in Argentina will continue contracting, though at a slower pace, while import compression will recede. Ultimately, the economy is expected to experience three years of contraction, and growth to revert to a positive rate only in 2021.

In Colombia, investment is expected to accelerate as planned infrastructure projects are carried out. Favorable financing conditions are envisioned to support domestic demand more broadly. These factors will support a rise in growth to 3.6 percent in 2020 and about 3.9 percent in 2021-22.

Growth in Chile is projected to recover after interruptions from social unrest in late 2019, to 2.5 percent in 2020 and 3.0 percent in 2021. This assumes a higher volume of copper exports after mine disruptions in 2019, improved private sector sentiment as business sector reforms are rolled out, and a boost from fiscal stimulus.

Aggregate growth in Central America is projected to firm over the forecast horizon. Easing credit conditions (especially in Costa Rica) and an unwinding of temporary setbacks to construction and infrastructure projects (Panama) will help boost output. The subregion is also expected to benefit from trade and business environment reforms in recent years, including an expanded customs union between Guatemala and Honduras.

Growth in the Caribbean is forecast to accelerate in the near term, predominantly due to major offshore oil production developments in Guyana, while growth in the largest Caribbean economy, the Dominican Republic, is projected to be stable at about 5 percent as the tourism sector stabilizes following disruptions in 2019 linked to health concerns.

Risks

LAC continues to face predominantly downside risks to growth. External risks, particularly those linked to trade and finance, are elevated. A further growth slowdown in China, should the bilateral U.S.-China trade dispute reescalate, could expose LAC to additional negative spillovers through trade, commodity price, and confidence channels. This risk is particularly acute for countries highly reliant on China as an export destination (Brazil, Chile, Peru, and Uruguay). Likewise, sluggish U.S. growth could be a greater-than-expected hindrance for Mexico and other countries reliant on the United States. Continued weak export growth would contribute to a rise in already-large current account deficits in some countries (Bolivia, Colombia, El Salvador, Honduras, and Panama, among others). The financing of large external imbalances could become more challenging should countries experience severe currency pressures or an unexpected rise in borrowing costs.

Adverse market responses to domestic market conditions within the region, including weak fiscal profiles, could dent capital inflows and investment. Investment growth is projected to firm in the baseline outlook but has been repeatedly buffeted by unanticipated developments during the past year and could continue to be hindered by policy uncertainty (Figures 2.3.2.D).

Adverse intraregional spillovers from the market volatility and sharp recession in Argentina could take a further toll if restoring the country's economic stability takes longer than expected. Negative repercussions are especially a risk for Bolivia, Paraguay, and Uruguay. Moreover, for Argentina, another bout of severe financial market stress could further inhibit debt sustainability and set back an already protracted economic recovery.

Should easing monetary policy be insufficient to counter weak growth, commitments to public spending prudence in the region could come under pressure. Though a return to an expansionary fiscal stance would provide a temporary boost to growth, it could have negative consequences for financial stability and fiscal sustainability. Fiscal positions are already on track to deteriorate somewhat during the forecast horizon as a result of sustained budget deficits (Figure 2.3.2.E). Weak growth could make it

more politically challenging to implement structural reforms, which are key to boosting longstanding low productivity (Box 2.3.1).

Social tensions in several countries in late 2019 could become more widespread, with negative economic repercussions. Discontent about lack of opportunities is a significant underlying risk for social stability, and ultimately for growth, in the region. Although inequality in many LAC countries has fallen in recent years, due in large part to gains at the low end of the income distribution, it remains high relative to other regions (World Bank 2016e, 2020; Messina and Silva 2019). The share of income going to the bottom 40 percent of households in LAC economies is lower, on average, than in all EMDEs and in advanced economies, while the share going to the top 10 percent is higher, at 35 percent, versus 25 percent in advanced economies and 31 percent in EMDEs (Figure 2.3.2.F).

Disruptions related to natural disasters, including the heightened frequency, duration, and force of climate events, are a persistent and growing downside risk for a host of LAC economies. The human and economic toll of Hurricane Dorian in The Bahamas in September 2019 is the latest example of the Caribbean's vulnerability to hurricanes, and illustrates the devastating consequences of natural disasters in the region. In Brazil, the large-scale fires in the Amazon rainforest last year have had widespread environmental consequences. They have also presented a policy risk, in that the authorities' sluggish response has complicated the political task of completing the EU-Mercosur trade agreement.

The EU-Mercosur agreement has the potential to significantly boost the depth of global trade integration in LAC if it passes in its current form, especially as the region has long been less open to trade than most other EMDE regions (World Bank 2019p). Completion of the agreement in its current form is an upside risk for the outlook. Deeper trade linkages and participation in global value chains have the potential to stimulate productivity through increased investment and deeper participation in global value chains.

TABLE 2.3.1 Latin America and the Caribbean forecast summary

(Real GDP growth at market prices in percent, unless indicated otherwise)

Percentage point differences from June 2019 projections

	2017	2018	2019e	2020f	2021f	2022f	2019e	2020f	2021f
EMDE LAC, GDP[1]	1.9	1.7	0.8	1.8	2.4	2.6	-0.9	-0.8	-0.3
(Average including countries with full national accounts and balance of payments data only)[2]									
EMDE LAC, GDP[2]	1.9	1.7	0.8	1.8	2.4	2.6	-0.9	-0.7	-0.3
GDP per capita (U.S. dollars)	0.7	0.6	-0.3	0.8	1.5	1.8	-1.1	-0.8	-0.2
PPP GDP	2.0	1.7	0.8	1.8	2.5	2.7	-1.0	-0.8	-0.2
Private consumption	2.7	2.1	1.1	2.1	2.7	2.9	-0.7	-1.1	-0.2
Public consumption	0.7	0.9	-0.3	0.9	1.0	1.2	-0.1	-0.3	-0.2
Fixed investment	-0.2	2.1	-0.3	2.6	4.0	3.6	-1.6	-0.5	-0.4
Exports, GNFS[3]	3.8	4.2	1.1	2.8	3.1	3.5	-3.0	-0.9	-0.7
Imports, GNFS[3]	6.3	5.5	0.4	3.3	3.8	4.0	-2.6	-1.4	-0.8
Net exports, contribution to growth	-0.5	-0.3	0.1	-0.1	-0.2	-0.1	0.1	0.1	0.0
Memo items: GDP									
South America[4]	1.6	1.4	0.9	1.9	2.6	2.7	-0.7	-0.7	-0.1
Central America[5]	3.8	2.7	2.5	3.0	3.3	3.4	-0.6	-0.4	-0.3
Caribbean[6]	3.3	5.0	3.8	5.6	3.9	4.3	0.0	1.1	-0.5
Brazil	1.3	1.3	1.1	2.0	2.5	2.4	-0.4	-0.5	0.2
Mexico	2.1	2.1	0.0	1.2	1.8	2.3	-1.7	-0.8	-0.6
Argentina	2.7	-2.5	-3.1	-1.3	1.4	2.3	-1.9	-3.5	-1.8

Source: World Bank.

Note: e = estimate; f = forecast. EMDE = emerging market and developing economies. World Bank forecasts are frequently updated based on new information and changing (global) circumstances. Consequently, projections presented here may differ from those contained in other Bank documents, even if basic assessments of countries' prospects do not differ at any given moment in time. The World Bank has ceased producing a growth forecast for Venezuela and has removed Venezuela from all growth aggregates in which it was previously included.

1. GDP and expenditure components are measured in 2010 prices and market exchange rates.

2. Aggregate includes all countries in Table 2.3.2 except Dominica, Grenada, Guyana, Haiti, St. Kitts and Nevis, St. Lucia, St. Vincent and the Grenadines, and Suriname.

3. Exports and imports of goods and non-factor services (GNFS).

4. Includes Argentina, Bolivia, Brazil, Chile, Colombia, Ecuador, Paraguay, Peru, and Uruguay.

5. Includes Costa Rica, El Salvador, Guatemala, Honduras, Nicaragua, and Panama.

6. Includes Antigua and Barbuda, The Bahamas, Barbados, Belize, Dominica, Dominican Republic, Grenada, Guyana, Haiti, Jamaica, St. Kitts and Nevis, St. Lucia, St. Vincent and the Grenadines, and Suriname.

To download the data in this table, please visit www.worldbank.org/gep.

TABLE 2.3.2 **Latin America and the Caribbean country forecasts**[1]

(Real GDP growth at market prices in percent, unless indicated otherwise)

Percentage point differences
from June 2019 projections

	2017	2018	2019e	2020f	2021f	2022f	2019e	2020f	2021f
Argentina	2.7	-2.5	-3.1	-1.3	1.4	2.3	-1.9	-3.5	-1.8
Belize	1.9	2.1	2.7	2.1	1.8	1.8	0.4	0.0	-0.1
Bolivia	4.2	4.2	2.2	3.0	3.2	3.4	-1.8	-0.6	-0.2
Brazil	1.3	1.3	1.1	2.0	2.5	2.4	-0.4	-0.5	0.2
Chile	1.3	4.0	1.3	2.5	3.0	3.0	-2.2	-0.6	0.0
Colombia	1.4	2.6	3.3	3.6	3.9	3.9	-0.2	-0.1	0.2
Costa Rica	3.4	2.6	2.0	2.5	3.0	3.2	-1.0	-0.6	-0.4
Dominican Republic	4.7	7.0	5.3	5.0	5.0	5.0	0.1	0.0	0.0
Ecuador	2.4	1.4	-0.3	0.2	0.8	1.2	-0.3	-0.2	0.0
El Salvador	2.3	2.5	2.4	2.5	2.5	2.5	-0.2	0.0	0.1
Grenada	4.4	4.2	3.5	2.9	2.9	3.2	-0.4	-0.8	-0.8
Guatemala	2.8	3.1	3.4	3.0	3.2	3.2	0.1	0.3	0.2
Guyana	2.1	4.1	4.5	86.7	10.5	14.6	-0.1	53.2	-12.4
Haiti[2]	1.2	1.5	-0.9	-1.4	-0.5	1.4	-1.3	-3.0	-1.8
Honduras	4.8	3.7	3.3	3.5	3.5	3.5	-0.3	-0.3	-0.4
Jamaica	1.0	1.9	1.0	1.1	1.2	2.0	-0.6	-0.6	-0.7
Mexico	2.1	2.1	0.0	1.2	1.8	2.3	-1.7	-0.8	-0.6
Nicaragua	4.7	-3.8	-5.0	-0.5	0.6	1.0	0.0	-1.6	-0.7
Panama	5.6	3.7	3.5	4.2	4.6	4.8	-1.5	-1.2	-0.6
Paraguay	5.0	3.7	0.7	3.1	3.9	3.8	-2.6	-0.9	-0.1
Peru	2.5	4.0	2.6	3.2	3.5	3.6	-1.2	-0.7	-0.5
St. Lucia	2.6	0.9	1.8	3.2	3.0	2.4	-1.6	-0.3	0.6
St. Vincent and the Grenadines	1.0	2.2	2.3	2.3	2.3	2.3	0.2	0.0	0.0
Suriname	1.8	2.6	2.2	2.5	2.1	2.1	0.2	0.4	0.0
Uruguay	2.6	1.6	0.5	2.5	3.5	3.2	-1.0	0.2	1.0

Source: World Bank.

Note: e = estimate; f = forecast. World Bank forecasts are frequently updated based on new information and changing (global) circumstances. Consequently, projections presented here may differ from those contained in other Bank documents, even if basic assessments of countries' prospects do not significantly differ at any given moment in time.

1. GDP and expenditure components are measured in 2010 prices and market exchange rates.
2. GDP is based on fiscal year, which runs from October to September of next year.

To download the data in this table, please visit www.worldbank.org/gep.

BOX 2.3.1 Labor productivity in Latin America and the Caribbean: Trends and drivers

Labor productivity growth in Latin America and the Caribbean (LAC) slowed to near zero during 2013-18, among the lowest of the six emerging market and developing economy (EMDE) regions. This rate is well below the 1.7 percent average during the pre-crisis period (2003-08) and a return to the average during the preceding four decades. In two-fifths of LAC economies, productivity growth was negative during 2013-18. Sluggish productivity growth during 2013-18 mainly reflects negative total factor productivity (TFP) growth in some large LAC economies, as the commodity price slump and intensifying market distortions allowed unproductive firms to continue operating. Despite anemic productivity growth, the level of productivity remains higher than the EMDE average, albeit still less than one-quarter of the level in advanced economies. Many countries in the region would benefit from reforms to improve competition and innovation, deepen trade linkages, improve the quality of education, reduce labor market inefficiencies, strengthen institutional quality, and increase the volume and efficiency of infrastructure investment.

Introduction

For decades, productivity growth in Latin America and the Caribbean (LAC) has been anemic (Fernández-Arias and Rodríguez-Apolinar 2016). After a brief pre-crisis burst, productivity growth fizzled out again after the global financial crisis. Relative to a pre-crisis (2003-08) average of 1.7 percent, productivity growth in the region dropped to 0.4 percent during 2013-18—a slowdown broadly in line with the emerging market and developing economy (EMDE) average but from lower starting rates (Figure 2.3.1.1.A). Although the level of productivity in LAC is still higher than in most other EMDE regions, sluggish productivity growth in the post-crisis period has slowed the region's progress toward the level of productivity in advanced economies (Figure 2.3.1.1.B). The productivity slowdown during 2013-18 was broad based, affecting three-fifths of LAC countries (Figure 2.3.1.1.C).

Within LAC, productivity growth has been heterogeneous across the three geographical subregions. South America, which was hard hit by the 2011-16 commodity price slide, political uncertainty, and challenging macroeconomic conditions in the largest economies, had the lowest productivity growth during 2013-18, at an average of just 0.1 percent per year, and the Caribbean had the highest, at 2.5 percent. Productivity growth in the Mexico and Central America subregion was 1.2 percent during 2013-18, higher than in 2003-08, although this occurred in the context of weak long-term productivity growth in Mexico.

Against this backdrop, this Box addresses the following questions:

- How has productivity growth evolved in the region?

- What factors have been associated with productivity growth in the region?

- What policy options are available to boost productivity growth?

This Box defines productivity as labor productivity, represented by real GDP per person employed (at 2010 prices and exchange rates). This definition deviates from some previous work on productivity in the region, which focused on total factor productivity (TFP). Labor productivity data used in this Box are available for nine EMDEs in South America (Argentina, Bolivia, Brazil, Chile, Colombia, Ecuador, Paraguay, Peru, and Uruguay), seven EMDEs in North and Central America (Costa Rica, El Salvador, Guatemala, Honduras, Mexico, Nicaragua, and Panama), and nine EMDEs in the Caribbean (Barbados, Belize, the Dominican Republic, Guyana, Haiti, Jamaica, St. Lucia, St. Vincent and the Grenadines, and Suriname). Data availability further restricts the sample in the two decomposition exercises below.

Evolution of regional productivity

Post-crisis productivity growth slowdown to near zero. Like other EMDE regions, productivity growth in LAC has slowed since the global financial crisis. At 0.4 percent during 2013-18, the post-crisis average returned productivity growth to its long-term average of near zero (0.3 percent; Figure 2.3.1.1.D). This rate is well below average post-crisis productivity growth in EMDEs (2.6 percent). Negative productivity growth occurred 9 of 25 countries, nearly all of which are in South America and the Caribbean, in 2013-18. In most cases, productivity growth was also lower than both the pre-crisis and long-term averages, as major economies in the region struggled with poor business climates, political tensions, regulatory burdens, and plunging commodity prices. Over the course of the past four decades, troughs in productivity growth have broadly coincided with major adverse economic events, including a series of severe debt crises in the 1980s that spawned the region's "lost decade," the global financial crisis, and periodic commodity price slumps. A brief pre-crisis burst in productivity growth to 1.7 percent

Note: This box was prepared by Dana Vorisek, building upon analysis in Chapter 3. Research assistance was provided by Vanessa Arellano Banoni and Shijie Shi.

BOX 2.3.1 Labor productivity in Latin America and the Caribbean: Trends and drivers (*continued*)

FIGURE 2.3.1.1 Evolution of labor productivity growth in LAC

Productivity growth in LAC fell from 1.7 percent in 2003-08 to 0.4 percent in 2013-18. The level of productivity in LAC is still higher than that in other EMDE regions, yet sluggish productivity growth in the post-crisis period has resulted in the region's losing ground in converging toward the level of productivity in advanced economies. Despite weak aggregate productivity growth in the region, some countries, including Bolivia, Costa Rica, the Dominican Republic, and Paraguay, achieved productivity growth in line with the EMDE average during 2013-18.

A. Productivity growth

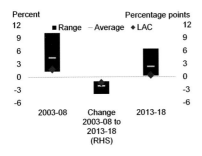

B. Level of productivity and rate of convergence

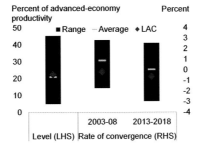

C. Share of economies with 2013-18 productivity growth below previous averages

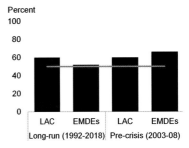

D. Productivity growth

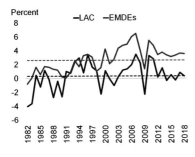

E. Productivity growth, by country

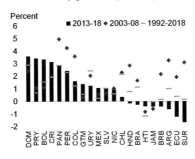

F. Productivity levels, 2018

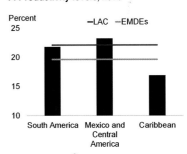

Source: Conference Board; Penn World Tables; World Bank (World Development Indicators).

A.-E. Productivity is defined as labor productivity (real GDP per person employed). Country group aggregates for a given year are calculated using constant 2010 U.S. dollar GDP weights. Data for multiyear spans shows simple averages of the annual data. Sample includes 25 LAC countries and 127 EMDEs.

A. Blue bars show the range of average productivity across the six EMDE regions: East Asia Pacific (EAP), Europe and Central Asia (ECA), Latin America and the Caribbean (LAC), the Middle East and North Africa (MENA), South Asia (SAR), and Sub-Saharan Africa (SSA). Orange dashes show the average of the six regional aggregates.

B. Rate of convergence is calculated as the difference in productivity growth rates over the log difference in productivity levels between LAC and advanced economies (AEs). Blue bars and orange dashes show the range and average of the six EMDE regional aggregates. "Level" of productivity refers to the GDP-weighted average of regional productivity as a share of the average advanced economy during 2013-18.

C. Orange line represents a 50 percent threshold.

D. Dotted lines show 1981-2018 averages.

E. Data for multiyear spans shows simple averages of the annual data. DOM = the Dominican Republic, PRY = Paraguay, BOL = Bolivia, CRI = Costa Rica, PAN = Panama, PER = Peru, COL = Colombia, GTM = Guatemala, URY = Uruguay, MEX = Mexico, SLV = El Salvador, NIC = Nicaragua, CHL = Chile, HND = Honduras, BRA = Brazil, HTI = Haiti, JAM = Jamaica, BRB = Barbados, ARG = Argentina, ECU = Ecuador, and SUR = Suriname.

F. Productivity is measured in 2010 U.S. dollars. Country group aggregates are calculated using 2010 U.S. dollar GDP weights. Sample includes 25 LAC economies (9 in South America, 7 in Mexico and Central America, and 9 in the Caribbean) and 127 EMDEs.

during 2003-08 comprised LAC's second-longest period of positive productivity growth since 1980.

Within-region heterogeneity of labor productivity growth. Notwithstanding weak labor productivity growth at the aggregate level in LAC during 2013-18, there was considerable heterogeneity across countries. Bolivia, Costa Rica, the Dominican Republic, and Paraguay featured the

highest labor productivity growth in the region, measuring well above pre-crisis and long-term averages (Figure 2.3.1.1.E). The improvement in the Dominican Republic reflects greater contribution from capital deepening and higher TFP growth; this arose from increased foreign direct investment (FDI) inflows, which were encouraged by the reforms that opened most sectors to foreign

BOX 2.3.1 Labor productivity in Latin America and the Caribbean: Trends and drivers (*continued*)

investment and by tax incentives for foreign investment (World Bank 2018i). Bolivia and Paraguay benefited from population migration from rural to urban areas, which coincided with a shrinking share of agriculture as a share of employment (IMF 2016b; World Bank 2018j). In Costa Rica, the rise in productivity growth was broad-based across sectors, supported by continued policy reforms and positive spillovers from FDI inflows (OECD 2018a). In four of the six LAC economies with the highest productivity growth during 2013-18 (Bolivia, the Dominican Republic, Panama, and Peru), productivity growth benefited from the steepest declines in the share of informal activity in the region during the decade to 2016 (World Bank 2019f).

High productivity levels relative to EMDEs but slowing convergence with advanced economies. Despite low productivity growth in the region over an extended period, the level of productivity in LAC (22 percent of the advanced-economy average) is above the EMDE average (19 percent of the advanced-economy average; Figure 2.3.1.1.F). High productivity levels in LAC are a legacy of the mid-20th century. Since the 1980s, labor productivity in LAC relative to the level in advanced economies has fallen (Ferreira, de Abreu Pessôa, and Veloso 2013; Fernández-Arias and Rodríguez-Apolinar 2016). The pre-crisis rise in productivity growth halted this divergence only briefly. This is in stark contrast to the narrowing labor productivity gap between the broader group of EMDEs and advanced economies since the 1990s.

Sources of regional productivity growth

Labor productivity can be decomposed into three sources—human capital accumulation, physical capital accumulation, and TFP, or the efficiency with which labor and capital are used during production. The post-crisis productivity growth slowdown predominantly reflected a return to negative TFP growth rates, as had prevailed in LAC during the 1990s (Figure 2.3.1.2.A; Busso, Madrigal, Pagés 2013). However, the post-crisis (2013-18) average disguises a steep slowdown in investment growth during 2016-18, as Brazil struggled to exit a deep recession, the effects of the commodity price slump rippled through the region's many commodity-reliant economies, and numerous economies experienced bouts of policy uncertainty.

- *South America.* The post-crisis labor productivity slowdown was most pronounced in South America. which was deeply impacted by the commodity price slump and country-specific constraints in large

economies (Figure 2.3.1.2.B). TFP growth in South America was continually negative during 2013-18, in part reflecting growing directed credit in Brazil (Dutz 2018; Calice, Ribiero, and Byskov 2018). It also reflected intensifying economic distortions (such as trade restrictions and price controls) in Argentina during the early part of the period, which allowed unproductive firms to survive.

- *Mexico and Central America.* In Mexico and Central America, the early impacts of the global financial crisis in 2007 and 2008 weighed on TFP in Mexico during 2003-08. Although post-crisis TFP growth was subdued, and capital deepening weakened during this period in the context of the repeated bouts of policy uncertainty, the removal of the crisis effects in Mexico allowed higher productivity growth in the subregion during 2013-18.

- *The Caribbean.* In the Caribbean, TFP growth accelerated during the post-crisis period, largely reflecting capital deepening in the largest economy in the subregion, the Dominican Republic.

Post-crisis productivity growth slowdown across sectors. As in the average EMDE, manufacturing made the largest sectoral contribution to productivity growth in LAC during the 1990s and the pre-crisis period. Relative to the pre-crisis period, the post-crisis period in LAC was marked by a broad-based slowdown in productivity growth across sectors, particularly in manufacturing, trade, and finance.

Stalling within-sector labor productivity growth. For countries with available sectoral data, the within-sector contribution to productivity growth has historically been greater than the between-sector contribution from labor reallocation from low-productivity to higher-productivity sectors (Figure 2.3.1.3.A). This is consistent with other studies of the region (Brown et al. 2016; Diao, McMillan, and Rodrik 2017). During the 1990s, a substantial part of labor productivity growth was due to within-sector growth as LAC countries liberalized trade policy in the second half of the 1980s and the early 1990s (Rodrik 2016a). The 1990s and early 2000s were a period of significant change in LAC's manufacturing industry. Faced with increasing foreign competition as the result of globalization, domestic manufacturing firms implemented more efficient processes that required less labor, and uncompetitive firms ceased operating. As workers were displaced from manufacturing, they shifted toward lower-productivity services and informal activities (Pagés-Serra 2010; McMillan, Rodrik, and Verduzco-Gallo 2014). In Argentina and Brazil, two

BOX 2.3.1 Labor productivity in Latin America and the Caribbean: Trends and drivers (*continued*)

of the largest economies in the region, labor shifted in the 1990s from manufacturing into less-productive non-tradable sectors, such as personal services and wholesale and retail trade, limiting between-sector productivity growth. Of the six LAC countries with available sectoral data, only Costa Rica and Mexico have consistently experienced positive between-sector productivity growth, and even in those cases the within-sector contribution has been smaller than the between-sector contribution.

As the manufacturing sector in LAC transformed during the 1990s and early 2000s, the agricultural sector became more productive relative to other sectors, with a shrinking share of agricultural employment accounting for a stable share of output between 1995 and 2008 (Figures 2.3.1.3.B and 2.3.1.3.C). The government sector, however, became less productive, accounting for a growing share of employment and the same share of output.

Since 2013, between-sector productivity gains have stalled in several large economies (Argentina, Brazil, Colombia). Within-sector productivity growth has collapsed to near zero as multiple structural constraints (e.g., inefficient provision of credit in Brazil and trade restrictions and price controls in Argentina) were compounded by an inability to adjust to adverse events, including unfavorable policy choices, a commodity price collapse, and financial stress episodes.

Sectoral productivity levels in LAC relative to EMDEs. In most sectors, and particularly in mining, productivity levels in LAC are higher than the EMDE average. However, LAC lags notably in trade and finance. Removing productivity barriers in these sectors would benefit aggregate regional productivity.

Key drivers of productivity. LAC has long lagged other EMDE regions in several key drivers of productivity—investment, innovation, and trade—and performs only about average in other drivers (Figure 2.3.1.4.A). Over time, the drivers of productivity in LAC have improved but the improvement has not kept pace with that in EMDEs (Figure 2.3.1.4.B). Cyclical factors, such as weak investment in large economies in the region and gyrations in global commodity price trends, are also linked to weak productivity growth in LAC. Investment growth has weakened substantially in the post-crisis period (Figure 2.3.1.4.C).

Limited innovation and technology adoption. Innovation, achieved through dedicating resources to research and development (R&D) or introducing new processes or

FIGURE 2.3.1.2 Sources of productivity growth in LAC

Sluggish productivity growth in LAC during the post-crisis period predominantly reflected a negative contribution from total factor productivity (TFP). The TFP contraction was especially pronounced in South America. In recent years, capital deepening has made a slowing contribution to productivity growth.

A. Contributions to productivity growth

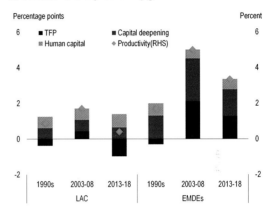

B. Contributions to productivity growth, by subregion

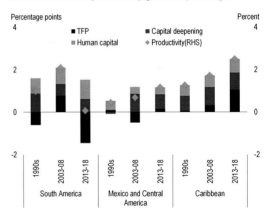

Source: Barro and Lee (2015); International Monetary Fund; Penn World Tables; United Nations (*Human Development Reports*), Wittgenstein Centre for Demography and Global Human Capital; World Bank.
A.-B. Country groups aggregated using constant 2010 U.S. dollar GDP weights.
A. Samples include 25 LAC economies and 92 EMDEs.
B. Samples include 9 economies in South America, 7 economies in Mexico and Central America, and 9 economies in the Caribbean.

BOX 2.3.1 **Labor productivity in Latin America and the Caribbean: Trends and drivers (*continued*)**

FIGURE 2.3.1.3 **Sectoral productivity in LAC**

Within-sector productivity growth, the main driver of productivity growth in LAC during the pre-crisis period, was much lower during the post-crisis period in several large economies, while between-sector productivity growth slowed in all economies with available sectoral data.

A. Within-sector and between-sector contributions to productivity growth

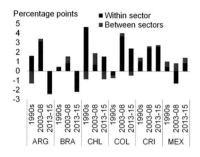

B. Composition of employment, by sector

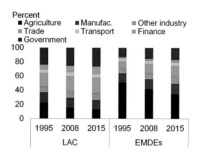

C. Composition of GDP, by sector

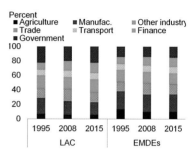

Source: Groningen Growth Development Center database, Haver Analytics, ILOSTAT, OECD STAN, United Nations, World KLEMS, World Bank.
A. The within-sector productivity contribution shows the initial real value added-weighted productivity growth; the between-sector contribution measures the productivity growth from a cross-sectoral shift of employment. ARG = Argentina, BRA = Brazil, CHL = Chile, COL = Colombia, CRI = Costa Rica, and MEX = Mexico.
B.C. "Other industry" includes construction, mining, and utilities; "finance" includes business services; "government" includes personal services. Samples include 6 LAC economies (Argentina, Brazil, Chile, Colombia, Costa Rica, and Mexico) and 46 EMDEs.

products, has been a key driver of labor and firm productivity in LAC (Crespi and Zuniga 2011; Grazzi and Jung 2016). Likewise, adoption of new technologies can reduce information costs and facilitate market access, thereby increasing productivity and expanding output in the region (Dutz, Almeida, and Packard 2018). LAC is missing key opportunities to raise productivity through these channels. R&D expenditure as a share of GDP is low in LAC relative to that in comparator EMDEs, as is the likelihood of firms in LAC introducing product innovations (Lederman et al. 2014; Figure 2.3.1.4.D).

Weak trade linkages. In three large economies in the region (Argentina, Chile, Mexico), deeper participation in global value chains is associated with positive effects on firm productivity (Montalbano, Nenci, and Pietrobelli 2018). Yet nearly all LAC economies trade less (as a share of their GDP) than EMDEs overall, and global value chain participation is lower than in the East Asia and Pacific region and in Europe and Central Asia (Figure 2.3.1.4.E). Even the LAC countries most integrated in global value chains (Chile, Costa Rica, and Mexico) are not among the most integrated EMDEs (OECD 2018b). The opportunity for regional productivity gains through trade is further hindered by the structure of intra- and extraregional trade relationships. Although LAC countries are party to numerous trade agreements, there is little

harmonization of rules of origin and non-tariff measures across agreements, and there is no region-wide trade agreement. These characteristics result in fragmentation of trading priorities and, together with weak diversification of traded goods in many countries, limit the development of intraregional global value chains. Rules of origin imposed under preferential trade agreements in the region are estimated to negate more than 15 percent of the positive trade effect of the agreements, while the costs of non-tariff measures imposed by LAC countries are estimated to equate to a 15 percent tariff for intermediate goods (Cadestin, Gourdon, and Kowalski 2016).

Poor-quality education and labor market constraints. At a median of 9.2 years in 2018, the duration of schooling in LAC compares favorably with 7.7 years in the average EMDE. In addition, the gap between the median years of schooling in LAC and advanced economies narrowed during the past decade, from 3.5 years in 2008 to 2.9 years in 2018. However, learning outcomes in LAC fall short of their potential, as indicated by international standardized test results and high dropout rates at the tertiary level (World Bank 2017b). Moreover, in most LAC countries, education outcomes are highly correlated with socioeconomic conditions, a scenario reinforced by persistently elevated income inequality (World Bank 2018k). Ultimately, skills deficiencies and mismatches and

BOX 2.3.1 Labor productivity in Latin America and the Caribbean: Trends and drivers (*continued*)

FIGURE 2.3.1.4 Drivers of labor productivity growth in LAC

Multiple structural constraints contribute to low productivity growth in LAC. The region performs particularly poorly relative to other EMDE regions in measures of investment, innovation, and trade. In other drivers, LAC is a mediocre performer relative to other regions. The drivers of productivity growth have become more supportive over time but at a slower pace than the EMDE average.

A. Drivers of productivity growth, 2017

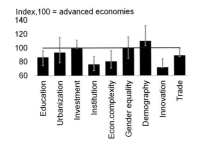

B. Index of productivity drivers

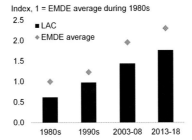

C. Investment growth

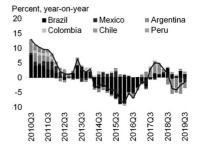

D. R&D spending

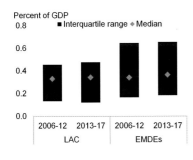

E. Trade

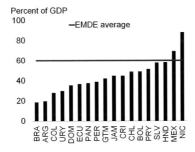

F. Firms indicating inadequately educated workers as their biggest obstacle

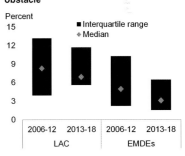

Source: Freedom House; Haver Analytics; International Country Risk Guide; Organisation for Economic Co-operation and Development; Observatory of Economic Complexity; Penn World Tables; United Nations Educational, Scientific, and Cultural Organization (Institute for Statistics); United Nations Population Prospects; World Integrated Trade Solution; World Bank (Doing Business, Enterprise Surveys, and Global Financial Development Database).
A. Unweighted average levels of drivers, normalized as average of AEs (index =100) and standard deviation of EMDEs as 10. Blue bars represent average of LAC economies in 2017. Orange whiskers represent range of averages for the six EMDE regions in 2017. Variables are defined as: Education=years of education, Urbanization=share of population living in urban areas, Investment=share of investment to GDP, Institutions=government effectiveness, Economic complexity=Economic Complexity Index of Hidalgo and Hausmann (2009), Gender equality=share of years of schooling for females to males, Demography=share of population under age 14, Innovation=log patents per capita, and Trade=(exports+imports)/GDP. Samples include 17-31 LAC economies, depending on the driver, and 63-150 EMDEs.
B. For each country, index is a weighted average—weighted by the normalized coefficients shown in Annex 3.3—of the normalized value of each driver of productivity. Drivers include the ICRG rule of law index, patents per capita, non-tropical share of land area, investment in percent of GDP, ratio of female average years of education to male average years, and share of population in urban area, Economic Complexity Index, years of schooling, working-age share of population, and inflation. Regional and EMDE indexes are GDP-weighted averages for single years and simple averages for time periods. Samples includes 17 LAC economies and 77 EMDEs.
C. Bars show investment-weighted averages. Last observation is 2019Q3. Data for Mexico for Q3 is estimated.
D. Sample includes 16 economies for LAC and 94 for EMDEs.
E. Bars show 2015-17 average of exports plus imports as a share of GDP. BRA = Brazil, ARG = Argentina, COL = Colombia, URY = Uruguay, DOM = the Dominican Republic, ECU = Ecuador, PAN = Panama, PER = Peru, GTM = Guatemala, JAM = Jamaica, CRI = Costa Rica, CHL = Chile, BOL = Bolivia, PRY = Paraguay, SLV = El Salvador, HND = Honduras, MEX = Mexico, NIC = Nicaragua. Sample includes 96 EMDEs.
F. Sample includes 30 LAC economies and 113 EMDEs.

low-quality education have negative implications for labor productivity and the functioning of labor markets. The incidence of youth who are neither in school nor working is high (de Hoyos, Rogers, and Székely 2016). An estimated half of firms are unable to find local workers with the skills they need, and consequently turn to foreign labor (OECD 2018b). Firm-level survey data for 2013-18

indicate that 7 percent of firms in LAC perceive an inadequately educated workforce as their biggest obstacle, more than double the share in all EMDEs (Figure 2.3.1.4.F). The poor functioning of labor markets due to skills deficiencies are compounded by longstanding regulatory rigidities that prevent efficient allocation and mobility of workers (Kaplan 2009).

BOX 2.3.1 Labor productivity in Latin America and the Caribbean: Trends and drivers (*continued*)

High informality. The informal sector averages slightly more than one-third of GDP, higher than in all other EMDE regions except Sub-Saharan Africa (World Bank 2019f). In LAC, high informality has been associated with lower aggregate and firm-level productivity (Loayza, Servén, and Sugawara 2010; de Paula and Sheinkman 2011; Chong, Galdo, and Saavedra 2008). In Paraguay, informal firms are not only less productive than formal firms, but have negative spillovers on formal firms' productivity (Vargas 2015).

Policy options

A range of options, targeted to country experiences, can be pursued to boost productivity in LAC and put the region on a path toward closing the productivity gap with advanced economies. Productivity in the region stands to benefit most from policy reforms to boost TFP, rather than to improve factors of production.

Improving factors of production

Increase the volume and efficiency of infrastructure investment. Relative to the pre-crisis period, capital deepening has been the main source of productivity growth in large parts of the region during the post-crisis period. However, it has slowed sharply in the past three years, and large infrastructure gaps remain. Access to water and electricity in LAC is high relative to all EMDEs; however, the region underperforms in transportation and sanitation (Fay et al. 2017). To address this, transportation development is underway in several countries. Colombia, for instance, is implementing 4G, a major public road infrastructure program. In addition, across the region, there is significant capacity to reduce infrastructure gaps by improving infrastructure spending efficiency—in particular, through improvements at the appraisal and evaluation stages of public investment projects and in public procurement systems.

Boosting firm productivity

Pursue well-targeted competition and innovation policies. Reducing barriers to entry for firms and the rigidity of labor regulations, on which LAC performs poorly compared to other EMDE regions and which encourages informal operation, is critical for promoting entrepreneurship and productivity. In Peru, for example, the elimination of subnational barriers to entry is found to have boosted firm productivity (Schiffbauer and Sampi 2019). Boosting low R&D spending and low technology-related innovations can also improve financial inclusion

through development of secure digital payment systems and fintech regulatory frameworks (World Bank 2017c). Improving the speed of uptake of new technologies in LAC, where firms adopt new technologies with a significant lag relative to the United States, would also boost productivity (Eden and Nguyen 2016).

Deepen trade linkages and reduce trade barriers. Trade relationships can boost productivity by facilitating knowledge exchange and innovation for the participating firms (Bown et al. 2017). Significant productivity gains could be made by reducing barriers to trade in LAC. The landmark European Union-Mercosur trade agreement, finalized by negotiators in June 2019 but not yet ratified, holds significant promise for decreasing trade barriers and deepening trade flows between Latin America and Europe. In addition, there have been some recent efforts to reduce trade barriers within the region; for instance, the Pacific Alliance eliminated tariffs among its members (Chile, Colombia, Mexico, and Peru) in May 2016.

Boost quality of education and implement labor market reforms. With the working-age share of the population in the region now at a peak and on track to begin the long-term downward trajectory that East Asia and Pacific and Europe and Central Asia have already begun, the contribution of additional labor to productivity growth in LAC will fall in the years ahead. Advancing human capital through education and skills development will become increasingly important. For many countries in the region, including Brazil, adapting labor markets to shifting economic opportunities in the strongly integrated global economy will require revision of dated labor market regulation (Dutz 2018). For firms, additional use of on-the-job training is an important element of boosting the productivity of their workers, especially in the context of rapidly changing technologies. Implementing programs that engage youth who are neither working nor studying is a critical policy concern in the region (Almeida and Packard 2018). Skills training programs such as Jovenes en Acción in Colombia and ProJoven in Peru have had positive impacts on employment and productivity among the target populations and could be replicated elsewhere (Attanasio et al. 2015; Diaz and Rosas 2016). Apprenticeship programs, which have been successful in several advanced economies, could also be explored. Reducing labor market rigidities (such as restrictions on use of term contracts, restrictions on working hours, use of minimum wages above market equilibrium, and imposition of high costs and penalties for redundancy) can boost productivity.

BOX 2.3.1 Labor productivity in Latin America and the Caribbean: Trends and drivers (*continued*)

Encouraging sectoral reallocation

Given that within-sector productivity gains in several large economies in LAC have stalled since the global financial crisis, countries in the region should rekindle efforts to implement policies that reallocate capital and labor towards more productive firms within the sectors. Policies could aim to strengthen competition, including through trade, and reform labor markets to facilitate the movement and productivity of labor. At the same time, the longstanding weakness in the region's between-sector productivity growth in the region calls for policies that reduce misallocation of capital and labor toward sectors with low productivity. In particular, with limited opportunity for further industrialization, LAC countries should target lack of competition in services industries, including transport, finance, trade, and information and communications technology, and ensure that workers have sufficiently strong skills to thrive in occupations being transformed by technology (Araujo, Vostroknutova, and Wacker 2017; World Bank forthcoming).

Creating a business-friendly environment

Implement supportive governance and business climate reforms. Institutional quality is a key driver of productivity over the long term. For instance, fair contract enforcement, straightforward and transparent legal processes, and contained political risk have all been shown to support productivity gains (Acemoglu et al. 2019; Rodrik 1999; Rodrik, Subramanian, and Trebbi 2004). Relative to other regions, however, LAC is a mediocre performer on measures of governance (Figure 2.3.1.4.A). Moreover, the region's performance has deteriorated during the post-crisis period in measures of government effectiveness, control of corruption, and regulatory quality (Kaufmann, Kraay, and Mastruzzi 2010). Especially when the burden of regulation is high, as it tends to be in LAC, corruption is detrimental for productivity (Amin and Ulku 2019). On measures of doing business, no country in LAC is among the top 50 performers in the world (World Bank 2020). Business environment reforms can also help reduce the size of the informal sector, where productivity is lower than in the formal sector. The process of institutional reforms could be spearheaded through productivity commissions such as those created in Chile, Colombia, and Mexico. Colombia, for example, is implementing a series of structural reforms as part of its Productive Development Policy 2016-2025.

MIDDLE EAST and NORTH AFRICA

Regional growth in the Middle East and North Africa decelerated to an estimated 0.1 percent in 2019. Geopolitical and policy constraints on oil sector production slowed growth in oil-exporting economies, despite support from public spending. Growth in oil importers remained stable, as reform progress and resilient tourism activity were offset by structural and external headwinds. Regional growth is projected to pick up to 2.4 percent in 2020 and to about 2.8 percent in 2021-22, as infrastructure investment and business climate reforms proceed. Risks are tilted firmly to the downside—geopolitical tensions, escalation of armed conflicts, slower-than-expected pace of reforms, or weaker-than-expected growth in key trading partners could heavily constrain activity. Sustained proliferation of these risks could also hamper long-term productivity prospects.

Recent developments

Growth in the Middle East and North Africa (MENA) slowed to an estimated 0.1 percent in 2019, down from 0.8 percent the previous year (Table 2.4.1; Figure 2.4.1.A).[1] The slowdown largely reflected the sharp growth contraction in the Islamic Republic of Iran, following the tightening of U.S. sanctions, geopolitical tensions in the Strait of Hormuz, and diplomatic setbacks. Weakened global growth weighed on demand for oil and other exports, further hindering activity in the region generally (Figure 2.4.1.B).

Public spending has been robust in some oil exporters, including those in the Gulf Cooperation Council (GCC). Non-oil activity has also shown supportive signs (Figure 2.4.1.C). However, these developments were insufficient to offset weak activity in the oil sector. In addition

to less supportive global demand, commitments to the oil production-cut agreement of the Organization of the Petroleum Exporting Countries and other signatory countries (OPEC+) and regional geopolitical events further constrained the oil sector.

Among oil importers, growth has been more stable. In Egypt, the subregion's largest economy, net exports as well as investment, partly supported by more accommodative monetary stance, continued to support growth. The maturity of its external debt has also shifted towards long-term instruments (Figure 2.4.1.D). Favorable tourism activity continues to support growth in oil importers, such as Morocco and Tunisia. However, agricultural production has become less favorable and weighed on activity in Morocco. Export growth potential in oil importers was weighed by weakened global demand, including from the Euro Area.

Inflation in the region generally eased. In GCC economies in 2019, it registered less than 1 percent on average (Figure 2.4.1.E). Inflation in Egypt subsided substantially in the second half of the year, allowing the central bank to cut interest rates three times since August. In smaller oil importers (e.g., Jordan), inflation has also moderated generally. In Iran, however, inflation rose sharply to more than 50 percent in mid-2019, partly reflecting the earlier depreciation of the rial

---

Note: This section was prepared by Lei Sandy Ye. Research assistance was provided by Vanessa Arellano Banoni.

[1] The World Bank's Middle East and North Africa aggregate includes 16 economies and is grouped into three subregions. Bahrain, Kuwait, Oman, Qatar, Saudi Arabia, and the United Arab Emirates comprise the Gulf Cooperation Council (GCC); all are oil exporters. Other oil exporters in the region are Algeria, the Islamic Republic of Iran, and Iraq. Oil importers in the region are Djibouti, the Arab Republic of Egypt, Jordan, Lebanon, Morocco, Tunisia, and West Bank and Gaza. Syrian Arab Republic, the Republic of Yemen, and Libya are excluded from regional growth aggregates due to data limitations.

FIGURE 2.4.1 MENA: Recent developments

Growth in the MENA region fell in 2019, for the third consecutive year, to an estimated 0.1 percent. In the large oil-exporting economies, oil production cuts, weak global economic momentum, and U.S. sanctions on Iran weighed on activity, despite signs of non-oil activity improvement. Activity among oil importers was supported by improved conditions in Egypt. Inflation rose sharply in Iran, while remaining generally low elsewhere. Easier financing conditions in advanced economies have supported international capital raising.

A. Growth

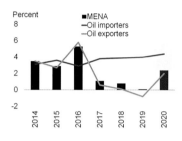

B. Global oil demand growth and prices

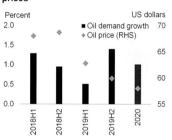

C. Composite PMI

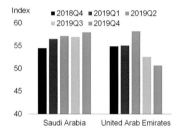

D. Egypt: Inflation, policy rate, and external debt maturity

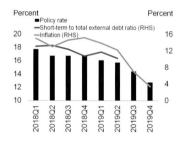

E. Inflation

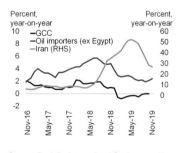

F. International debt securities outstanding

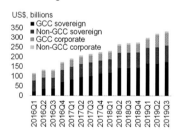

Source: Bank for International Settlements; Haver Analytics; International Energy Agency; International Monetary Fund; World Bank.
A. Weighted average growth rates of real GDP. Gray shaded area denotes forecasts.
B. Left panel denotes year-on-year growth of period average global oil demand in millions of barrels a day. Right panel denotes average oil price during the periods shown. Oil price denotes average of Brent, Dubai, and WTI. 2019H2 denotes latest data as of Dec 19. 2020 denote World Bank forecast for oil price and IEA forecast for global oil demand. 2019 global oil demand data are estimates.
C. Above 50 denotes expansion; below 50 contraction. 2019Q4 denotes average of October and November.
D. Averages over the period denoted. Policy rate refers to the overnight lending rate. Inflation refers to CPI inflation. 2019Q4 data for inflation and policy rate denote average of October and November.
E. CPI inflation (year-on-year monthly rate). Last observation is November 2019 for Iran and oil importers and October for the GCC. GCC include 6 economies. Oil importers include 4 economies.
F. Includes 5 GCC and 6 non-GCC economies. Sum of international debt securities outstanding. "Corporates" include non-financial and financial corporations.

in the parallel market, although inflation has subsided in late 2019 to below 30 percent.

Financial sector conditions in MENA have been supportive to activity. Banking systems in the GCC economies remain broadly resilient, with capital adequacy ratios generally sound and non-performing loan ratios contained. Benign global financing conditions associated with more accommodative advanced economies' monetary policy have supported equity flows in the region and encouraged investor risk appetite in the large economies (e.g., GCC and Egypt). In the GCC, new bonds were issued in international capital markets in both the corporate and sovereign sectors, and bank credit growth has shown improvement (Figure 2.4.1.F). However, access to finance elsewhere remains a major obstacle to investment, especially for small and medium-sized enterprises (SMEs; Ghassibe, Appendino, and Mahmoudi 2019).

Outlook

Growth in the region is projected to accelerate in 2020 to 2.4 percent, supported by higher investment, promoted by both infrastructure initiatives and stronger business climates. The forecasted stabilization in Iran assumes that the impact of sanctions tapers somewhat (Table 2.4.2). Regional growth is expected to remain stable over 2021-22, at about 2.8 percent. Continued reform efforts and strengthening domestic demand in key economies should provide support to activity. Despite the projected growth acceleration, long-standing challenges, such as high unemployment rates among youth and women and high poverty rates in some countries, will remain. In particular, for economies affected by fragility, conflict, and violence, armed conflicts imposed further setbacks to poverty via lower provision of public services and social safety nets. More sustained growth will be needed to resolve these challenges.

Among oil exporters, growth is expected to pick up to 2 percent in 2020. Infrastructure investment, along with an improved regulatory environment backed by business climate reforms, are expected to support activity in the GCC

(World Bank 2019q, Figure 2.4.2.A). Iran's economy is expected to stagnate at a lower base, as the initial intensive impact of sanctions on oil production and exports is assumed to taper somewhat. Algeria's growth is expected to pick up modestly, as policy uncertainty abates somewhat and investment improves. Investment associated with reconstruction and fiscal easing is expected to support Iraq's growth. Facilities and capacity expansion in oil and gas sectors is also expected to support activity in many oil exporters. Over the medium term, growth in GCC economies is expected to remain steady, underpinned by planned diversification programs, longer-term infrastructure programs, and measures to ease foreign investment restrictions.

Growth in oil importers is expected to rise slightly in 2020, to 4.4 percent, led by improvements in larger economies. Growth in oil importers is contingent upon the materialization of reform plans and no escalation of political risks. Tourism, aided by government promotion initiatives and improved security, is expected to continue supporting activity in Egypt, Morocco, and Tunisia. However, for smaller oil importers, banking sector fragility and high public debt are significant constraints on growth (Figure 2.4.2.B). Moreover, the sustainability of debt or external position in these economies often depends on the materialization of expected multilateral and bilateral financing flows or on the strength of sovereign credit; and are vulnerable to sudden shifts in market confidence. Modest growth in smaller oil importers weighs further on the high budgetary financing pressures of these economies and the sustainability of their high debt.

Medium-term growth prospects for the MENA region are contingent on an attenuation of armed conflicts, and on limiting their regional spillovers. Structural reforms, such as those to provide stronger fiscal management and to enhance the investment climate, are underway in many GCC and non-GCC economies. New financial reforms, such as investment law and stronger minority investor protection in Egypt; the relaxation of foreign investment restrictions across 13 sectors and in SME licensing in the United Arab Emirates; and a new secured transactions law in

FIGURE 2.4.2 MENA: Outlook and risks

Stronger momentum in the non-oil sector in the GCC, aided by business climate reforms, is expected to support activity. Oil importers' growth prospects are also supported by policy reforms but are challenged by high debt levels and structural issues. Geopolitical risks are acute and have prolonged the refugee crisis in fragile areas. Political instability hampers reform progress and poses a major constraint to productivity. Lower-than-expected growth in the Euro Area would constrain external demand for the region, especially oil importers.

A. Improvement in business climate: 2018-19

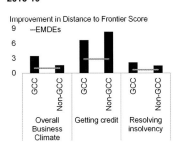

B. Public debt in MENA

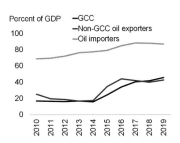

C. Labor market competitiveness

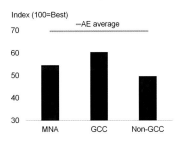

D. Syrian refugees' intention to return

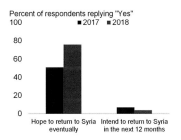

E. Political instability as biggest obstacle to firm operations

F. Euro Area growth forecasts

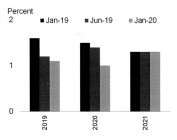

Source: Bank for International Settlements,; Haver Analytics; International Monetary Fund; United Nations; World Bank; World Economic Forum.

A. Includes 6 GCC and 9 non-GCC economies. Unweighted average of each economy's change in Distance to Frontier Score in the denoted measures between 2018-19 (2020 DoingBusiness edition).

B. Unweighted averages. 2019 data are estimates.

C. Index of labor market competitiveness based on the Global Competitiveness Index. Index constructed based on data on labor market entry/exit, wage flexibility and skills match. Unweighted averages. AE denotes advanced economies. Based on 2019 data edition.

D. Based on United Nation's Annual Surveys on Syrians' Refugees' Perceptions and Intentions to Return to Syria. Survey respondents include Syrian refugees in Egypt, Iraq, Lebanon, and Jordan. X-axis denotes two questions to survey respondents on whether they "hope to return to Syria one day" and whether they "intend to return to Syria in the next 12 months ("Yes", "No", "Do not know"). 2018 data denote survey conducted between Nov 2018 and Feb 2019.

E. Percent of firms citing political instability as biggest obstacle to business operations, based on the World Bank's Enterprise Surveys data. Unweighted averages across economies. Data for latest available year across 9 MENA economies.

F. Legend denotes month-year for which World Bank forecast is published. Columns denote the growth forecast year.

Jordan have been adopted. They are expected to help relieve financial constraints in the corporate sector, support investor confidence, and raise foreign direct investment (FDI). Structural reforms of this nature could help raise the historically weak long-term productivity performance in these countries (Arezki et al. 2019a,b; Youssef et al. 2019; Box 2.4.1). Nonetheless, the scope for improvements in many areas remains large – for instance, limited churn of firms, barriers to competition, and labor market inefficiencies hinder MENA firms' ability to generate private sector jobs (Figure 2.4.2C; Arezki et al. 2019a).

Risks

Risks are firmly tilted to the downside. These include the long-standing risks from geopolitical conflicts, political uncertainty, and volatility in oil prices as well as more recent risks associated with reescalation of global trade tensions.

Geopolitical risks have increased substantially. Syria and surrounding countries remain filled with high uncertainties and diverse intra– and interregional developments. Armed conflicts in Syria have held back refugees' short-term intention to return, despite greater desire to ultimately resettle in their home country (Figure 2.4.2.D). In Yemen, the near-term prospects remain highly uncertain due to the active conflict, now in its fifth year. Yemen's socioeconomic outlook depends critically on a cessation of hostilities and a renewed political vision for the country. An escalation of U.S.-Iran tensions would pose difficulties for other regional economies as well as Iran itself.

Political uncertainty also clouds MENA's growth prospects, particularly in non-GCC economies. While political impasse and some previously delayed reforms have been partly resolved, policy uncertainty in Algeria remains significant. Reconstruction in Iraq had already experienced some delays, and a lack of political consensus on economic reforms continues to challenge the

government (Mansour, Maseeh, and Celiku 2019). Such uncertainties and delays could hinder productivity and private sector development – survey evidence shows that political instability is by far a bigger obstacle to firm operations in MENA than any other EMDE regions (Figure 2.4.2.E; World Bank 2016f).

Geopolitical factors related to U.S.-Iran tensions, as well as the recent attack on Saudi Aramco's oil facilities, have raised volatility in oil prices. This volatility may rise further. A sharp rise in oil price volatility may complicate or stall fiscal adjustments in both oil exporters and importers. It could also set back investment programs in oil exporters and cause difficulties for subsidy reforms in oil importers by increasing the uncertainty associated with future revenue and income streams.

Renewed escalation of global trade tensions may further weaken growth prospects in advanced economies and several large EMDEs. This may translate into further setback to growth in the Euro Area, to which the MENA region and especially the Maghreb region have significant trade exposure (Figure 2.4.2.F). Oil importers are subject to risks from the GCC, a significant source of remittances and FDI flows. Global trade tensions may also affect the MENA region through the oil price channel (IEA 2019). Sharp oil price declines via weaker global oil demand would significantly affect activity in MENA oil exporters.

Volatility in external financing conditions could destabilize MENA's financial markets. For example, higher uncertainty about the path of advanced economy's monetary easing stance could present a downside risk to capital flows to GCC economies, which have low debt levels relative to oil importers but rising exposure to international financial markets. Moreover, it could raise their difficulties in financing contingent liabilities in public spending projects through large bond issuances. For oil importers, volatility in global interest rates could raise the debt service costs of their high levels of public debt.

TABLE 2.4.1 Middle East and North Africa forecast summary

(Real GDP growth at market prices in percent, unless indicated otherwise)

Percentage point differences
from June 2019 projections

	2017	2018	2019e	2020f	2021f	2022f	2019e	2020f	2021f
EMDE MENA, GDP[1]	1.1	0.8	0.1	2.4	2.7	2.8	-1.2	-0.8	0.0
(Average including countries with full national accounts and balance of payments data only)[2]									
EMDE MENA, GDP[2]	1.4	0.9	-0.4	2.3	2.7	2.8	-1.5	-0.6	0.0
GDP per capita (U.S. dollars)	-0.4	-0.8	-2.0	0.7	1.2	1.4	-1.6	-0.8	-0.2
PPP GDP	1.7	0.9	-0.4	2.4	2.9	2.9	-1.5	-0.6	0.1
Private consumption	2.6	0.7	1.4	1.9	2.2	2.2	0.1	0.0	0.1
Public consumption	4.9	2.9	0.4	2.1	2.3	2.4	-1.0	0.7	1.3
Fixed investment	1.7	0.2	2.4	5.2	5.7	6.1	-2.0	-0.5	-0.7
Exports, GNFS[3]	4.5	2.4	-1.7	3.0	3.6	3.7	-2.1	-0.9	0.0
Imports, GNFS[3]	7.7	-2.0	1.1	3.4	4.0	4.0	-0.8	0.1	0.2
Net exports, contribution to growth	-0.5	2.0	-1.3	0.3	0.4	0.4	-0.8	-0.5	0.0
Memo items: GDP									
Oil exporters[4]	0.6	0.1	-0.8	2.0	2.3	2.3	-1.5	-0.9	0.1
GCC countries[5]	-0.3	2.0	0.8	2.2	2.6	2.7	-1.3	-1.0	-0.1
Saudi Arabia	-0.7	2.4	0.4	1.9	2.2	2.4	-1.3	-1.2	-0.1
Iran	3.8	-4.9	-8.7	0.0	1.0	1.0	-4.2	-0.9	0.0
Oil importers[6]	3.8	3.9	4.0	4.4	4.6	4.6	-0.1	-0.1	-0.1
Egypt	4.8	5.5	5.7	5.9	6.0	6.0	0.0	0.0	0.0
Fiscal year basis[7]	4.2	5.3	5.6	5.8	6.0	6.0	0.1	0.0	0.0

Source: World Bank.

Note: e = estimate; f = forecast. EMDE = emerging market and developing economies. World Bank forecasts are frequently updated based on new information and changing (global) circumstances. Consequently, projections presented here may differ from those contained in other Bank documents, even if basic assessments of countries' prospects do not differ at any given moment in time.

1. GDP and expenditure components are measured in 2010 prices and market exchange rates. Excludes Libya, Syria, and Yemen due to data limitations.
2. Aggregate includes all countries in notes 4 and 6 except Djibouti, Iraq, Qatar, and West Bank and Gaza, for which data limitations prevent the forecasting of GDP components.
3. Exports and imports of goods and non-factor services (GNFS).
4. Oil exporters include Algeria, Bahrain, Iran, Iraq, Kuwait, Oman, Qatar, Saudi Arabia, and the United Arab Emirates.
5. The Gulf Cooperation Council (GCC) includes Bahrain, Kuwait, Oman, Qatar, Saudi Arabia, and the United Arab Emirates.
6. Oil importers include Djibouti, Egypt, Jordan, Lebanon, Morocco, Tunisia, and West Bank and Gaza.
7. The fiscal year runs from July 1 to June 30 in Egypt; the column labeled 2018 reflects the fiscal year ended June 30, 2018.
To download the data in this table, please visit www.worldbank.org/gep.

TABLE 2.4.2 Middle East and North Africa economy forecasts[1]

(Real GDP growth at market prices in percent, unless indicated otherwise)

Percentage point differences from June 2019 projections

	2017	2018	2019e	2020f	2021f	2022f	2019e	2020f	2021f
Algeria	1.3	1.4	1.3	1.9	2.2	2.2	-0.6	0.2	0.8
Bahrain	3.8	2.2	2.0	2.1	2.4	2.4	0.0	-0.1	-0.4
Djibouti	5.1	5.5	7.2	7.5	8.0	8.4	0.2	0.0	0.0
Egypt	4.8	5.5	5.7	5.9	6.0	6.0	0.0	0.0	0.0
Fiscal year basis[2]	4.2	5.3	5.6	5.8	6.0	6.0	0.1	0.0	0.0
Iran	3.8	-4.9	-8.7	0.0	1.0	1.0	-4.2	-0.9	0.0
Iraq	-2.5	-0.6	4.8	5.1	2.7	2.5	2.0	-3.0	0.4
Jordan	2.1	1.9	2.0	2.2	2.4	2.5	-0.2	-0.2	-0.2
Kuwait	-3.5	1.2	0.4	2.2	2.0	2.0	-1.2	-0.8	-0.9
Lebanon	0.6	0.2	-0.2	0.3	0.4	0.5	-1.1	-1.0	-1.1
Morocco	4.2	3.0	2.7	3.5	3.6	3.8	-0.2	0.0	0.0
Oman	0.3	1.8	0.0	3.7	4.3	4.3	-1.2	-2.3	1.5
Qatar	1.6	1.5	0.5	1.5	3.2	3.2	-2.5	-1.7	-0.2
Saudi Arabia	-0.7	2.4	0.4	1.9	2.2	2.4	-1.3	-1.2	-0.1
Tunisia	1.8	2.5	1.6	2.2	2.6	2.6	-1.1	-1.0	-0.9
United Arab Emirates	0.5	1.7	1.8	2.6	3.0	3.0	-0.8	-0.4	-0.2
West Bank and Gaza	3.1	0.9	0.5	2.5	2.6	2.7	0.0	1.5	1.0

Source: World Bank.
Note: e = estimate; f = forecast. World Bank forecasts are frequently updated based on new information and changing (global) circumstances. Consequently, projections presented here may differ from those contained in other Bank documents, even if basic assessments of economies' prospects do not significantly differ at any given moment in time.
1. GDP at market prices and expenditure components are measured in 2010 prices and market exchange rates. Excludes Libya, Syria, and Yemen due to data limitations.
2. The fiscal year runs from July 1 to June 30 in Egypt; the column labeled 2018 reflects the fiscal year ended June 30, 2018.
To download the data in this table, please visit www.worldbank.org/gep.

BOX 2.4.1 Labor productivity in the Middle East and North Africa: Trends and drivers

Labor productivity growth in the Middle East and North Africa (MENA) has been the weakest among emerging market and developing economy (EMDE) regions, both pre-crisis and post-crisis. It averaged 0.3 percent between 2013-18, although with wide heterogeneity. Weak productivity growth had widened the productivity gap between advanced economies and MENA EMDEs. Large public sectors, underdeveloped private sectors, and lack of economic diversification hold back productivity growth, although recent reform initiatives in many countries in the region are promising.

Introduction

Labor productivity growth in the Middle East and North Africa (MENA) has been the weakest among emerging market and developing economy (EMDE) regions, averaging 0.3 percent during 2013-18 (Figure 2.4.1.1). There is wide heterogeneity across the region in productivity growth, but on average, the productivity gap between MENA EMDEs and advanced economies has widened. In energy exporters, labor productivity growth has been severely constrained by weak investment, while in energy importers, it has stagnated below the EMDE average rate. Moreover, the continuing importance of commodity exports in many economies means that they have not experienced the diversification or expansion of other sectors that helped drive high productivity growth in regions like East Asia and the Pacific.

Against this backdrop, this box addresses the following questions for the MENA region:

- How has productivity growth evolved?

- What factors have been associated with productivity growth?

- What policy options are available to boost productivity growth?

Unless otherwise noted, discussion of productivity in this box refers to labor productivity, measured as output per worker. The primary sample under which regional labor productivity trends are discussed is based on 14 MENA economies: Algeria, Bahrain, Egypt, Iran, Iraq, Jordan, Kuwait, Lebanon, Morocco, Oman, Qatar, Saudi Arabia, Tunisia, and the United Arab Emirates.

Evolution of regional productivity

Low labor productivity growth. From already weak pre-crisis rates (1.3 percent during 2003-08), labor productivity growth in MENA decelerated further, to

about 0.3 percent during 2013-18. This slowdown affected about half of EMDEs in the region, especially energy exporters (Figure 2.4.1.2). Weak post-crisis productivity growth in the region continues a long-standing trend that featured productivity growth below the EMDE average for the past two decades.

Within-region heterogeneity. Productivity trends in the MENA region differ considerably by country. Among energy exporters, productivity growth averaged about 0 percent in 2013-18 amid a 50 percent oil price collapse from its mid-2014 peak. The oil price collapse also did not greatly benefit energy importers in the region – productivity growth remained flat at about 1.5 percent during both 2003-08 and 2013-18, well below the EMDE average.

Wide dispersion in labor productivity levels. At nearly half of advanced-economy productivity, MENA has the highest productivity level of any EMDE region. However, productivity levels in MENA differ widely within region, with substantially higher levels in the Gulf Cooperation Council (GCC) economies than in energy importers. This disparity reflects the variation in natural resource endowments between lower-middle-income energy importers such as Egypt, Morocco, and Tunisia, and high-income energy exporters such as Saudi Arabia and United Arab Emirates. MENA's convergence towards advanced economy productivity levels has decelerated further from the 2003-08 to 2013-18 periods due to weak productivity growth.

Sources of labor productivity growth. In the two decades prior to the oil price collapse of 2014-16, labor productivity growth in the region was primarily supported by capital deepening, driven by capital investment by energy exporters (IMF 2012, 2015; Malik and Masood 2018). In an alternative labor productivity decomposition that also incorporates natural resources (Brandt, Schreyer and Zipperer 2017), natural resource activity appears to drive MENA productivity growth significantly. Its average contribution to productivity growth shrank from about 1.2 percentage points during 2003-08 to 0.2 percentage point during 2013-14, the last year for which natural resources data are available (Figure 2.4.1.2).

Note: This box was prepared by Lei Sandy Ye, building upon analysis in Chapter 3. Research assistance was provided by Vanessa Arellano Banoni and Shijie Shi.

BOX 2.4.1 Labor productivity in the Middle East and North Africa: Trends and drivers (*continued*)

FIGURE 2.4.1.1 Productivity in MENA in regional comparison

Labor productivity growth in the Middle East and North Africa (MENA) has been the weakest among emerging market and developing economy (EMDE) regions, both pre-crisis and post-crisis. It averaged 0.3 percent between 2013-18. Despite high average productivity level relative to other EMDE regions, weak productivity growth has recently widened its productivity gap with advanced economies.

A. Average productivity growth

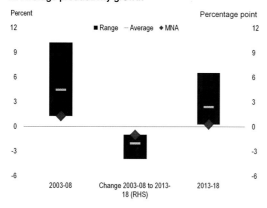

B. Productivity levels and convergence

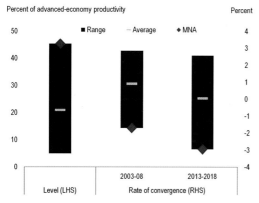

Source: Penn World Table; The Conference Board; World Bank.
Note: Productivity is defined as labor productivity (real GDP per person employed). Sample includes 35 advanced economies and 127 EMDEs: 16 in East Asia and the Pacific (EAP), 21 in Eastern Europe and Central Asia (ECA), 25 in Latin America and the Caribbean (LAC), 14 in Middle East and North Africa (MNA), 7 in South Asia (SAR), and 44 in Sub-Saharan Africa (SSA). The 14 MNA economies in the sample are Algeria, Bahrain, Egypt, Iran, Iraq, Jordan, Kuwait, Lebanon, Morocco, Oman, Qatar, Saudi Arabia, Tunisia, and the United Arab Emirates.
A. Aggregate growth rates in 2010 U.S. dollars at 2010 prices and exchange rates.
B. Rate of convergence is calculated as the difference in productivity growth rates over the log difference in productivity levels between MNA and advanced economies (AE). Blue bars and orange dashes show the range and average of the six EMDE regional aggregates. "Level" of productivity refers to the GDP weighted average of regional productivity as a share of the average advanced economy during 2013-2018.

The commodity sector is capital-intensive. As a result, oil prices and capital expenditures are closely linked in the MENA region (IMF 2018b; Albino-War et al. 2014). Foreign direct investment is also highly undiversified and heavily concentrated in the commodity sector (World Bank 2003). After the global financial crisis, investment growth in the region slowed sharply. Among energy exporters, this slower growth has been attributed to tight financial constraints associated with lower oil prices. Among energy importers, the legacies of the Arab Spring movements led many economies to increase investment on defense at the expense of infrastructure and other productivity-enhancing projects and initiatives (Baffes et al. 2015; Ianchovichina 2017).

Pre-crisis capital deepening was partly offset by contractionary total factor productivity (TFP) growth, the weakness of which has been widely documented for the region over the past three decades.[1] The inverse relationship between capital accumulation and TFP growth suggests inefficient investment, and may be attributed to two factors. First, predominantly public investment combined with the large economic role of state-owned enterprises crowds out private investment and job creation. Second, fiscal policy tends to be procyclical—just like public investment—as countries often pursue expansionary fiscal policy during oil price booms (Abdih et al. 2010). During periods of high capital investment and oil price booms, technology-enhancing-oriented reform momentum tends to be weaker, weighing on TFP growth. Negative TFP growth in MENA before the global financial crisis stands in sharp contrast to the robust pre-crisis TFP growth in the broader group of EMDEs. TFP growth started to pick up as oil prices bottomed out in 2016, although it remained low at 1 percent on average during 2016-18.[2]

Heterogeneity in sources of labor productivity growth. While labor productivity growth in the MENA region as a whole has long been anemic and continues to be weak, there has been wide divergence within the region in its

---

[1] Weak or negative TFP growth is found to be a prevalent feature in the MENA region during the past three decades. For regional and country-specific studies that highlight TFP growth in MENA, see Baier, Dwyer, and Tamura (2006); Bisat, El-Erjan, and T. Helbling (1997); Callen et al. (2014); IMF (2012); Keller and Nabli (2002); Malik and Masood (2018); World Bank (2017d); and Yousef (2004).

[2] TFP growth can also be affected by non-technology factors, such as capital and labor utilization. Hence, TFP growth estimates may over- or understate the true change in the influence of technology on productivity (Dieppe, Kindberg-Hanlon, and Kiliç Çelik, forthcoming).

BOX 2.4.1 Labor productivity in the Middle East and North Africa: Trends and drivers (*continued*)

FIGURE 2.4.1.2 Evolution of labor productivity growth in MENA

The post-crisis productivity growth slowdown was concentrated in energy exporters and affected about half of the region's economies. During 2013-18, average productivity growth was around zero percent in energy exporters and about 1.5 percent (still below the EMDE average) in energy importers. Productivity growth has been largely driven by declining capital stock amid weak TFP growth, especially in energy exporters. Productivity levels in energy exporters are much higher than in energy importers. The contribution of natural resources to productivity growth fell significantly from the 2003-08 to 2013-18 periods.

A. Productivity growth in MENA

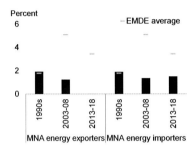

B. Share of economies with productivity growth below long-run and pre-crisis averages

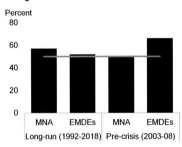

C. Productivity relative to advanced economies

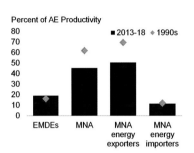

D. Contributions to regional productivity growth

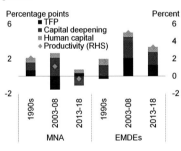

E. Contributions to productivity growth

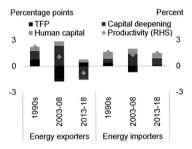

F. Role of natural resources

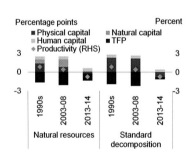

Source: Barro and Lee (2015); Haver Analytics; International Monetary Fund; Penn World Tables; United Nations (Human Development Reports), Wittgenstein Centre for Demography and Global Human Capital; World Bank.
Note: Productivity is defined as labor productivity (real GDP per person employed). Aggregate growth rates calculated using GDP weights at 2010 prices and market exchange rates.
A-C. The sample includes 14 MNA economies: Algeria, Bahrain, Egypt, Iran, Iraq, Jordan, Kuwait, Lebanon, Morocco, Oman, Qatar, Saudi Arabia, Tunisia, and the United Arab Emirates. Includes 127 EMDEs.
A. Dashed lines indicate the average EMDE labor productivity growth.
B. Share of countries for which productivity growth average over 2013-18 is lower compared to a long-run (1992-2018) and pre-crisis (2003-08) average.
D.E. MNA Sample in decomposition is the same as in A but excludes Algeria and UAE due to data availability. Includes 92 EMDEs in D.
F. The sample includes 10 MNA economies with available data on natural resources capital: Bahrain, Egypt, Jordan, Kuwait, Lebanon, Morocco, Oman, Qatar, Saudi Arabia, and Tunisia.

driving forces. For energy exporters, productivity growth decelerated markedly from 2003-08 to the post-crisis period of 2013-18 due to sharply declining investment activity. For energy importers, productivity growth improved modestly from a weak base, largely due to the recovery from negative average TFP growth rates during 2003-08 to slightly above zero percent during 2013-18.

Sources of regional labor productivity growth

High barriers to factor reallocation. Factor reallocation toward more productive activity has played only a limited role in driving productivity growth in MENA. This muted influence has reflected high barriers to entry and distortions such as the lack of competitive markets (Arezki

BOX 2.4.1 Labor productivity in the Middle East and North Africa: Trends and drivers (*continued*)

FIGURE 2.4.1.3 Factors supporting productivity growth in MENA

Productivity levels relative to advanced economies are the highest in MENA for the capital-intensive industrial sector, while employment is concentrated in the services sector. Evidence for Egypt and Morocco suggests that productivity growth in North Africa has been limited to within-sector productivity gains.

A. Sectoral productivity

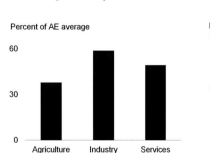

B. Sectoral employment

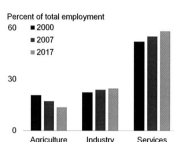

C. Within versus between sector contribution to productivity growth

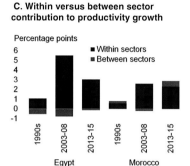

Source: Groningen Growth Development Center Database; Haver Analytics; International Labour Organization; Penn World Tables; World Bank.
Note: Productivity is defined as labor productivity (real GDP or value-added per person employed).
A.B. Medians across economies in each sector. Includes 12 MENA economies. Panel A based on 2017 data. AE average denotes weighted average across advanced economies.
C. The within-sector productivity contribution shows the initial real value added-weighted productivity growth; the between-sector contribution measures the productivity growth from a cross-sectoral shift of employment. Based on nine-sector decomposition.

et al. 2019a). Small exporting firms are hesitant to scale up their operations and benefit little from global value chain integration (World Bank 2016f). For the North Africa region, evidence from Egypt and Morocco suggests that within-sector productivity gains were the main source of productivity growth for their economies (Figure 2.4.1.3). In Saudi Arabia, employment appears to have moved towards sectors with relatively low productivity in the past (Fayad and Rasmussen 2012). These trends imply distortions in the economy exist that prevent more efficient reallocation of resources across sectors. High capital intensity of the commodity sector accounted for high average productivity levels in MENA, and scope for productivity improvement in the private sector remains large. Moreover, the majority of employment is concentrated in the services sector, reflecting an exceptionally high proportion of the workforce (about one-fifth) employed in the public sector (Tamirisa and Duenwald 2018).

Other drivers of labor productivity growth. Weak productivity in the MENA region has been associated with underdevelopment of the private sector, overreliance on the public sector, and lack of economic diversification (Devarajan and Mottaghi 2015).

- *Large public sector.* On average, about one-fifth of the region's workforce is employed in the public sector, and public-private sector wage gaps are among the highest in the world (Purfield et al. 2018; Tamirisa and Duenwald 2018). The education system is targeted towards government employment, with few high-quality private sector jobs (World Bank 2018l). These dynamics hold back the adoption of technology from abroad (Mitra et al. 2016; Raggl 2015; Samargandi 2018). In the Gulf Cooperation Council, weak productivity growth has been associated with low mobility of high-skilled foreign workers (Callen et al. 2014).

- *Restrictive business climate.* Poor governance quality, large informal sectors, and cumbersome tax policy and administration hampered the reallocation of resources from low-productivity to higher-productivity firms (Nabli 2007; World Bank 2016f). Non-GCC economies in MENA rank especially low in the World Bank's Worldwide Governance Indicators, such as regulatory quality and government effectiveness. Private firms often face challenges in access to finance; yet, providing access to formal finance is associated with labor productivity growth being 2 percentage points higher in MENA firms (Blancher et al. 2019).

BOX 2.4.1 Labor productivity in the Middle East and North Africa: Trends and drivers (*continued*)

FIGURE 2.4.1.4 Policy challenges

Multipronged and sustainable reforms that improve governance and boost private sector development are crucial in MENA. Reforms could lift the potential of its young population and relieve constraints to firm productivity, such as access to finance.

A. Access to finance as an obstacle to productivity	B. Youth unemployed or not in education	C. Governance: Non-GCC economies
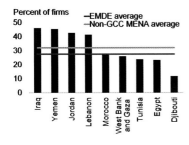	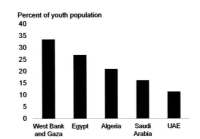	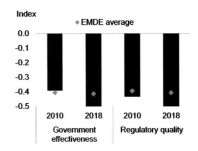

Source: World Bank.

A. Percent of firms citing access to finance as a major obstacle to firm operations. Based on World Bank's Enterprise Surveys. Latest available survey year for each economy denoted. Non-GCC MENA denotes average of all economies shown in the figure.

B. Share of youth not in education, employment, or training, as a percent of youth population. UAE stands for United Arab Emirates. Latest available data since 2015.

C. Includes 10 non-GCC economies. Unweighted averages. Based on 2018 data (or latest available year). Index, based on Worldwide Governance Indicators, ranges from -2.5 to 2.5. A lower index denotes worse rating.

- *Anemic private sector.* Firm productivity in MENA has been restricted by low firm turnover and creation. Only six limited liability companies were created annually for every 10,000 working-age people in MENA during 2009-12—considerably less than in other EMDEs (Schiffbauer et al. 2015).

- *Lack of diversification.* Trade openness and export diversification in MENA remain low among EMDE regions. This lack of diversification is partly the result of exchange rate misalignments associated with high reliance on extractive industries or low technological content of exports (Benhassine et al. 2009). In the large EMDEs of the region, low export diversification has been found to hinder productivity growth.[3] Research and development, as measured by the number of patent applications per capita, has been above the EMDE average. However, it remains well below advanced-economy averages and has held back productivity growth and diversification (Samargandi 2018, Rahmati and Pilehvari 2017).

Recent reforms. A number of large economies in the region have adopted reform plans in the past five years that

may have begun to support productivity growth. In the GCC, a series of plans include measures to improve productivity and diversify away from the energy sector. Efforts to boost small and medium-sized enterprise (SME) growth and encourage private-sector development include the establishment of an SME agency in Saudi Arabia and SME delicensing in the United Arab Emirates. Among energy importers, measures to improve the business and private sector climate have been enacted in Egypt, Morocco, and Tunisia (World Bank 2019r). Initial market responses to these developments suggest that efficiency gains have been generated. For instance, Saudi Arabia was included in the MSCI Emerging Markets Index recently, and many GCC economies established policies to relax foreign investment restrictions (e.g., UAE's relaxation of restriction in 13 sectors in 2019). These changes have been associated with foreign investment inflows, which in EMDEs often catalyze productivity-enhancing private investment (Henry 2007). These policies have also made it easier to raise international capital, which has already helped finance fiscal and balance-of-payments needs in MENA (IMF 2019d). Egypt's macroeconomic reforms since 2016 include the liberalization of the exchange rate, business climate reforms, and energy subsidy reforms. These reforms have been positively perceived by investors and may have raised the country's export and investment prospects (Youssef et al. 2019).

---

[3] See IMF (2013, 2015); Morsey, Levy, and Sanchez (2014); Samargandi (2018).

BOX 2.4.1 Labor productivity in the Middle East and North Africa: Trends and drivers (*continued*)

Prospects for labor productivity growth. Recent broad-based reform commitments across the region are promising for labor productivity growth. However, many reforms are subject to high risk of delays in implementation, especially in non-GCC economies where political fragmentation and budget irresolution have frequently held back multiyear reform plans. In some non-GCC economies, recent protests related to social tensions and political developments underscore the fragility associated with reform progress. Armed conflicts in economies like Yemen continue to challenge the peace that these economies need in order to work toward higher productivity.

Policy options

Concerted and multipronged efforts are required to reliably raise productivity growth. Policies need to be directed at raising the quality of human capital and boosting private sector investment, increasing firm productivity, removing obstacles to sectoral reallocation, and creating business-friendly environments. Within these broad themes, specific policies need to be tailored to a country's specific circumstances.[4]

The effectiveness of reform in practice is contingent on the health of each economy and the timing of political events (Alesina, et al. 2019). Under some circumstances, a targeted approach that leverages synergies may be warranted. Deep institutional reforms to raise market contestability, for example, may also bring a variety of collateral benefits like higher technological progress (Arezki et al. 2019a). Similarly, well-designed deployment of FinTech could help garner broad-based support for institutional reforms (World Bank 2019r).

Improving factors of production

Boosting private investment. While capital deepening has been a main driver of productivity growth in MENA, it has been primarily supported by large public spending (for example, in the commodity sector in the GCC; IMF 2018b). This suggests large scope to boost private investment. A wide range of reforms is needed to encourage private investment, including expanding access to finance, improving business climates and governance, reducing the wage premium of government employment, and leveling the playing field with state-controlled enterprises (Arezki, et al. 2019a).

---

[4] Higher labor productivity gains in the region could in turn help reduce external imbalances in the region (Arezki et al. 2019b).

Raise human capital. The contribution of human capital to labor productivity growth has been modest in the past two decades, amounting to only about half a percentage point. The region's human capital challenge is to improve educational access for youth and women, improve the connection between educational attainment and private sector jobs, and to shift its bias in educational training away from the public sector (World Bank 2018l). These measures would help the productivity potential of its large youth population. More educational programs to improve the skills match between workers and employers can enhance the quality of jobs in MENA (Gatti et al. 2013).

Boost firm productivity

Disincentives for innovation and factor reallocation between firms discourages labor productivity in MENA.

Improve access to finance. Access to finance is a large obstacle for firms in MENA, particularly for non-GCC economies, as lack of financing hinders their ability to invest and innovate (Figure 2.4.1.4). Better access to credit, supported by broader credit bureau coverage and stronger insolvency resolution regimes, appears to yield sizable benefits to productivity growth in MENA (Ghassibe, Appendino, and Mahmoudi 2019). New insolvency resolution laws adopted in Djibouti, Egypt, Saudi Arabia, and Jordan are promising for facilitating debt resolution between creditors and debtors. New minority investor protection regulation in Egypt helps improve corporate governance and investor confidence by requiring shareholder approval in issuing new shares.

Address informality. Informality, although low by average EMDE standards, presents a challenge to businesses in non-GCC economies. Competition from the informal sector is a major obstacle for formal sector businesses in several large economies (Morocco, Tunisia), and a higher share of informal workers in SMEs is associated with lower wages and more limited export potential (Elbadawi and Loayza 2008). Aligning tax systems to international best practices (e.g., harmonized electronic filing systems in Morocco) and reducing regulatory hurdles for firms can help attract informal firms to more productive formal activity while raising revenue collection.

Encouraging efficient resource reallocation

Reallocation towards more productive private sector activities has made limited contributions to productivity growth in MENA. In energy exporters, policies to encourage diversification of exports and output can

BOX 2.4.1 Labor productivity in the Middle East and North Africa: Trends and drivers (*continued*)

generate new opportunities for labor to move into more productive private sector opportunities. In energy importers, such as Egypt and Morocco, expanding exporters' global market reach and improving the quality of exports could help improve productivity (World Bank 2016f).

Diversification through trade. Reforms in investment, trade, and tariff policies will help MENA economies move up the export value chain and encourage greater product variety, which currently lags behind international benchmarks. Regional integration efforts (e.g., Compact with Africa) could provide an avenue to promote diversification and raise productivity.

Diversification from commodity dependence. For energy exporters, including the GCC, stronger fiscal management could help promote diversification by broadening the revenue base (Diop and Marotta 2012; World Bank 2019q). For energy importers, options for diversification may include investment in renewable energies via public-private partnerships (e.g., Egypt; Vagliasindi 2013), or initiatives to boost the private services sector (e.g., tourism initiatives in oil importers). Efforts to expand the reach of firms to the global market can also help boost productivity growth (World Bank 2016f).

Creating a growth friendly environment

Improve business climates. Business climate reforms, such as the reduction of regulatory hurdles to start businesses or the removal of particularly distortionary taxes, can help boost private investment and productivity. They can also provide firms easier access to critical inputs, such as improved electricity supply. They can support productivity through better allocation of resources (e.g., more efficient

taxation systems) and stronger entrepreneurship activities (e.g., lower cost to start a business). In MENA, reforms that move an economy one unit higher in the Global Competitiveness Index have been estimated to raise productivity growth significantly (Mitra et al. 2016). Many MENA economies have adopted broad-based business climate reforms recently, including improved electricity connection in Bahrain, enhanced electronic tax filing in Jordan, and easier property registration in Kuwait.

Improve governance. Governance quality in MENA, especially non-GCC economies, lags behind other EMDEs and has exhibited little improvement over the past decade (Figure 2.4.1.4). Weak governance has discouraged private sector activity and investment (Nabli 2007). Governance reforms, such as streamlining public service delivery and strengthening legal frameworks in areas like procurement laws can increase productivity growth by encouraging more efficient allocation of resources. They can also increase investment prospects through improved investor confidence. Reforms for state-owned enterprises in telecom industries can also enhance productivity via higher efficiency (Arezki et al. 2019b).

Improve gender equality. Women comprise only about one-fifth of the labor force in MENA. Bridging the gender gap in a number of areas, including workforce development and access to digital and financial services, is especially relevant for MENA. Closing these gaps can raise productivity growth through more vibrant entrepreneurship and private sector participation. Legislation to reduce economic discrimination against women in Tunisia is an example of recent reform in this area.

SOUTH ASIA

Growth in South Asia is estimated to have decelerated to 4.9 percent in 2019, reflecting a sharper-than-expected and broad-based weakening in domestic demand. In India, activity was constrained by insufficient credit availability, as well as by subdued private consumption. Regional growth is expected to pick up gradually, to 6 percent in 2022, on the assumption of a modest rebound in domestic demand. While growth in Bangladesh is projected to remain above 7 percent through the forecast horizon, growth in Pakistan is projected to languish at 3 percent or less through 2020 as macroeconomic stabilization efforts weigh on activity. Growth in India is projected to decelerate to 5 percent in FY2019/20 amid enduring financial sector issues. Policy measures such as enhancing foreign direct investment inflows and competitiveness, promoting access to finance for small enterprises, and improving infrastructure can deliver productivity gains and lift growth in the region. Key risks to the outlook include a sharper-than-expected slowdown in major economies, a reescalation of regional geopolitical tensions, and a setback in reforms to address impaired balance sheets in the financial and corporate sectors.

Recent developments

South Asia's growth is estimated to have decelerated to 4.9 percent in 2019, substantially weaker than 7.1 percent in the previous year (Figure 2.5.1.A). The deceleration was pronounced in the two largest economies, India and Pakistan. Weak confidence, liquidity issues in the financial sector (India), and monetary tightening (Pakistan) caused a sharp slowdown in fixed investment and a considerable softening in private consumption. Export and import growth for the region as a whole moderated, in line with a continued slowdown in global trade and industrial activity (World Bank 2019s). Business confidence was hampered by subdued consumer demand in India and security challenges in Sri Lanka.

Demand faltered amid credit tightening, reflecting structurally high non-performing assets (e.g., Bangladesh, India, Pakistan), liquidity shortages in the non-bank financial sector in India, and tightening policies in Pakistan. In India, activity slowed substantially in 2019, with the deceleration

most pronounced in the manufacturing and agriculture sectors, whereas government-related services subsectors received significant support from public spending. GDP growth decelerated to 5 percent and 4.5 percent (y/y) in the April-June and July-September quarters of 2019, respectively—the lowest readings since 2013. Sharp slowdowns in household consumption and investment offset the rise in government spending (Figure 2.5.1.B). High-frequency data suggest that activity continued to be weak for the rest of 2019 (Figure 2.5.1.C).

In Pakistan, growth decelerated to an estimated 3.3 percent in FY2018/19, reflecting a broad-based weakening in domestic demand. Significant depreciation of the Pakistani rupee (the nominal effective exchange rate depreciated about 20 percent over the past year) resulted in inflationary pressures (SBP 2019). Monetary policy tightening in response to elevated inflation restricted access to credit. The government retrenched, curtailing public investment, to deal with large twin deficits and low international reserves.

Bangladesh, the third-largest economy in the region, fared better than India and Pakistan, with growth officially estimated at 8.1 percent in

Note: This section was prepared by Temel Taskin. Research assistance was provided by Jankeesh Sandhu.

FIGURE 2.5.1 **SAR: Recent developments**

Regional growth is estimated to have decelerated to 4.9 percent in 2019. In India, the combination of funding issues in non-banking financial companies (NBFC) and uncertainty weighed on growth. Industrial production points to continuing weakness in activity. While regional exports softened in aggregate, Bangladesh's export growth accelerated, partly reflecting trade diversion amid trade tensions between major economies. Monetary policy was broadly accommodative amid weak activity and subdued inflation. Current account deficits narrowed with weakening imports.

A. Growth

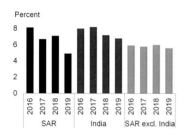

B. Private consumption and investment in India

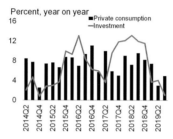

C. Industrial production growth

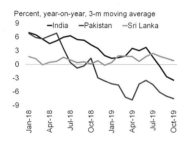

D. Bangladesh: Goods exports growth

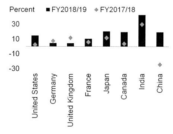

E. Inflation

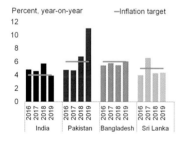

F. Monetary policy rates

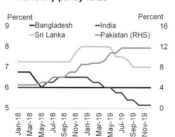

Source: Bangladesh Bureau of Export Promotion; Haver Analytics; World Bank.
A. SAR = South Asia region. Aggregate growth rates calculated using constant 2010 U.S. dollar GDP weights. Data for 2019 are estimates.
B. Last observation is 2019Q3.
C. Last observation is October 2019.
D. Exports data are merchandise exports and in current U.S. dollars.
E. Bangladesh, India, and Pakistan data reflects fiscal years. 2019 data reflects November for Bangladesh, India, Pakistan, and Sri Lanka.
F. Data represent monetary policy rates of Reserve Bank of India, State Bank of Pakistan, Bangladesh Bank, and Central Bank of Sri Lanka. Last observation is December 2019.

FY2018/19. A moderation in domestic demand was more than offset by a pickup in exports, partly as a result of trade diversion following bilateral tariff increases between China and the United States. Bangladesh's exports showed signs of softening in recent months, after a substantial increase in exports to major trade partners in the last fiscal year (Figure 2.5.1.D).

Growth in Sri Lanka continued to soften in 2019, to an estimated 2.7 percent, as tourist arrivals collapsed following terror attacks in April (World Bank 2019t). The Central Bank of Sri Lanka eased its policy stance with cuts in interest rates and reserve requirements in response to subdued economic activity. In Afghanistan, growth recovered to an estimated 2.5 percent in 2019, benefiting from a pickup in agriculture thanks to benign weather conditions. However, political uncertainty and security challenges weighed on the manufacturing and services sectors.

Growth in Nepal is estimated at 7.1 percent in FY2018/19, the third consecutive year of over 6 percent growth. Activity was underpinned by solid remittance inflows, buoyant tourist arrivals, and good monsoons. In Bhutan, activity remained subdued as underlying drivers—hydropower and tourism—have not picked up significantly in FY2018/19, resulting in 3.9 percent GDP growth. While tourist arrivals increased, tourism receipts declined reflecting lower average spending by tourists. Growth in Maldives moderated, despite an increase in tourism, amid softening construction activity, which partly reflected the completion of infrastructure projects and delays in the implementation of new ones. Accordingly, activity is estimated to have expanded by 5.2 percent in 2019.

Inflation has been mostly stable in the region on the back of weak domestic demand and broadly stable currency markets, with the notable exception of Pakistan (Figure 2.5.1.E). Central banks in other major economies were able to cut policy rates several times amid negative output gaps and persistently below-target inflation (India, Sri Lanka; Figure 2.5.1.F).

Progress in fiscal consolidation has broadly weakened. Pakistan's budget deficit rose more sharply than expected. Contributing factors were a shortfall in revenue collection, combined with a sizable increase in interest payments. In Sri Lanka, weaker-than-expected tax revenues and increased public spending resulted in a widening budget deficit. Current account deficits have generally narrowed over the past year, on the back of softening imports in the region.

Outlook

Growth in South Asia is projected to gradually pick up over the forecast period, from 4.9 percent in 2019 to 6 percent in 2022 (Figure 2.5.2.A; Tables 2.5.1, 2.5.2). This projection assumes a modest rebound in domestic demand. The weak global trade outlook will continue to weigh on regional export growth in the near term. Regional economic activity is expected to benefit from policy accommodation (India, Sri Lanka), improvement in business confidence and support from infrastructure investments (Afghanistan, Bangladesh, Pakistan).

In India, weakness in credit from non-bank financial companies is expected to linger. Although a gradual growth recovery is expected in the second half of the fiscal year, the challenges faced by the economy over the first half should contribute to a third consecutive year of slowing growth in FY2019/20 (April 2019-March 2020). Thereafter, growth is expected to gradually recover, to 6.1 percent in FY2021/22. This forecast is predicated on the monetary policy stance remaining accommodative. It also assumes that stimulative fiscal and structural measures already taken—including corporate tax cuts, income transfers to farmers, spending on rural development, support measures to the automobile industry, and further liberalization of foreign direct investment (FDI)—will begin to pay-off. The scope for more proactive support from fiscal and monetary policies is limited, as inflation has recently crossed the midpoint of the target range, and weaker-than-expected tax revenues are being accompanied by increased public spending.

Macroeconomic adjustment in Pakistan, including a continuation of tight monetary policy and fiscal consolidation, is expected to continue. Growth is

FIGURE 2.5.2 **SAR: Outlook and risks**

Growth is projected to increase gradually, reflecting a modest rebound in domestic demand. The regional outlook for 2020 has deteriorated recently, and risks are tilted to the downside. Financial sector weakness will likely weigh on activity unless balance sheet vulnerabilities are addressed. NBFCs represent a significant share of total loans, and their linkages with the banking sector imply broad-based contagion risks in India. Lack of progress in reforms to improve tax collection could exacerbate fiscal deficits.

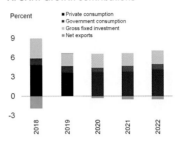

A. SAR: Growth contributions

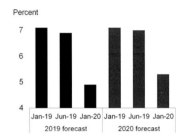

B. SAR: Growth forecasts

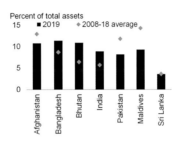

C. Non-performing assets

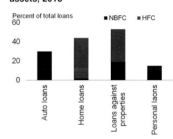

D. India: Non-bank financial system assets, 2018

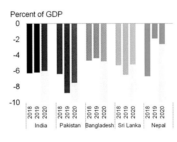

E. Fiscal balances

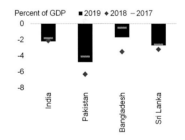

F. Current account balances

Source: Haver Analytics; Consensus Economics; Reserve Bank of India; World Bank.
A. SAR= South Asia region. Aggregate growth rates are calculated using constant 2010 U.S. dollar GDP-weights. Data for 2019 are estimates. Shaded areas are forecasts.
B. Blue bars represent World Bank forecasts. Last observation is December 2019.
C. Last observation is 2019Q2 for Afghanistan, Bhutan, India, Pakistan, and Maldives, and 2019Q1 for Sri Lanka. Bangladesh observation is for 2018.
D. Data obtained from RBI (2019) and represent December 2018.
E. Shaded areas indicate forecasts. Data for 2019 are estimates. The data refer to fiscal years of countries except for Sri Lanka, as described in Table 2.5.1.
F. Data for 2019 are estimates. The data refer to fiscal years of countries except for Sri Lanka, as described in Table 2.5.1.

projected to bottom-out at 2.4 percent in FY2019/20 (July 2019-June 2020). Thereafter, as macroeconomic conditions improve and structural reforms support investment, growth is projected to steadily advance, reaching 3.9 percent by FY2021/22.

Growth in Bangladesh is projected to remain above 7 percent throughout the forecast horizon. A solid macroeconomic framework, political stability, implementation of planned public infrastructure projects, and ongoing reforms to improve the business environment underlie this projection (World Bank 2019u).

Sri Lanka's growth is projected to advance to 3.3 percent in 2020. The acceleration afterwards will be supported by recovering investment and exports, as long as the security challenges and political uncertainty of 2019 dissipate. Growth is seen to stabilize around 3.7 percent over the rest of the forecast horizon, in line with potential growth.

In Afghanistan, activity is expected to continue accelerating, assuming a stable political transition after elections and a subsequent improvement in business confidence. Nepal's economy is projected to grow at about 6.5 percent through 2022, supported by strong services and construction sector activities, amid buoyant tourist arrivals and rising public spending. Growth in Bhutan and Maldives will continue to be underpinned by tourism and infrastructure projects, over the forecast horizon averaging 6.5 percent and 5.6 percent, respectively.

Over the medium term, regional growth is expected to rise toward potential. Trends in urbanization, progress in human capital accumulation, and demographic developments will support potential growth and productivity. Policy measures such as enhancing FDI inflows and competitiveness, promoting access to finance for small enterprises, and improving infrastructure can deliver productivity gains in the region (World Bank 2019d; Kochhar et al. 2006; Box 2.5.1). South Asia's participation in international trade remains substantially below that of other regions. While both imports and exports as a share of GDP in South Asian countries are below levels of comparable economies, the gap in exports—

both within region and across major destinations—is much larger (World Bank 2019v). Greater participation in global and regional value chains would lift growth, convey positive productivity and technology spillovers, and narrow current account deficits in the region.

Risks

South Asia's growth outlook has deteriorated considerably over the past six months. Private consumption and investment weakened sharply amid challenges in the financial sector, which hampered confidence (Figure 2.5.2.B). Risks to the growth outlook remain tilted to the downside and relate primarily to financial sector vulnerabilities, geopolitical tensions, and lack of progress on reforms. Although recent tensions between India and Pakistan have abated, a reescalation would damage confidence and weigh on investment in the region.

Non-performing assets in the financial sector remain high amid weakening regional growth (Figure 2.5.2.C). Further deterioration of balance sheets of banks and corporates would threaten the funding of productive investments (Behera and Sharma 2019). Failure to close the infrastructure gaps would hold back output and employment (World Bank 2020). Announced initiatives, such as the recapitalization and consolidation of public sector banks and measures to foster FDI inflows, are expected to support activity. Insufficient progress in implementing these reforms would set back growth in the region.

The non-bank financial system in India remains vulnerable to stress. A major idiosyncratic default could trigger a broader liquidity shortage in the sector, as it did over the past year (RBI 2019). Non-banks represent a significant share of total loans, and their linkages with the banking sector imply that contagion risks are material (Figure 2.5.2.D).

Lack of progress in reforms to improve tax collection could result in more acute revenue shortfalls (Bangladesh, Sri Lanka) and put further pressure on elevated fiscal deficits (Pakistan; Figure 2.5.2.E). This could have negative consequences for infrastructure investment, and hence for projected growth, as well as for the fiscal space available to respond to a future cyclical downturn.

With respect to external risks, a sharper-than-expected slowdown in major external markets such as the United States and the Euro Area, would affect South Asia through trade, financial, and confidence channels, especially for countries with strong trade links to these economies (Chapter 1). For countries with elevated debt levels and large current account deficits (Figure 2.5.2.F; Pakistan, Sri Lanka), an unexpected tightening in global financing conditions could sharply raise borrowing costs and lead to stops in capital inflows (Sengupta and Gupta 2015).

TABLE 2.5.1 **South Asia forecast summary**

(Real GDP growth at market prices in percent, unless indicated otherwise)

Percentage point differences from June 2019 projections

	2017	2018	2019e	2020f	2021f	2022f		2019e	2020f	2021f
EMDE South Asia, GDP[1, 2]	6.7	7.1	4.9	5.5	5.9	6.0		-2.0	-1.5	-1.2
(Average including countries with full national accounts and balance of payments data only)[3]										
EMDE South Asia, GDP[3]	6.7	7.1	4.9	5.5	5.9	6.0		-2.0	-1.5	-1.2
GDP per capita (U.S. dollars)	5.5	5.9	3.7	4.3	4.8	4.8		-2.0	-1.5	-1.1
PPP GDP	6.7	7.1	4.9	5.5	5.9	5.9		-2.0	-1.5	-1.2
Private consumption	6.7	7.9	4.4	5.8	6.3	6.8		-2.6	-1.1	-0.7
Public consumption	12.4	10.3	10.2	7.8	7.6	7.6		2.6	0.9	0.5
Fixed investment	8.5	10.3	4.0	6.4	6.5	6.5		-4.3	-1.4	-1.4
Exports, GNFS[4]	5.5	10.3	4.9	5.2	5.9	6.0		-0.5	0.0	0.4
Imports, GNFS[4]	15.5	15.1	3.4	4.8	6.1	6.2		-2.8	-1.0	0.0
Net exports, contribution to growth	-2.7	-1.9	0.1	-0.3	-0.5	-0.5		0.8	0.3	0.1

Memo items: GDP[2]	16/17	17/18	18/19e	19/20f	20/21f	21/22f		18/19e	19/20f	20/21f
South Asia excluding India	5.8	6.0	5.6	4.8	4.7	5.1		0.1	0.0	-0.3
India	8.2	7.2	6.8	5.0	5.8	6.1		-0.4	-2.5	-1.7
Pakistan (factor cost)	5.2	5.5	3.3	2.4	3.0	3.9		-0.1	-0.3	-1.0
Bangladesh	7.3	7.9	8.1	7.2	7.3	7.3		0.8	-0.2	0.0

Source: World Bank.

Note: e – estimate; f – forecast. EMDE – emerging market and developing economies. World Bank forecasts are frequently updated based on new information and changing (global) circumstances. Consequently, projections presented here may differ from those contained in other Bank documents, even if basic assessments of countries' prospects do not differ at any given moment in time.

1. GDP and expenditure components are measured in 2010 prices and market exchange rates.

2. National income and product account data refer to fiscal years (FY) for the South Asian countries, while aggregates are presented in calendar year (CY) terms. The fiscal year runs from July 1 through June 30 in Bangladesh, Bhutan, and Pakistan, from July 16 through July 15 in Nepal, and April 1 through March 31 in India.

3. Subregion aggregate excludes Afghanistan, Bhutan, and Maldives, for which data limitations prevent the forecasting of GDP components.

4. Exports and imports of goods and non-factor services (GNFS).

To download the data in this table, please visit www.worldbank.org/gep.

TABLE 2.5.2 South Asia country forecasts

(Real GDP growth at market prices in percent, unless indicated otherwise)

Percentage point differences from June 2019 projections

Calendar year basis[1]	2017	2018	2019e	2020f	2021f	2022f	2019e	2020f	2021f
Afghanistan	2.7	1.8	2.5	3.0	3.5	3.5	0.1	-0.2	-0.1
Maldives	6.9	6.7	5.2	5.5	5.6	5.6	-0.5	0.3	0.3
Sri Lanka	3.4	3.2	2.7	3.3	3.7	3.7	-0.8	-0.3	0.0

Fiscal year basis[1]	16/17	17/18	18/19e	19/20f	20/21f	21/22f	18/19e	19/20f	20/21f
Bangladesh	7.3	7.9	8.1	7.2	7.3	7.3	0.8	-0.2	0.0
Bhutan	6.3	3.8	3.9	5.6	7.6	6.2	-1.5	0.2	2.4
India	8.2	7.2	6.8	5.0	5.8	6.1	-0.4	-2.5	-1.7
Nepal	8.2	6.7	7.1	6.4	6.5	6.6	0.0	0.0	0.0
Pakistan (factor cost)	5.2	5.5	3.3	2.4	3.0	3.9	-0.1	-0.3	-1.0

Source: World Bank.

Note: e = estimate; f = forecast. World Bank forecasts are frequently updated based on new information and changing (global) circumstances. Consequently, projections presented here may differ from those contained in other Bank documents, even if basic assessments of countries' prospects do not significantly differ at any given moment in time.

1. Historical data is reported on a market price basis. National income and product account data refer to fiscal years (FY) for the South Asian countries with the exception of Afghanistan, Maldives, and Sri Lanka, which report in calendar year. The fiscal year runs from July 1 through June 30 in Bangladesh, Bhutan, and Pakistan, from July 16 through July 15 in Nepal, and April 1 through March 31 in India.

To download the data in this table, please visit www.worldbank.org/gep.

BOX 2.5.1 Labor productivity in South Asia: Trends and drivers

In contrast to other emerging market and developing (EMDE) regions, labor productivity growth in South Asia (SAR) has slowed only mildly since the global financial crisis. In 2013-18, SAR productivity growth remained the second fastest (after East Asia and Pacific) among EMDE regions, at 5.3 percent a year. Rapid growth has helped reduce the region's wide productivity gap with the advanced-economy average. But the level of productivity in SAR remains the lowest among EMDE regions, in part reflecting widespread informal economic activity and struggling manufacturing sectors. Low human capital, poor business environments, inefficient resource allocation, and limited exposure to foreign firms and foreign investment weigh on productivity. Opening up SAR economies by enhancing foreign direct investment inflows and participation in global and regional value chains could support technology and information transfer to the region. Promoting access to finance and improving infrastructure could unlock growth bottlenecks for firms and lift productivity in the region.

Introduction

In contrast to other emerging market and developing (EMDE) regions, productivity growth in South Asia (SAR) slowed only mildly after the global financial crisis from pre-crisis rates, to 5.3 percent a year during 2013-18 (Figure 2.5.1.1.A). This followed a steady rise from anemic rates in the mid-1980s when heavily state-directed economic policy strategies dampened investment and innovation. As a result, the region's convergence towards advanced-economy productivity levels was the second-fastest over 2013-18 (after East Asia and the Pacific). Despite this, the region had the lowest average productivity level of any EMDE region, at 5 percent of the advanced-economy average in the post-crisis period (Figure 2.5.1.1.B).

Against this backdrop, this box will discuss the following questions about the evolution of productivity growth in the SAR region:

- How has productivity evolved in the region?

- What have been the factors associated with productivity growth?

- What policy options are available to boost productivity growth?

This box defines productivity as labor productivity, measured as real GDP per worker at constant (2010) local currency prices. Cross-country comparisons of labor productivity levels use average 2010 market exchange rates. Data for labor productivity at the national level, as well as for the three main production sectors (agriculture, manufacturing and mining, and services) are available for all EMDEs in SAR: Afghanistan, Bangladesh, Bhutan, India, Maldives, Nepal, Pakistan, and Sri Lanka. However, the analysis in some cases uses only limited samples

because of limited data availability: India and Sri Lanka for growth accounting decompositions, and India, Pakistan, and Sri Lanka for sectoral analysis using nine-sector data.

Evolution of regional productivity

Robust productivity growth. Productivity growth in SAR remained robust, at 5.3 percent a year, in 2013-18, only narrowly below the pre-crisis average of 6.4 percent in 2003-08 (Figure 2.5.1.1.C). In the post-crisis period, a slight moderation in India's productivity growth, and larger declines in the smaller economies of Afghanistan, Bhutan and Sri Lanka, were partially offset by pickups in Bangladesh and Pakistan (Figure 2.5.1.1.D). The region's resilience reflected three main elements: (1) SAR's limited exposure to external headwinds, (2) continued rapid urbanization, and (3) an improving business environment that supported productivity gains from the continuing shift away from agriculture toward more productive services sectors (World Bank 2016a; APO 2018). As a result, in the post-crisis period, the share of economies with productivity growth below long-run and pre-crisis averages weas lower than in other EMDEs (Figure 2.5.1.1.E).

- In **India**, disruptions to economic activity due to cash shortages in 2016 and transitional costs related to the introduction of the new Goods and Services Tax (GST) system in 2017 contributed to a slowing of productivity growth to 5.6 percent a year during 2013-18, from the 2003-08 average of 7.1 percent a year. Nevertheless, India's post-crisis productivity growth remained in the highest decile among EMDEs. It was supported by investments in the energy and transport sectors, improvements in the ease of doing business, and ongoing structural reforms.

- In **Pakistan**, annual productivity growth picked up from a pre-crisis average of 2.4 percent to 3.1 percent during 2013-18, slightly below the EMDE average of 3.4 percent. During the post-crisis period, productivity growth benefited from strong foreign

---

Note: This section was prepared by Temel Taskin, building upon analysis in Chapter 3. Research assistance was provided by Jankeesh Sandhu and Shijie Shi.

BOX 2.5.1 Labor productivity in South Asia: Trends and drivers (*continued*)

FIGURE 2.5.1.1 Evolution of productivity growth in SAR

On average labor productivity expanded by 5.3 percent a year over the last ten years, significantly higher than the EMDE average. The catch-up to advanced economies starts from a low base, as productivity levels in SAR are just one-quarter of levels in the average EMDE. The increasing trend in productivity growth was broad-based in larger economies of the region. However, there is significant dispersion in the level of productivity across the region.

A. Productivity growth

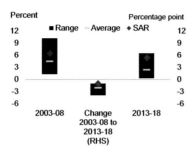

B. Productivity gap and convergence

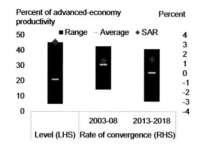

C. Productivity growth in SAR and EMDEs

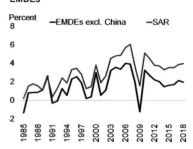

D. SAR: Productivity growth distribution

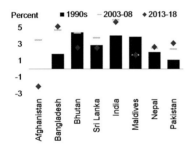

E. Share of economies with productivity growth below long-run and pre-crisis averages, 2013-18

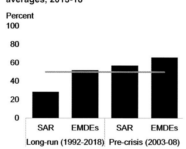

F. Relative productivity levels in SAR

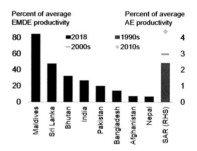

Source: Haver Analytics; Penn World Tables; World Bank.
Note: SAR = South Asia region. EMDE = emerging and developing economy. AE = advanced economy. Productivity refers to labor productivity unless otherwise indicated. Sample includes 127 EMDEs and 7 SAR economies unless otherwise indicated.
A.B. Range indicates interquartile range of country-level productivity distribution. Rate of convergence calculated as the difference in productivity growth rates with the average advanced economy divided by the log difference in productivity levels with the average advanced economy.
C.E.F. Aggregate growth rates calculated using U.S. dollar GDP weights at 2010 prices and exchange rates.
D. The year brackets refer to the average growth within the corresponding periods.

direct investment (FDI) inflows and infrastructure projects which supported private sector activity.

- In **Bangladesh**, post-crisis productivity growth benefited from improved macroeconomic and political stability which supported both public and private fixed investment. As a result, productivity growth in Bangladesh was robust during 2013-18 at 5.1 percent, slightly above the pre-crisis average of 4.7 percent and in the top decile of EMDEs.

- Productivity growth in the rest of the region either stalled or declined in the post-crisis episode in line

with the global trend (Chapter 3). The factors behind the slowdown included natural disasters, macroeconomic and political instability, and weaker growth of global trade and manufacturing activity.

SAR's robust productivity growth through the 2000s is in stark contrast to its weakness during the 1980s and 1990s, even though in those decades also it was mostly stronger than in other EMDEs. In the 1980s, India's state-directed economy generated minimal productivity growth as heavy regulation and widespread corruption (the "license raj") stifled manufacturing, investment, and technology adoption. In the wake of India's 1991 balance of payments

BOX 2.5.1 Labor productivity in South Asia: Trends and drivers (*continued*)

crisis, major reforms reduced restrictions on product and factor markets and allowed more trade, catalyzing a surge in productivity growth (Rodrik and Subramanian 2004; Virmani and Hashim 2011). In Pakistan, productivity growth was limited by macroeconomic instability (Lopez-Calix et al. 2012; Amjad and Awais 2016).

Low productivity levels. Despite its strong growth over the past three decades, labor productivity in SAR in 2013-18 was still only 5 percent of the advanced economy average, the lowest among EMDE regions and significantly below the EMDE average, which was around 20 percent of the advanced-economy average. In contrast to other EMDE regions, however, the pace of convergence has picked up since the global financial crisis. At the recent rate of convergence, about half of economies in South Asia would halve their productivity gap with advanced economies over the next 40 years.

Within-region dispersion in productivity levels. Productivity differences across countries are very large in SAR. Afghanistan and Nepal have the lowest productivity levels, at around 7 percent of the EMDE average, partly reflecting political instability, including prolonged armed conflict in Afghanistan, and natural disasters. Bhutan, Maldives, and Sri Lanka have higher productivity levels, in the range of 32-85 percent of the EMDE average, reflecting the benefit of relatively large service sectors, in particular tourism activity. Productivity levels in the three largest economies of SAR—India, Bangladesh, and Pakistan—are lower, ranging between 14 and 27 percent of the EMDE average, reflecting their relatively large informal sectors, low urbanization rates, and weak financial development (Figure 2.5.1.1.F).

Slowing contribution from capital deepening. Labor productivity growth can be decomposed into contributions from increases in other factors of production (human and physical capital) and advances in the effectiveness of their use (total factor productivity, TFP). Estimates for this decomposition are available for India and Sri Lanka. In these economies, a slowdown in investment growth accounted for all of the post-crisis slowdown in productivity growth, and thus for more than the average contribution of investment to productivity slowdowns in all EMDEs. The contributions to labor productivity growth of total factor productivity growth and human capital growth remained the same as in the pre-crisis period (Figure 2.5.1.2.A). The weakening of investment growth in part reflected the economic disruptions in India around the currency exchange of 2016 and the introduction of the GST in 2017. Slower growth of global

trade in recent years has weighed further on investment as well as exports. The slowdown of investment growth was from high pre-crisis rates that were fueled partly by large foreign direct investment inflows after financial liberalization reforms in the 1990s (Fujimori and Sato 2015; Park 2010).

Sources of regional productivity growth

The slight moderation in SAR's post-crisis productivity growth was accounted for mainly by India, and mainly by weaker growth in the industrial sector, as in other EMDEs. The median productivity level of the industrial sector in SAR is just slightly more than one half of the EMDE median (Figure 2.5.1.2.B). Poor manufacturing productivity in part reflects limited integration into international trade networks and global value chains, which has constrained the region's interaction with more productive foreign firms and reduced opportunities to benefit from technology transfer from other countries (Figure 2.5.1.2.C). This said, post-crisis productivity growth in this sector remained higher than the EMDE average reflecting improvements in the business environment as well as ongoing public investment in transportation and energy infrastructure.

Growing productivity gains from between-sector reallocation. Factor reallocation from low- productivity to high-productivity sectors and firms has historically not been an important source of productivity gains in SAR (World Bank 2017e; Mallick 2017; Doughtery et al. 2009; Goretti, Kihara, and Salgado 2019). However, since the global financial crisis, between-sector reallocation accounted for more than one-third of productivity growth in 2013-15, up from one-tenth in 2003-08. Meanwhile, within-sector productivity growth slowed sharply, by more than one-third from pre-crisis rates (Figure 2.5.1.2.D).

Most of the post-crisis productivity gains from sectoral reallocation reflected a shift from agriculture, which accounted for about 10 percent of SAR GDP in 2015 but almost half of employment, into services, which accounted for about half of GDP but roughly one-third of employment (Figure 2.5.1.2.E). Agriculture, the region's lowest-productivity sector (with average productivity 22 percent of the advanced-economy average), has roughly one-tenth the productivity of financial services (68 percent of the advanced-economy average) which is the region's most productive sector. In the post-crisis episode, the contribution of services sectors to economy-wide productivity in SAR has declined while that of agriculture has increased, as in other EMDEs (Figure 2.5.1.2.F).

BOX 2.5.1 Labor productivity in South Asia: Trends and drivers (*continued*)

FIGURE 2.5.1.2 Sectoral productivity and employment in SAR

The gains in productivity of the region are mostly accounted for by improvements in TFP growth and capital deepening. Productivity levels in industry and services sectors are much higher relative to the agriculture sector, and have grown significantly over the past three decades. Progress in within-sector productivity growth has played a much larger role in South Asia relative to other EMDEs. The share of employment in trade and financial services increased over time as workers have shifted away from low-productivity agricultural production to these sectors.

A. Productivity decomposition

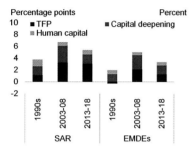

B. Sectoral productivity trends in SAR

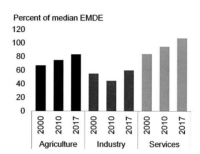

C. Sectoral productivity levels, 2015

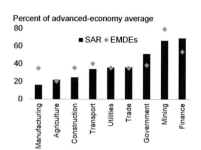

D. Within- and between-sector contributions to productivity growth

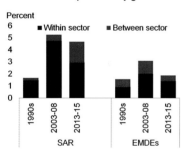

E. Sectoral employment shares

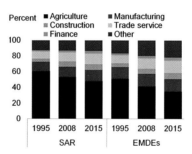

F. Sectoral contribution to productivity

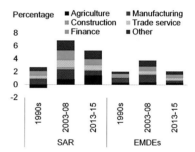

Sources: APO productivity database; Expanded African Sector; Groningen Growth Development Center database; ILOSTAT; OECD STAN; United Nations; World KLEMS.
Note: SAR = South Asia region, EMDE = emerging and developing economy. Productivity refers to labor productivity unless otherwise indicated.
A. SAR sample includes India and Sri Lanka. EMDE sample includes 92 countries.
B. The year brackets refer to the average growth within the corresponding periods. SAR sample includes Afghanistan, Bangladesh, Bhutan, India, Maldives, Nepal, Pakistan, and Sri Lanka. EMDE sample includes 127 EMDEs.
C.-F. EMDE sample includes 46 countries. SAR sample includes 3 countries: India, Pakistan, Sri Lanka.
D. Growth within sector shows the contribution of initial real value added-weighted productivity growth rate of each sector, holding employment shares fixed, and 'between sector' effect shows the contribution arising from changes in sectoral employment shares. Median of the county-specific contributions.
E.-F. "Other" includes transport services and government services. "Manufacturing" includes mining and utilities; "Finance" includes business services.

Other drivers of productivity. In SAR, the contributions of most of the long-run drivers of productivity to productivity growth have remained low compared to other EMDEs and advanced economies despite substantial progress since the early 1990s in a range of these variables (Figure 2.5.1.3.A). Measures of gender equality and trade openness are below other EMDE regions, as demonstrated by very low female participation rates and weak integration with global value chains. In the post-crisis period, the pace

of improvement in several of the long-run determinants of productivity slowed, including average years of schooling, labor force participation, investment, urbanization and economic complexity. Nonetheless, improvements in these drivers did continue. Despite a slowdown in the post-crisis episode, investment continued to contribute to productivity growth more than in other EMDEs and advanced economies (Figure 2.5.1.3.B). By contrast, limited global integration, weakness in control of

BOX 2.5.1 Labor productivity in South Asia: Trends and drivers (*continued*)

FIGURE 2.5.1.3 Drivers of productivity growth in SAR

Many of the drivers remain at the low end of the EMDE regional range suggesting scope for further improvements. While investment consistently supports economic activity, research and development lag significantly behind other regions.

A. Level of drivers of productivity in SAR

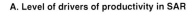
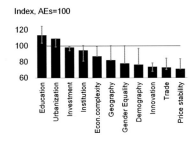

B. Investment

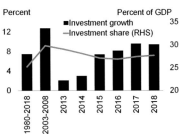

C. Research and development, 2017

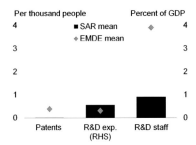

Source: Haver Analytics; United Nations; World Bank.
Note: EMDE = emerging and developing economy. AE = advanced economy. SAR = South Asia region.
A. Unweighted average levels of drivers normalized as average of AEs as 100 and standard deviation is 10. Blue bars represent average within SAR economies in 2018. Orange lines represent range of the average drivers for six regions in 2018. Variables corresponding to the concepts are as follows: Education = years of education, Urbanization = share of population living in urban area, Investment = share of investment to GDP, Institution = WGI Government Effectiveness Index, Econ. Complexity = Economic complexity index, Geography=share of land area which are not in tropical region, Gender equality=female average years of education minus male average years, Demography = share of population under 14, Innovation = Log patent per capita, Trade = (Export+Import)/GDP, Price stability = (-1)*log inflation rate. Numbers of countries are 7 for SAR. See Annex 3.3 for details.
B. Investment growth: growth in gross fixed capital formation; investment share: change in gross fixed capital formation as a share of GDP.
C. R&D exp: research and development expenditures. Aggregates are calculated using constant 2010 U.S. dollar GDP weights.

corruption, low research and development activity, and pervasive informality continued to weigh on SAR's productivity growth (Figure 2.5.1.3.C).

- *Limited global integration.* Export-oriented firms have been more productive than non-exporters in SAR (Figure 2.5.1.4.A). However, SAR's largest economies are less open to trade than the average EMDE or advanced economy (Figure 2.5.1.4.B). Similarly, while FDI inflows have grown, they remain below the EMDE average (Figure 2.5.1.4.C). SAR's limited contacts with more productive foreign firms reduce the potential for technology and information transfer (Figure 2.5.1.4.D; Maiti 2019; Fujimori and Sato 2015; Topalova and Khandelwal 2011).

- *Lack of supporting infrastructure.* Many firms cite infrastructure gaps as important obstacles to their business activities. Firms that cited infrastructure obstacles were found to be less productive in Pakistan and Bangladesh (Grainger and Zhang 2017; Fernandes 2008). The environment has also been less supportive in terms of access to finance (Figure 2.5.1.4.E), with state-owned banks dominating banking system assets (e.g. roughly 70 percent in India) and their balance sheets encumbered by elevated nonperforming loan ratios (usually around 10 percent).

- *Firm characteristics.* Heavy regulatory restrictions have deterred firm growth and prevented firms from becoming more productive, including through productivity-improving investment (Cirera and Cusolito 2019; Kanwar and Sperlich 2019). Complicated tax systems, labor regulations, and licensing requirements have been factors containing the productivity of smaller firms (Figure 2.5.1.4.F). Such factors have encouraged widespread informality, with the informal sector accounting for roughly one-third of GDP and self-employment accounting for 70 percent of total employment in SAR (World Bank 2019f). The potential for productivity gains in SAR from resource reallocation from less productive to more productive firms has been estimated to be large (Lall, Shalizi and Deichmann 2003).[1]

---

[1] For example, equalizing the efficiency of capital and labor allocation across firms to the level of United States could have increased TFP in India as much as 50 percent in the 1990s (Hsieh and Klenow 2009). Similarly, a one-standard deviation decrease in the misallocation of land and buildings in India was estimated to have improved labor productivity by 25 percent between 1989 and 2010 (Duranton et al. 2015). Direct and indirect contribution of services to the total value added of manufacturing sector varies between 33 percent and 50 percent as of 2017 in South Asia (Mercer-Blackman and Ablaza 2018).

BOX 2.5.1 Labor productivity in South Asia: Trends and drivers (*continued*)

FIGURE 2.5.1.4 Policy options in SAR

Low trade openness remains a major constraint for productivity growth in SAR. Continued urbanization in the region can bring agglomeration benefits and enhance productivity if it is accompanied with doing-business reforms given that firms in larger cities tend to be more productive. Low FDI inflows to SAR, compared to other EMDEs, hold back positive spillovers from productive foreign firms. Given their low productivity, state banks weigh on financial sector productivity. Small firms face more severe obstacles to access to finance and their TFP is lower than large firms in South Asia.

A. Export status, location scale, and TFP in SAR

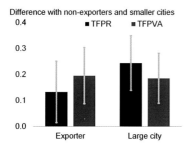

B. Trade openness

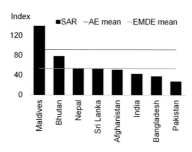

C. FDI inflows

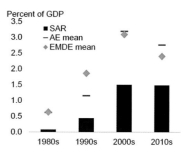

D. Ownership status and TFP in SAR

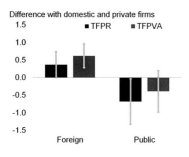

E. Access to finance

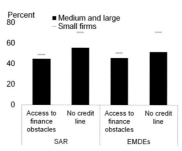

F. Firm size and TFP in SAR

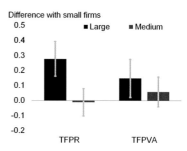

Source: World Bank.

Note: Firm-level TFP is computed using a Cobb-Douglas production function, assuming elasticities of output with respect to inputs are the same across countries in a given income group. See Chapter 3 Appendix 3.3 for a detailed description of calculation and sample coverage. SAR = South Asia region. EMDE = emerging and developing economy. AE = advanced economy.

A.D.E.F. Calculations are based on World Bank Enterprise Surveys. TFPR = Log Total Factor Productivity based on Revenues. TFPVA = Log Total Factor Productivity based on Value Added. The bars represent estimated coefficients of dummy variables for "exporter", "located in a city with population larger than 1 million", "foreign owner", and "public enterprise" in a regression where dependent variable is log TFP and independent variables are the aforementioned dummy variable (large, exporter, etc.), country dummy variables, and year dummy variables. Survey weights are used in all calculations. Sample includes 15,248 firms in 109 EMDEs, including 20 LICs, for the period 2007-17.

B. Trade openness index is described as the ratio of imports and exports to GDP. Aggregates are calculated using constant 2010 U.S. dollar GDP weights. Sample includes 155 EMDEs and 35 AEs.

C. FDI = Foreign direct investment. Aggregates are calculated using constant 2010 U.S. dollar GDP weights. Sample includes 155 EMDEs and 35 AEs.

E. The vertical axis shows the percentage of responses which indicate "access to finance" as a moderate/major/very severe obstacle.

- *Weak human capital.* SAR has lagged most EMDE regions in educational enrolment and attainment, as well as in mortality indicators. In addition, poor operations and human resource management quality has reduced the productivity of firms (Bloom et al. 2012).

- *Gender gaps.* South Asia's female labor force participation rate is far below comparable economies,

and progress in this area is mixed across the region (Goretti, Kihara, and Salgado 2019). Gender gaps in workforce participation, education, and financial inclusion restrain the region's long-term growth potential (Khera 2018).

Robust productivity outlook. Looking ahead, the fact that many of the drivers of productivity have remained at the low end of the EMDE range indicates scope for substantial

BOX 2.5.1 Labor productivity in South Asia: Trends and drivers (*continued*)

FIGURE 2.5.1.5 Productivity prospects in SAR

Rising working-age population shares, educational attainment and life expectancy will improve human capital. Increasing urbanization, accompanied by sectoral reallocation, could support productivity in the region. On the other hand, the region is highly vulnerable to natural disasters, environmental deterioration and climate change risks.

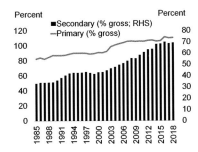

A. School enrollment projections

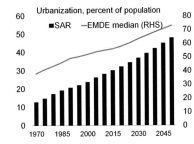

B. Urbanization projections

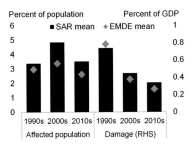

C. Damage from natural disasters

Source: Centre for Research on the Epidemiology of Disasters; United Nations; World Bank.
Note: SAR = South Asia Region. EMDE = Emerging and Developing Economy.
A.-C. Aggregates are calculated using constant 2010 U.S. dollar GDP weights.
A. Last observation is 2018.
B. SAR sample includes 8 South Asian countries. EMDE sample includes 159 countries. Last projection year is 2050.
C. Simple average of aggregate regional damages per year.

improvements. Increasing rates of school enrolment would lift human capital and improve productivity (Figure 2.5.1.5.A). Low urbanization rates compared to other EMDEs limit the benefits from agglomeration in SAR in the near term, but longer-term trends may be expected to raise the contribution of urbanization to productivity growth (Figure 2.5.1.5.B). Recent reforms, such as the new GST system in India and the Inland Revenue Act in Sri Lanka are expected to broaden the tax base and make resources available for human capital and infrastructure investments (World Bank 2018m). Business climates have improved significantly in recent years, as shown for example by shortening approval times for trademarks and patents, lowering restrictions on foreign direct investment, and accelerating investment in energy and transport infrastructure (World Bank 2017f). On the other hand, the region is highly vulnerable to natural disasters, and environmental deterioration and climate change risks weigh on the productivity growth outlook (Figure 2.5.1.5.C). An improved productivity outlook will require the resolution of financial sector issues to unlock credit for investment along with further improvements in the ease of doing business.

The working-age share of the population is expected to increase in SAR until 2045, providing a larger and more prolonged demographic dividend than in most other regions. Against the backdrop of improving human capital, and continued urbanization, this increase in the labor force is expected to contribute to productivity growth in the years ahead (Annex 3.3).

Policy options

Many drivers of productivity are still much lower in SAR than in advanced economies and other EMDE regions, indicating significant room for policy reforms that reduce obstacles to faster productivity growth. Such policies need to be directed at improving the quality as well as quantity of human and physical capital, increasing firm productivity, encouraging efficient sectoral reallocation, and creating business-friendly environments.

Improving factors of production

Support physical capital accumulation, especially infrastructure investment. The post-crisis slowdown in SAR productivity growth mostly reflected weaker capital accumulation. Many firms cite infrastructure gaps as important obstacles to their business activities (Figure 2.5.1.6.A). Moreover, firms facing infrastructure obstacles have been found to be less productive than others in Pakistan and Bangladesh (Grainger and Zhang 2017; Fernandes 2008). Improved infrastructure in the energy

BOX 2.5.1 Labor productivity in South Asia: Trends and drivers (*continued*)

and transportation sectors, as well as technology-oriented capital accumulation, can promote productivity growth and boost international competitiveness (Calderón, Moral-Benito, and Serven 2015).

Strengthen investment in human capital. While the region has benefited from raising life expectancy, reducing mortality, and expanding access to education over the past three decades, there is still significant room for further human capital development (Figure 2.5.1.6.B). With the increasing working-age share of the population in the region, delivering strong output growth and improvements in human capital will be key to progress in productivity growth (Goretti, Kihara, and Salgado 2019). A better educated and healthier workforce can have better and more stable jobs and be more productive (World Bank 2018a). Policies to expand school attendance and support nutrition programs for early childhood development can boost educational outcomes in SAR (Beteille 2019; Torlese and Raju 2018; World Bank 2018n).

Tackle gender gaps. Addressing constraints on economic opportunities for women can provide significant gains in long-term growth (Khera 2018). Key policies such as increasing access to childcare, improving financial inclusion, and ensuring public safety and sanitation can promote gender equality and boost productivity in SAR (Sharafudheen 2017; World Bank 2016g).

Enhancing firm productivity

Increase the region's integration into the global economy. SAR's participation in international trade remains substantially less than that of other regions (Gould, Tan, and Emamgholi 2013). While both imports and exports in SAR, relative to GDP, are lower than in comparable economies, the gap in exports—both within and outside the region—is much larger than that in imports (World Bank 2019v). The empirical evidence on positive productivity spillovers from international trade and FDI inflows indicates that measures to foster FDI and participation in global and regional value chains can lift productivity in SAR. SAR may benefit from shifting FDI flows in the context of recent shifts in global manufacturing activity.

Bangladesh's apparel sector benefited substantially from tailored policies during the 1990s and 2000s, which lifted barriers to international trade and investment and enhanced participation in global value chains. The interaction with foreign firms lifted productivity of local suppliers through the demand for inputs with higher standards and quality. Similarly, Bangladesh's duty-free access to the European Union (EU) from 2001 boosted knitwear exports to the EU between 2000 and 2004, enhanced the productivity of producers, and helped them expand to other export markets (World Bank 2019d).

Improve corporate management practices. Lack of information and training on best management practices seems to limit progress in productivity at the firm level. Governments can help improve the quality of management in the region by organizing training programs and workshops to disseminate information on best management practices. In India, for example, productivity in firms that provided management training increased by 17 percent in the first year of the intervention (Bloom et al. 2013). The low number of patents granted and the limited number of staff engaged in research and development in South Asian firms have also been in part attributed to limited management capacity (Cirera and Maloney 2017). Policies that ensure property rights and create technology hubs can increase firm participation in product innovation and expand their business in foreign markets (Cirera and Maloney 2017).

Address informality. Self-employment accounts for around 70 percent of employment in SAR (Figure 2.5.1.6.C). The level of output informality (DGE and MIMIC) and some obstacles related to business operations are comparable to other EMDEs (Figure 2.5.1.6.D). This sector is associated with lower productivity and weaker access to finance, a barrier to productive investment and a constraint on firms. Encouraging participation in global value chains and enhancing a business-friendly regulatory and tax environment can promote resource reallocation from less productive informal activities to more productive formal ones in SAR (Artuc et al. 2019; Amin, Ohnsorge, and Okou 2019).

With sizable rural populations employed informally in agriculture and large shares of self-employment in the workforce, productivity in the region could benefit significantly from improvements in the productivity of the informal sector. Policies to promote such improvements could include efforts to by improve labor force skills and enhance the functioning of agricultural markets (Goretti, Kihara, and Salgado 2019).

Promoting efficient sectoral reallocation of resources

Promote productivity-enhancing sectoral reallocation and improvements in within-sector allocation of resources.

BOX 2.5.1 Labor productivity in South Asia: Trends and drivers (*continued*)

FIGURE 2.5.1.6 Constraints to productivity growth in SAR

Many firms experience obstacles in their operations due to infrastructure gaps and political instability. The region is behind other EMDEs in terms of some doing business indicators, as well as human capital development, limiting opportunities to improve productivity. Financial development is also weaker compared to other EMDEs, which is reflected in low credit to GDP ratios. Many of these obstacles to doing business contribute to the high levels of informality in the region.

A. Biggest obstacles in SAR

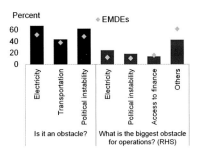

B. Human capital

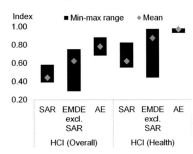

C. Informality

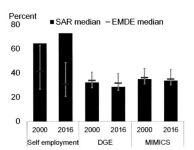

D. Obstacles related to regulations

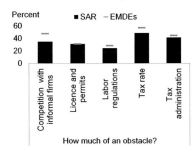

E. Financial development

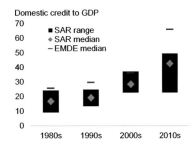

F. Doing business, distance to frontier

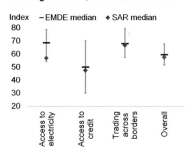

Source: Elgin et al. (2012); United Nations; World Bank.
Note: SAR = South Asia region. EMDE = emerging and developing economy. AE = advanced economy.
A. Calculations are based on World Bank Enterprise Surveys. Survey weights are used in calculations. Left section represents the responses to "How much of an obstacle?" question in World Bank Enterprise Survey. The vertical axis shows the percentage of responses which indicate moderate/major/very severe obstacle. Right section represents the responses to "What is the biggest obstacle affecting the operations of this establishment?" question. Vertical axis shows the percentage of responses. Others include: Access to land, business licensing and permits, corruption, courts, crime/theft/disorder, customs and trade regulations, inadequately educated workforce, labor regulations, practices of competitors in the informal sector, tax administration, tax rates.
B. HCI = Human Capital Index. Range reflects the minimum and maximum of the distribution across countries. Higher values of the index reflect better human capital development. See World Bank (2018a) for details of the methodology. Aggregates are calculated using U.S. dollar GDP weights at 2010 prices and exchange rates.
C. DGE = dynamic general equilibrium model. MIMIC = multiple indicators multiple causes model. Both DGE and MIMIC estimates measure the informal output in percent of official GDP.
D. Calculations are based on World Bank Enterprise Surveys and represents the responses to "How much of an obstacle?" question. The vertical axis shows the percentage of responses which indicate moderate/major/very severe obstacle.
F. SAR sample includes 8 South Asian countries. EMDE sample includes 159 countries. The orange whiskers indicate interquartile range of EMDEs.

SAR has received a welcome boost to productivity from intersectoral reallocation of resources since the global financial crisis. A policy challenge will be to maintain this momentum. The productivity gains from sectoral reallocation from agriculture to more productive sectors can be increased if accompanied by improved local services and urban planning (Ellis and Roberts 2016; World Bank 2019s). Such policies should be complemented by measures to increase the productivity of the agriculture sector (Cusolito and Maloney 2018).

The contribution of within-sector productivity growth has weakened substantially since the global financial crisis. This calls for a renewed effort to promote the reallocation of capital and labor to more productive firms within sectors. By one estimate, such interfirm reallocation could unlock 40-60 percent productivity gains in India (Hsieh and Klenow 2009). Productivity-enhancing interfirm reallocation could be encouraged by policies to foster competition and by reducing regulatory burdens that discourage firm growth (Duranton et al. 2016).

BOX 2.5.1 Labor productivity in South Asia: Trends and drivers (*continued*)

Encourage intersectoral linkages. Intersectoral linkages play an important role in improving productivity through value chains in South Asia. For instance, progress in information and communication technologies provides positive productivity spillovers to broader services sectors (Krishna et al. 2016). Reducing barriers to trade and encouraging intersectoral and regional linkages can lift productivity through technology spillovers. For example, in India, Bangladesh, and Sri Lanka the creation of special economic zones has helped expand exports and product diversification (Aggarwal, Hoppe, and Walkenhorst 2019).

Creating a growth-friendly environment

Unlock access to finance. Infrastructure spending in recent years has eased supply-side bottlenecks in SAR. However, poor access to finance remains a hindrance for the region, particularly given the weaknesses on corporate and financial sector balance sheets. Weak access to finance constrains small and medium-sized firms—especially women-owned businesses—and holds back firm-level productivity gains in India (Figure 2.5.1.6.E; World Bank 2013a; Schiantarelli and Srivastava 1997).

Improve the ease of doing business. Despite improvements in recent years, SAR is still among the least business-friendly EMDE regions, reflected in distance-to-frontier scores in doing business statistics (2.5.1.6.F). India's economic reforms during the early 1990s enhanced openness and eased regulatory burdens in the services sector, and these were followed by a significant expansion in domestic and foreign investment. In India also, the entry of foreign service providers was associated with more competitive business services, which supported productivity gains in the manufacturing sector (Arnold et al. 2016).

Ensure macroeconomic and political stability. Economic and financial crises have proven to hold back productivity in the region, as observed after the global financial crisis and in economic downturns in India and Pakistan in the 1990s. Political instability seems to be a more severe obstacle to the operations of South Asian firms than in other EMDE regions (World Bank 2013b, 2013c). Strengthening economic policy institutions, improving monetary and fiscal policy frameworks, and enhancing financial regulation and supervision can help to provide a stable macroeconomic framework for firms, reduce uncertainty, and boost productivity.

SUB-SAHARAN AFRICA

Growth in Sub-Saharan Africa moderated to a slower-than-expected 2.4 percent in 2019. Activity was dampened by softening external demand, heightened global policy uncertainty, and falling commodity prices. Domestic fragilities in several countries further constrained activity. Growth is projected to firm to 2.9 percent in 2020 and strengthen to 3.2 percent in 2021-22—notably weaker than previous projections. The growth pickup is predicated on improving investor confidence in some large economies, a strengthening cyclical recovery among industrial commodity exporters along with a pickup in oil production, and robust growth among several exporters of agricultural commodities. Nonetheless, these growth rates will be insufficient to make significant progress in reducing poverty in many countries in the region, highlighting the need for lasting improvements in labor productivity to bolster growth over the medium term. Downside risks to the outlook include a sharper-than-expected deceleration in major trading partners; increased investor risk aversion and capital outflows triggered by elevated debt burdens; and growing insecurity.

Recent developments

The feeble economic recovery in Sub-Saharan Africa has lost momentum, with growth in 2019 estimated to have edged down to 2.4 percent, from 2.6 percent in 2018. This was a weaker pace than anticipated in June (Figure 2.6.1.A). Intensifying global headwinds such as decelerating activity in major trading partners, elevated policy uncertainty, and falling commodity prices, have been compounded by domestic fragilities in several countries.

In Angola, Nigeria, and South Africa—the three largest economies in the region—growth was subdued in 2019, remaining well below historical averages and contracting for a fifth consecutive year on a per capita basis. Activity in Nigeria was lackluster, as both macroeconomic policy and the business environment remain unconducive to strong domestic demand. Growth in 2019 is estimated to have remained broadly unchanged at 2 percent, as the agricultural sector continued to underperform due to lingering insurgency in the Northeast and farmers-herdsmen clashes, while

unreliable electricity supply constrained manufacturing activity. Some of this weakness was, however, offset by increased oil production.

In South Africa, growth remained anemic in 2019 as it fell to an estimated 0.4 percent. Weak growth momentum has reflected an array of overlapping constraints. These include persistent policy uncertainty, constrained fiscal space, subdued business confidence, infrastructure bottlenecks—especially in electricity supply—and weakening external demand, particularly from the Euro Area and China. In addition, financial stresses at the public energy utility have worsened the government budget balance and raised debt sustainability concerns, weighing further on sentiment (Figure 2.6.1.B).

Activity in Angola is estimated to have contracted by 0.7 percent in 2019, as oil output declined for the fourth consecutive year due to lower yields from aging fields and postponed investment in new capacity. Nonetheless, growth in the non-oil sector strengthened further as several key reforms continued to improve the business environment.

In Sudan, the fourth largest economy in the region, political instability, alongside an ongoing currency crisis, has caused activity to contract

Note: This section was prepared by Rudi Steinbach. Research assistance was provided by Jankeesh Sandhu.

FIGURE 2.6.1. SSA: Recent developments

The recovery in Sub-Saharan Africa has stalled, as intensifying global headwinds have compounded domestic weakness in several economies. In South Africa, power cuts and financial stress constrained growth and worsened fiscal deficits. More broadly, lower commodity prices are weighing on activity in commodity exporters and contributing to deteriorating current account balances. Inflation has been mostly subdued—helped in part by lower oil prices. Persistent budget deficits have partly reflected weaker commodity revenues and growing interest burdens.

A. Growth

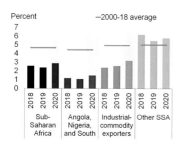

B. South Africa budget deficit and support for Eskom

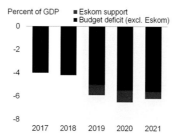

C. Commodity price changes

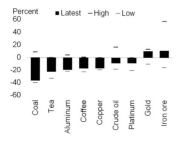

D. Current account balances

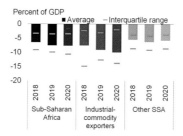

E. Inflation, annual rate

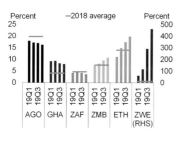

F. Fiscal balances

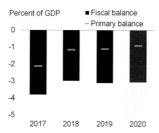

Source: Haver Analytics; National Treasury, Republic of South Africa; *World Economic Outlook*, International Monetary Fund; World Bank; World Bank Pink Sheet; Zimbabwe National Statistics.
Note: "Industrial-commodity exporters" represents oil and metal exporting countries. "Other SSA" includes agricultural commodity exporting and commodity importing countries.
A. Aggregate growth rates calculated using GDP weights at 2010 prices and market exchange rates. "Industrial-commodity exporters" excludes Angola, Nigeria, and South Africa.
B. Eskom is the South African public energy utility. Years represent fiscal years; for example, the year 2017 is the 2017/18 fiscal year.
C. Bars represent the percentage change in the November 2019 monthly price relative to January 2018. "High" and "Low" represent the respective peaks and troughs of price changes, in percent, since January 2018.
D. Unweighted averages of country groupings.
E. AGO = Angola, GHA = Ghana, ZAF = South Africa, ZMB = Zambia, ETH = Ethiopia, ZWE = Zimbabwe. 2019Q4 reflects the average of October and November.
F. Unweighted averages.

sharply. However, the formation of a three-year interim government to oversee the country's transition to democracy helped improve stability in the second half of last year.

Beyond the large economies, growth deteriorated in several industrial commodity exporters in 2019 as weaker prices and softer demand dampened activity in extractives sectors (Democratic Republic of Congo, Liberia, Namibia; Figure 2.6.1.C). In contrast, growth accelerated in some countries as investments in new oil and mining capacity boosted activity (Ghana, Guinea, Mauritania).

Among exporters of agricultural commodities, growth rates have been more robust, notwithstanding some mild slowdowns. Estimates for 2019 indicate that growth averaged in excess of 5 percent, as sustained public investment in infrastructure continued to support activity (Togo, Uganda). Yet, growth softened in some other countries as decelerating external demand and lower commodity prices constrained export revenues (Madagascar, Rwanda). In others, agricultural production suffered from severe drought (Senegal, Zimbabwe), or late rains (Kenya). Zimbabwe also suffered a sharp rise in inflation that continued to squeeze real incomes, resulting in a large contraction in economic activity, estimated at 7.5 percent. Activity has been further constrained by persistent shortages of food, fuel, electricity, and foreign exchange.

Current account deficits are estimated to have widened, on average, across the region (Figure 2.6.1.D). In several countries, capital imports related to large infrastructure projects underpinned deficits (Mauritania, Mozambique, Niger, Uganda). In others, weaker export performances, due to softening external demand and lower commodity prices, were responsible for larger external balances (Angola, Chad, Republic of Congo). In some countries, current account balances improved as a result of import compression due to weak domestic demand (Namibia, South Africa, Zambia). In others, infrastructure improvements and reforms in export-oriented industries led to increased exports and an improved trade balance (Burkina Faso, Côte d'Ivoire). Current account financing was more challenging for most of 2019, as growing concerns over global growth prospects and heightened trade tensions weighed on investor sentiment and capital inflows. Eurobond issuances during the first ten months of 2019 were down by one-third compared to the same period in 2018.

Inflation continued to moderate in most of the region last year, partly reflecting lower oil prices as well as earlier monetary policy tightening in some countries (Figure 2.6.1.E). This allowed authorities in several countries to adopt more accommodative monetary policy stances (Angola, Botswana, Kenya, Mauritius, Mozambique, Namibia, South Africa). In some countries, however, inflation accelerated amid rising food prices (Ethiopia, Zambia, Zimbabwe) and exchange rate pressures (Zambia, Zimbabwe).

Large and persistent budget deficits have reflected growing interest burdens, as well as weaker commodity revenues among industrial-commodity exporters and sustained public investment among exporters of agricultural commodities (Figure 2.6.1.F). In several countries, budget balances have improved due to a combination of fiscal discipline, more efficient domestic resource mobilization, tax administration reforms, and reforms of energy subsidies (Benin, Cabo Verde, Cote d'Ivoire, Gabon, Mali, Sierra Leone).

Outlook

Growth in the region is expected to firm to 2.9 percent in 2020, and accelerate further to an average of 3.2 percent in 2021-22 (Figure 2.6.2.A). The pickup assumes that investor confidence improves in some large economies, that energy bottlenecks ease, that a pickup in oil production contributes to a cyclical recovery among industrial commodity exporters, and that robust growth continues among exporters of agricultural commodities. However, the forecast for 2020-22 is 0.4 percentage point lower than previously projected, reflecting weaker demand from key trading partners, lower commodity prices, and adverse domestic developments in several countries.

On a per capita basis, the outlook translates into Sub-Saharan Africa growth of 0.3 percent in 2020,

firming to an average of 0.7 percent in 2021-22. In the projection, per capita incomes rise by more than 4 percent per year in several countries that, together, account for one-tenth of the region's poor (e.g., Côte d'Ivoire, Ethiopia, Rwanda, Senegal). However, per capita incomes contract among some of the largest economies that account for one-third of the region's poor (Angola, Nigeria, Sudan). Projected per capita growth for the region is insufficient to yield significant progress in poverty alleviation. Lasting improvements in labor productivity are needed to bolster growth over the medium term (Box 2.6.1; Figure 2.6.2.B).

Growth in Nigeria is expected to remain subdued. The macroeconomic framework—characterized by multiple exchange rates, foreign exchange restrictions, high persistent inflation, and a central bank targeting manifold objectives—does not provide a firm anchor for confidence. Growing uncertainty about the direction of government policies is expected to further dampen the outlook. Growth is projected to remain broadly unchanged, rising only to an average of 2.1 percent in 2020-22. This is weaker than previous projections, reflecting softer external demand, lower oil prices, and a slower-than-previously-expected improvement in oil production in view of the lack of much-needed reforms.

In South Africa, growth is expected to firm to 0.9 percent in 2020, before strengthening to an average of 1.4 percent in 2021-22. This assumes that the new administration's structural reform agenda gathers pace, that policy uncertainty wanes, and that investment—both public and private—gradually recovers. The outlook is, however, markedly weaker than previous projections. Increasingly binding infrastructure constraints—notably in electricity supply—are expected to inhibit domestic growth, while export momentum will be hindered by weak external demand.

Growth in Angola is projected to rise to 1.5 percent in 2020 and to average 2.7 percent in 2021-22. This projection assumes that ongoing structural reforms—supported by prudent monetary policy and fiscal consolidation—provide greater macroeconomic stability, continue to

FIGURE 2.6.2 SSA: Outlook and risks

Growth in the region is projected to firm somewhat as investor confidence in some of the large economies improves and oil production in major oil exporters picks up, while activity among exporters of agricultural commodities remains solid. Per capita growth, however, will remain below 1 percent. Several downside risks could materialize, including slower-than-expected growth in major trading partners, episodes of financial stress given rising debt vulnerabilities, and disruptions to activity amid increased displacement of populations and growing climate risks.

A. GDP growth

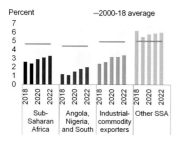

B. GDP growth per capita

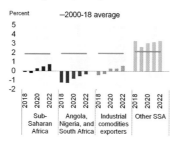

C. Cumulative revisions to 2020 growth in key trading partners

D. Government debt in SSA

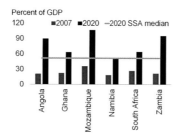

E. Internally displaced populations and countries requiring external assistance for food

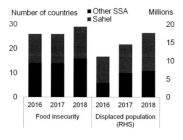

F. Extreme weather events in SSA

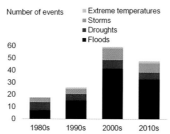

Source: The Emergency Events Database; Université Catholique de Louvain; United Nations Food and Agricultural Organization; United Nations High Commissioner for Refugees (UNHCR); World Bank; *World Economic Outlook*, International Monetary Fund.

A.-B. Aggregate growth rates calculated using GDP weights at 2010 prices and market exchange rates. "Industrial-commodity exporters" excludes Angola, Nigeria, and South Africa.

C. Cumulative revisions to the 2020 growth forecasts since the June 2018 *Global Economic Prospects* report.

D. "2020 SSA median" reflects the median of 47 countries.

E. "Food insecurity" reflects countries in SSA requiring external assistance for food. These countries are expected to lack the resources to deal with reported critical problems of food insecurity. The sample includes countries with a lack of food availability, widespread lack of access to food, or severe but localized problems. "Displaced population" reflects only internally displaced populations (IDPs) who are protected or assisted by UNHCR. These are also not necessarily representative of the entire IDP population in a given country.

F. Data reflect annual averages of extreme weather events in SSA as of October 31, 2019.

improve the business environment and bolster private investment. In particular, recently announced oil-sector reforms are expected to support a recovery in oil production.

Elsewhere in the region, growth is forecast to strengthen, stabilizing just below 5 percent in 2021-22. In the West African Economic and Monetary Union (WAEMU), growth is expected to average 6.7 percent. Among the region's exporters of agricultural commodities, sustained strong public infrastructure spending, combined with increased private sector activity (Madagascar, Rwanda, Uganda), or continued reforms to raise the productivity and competitiveness of export-oriented sectors (Burkina Faso, Côte d'Ivoire), will continue to support output. In Kenya, growth is expected to remain solid, but soften somewhat as accommodative monetary policy does not fully offset the impact of a fiscal tightening.

In contrast, the ongoing cyclical recovery among oil and metals exporters will be more sluggish, reflecting weaker external demand and softer commodity prices. In some countries, growth is projected to moderate somewhat over the forecast, in part due to slowing resource production (Democratic Republic of Congo, Ghana). Activity in Ghana—the region's fifth largest economy—is expected to soften from the 7 percent growth of 2019 partly due to slowing oil production as much-needed maintenance on various oil fields is carried out to ensure their long-term viability. Longer-term growth prospects will, however, be supported by the improved strength of the financial sector following much-needed reforms implemented during 2018-19. Despite the global headwinds, investments in new oil and mining capacity are expected to support faster growth in several oil and metals exporters (Botswana, Cameroon, Chad, Guinea, Mozambique, Namibia). In Sudan, the business climate is expected to improve if tensions continue their recent easing during the 3-year political transition.

Risks

The balance of risks for Sub-Saharan Africa is firmly to the downside. A sharper-than-expected deceleration in major trading partners such as

China, the Euro Area, or the United States, would substantially lower export revenues and investment. Together these economies account for 40 percent of the region's goods exports and one-third of FDI inflows, and their growth prospects continue to be downgraded (Figure 2.6.2.C). China, in particular, accounts for one-half of global metals demand and one-quarter of global oil demand (World Bank 2018o). A faster-than-expected slowdown in China would cause a sharp fall in commodity prices and, given Sub-Saharan Africa's heavy reliance on extractive sectors for export and fiscal revenues, weigh heavily on regional activity.

Government debt in the region is expected to reach 62 percent of GDP, on average, in 2020, up from its trough of 39 percent of GDP in 2011. This broad-based rise in government debt has led to sharp increases in interest burdens, crowding out non-interest expenditure and raising concerns about debt sustainability. Countries with elevated debt burdens are susceptible to sudden increases in investor risk aversion (Angola, Ghana, Mozambique, Namibia, South Africa, Zambia; Figure 2.6.2.D). This can lead to sizable currency depreciations, capital outflows, and increases in borrowing costs as risk premia rise sharply. Where debt is largely denominated in foreign currency, sharp currency depreciations would make servicing debt more challenging.

Ballooning debt burdens of state-owned enterprises represent substantial contingent liability risks in several countries (Ethiopia, Ghana, South Africa, The Gambia); materialization of these risks could damage already-fragile fiscal outlooks (Bachmair and Bogoev 2018; Bova et al. 2016). In addition to raising fiscal sustainability concerns, economic activity can be directly affected by potential disruptions at state-owned enterprises, particularly if they provide essentials such as electricity. Some countries are, however, implementing reforms to improve the functioning of state-owned enterprises and to alleviate their government's exposure to contingent liabilities (Ethiopia, Ghana, The Gambia).

Insecurity, conflicts, and insurgencies—particularly in the Sahel—would weigh on economic activity and food security in several economies (Burkina Faso, Chad, Ethiopia, Mali, Niger, Nigeria), if they were to intensify further or spread geographically (Figure 2.6.2.E; FAO 2019; UNHCR 2019). Moreover, the large populations that are forcibly displaced by these conflicts cluster in areas that often become a source of further instability, with poverty rates being worse than in their places of origin (Beegle and Christiaensen 2019).

Extreme weather events are becoming more frequent as the climate changes, posing a significant downside risk to activity due to the disproportionate role played by agriculture in many economies in the region (Figure 2.6.2.F). The devastation caused by the tropical cyclones that hit low-income countries in East and Southern Africa in 2019 bear testimony to this, as do persistent drought conditions, particularly in the Sahel and Southern Africa. As droughts continue to suppress agricultural output, they increase food insecurity, raise food price inflation, exacerbate poverty levels, and often contribute to forced displacement of populations (IPCC 2019).

TABLE 2.6.1 Sub-Saharan Africa forecast summary

(Real GDP growth at market prices in percent, unless indicated otherwise)

Percentage point differences
from June 2019 projections

	2017	2018	2019e	2020f	2021f	2022f	2019e	2020f	2021f
EMDE SSA, GDP[1]	2.7	2.6	2.4	2.9	3.1	3.3	-0.5	-0.4	-0.4
(Average including countries with full national accounts and balance of payments data only)[2]									
EMDE SSA, GDP[2,3]	2.7	2.6	2.5	2.9	3.1	3.3	-0.4	-0.4	-0.4
GDP per capita (U.S. dollars)	-0.1	-0.1	-0.2	0.3	0.5	0.7	-0.4	-0.4	-0.4
PPP GDP	2.9	2.8	2.7	3.1	3.3	3.5	-0.4	-0.4	-0.4
Private consumption	2.5	2.4	2.1	2.6	2.8	2.8	-0.1	-0.1	0.0
Public consumption	1.2	2.5	2.7	2.4	2.5	2.6	0.1	-0.1	-0.2
Fixed investment	4.5	6.2	3.1	3.1	4.1	5.5	-2.8	-3.0	-2.6
Exports, GNFS[4]	6.1	3.1	1.6	1.5	2.6	3.0	-0.7	-1.6	-0.4
Imports, GNFS[4]	1.0	5.9	2.4	2.5	3.1	3.6	-0.6	-0.9	-0.6
Net exports, contribution to growth	1.5	-0.7	-0.2	-0.3	-0.1	-0.1	0.0	-0.2	0.1
Memo items: GDP									
SSA excluding Nigeria, South Africa, and Angola	4.8	4.4	4.1	4.6	4.7	4.8	-0.5	-0.3	-0.3
Oil exporters[5]	1.5	1.4	1.7	2.3	2.3	2.4	-0.4	-0.2	-0.3
CFA countries[6]	3.5	4.2	4.6	5.1	5.2	5.2	-0.4	0.1	0.1
CEMAC	0.0	1.4	2.3	3.3	3.4	2.9	-0.8	0.2	0.1
WAEMU	6.6	6.6	6.4	6.4	6.5	6.9	-0.2	-0.1	0.0
SSA3	1.0	1.2	1.1	1.5	1.8	2.0	-0.5	-0.5	-0.4
Nigeria	0.8	1.9	2.0	2.1	2.1	2.1	-0.1	-0.1	-0.3
South Africa	1.4	0.8	0.4	0.9	1.3	1.5	-0.7	-0.6	-0.4
Angola	-0.1	-1.2	-0.7	1.5	2.4	3.0	-1.7	-1.4	-0.4

Source: World Bank.
Note: e = estimate; f = forecast. EMDE = emerging market and developing economies. World Bank forecasts are frequently updated based on new information and changing (global) circumstances. Consequently, projections presented here may differ from those contained in other Bank documents, even if basic assessments of countries' prospects do not differ at any given moment in time.
1. GDP and expenditure components are measured in 2010 prices and market exchange rates. Excludes Central African Republic, São Tomé and Príncipe, Somalia, and South Sudan.
2. Subregion aggregate excludes Central African Republic, São Tomé and Príncipe, Somalia, and South Sudan, for which data limitations prevent the forecasting of GDP components.
3. Subregion growth rates may differ from the most recent edition of Africa's Pulse (https://www.worldbank.org/en/region/afr/publication/africas-pulse) due to data revisions and the inclusion of the Central African Republic and São Tomé and Principe in the subregion aggregate of that publication.
4. Exports and imports of goods and non-factor services (GNFS).
5. Includes Angola, Cameroon, Chad, Republic of Congo, Gabon, Ghana, Nigeria, and Sudan.
6. Includes Benin, Burkina Faso, Cameroon, Central African Republic, Chad, Republic of Congo, Côte d'Ivoire, Equatorial Guinea, Gabon, Mali, Niger, Senegal, and Togo.
To download the data in this table, please visit www.worldbank.org/gep.

TABLE 2.6.2 **Sub-Saharan Africa country forecasts**[1]

(Real GDP growth at market prices in percent, unless indicated otherwise)

Percentage point differences
from June 2019 projections

	2017	2018	2019e	2020f	2021f	2022f	2019e	2020f	2021f
Angola	-0.1	-1.2	-0.7	1.5	2.4	3.0	-1.7	-1.4	-0.4
Benin	5.8	6.7	6.4	6.7	6.7	6.7	-0.1	0.2	0.2
Botswana	2.9	4.5	4.0	4.1	4.2	4.2	-0.2	0.2	0.2
Burkina Faso	6.3	6.8	6.0	6.0	6.0	6.0	0.0	0.0	0.0
Burundi	0.5	1.6	1.8	2.0	2.1	2.2	0.0	-0.1	0.1
Cabo Verde	3.7	5.1	5.0	5.0	5.0	5.0	0.6	0.4	0.3
Cameroon	3.5	4.1	4.0	4.2	4.3	4.5	-0.2	-0.2	-0.3
Chad	-3.0	2.6	3.0	5.5	4.8	4.8	-0.4	-0.1	0.0
Comoros	3.8	3.4	1.7	4.8	3.7	3.6	-1.4	1.6	0.5
Congo, Dem. Rep.	3.7	5.8	4.3	3.9	3.4	3.6	-1.6	-2.6	-3.4
Congo, Rep.	-1.8	1.6	2.2	4.6	1.9	2.4	-3.2	3.1	0.0
Côte d'Ivoire	7.7	7.4	7.3	7.0	7.1	7.1	-0.1	-0.3	-0.2
Equatorial Guinea	-4.7	-6.1	-4.3	-2.3	1.0	-4.8	-2.1	-0.4	2.8
Eswatini	2.0	2.4	1.3	2.6	2.5	2.5	0.2	1.0	0.8
Ethiopia[2]	10.0	7.9	9.0	6.3	6.4	7.1	1.1	-1.9	-1.8
Gabon	0.5	0.8	2.9	3.0	3.2	3.3	0.1	-0.7	-0.7
Gambia, The	4.8	6.6	6.0	6.3	5.8	5.5	0.6	1.1	0.8
Ghana	8.1	6.3	7.0	6.8	5.2	4.6	-0.6	-0.2	-0.6
Guinea	10.0	5.8	5.9	6.0	6.0	6.0	0.0	0.0	0.0
Guinea-Bissau	5.9	3.8	4.6	4.9	5.0	5.0	0.3	0.1	-0.5
Kenya	4.9	6.3	5.8	6.0	5.8	5.8	0.1	0.1	-0.2
Lesotho	-0.4	1.5	2.6	0.7	2.1	2.8	1.1	0.3	-2.0
Liberia	2.5	1.2	-1.4	1.4	3.4	4.2	-1.8	-0.2	2.1
Madagascar	4.3	5.1	4.7	5.3	4.4	5.0	-0.5	0.0	-0.7
Malawi	4.0	3.5	4.4	4.8	5.2	5.3	-0.1	0.1	0.1
Mali	5.3	4.7	5.0	5.0	4.9	4.9	0.0	0.1	0.1
Mauritania	3.0	3.6	6.4	5.7	5.8	8.7	-0.3	-0.1	-0.2
Mauritius	3.8	3.8	3.9	3.9	4.0	4.0	0.0	0.0	0.5
Mozambique	3.7	3.4	2.0	3.7	4.2	4.4	0.0	0.2	0.0
Namibia	-0.9	-0.1	-0.5	0.9	1.7	1.9	-1.4	-0.6	-0.2
Niger	4.9	6.5	6.3	6.0	5.6	11.9	-0.2	0.0	0.0
Nigeria	0.8	1.9	2.0	2.1	2.1	2.1	-0.1	-0.1	-0.3
Rwanda	6.1	8.6	8.5	8.1	8.0	8.0	0.7	0.1	0.5
Senegal	7.1	6.8	6.3	6.8	7.0	7.0	-0.5	-0.2	0.0
Seychelles	4.3	4.1	3.5	3.3	3.3	3.4	0.1	0.3	0.1
Sierra Leone	3.8	3.5	4.8	4.9	4.9	5.0	-0.6	-0.5	-0.3
South Africa	1.4	0.8	0.4	0.9	1.3	1.5	-0.7	-0.6	-0.4
Sudan	4.3	-2.3	-2.6	-1.4	-0.6	0.2	-0.7	-0.1	0.2
Tanzania	6.8	5.4	5.6	5.8	6.1	6.2	0.2	0.1	0.0
Togo	4.4	4.9	5.3	5.5	5.5	5.5	0.3	0.3	0.4
Uganda[2]	3.9	5.9	6.1	6.5	5.9	6.0	0.0	0.0	0.1
Zambia	4.1	3.1	1.8	2.6	2.6	4.0	-0.7	-0.2	-0.2
Zimbabwe	4.7	3.5	-7.5	2.7	2.5	2.8	-4.4	-0.8	-2.4

Source: World Bank.

Note: e = estimate; f = forecast. World Bank forecasts are frequently updated based on new information and changing (global) circumstances. Consequently, projections presented here may differ from those contained in other Bank documents, even if basic assessments of countries' prospects do not significantly differ at any given moment in time.

1. GDP and expenditure components are measured in 2010 prices and market exchange rates. Excludes Central African Republic, São Tomé and Príncipe, Somalia, and South Sudan.
2. Fiscal-year based numbers.
To download the data in this table, please visit www.worldbank.org/gep.

BOX 2.6.1 Labor productivity in Sub-Saharan Africa: Trends and drivers

Since 2013, Sub-Saharan Africa has experienced a broad-based slowdown in labor productivity growth. Productivity growth has all but stalled amid falling commodity prices, weakening external demand, and growing domestic fragilities. In the decade prior to the global financial crisis, productivity growth benefited from strengthening institutions, stronger investment, infrastructure development, improving human capital, and better macroeconomic policy frameworks, but the pace of improvement has stagnated. Productivity in the region is still only one-half of that in EMDEs and roughly one-tenth of that in advanced economies. Ambitious policy efforts will be needed to generate the productivity growth required for per capita incomes in Sub-Saharan Africa to reach those of its EMDE peers, let alone those of advanced economies. To stimulate labor productivity growth, the region needs to implement policies that boost agricultural productivity, increase resilience to climate change, broaden economic diversification, and continue human capital development.

Introduction

In one of the steepest declines of any emerging market and developing economy (EMDE) region, labor productivity growth has slowed sharply in Sub-Saharan Africa (SSA) since the global financial crisis, from about 2.9 percent during the pre-crisis period of 2003-2008 to 0.5 percent during 2013-18 (Figure 2.6.1.1.A). The slowdown was particularly sharp among industrial commodity exporters—exporters of oil and metals account for roughly 80 percent of the region's GDP—whereas productivity growth continued to accelerate among several agricultural commodity exporters.[1] This deceleration returns productivity growth to near its 1990s average (-0.4 percent) and ends a period of solid growth of 2-3 percent throughout the pre-crisis period, when it was supported by a favorable external environment, strengthening institutions, improving human capital, and better macroeconomic policy frameworks.

SSA's productivity levels are low, at around one-half of the EMDE average and 11 percent of the advanced-economy average in 2018 (Figure 2.6.1.1.B). However, if a few high-productivity countries are excluded, SSA's productivity levels are far lower, at a mere 3 percent of the advanced-economy average. At near-nil productivity growth, SSA's productivity levels have now started to further diverge from advanced-economy averages. Among EMDE regions, only the Middle East and North Africa has a slower pace of convergence, but starting from productivity levels that average about four times those of Sub-Saharan Africa. Absent major policy efforts to lift productivity growth, its

stagnation offers dim prospects for the nearly 60 percent of the global extreme poor that currently reside in SSA.

Against this backdrop, this box addresses the following questions:

1. How has productivity evolved in the region?

2. What are the factors associated with productivity growth in the region?

3. What policy options are available to boost productivity growth?

This box defines productivity as labor productivity, represented by real GDP per person employed (at 2010 prices and exchange rates). Growth in labor productivity is decomposed into the contributions made by changes in the standard factor inputs (human and physical capital per worker) and the effective use of these inputs, as captured by total factor productivity, assuming a Cobb-Douglas production function. Cross-country comparisons of labor productivity use market exchange rates in 2010 to convert national currency units into U.S. dollars. Data are available for 44 EMDEs in SSA, of which 21 are oil or metals exporters, 19 are exporters of agricultural commodities, and 5 are commodity importers.[2]

Evolution of regional productivity

Robust pre-crisis productivity growth. Productivity growth in SSA started improving in the mid-1990s, as the region recovered from some of the adverse factors that had weighed heavily on activity in the 1980s and early 1990s.[3] Prior to the crisis, productivity growth rose sharply, to 2.9

Note: This box was prepared by Rudi Steinbach, with contributions from Sinem Kilic Celik, and builds upon analysis in Chapter 3. Research assistance was provided by Jankeesh Sandhu and Shijie Shi.

[1] An economy is defined as a commodity exporter when, on average in 2012-14, either (1) total commodities exports accounted for 30 percent or more of total goods exports or (2) exports of any single commodity accounted for 20 percent or more of total goods exports. Economies for which these thresholds are met as a result of reexports are excluded. Commodity importers are economies not classified as commodity exporters.

[2] One country, Chad, is classified as both an oil and an agricultural-commodity exporter.

[3] Adverse developments in the 1980s and early 1990s included a multitude of sovereign debt, banking, and currency crises, debt overhang, low commodity prices, weak investment, and severe conflicts and political instability in several countries (Calderón and Boreux 2016; Reinhart and Rogoff 2009; Straus 2012).

BOX 2.6.1 Labor productivity in Sub-Saharan Africa: Trends and drivers (*continued*)

percent, on average during 2003-08. Growth was supported by a favorable external environment, including a commodity price boom between 2001-11 that fueled an inflow of foreign capital and unprecedented investment and benefited many of the region's low-income countries (Figure 2.6.1.2.A; Khan et al. 2016; Steinbach 2019; World Bank 2019a). Faster productivity growth was also supported by improvements in education, health care, infrastructure, financial access, and trade openness (Calderón and Servén 2010; Cole and Neumayer 2006; Shiferaw et al. 2015; World Bank 2018k, 2019z).

In the 2000s, productivity growth in the region's industrial commodity-exporting countries picked up sooner and more sharply than in agricultural commodity exporters and commodity importers. In addition to the higher export revenues brought about by rising commodity prices, oil and metal exporting countries benefited from substantial investments in commodity production and exploration (Khan et al. 2016; Schodde 2013). The productivity growth pick-up in industrial-commodity exporters was also driven by country-specific developments. In South Africa—the region's largest metal exporter—productivity growth accelerated sharply after the country's transition to democracy in 1994, thanks in part to improving policy frameworks, increased trade openness and foreign capital inflows (Arora 2005; Du Plessis and Smit 2007). By the mid-2000s, the more than 20 percent decline in productivity during the final decade of Apartheid had been fully reversed.

Stalling post-crisis productivity. Since the global financial crisis, productivity growth has fallen sharply in SSA, to near-nil (0.5 percent) on average during the post-crisis period (2013-18). Productivity growth slowed in a broad range of economies, with post-crisis productivity growth falling below its pre-crisis average in over 60 percent of countries. Oil- and metal-exporting countries experienced the steepest slowdowns amid the commodity price slump of 2014-16, as productivity growth fell to 0 percent in the post-crisis period, from 3.2 percent growth pre-crisis.

Post-crisis productivity growth in agricultural commodity-exporters and commodity importers was more resilient, particularly among the former for whom it strengthened to 2.3 percent. Despite the sharp fall in agricultural commodity prices during the commodity price slump—albeit less severe than the drop in industrial commodity prices—sustained productivity growth was supported by improving macroeconomic policy frameworks, investment in infrastructure, and continuous efforts to improve business environments. Doing Business rankings improved

FIGURE 2.6.1.1 Productivity in SSA in regional comparison

Productivity growth in Sub-Saharan Africa (SSA) rose sharply in the pre-crisis period, reflecting a favorable external environment and improvements in key drivers of productivity. Stronger productivity growth also allowed a large productivity gap between advanced economies and SSA EMDEs to narrow slightly over this period. Since then, productivity growth in the region has slowed sharply. At near-zero productivity growth, the region's productivity levels have, on average, diverged from advanced economy levels during the post-crisis period.

A. Productivity growth

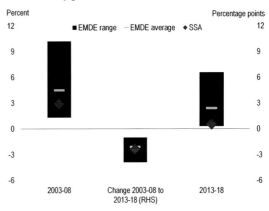

B. Productivity gap and convergence

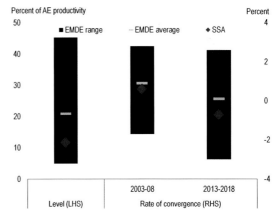

Source: Penn World Table; The Conference Board; *World Development Indicators*, World Bank.
Note: Unless specified otherwise, productivity is defined as labor productivity, (real GDP per person employed).
A. Sample includes range and simple average for the 127 EMDEs and simple average for 44 Sub-Saharan Africa countries.
B. Sample includes 35 advanced economies (AE) and 127 EMDEs. Rate of convergence is calculated as the difference in productivity growth rates over the log difference in productivity levels between SSA and advanced economies. Blue bars and orange dashes show the range and average of the six EMDE regional aggregates. "Level" of productivity refers to the GDP-weighted average of regional productivity as a share of the average advanced economy during 2013-2018.

BOX 2.6.1 Labor productivity in Sub-Saharan Africa: Trends and drivers (*continued*)

FIGURE 2.6.1.2 Evolution of labor productivity growth in SSA

The sharp slowdown in SSA's productivity growth relative to the pre-crisis period is concentrated among exporters of industrial commodities, in part reflecting the commodity-price slump of 2014-16. Excluding five high-productivity countries, productivity levels in the region are, on average, 3 percent that of advanced economies. Rapid productivity growth between the 1990s and 2008 reflected improvements in human capital, the deepening of physical capital, as well as a rise in total factor productivity (TFP). Following the commodity price slump, TFP slowed sharply among industrial-commodity exporters. Among exporters of agricultural commodities, capital deepening has reflected continued investment in infrastructure. TFP has contracted in recent years, mostly among industrial-commodity exporters. However, the fall in TFP was likely less severe when the contribution from slowing extraction of natural capital is accounted for.

A. SSA and EMDE labor productivity growth

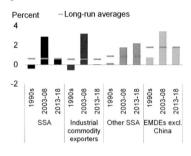

B. Productivity relative to advanced economies

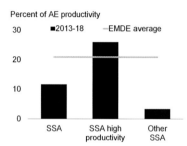

C. Contributions to productivity growth

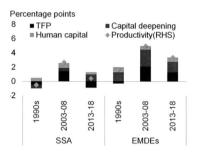

D. Contributions to productivity growth, by export composition

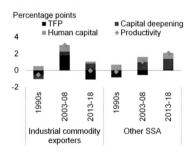

E. Contributions to productivity growth in Nigeria

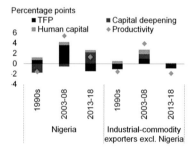

F. Contribution to productivity growth, by natural capital

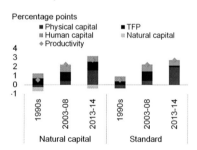

Source: Penn World Table; *Wealth Accounting*, World Bank.
Note: Unless specified otherwise, productivity is defined as labor productivity (real GDP per person employed).
A. Aggregate growth rates calculated using GDP weights at 2010 prices and market exchange rates. Dashed lines indicate average long-term labor productivity growth (1981-2018 for SSA; 1990-2018 for EMDEs excl. China). Samples include 44 Sub-Saharan African economies and 126 EMDEs. "Other SSA" includes agriculture exporters and commodity importers.
B. GDP-weighted averages calculated using GDP weights at 2010 prices and market exchange rates. Sample includes 127 EMDEs and 44 Sub-Saharan African economies. "SSA high productivity" includes Equatorial Guinea, Gabon, Mauritius, Seychelles, and South Africa.
C.-F. Aggregate growth rates calculated using GDP weights at 2010 prices and market exchange rates. Samples include 26 Sub-Saharan African economies and 92 EMDEs.
D. "Industrial-commodity exporters" includes metals and oil exporters. "Other SSA" includes agricultural commodity exporters and commodity importers.
F. For comparability, the sample for both the natural and standard decomposition includes 22 countries.

by three positions in the median agricultural commodity-exporter between the pre- and post-crisis periods, compared to a median deterioration of seven positions among industrial commodity exporters. Several country-specific reasons also helped lift productivity among agricultural commodity exporters. In Rwanda, productivity growth was boosted by continued reforms to strengthen institutions and governance, upgrade infrastructure, increase access to education, and improve

the business environment, to attract private investment (World Bank 2019w). In 2018, the country led SSA in its ease of doing business, ranking 29th globally. In Côte d'Ivoire, a return to stability following the end of decade-long civil strife in 2011 has since enabled a sharp rise in productivity, amid increased public investment, recovering foreign direct investment (FDI) inflows, an improving business environment and rising export activity (Klapper, Richmond, and Tran 2013; World Bank 2015c).

BOX 2.6.1 Labor productivity in Sub-Saharan Africa: Trends and drivers (*continued*)

Low productivity levels. Productivity in SSA is the second-lowest of all EMDE regions, after South Asia. However, if the five most productive economies are excluded (Equatorial Guinea, Gabon, Mauritius, Seychelles, South Africa), SSA has the lowest productivity of all EMDE regions, at 3 percent of the advanced-economy average in 2018 (Figure 2.6.1.2.B). Higher productivity levels in these five economies—at 24 percent of the advanced-economy average—is roughly one-quarter above the EMDE average. It exceeds productivity in other SSA economies, in part due to significant oil wealth (Equatorial Guinea, Gabon), dominant tourism sectors in island states (Mauritius, Seychelles), and a considerably higher capital stock combined with mineral wealth (South Africa). The post-crisis slowdown in productivity growth has dimmed prospects for SSA's continued convergence with advanced economies and other EMDEs. If recent rates of productivity growth persist, less than 5 percent of economies in SSA are on course to halve their productivity gap with advanced economies over the next 40 years.

Post-crisis total factor productivity decline. The post-crisis slowdown in SSA's productivity growth reflected less effective use of factor inputs, as captured by total factor productivity (TFP; Figure 2.6.1.2.C).[4] TFP growth, which accounted for the majority (three-fifths) of productivity growth pre-crisis, plunged from 1.4 percent pre-crisis to -0.9 percent post-crisis in the sharpest deterioration of any EMDE region. Rapid pre-crisis TFP growth, especially in industrial commodity exporters, reflected heavy resource investment and exploration during the commodity boom, large FDI inflows, communication infrastructure improvements (including the increased use of mobile phones), expanded access to finance, and better business climates (Figure 2.6.1.2.D; Aker and Mbiti 2010; Goedhuys, Janz, and Mohnen 2008; Keefer and Knack 2007; Wamboye, Tochkov, and Sergi 2015). The sharp post-crisis decline in TFP was most pronounced in industrial commodity exporters, following the commodity price collapse of 2014-16 and the accompanying collapse

in investment, FDI inflows, and exports, compounded by somewhat weaker business environments.[5] In Liberia and Sierra Leone, the post-crisis fall in TFP was exacerbated by the devastating Ebola outbreak of 2014-16 (World Bank 2019x).

In contrast, TFP has remained resilient, or even strengthened, among some exporters of agricultural commodities and commodity importers (Côte d'Ivoire, Kenya, Mauritius, Togo). Agricultural commodity prices fell less steeply, on average, than industrial commodity prices during the 2011-16 commodity price slump, and beneficial terms of trade supported activity among commodity importers. Faster TFP growth in these economies was also underpinned by sustained public investment in infrastructure, continued efforts to improve business environments, and more robust macroeconomic policy frameworks.

Post-crisis acceleration of capital deepening. The contraction in TFP growth offset the post-crisis boost to productivity growth generated from capital deepening. Labor productivity in agricultural commodity exporters benefited from heavy public investment.[6] In Nigeria, investment was fueled by large FDI inflows into the energy, banking, manufacturing, and telecommunications sectors (although investment slowed sharply after 2014 as oil prices collapsed; Figure 2.6.1.2.E; World Bank 2019y). In contrast, investment has fallen sharply in other industrial commodity exporters in SSA—by 7 percentage points of GDP in the median economy—following the 2014-16 commodity price slump, compounding the already slowing TFP growth.

Impact of natural resource extraction on productivity measurement. Natural capital accounts for an economy's natural resources, such as oil, metals, and agricultural land, and is particularly relevant given SSA's commodity reliance. Standard productivity decompositions fold the extraction of natural capital into total factor productivity and, to a lesser extent, physical capital, biasing their estimated contributions to productivity growth (Brandt, Schreyer and Zipperer 2017; Calderón and Cantu 2019; World Bank 2019z). During the pre-crisis commodity

---

[4] The standard productivity growth decomposition does not explicitly account for the contribution of natural capital as a factor of production. As a result, the TFP estimates produced here are potentially biased as they implicitly include the productivity contribution from natural capital. From a longer-term perspective, World Bank (2019z) finds that the significant difference between productivity in SSA and that of the productivity frontier (United States) largely reflected weak factor accumulation between 1960 and the 1990s, as the index of human capital in SSA relative to that of the United States declined sharply from 1960 to 1980, while the relative accumulation of physical capital remained subdued. In contrast, from 2000, the gap in efficiency (or TFP) became the major contributor to difference in productivity between SSA and the frontier. This TFP gap widened further from 2010 onwards.

[5] TFP declines have been most severe in oil-exporting Angola, Nigeria, and Chad, as well as in metal-exporting countries such as Botswana, Mozambique, Sierra Leone and South Africa.

[6] Greater fiscal space, partly due to the Multilateral Debt Relief Initiative (MDRI) and Heavily-Indebted Poor Countries (HIPC) initiative, supported increased investment in infrastructure and human capital which resulted in an 18-percentage-point rise in average secondary school enrollment rates from 33 percent in 2000 to 51 percent in 2014.

BOX 2.6.1 Labor productivity in Sub-Saharan Africa: Trends and drivers (*continued*)

FIGURE 2.6.1.3 Sectoral productivity growth in SSA

The sectoral reallocation of labor in Sub-Saharan Africa has been an important driver of regional productivity growth; however, its contribution has dwindled more recently. Agriculture in SSA has the lowest productivity, while productivity is highest in mining and finance. Low aggregate productivity in the region is partly explained by the agricultural sector's significant contribution to value added, combined with the disproportionate share of employment devoted to the sector.

A. Within-sector and structural contributions to productivity growth

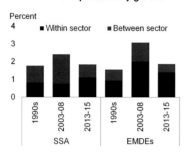

B. Sectoral productivity, 2015

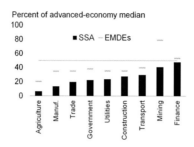

C. Employment by sector

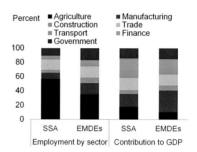

Source: APO productivity database; de Vries, Timmer, and de Vries 2013; Expanded Africa Sector Database; Groningen Growth Development Center database; Haver Analytics; ILOSTAT; Mensah and Szirmai (2018); Mensah et al. (2018); OECD STAN; United Nations; World Bank; World KLEMS.
Note: Unless specified otherwise, productivity is defined as labor productivity (real GDP per person employed).
A. Growth within sector shows the contribution of initial real value added-weighted productivity growth rate of each sector and 'between sector' effect shows the contribution arising from changes in sectoral employment shares. Median of the county-specific contributions. Sample includes 19 Sub-Saharan African economies and 46 EMDEs.
B. Figure shows the median of country groups. The sample includes 19 SSA economies and 46 EMDEs.
C. Sample includes 19 SSA countries and 46 EMDEs.

price boom and the accompanying boom in resource exploration and development, the increased extraction of natural capital lifted productivity growth in SSA (Figure 2.6.1.2.F; Khan et al. 2016). However, as the boom ended and commodity prices began to fall, natural capital extraction declined accordingly, and its contribution detracted from overall productivity growth. Data for natural capital is available until 2014, the year the commodity price slide intensified, but well before prices reached their early-2016 troughs. Even during these early years (2013-14), it appears that the post-crisis fall in TFP was likely less severe than the standard decomposition suggests, as the decline in natural capital potentially accounted for a large share of the slowdown in TFP growth from pre-crisis years.[7]

Sources of regional productivity growth

Productivity growth through sectoral reallocation. The

post-crisis slowdown in productivity growth from pre-crisis rates reflects slowing gains brought by the reallocation of labor from low-productivity sectors (mostly agriculture) to higher-productivity sectors. In contrast, within-sector productivity growth has continued apace (Figure 2.6.1.3.A).[8]

Productivity has differed widely across sectors in SSA (Figure 2.6.1.3.B). Productivity in agriculture—the least productive sector that employs more than half of the workforce and accounts for 18 percent of GDP—is between 4 and 7 percent of the productivity in mining and finance, the two most productive sectors at the nine-sector level (Figure 2.6.1.3.C).[9] Relative to the wider EMDE sample, agricultural productivity in SSA is about three times lower, on average. Low agricultural productivity in SSA reflects the prevalence of subsistence farming, sub-optimal crop selection, poor land quality amid unfavorable climates, limited uptake of modern technologies and production methods to improve yields, and small farm sizes (Adamopoulos and Restuccia 2014, 2018; Caselli 2005; Sinha and Xi 2018). Moreover, the use of price

---

[7] Direct comparisons between the standard decomposition and that including natural capital are complicated by the smaller country sample in the natural capital decomposition, as it includes 22 countries (72 percent of SSA GDP) compared to 26 countries (83 percent of SSA GDP) in the standard decomposition. Furthermore, the decline in natural capital may capture a lower valuation of the stock of natural capital.

[8] Sectoral productivity data are available for only about half the SSA economies with data for aggregate productivity.

[9] The sample includes 19 SSA economies at the nine-sector level.

BOX 2.6.1 Labor productivity in Sub-Saharan Africa: Trends and drivers (*continued*)

controls—a widespread practice across particularly low-income countries in the region—often distort the allocation of resources and inputs in agricultural sectors and weigh further on productivity by adversely affecting incentives to invest in human capital or adopt modern technologies and production methods (Special Focus 1; Chen 2017; Chen and Restuccia 2018; World Bank 2019z). The agricultural sector's significant contribution to value added, combined with the disproportionate share of employment devoted to the sector, helps explain SSA's low aggregate productivity relative to other EMDE regions.

Pre-crisis, sectoral reallocation accounted for more than half of aggregate productivity growth as labor moved from agriculture to services sectors and, to a lesser extent, manufacturing (Chapter 3; Enache, Ghani, and O'Connell 2016; Haile 2018; Rodrik 2016b). This process was facilitated by rapid urbanization as the urban share of population rose by 5 percentage points, to 39 percent, between 2000 and 2010. Since the crisis, however, the sectoral reallocation of labor to more productive sectors has slowed. As growth in commodity-exporting economies fell sharply during the commodity price slump of 2014-16, construction stalled, consumption eased, and credit contracted. Real-income losses in industrial sectors spilled over to weaker demand in the broader economy. As a result, services sectors were no longer able to absorb as much labor as they did pre-crisis.

Other drivers of productivity growth. Rapid improvements in the key drivers of productivity during the pre-crisis period supported productivity growth until the global financial crisis; however, the pace of improvement has since lost momentum. Productivity drivers with particularly prominent slowdowns in improvements include innovation, gender equality, education, health, trade openness, institutional quality, and investment (Figure 2.6.1.4.A and 2.6.1.4.B). Moreover, SSA continues to lag well behind other EMDEs in most drivers of productivity (Figure 2.6.1.4.C).

Institutional quality and the business environment. Although various aspects of governance and institutional quality improved in the region from the late 1990s into the pre-crisis period, this progress has mostly stalled, and even deteriorated in some instances. On average, business climates have also regressed during the post-crisis period; today, almost two-thirds of SSA countries still rank in the lowest quartile of countries by business climates, and one-half do so for poor governance (Figure 2.6.1.4.D). Poor business climates and governance, as well as distortions

caused by price controls, have not only constrained productivity by distorting the efficient allocation of resources, but have also deterred private sector investment (Cirera, Fattal Jaef, and Maemir 2017; World Bank 2019z).

Integration with the global economy. Between the mid-1990s and 2008, the region's openness to trade—that is, the sum of imports and exports relative to the size of the economy—rose 16 percentage points to 81 percent of GDP, helping to boost productivity. However, alongside falling commodity prices and slowing external demand, particularly from China and the Euro Area (the region's two largest trading partners), trade integration has partially unwound in the post-crisis period, with openness falling to 74 percent of GDP by 2017. The region's heavy dependence on commodity extraction sectors manifests in a smaller share of exporting firms compared to the EMDE average (Figure 2.6.1.4.E). Although the share of foreign-owned firms—which are generally more productive than their domestically owned counterparts—is high, such firms tend to cluster in extractives sectors with limited links to other sectors (Figure 2.6.1.4.F; Liu and Steenbergen 2019; World Bank 2018p). SSA's participation in global value chains is mostly limited to exports of raw agricultural commodities and natural resources used as inputs in other countries' exports (World Bank 2019d). Greater manufacturing sector participation in international trade and global value chains has been constrained by the sector's relative lack of international competitiveness, in part due to high productivity-adjusted labor costs (Gelb et al. 2017) and an array of non-tariff barriers, including the region's disadvantageous geography (Christ and Ferrantino 2011; Raballand et al. 2012).

Prospects for productivity growth slowdown. Although wide sectoral productivity differentials offer ample productivity growth potential through sectoral reallocation away from the agriculture sector, headwinds to productivity growth are substantial and expected to persist.

- *Weather-related shocks.* Given agriculture's prominence in economic activity in SSA, climate change presents severe challenges to productivity growth prospects in agricultural sectors as mean temperatures continue to rise and extreme weather events occur more frequently (IPCC 2014; Steinbach 2019; World Bank 2019a, 2019f).

- *Constraints to public investment.* Government indebtedness in SSA has increased sharply since 2013, rising by 20 percentage points, on average, to 60

BOX 2.6.1 Labor productivity in Sub-Saharan Africa: Trends and drivers (*continued*)

FIGURE 2.6.1.4 Drivers of productivity growth in SSA

Despite significant improvements, key productivity drivers remain significantly below those of advanced economies and EMDEs. Moreover, their pace of improvement has slowed in recent years. On average, business environments in Sub-Saharan Africa are more challenging than in other countries. While the region boasts the largest share of higher-productivity foreign-owned firms, its firms export less than their counterparts in other EMDEs.

A. Index of productivity growth drivers

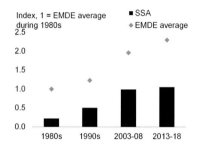

B. Share of SSA economies with slower improvements in drivers 2013-18 relative to 2003-08

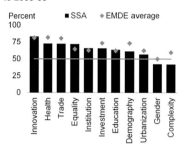

C. Levels of drivers across regions, 2018

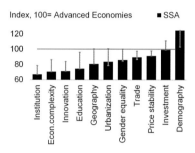

D. Obstacles to doing business

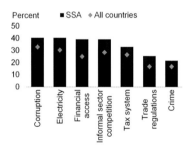

E. Share of exporting firms

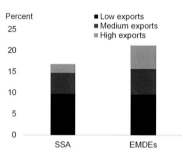

F. Ownership status

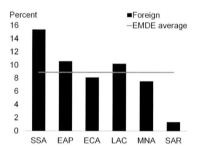

Source: Penn World Table; United Nations (2015); World Bank (Enterprise Surveys, Wealth Accounting, and World Development Indicators).

Note: Unless specified otherwise, productivity is defined as labor productivity (real GDP per person employed).

A. For each country, index is a weighted average (the normalized coefficients appearing in Annex 3.3) of the normalized value of each driver of productivity. Drivers include the International Country Risk Guide rule of law index, patents per capita, share of non-tropical area, investment as a percent of GDP, ratio of female average years of education to male average years, share of population in urban areas, Economic Complexity Index, years of schooling, share of working-age population, and inflation. See Chapter 3 (Annex 3.3) for details. Regional and EMDE indexes are GDP-weighted averages. Samples include 54 EMDEs and 11 economies in SSA.

B. Blue bars represent share of 48 economies in Sub-Saharan African economies where improvements in each driver of productivity were lower during 2008-17 than in the pre-crisis period 1998-2007, or changes in 2008-17 were below zero. Orange diamond is the corresponding values for 152 EMDE countries. Variables are defined as: Institutions = Government effectiveness; Innovation = patents per capita; Investment = investment to GDP ratio; Income equality = (-1) * Gini; Urbanization = urban population percentage; Economic complexity = Hidalgo and Hausmann (2009)'s Economic Complexity Index; Education = years of schooling; Demography = share of working-age population; and Gender equality = female average years of education divided by male average years. Samples include 26-48 SSA economies, depending on the driver, and 98-151 EMDEs.

C. Unweighted average levels of drivers, normalized as average of advanced economies as 100. Blue bar represents average within SSA. Orange lines represent range of the average drivers for six regions in 2017. Variables corresponding to the concepts are follows: Education = years of education; Urbanization = share of population living in urban area; Investment = share of investment to GDP; Institution = Government Effectiveness; Economic Complexity = Economic Complexity Index+; Geography = share of land area which are outside of tropical region; Gender Equality = Share of the year of schooling for female to male; Demography = share of population under 14; Innovation = Log patent per capita; Trade = Exports + Imports/GDP; and Price stability = (-1)* inflation rate.

D. Unweighted averages. Variables corresponding to the concepts are follows: Corruption = percent of firms identifying corruption as a major constraint; Electricity = Percent of firms identifying electricity as a major constraint; Financial access = percent of firms identifying access to finance as a major constraint; Informal sector competition = percent of firms identifying practices of competitors in the informal sector as a major constraint; Tax system is the average of tax rates (percent of firms identifying tax rates as a major constraint) and tax administration (percent of firms identifying tax administration as a major constraint); Trade regulations = percent of firms identifying customs and trade regulations as a major constraint; Crime = percent of firms identifying crime, theft and disorder as a major constraint.

E. Share of exporting firms. Firms classified as high, medium, and low export more than 75 percent, between 50 and 75, and up to 25 percent of their sales, respectively.

F. Share of firms with foreign ownership.

BOX 2.6.1 Labor productivity in Sub-Saharan Africa: Trends and drivers (*continued*)

percent of GDP in 2019. Reduced fiscal space could weigh on future productivity growth as it will likely constrain investment in productivity-enhancing infrastructure, health, and education as well as research and development. It can also make countries more vulnerable to financial crises (Box 3.4).

- *Commodity-reliance.* Growth prospects for commodity sectors that could encourage capital deepening are dim. Long-term commodity demand growth is expected to moderate as growth in China—the largest source of commodity demand—slows and shifts toward less resource-intensive sectors (World Bank 2018o).

- *High informality.* High informality in the region—around 40 percent of official GDP and 90 percent of total employment—may inhibit faster aggregate productivity growth, as productivity among informal firms are only one-seventh of that in their formal counterparts (La Porta and Shleifer 2014; World Bank 2019f). In addition, much-needed productivity-enhancing government spending is constrained because informal firms do not pay taxes.

Policy options

Coordinated policy efforts are required to achieve stronger productivity growth, notable reductions in extreme poverty, and a narrowing of the significant income gap with the rest of the world. There are four strands of policy options that emerge from the findings of this box.

Improving factors of production

Boosting human capital and leveraging demographic dividends. Improving human capital has been an important source of productivity growth in SSA. Continued investment and increased spending on health care, including greater provision of treatment for highly prevalent conditions such as malaria and HIV/AIDS, could raise productivity of the labor force and life expectancy in general (Figure 2.6.1.5.A; Asiki et al. 2016; Barofsky, Anekwe and Chase 2015; Ferreira, Pessôa and Dos Santos 2011). Increased life expectancy due to improved health care also generates incentives to invest in education (Cervellati and Sunde 2011). In Ethiopia, a rapid decline in fertility rates between 1995-2015, rising incomes, and falling poverty rates reflected an approach combining improvements in education and health, family planning, and increased economic opportunity (World Bank 2019aa). Harnessing the region's potential demographic dividend from declining fertility rates and

falling dependency ratios requires policies that support female empowerment, including education, health care, and greater labor market access for women (Figure 2.6.1.5.B; Bloom, Kuhn and Prettner 2017; Groth and May 2017; Kalemli-Ozcan 2003). As the ratio of the young dependent population to the working-age population declines in SSA, resources could be freed up to invest in the health and education of the young, boosting the productivity of the future labor force and spurring per capita growth (Ashraf, Weil and Wilde 2013).

Narrowing the gender gap. Despite some improvements, gender gaps remain large in SSA (World Bank 2012). Although the gender gap in labor force participation has been narrowing, on average, significant gaps in earnings of women relative to men persist. This reflects gender disparity in secondary and tertiary education, differing occupations, and greater time devoted by women to housework and childcare (World Bank 2019aa). Moreover, improvements in the ratio of average years of education of females to males have been slowing in the post-crisis period. This is reflected by lower productivity of females in agriculture, as well as female entrepreneurs—crops tended by women yield one-third less per hectare than those of men, and a similar margin applies to profits earned by female entrepreneurs (Figure 2.6.1.5.C; O'Sullivan et al. 2014; Campos et al. 2019). Policies to empower women and boost their productivity include those promoting skills building beyond traditional training programs, such as a greater focus on developing an entrepreneurial mindset; this approach has been found to lift sales and profits in Togo (Campos et al. 2017, World Bank 2019aa). Other policies include relieving capital constraints faced by females due to lower asset holdings offering limited collateral; and addressing social norms that constrain women's economic opportunities and earnings, such as perceptions about the type of work that is suitable to men or women.

Closing infrastructure gaps. Although capital deepening has continued apace among the region's agricultural commodity exporters and commodity importers, it has slowed considerably among most industrial commodity exporters, and severe infrastructure deficiencies remain throughout the region. Meeting the infrastructure-related Sustainable Development Goals in 2030 will require additional investment spending between 2015-30 of roughly 7 percent of GDP per year in SSA (excluding maintenance spending)—the highest of all EMDE regions (Figure 2.6.1.5.D; Rozenberg and Fay 2019). Stronger productivity growth—through both capital-deepening investment and improved TFP—is contingent on

BOX 2.6.1 Labor productivity in Sub-Saharan Africa: Trends and drivers (*continued*)

FIGURE 2.6.1.5 Prospects for productivity growth in SSA

Continued improvements in health care could raise life expectancy and the overall productivity of the labor force, as increased life expectancy also generates incentives to invest in education. Sub-Saharan Africa could harness a significant demographic dividend, as falling fertility rates lead to a lower dependency ratio. Owing to limited access to resources and training, crops tended by women yield one-third less per hectare than those of men; a similar margin applies to profits earned by female entrepreneurs. To meet the SDGs by 2030 will require investment spending of about 7 percent of GDP per year. Reducing trade costs in SSA will help accelerate regional and global integration. Conflicts have been rising in the region, particularly acts of violence against civilians.

A. Human capital development

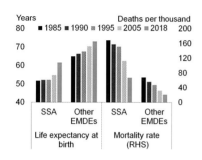

B. Dependency ratios and fertility rates

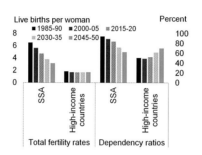

C. Shortfalls in profits and agricultural output of females relative to males

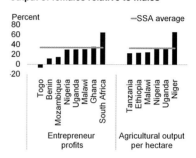

D. Infrastructure spending needs

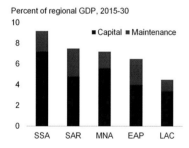

E. Import and export compliance costs

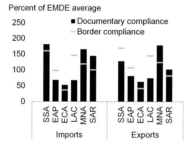

F. Conflict events

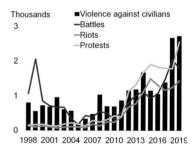

Source: Armed Conflict Location and Event Data Project database; Campos et al. (2019); O'Sullivan et al. (2014); Rozenberg and Fay (2019); World Bank Doing Business 2020; United Nations.

Note: Unless specified otherwise, productivity is defined as labor productivity (real GDP per person employed).

A. Unweighted averages. "Mortality rate" refers to under-five mortality.

B. The dependency ratio is calculated as the ratio of the population at ages 0–14 plus the population aged 65+ to the population at ages 15–64.

C. Bars for "Entrepreneur profits" show the extent to which profits for male-owned firms exceed those of female-owned firms using data from impact evaluations. Bars for "Agricultural output per hectare" show the extent to which agricultural output per hectare on male-managed plots exceeds that of female-managed plots. Entrepreneur profits in Ghana reflect the average of both the Grants for Micro-Enterprises Survey and the Tailoring Survey; Entrepreneur profits in Nigeria reflect the average of both the Growth and Employment Survey and the Business Plan Competition Survey. Agricultural output per hectare accounts for differences in plot size and geographic factors. Agricultural output in Nigeria reflects a simple average of gaps for northern Nigeria (46 percent) and southern Nigeria (17 percent).

D.E. Bars show average annual spending needs during 2015-30. Estimates are generated using policy assumptions that cap investment needs at 4.5 percent of LMICs' GDP per year. SSA=Sub-Saharan Africa, SAR=South Asia, MNA=Middle East and North Africa, EAP=East Asia and Pacific, LAC=Latin America and the Caribbean.

E. Unweighted averages. Sample includes 156 EMDEs and 47 SSA economies. EMDE average excludes SSA.

F. Sample includes 30 SSA economies. Last observation is November 9, 2019.

infrastructure deficiencies being addressed. Access to electricity is a critical obstacle to achieving development goals in SSA, and reforms to improve access in a sustainable manner need to strike a balance between affordable provision for consumers, particularly the poor, and cost recovery for utilities (Blimpo and Cosgrove-Davies 2019; Vorisek and Yu (forthcoming). In addition to closing infrastructure gaps, improvements to the resilience of existing infrastructure are needed to limit frequent disruptions, particularly in power, water and sanitation, transport, and telecommunications (World Bank 2019ab). To ensure public investment is efficient in boosting growth and productivity, it should be supported by adequate public investment management frameworks that encompass strong cash management and procurement processes.

BOX 2.6.1 Labor productivity in Sub-Saharan Africa: Trends and drivers (*continued*)

Boosting firm productivity

Boosting productivity in agriculture. Given the large share of activity and employment accounted for by agriculture, measures to raise agricultural productivity at the farm level—especially in staple crops—can yield significant development gains (Beegle and Christiaensen 2019). These include ensuring secure land tenures, better access to markets and finance, better crop choices, more effective and increased use of fertilizers, improved irrigation, diffusion and adoption of new technologies, as well as targeted trainings to help small farmers reap the benefits of cutting-edge knowledge and practices specific to the area and product (Chen 2017; Fuglie et al. 2019; Sinha and Xi 2018; World Bank 2019aa). For example, text messages providing advice and reminders to sugarcane farmers in Kenya helped boost fertilizer use and crop yields (Casaburi et al 2014; Fuglie et al. 2019). Ensuring gender equality in access to resources could further boost agricultural productivity; giving women in Malawi and Ghana the same access to fertilizers and other inputs as men could boost maize yields by one-sixth (World Bank 2012). Gains from faster productivity growth in agriculture will free up workers to transition to other, more productive, sectors.

Addressing informality. Although informality is higher in SSA than in other EMDE regions, informal firms often brim with potential—more formal firms in SSA started as informal firms, and this period of transition is found to be shorter than in other EMDEs (World Bank 2019f). Policies to unlock informal firms' potential include upgrading skills of workers, ensuring better access to inputs and resources like financial services, transport and communications connectivity, health services, land and property rights, and product markets (Oosthuizen et al. 2016). Removing barriers to enter the formal sector can further accelerate the transition out of informality: lowering registration costs by half could double the share of formal enterprises through formalization of informal firms and new entrants (Nguimkeu 2015; World Bank 2019aa). Regulatory and institutional reforms to build public trust can strengthen incentives for firms to operate formally. Policies aimed directly at the youth can bolster the prospects of the future workforce and help alleviate youth unemployment. In Rwanda, entrepreneurship has been introduced as a secondary school subject to help prepare the youth to be successful entrepreneurs or to compete in the formal labor market (Choi, Dutz, and Usman 2019).

Leveraging digital technologies. Firm productivity in SSA could also benefit significantly from the proliferation of digital technologies—more so than other regions (Choi, Dutz, and Usman 2019; Hjort and Poulsen 2019). SSA's comparatively low levels of human capital and high degree of informality are ideally suited for the adoption and development of productivity-enhancing, low-skill-biased digital technologies in the agriculture, manufacturing and services sectors. In some countries, the use of digital technologies has been found to boost firm productivity by facilitating process and product innovation (Democratic Republic of Congo, Tanzania; Cirera, Lage, and Sabetti 2016). Digital technologies can also help in banking the unbanked and transform lending in SSA. Kenya's mobile money service, M-Pesa, boosted the financial savings of female-headed households and enabled women to move out of agriculture into more productive sectors (Suri and Jack 2016). Digital loans offered through mobile money platforms are also growing in popularity and may grant financial inclusion to individuals without credit scores or sufficient collateral, as digital loan providers use alternative credit scores based on telecommunications data (Cook and McKay 2015; Francis, Blumenstock, and Robinson 2017; World Bank 2019aa). However, the use of digital credit has so far been largely concentrated in urban areas, at short maturities, and not as investment loans by the rural poor (Björkegren and Grissen 2018).

Accelerating trade openness and global integration. The African Continental Free Trade Area (AfCFTA) has the potential to boost regional trade and bolster firm productivity by facilitating investment, international competitiveness, the transfer of technology and new innovations, and participation in regional and global value chains (Berg and Krueger 2003; Calderon and Cantú 2019; Del Prete, Giovannetti, and Marvasi 2017; Laget et al. 2018; World Bank 2019d). To maximize the potential productivity gains from the free trade area, infrastructure needs to be expanded—particularly transport networks—and business climates improved. In addition, gains from AfCFTA depend on the implementation of trade facilitation measures and addressing of significant non-tariff barriers to trade—trade costs in SSA, such as border and documentary compliance costs, are roughly one-half higher than those of other EMDE regions (Figure 2.6.1.5.E; World Bank 2019d). Currently, most regional trade in SSA takes place among countries within existing regional economic communities, as high tariffs and non-tariff barriers limit trade between countries of different groupings.

Encouraging sectoral reallocation

Enabling factor mobility. Productivity gains from sectoral

BOX 2.6.1 Labor productivity in Sub-Saharan Africa: Trends and drivers (*continued*)

reallocation of labor in the region—a major driver of pre-crisis productivity growth—can be reignited by policies aimed at reducing the barriers to factor mobility. These barriers include low human capital of the labor force, weak infrastructure (such as inadequate transport systems in urban areas), low access to finance, and disadvantageous trade policies. In Nigeria, tariff structures have been shown to reduce incentives for sectoral reallocation to higher-productivity sectors, as the tariffs systematically boosted profitability of the least productive sectors but not that of higher-productivity sectors (World Bank 2017g).

Diversification. Countries with highly diversified economic activity across a broad range of sectors tend to have higher productivity levels (Chapter 3). SSA, however, remains heavily dependent on extractives sectors, particularly for export and fiscal revenues, with the latter dependence often a cause of procyclical fiscal policies. Policy measures aimed at broadening the production base toward a wider and more complex array of export goods, across a range of manufacturing and services sectors, will enable greater participation in value chains and help insulate economic activity from the destabilizing effects of large international commodity price swings. In Côte d'Ivoire—the world's largest supplier of cocoa beans—diversification along the cocoa value chain through the expansion of domestic grinding and processing facilities has allowed the country to also produce a diverse array of value-added cocoa products and to overtake the Netherlands as the world's leading cocoa-processing country (World Bank 2016h). AfCFTA could contribute to economic diversification if it leads to the establishment of regional value chains. However, successful economic diversification requires several supporting measures, including improved human capital, better infrastructure, stronger governance, and deeper financial markets with increased access to credit (Fosu and Abass 2019).

Creating a growth-friendly environment

Protection from climate change. Some of the adverse effects of climate change can be mitigated through appropriate land-use planning and investment in climate-smart infrastructure (Collier, Conway and Venables 2008; World Bank 2019a). Effective social protection policies, possibly financed with energy taxes or the removal of fuel subsidies, could provide resources to support livelihoods during extreme events (Hallegatte et al 2015). Climate adaptation policies can be strengthened by building

capacity in policy implementation, boosting access to adaptation financing, and raising public awareness of climate change (Adenle et al. 2017; World Bank 2019ac).

Stability. SSA has historically witnessed many conflicts, particularly between the 1970s and early 2000s, that not only took heavy human tolls, but also shook the stability of the affected countries by weakening institutions and severely damaging or destroying infrastructure. Conflicts in Burundi, the Democratic Republic of Congo, Liberia, Rwanda, and Sierra Leone inflicted losses of human life equivalent to between 1 and 10 percent of their populations (Steinbach 2019; World Bank 2019a). More recently, rising incidence of conflict—particularly acts of violence against civilians—has increasingly weighed on activity in several countries and forcibly displaced large populations (Figure 2.6.1.5.F). Efforts to achieve lasting peace can strengthen economic activity and boost productivity through stronger investment and increased TFP (Chen, Loayza, and Reynal-Querol 2008).

Strengthening institutional quality and business environments. Business environments stand to benefit from improved infrastructure; limited access to reliable electricity and poor transport infrastructure are often cited as key constraints to business in SSA. In addition, high non-infrastructure-related costs, such as high prices to transport goods within countries and across borders, tend to exacerbate the burden of weak infrastructure. In many instances, high road-transport costs reflect excessive market power of trucking companies. Competition-enhancing deregulation can help alleviate this business constraint and boost productivity. For example, in landlocked Rwanda, deregulation in the transport sector led to an abrupt fall in transport costs (Barrett et al. 2017) Business environment deficiencies can further be addressed by increasing access to finance, simplifying tax systems, reducing regulatory burdens and compliance requirements, improving judicial systems to address corruption and strengthen enforcement, and liberalizing labor and product markets (Bah and Fang 2015; World Bank 2019f). Strengthening institutional quality by improving judicial systems can help address corruption—a leading obstacle to doing business—and strengthen contract enforcement. Such structural reforms can bolster firm productivity (Kouamé and Tapsoba 2018). Reforms aimed at improving the business environment can also help lower the size of the informal sector, which tends to have lower productivity than the formal economy.

References

Abdih, Y., P. Lopez-Murphy, A. Roitman, and R. Sahay. 2010. "The Cyclicality of Fiscal Policy in the Middle East and Central Asia: Is the Current Crisis Different?" IMF Working Paper 10/68, International Monetary Fund, Washington, DC.

Acemoglu, D., S. Johnson, and J. Robinson. 2005. "Institutions as a Fundamental Cause of Long-Run Growth." In *Handbook of Economic Growth 1A,* edited by P. Aghion and S. Durlauf, 385–472. Amsterdam: North-Holland.

Acemoglu, D., S. Naidu, P. Restrepo, and J. Robinson. 2019. "Democracy Does Cause Growth." *Journal of Political Economy* 127 (1): 47–100.

Adamopoulos, T., and D. Restuccia. 2014. "The Size Distribution of Farms and International Productivity Differences." *American Economic Review* 107 (10): 1667-97.

Adamopoulos, T., and D. Restuccia. 2018. "Geography and Agricultural Productivity: Cross-Country Evidence from Micro Plot-Level Data." NBER Working Paper 24532, National Bureau of Economic Research, Cambridge, MA.

ADB (Asian Development Bank). 2019. *The Servicification of Manufacturing in Asia: Redefining the Sources of Labor Productivity.* Manila: Asian Development Bank.

Adenle, A. A., J. D. Ford, J. Morton, S. Twomlow, K. Alverson, A. Cattaneo, R. Cervigni, et al. 2017. "Managing Climate Change Risks in Africa—A Global Perspective." *Ecological Economics 141 (November): 190 -201.*

Adler, G., R. Duval, D. Furceri, S. K. Çelik, K. Koloskova, M. Poplawski-Ribeiro. 2017. "Gone with the Headwinds: Global Productivity." IMF Staff Discussion Note 17/04, International Monetary Fund, Washington, DC.

Aggarwal, A., M. Hoppe, and P. Walkenhorst. 2019. "Special Economic Zones in South Asia: Industrial Islands or Vehicles for Diversification?" Washington, DC: World Bank.

Ahluwalia, I. J., S. Chaudhuri, and S. Chaudri. 2003. "Trade Liberalization, Productivity, and Export Performance: A Study of the Indian Manufacturing Sector in the 1990s." South Asia Region Internal Discussion Paper. Report IDP-189. Washington, DC: World Bank.

Aiyar, S., B. Augustyniak, C. Ebeke, E. Ebrahimy, S. Elekdag, N. Klein, S. Lall, H. Zhao and D. Muir. 2013. "German-Central European Supply Chain – Cluster Report". IMF Country Report 13/263, International Monetary Fund, Washington, DC.

Aiyar, S., C. Ebeke, X. Shao. 2016. "The Impact of Workforce Aging on European Productivity." IMF Working Paper 16/238, International Monetary Fund, Washington, DC.

Aker, J. C., and I. M. Mbiti. 2010. "Mobile Phones and Economic Development in Africa." *Journal of Economic Perspectives* 24 (3): 207-32.

Albino-War, M., S. Cerovic, F. Grigoli, J. C. Flores, J. Kapsoli, H. Qu, Y. Said, B. Shukurov, M. Sommer, and S. Yoon. 2014. "Making the Most of Public Investment in MENA and CCA Oil Exporting Countries." IMF Staff Discussion Note 14/10, International Monetary Fund, Washington, DC.

Alesina, A., D. Furceri, J. Ostry, C. Papageorgiou, and D. Quinn. 2019. "Structural Reforms and Election: Evidence from a World-wide New Dataset." Harvard University Working Paper, Cambridge, MA.

Almeida, R., and T. Packard. 2018. *Competências e Empregos: uma Agenda para a Juventude.* Washington, DC: Grupo Banco Mundial.

Altinok, N., N. Angrist, and H. A. Patrinos. 2018. "Global Data Set on Education Quality (1965–2015)." Policy Research Working Paper 8314, World Bank, Washington, DC.

Amin, M., and H. Ulku. 2019. "Corruption, Regulatory Burden and Firm Productivity." Policy Research Working Paper 8911, World Bank, Washington, DC.

Amjad, R., and N. Awais. 2016. "Pakistan's Productivity Performance and TFP Trends, 1980-2015: Cause for Real Concern." *Lahore Journal of Economics* 21 (SE): 33-63.

Andrews, D., C. Criscuolo, and P. N. Gal. 2015. "Frontier Firms, Technology Diffusion and Public Policy: Micro Evidence from OECD Countries." In *The Future of Productivity. Main Background Papers.* Paris: Organization for Economic Co-operation and Development.

APO (Asian Productivity Organization). 2017. *Asian Productivity Databook.* Tokyo: Asian Productivity Organization.

———. 2018. *APO Productivity Databook. Tokyo: Asian Productivity Organization.*

Araujo, J. T., E. Vostroknutova, and K. Wacker. 2017. "Productivity Growth in Latin America and the Caribbean: Exploring the Macro-Micro Linkages." MFM Global Practice Discussion Paper 19, World Bank, Washington, DC.

Arezki, R., M. Ait Ali Slimane, A. Barone, K. Decker, D. Detter, R. Fan, H. Nguyen, G. Miralles, L. Senbet, 2019a. "Reaching New Heights: Promoting Fair Competition in the Middle East and North Africa." *MENA Economic Update.* October. Washington, DC: World Bank.

Arezki, R., D. Lederman, A. Harb, R. Fan, and H. Nguyen. 2019b. "Reforms and External Imbalances: The Labor-Productivity Connectivity Connection in the Middle East and North Africa." *MENA Economic Update.* April. Washington, DC: World Bank.

Arnold, J. M., B. S. Javorcik, M. Lipscomb, and A. Mattoo. 2016. "Services Reform and Manufacturing Performance: Evidence from India." *Economic Journal* 126 (590): 1–39.

Arnold, J. M., B. S. Javorcik, and A. Mattoo. 2011. "Does Services Liberalization Benefit Manufacturing Firms? Evidence from the Czech Republic." *Journal of International Economics* 85 (1): 136-146.

Arora, V. 2005. "Economic Growth in Post-Apartheid South Africa: A Growth-Accounting Analysis." In *Post-apartheid South Africa: The First Ten Years*, edited by L. A. Ricci and M. Nowak, 13-22. Washington, DC: International Monetary Fund.

Artuc, E., G. Lopez-Acevedo, R. Robertson, and D. Samaan. 2019. "Export to Jobs: Boosting the Gains from Trade in South Asia." South Asia Development Forum. Washington, DC: World Bank.

Ashraf, Q. H., D. N. Weil, and J. Wilde. 2013. "The Effect of Fertility Reduction on Economic Growth." *Population and Development Review* 39 (1): 97-130.

Asiki, G., G. Reniers, R. Newton, K. Baisley, J. Nakiyingi-Miiro, E. Slaymaker, I. Kasamba et al. 2016. "Adult Life Expectancy Trends in the Era of Antiretroviral Treatment in Rural Uganda (1991–2012)." Aids 30 (3): 487-493.

Aslam, A., S. Beidas-Strom, R. Bems, O. Celasun, S. K. Celik, and Z. Koczan. 2016. "Trading on Their Terms? Commodity Exporters in the Aftermath of the Commodity Boom." IMF Working Paper 16/27, International Monetary Fund, Washington, DC.

Attanasio, O., A. Guarin, C. Medina, and C. Meghir. 2015. "Long Term Impacts of Vouchers for Vocational Training: Experimental Evidence in Colombia." NBER

Working Paper 21390, National Bureau of Economic Research, Cambridge, MA.

Ayyagari, M., A. Demirgüç-Kunt, and V. Maksimovic. 2017. "SME Finance." Policy Research Working Paper 8241, World Bank, Washington, DC.

Ayyagari, M., P. F. Juarros, M. S. Martinez Peria, and S. Singh. 2016. "Access to Finance and Job Growth: Firm-level Evidence Across Developing Countries." Policy Research Working Paper 7604, World Bank, Washington, DC.

Bachmair, F. and J. Bogoev. 2018. "Assessment of Contingent Liabilities and Their Impact on Debt Dynamics in South Africa." MTI Discussion Paper 1, Macroeconomics, Trade and Investment Global Practice, The World Bank, Washington, DC.

Baffes, J., M. A. Kose, F. Ohnsorge, and M. Stocker. 2015. "The Great Plunge in Oil Prices: Causes, Consequences, and Policy Responses." Policy Research Note 1, World Bank, Washington DC.

Bah, E., and L. Fang. 2015. "Impact of the Business Environment on Output and Productivity in Africa." *Journal of Development Economics* 114 (May): 159-171.

Baier, S. L., G. P. Dwyer, and R. Tamura. 2006. "How Important Are Capital and Total Factor Productivity for Economic Growth." *Economic Inquiry* 44 (1): 23-49.

Baker, S. R., N. Bloom, and S. J. Davis. 2016. "Measuring Economic Policy Uncertainty." *The Quarterly Journal of Economics* 131 (4): 1593–1636.

Balabushko, O., O. Betliy, V. Movchan, R. Piontkivsky, and M. Ryzhenkov. 2018. "Crony Capitalism in Ukraine: Relationship between Political Connectedness and Firms' Performance." Policy Research Paper 8471, World Bank, Washington DC.

Baldwin, R. 2019. *The Globotics Upheaval: Globalization, Robotics and the Future of Work.* New York: Oxford University Press.

Baldwin, R., and J. Lopez-Gonzalez. 2013. "Supply-Chain Trade: A Portrait of Global Patterns and Several Testable Hypotheses." *The World Economy* 38 (11): 1682-1721.

Bank of England. 2018. *EU Withdrawal Scenarios and Monetary and Financial Stability: A Response to the House of Commons Treasury Committee.* November. London: Bank of England.

Barofsky, J., T. D. Anekwe, and C. Chase. 2015.

"Malaria Eradication and Economic Outcomes in Sub-Saharan Africa: Evidence from Uganda." *Journal of Health Economics* 44 (December): 118-136.

Barrett, C. B., L. Christiaensen, M. Sheahan, and A. Shimeles. 2017. "On the Structural Transformation of Rural Africa." Policy Research Working Paper 7938, World Bank, Washington, DC.

Barro, R. J., and J.-W. Lee. 2015. *Education Matters: Global Schooling Gains from the 19th to the 21st Century.* New York: Oxford University Press.

Bartelsman, E. J., and S. Scarpetta. 2007. "Reallocation and Productivity in Transition and Integration Phases." Policy Research Working Paper 6572, World Bank, Washington, DC.

Beck, T. 2018. "Finance and Resource Booms: A Complicated Relationship. Two Proposals." In *Rethinking the Macroeconomics of Resource-Rich Countries,* edited by Arezki, A, R. Boucekkine, J. Frankel, M. Laksaci, and R. van der Ploeg. CEPR's Policy Portal. https://voxeu.org/system/files/epubli cation/Resource_Rich_Countries_eBook.pdf.

Beegle, K., and L. Christiaensen. 2019. *Accelerating Poverty Reduction in Africa.* Washington, DC: World Bank.

Behera, H., and S. Sharma. 2019. "Does Financial Cycle Exist in India?" RBI Working Paper 03, Reserve Bank of India, Mumbai.

Benhassine, N., S. H. Youssef, P. Keefer, A. Stone, and S. N. Wahba. 2009. "From Privilege to Competition: Unlocking Private-led Growth in the Middle East and North Africa." *MENA Development Report.* Washington, DC: World Bank.

Berg, A., and A. O. Krueger. 2003. "Trade, Growth, and Poverty: A Selective Survey." IMF Working Paper 03/30, International Monetary Fund, Washington, DC.

Beteille, T. 2019. *Ready to Learn, Ready to Thrive: Before School, In School and Beyond School in South Asia.* Washington, DC: World Bank.

Beverelli, C., M. Fiorini, and B. Hoekman. 2017. "Services Trade Policy and Manufacturing Productivity: The Role of Institutions." *Journal of International Economics* 104 (January): 166–182.

Bisat, A., M. A. El-Erian, and T. Helbling. 1997. "Growth, Investment, and Saving in the Arab Economies." IMF Working Paper 97/85, International Monetary Fund, Washington, DC.

Björkegren, D., and D. Grissen. 2018. "The Potential of Digital Credit to Bank the Poor." *AEA Papers and Proceedings* 108 (May): 68-71.

Blancher, N., A. Bibolov, and A. Fouejieu. 2019. "Financial Inclusion of Small and Medium-Sized Enterprises in the Middle East and Central Asia." IMF Working Paper 19/02, International Monetary Fund, Washington, DC.

Blimpo, M. P., and M. Cosgrove-Davies. 2019. *Electricity Access in Sub-Saharan Africa: Uptake, Reliability, and Complementary Factors for Economic Impact.* Washington, DC: World Bank.

Bloom, D. E., M. Kuhn, and K. Prettner. 2017 "Africa's Prospects for Enjoying a Demographic Dividend." *Journal of Demographic Economics* 83 (1): 63-76.

Bloom, N., B. Eifert, A. Mahajan, D. McKenzie, and J. Roberts. 2013. "Does Management Matter? Evidence from India." *Quarterly Journal of Economics* 128 (1): 1-51.

Bouis, R., R. Duval, and J. Eugster. 2016. "Product Market Deregulation and Growth: New Country-Industry-Level Evidence." IMF Working Paper 16/114, International Monetary Fund, Washington, DC.

Bova, E., M. Ruiz-Arranz, F. Toscani, and H. E. Ture. 2016. "The Fiscal Costs of Contingent Liabilities; A New Dataset." IMF Working Paper 16/14, International Monetary Fund, Washington, DC.

Bown, C., D. Lederman, S. Pienknagura, and R. Robertson. 2017. *Better Neighbors: Toward a Renewal of Integration in Latin America.* Washington, DC: World Bank.

Brandt, N., P. Schreyer, and V. Zipperer. 2017. "Productivity Measurement with Natural Capital." *Review of Income and Wealth* 63 (S1): S7-S21.

Brenton, P., R. Newfarmer, and P. Walkenhorst. 2009. "Avenues for Export Diversification: Issues for Low-Income Countries." MPRA Paper 22758, University Library of Munich.

Brown, J. D., G. A. Crespi, L. Iacovone, and L. Marcolin. 2016. "Productivity Convergence at Firm Level: New Evidence from the Americas." In *Understanding the Income and Efficiency Gap in Latin America and the Caribbean*, edited by J. T. Araujo, E. Vostroknutova, K. Wacker, and M. Clavijo. Washington, DC: World Bank.

Brown, J. D., and J. S. Earle. 2007. "Firm-Level

Components of Aggregate Productivity Growth in ECA Economies." Background Paper, World Bank, Washington, DC.

Brown, J. D., J. S. Earle, and Á. Telegdy, "The Productivity Effects of Privatization: Longitudinal Estimates from Hungary, Romania, Russia, and Ukraine." *Journal of Political Economy* 114 (1): 61-99.

Bruszt, L., and N. Campos. 2016. "Deep Economic Integration and State Capacity: The Case of the Eastern Enlargement of the European Union." ADP Working Paper, Asian Development Bank, Manilla.

Busso, M., L. Madrigal, and C. Pagés. 2013. "Productivity and Resource Misallocation in Latin America." *B. E. Journal of Macroeconomics* 13 (1): 903–32.

Cadestin, C., J. Gourdon, and P. Kowalski. 2016. "Participation in Global Value Chains in Latin America: Implications for Trade and Trade-Related Policy." Trade Policy Paper No. 192, Organisation for Economic Co-operation and Development, Paris.

Caldara, D., M. Iacoviello, P. Molligo, A. Prestipino, and A. Raffo. 2019. "The Economic Effects of Trade Policy Uncertainty." International Finance Discussion Papers 1256, Board of Governors of the Federal Reserve System, Washington, DC.

Calderón, C., and S. Boreux. 2016. "Citius, Altius, Fortius: Is Growth in Sub-Saharan Africa More Resilient?" *Journal of African Economies* 25 (4): 502-528.

Calderón, C., and C. Cantú. 2019. "Trade Integration and Growth: Evidence from Sub-Saharan Africa." Policy Research Working Paper 8859, World Bank, Washington, DC.

Calderón, C., and L. Servén. 2010. "Infrastructure and Economic Development in Sub-Saharan Africa." *Journal of African Economies* 19 (S1): i13-i87.

Calderón, C. Moral-Benito, E. and L. Serven. 2015. Is Infrastructure Capital Productive? A Dynamic Heterogeneous Approach. *Journal of Applied Econometrics,* Vol 30(2): 177-198.

Calice, P., E. P. Ribiero, and S. Byskov. 2018. "Efficient Financial Allocation and Productivity Growth in Brazil." Policy Research Working Paper 8479, World Bank, Washington, DC.

Callen, T., R. Cherif, F. Hasanov, A. Hegazy, and P. Khandelwal. 2014. "Economic Diversification in the GCC: Past, Present, and Future." IMF Staff Discussion Note, International Monetary Fund, Washington, DC.

Campos, F., R. Coleman, A. Conconi, A. Donald, M. Gassier, M. Goldstein, Z. Chavez, et al. 2019. *Profiting from Parity: Unlocking the Potential of Women's Business in Africa.* Washington, DC: World Bank.

Campos, F., M. Frese, M. Goldstein, L. Iacovone, H. Johnson, D. McKenzie, and M. Mensmann. 2017. "Teaching Personal Initiative Beats Traditional Training in Boosting Small Business in West Africa." *Science* 357 (6357): 1287–90.

Casaburi, L., M. Kremer, S. Mullainathan, and R. Ramrattan. 2014. "Harnessing ICT to Increase Agricultural Production: Evidence from Kenya." Harvard University, Cambridge, MA.

Caselli, F. 2005. "Accounting for Cross-Country Income Differences." In *Handbook of Economic Growth 1,* edited by P. Aghion and S. N. Durlauf, 679-741. Amsterdam: Elsevier.

Cervellati, M., and U. Sunde. 2011. "Life Expectancy and Economic Growth: The Role of the Demographic Transition." *Journal of Economic Growth* 16 (2): 99-133.

Chen, C. 2017. "Technology Adoption, Capital Deepening, and International Productivity Differences." Department of Economics Working Paper 584, University of Toronto.

Chen, C. and D. Restuccia. 2018. "Agricultural Productivity Growth in Africa." Background paper prepared for the AFRCE project Boosting Productivity in Sub-Saharan Africa, World Bank, Washington, DC.

Chen, E. 2002. "The Total Factor Productivity Debate: Determinants of Economic Growth in East Asia." *Asian Pacific Economic Literature* 40 (1):18-38.

Chen, S., N. V. Loayza, and M. Reynal-Querol. 2008 "The Aftermath of Civil War." *The World Bank Economic Review* 22 (1): 63-85.

Choi, J., M. Dutz, and Z. Usman. 2019. *The Future of Work in Africa: Harnessing the Potential of Digital Technologies for All.* Washington, DC: World Bank.

Chong, A., J. Galdo, and J. Saavedra. 2008. "Informality and Productivity in the Labor Market in Peru." *Journal of Economic Policy Reform* 11 (4): 229–45.

Christ, N., and M. J. Ferrantino. 2011. "Land Transport for Export: The Effects of Cost, Time, and

Uncertainty in Sub-Saharan Africa." *World Development* 39 (10): 1749–59.

Chuah, L. L., Loayza, N. V. Nguyen, and H. Minh. 2018. "Resource Misallocation and Productivity Gaps in Malaysia." Policy Research Working Paper 8368, World Bank, Washington, DC.

Cirera, X., and A. P. Cusolito. 2019. "Innovation Patterns and Their Effects on Firm-Level Productivity in South Asia." Policy Research Working Paper 8876, World Bank, Washington, DC.

Cirera, X., R. N. Fattal Jaef, and H. B. Maemir. 2017. "Taxing the Good? Distortions, Misallocation, and Productivity in Sub-Saharan Africa." Policy Research Working Paper 7949, World Bank, Washington, DC.

Cirera, X., F. Lage, and L. Sabetti. 2016. "ICT Use, Innovation, and Productivity: Evidence from Sub-Saharan Africa." Policy Research Working Paper 7868, World Bank, Washington, DC.

Cirera, X., and W. F. Maloney. 2017. "The Innovation Paradox: Developing-Country Capabilities and the Unrealized Promise of Technological Catch-Up." World Bank, Washington, DC.

Cole, M. A., and E. Neumayer. 2006. "The Impact of Poor Health on Total Factor Productivity." *The Journal of Development Studies* 42 (6): 918-938.

Collier, P., G. Conway, and T. Venables. 2008. "Climate Change and Africa." *Oxford Review of Economic Policy* 24 (2): 337-353.

Colombia Departamento Nacional de Planeación. 2018. "Estrategia para la atención de la migración desde Venezuela." Colombia Departamento Nacional de Planeación, Bogotá.

Cook, T., and C. McKay. 2015. "How M-Shwari Works: The Story So Far." Consultative Group to Assist the Poor (CGAP) and Financial Sector Deepening (FSD) Kenya.

Crespi, G., and P. Zuniga. 2011. "Innovation and Productivity: Evidence from Six Latin American Countries." *World Development* 40 (2): 273-90.

Cusolito, A. P., W., and Maloney 2018. *Productivity Revisited: Shifting Paradigms in Analysis and Policy.* Washington, DC: World Bank.

Cusolito, A. P., R. Safadi, and D. Taglioni. 2017. "Inclusive Global Value Chains: Policy Options for Small and Medium Enterprises and Low-Income Countries." A co-publication of the World Bank Group

and the Organization for Economic Co-operation and Development.

Danforth, J., P. A. Medas, and V. Salins. 2016. *How to Adjust to a Large Fall in Commodity Prices.* Washington, DC: International Monetary Fund.

De Haas, R., and I. Van Lelyveld. "Foreign Banks and Credit Stability in Central and Eastern Europe. A Panel Data Analysis." *Journal of Banking & Finance* 30 (7): 1927-1952.

de Hoyos, R., H. Rogers, and M. Székely. 2016. *Out of School and Out of Work: Risk and Opportunities for Latin America's Ninis.* Washington, DC: World Bank.

De Nicola, F., V. V. Kehayova, and H. M. Nguyen. 2018. "On the Allocation of Resources in Developing East Asia and Pacific." Policy Research Working Paper 8634, Washington, DC: World Bank.

de Paula, A., and J. A. Scheinkman. 2011. "The Informal Sector: An Equilibrium Model and Some Empirical Evidence from Brazil." *Review of Income and Wealth* 57 (s1): s8-s26.

de Vries, G.J., M.P. Timmer, and K. de Vries 2013. "Structural Transformation in Africa: Static Gains, Dynamic Losses." GGDC Research Memorandum 136, Groningen Growth and Development Centre, University of Groningen, Netherlands.

Del Prete, D., G. Giovannetti, and E. Marvasi. 2017. "Global Value Chains Participation and Productivity Gains for North African firms." *Review of World Economics* 153 (4): 675-701.

Delogu, M., F. Docquier, and J. Machado. 2014. "The Dynamic Implications of Liberalizing Global Migration." CESifo Working Paper Series 4596, CESifo Group, Munich.

Devarajan, S., and L. Mottaghi. 2015. *MENA Economic Monitor. Towards a New Social Contract. April.* Washington, DC: World Bank.

Di Mauro, F., D. Hoang, A. Feng, S. J. Ong, and J. Pang. 2018. "Productivity Was Not that Sluggish in Developing Asia, Afterall. A Firm Level Perspective Using a Novel Dataset." Productivity Research Network, National University of Singapore mimeo.

Diao, X., M. McMillan, and D. Rodrik. 2017. "The Recent Growth Boom in Developing Economies: A Structural Change Perspective." NBER Working Paper 23132, National Bureau of Economic Research, Cambridge, MA.

Diaz, J. J., and D. Rosas. 2016. "Impact Evalation of the Job Youth Training Program Projoven." Working Paper 693, Inter-American Development Bank, Washington, DC.

Dieppe, A., G. Kindberg-Hanlon, and S. Kiliç Çelik. Forthcoming. "Global Productivity Trends: Looking Through the Turbulence." In *Productivity in Emerging and Developing Economies.* Washington, DC: World Bank.

Diop, N., and D. Marotta. 2012. *Natural Resource Abundance, Growth, and Diversification in the Middle East and North Africa: The Effects of Natural Resources and the Role of Policies.* Washington, DC: World Bank.

Divanbeigi, R., and R. Ramalho. 2015. "Business Regulations and Growth." Policy Research Working Paper 7299, World Bank, Washington, DC.

Du Plessis, S., and B. Smit. 2007. "South Africa's Growth Revival after 1994." *Journal of African Economies* 16 (5): 668-704.

Duranton, G., Ghani. E., Goswami, A. G., and W. Kerr. 2016. "A Detailed Anatomy of Factor Misallocation in India." Policy Research Working Paper 7547, World Bank, Washington, DC.

Dutz, M. A. 2018. *Jobs and Growth: Brazil's Productivity Agenda. Washington, DC: World Bank.*

Dutz, M. A., R. K. Almeida, and T. G. Packard. 2018. *The Jobs of Tomorrow: Technology, Productivity, and Prosperity in Latin America and the Caribbean.* Washington, DC: World Bank.

Dutz, M. A., and S. D. O'Connell. 2013. "Productivity, Innovation and Growth in Sri Lanka: An Empirical Investigation." Policy Research Working Paper 6354, World Bank, Washington, DC.

Easterly, W., and S. Fischer. 1994. "The Soviet Economic Decline Revisited." Policy Research Working Paper 1284, World Bank, Washington, DC.

EBRD (European Bank for Reconstruction and Development). 2014. *Transition Report 2013: Stuck in Transition?* London: European Bank for Reconstruction and Development.

———. *Transition Report 2017-18: Sustaining Growth.* London: European Bank for Reconstruction and Development.

———. 2018a. "The Western Balkans in Transition: Diagnosing the Constraints on the Path to a Sustainable Market Economy." Background paper for the Western Balkans Investment Summit, hosted by the EBRD, February 26, 2018, European Bank for Reconstruction and Development, London.

———. 2018b. *Transition Report 2018-19: Work in Transition.* London: European Bank for Reconstruction and Development.

———. 2019a. *Regional Economic Prospects in the EBRD Regions: Stalling Engines of Growth.* London: European Bank for Reconstruction and Development.

———. 2019b. *Transition Report 2019-20: Better Governance, Better Economies.* London: European Bank for Reconstruction and Development.

Eden, M., and H. Nguyen. 2016. "Reconciling Micro- and Macro-Based Estimates of Technology Adoption Lags in a Model of Endogenous Technology Adoption." In *Understanding the Income and Efficiency Gap in Latin America and the Caribbean,* edited by J. T. Araujo, E. Vostroknutova, K. Wacker, and M. Clavijo. Washington, DC: World Bank.

Elbadawi, I., and N. Loayza. 2008. "Informality, Employment and Economic Development in the Arab World." *Journal of Development and Economic Policies* 10 (2): 27-75.

Elekdag, S., D. Muir, and Y. Wu. 2015. "Trade Linkages, Balance Sheets, and Spillovers: The Germany-Central European Supply Chain." *Journal of Policy Modeling* 37 (2): 374-387.

Elgin, C., and O. Oztunali. 2012. "Shadow Economies Around the World: Model Based Estimates." Working Paper 2012/05, Department of Economics, Boğaziçi University, Istanbul.

Ellis, P., and M. Roberts. 2016. *Leveraging Urbanization in South Asia: Managing Spatial Transformation for Prosperity and Livability. South Asia Development Matters.* Washington, DC: World Bank.

Enache, M., E. Ghani, and S. O'Connell. 2016. "Structural Transformation in Africa: A Historical View." Policy Research Working Paper 7743, World Bank, Washington, DC.

Falcetti, E., T. Lysenko, and P. Sanfey. 2006. "Reforms and Growth in Transition: Re-examining the Evidence." *Journal of Comparative Economics* 34 (3): 421-445.

FAO (Food and Agriculture Organization of the United Nations). 2019. *Crop Prospects and Food Situation.* July. Food and Agriculture Organization of the United Nations: Rome.

Fay, M., L. Andres, C. Fox, U. Narloch, S. Straub, and M. Slawson. 2017. *Rethinking Infrastructure in Latin America and the Caribbean: Spending Better to Achieve More.* Washington, DC: World Bank.

Fayad, G., and T. Rasmussen. 2012. "Realizing Growth Objectives: Transitioning from Factor Accumulation to Productivity Improvement." In *Saudi Arabia: Selected Issues, IMF Country Report 12/272,* International Monetary Fund, Washington, DC.

Fernandes, A. M. 2008. "Firm Productivity in Bangladesh Manufacturing Industries." *World Development* 36 (10): 1725-1744.

Fernández-Arias, E., and S. Rodríguez-Apolinar. 2016. "The Productivity Gap in Latin America: Lessons from 50 Years of Development." Working Paper IDB-WP-692, Inter-American Development Bank, Washington, DC.

Ferreira, P. C., S. de Abreu Pessôa, and F. Veloso. 2013. "On the Evolution of Total Factor Productivity in Latin America." *Economic Inquiry* 51 (1): 16–30.

Ferreira, P. C., S. Pessôa, and M. R. Dos Santos. 2011. "The Impact of AIDS on Income and Human Capital." *Economic Inquiry* 49 (4): 1104-1116.

Flabbi, L., and R. Gatti. 2018. "A Primer on Human Capital." Policy Research Working Paper 8309, World Bank, Washington, DC.

Fosu, A. K., and A. F. Abass. 2019. *"Domestic Credit and Export Diversification: Africa from a Global Perspective."* Journal of African Business 20 (2): 160-179.

Francis, E., J. Blumenstock, and J. Robinson. 2017. "Digital Credit in Emerging Markets: A Snapshot of the Current Landscape and Open Research Questions." Digital Credit Observatory, Center for Effective Global Action, University of California, Berkeley.

Freund, C., M. J. Ferrantino, M. Maliszewska, and M. Ruta. 2018. "Impacts on Global Trade and Income of Current Trade Disputes." MTI Practice Note 2, World Bank, Washington, DC.

Fuglie, K., M. Gautam, A. Goyal, and W. Maloney. 2019. *Harvesting Prosperity: Technology and Productivity Growth in Agriculture.* Washington, DC: World Bank.

Fujimori, A., and T. Sato. 2015. "Productivity and Technology Diffusion in India: The Spillover Effects from Foreign Direct Investment." *Journal of Policy Modeling* 37 (4): 630-651.

Funke, N., A. Isakova, and M. Ivanyna. 2017. "Identifying Structural Reform Gaps in Emerging Europe, the Caucasus, and Central Asia." IMF Working Paper 17/82, International Monetary Fund, Washington, DC.

Gatti, R., M. Morgandi, E. Grun, S. Brodmann, D. Angel-Urdinola, J.M. Moreno, D. Marotta, M. Schiffbauer, and E. Mata Lorenzo. 2013. *Jobs for Shared Prosperity: Time for Action in the Middle East and North Africa.* Washington, DC: World Bank.

Gautam, M., and A. Mansur. 2018. "Too Small to be Beautiful? The Farm Size and Productivity Relationship in Bangladesh." *Food Policy* 84 (April): 165-175.

Gelb, A., C. J. Meyer, V. Ramachandran, and D. Wadhwa. 2017. "Can Africa Be a Manufacturing Destination? Labor Costs in Comparative Perspective." CGD Working Paper 466, Center for Global Development, Washington, DC.

Georgiev, Y., P. Nagy-Mohacsi, and A. Plekhanov. 2017. "Structural Reform and Productivity Growth in Emerging Europe and Central Asia." ADB Economics Working Paper Series 532, Asian Development Bank, Manila.

Ghani, E., W. R. Kerr, and S. D. O'Connell. 2013. "Input Usage and Productivity in Indian Manufacturing Plants." Policy Research Working Paper 6656. World Bank, Washington, DC.

Gharleghi, B., and V. Popov. 2018. "Farewell to Agriculture? Productivity Trends and the Competitiveness of Agriculture in Central Asia." MPRA Paper 89520, University Library of Munich, Germany.

Ghassibe, M., M. Appendino, and S.E. Mahmoudi. 2019. "SME Financial Inclusion for Sustained Growth in the Middle East and Central Asia." IMF Working Paper 19/209, International Monetary Fund, Washington, DC.

Goedhuys, M., N. Janz, and P. Mohnen. 2008. "What Drives Productivity in Tanzanian Manufacturing Firms: Technology or Business Environment?" *The European Journal of Development Research* 20 (2): 199-218.

Goretti, M., D. Kihara, R. Salgado, and A. M. Gulde. 2019. "Is South Asia Ready for Take Off?" Asia and Pacific Department Paper 19/18, International Monetary Fund, Washington, DC.

Gould, D. 2018. *Critical Connections: Promoting Economic Growth and Resilience in Europe and Central*

Asia. Europe and Central Asia Studies. Washington, DC: World Bank.

Gould, D. M., C. Tan, and A. S. S. Emamgholy. 2013. "Attracting Foreign Direct Investment: What Can South Asia's Lack of Success Teach Other Developing Countries?" Policy Research Working Paper 6696, World Bank, Washington, DC.

Gradzewicz, M., J. Growiec, M. Kolasa, Ł. Postek, and P. Strzelecki. 2018. "Poland's Uninterrupted Growth Performance: New Growth Accounting Evidence." *Post-Communist Economies* 30 (2): 238-272.

Grainger, C. A., and F. Zhang. 2017. "The Impact of Electricity Shortages on Firm Productivity: Evidence from Pakistan." Policy Research Working Paper 8130, World Bank, Washington, DC.

Grazzi, M., and J. Jung. 2016. "ICT, Innovation, and Productivity." In *Firm Innovation and Productivity in Latin America and the Caribbean: The Engine of Economic Development,* edited by M. Grazzi and C. Pietrobelli, 103-36. Washington, DC: Inter-American Development Bank.

Grigoli, F., A. Herman, A. J. Swiston. 2017. "A Crude Shock : Explaining the Impact of the 2014-16 Oil Price Decline Across Exporters." IMF Working Paper 17/160, International Monetary Fund, Washington, DC.

Groth, H., and J. F. May, eds. 2017. *Africa's Population: In Search of a Demographic Dividend. Cham.* Switzerland: Springer International.

Gylfason, T. 2018. "From Economic Diversification to Growth. Two Proposals." In *Rethinking the Macroeconomics of Resource-Rich Countries,* edited by Arezki, A, R. Boucekkine, J. Frankel, M. Laksaci, and R. van der Ploeg. CEPR's Policy Portal. https:// voxeu.org/system/files/epublication/Resource_Rich_Co untries_eBook.pdf.

H. M. Government. 2018. "EU Exit: Long-Term Economic Analysis." November. HM Government, London.

Ha, J., M. A. Kose, and F. Ohnsorge. 2019. *Inflation in Emerging and Developing Economies: Evolution, Drivers, and Policies.* Washington, DC: World Bank.

Haile, F. 2018. "Structural Change in West Africa: A Tale of Gain and Loss." Policy Research Working Paper 8336, World Bank, Washington, DC.

Hallegatte, S., M. Bangalore, L. Bonzanigo, M. Fay, T. Kane, U. Narloch, J. Rozenberg, D. Treguer, and A.

Vogt-Schilb. 2015. *Shock Waves: Managing the Impacts of Climate Change on Poverty.* Washington, DC: World Bank.

Hallward-Driemeier M., G. Iarossi, and K. L. Sokoloff. 2002. "Exports and Manufacturing Productivity in East Asia: A Comparative Analysis with Firm-Level Data." NBER Working Paper 8894, National Bureau of Economic Research, Cambridge, MA.

Hallward-Driemeier, M., and G. Nayyar. 2018. *Trouble in the Making? The Future of Manufacturing-Led Development.* Washington, DC: World Bank.

Helble, M., T. Long, and T. Le. 2019. "Sectoral and Skill Contributions to Labor Productivity in Asia." ADBI Working Paper 929, Asian Development Bank Institute, Tokyo.

Henry, P. 2007. "Capital Account Liberalization: Theory, Evidence, and Speculation." *Journal of Economic Literature* 45 (4): 887-935.

Hesse, H. 2008. "Export Diversification and Economic Growth." Working Paper 21, Commission on Growth and Development, World Bank, Washington, DC.

Hjort, J., and J. Poulsen. 2019. "The Arrival of Fast Internet and Employment in Africa." *American Economic Review* 109 (3): 1032-79.

Hodge, A., S. Shankar, D. S. Prasada Rao, and A. Duhs. 2011. "Exploring the Links between Corruption and Growth." *Review of Development Economics* 15 (3): 474-90.

Hsieh, C., and P. J. Klenow. 2009. "Misallocation and Manufacturing TFP in China and India." *Quarterly Journal of Economics* 124 (4): 1403-1448.

Hu A. G. Z., G. H. Jefferson and Q. Jinchang. 2005. "R&D and Technology Transfer: Firm-Level Evidence from Chinese Industry." *Review of Economics and Statistics* 87 (4): p.780-786.

Ianchovichina, E. 2017. *Eruptions of Popular Anger: The Economics of the Arab Spring and Its Aftermath. MENA Development Report.* Washington, DC: World Bank.

IDB (Inter-American Development Bank). 2016. *Time to Act: Latin America and the Caribbean Facing Strong Challenges.* Washington, DC: Inter-American Development Bank.

IEA (International Energy Agency). 2019. *Oil Market Report.* Paris: IEA.

ILO (International Labour Office). 2017. *What Future for Decent Work in Europe and Central Asia:*

Opportunities and Challenges. Geneva: International Labour Office.

IMF (International Monetary Fund). 2006. World Economic Outlook. Financial Systems and Economic Cycles. Chapter 3. Asia Rising: Patterns of Economic Development and growth.

———. 2012. "Saudi Arabia Article IV Consultation." IMF Country Report 12/271, International Monetary Fund, Washington, DC.

———. 2013. "Labor Market Reforms to Boost Employment and Productivity in the GCC." Annual Meeting of the Gulf Cooperation Council Ministers of Finance and Central Bank Governors, Riyadh, October 5. International Monetary Fund, Washington, DC.

———. 2014. *The Caucasus and Central Asia: Transitioning to Emerging Markets.* Washington, DC: International Monetary Fund.

———. 2015. "Islamic Republic of Iran Consultation." IMF Country Report No. 15/349, International Monetary Fund, Washington, DC.

———. 2016a. "Economic Diversification in Oil-Exporting Arab Countries." Annual Meeting of Arab Ministers of Finance.

———. 2016b. "Bolivia: 2016 Article IV Staff Report." IMF Country Report 16/387, International Monetary Fund, Washington, DC.

———. 2017. *Asia and Pacific: Preparing for Choppy Seas.* Regional Economic Outlook series. May. Washington, DC: International Monetary Fund.

———. 2018a. "Productivity Growth in Asia: Boosting Firm Dynamism and Weeding out the Zombies." In *Asia at the Forefront: Growth Challenges for the Next Decade and Beyond.* Regional Economic Outlook series. October. Washington, DC: International Monetary Fund.

———. 2018b. *Middle East and Central Asia.* Regional Economic Outlook series. November. Washington, DC: International Monetary Fund.

———. 2019a. *Promoting Inclusive Growth in the Caucasus and Central Asia.* Washington, DC: International Monetary Fund.

———. 2019b. "Financial Inclusion of Small and Medium-Sized Enterprises in the Middle East and Central Asia." IMF Departmental Paper 19/02, International Monetary Fund, Washington, DC.

———. 2019c. Fiscal *Monitor: Curbing Corruption. April.* Washington, DC: International Monetary Fund.

———. 2019d. *Middle East and Central Asia Economic Outlook.* October. Washington, DC: International Monetary Fund.

Iootty, M., J. Pena, and D. De Rosa. 2019. "Productivity Growth in Romania: A Firm-Level Analysis." Policy Research Working Paper 9043, World Bank, Washington, DC.

IPCC (Intergovernmental Panel on Climate Change). *2014. Climate Change 2014: Impacts, Adaptation, and Vulnerability. IPCC Working Group II.* Geneva: Intergovernmental Panel on Climate Change.

———. 2019. *Climate Change and Land: an IPCC Special Report on Climate Change, Desertification, Land Degradation, Sustainable Land Management, Food Security, and Greenhouse Gas Fluxes in Terrestrial Ecosystems.* Geneva: Intergovernmental Panel on Climate Change.

ITF (International Transport Forum). 2018. "The Billion Dollar Question: How Much Will It Cost to Decarbonise Cities' Transport Systems?" Discussion Paper, Paris.

Jirasavetakul, L. B. F., and J. Rahman. "Foreign Direct Investment in New Member States of the EU and Western Balkans: Taking Stock and Assessing Prospects." IMF Working Paper 18/187, International Monetary Fund, Washington, DC.

Kalemli-Ozcan, S. 2003. "A Stochastic Model of Mortality, Fertility, and Human Capital Investment." *Journal of Development Economics* 70 (1): 103-118.

Kanwar, S., and S. Sperlich. 2019. "Innovation, Productivity and Intellectual Property Reform in an Emerging Market Economy: Evidence from India." *Empirical Economics.* https://doi.org/10.1007/s00181-019-01707-3.

Kaplan, D. 2009. "Job Creation and Labor Reform in Latin America." *Journal of Comparative Economics* 37 (1): 91-105.

Kaufmann, D., A. Kraay, and M. Mastruzzi. 2010. "The Worldwide Governance Indicators: Methodology and Analytica Issues." Policy Research Working Paper 5430, World Bank, Washington, DC.

Kaufmann, D., A. Kraay, and M. Mastruzzi. 2010. "Response to 'What Do the Worldwide Governance Indicators Measure?'" *The European Journal of Development Research* 22 (1): 55-58.

Keefer, P., and S. Knack. 2007. "Boondoggles, Rent-seeking, and Political Checks and Balances: Public Investment under Unaccountable Governments." *The Review of Economics and Statistics* 89 (3): 566-572.

Keller, J., and M. K. Nabli. 2002. "The Macroeconomics of Labor Market Outcomes in MENA over the 1990s: How Growth Has Failed to Keep Pace with a Burgeoning Labor Market." Working Paper 71, Egyptian Center for Economic Studies, Cairo.

Khan, T., T. Nguyen, F. Ohnsorge, and R. Schodde. 2016. "From Commodity Discovery to Production." Policy Research Working Paper 7823, World Bank, Washington, DC.

Khera, P. 2018. "Closing Gender Gaps in India: Does Increasing Women's Access to Finance Help?" IMF Working Paper 18/212, International Monetary Fund, Washington, DC.

Kim, Y. E., and N. V. Loayza. 2017. "Productivity Determinants: Innovation, Education, Efficiency, Infrastructure, and Institutions." World Bank, Washington, DC.

Kim, Y. E., and N. V. Loayza. 2019. "Productivity Growth: Patterns and Determinants Across the World." Policy Research Working Paper 8852, World Bank, Washington, DC.

Kim, Y. E., N. V. Loayza, and C. Meza-Cuadra. 2016. "Productivity as the Key to Economic Growth and Development." Research & Policy Brief 3, World Bank, Washington, DC.

Kinda, T. 2019. "E-commerce as a Potential New Engine for Growth in Asia." IMF Working Paper 19/135, International Monetary Fund, Washington, DC.

Klapper, L., C. Richmond, and T. Tran. 2013. "Civil Conflict and Firm Performance: Evidence from Cote d'Ivoire." Policy Research Working Paper 6640, World Bank, Washington, DC.

Kochhar, K., K. Utsav, R. Rajan, A. Subramanian, and I. Tokatlidis. 2006. "India's Pattern of Development: What Happened, What Follows?" *Journal of Monetary Economics* 53 (5): 981-1019.

Kose, M. A., and F. Ohnsorge. 2019. *A Decade since the Global Recession: Lessons and Challenges for Emerging and Developing Economies.* Washington, DC: World Bank.

Kouamé, W., and S. Tapsoba. 2018. "Structural Reforms and Firms' Productivity: Evidence from

Developing Countries." Policy Research Working Paper 8308, World Bank, Washington, DC.

Krishna, K. L., D. K. Das, A. A. Erumdan, S. Aggarwal, and P. C. Das. 2016. "Productivity Dynamics in India's Service Sector: An Industry-Level Perspective." Working Paper 261. Center for Development Economics, Delhi School of Economics, Delhi.

Kraay, A. 2018. "Methodology for a World Bank Human Capital Index." Policy Research Working Paper 8593, World Bank, Washington, DC.

La Porta, R., and A. Scheifler. 2014. "Informality and Development." *Journal of Economic Perspectives* 28 (3): 109-126.

Laget, E., A. Osnago, N. Rocha, and M. Ruta. 2018. "Deep Trade Agreements and Global Value Chains." Policy Research Working Paper 8491, World Bank, Washington, DC.

Lall, S., Z. Shalizi, and U. Deichmann. 2001. "Agglomeration Economies and Productivity in Indian Industry." *Journal of Development Economics* 73 (2): 643-673.

Lederman, D., and W. F. Maloney. 2007. *Natural Resources: Neither Curse nor Destiny.* Palo Alto, CA: Stanford University Press.

Lederman, D., J. Messina, S. Pienknagura, and J. Rigolini. 2014. *Latin American Entrepreneurs: Many Firms but Little Innovation.* Washington, DC: World Bank.

Lehne, J., J. Mo, and A. Plekhanov. 2014. "What Determines the Quality of Economic Institutions? Cross-Country Evidence." EBRD Working Paper 171, European Bank for Reconstruction and Development, London.

Levenko, N., K. Oja, and K. Staehr. 2019. "Total Factor Productivity Growth in Central and Eastern Europe Before, During and After the Global Financial Crisis." *Post-Communist Economies* 31 (2): 137-160.

Liu, Y., and V. Steenbergen. 2019. "The Role of FDI in Global Value Chains (GVCs): Implications for SubSaharan Africa." Unpublished working paper, World Bank, Washington, DC.

Loayza, N. V., L. Servén, and N. Sugawara. 2010. "Informality in Latin America and the Caribbean." In *Business Regulation and Economic Performance,* edited by N. Loayza and L. Servén, 157–196. Washington, DC: World Bank.

Lopez-Calix, J., T. G. Srinivasan, and M. Waheed. 2012. "What Do We Know About Growth Patterns in Pakistan?" Policy Paper Series on Pakistan (PK 05/12), World Bank, Washington, DC.

Lovász, A. 2016 "Childcare Expansion and Mothers' Employment in Post-Socialist Countries." IZA World of Labor, Bonn, Germany. https://wol.iza.org/articles/childcare-expansion-and-mothers-employment-in-post-socialist-countries/long.

Lovász, A., and A. Szabó-Morvai 2013. "Does Childcare Matter for Maternal Labor Supply? Pushing the Limits of the Regression Discontinuity Framework." Budapest Working Papers on the Labour Market 1313, Hungarian Academy of Sciences, Budapest.

Maiti, D. 2019. "Trade, Labor Share, and Productivity in India's Industries." ADBI Working Paper 926, Asian Development Bank Institute, Tokyo.

Malik, M., and T. Masood. 2018. "Economic Growth, Productivity and Convergence of the Middle East and North African Countries." MPRA Paper 87882, Munich Personal RePEc Archive, Munich.

Mallick, J. 2017. "Structural Change and Productivity Growth in India and the People's Republic of China." ADBI Working Paper 656, Asian Development Bank Institute, Tokyo.

Mansour, W., A. N. Maseeh, and B. Celiku. 2019. "Iraq Economic Monitor: Turning the Corner - Sustaining Growth and Creating Opportunities for Iraq's Youth." World Bank, Washington, DC.

Mason, A. D., and S. Shetty. 2019. *A Resurgent East Asia: Navigating a Changing World. World Bank East Asia and Pacific Regional Report*. Washington, DC: World Bank.

McMillan, M., D. Rodrik, and I. Verduzco-Gallo. 2014. "Globalization, Structural Change, and Productivity Growth, with and Update on Africa." *World Development* 63 (C): 11-32.

Mensah, E. B., S. Owusu, N. Foster-McGregor, and A. Szirmai. 2018. "Structural Change, Productivity Growth and Labor Market Turbulence in Africa." UNU-MERIT Working Paper 2018-25, University in Maastricht, Netherlands.

Mensah, E. B., and A. Szirmai. 2018. "Africa Sector Database (ASD): Expansion and Update". UNU-MERIT Working Paper 2018-20, University in Maastricht, Netherlands.

Mercer-Blackman, V., and C. Ablaza. 2018. "The Servicification of Manufacturing in Asia: Redefining the Sources of Labor Productivity." ADBI Working Paper 902, Asian Development Bank Institute, Tokyo.

Messina, J., and J. Silva. 2019. "Twenty Years of Wage Inequality in Latin America." Policy Research Working Paper 8995, World Bank, Washington, DC.

Mitra, A. 2016. "Productivity Growth in India: Determinants and Policy Initiatives Based on the Existing Literature." United Nations Working Paper 16/08, United Nations, New York.

Mitra, P., A. Hosny, G. Minasyan, M. Fischer, and G. Abajyan. 2016. "Avoiding the New Mediocre: Raising Long-Term Growth in the Middle East and Central Asia." Middle East and Central Asia Departmental Paper 16/1, International Monetary Fund, Washington, DC.

Montalbano, P., S. Nenci, and C. Pietrobelli. 2018. "Opening and Linking Up: Firms, GVCs, and Productivity in Latin America." *Small Business Economics* 50 (4): 917–35.

Morsy, H., A. Levy, and C. Sanchez. 2014. "Growing Without Changing: A Tale of Egypt's Weak Productivity Growth." EBRD Working Paper 172, European Bank for Reconstruction and Development, London.

Munoz, M. R., V. Perotti, J. Revilla, N. V. Loayza, T. Sharifuddin, S. Binti, J. Kunicova, et al. 2016. "The Quest for Productivity Growth." *Malaysia Economic Monitor*. Washington, DC: World Bank.

Nabli, M. 2007. *Breaking the Barriers to Higher Economic Growth: Better Governance and Deeper Reforms in the Middle East and North Africa*. Washington, DC: World Bank.

Nguimkeu, P. E. 2015. "An Estimated Model of Informality with Constrained Entrepreneurship." Working Paper, Georgia State University.

Nicoletti, G., and S. Scarpetta. 2005. "Regulation and Economic Performance: Product Market Reforms and Productivity in the OECD," OECD Economics Department Working Paper 460, Organisation for Economic Co-operation and Development, Paris.

O'Sullivan, M., A. Rao, R. Banerjee, K. Gulati, and M. Vinez. 2014. "Levelling the Field: Improving Opportunities for Women Farmers in Africa." World Bank and ONE Campaign, Washington, DC.

OECD (Organisation for Economic Co-operation and Development). 2016. "The Best Versus the Rest: The Global Productivity Slowdown, Divergence Across Firms and the Role of Public Policy." OECD Productivity Working Paper 5, Organisation for Economic Co-operation and Development, Paris.

————. 2018a. *OECD Economic Survey of Costa Rica: Research Findings on Productivity.* Paris: Organisation for Economic Co-operation and Development.

————. 2018b. *Boosting Productivity and Inclusive Growth in Latin America.* Paris: Organisation for Economic Co-operation and Development.

Oosthuizen, M., K. Lilenstein, F. Steenkamp, and A. Cassim. 2016. "Informality and Inclusive Growth in Sub-Saharan Africa." ELLA Regional Evidence Paper, ELLA Network, Lima.

Orlic, E., I. Hashi, and M. Hisarciklilar. 2018. "Cross Sectoral FDI Spillovers and Their Impact on Manufacturing Productivity." *International Business Review* 27 (4): 777-796.

Page, J. 1994. "The East Asian Miracle: Four Lessons for Development Policy." *NBER Macroeconomics Annual 1994* 9: 219-282.

Pagés-Serra, C., ed. 2010. *The Age of Productivity: Transforming Economies from the Bottom Up.* Washington, DC: Inter-American Development Bank.

Papageorgiou, C., and N. Spatafora. 2012. "Economic Diversification in LICs: Stylized Facts and Macroeconomic Implications." IMF Staff Discussion Note 12/13, International Monetary Fund, Washington, DC.

Park, J. 2010. "Projection of Long-Term Total Factor Productivity Growth for 12 Asian Economies." ADB Economics Working Paper 227, Asian Development Bank, Manila.

Peralta-Alva, A., and A. Roitman. 2008. "Technology and the Future of Work." IMF Working Paper 19/207, International Monetary Fund, Washington, DC.

Purfield C., H. Finger, K. Ongley, B. Baduel, C. Castellanos, G. Pierre, V. Stepanyan, and E. Roos. 2018. "Opportunity for All: Promoting Growth and Inclusiveness in the Middle East and North Africa." IMF Departmental Paper 18/11, International Monetary Fund, Washington, DC.

Raballand, G., S. Refas, M. Beuran, and G. Isik. 2012. *Why Does Cargo Spend Weeks in Sub-Saharan African Ports? Lessons from Six Countries.* Washington, DC: World Bank.

Raggl, A. 2015. "Determinants of Total Factor Productivity in the Middle East and North Africa." *Review of Middle East Economic and Finance* 11 (2): 119-143.

Rahmati, M., and A. Pilehvari. 2017. "The Productivity Trend in Iran: Evidence from Manufacturing Firms." *Economics of Transition and Institutional Change* 27 (1): 395-408.

RBI (Reserve Bank of India). 2019. *Financial Stability Report. July 2019. Mumbai: Reserve Bank of India.*

Reinhart, C. M., and K. S. Rogoff. 2009. *This Time is Different: Eight Centuries of Financial Folly.* Princeton, NJ: Princeton University Press.

Rodríguez-Pose, A., and T. Ketterer. 2019. "Institutional Change and the Development of Lagging Regions in Europe." *Regional Studies.* https://doi.org/10.1080/00343404.2019.1608356.

Rodrik, D. 1999. "Where Did All the Growth Go? External Shocks, Social Conflict, and Growth Collapses." *Journal of Economic Growth* 4 (4): 385–412.

————. 2016a. "Premature Deindustrialization." *Journal of Economic Growth* 21 (1): 1–33.

————. 2016b. "An African Growth Miracle?" *Journal of African Economies* 27 (1): 10-27.

Rodrik, D. and A. Subramanian. 2004. "From 'Hindu Growth' to Productivity Surge: The Mystery of the Indian Growth Transition." IMF Working Paper 04/77, International Monetary Fund, Washington, DC.

Rodrik, D., A. Subramanian, and F. Trebbi. 2004. "Institutions Rule: The Primacy of Institutions Over Geography and Integration in Economic Development." *Journal of Economic Growth* 9 (2): 131–65.

Rovo, N. 2019. "Structural Reforms to Set the Growth Ambition: New Growth Agenda." World Bank, Washington DC.

Rozenberg, J., and M. Fay, eds. 2019. *Beyond the Gap: How Countries Can Afford the Infrastructure They Need While Protecting the Planet.* Washington, DC: World Bank.

Russell, M. 2018. "Seven Economic Challenges for Russia: Breaking Out of Stagnation?" European Parliament Think Tank In-Depth Analysis Paper, European Parliament, Brussels.

Ruta, M., I. C. Constantinescu, and A. Mattoo. 2017. "Does Vertical Specialization Increase Productivity?" Policy Research Working Paper 7978, World Bank, Washington DC.

Ryzhenkov, M. 2016. "Resource Misallocation and Manufacturing Productivity: The Case of Ukraine," *Journal of Comparative Economics* 44 (1): 41-55.

Saleem, H., M. Shahzad, M. B. Khan, and B. A. Khiliji. 2019. "Innovation, Total Factor Productivity and Economic Growth in Pakistan: A Policy Perspective." *Journal of Economic Structures.* 8 (1): 1-18.

Samargandi, N. 2018. "Determinants of Labor Productivity in MENA Countries." *Emerging Markets Finance and Trade* 54 (5): 1063–81.

Satpathy, L., B. Chatterjee, and J. Mahakud. 2017. "Financial Constraints and Total Factor Productivity: Evidence from Indian Manufacturing Companies." *Journal of Management Research* 17 (3): 146-162.

SBP (State Bank of Pakistan). 2019. *The State of Pakistan's Economy—Third Quarterly Report 2018-2019.* Islamabad: State Bank of Pakistan.

Schiantarelli, F., and V. Srivastava. 1997. "Debt Maturity and Firm Performance: A Panel Study of Indian Companies." Policy Research Working Paper 1724, World Bank, Washington, DC.

Schiffbauer, M., and J. Sampi. 2019. "Enforcing Competition and Firm Productivity: Evidence from 1,800 Peruvian Municipalities." Policy Research Working Paper 8714, World Bank, Washington, DC.

Schiffbauer, M., A. Sy, S. Hussain, H. Sahnoun, and P. Keefer. 2015. "Jobs or Privileges: Unleashing the Employment Potential of the Middle East and North Africa." *MENA Development Report.* Washington, DC: World Bank.

Schneider, F., A. Buehn, and C. Montenegro. 2010. "Shadow Economies All over the World: New Estimates for 162 Countries from 1999 to 2007." Policy Research Working Paper 5356, World Bank, Washington, DC.

Schodde, R. 2013. "The Impact of Commodity Prices and Other Factors on the Level of Exploration." Minex Consulting seminar series, South Yarra, Australia.

Sengupta, R., and A. S. Gupta. 2015. "Capital Flows and Capital Account Management in Selected Asian Economies." New Thinking and the New G20 *series. No. 9.* Waterloo, Canada: The Centre for International Governance Innovation.

Sharafudheen, T. 2017. *South Asia Gender Initiative.* Washington, DC: World Bank.

Shepotylo, O., and V. Vakhitov. 2015. "Services Liberalization and Productivity of Manufacturing Firms: Evidence from Ukraine." *Economics of Transition* 23 (1): 1-44.

Shiferaw, A., M. Söderbom, E. Siba, and G. Alemu. 2015. "Road Infrastructure and Enterprise Dynamics in Ethiopia." *The Journal of Development Studies* 51 (11): 1541-1558.

Sinha, R., and X. Xi. 2018. "Agronomic Endowment, Crop Choice and Agricultural Productivity." Background paper prepared for the AFRCE project Boosting Productivity in Sub-Saharan Africa, World Bank, Washington, DC.

Steinbach, M. R. 2019. "Growth in Low-Income Countries: Evolution, Prospects, and Policies." Policy Research Working Paper 8949, World Bank, Washington, DC.

Stocker, M., J. Baffes, Y. Some, D. Vorisek, and C. Wheeler. 2018. "The 2014-16 Oil Price Collapse in Retrospect: Sources and Implications." Policy Research Working Paper 8419, World Bank, Washington, DC.

Straus, S. 2012. "Wars Do End! Changing Patterns of Political Violence in Sub-Saharan Africa." *African Affairs* 111 (443): 179-201.

Subramanian, A., and M. Kessler. 2013. "The Hyperglobalization of Trade and Its Future," Working Paper 13-6, Peterson Institute for International Economics, Washington.

Suri, T., and W. Jack. 2016. "The Long-Run Poverty and Gender Impacts of Mobile Money." *Science* 354 (6317): 1288–92.

Tamirisa, N., and C. Duenwald. 2018. "Public Wage Bills in the Middle East and North Africa." Middle East and Central Asia Department, International Monetary Fund, Washington, DC.

Timmer, M. P., and A. Szirmai. 2000. "Productivity Growth in Asian Manufacturing: The Structural Bonus Hypothesis Examined." *Structural Change and Economic Dynamics* 11 (4): 371-392.

Topalova, P., and A. Khandelwal. 2011. "Trade Liberalization and Firm Productivity: The Case of India." *The Review of Economics and Statistics* 93 (3): 995-1009.

Torlese, H., and D. Raju. 2018. "Feeding of Infants

and Young Children in South Asia." Policy Research Working Paper 8655, World Bank, Washington, DC.

Transparency International. 2019. Corruption Perceptions Index 2018. Accessed July 23. https://www.transparency.org/cpi2018.

Trushin, E. 2018. "Growth and Job Creation in Uzbekistan: An In-Depth Diagnostic." World Bank, Washington, DC.

Tuan, T., L. F. Y. Ng, and B. Zhao. 2009. "China's Post-Economic Reform Growth: The Role of FDI and Productivity Progress." *Journal of Asian Economics* 20 (3): 280-293.

UNCTAD (United Nations Conference on Trade and Development). 2019. "Trade and Trade Diversion Effects of United States Tariffs on China." Research Paper 37, Geneva, UNCTAD.

Unel, B. 2003. "Productivity Trends in India's Manufacturing Sectors in the Last Two Decades." IMF Working Paper 03/22, International Monetary Fund, Washington, DC.

UNHCR (United Nations High Commissioner for Refugees). 2019. *Global Trends: Forced Displacement in 2018.* Geneva: United Nations High Commissioner for Refugees.

UNICEF (United Nations Children's Fund). 2019. Primary Education. Accessed November 12, 2019. https://data.unicef.org/topic/education/primary-education/.

Vagliasindi, M. 2013. *Revisiting Public-Private Partnerships in the Power Sector.* Washington, DC: World Bank.

Van Eyden, R., M. Difeto, R. Gupta, and M. E. Wohar. 2019. "Oil Price Volatility and Economic Growth: Evidence from Advanced Economies Using More than a Century's Data." *Applied Energy* 233-234 (January): 612-621.

Vargas, M. 2015. "Informality in Paraguay: Macro-Micro Evidence and Policy Implications." IMF Working Paper 15/245, International Monetary Fund, Washington, DC.

Virmani, A., and D. Hashim. 2011. "J-Curve of Productivity and Growth: Indian Manufacturing Post-Liberalization." IMF Working Paper 11/163, International Monetary Fund, Washington, DC.

Vorisek, D., and S. Yu. Forthcoming. "Understanding the Cost of Achieving the Sustainable Development Goals: The World Bank Group's Contributions." Policy Research Working Paper, World Bank, Washington, DC.

Wamboye, E., K. Tochkov, and B. S. Sergi. 2015. "Technology Adoption and Growth in Sub-Saharan African Countries." *Comparative Economic Studies* 57 (1): 136-167.

Wang, Y. 2016. "What Are the Biggest Obstacles to Growth of SMEs in Developing Countries?—An Empirical Evidence from an Enterprise Survey." *Borsa Istanbul Review* 16 (3): 167-176.

World Bank. 1995. *Bureaucrats in Business: The Economics and Politics of Government Ownership.* Washington, DC: World Bank.

———. 2003. *Trade, Investment and Development in the Middle East and North Africa—Engaging with the World.* Washington, DC: World Bank.

———. 2008. *Unleashing Prosperity: Productivity Growth in Eastern Europe and the Former Soviet Union.* Washington, DC: World Bank.

———. 2012. *World Development Report 2012: Gender Equality and Development.* Washington, DC: World Bank.

———. 2013a. *Micro, Small, and Medium Enterprise Finance: Women-Owned Business in India.* Washington, DC: World Bank.

———. 2013b. *Enterprise Surveys: Nepal Country Highlights 2013.* Enterprise Surveys Country Highlights. Washington, DC: World Bank.

———. 2013c. *Enterprise Surveys: Bangladesh Country Highlights 2013.* Enterprise Surveys Country Highlights. Washington, DC: World Bank.

———. 2014. *Turkey's Transition.* Washington, DC: World Bank.

———. 2015a. *East Asia's Changing Urban Landscape: Measuring a Decade of Spatial* Growth. Washington, DC: World Bank.

———. 2015b. *Golden Aging: Prospects for Healthy, Active, and Prosperous Aging in Europe and Central Asia.* Europe and Central Asia Studies. June. Washington DC: World Bank.

———. 2015c. *Côte d'Ivoire Systematic Country Diagnostic: From Crisis to Sustained Growth—Priorities for Ending Poverty and Boosting Shared Prosperity.* Washington, DC: World Bank.

———. 2016a. *Global Economic Prospects: Spillovers amid Weak Growth.* January. Washington, DC: World Bank.

———. 2016b. *Thailand Economic Monitor. Aging Society and Economy.* Washington, DC: World Bank.

———. 2016c. *World Development Report 2016: Digital Dividends.* Washington, DC: World Bank.

———. 2016d. *Russian Federation—Systematic Country Diagnostic: Pathways to Inclusive Growth.* Washington, DC: World Bank.

———. 2016e. *Poverty and Shared Prosperity 2016: Taking on Inequality.* Washington, DC: World Bank.

———. 2016f. *What's Holding Back the Private Sector in MENA? Lessons from the Enterprise Survey.* Washington, DC: World Bank.

———. 2016g. *South Asia Regional Gender Action Plan (RGAP): FY16-FY21—June 2016.* Washington, DC: World Bank.

———. 2016h. *Africa's Pulse: An Analysis of Issues Shaping Africa's Economic Future.* October. Washington, DC: World Bank.

———. 2017a. "Cities in Eastern Europe and Central Asia: A Story of Urban Growth and Decline." World Bank, Washington, DC.

———. 2017b. *At a Crossroads: Higher Education in Latin America and the Caribbean.* Washington, DC: World Bank.

———. 2017c. *The Global Findex Database 2017: Measuring Financial Inclusion and the Fintech Revolution.* Washington, DC: World Bank.

———. 2017d. *Gulf Economic Monitor. Sustaining Fiscal Reforms in the Long Term.* June. Washington, DC: Washington DC.

———. 2017e. *South Asia's Turn: Policies to Boost Competitiveness and Create the Next Export Powerhouse. South Asia Development Matters.* Washington, DC: World Bank.

———. 2017f. *Doing Business 2018: Reforming to Create Jobs.* Washington, DC: World Bank.

———. 2017g. *Nigeria Bi-Annual Economic Update: Fragile Recovery.* April. Washington, DC: World Bank.

———. 2018a. *Global Economic Prospects: Broad-Based Upturn, but for How Long?* January. Washington, DC: World Bank.

———. 2018b. *East Asia and Pacific Economic Update: Enhancing Potential.* April. Washington, DC: World Bank.

———. 2018c. *Growth and Productivity in the Philippines: Winning the Future.* Washington, DC: World Bank Group.

———. 2018d. *China—Systematic Country Diagnostic: Towards a More Inclusive and Sustainable Development.* Washington, DC: World Bank.

———. 2018e. "Productivity Unplugged: The Challenges of Malaysia's Transition into a High-Income Country." *The Malaysian Development Experience Series.* Washington, DC: World Bank Group.

———. 2018f. *Europe and Central Asia Economic Update: Cryptocurrencies and Blockchain.* May. Washington, DC: World Bank.

———. 2018g. *Jobs in the Kyrgyz Republic.* Washington, DC: World Bank.

———. 2018h. *Poverty and Shared Prosperity 2018: Piecing Together the Poverty Puzzle.* Washington, DC: World Bank.

———. 2018i. "Dominican Republic: Systemic Country Diagnostic." World Bank, Washington, DC.

———. 2018j. "Paraguay Systemic Country Diagnostic." World Bank, Washington, DC.

———. 2018k. *World Development Report 2018: Learning to Realize Education's Promise.* Washington, DC: World Bank.

———. 2018l. *Expectations and Aspirations: A New Framework for Education in the Middle East and North Africa.* Washington, DC: World Bank.

———. 2018m. *World Development Report 2019: The Changing Nature of Work.* Washington, DC: World Bank.

———. 2018n. *India Gender Portfolio Review* 2018. Part-2: Sectoral Findings Vol. 2. Washington, DC: World Bank.

———. 2018o. *Global Economic Prospects: The Turning of the Tide?* June. World Bank: Washington, DC.

———. 2018p. *Global Investment Competitiveness Report 2017/2018: Foreign Investor Perspectives and Policy Implications.* Washington, DC: World Bank.

———. 2019a. *Global Economic Prospects: Heightened Tensions, Subdued Investment.* June. Washington, DC: World Bank.

———. 2019b. *East Asia and Pacific Economic Update: Weathering Growing Risks.* October. Washington, DC: World Bank.

———. 2019c. *China Economic Update.* December. Washington, DC: World Bank.

———. 2019d. *World Development Report 2020: Trading for Development in the Age of Global Value Chains.* Washington DC: World Bank.

———. 2019e. *A Decade Since the Global Recession: Lessons and Challenges for Emerging and Developing Economies.* Washington, DC: World Bank.

———. 2019f. *Global Economic Prospects: Darkening Skies.* January. Washington DC: World Bank.

———. 2019g. *Europe and Central Asia Economic Update, Fall 2019: Migration and Brain Drain.* October. Washington, DC: World Bank.

———. 2019h. *Western Balkans Regular Economic Report: Rising Uncertainty. Fall.* October. Washington, DC: World Bank.

———. 2019i. *Country Economic Memorandum: Firm Productivity and Economic Growth in Turkey.* Washington, DC: World Bank.

———. 2019j. *Kazakhstan: Reversing Productivity Stagnation-Country Economic Memorandum.* Washington, DC: World Bank.

———. 2019k. Enterprise Surveys. Accessed November 4, 2019. https://www.enterprisesurveys.org/en/enterprisesurveys.

———. 2019l. *Moldova: Rekindling Economic Dynamism.* Washington, DC: World Bank.

———. 2019m. *Ukraine Growth: Faster, Lasting and Kinder.* Washington, DC: World Bank.

———. 2019n. *Western Balkans Regular Economic Report: Reform Momentum Needed.* Spring. Washington DC: World Bank.

———. 2019o. "Global Trade Watch 2018: Trade amid Tensions." World Bank, Washington, DC.

———. 2019p. *Trade Integration as a Pathway to Development?: LAC Semiannual Report.* Washington, DC: World Bank.

———. 2019q. *Gulf Economic Update: Economic Diversification for a Sustainable and Resilient GCC.* World Bank, Washington, DC.

———. 2019r. *The Middle East and North Africa: From Transition to Transformation.* Washington, DC: World Bank.

———. 2019s. *South Asia Economic Focus. Making (De)centralization Work.* Fall. Washington, DC: World Bank.

———. 2019t. *Sri Lanka Development Update.* October. Washington, DC: World Bank.

———. 2019u. *Bangladesh Development Update.* October. Washington, DC: World Bank.

———. 2019v. *South Asia Economic Focus. Exports Wanted.* Spring. Washington, DC: World Bank.

———. 2019w. *Rwanda Systematic Country Diagnostic.* Washington, DC: World Bank.

———. 2019x. *Liberia Growth and Economic Diversification Agenda Productivity-driven Growth and Diversification.* Washington, DC: World Bank.

———. 2019y. *Nigeria Bi-Annual Economic Update: Jumpstarting Inclusive Growth—Unlocking the Productive Potential of Nigeria's People and Resource Endowments.* Fall. Washington, DC: World Bank.

———. 2019z. *Boosting Productivity in Sub-Saharan Africa.* Washington, DC: World Bank.

———. 2019aa. *Africa's Pulse: An Analysis of Issues Shaping Africa's Economic Future.* October. Washington, DC: World Bank.

———. 2019ab. *Lifelines: The Resilient Infrastructure Opportunity.* Washington, DC: World Bank.

———. 2019ac. *The World Bank Group's Action Plan on Climate Change Adaptation and Resilience.* Washington, DC: World Bank.

———. 2020. *Doing Business 2020. Comparing Business Regulation in 190 Economies.* Washington, DC: World Bank.

———. Forthcoming. *Economic Transformation and the Future of Work in LAC.* Washington, DC: World Bank.

World Bank and DRCSC (Development Research Center of the State Council, the People's Republic of China). 2014. *Urban China: Toward Efficient, Inclusive, and Sustainable Urbanization. Washington, DC: World Bank.*

World Bank and DRCSC (Development Research Center of the State Council, the People's Republic of China). 2019. *Innovative China: New Drivers of Growth.* Washington, DC: World Bank.

World Bank and MPIV (Ministry of Planning and Investment of Vietnam). 2016. *Vietnam 2035: Toward Prosperity, Creativity, Equity, and Democracy.* Washington, DC: World Bank.

Xu, X., and Y. Sheng. 2012. "Productivity Spillovers from Foreign Direct Investment: Firm-Level Evidence from China." *World Development* 40 (1): 62-74.

Yousef, T. 2004. "Development, Growth and Policy Reforms in the Middle East and North Africa." *Journal of Economic Perspectives* 18 (3): 91-116.

Youssef, H., S. Alnashar, J. Erian, A. Elshawarby, and C. Zaki. 2019. *Egypt Economic Monitor: From Floating to Thriving—Taking Egypt's Exports to New Levels.* Washington, DC: World Bank.

Zettelmeyer, J., E. Berglöf, L. Bruynooghe, H. Harmgart, P. Sanfey, and H. Schweiger. 2010. "European Transition at Twenty: Assessing Progress in Countries and Sectors." Working Paper 91, United Nations University—World Institute for Development Economics Research, Helsinki.

SPECIAL FOCUS 2

Low for How Much Longer?
Inflation in Low-Income Countries

Inflation in low-income countries (LICs) has declined sharply to a median of 3 percent in mid-2019 from a peak of 25 percent in 1994. The drop has been supported by the move to more flexible exchange rate regimes, greater central bank independence, and a generally more benign external environment since the 1990s. However, low LIC inflation cannot be taken for granted amid mounting fiscal pressures and the risk of exchange rate shocks. To maintain low and stable inflation, monetary and fiscal policy frameworks need to be strengthened and supported by efforts to replace price controls with more efficient policies.

Introduction

The number of low-income countries (LICs) has more than halved since 2001. As of 2019, 31 countries are classified as "low income" according to the World Bank definition, down from 64 in 2001, following the graduation of 35 mostly metals-exporting and transition economies to middle-income status.[1] Today, LICs are predominantly agriculture-based, small, and fragile, and they tend to have weak institutions (World Bank 2015). All but six are in Sub-Saharan Africa.

LICs have made large strides in price stabilization over the past five decades, with sharp declines in inflation levels and volatility (Figure SF2.1). That said, the level and volatility of inflation in LICs has remained higher than in advanced economies and other emerging market and developing economies (EMDEs) over the past two decades (Ha, Ivanova et al. 2019a). Reasons include monetary policy challenges that arise in LICs due to their volatile economies, pervasive use of administered pricing, conflicts among central bank policy objectives, weaknesses in monetary policy transmission, and limited analytical capacity at central banks. The disinflation in today's LICs was also considerably less pronounced than in the (larger number of) EMDEs that were classified as LICs in 2000 but have since achieved middle-income status.

Low inflation has typically been associated with more stable output and employment, higher output growth and investment, and falling poverty rates. Low and stable inflation makes relative price

changes more apparent, provides confidence for long-term savers and investors, protects the purchasing power of household income and wealth, and enhances financial stability (Easterly 2019; Ha, Kose, and Ohnsorge 2019a).[2] By contrast, economies that have experienced high inflation have suffered significantly lower economic growth (Kremer, Bick, and Nautz 2013).

Low and stable inflation is especially important for LICs, where a large number of the world's poor reside. Those most at risk are the "near poor"— those living on incomes just above $1.90 per day, the World Bank's threshold for extreme poverty. (The very poorest households hold few nominal assets or incomes that would be affected by inflation.) Poorer households—which are more prevalent in LICs than in the EMDEs—may suffer greater welfare losses from inflation than wealthier households because they are less able to protect the real value of their income and assets from the impact of inflation (Ha, Ivanova et al. 2019b). An erosion of their real incomes and assets through inflation could tip these households into extreme poverty.[3] In addition, by stabilizing output fluctuations that disproportionally hurt the poor, the adoption of a credible monetary policy regime that maintains low and stable inflation may help reduce poverty and inequality (Romer and Romer 1999).

Note: This Special Focus was prepared by Jongrim Ha and Franziska Ohnsorge.

[1] In addition, there are two countries (South Sudan and Syrian Arab Republic) that are newly grouped as LICs in 2019.

---

[2] Several policy outcomes have improved considerably since the 1990s, including lower inflation, smaller black market premiums, and lesser currency overvaluation (Easterly 2019).

[3] Although the evidence of a positive correlation between inflation and inequality or poverty is mixed at the aggregate level, the links are better established at the household level (Ha, Ivanova et al. 2019b). For example, single-country studies on EMDEs, such as India (Datt and Ravallion 1998), the Philippines (Blejer and Guerrero 1990), and Brazil (Ferreira and Litchfield 2001), find that higher inflation is associated with a lower share of income held by the poor or higher inequality. Using panel data of 24 developed and 66 developing countries over 1990–2014, Siami-Namini and Hudson (2019) similarly find bi-directional Granger causality between inflation and income inequality in both groups.

FIGURE SF2.1 Inflation in low-income countries and poverty

Inflation and inflation volatility in LICs have declined since 1970, broadly in line with other EMDEs. The decline has been broad-based across countries, as well as across components of inflation. Those that have grown to middle-income status have had faster declines in inflation. The remaining LICs feature higher poverty than EMDEs. Those just above the extreme poor level are at risk of being tipped back into poverty when inflation erodes the real value of their assets and incomes.

A. Inflation

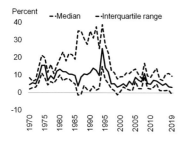

B. Number of LICs by inflation bracket

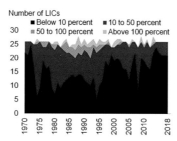

C. Inflation

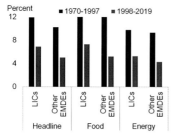

D. Inflation volatility

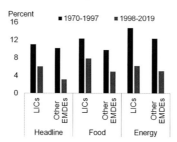

E. Inflation in former and current LICs

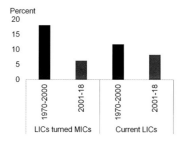

F. Poverty

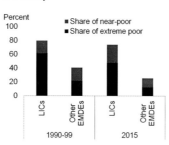

Source: Haver Analytics; International Monetary Fund; World Bank.
Note: Data for 26 low-income countries and 99 other EMDEs. Inflation refers to year-on-year inflation. EMDEs = emerging market and developing economies; LICs = low-income countries.
A. Blue lines are cross-country medians of inflation; dashed lines indicate the interquartile range across 26 LICs. 2019 inflation rates are based on year-on-year inflation during the first half of 2019 in 19 LICs.
B. Number of LICs in which inflation was in the bracket indicated. Data for 2019 are not yet available for some LICs and was not included.
C.D. Cross-country medians of inflation (C) or standard deviations of inflation (D). The differences across sample periods are all statistically significant.
E. Median inflation across countries. "LICs turned MICs" indicates 33 countries classified as low-income countries in 2000 but classified as middle-income countries as of 2019. "Current LICs" indicates 29 low-income countries as of 2019.
F. Median share of population in extreme poverty (living on less than $1.90 per day) and near-poverty (living on $1.90-$3.20 per day) in 27 LICs and 109 other EMDEs.

Against this backdrop, this Special Focus delves into the characteristics of LIC inflation, quantifies its drivers, and examines related monetary policy challenges. Specifically, it discusses the following questions:

- How has inflation evolved in LICs?

- What factors have supported inflation developments in LICs?

- What policy challenges do LIC central banks face in managing inflation?

Evolution of inflation

Among LICs, median inflation has fallen by two-thirds since 1970, to 3.2 percent in mid-2019—broadly in line with inflation developments in other EMDEs). The inflation decline has been broad-based across countries as well as inflation components (e.g., food, energy). As a result, the wide heterogeneity of inflation among LICs in the 1990s has narrowed sharply.

1970s to 1990s. Median inflation among LICs was 9-10 percent over this period. Although broadly in line with inflation in other EMDEs, LIC inflation underwent several spikes (up to 25 percent), especially in the early 1990s, amid currency crises. In half the years between 1970 and 2000, the majority of LICs had double-digit inflation.

Post-2000. Median inflation in LICs has fallen rapidly—to 3.2 percent in mid-2019 from a peak of 25.2 percent in 1994 (Figure SF2.1.A). This decline was broad-based and narrowed some of the wide heterogeneity in inflation among LICs. In one-third of LICs, inflation in mid-2019 was less than one-third of its level in 1970. In an even larger number (63 percent) of LICs, inflation in mid-2019 was less than one-third of its 1994 level. By 2008, hyperinflation episodes in LICs (inflation in excess of 1,000 percent) had also subsided.[4] In mid-2019, inflation was in the single

---

[4] In the 1990s Democratic Republic of Congo and Tajikistan experienced inflation over 1,000 percent.

digits in more than three-quarters of LICs, compared with less than one-fifth in 1994 (Figure SF2.1.B).

Since 1970, core, food price, and energy price inflation have also declined, as has inflation volatility (Figures SF2.1.C and SF2.1.D).

Inflation in non-LIC EMDEs. Although the inflation decline in LICs has been broadly in line with developments in other EMDEs, its level remains well above its counterparts.[5] Disinflation in today's LICs has also fallen short of that among (the larger number of) EMDEs that used to be LICs in 2000 but that have since achieved middle-income status, even though these countries started with lower levels of inflation (Figure SF2.1.E).

Factors supporting inflation developments

Since 2000, improvements in LIC policies and a benign global macroeconomic environment have supported the decline in LIC inflation. That said, policy frameworks in the median LIC remain generally weaker than those in other EMDEs.

Improved policies. The adoption of more resilient monetary, exchange rate, and fiscal policy frameworks has facilitated more effective control of inflation (Hammond, Kanbur, and Prasad 2009; Taylor 2014). Inflation has tended to be lower in LICs with higher degrees of central bank independence and transparency, lower central bank head turnover, and lower public debt ratios (Easterly 2019; Ha, Kose, and Ohnsorge 2019a). Since 1970, monetary policy frameworks have strengthened in LICs. For example, the index of central bank transparency by Dincer, Eichengreen, and Geraats (2019) (available for 9 LICs) doubled between 1998, when the series starts, and 2015, when the series ends (Figure SF2.2.A). In 1970, all but three LICs had pegged exchange rates whereas, in 2019, less than half (14 of 29 LICs with

FIGURE SF2.2 Factors supporting falling inflation in LICs

The decline in LIC inflation has been supported by the move to more flexible exchange rate regimes, greater central bank independence, lower government debt, and a more benign external environment.

A. Central bank transparency index

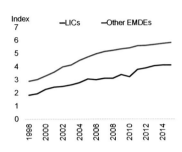

B. Number of LICs, by exchange rate regime

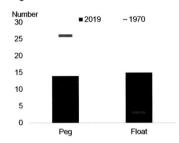

C. Government debt

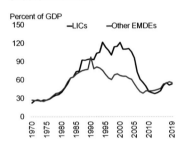

D. Financial and trade openness

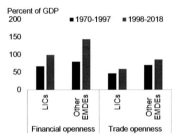

E. Inflation, by country characteristics

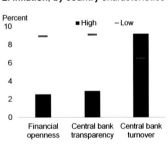

F. Exchange rate volatility

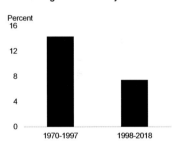

Source: Dincer, Eichengreen, and Geraats (2019); Dreher, Stum, and De Haan (2010); Haver Analytics; International Monetary Fund (IMF); Shambaugh (2004); World Bank.
Note: Data for 28 low-income countries and 96 other EMDEs. EMDEs = emerging markets and developing economies; GDP = gross domestic product; LICs = low-income countries.
A.C. Unweighted averages.
A. Central bank transparency index as defined in Dincer, Eichengreen, and Geraats (2019). Data for 9 LICs and 83 other EMDEs.
B. Exchange rate regime as defined in Shambaugh (2004).
C. Data for 2019 are based on IMF (2019).
D. Median trade openness (measured by trade-to-GDP ratio) and financial openness (international asset and liabilities to GDP) across countries.
E. Median year-on-year inflation in LICs during 1998-2018, by country characteristics. "High" indicates above-median financial openness, central bank transparency, and turn-over rate of central bank governors. "Low" indicates below-median financial openness, central bank transparency, and turn-over rate.
F. Exchange rate volatility is the cross-country average of the standard deviation of nominal effective appreciation in 28 low-income countries during each time period.

---

[5] For instance, inflation remains in double-digits in Ethiopia, mainly due to recent currency depreciation and surging food prices after road disruptions and a drought.

available data) did (Figure SF2.2.B).[6] In addition, fiscal pressures on monetary policy also appear to have eased. In part as a result of debt relief initiatives, government debt has declined from a peak of 121 percent of GDP in 2000, on average, to 53 percent of GDP in 2019— broadly in line with the average non-LIC EMDE (Figure SF2.2.C).[7]

More benign external environment. LIC economies, on average, have become more open to trade and finance since the 1970s, although they remain less open than other EMDEs (Figure SF2.2.D; IMF 2011a). Higher capital account openness, in particular, has been associated with lower inflation, whereas there appears to be little difference between LICs that have been highly open to trade and those that have not (Figure SF2.2.E). Despite a growing number of LICs switching to floating exchange rate regimes, exchange rates have been considerably more stable since 1998 than in the preceding two decades (Figure SF2.2.F). This has helped lower LIC inflation volatility and inflation.

Global inflation cycle. LICs are now more integrated into the global economy. As a result, LIC inflation has become increasingly synchronized with the global inflation cycle. What was once a negligible contribution to LIC inflation, global inflation's impact on domestic inflation has become sizeable, especially since 2000 (Ha, Kose, and Ohnsorge 2019b; Parker 2018).[8] Over the past decade, the global

disinflation around the global financial crisis and oil price plunges in 2014-16 may have added downward pressure to inflation in LICs.

Monetary policy challenges

The level and volatility of inflation in LICs have remained higher than in advanced economies and other EMDEs over the past two decades. This difference may reflect monetary policy challenges particular to LICs arising from higher economic volatility and pervasive use of administered pricing, conflicts among central bank policy objectives, weaknesses in monetary policy transmission, and limited analytical capacity at central banks (Ha, Ivanova, et al. 2019a).

Volatile economies. Policymakers in LICs must contend with greater economic volatility than their counterparts in other countries. This in part reflects the greater frequency of supply shocks and the poorer anchoring of inflation expectations that allow exchange rate fluctuations to spill over into inflation.

- *Supply shocks.* LIC economies are particularly vulnerable to supply shocks, especially weather-related ones. Agriculture sectors tend to be large, poor transport links prevent risk sharing, and food comprises a large share of household consumption (Bleaney and Francisco 2018; Cachia 2014). As a result, rainfall appears to have the most pronounced effect on economic growth in EMDEs in Sub-Saharan Africa (Barrios, Bertinelli, and Strobl 2010).

- *Exchange rate volatility.* Exchange rates in LICs tend to be more volatile than those in other EMDEs, in part reflecting their greater frequency of supply shocks. With inflation expectations poorly anchored, exchange rate pass-through also tends to be higher in LICs than in other EMDEs (Ha, Ivanova et al. 2019a).

Conflicts among policy objectives. LICs frequently have multiple monetary policy objectives, with inflation being only one among several. This in part reflects challenges in

---

[6] Several Sub-Saharan African LICs (as well as some recent low- and middle-income countries) belong to monetary unions (e.g., the West African Economic and Monetary Union, and the Central African Economic and Monetary Community). Many of these LICs have also experienced low levels of inflation over the recent decades (Ha, Kose and Ohnsorge 2019a).

[7] In addition, the relationship between fiscal position and inflation appears to be non-linear: in a low-inflation environment, fiscal deficits tend to be less inflationary (Catão and Terrones 2005; Lin and Chu 2013). As a result, the current low-inflation environment may help further mute the pressures from fiscal dominance on inflation in LICs.

[8] Using a dynamic factor model for 99 countries (including 16 LICs), Ha, Kose, and Ohnsorge (2019b) find that the contribution of global inflation factor to domestic inflation variation increased to 17 percent in 2001-17 from a 3-4 percent in 1970s to 1990s. Parker (2018) similarly finds that global inflation accounted for around a quarter of inflation variation in LICs over 2001-2012, compared to its contribution (10-20 percent) in the earlier periods.

formulating an appropriate numerical inflation target for LICs. The threshold at which inflation has clear negative effects on output is significantly higher for EMDEs than for advanced economies and varies widely depending on country characteristics (Khan and Senhadji 2001). A survey of low- and lower-middle-income countries that listed price stability as a central bank objective, found that most countries did not have a numerical inflation target, and those that had such a target simply tended to align it with the bank's inflation forecast (IMF 2015). LICs central banks are thus likely to have a broader set of objectives; the exchange rate is more likely to be a separate and important policy objective (Berg and Miao 2010; Rodrik 2018).[9] Other objectives may include supporting activity or fiscal sustainability.

- *Conflicts between inflation and output objectives.* To lower inflation after a history of high inflation, the central bank must be willing to tolerate weak activity perhaps for an extended period. A commitment to lowering inflation from a history of high inflation will require the central bank to be willing to tolerate weak activity perhaps for an extended period (Kasa 2001; Gemayel, Jahan, and Peter 2011). However, frequent supply shocks in LIC, for example from the effects of weather events on agricultural production, may raise inflation while depressing output (Frankel 2011).[10] Stabilizing inflation in response to such supply shocks may thus require failing to maintain output (Adam 2011; Bashar 2011; Nguyen et al. 2017).

- *Conflicts between inflation and exchange rate objectives.* In LICs (as in some other EMDEs)

the exchange rate may be an important policy objective (Buffie et al. 2004; IMF 2015; Mishkin and Savastano 2001; Taylor 2001). A declared strategy of stabilizing the exchange rate against currencies of trading partners with a track record of low and stable inflation may well be compatible with achieving domestic price stability and the limited international financial integration of many LICs may still afford some room for active monetary policy (Ostry, Ghosh, and Chamon 2012). However, when currency exposures are high, exchange rate pressures may prevent central banks from acting to preserve low and stable inflation.

- *Conflicts between inflation and fiscal objectives.* For LIC governments with weak revenue-raising capabilities and an absence of well-functioning capital markets, inflation may become an important source of financing fiscal deficits (Baldacci, Hillman, and Kojo 2004). The presence of large fiscal deficits or high government debt in LICs can cause fiscal policy to rely on accommodative monetary policy to ensure fiscal sustainability (Baldini and Poplawski-Ribeiro 2011; Weidmann 2013). In almost every year between 1992 and 2002, two-thirds of LICs had higher debt-to-GDP ratios than the one-third of non-LIC EMDEs with the highest debt levels. In half the years between 1995 and 2017, the median fiscal deficit in LICs was above that in non-LIC EMDEs. Weak institutions (Bleaney, Morozumi, and Mumuni 2016) and political instability (Aisen and Veiga 2006) may reinforce the negative association between budget deficits and price stability. Central banks in LICs are therefore more likely to face conflicts between price stability and pressures to maintain low interest rates or provide outright fiscal financing (Mas 1995; Prasad 2010).

Widespread price controls. Price controls—typically imposed to protect vulnerable groups—are more common in LICs than in other EMDEs (Special Focus 1). The most frequently used price controls in LICs are on basic food stuffs and petroleum. Since food expenditures represent

---

[9] Using a heterogeneous structural vector autoregressive model for 105 countries, Ha, Ivanova et al. (2019a) find that core inflation in LICs with a floating exchange rate regime is less robust in the face of external shocks than in countries that fixed exchange rates. In advanced economies and other EMDEs, shocks to global core inflation account for a much larger fraction of the variance of domestic core inflation in fixed regimes than in floating regimes.

[10] For instance, a poor harvest will tend to increase inflation in the short term while depressing economic activity. Supply shocks thus push inflation and output growth in opposite directions, giving rise to a conflict between monetary policy's primary objective of stabilizing prices and its secondary objectives of supporting growth and maintaining a narrow output gap.

nearly 60 percent of the consumption basket in LICs, compared with 42 percent in other EMDEs, a significant portion of the basket is therefore subject to administered pricing (Laborde, Lakatos and Martin 2019).[11] Price controls can temporarily contribute to price stabilization in LICs, especially for key commodities subject to perceived excessive volatility in international markets.[12] However, this poses monetary policy challenges, as well as fiscal and growth challenges that can heighten conflicts between monetary policy objectives.

Weaknesses in the instruments and transmission mechanism of monetary policy. In advanced economies and many EMDEs, the key monetary policy instrument is a short-term interest rate, most often an interbank rate. An advanced-economy central bank can guide the interbank rate through bank reserves and standing facilities. In LICs, however, interbank markets are typically absent, as are liquid secondary markets in government securities, which the central bank could seek to influence through open-market operations (Mishra, Montiel, and Spilimbergo 2012). The government securities market in LICs tends to be a primary market in which counterparties are commercial banks that buy and hold government securities. Thus, the central bank often conducts monetary policy by directly lending to and borrowing from the commercial banking system. However, even the bank lending channel can be impaired in LICs.

- *Limited financial inclusion.* LICs tend to have large informal sectors but small formal financial sectors (World Bank 2019). Broad money and domestic credit by financial sector

in LICs are half the share of GDP of other EMDEs (Figure SF2.3.A). Only one-third of adults have a bank account in LICs, compared with 57 percent in other EMDEs (Figure SF2.3.B). As a result, the financial system has only weak links to overall economic activity. Around 80 percent of investment in LICs is financed internally and three-quarters of firms do not tap banks to finance investment (Figures SF2.3.C and SF2.3.D).

- *Weak institutions.* The institutional and legal environment in LICs—including property rights, accounting and disclosure standards, and contract enforcement—tends to be weak (Beck, Demirgüç-Kunt, and Levine 2004). This makes financial intermediation from private savers to private borrowers costly and risky, inducing banks to limit this activity and to hold safer government securities.

- *Preponderance of large firms.* Productive activity in LICs is often characterized by a few large, well-established firms and many very small, opaque, and often unstable ones. The marginal cost of bank lending to large firms tends to be lower than that of extending credit to small firms. As a result, the volume of lending to large firms may be very insensitive to fluctuations in bank funding costs induced by monetary policy (Mishra and Montiel 2013; Mishra et al. 2014).

- *Widespread informality.* The informal sector accounts for about almost two-fifths of GDP and 90 percent of employment in the average LIC, in part reflecting large agricultural sectors and a high share of unskilled workers (World Bank 2019). Firms in the informal sector have limited access to credit from the banking sector and capital markets, and thus have limited interactions with the formal financial sector. This dampens monetary policy transmission through the formal financial system.

- *Other factors.* In addition, the strength of monetary transmission in LICs has proven difficult to estimate because of data limitations (Li et al. 2016). What empirical evidence has been estimated suggests that the

---

[11] In addition, LICs suffer collateral damage from other countries' administered prices on food and energy because of the high share of food and energy in LIC consumption baskets and trade. Volatility in global food and energy commodity prices is amplified when other countries respond to rising global commodity prices by imposing price and other controls to suppress prices in local markets (Laborde, Lakatos, and Martin 2019). The resulting higher volatility of import prices in LICs complicates central banks' efforts to maintain low and stable inflation.

[12] Median food and headline inflation were lower in the 52 EMDEs with food price controls than in the 23 EMDEs without such controls. However, the relative price distortions introduced by highly restricted food price controls have been associated with high inflation in LICs (Special Focus 1).

transmission is weak for several reasons: credit and other financial markets tend to be shallow; contract enforceability is limited; information asymmetries are pervasive; and many LICs retain elements of financial repression in the form of interest rate controls.[13] For example, while changes in policy rates tended to be transmitted almost one-for-one into retail bank lending rates in advanced economies, pass-through in EMDEs was only in the range of 30-45 percent (Abuka et al. 2015; Saborowski and Weber 2013).

Shortcomings in the analytical capacity of central banks. Because monetary policy affects the economy with lags, an important component of any monetary policy regime is the ability of the central bank to accurately forecast its target variables on the assumption of unchanged policies as well as to assess the effects of policy changes on those variables. Few LIC central banks have the structural models with proven track records required for such forecasts (IMF 2015). This reflects in part lack of relevant historical data, insufficient knowledge about the macroeconomic structure of the economies concerned, rapid structural change in the economy, and shortages of research expertise (Gemayel, Jahan, and Peter 2011; IMF 2015).

Complications introduced by globalization. Globalization is likely to alter the monetary transmission mechanism in complicated ways (Abuka et. al. 2015; Montiel and Pedroni 2018). It increases the economy's exposure to external shocks, in the form of exogenous changes in the foreign-currency prices of traded goods, remittance flows, and capital flows. It may also alter the trade-offs between different central bank objectives.

Policy options going forward

Going forward, the achievements of low and stable inflation in many LICs cannot be taken for granted. If the external environment turns less

---

¹³ For details, see Mishra, Montiel, and Spilimbergo (2012); IMF (2015); and Mishra and Montiel (2013).

FIGURE SF2.3 Monetary policy challenges in LICs

Financial systems are small and have narrow reach in LICs, and this limits monetary policy transmission through the financial sector. Broad money and domestic credit by the financial sector in LICs are half the share of GDP than in other EMDEs. Only a third of adults have bank accounts in LICs, compared with 60 percent in other EMDEs. Around 80 percent of investment in LICs is financed internally, while less than 20 percent is financed by the banking sector.

A. Broad money and domestic credit

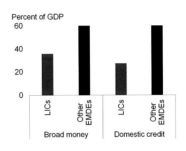

B. Fraction of adults with bank accounts

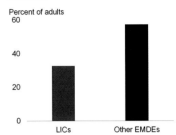

C. Share of investment that is internally financed

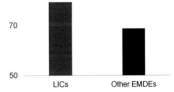

D. Share of firms that approach banks to finance investment

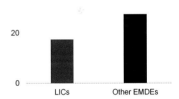

Source: Enterprise Survey; Global Findex Database; World Development Indicators.
Note: EMDEs = emerging markets and developing economies; LICs = low-income countries. Unweighted averages across countries.
A. Broad monetary and domestic credit provided by financial sector (both percent of GDP) in 2017, based on 20 LICs and 110 other EMDEs.
B. Proportion of adults (age over 15) holding a bank account in 2017. Survey based on 23 LICs and 86 other EMDEs.
C. Proportion of investment financed internally. Enterprise survey based on 15 LICs and 47 other EMDEs.
D. Proportion of firms using banks to finance investments. Enterprise survey based on 15 LICs and 47 other EMDEs.

---

benign or fiscal pressures mount, the ability of central banks in LICs to maintain low inflation may be tested. Since 2013, government debt has risen rapidly, by almost 15 percentage points of GDP in the median LIC; about half of LIC debt is external and, hence, predominantly foreign-currency-denominated (World Bank 2019). This increases LIC governments' vulnerability to financial market disruptions that raise borrowing costs. Mounting fiscal pressures could heighten tensions between the multiple objectives of LIC central banks. Separately, because of poorly anchored inflation expectations, exchange rate depreciations following financial market stress could raise LIC inflation. Broader policy efforts aimed at strengthening fiscal and monetary policy frameworks, and improving debt management, are therefore required in LICs to safeguard low and stable inflation.

Many of the monetary policy challenges facing LICs are related to their level of economic and financial development. Addressing these challenges requires a broader development process and includes: the development of financial markets to provide the central bank with more effective policy instruments; the improvement of systems compiling economic statistics; and capacity development in central banks and economic ministries, including strengthening economic expertise.

- *Strengthening central bank independence.* Central bank independence has increased among LICs since the early 1990s, partly as a means to allow central banks to give primacy to price stability over other objectives and enhance their credibility (Dincer and Eichengreen 2014; Garriga 2016). However, central bank independence of lower- and middle-income countries remains less than in other EMDEs and advanced economies, and de jure independence does not necessarily translate into de facto independence (IMF 2019).

- *Clarifying priorities in central banks' objectives.* A transparent prioritization of central bank objectives in the event of conflicts between different objectives could help central banks achieve their primary targets. Other policy options could be developed to help achieving central banks' secondary objectives— including for output or financial stability—of monetary policy. Such policies could include the judicious use of budgetary policy when there is fiscal space, and structural reforms

that reduce the economy's vulnerability to shocks, strengthen automatic fiscal stabilizers, increase the flexibility and effectiveness of discretionary fiscal policy, and increase the flexibility of labor markets. Institutional changes could include entrusting responsibility for financial stability to a separate supervisory and regulatory authority, associated with a well-capitalized deposit insurance agency.

- *Expanding central bank tools.* The central bank could develop or strengthen instruments separate from monetary policy to address its objective of financial stability, including capital flow management measures and macroprudential policies.

- *Considering best suitable nominal anchors for monetary policy.* Although inflation targeting, with its usual focus on the CPI, has been the most popular among advanced economies and larger EMDEs, other EMDEs and LICs could consider alternative nominal anchors for monetary policy that best suit their economic structures. For example, countries that produce commodities that are subject to volatile global commodity prices, and have procyclical access to global capital markets, could target export prices or producer prices. These targets may stabilize output better than CPI targeting in the presence of frequent terms of trade or financial shocks (Frankel 2011).

- *Building and maintaining central bank credibility.* The central bank could strengthen its efforts to convince the public of the primacy it gives to the low-inflation objective (Mishkin 1997). Declaration of a specific inflation target could serve this purpose, but this strategy may not yet suit LICs with weak and uncertain monetary transmission, data deficiencies, and limited analytical capacity.

References

Abuka, C., R. Alinda, C. Minoui, J. L. Peydro, and A. Presbitero. 2015. "The Bank Lending Channel in a Frontier Economy: Evidence from Loan-Level Data." https://www.rieti.go.jp/jp/events/15061501/pdf/7-2_pr esbitero.pdf.

Adam, C. 2011. "On the Macroeconomic Management of Food Price Shocks in Low-Income Countries." *Journal of African Economies* 20 (1): i63-i99.

Aisen, A., and F. J. Veiga. 2006. "Does Political Instability Lead to Higher Inflation? A Panel Data Analysis." *Journal of Money, Credit and Banking* 38 (5): 1379-89.

Baldacci, E., A. L. Hillman, and N. C. Kojo. 2004. "Growth, Governance, and Fiscal Policy Transmission Channels in Low-Income Countries." *European Journal of Political Economy* 20 (3): 517-49.

Baldini, A., and M. Poplawski-Ribeiro. 2011. "Fiscal and Monetary Determinants of Inflation in Low-Income Countries: Theory and Evidence from Sub-Saharan Africa." *Journal of African Economies* 20 (3): 419-62.

Barrios, S., L. Bertinelli, and E. Strobl. 2010. "Trends in Rainfall and Economic Growth in Africa: A Neglected Cause of the African Growth Tragedy." *Review of Economics and Statistics* 92 (2): 350-66.

Bashar, O. H. M. N. 2011. "The Role of Aggregate Demand and Supply Shocks in a Low-Income Country: Evidence from Bangladesh." *Journal of Developing Areas* 44 (2): 243-64.

Beck, T., A. Demirgüç-Kunt, and R. Levine. 2004. "Finance, Inequality and Poverty: Cross-Country Evidence." Policy Research Working Paper 3338, World Bank, Washington, DC.

Berg, A., and Y. Miao. 2010. "The Real Exchange Rate and Growth Revisited: The Washington Consensus Strikes Back?" IMF Working Paper 10/58, International Monetary Fund, Washington, DC.

Bleaney, M., and M. Francisco. 2018. "Is the Phillips Curve Different in Poor Countries?" *Bulletin of Economic Research* 70 (1): E17-E28.

Bleaney, M., A. Morozumi, and Z. Mumuni. 2016. "Fiscal Deficits and Inflation: Institutions Matter." University of Nottingham, U.K.

Blejer, M., and I. Guerrero. 1990. "The Impact of Macroeconomic Policies on Income Distribution: An Empirical Study of the Philippines." *Review of Economics and Statistics* 72 (3): 414-23.

Buffie, E., C. Adam, S. O'Connell, and C. Pattillo. 2004. "Exchange Rate Policy and the Management of Official and Private Capital Flows in Africa." *IMF Staff Papers* 51 (s1): 126-60.

Cachia, F. 2014. "Regional Food Price Inflation Transmission." FAO Working Paper ESS/14-01, Food and Agriculture Organization of the United Nations, Rome.

Catão, L., and M. Terrones. 2001. "Fiscal Deficits and Inflation—A New Look at the Emerging Market Evidence." IMF Working Paper 01/74, International Monetary Fund, Washington, DC.

Datt, G., and M. Ravallion. 1998. "Why Have Some Indian States Done Better Than Others at Reducing Rural Poverty?" *Economica* 65 (257): 17-38.

Dincer, N., and B. Eichengreen. 2014. "Central Bank Transparency and Independence: Updates and New Measures." *International Journal of Central Banking* 10 (1): 189-259.

Dincer, N., B. Eichengreen, and P. Geraats. 2019. "Transparency of Monetary Policy in the Post Crisis World." In *Oxford Handbook of the Economics of Central Banking*, edited by D. Mayes, P. Siklos, and J.-E. Sturm. New York: Oxford University Press.

Dreher, A., J. Sturm, and J. de Haan. 2010. "When Is a Central Bank Governor Replaced? Evidence Based on a New Data Set." *Journal of Macroeconomics* 32 (3) 766-781.

Easterly, W. 2019. "In Search of Reforms for Growth: New Stylized Facts on Policy and Growth Outcomes." NBER Working Paper 26318, National Bureau of Economic Research, Cambridge, MA.

Frankel, J. A. 2011. "Monetary Policy in Emerging Markets: A Survey." In *Handbook of Monetary Economics 3B*, edited by B. M. Friedman and M. Woodford. New York: Elsevier.

Garriga, A. C. 2016. "Central Bank Independence in the World: A New Data Set." *International Interactions* 42 (5): 849-68.

Ha, J., A. Ivanova, P. Montiel, and P. Pedroni. 2019a. "Inflation in Low-Income Countries." Policy Research Working Paper 8934. World Bank, Washington, DC.

Ha, J., A. Ivanova, F. Ohnsorge, and D. F. Unsal. 2019b. "Inflation: Concepts, Evolution, and Correlates." Policy Research Working Paper 8738, World Bank, Washington, D.C.

Ha, J., M. A. Kose, and F. Ohnsorge, eds. 2019a. *Inflation in Emerging and Developing Economies: Evolution, Drivers, and Policies*. Washington, DC: World Bank.

————. 2019b. "Global Inflation Synchronization." Policy Research Working Paper 8768. World Bank, Washington, DC.

Hammond, G., R. Kanbur, and E. Prasad. 2009. "Monetary Policy Challenges for Emerging Market Economies." In *New Monetary Policy Frameworks for Emerging Markets: Coping with the Challenges of Financial Globalization*, edited by G. Hammond, R. Kanbur, and E. Prasad. Cheltenham, U.K.: Edward Elgar Publishing.

IMF (International Monetary Fund). 2015. *Evolving Monetary Policy Frameworks in Low-Income and Other Developing Countries*. Washington, DC: International Monetary Fund.

————. 2019. *World Economic Outlook: Growth Slowdown, Precarious Recovery*. April. Washington, DC: International Monetary Fund.

Kasa, K. 2001. "Will Inflation Targeting Work in Developing Countries?" *FRBSF Economic Letter* 2001 (1), Federal Reserve Bank of San Francisco, San Francisco, CA.

Khan, M., and A. Senhadji. 2001. "Threshold Effects in the Relationship between Inflation and Growth." *IMF Staff Papers* 48 (1): 1-21.

Kremer, S., A. Bick, and D. Nautz. 2013. "Inflation and Growth: New Evidence from a Dynamic Panel Threshold Analysis." *Empirical Economics* 44 (2): 861-78.

Laborde, D., C. Lakatos, and W. Martin. 2019. "Poverty Impact of Food Price Shocks and Policies." Policy Research Working Paper 8724. World Bank, Washington, DC.

Li, B. G., S. A. O'Connell, C. Adam, A. Berg, and P. Montiel. 2016. "VAR Meets DSGE: Uncovering the Monetary Transmission Mechanism in Low-Income Countries." IMF Working Paper 16/90, International Monetary Fund, Washington, DC.

Lin, H.-Y., and H.-P. Chu. 2013. "Are Fiscal Deficits Inflationary?" *Journal of International Money and Finance* 32 (C): 214-33.

Mas, I. 1995. "Central Bank Independence: A Critical View from a Developing Country Perspective." *World Development* 23 (10): 1639-52.

Mishkin, F. 1997. "Strategies for Controlling Inflation." NBER Working Paper 6122, National Bureau of Economic Research, Cambridge, MA.

Mishkin, F. S., and M. A. Savastano. 2001. "Monetary Policy Strategies for Latin America." *Journal of Development Economics* 66 (2): 415-444.

Mishra, P., P. Montiel, and A. Spilimbergo. 2012. "Monetary Transmission in Low-Income Countries: Effectiveness and Policy Implications." *IMF Economic Review* 60 (2): 270-302.

Mishra, P., and P. Montiel. 2013. "How Effective Is Monetary Transmission in Low-Income Countries? A Survey of the Empirical Evidence." *Economic Systems* 37 (2): 187-216.

Mishra, P., P. J. Montiel, P. Pedroni, and A. Spilimbergo. 2014. "Monetary Policy and Bank Lending Rates in Low-Income Countries: Heterogeneous Panel Estimates." *Journal of Development Economics* 111 (November): 117-31.

Nguyen, A. D. M., J. Dridi, F. Unsal, and O. H. Williams. 2017. "On the Drivers of Inflation in Sub-Saharan Africa." *International Economics* 151 (October): 71-84.

Ostry, J. D., A. R. Ghosh, and M. Chamon. 2012. "Two Targets, Two Instruments: Monetary and Exchange Rate Policies in Emerging Economies." Staff Discussion Note 12/01, International Monetary Fund, Washington, DC.

Parker, M. 2018. "How Global Is 'Global Inflation'?" *Journal of Macroeconomics* 58 (December): 174-97.

Prasad, E. S. 2010. "Financial Sector Regulation and Reforms in Emerging Markets: An Overview." NBER Working Paper 16428, National Bureau of Economic Research, Cambridge, MA.

Rodrik, D. 2018. "The Real Exchange Rate and Economic Growth." *Brookings Papers on Economic Activity* (Fall): 365-439.

Saborowski, C., and S. Weber. 2013. "Assessing the Determinants of Interest Rate Transmission through Conditional Impulse Response Functions." IMF Working Paper 13/23, International Monetary Fund, Washington, DC.

Shambaugh, J. C. 2004. "The Effect of Fixed Exchange Rates on Monetary Policy." *Quarterly Journal of Economics* 119 (1): 301-52.

Siami-Namini, S., and D. Hudson. 2019, "Inflation and Income Inequality in Developed and Developing Countries." *Journal of Economic Studies* 46 (3): 611-632.

Taylor, J. 2001. "The Roles of Exchange Rates in Monetary-Policy Rules." *American Economic Review* 91 (2): 263-67.

————. 2014. "Inflation Targeting in Emerging Markets: Le Global Experience." Speech at the Conference on Fourteen Years of Inflation Targeting in South Africa and the Challenge of a Changing Mandate, South African Reserve Bank, Pretoria, December 19.

Weidmann, J. 2013. "Who Calls the Shots? The Problem of Fiscal Dominance." Speech at the BdF-BBk Macroeconomics and Finance Conference, Deutsche Bundesbank Eurosystem, Paris.

World Bank. 2015. *Global Economic Prospects: Having Fiscal Space and Using It.* January. Washington, DC: World Bank.

————. 2019. *Global Economic Prospects: Darkening Skies.* January. Washington, DC: World Bank.

CHAPTER 3

FADING PROMISE

How to Rekindle Productivity Growth

A broad-based slowdown in labor productivity growth has been underway since the global financial crisis. In emerging market and developing economies (EMDEs), the slowdown has reflected weakness in investment and moderating efficiency gains as well as dwindling resource reallocation between sectors. The pace of improvements in key drivers of labor productivity—including education, urbanization, and institutions—has slowed or stagnated since the global financial crisis and is expected to remain subdued. To rekindle productivity growth, a comprehensive approach is necessary: facilitating investment in physical, intangible, and human capital; encouraging reallocation of resources towards more productive sectors; fostering firm capabilities to reinvigorate technology adoption and innovation; and promoting a growth-friendly macroeconomic and institutional environment. Specific policy priorities will depend on individual country circumstances.

Introduction

Productivity growth is the primary source of lasting income growth, which in turn is the main driver of poverty reduction. Most cross-country differences in income per capita have been attributed to differences in productivity (Figure 3.1).[1] Whereas the one-quarter of emerging market and developing economies (EMDEs) with the fastest productivity growth have reduced their extreme poverty rates by an average of more than 1 percentage point per year since 1981, poverty rates rose in EMDEs with productivity growth in the lowest quartile.

The broad-based slowdown in labor productivity growth over the past decade has raised concerns about progress in achieving development goals. In EMDEs, the slowdown puts at risk hard-won gains in productivity catch-up to advanced economies prior to the 2007-09 global financial crisis. Labor productivity gaps with advanced economies remain substantial, with workers in the average EMDE producing less than one-fifth of the output of those in advanced economies. Against this backdrop, this chapter presents a comprehensive examination of the evolution of productivity, the correlates of productivity improvements, and policy options to rekindle productivity growth. Specifically, the chapter addresses the following questions:

- How has productivity growth evolved over the last four decades?

- How has the pace of productivity convergence changed?

- What are the underlying factors associated with productivity growth?

- What policy options are available to boost productivity growth?

Contribution and framework. The chapter makes several contributions to the literature and policy debate on labor productivity. The framework of the analysis in this chapter is as follows:

- *EMDE focus.* Thus far, the literature has focused on trends in subsets of countries such as advanced economies, OECD countries or specific regions.[2] The chapter is the first to provide both an overarching global and in-depth EMDE view of productivity trends alongside detailed regional analysis. To achieve this, it utilizes a comprehensive dataset of multiple measures of productivity growth for up to 29 advanced economies and 74 EMDEs during 1981-2018.

- *Multiple approaches.* The chapter synthesizes findings from empirical exercises using macroeconomic, sectoral, and firm-level data on productivity. Previous studies have typically analyzed productivity using data for only one of these three dimensions.[3] This

---

Note: This chapter was prepared by Alistair Dieppe and Gene Kindberg-Hanlon, with contributions from Atsushi Kawamoto, Sinem Kilic Celik, Hideaki Matsuoka, Yoki Okawa, and Cedric Okou. Research assistance was provided by Khamal Clayton, Aygul Evdokimova, Awais Khuhro, Xinyue Wang, and Heqing Zhao.

[1] See for details Caselli (2005) and Hall and Jones (1999).

[2] For details, see Fernald (2012), Adler et al. (2017), OECD (2015), ADB (2017), Dabla-Norris et al. (2015), Cusolito and Maloney (2018), World Bank (2018a).

[3] For macroeconomic analysis, see Adler et al. (2017) and Kim and Loayza (2019). For sectoral analysis, see McMillan, Rodrik, and Verduzco-Gallo (2014); and McMillan, Rodrik, and Sepulveda (2017). For firm-level analysis, see Cirera and Maloney (2017); Cusolito and Maloney (2018); and Fuglie et al. (2019).

FIGURE 3.1 Labor productivity, per capita income and poverty reduction

Cross-country differences in labor productivity explain most of the variation in income per capita. Poverty declined by more than 1 percentage point on average per year in the one-quarter of EMDEs with the highest productivity growth during 1981-2015, while poverty rose in EMDEs with the lowest productivity growth.

A. Labor productivity and per capita income

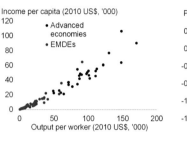

B. Annual change in the poverty rate in EMDEs, by productivity growth

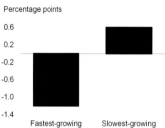

Source: PovcalNet; World Bank.
Note: Sample includes 29 advanced economies and 74 EMDEs.
A. Income per capita and output per worker measured in US dollars at 2010 prices and exchange rates.
B. Unweighted averages using annual data during 1981-2015. Fastest-growing EMDEs are those in the top quartile by productivity growth; slowest-growing EMDEs are those in the bottom quartile of labor productivity growth. Poverty rate defined as the share of the population living on less than $1.90 a day (2011 PPP).

chapter combines these approaches and includes a thorough review of the literature in each area.

- *Comprehensive assessment of correlates of productivity growth.* The chapter reviews a large body of literature on the correlates of productivity growth. It undertakes an empirical exercise that expands upon previous work, whose data typically use either a shorter sample or a narrower set of correlates.[4] The chapter also quantifies the damage that financial crises inflict on productivity growth.[5]

Main findings. The following findings emerge from the chapter.

- *Broad-based post-crisis decline in labor productivity growth.* Global labor productivity growth slowed from its pre-crisis peak of 2.7 percent in 2007 to a trough of 1.5 percent in

2016 and since then has remained low, at 1.9 percent in 2018. The post-crisis slowdown has been broad-based, affecting nearly 70 percent of advanced economies and EMDEs and over 80 percent of the global extreme poor and has affected all EMDE regions (Figure 3.2). In advanced economies, the slowdown continues a trend that has been underway since the late 1990s. In EMDEs, which have a history of recurring multi-year productivity growth surges and setbacks, the productivity growth slowdown from peak (6.6 percent in 2007) to trough (3.2 percent in 2015) has been the steepest, longest, and broadest yet. Commodity-exporting EMDEs—which account for almost two-thirds of EMDEs—have been the worst affected.[6]

- *Large labor productivity gaps, slow convergence in EMDEs.* Average output per worker in EMDEs is less than one-fifth of that in the average advanced economy, and just 2 percent in LICs. Although EMDE productivity convergence improved ahead of the global financial crisis, it is now progressing at rates that would require over a century to halve the current productivity gap with the average advanced economy. However, the pace of convergence differs across regions: more than half of EMDEs in East Asia and Pacific (EAP) are on course to halve their productivity gap in less than 40 years, while fewer than 20 percent of economies in the Middle East and North Africa (MNA), Latin America and the Caribbean (LAC), and Sub-Saharan Africa (SSA) will likely achieve the same reduction over this timeframe.

- *Accounting for the slowdown.* Slower capital deepening has accounted for the lion's share of the post-crisis (2013-18) slowdown in productivity growth in advanced economies from pre-crisis averages (2003-08). In EMDEs, subdued investment and slowing total factor productivity (TFP) growth have

---

[4] Durlauf, Kourtellos, and Tan (2008); Kim and Loayza (2019); Adler et al. (2017).

[5] This complements earlier work documenting damage from financial crises to the level of potential output (Cerra and Saxena 2008) and to potential growth (Furceri and Mourougane 2012a).

---

[6] In commodity-exporting EMDEs, productivity growth slowed by 4.1 percentage points between 2007 and 2015 to around 0, compared with 3.5 percentage points in commodity-importing EMDEs.

accounted, in approximately equal measure, for the post-crisis productivity growth slowdown. About one-half of the slowdown in EMDEs reflects fading gains from the reallocation of resources towards more productive sectors. Reallocation previously drove more than one-third of pre-crisis productivity growth in EMDEs, and three-quarters in LICs.

- *Challenging prospects for labor productivity growth.* Since the global financial crisis, improvements in many key correlates of productivity growth in EMDEs have slowed or gone into reverse. Working-age population growth has slowed, educational attainment has stabilized, and the pace of expansion into more diverse and complex forms of production has lost momentum as the growth of global value chains stalled. At the firm level, EMDE firms that are large and export-oriented are closest to the productivity frontier, suggesting that continued global trade weakness and slower global production integration could be particularly damaging to productivity growth in EMDEs. In addition, the global financial crisis dented productivity growth and momentum has yet to be rebuilt.

- *Policy priorities.* The broad-based nature of the labor productivity growth slowdown can be addressed with a comprehensive set of policies. Policies can lift labor productivity economy-wide by stimulating private and public investment, and improving human capital; fostering firm productivity, including by upgrading workforce skills; exposing firms to trade and foreign investment; facilitating the reallocation of resources towards more productive and a more diversified set of sectors; and creating a generally growth-friendly macroeconomic and institutional environment.

Concepts. Throughout this chapter, productivity is defined as output (GDP) per input of a unit of labor. To ensure as large and comparable a sample as possible over time and across countries, this chapter uses the number of people employed rather than the number of hours worked as the

FIGURE 3.2 Global productivity developments

A broad-based slowdown in productivity growth has been underway, affecting the majority of advanced economies and EMDEs. In EMDEs, productivity growth slowed from its most recent peak of 6.6 percent in 2007 to 3.2 percent in 2015, the steepest, longest, and broadest slowdown in 40 years. Productivity levels in EMDEs are less than 20 percent of the advanced-economy average, and just 2 percent in LICs. The productivity slowdown has coincided with lower gains from sectoral reallocation and a slowdown in improvements in many drivers of productivity growth.

A. Global, advanced-economy, and EMDE productivity growth

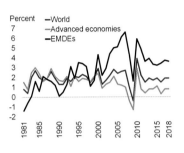

B. Share of economies and global poor with 2013-18 productivity growth below historical averages

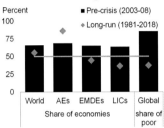

C. Magnitude and extent of multi-year productivity slowdowns and recoveries

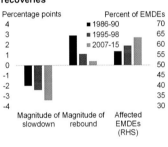

D. EMDE productivity levels, 2013-18

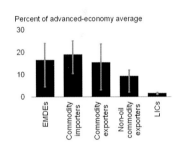

E. Within and between sector contributions to productivity growth

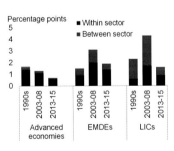

F. Share of EMDEs with a post-crisis slowdown in the growth of underlying drivers of productivity

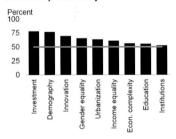

Source: World Bank (full sources in subsequent figures).
Note: Productivity is defined as output per worker. Unless otherwise indicated, data are from a sample of 29 advanced economies (AEs) and 74 emerging market and developing economies (EMDEs). Aggregates are GDP-weighted at constant 2010 prices and exchange rates.
B. Percent of economies, or share of global extreme poor (population living on less than $1.90 per day), with productivity growth in 2013-18 below pre-crisis (2003-08) or long-term (1981-2018) average productivity growth. Grey line indicates 50 percent.
C. "Magnitude of slowdown" is the cumulative decline in EMDE productivity growth from the peak of the episode to the trough for episodes lasting more than two years. "Magnitude of rebound" is the cumulative increase in EMDE productivity growth from the trough (end) of the episode to three years later. "Affected EMDEs" is the share of EMDEs that experienced a slowdown.
D. Blue bars show unweighted average output per worker during 2013-18 relative to the advanced-economy average. Whiskers indicate interquartile range relative to the advanced-economy average.
E. Sample includes 80 economies, including 46 EMDEs (of which 8 are LICs), using data for 1995-2015. Growth "within sector" shows the contribution to aggregate productivity growth of each sector holding employment shares fixed. The 'between sector' effect shows the contribution arising from changes in sectoral employment shares.
F. Post-crisis slowdown defined as the share of economies where improvements in each underlying driver of productivity during 2008-2017 was less than zero or the pace of improvement during the pre-crisis period 1998-2007. Variables definitions in Chart 3.9.A.

measure of labor input.[7] A second measure, total factor productivity (TFP), is also featured in the chapter. TFP measures the efficiency with which factor inputs are combined and is often used to proxy technological progress (Annex 3.2).

Evolution of labor productivity growth

Since 2007, a broad-based slowdown in labor productivity growth has been underway that has reached the majority of advanced economies and EMDEs. For EMDEs, this has partly reversed a pre-crisis productivity growth surge, although productivity growth remains above the very weak rates of the 1980s and 1990s. Some low-income countries have escaped the productivity growth slowdown but productivity growth has regressed in some fragile and conflict-afflicted low-income countries.

Global productivity. From its peak in 2007, global productivity growth has slowed by 0.8 percentage point, to 1.9 percent in 2018. The post-crisis (2013-18) average of 1.8 percent was 0.5 percentage point below the pre-crisis (2003-08) average and slightly below the long-term (1981-2018) average (Figure 3.3). This post-crisis slowdown from pre-crisis averages was broad-based, affecting two-thirds of economies, both advanced economies and EMDEs. Those economies with slower post-crisis productivity growth than during the pre-crisis period account for over 80 percent of global GDP and the extreme poor.

Advanced economies. The post-crisis slowdown in advanced-economy productivity growth continues a trend that has been underway since the late 1990s, following a brief resurgence from an even longer-running negative trend. The slowdown has been attributed to a declining contribution from information and communication technology (ICT) intensive sectors in the United States, and slow adoption of ICT technologies, and restrictive

product market regulations in parts of Europe.[8] During the global financial crisis, productivity growth in advanced economies plunged and never recovered to pre-crisis levels. At 0.8 percent on average during 2013-18, it was one-half its long-term average and 0.4 percentage points below its pre-crisis average. This slowdown relative to long-run averages affected nearly 90 percent of advanced economies.

EMDEs. Productivity growth in EMDEs has slowed sharply from its 2007 peak of 6.6 percent to a low of 3.2 percent in 2015 and, since then, has inched up to 3.6 percent in 2018. The post-crisis slowdown from pre-crisis averages affected nearly 70 percent of EMDEs and, in around half of EMDEs, productivity growth has now fallen below its long-term (1981-2018) average. The slowdown has been particularly pronounced in China, where a policy-guided decline in public investment growth has been underway for several years, and in commodity exporters, which have been hit hard by the commodity price plunge of 2014-16. Weak post-crisis productivity growth follows on the heels of a major productivity surge during 2003-08 when EMDE productivity growth more than doubled from 1990s averages, in part reflecting a strong cyclical rebound from the 1997-98 Asian financial crisis.

Since 1980, EMDE productivity growth has gone through three multi-year surges and setbacks in productivity growth. Previous multi-year slowdowns—in 1986-1990 and 1995-1998—preceded global recessions (1991) or global slowdowns and EMDE crises (1998). However, the slowdown since 2007 has been the most prolonged, steepest and broadest-based yet.[9] In

---

[7] Number of people engaged includes employees and self-employed. Alternative measures might better capture labor input but have insufficient coverage for EMDEs (Annex 3.1). In countries with large informal sectors, both employment and output may be subject to sizable measurement error (World Bank 2019a, Annex 3.1).

[8] For a summary of the effects of the ICT slowdown on U.S. productivity in the 2000s, see Duval, Hong, and Timmer (2017), Jorgenson, Ho, and Stiroh (2008), and Fernald (2012). In Europe, the trend decline in productivity has been ascribed to sectoral misallocation due to cheap credit in southern Europe (Gopinath et al. 2017), a failure to adopt ICT and associated technology to the same extent as the United States (van Ark, O'Mahony, and Timmer 2008), and restrictive product market regulations (Haltiwanger, Scarpetta, and Schweiger 2014).

[9] The most recent slowdown in productivity growth has lasted eight years—compared with the four years of 1986-90 and the three years of 1995-98—and, from peak to trough, has been around 50 percent steeper than the slowdowns in the late 1980s and the late 1990s. It has reached 64 percent of EMDEs, slightly more than the slowdown in the 1990s (59 percent) and 1980s (57 percent).

contrast to previous episodes, the current productivity slowdown has yet to be marked by a strong rebound.

EMDE productivity growth remains slightly above its average in the 1980s and 1990s, which was well below the pre-crisis surge in productivity growth. In commodity importers, average productivity growth in 2013-18 has remained more than twice its 1980s average and one-third above its 1990s average. However, in commodity-exporting EMDEs, the post-crisis commodity price plunge has returned productivity growth to just 0.6 percent, rates which are weak but still above the growth rates of the 1980s.

LICs. On average, LIC productivity growth has fallen only modestly to 2.4 percent during 2013-18, substantially above the negative rates of the 1980s and early 1990s. However, productivity growth has again slowed sharply or turned negative in some fragile and conflict-afflicted states (Burundi, Mozambique).

Regions. Productivity growth decelerated in all EMDE regions during 2013-18 from their pre-crisis (2003-08) averages (Box 3.1). This slowdown occurred amid heightened debt levels which increase the probability of financial crises and crowd out productive investments. The most pronounced slowdown (by 3.8 percentage points to 1.5 percent in 2013-18) occurred in Europe and Central Asia (ECA), where the global financial crisis and subsequent Euro Area debt crisis caused severe economic disruptions. Productivity growth has also fallen steeply in Latin America and the Caribbean (LAC), the Middle East and North Africa (MNA), and Sub-Saharan Africa (SSA), to near zero. Productivity growth declined substantially in East Asia and Pacific (EAP) and more modestly in South Asia (SAR) from pre-crisis levels, but it continued to be robust, remaining above 5 percent in both regions.

Missed opportunities. The steep productivity growth slowdown since the global financial crisis implies considerable output losses relative to a counterfactual of productivity growth continuing at its pre-crisis trend. Output per worker in advanced economies would be 5 percent higher today had productivity growth continued at its

FIGURE 3.3 Evolution of global productivity growth

In EMDEs, productivity growth has declined from pre-crisis levels, although it remains strong relative to longer-run averages in half of EMDEs. At 0.6 percent, EMDE commodity exporters have had the weakest average productivity growth since 2013. Productivity growth in EMDE commodity importers and LICs has been more resilient.

A. Global, advanced-economy, and EMDE productivity growth

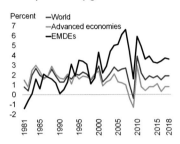

B. EMDE productivity growth

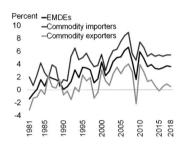

C. Economies with 2013-18 productivity growth below historical averages

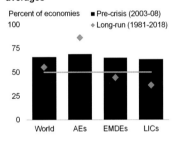

D. EMDE average productivity growth, pre- and post-crisis

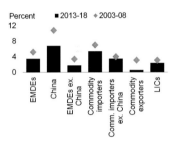

E. Productivity growth in EMDE regions

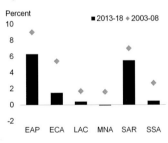

F. Cumulative productivity losses relative to 2003-08 trend

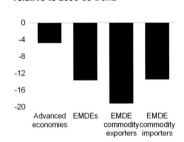

Source: Penn World Table; The Conference Board; World Bank, World Development Indicators.
Note: Productivity is defined as output per worker. Data are from a balanced sample between 1981-2018 and includes 29 advanced economies (AEs), and 74 emerging market and developing economies (EMDEs) including 11 low-income countries (LICs), as of 2019 World Bank classifications, 52 commodity exporters and 22 commodity importers. GDP-weighted (at constant 2010 prices and exchange rates) aggregates.
A.B. GDP weighted averages (at 2010 prices and exchange rates).
C. Share of economies for which average productivity growth during 2013-18 was lower than the long-run (1981-2018) average or the pre-crisis (2003-2008) average.
E. GDP-weighted productivity growth for 8 EMDEs in East Asia and the Pacific (EAP), 10 EMDEs in Eastern Europe and Central Asia (ECA), 18 EMDES in Latin America and the Caribbean (LAC), 10 EMDEs in Middle East and North Africa (MNA), 2 EMDEs in South Asia (SAR), and 26 EMDEs in Sub-Saharan Africa (SSA).
F. Percent fall in productivity level by 2018 relative to a counterfactual scenario where productivity continued to grow at its 2003-08 average growth rate from 2009 onwards.

BOX 3.1 EMDE regional labor productivity trends and bottlenecks

The post-crisis slowdown in productivity growth was particularly severe in East Asia and Pacific, Europe and Central Asia, and Sub-Saharan Africa amid slowing investment growth, financial market disruptions, and a post-crisis commodity price slide. Meanwhile, productivity growth in Latin America and the Caribbean and the Middle East and North Africa—the slowest even before the global financial crisis—has fallen to near-zero as investment collapsed amid political uncertainty, episodes of financial stress in major economies, and falling commodity prices. As a result, the pace of catch-up to advanced-economy productivity levels has slowed in most regions since the global financial crisis and, in some regions, productivity is even falling further behind. In almost all regions, productivity gains from the reallocation of labor from low-productivity to higher-productivity sectors have slowed sharply. To boost productivity, policies are needed to address key obstacles to productivity growth. Some of these obstacles are shared across EMDE regions, including resource-reliant economies, widespread informality, shortcomings in education, and weak governance, and some are region-specific bottlenecks.

Introduction

Although common across all EMDE regions, the post-crisis productivity growth slowdown has differed markedly in severity. Generally, it was more pronounced in more open EMDE regions that are closely integrated into advanced-economy supply chains. Meanwhile, in regions with a large number of commodity exporters, productivity growth has fallen close to zero. As a result, to varying degrees, the catch-up to advanced-economy productivity levels has slowed since the global financial crisis and, in some regions, productivity is even falling further behind. Policy priorities to reignite productivity growth differ across regions.

This box draws out differences in regional productivity trends and policy priorities (summarizing Boxes 2.1-2.6).[1] Specifically, it addresses the following questions:

- How has the evolution of productivity varied across regions?

- What factors were associated with stronger productivity growth?

For the purposes of this box, productivity is defined as labor productivity—that is, real GDP per worker (at 2010 prices and exchange rates).

Evolution of productivity

Post-crisis labor productivity growth slowdown. An exceptional pre-crisis surge in productivity growth was broad-based across regions, with productivity in more than 50 percent of economies in each region except The Middle

East and North Africa (MENA) growing faster than the advanced economy average (Rodrik 2011; Roy, Kessler and Subramanian 2016; Figure 3.1.1). Since the global financial crisis (2013-18), however, productivity growth has slowed from pre-crisis (2003-08) rates in all EMDE regions.

The slowdown was particularly steep in East Asia and the Pacific (EAP), especially in China, as well as in Europe and Central Asia (ECA) and Sub-Saharan Africa (SSA). In these regions, investment growth has declined sharply from pre-crisis levels amid a policy-guided public investment slowdown in China (EAP), financial system disruptions associated with the Euro Area crisis (ECA), and the commodity price collapse of 2014-16 (ECA, SSA). However, in all three regions, there were important exceptions to the sharp slowdown. In EAP, the slowdown was concentrated in China while productivity growth continued to be robust in other major EAP economies, especially some ASEAN economies (the Philippines and Vietnam), as FDI and investment growth remained robust (Box 2.1). In ECA, the slowdown was muted in agricultural economies in Central Asia that shifted their economic ties towards China and in Central European economies that continued to integrate into Western European supply chains and benefited from investment financed by European Union structural funds. In SSA, productivity growth accelerated in agricultural commodity exporters.

The slowdown was mildest in South Asia (SAR), in part because the region is the least open EMDE region to global trade and finance, continued to urbanize rapidly, and, as a predominantly commodity-importing region, benefited from the commodity price slide. In MENA, the slowdown was mild since limited links to global financial markets insulated commodity-importing economies from global financial stress.

Post-crisis productivity growth across regions. Productivity growth in Latin America and the Caribbean

---

Note: This box was prepared by Gene Kindberg-Hanlon with research assistance from Shijie Shi.

[1] To be as representative of each region as possible, this box uses a broader sample than the main text in Chapter 3, resulting in a shorter time horizon under consideration. This box and the regional boxes cover a sample containing 127 EMDE economies, compared to 74 in the main text.

BOX 3.1 EMDE regional labor productivity trends and bottlenecks (*continued*)

FIGURE 3.1.1 Evolution of regional labor productivity

The post-crisis slowdown in labor productivity growth was particularly severe in EAP, ECA and SSA as these regions struggled with slowing investment growth, financial market disruptions, and weaker commodity prices. In EAP and ECA, the slowdown in productivity growth has reflected both a slower pace of capital deepening and weaker TFP growth. In MENA and SAR, TFP has continued growing or stabilized after earlier contractions (MENA).

A. Labor productivity growth in EMDE regions

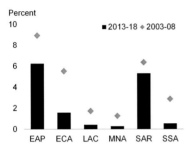

B. Share of economies growing faster than the average advanced economy

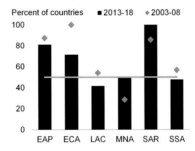

C. Annual rate of productivity convergence, 2003-08 and 2013-18

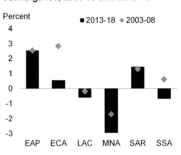

D. Regional average productivity differentials, GDP-weighted, 2018

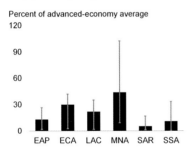

E. Contributions to regional productivity growth; EAP, ECA, LAC

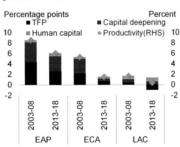

F. Contributions to regional productivity growth: MNA, SAR, SSA

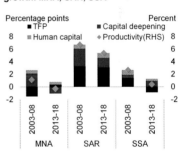

Source: International Monetary Fund; Penn World Table; The Conference Board; World Bank, World Development Indicators.

A.B.C.D. Productivity refers to output per worker at 2010 prices and exchange rates. Sample includes 35 advanced economies (AE) and 16 EMDEs in East Asia and the Pacific (EAP), 21 EMDEs in Eastern Europe and Central Asia (ECA), 25 EMDES in Latin America and the Caribbean (LAC), 14 EMDEs in Middle East and North Africa (MNA), 7 EMDEs in South Asia (SAR), and 44 EMDEs in Sub-Saharan Africa (SSA).

A. GDP-weighted average labor productivity growth.

B. Share of economies with faster productivity growth than the advanced-economy average in each period.

C. Rate of convergence calculated as the difference in productivity growth rates with the average advanced economy divided by the log difference in productivity levels with the average advanced economy. Regional rate of convergence is the GDP-weighted average of EMDE members of each region.

D. Whiskers show the range within the region as a percent of the advanced economy average while bars show the GDP-weighted average level of productivity relative to advanced economies. Productivity reflects output per worker measured in US dollars at 2010 prices and exchange rates.

E.F Aggregates calculated using GDP weights at 2010 prices and exchange rates. The sample includes 92 emerging market and developing economies (EMDEs), including 8 East Asia and Pacific, 21 Europe and Central Asia, 19 Latin America and the Caribbean, 12 Middle East and North Africa, 2 South Asia, and 30 Sub-Saharan Africa economies.

(LAC), MNA, and SSA—even before the crisis, the slowest—has fallen to near zero as investment collapsed amid political uncertainty, episodes of financial stress in major economies, and falling commodity prices (Box 2.3). As a result, productivity growth in the majority of EMDEs in LAC, MNA, and SSA now lags that in advanced economies and, on average in these regions, productivity levels are diverging from those in advanced economies. In contrast, productivity growth continues above 5 percent in

EAP and SAR, where investment growth is still higher than in other EMDE regions (EAP, SAR) or the shift towards more productive sectors has accelerated (SAR). In these two regions, productivity continues to converge towards advanced-economy levels at approximately the pre-crisis pace.

Regional dispersion of productivity. On average, productivity in EMDEs was just 19 percent of the

BOX 3.1 EMDE regional labor productivity trends and bottlenecks (*continued*)

advanced-economy average in 2018.[2] Among EMDE regions, average labor productivity is highest in the MNA (45 percent of the advanced-economy average), LAC and ECA (about 22-30 percent, respectively) and lowest in SAR (6 percent) and SSA (11 percent). However, these regional averages disguise wide dispersion within some regions, especially MNA, ECA, and SSA. In some Gulf Cooperation Council (GCC) countries in MNA, for example, productivity is near advanced-economy averages whereas in heavily agricultural economies, such as the Arab Republic of Egypt and Morocco, it amounted to 10 percent of the advanced-economy average (Box 2.4). Similarly, close trade integration with Western Europe and, increasingly, China and major reforms since the collapse of the Soviet Union have helped raise average productivity levels in ECA to the second-highest among EMDE regions (30 percent). However, there is wide heterogeneity, with Poland producing around 38 percent of the advanced economy average worker, while some agricultural economies in Central Asia produce just 3 percent (Box 2.2). In SSA, LICs produce about 2 percent of the advanced economy average whereas oil exporters such as Gabon produce 33 percent (Box 2.6). In contrast, closely integrated EAP has a narrower range of productivity levels (2-25 percent of the advanced-economy average).

Capital deepening versus total factor productivity growth. Productivity growth can be decomposed into the use of factor inputs (human or physical capital) or the effectiveness of their use (total factor productivity, or TFP, Figure 3.1.1). In EAP and ECA, the post-crisis slowdown in productivity growth has reflected both a slower pace of capital deepening and weaker TFP growth, albeit to varying degrees. Two-fifths of the slowdown in EAP reflected slowing capital deepening, the remainder slowing TFP growth. In EAP, a policy-guided move towards more sustainable growth in China and trade weakness weighed on investment and capital deepening. In ECA, most (two-thirds) of the productivity growth slowdown reflected a collapse in investment growth as conflict erupted in parts of the region, sanctions were imposed on the Russian Federation, political and economic shocks unfolded in Turkey, financial systems transformed after the Euro Area debt crisis, and the commodity price collapse hit commodity exporters (Arteta and Kasyanenko 2019).

In MNA and SAR, in contrast, TFP continued growing at the pre-crisis pace (SAR) or stabilized after earlier contractions (MNA), even as capital deepening slowed sharply (SAR) or reversed (MNA). In MNA, the oil price collapse of 2014-16 weighed heavily on investment in oil exporters and political tensions discouraged investment in commodity importers. However, macroeconomic and structural reform efforts helped stem pre-crisis contractions in TFP. In SAR, persistent post-crisis investment weakness—in part due to disruptive policy changes and tapering growth of FDI inflows—was offset by productivity-enhancing sectoral reallocation, as labor moved out of agriculture into more productive sectors amid rapid urbanization (Box 2.5).

Conversely, in SSA and LAC, TFP contracted. In major LAC economies, continued post-crisis credit extension or intensifying economic distortions (such as trade restrictions and price controls) allowed unproductive firms to survive to a greater extent than pre-crisis. In SSA, the contraction in TFP was partly offset by accelerating capital deepening as a number of countries invested heavily in public infrastructure, typically financed by debt.

Regional sources of productivity growth and bottlenecks

A wide range of factors have weighed on productivity growth since the global financial crisis, but their relative role has differed across regions. In all regions other than SAR, productivity gains from the reallocation away from low-productivity (usually agriculture) sectors to higher-productivity sectors have slowed (Enache, Ghani, and O'Connell 2016). In addition, the pre-crisis pace of improvements in various aspects of the supporting environment for productivity growth has slowed. Productivity levels in all regions remain less than half of those in advanced economies, providing significant scope for faster productivity growth. However, significant bottlenecks to productivity convergence remain, many of which differ across regions.

Sectoral reallocation

Declining gains from sectoral reallocation. In all regions except MNA, switching employment from low-productivity sectors to sectors with above-average productivity levels supported productivity growth during 2003-08, especially in EAP, ECA, and SSA (Figure 3.1.2). In SSA, it accounted for more than half of growth in the median economy during 2003-2008 (Diao, McMillan, and Rodrik 2017).

---

[2] In this section, GDP-weighted averages of productivity are used to compare productivity levels across economies—in the main text, simple averages are used.

BOX 3.1 EMDE regional productivity trends and bottlenecks (*continued*)

FIGURE 3.1.2 Sectoral contributions to regional productivity growth

Since the global financial crisis productivity gains from sectoral reallocation have faded across all regions (with the exception of SAR). In SAR and SSA, around half of employment is in the agricultural sector, which only accounts for around 20 percent of output, reflecting low productivity in this sector. The wide dispersion of sectoral productivity levels within regions demonstrates the importance of introducing measures to reduce misallocation and boost productivity in the weakest sectors.

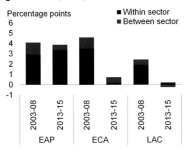

A. Within and between sector contributions to regional productivity growth: EAP, ECA, LAC

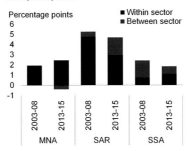

B. Within and between sector contributions to regional productivity growth: MNA, SAR, SSA

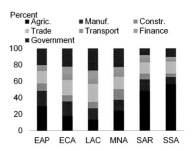

C. Composition of employment by sector, 2015

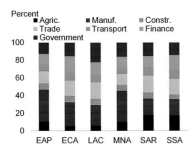

D. Composition of value-added by sector, 2015

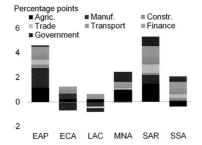

E. Sectoral contribution to aggregate productivity growth, 2013-15

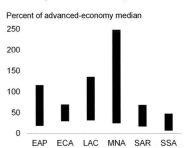

F. Sectoral productivity levels dispersion within regions, 2015

Source: APO productivity database; Expanded African Sector Database; Groningen Growth Development Center Database; Haver Analytics; ILOSTAT; OECD STAN; United Nations; World KLEMS.

Note: Sample includes 46 EMDEs, of which 8 are LICs and 9 East Asia and Pacific, 6 Europe and Central Asia, 6 Latin America and the Caribbean, 3 Middle East and North Africa, 3 South Asia, and 19 Sub - Saharan African economies.

A.B. Median contribution for each region. Growth within sector shows the contribution of initial real value added-weighted productivity growth rate of each sector and 'between sector' effect shows the contribution arising from changes in sectoral employment shares.

E. Median contribution to productivity growth.

F. Range of (regional averages of) sector-specific productivity levels relative to advanced-economy average productivity for the same sector in 2015, valued at 2011 purchasing power adjusted exchange rates. The range for MNA excludes sectoral productivity for mining which exceeds 1000 percent of the advanced-economy average.

Since the global financial crisis, however, productivity gains from sectoral reallocation have faded across all regions (with the exception of SAR). In commodity-reliant regions such as LAC, MNA, and SSA, this in part reflected lower absorption of labor by services and construction sectors as real income losses in resource sectors spilled over into weaker demand. In EAP, it reflected slowing labor reallocation as overcapacity was gradually being unwound. In ECA, high-productivity manufacturing, financial, and mining sectors suffered during the Euro Area debt crisis and the post-crisis commodity price collapse. Meanwhile,

in SAR, the move of labor out of low-productivity agriculture into more productive sectors accelerated as rapid urbanization continued and strong consumption growth fueled employment in higher-productivity trade services.

Looking ahead, further sectoral reallocation continues to have a high potential to lift productivity growth in SSA and SAR, where low-productivity agriculture accounts for around 50 percent of employment and 20 percent of output. Substantial gaps in productivity between sectors

BOX 3.1 EMDE regional productivity trends and bottlenecks (*continued*)

remain, offering the potential for further aggregate productivity gains from resource reallocation between sectors.

Bottlenecks to productivity growth

Several bottlenecks to higher productivity are shared, to varying degrees, by multiple EMDE regions. These include commodity-reliance, widespread informality, poor education, and weak governance. Other bottlenecks are mostly region-specific.

Reliance on commodity exports. In LAC, MNA, and SSA, commodities account for over 20 percent of exports on average. In ECA, they account for 30 percent of exports, largely due to Russia, where around 60 percent of exports are (mostly energy) commodities. Economies that are highly reliant on a narrow range of commodity exports can also suffer from misallocation and procyclical trends for productivity growth (Frankel 2010). Conversely, producing across a broad range of sectors can insulate economies from external shocks, and can facilitate knowledge transfer to strengthen productivity (Kraay, Soloaga, and Tybout 2002; Schor 2004). In EAP, for example, high pre-crisis productivity growth was spurred by rapid integration into global supply chains and attraction of FDI which enabled a substantial increase in the range and sophistication of production in the region (Wei and Liu 2006).

Weak governance and institutions. In most EMDE regions, governance and business climates are less business-friendly than in advanced economies. The largest distances to the frontier (the most business-friendly climates) are in SSA, SAR, and LAC, but also in pockets of ECA (Central Asia and Eastern Europe) and MNA (North Africa). In all regions, a large majority of EMDEs fall below the global average for tackling corruption. Poor institutions have been associated with weak firm productivity and inefficient government investment in productivity-augmenting infrastructure (Cirera, Fattal-Jaef, and Maemir 2019). In EAP, poor corporate governance in some sectors contributes to resource misallocation and weighs on productivity.

Informality. Informality is pervasive in EMDEs, although there are large differences in the productivity of informal sectors across regions. Informal firms are less productive than those in the formal sector and, by competing on more favorable terms, can deter investment and erode the productivity of formal firms (Amin, Ohnsorge, and Okou 2019). In all regions except MNA, the informal sector

accounts for 25-40 percent of official GDP (22 percent of GDP in MNA); however, reflecting heterogeneity in productivity levels, informal employment (measured as self-employment) varies widely from 22 percent (MENA) to 62 percent (SSA) of total employment (World Bank 2019a).

Limited human capital. Higher-skilled and better-educated labor forces tend to adopt new technologies, including new ICT and manufacturing technologies, more readily and more effectively (World Bank 2019c). In EAP and ECA, expected years of schooling for children are now within one year of advanced economies on average, but SAR and SSA lag more than 3 years behind the advanced-economy average (Figure 3.1.3). Even where years of schooling are on par with advanced economies, education can be ineffective where learning outcomes are poor (World Bank 2018a). In learning-adjusted terms, which controls for the quality of education in addition to years of attainment, SAR and SSA lag substantially (six or more learning-adjusted years) behind advanced economies.

Region-specific factors. In each region, some challenges to improving or sustaining productivity growth are notable:

- In **EAP**, the region faces challenges in sustaining productivity growth as rapid trade integration, which spurred productivity growth in the 2000s, fades. With maturing supply chains and weak global trade, the priority has shifted towards improving the allocation and efficiency of investment, including in a wider range of sectors (World Bank and DRCSC 2019).

- In **ECA**, reform momentum has stalled in many economies since the global financial crisis. This follows on the heels of a period of rapid progress in the 1990s and 2000s in the transition to market-based economies and, in Central Europe, in the accession to the European Union (Georgiev, Nagy-Mohacsi, and Plekhanov 2018). Restrictive product market and services regulations now hinder competition and deter foreign investment.

- In **MNA**, the government accounts for a large share of employment relative to other regions. About one-fifth of the workforce is employed in the public sector. This is in part driven by a sizable wage premium for public-sector workers and a bias in the education system toward training for public sector employment. The non-GCC private sector is anemic, with lower firm turnover than in other EMDE regions.

BOX 3.1 EMDE regional productivity trends and bottlenecks (*continued*)

FIGURE 3.1.3 Potential bottlenecks to productivity growth

Several bottlenecks to higher productivity are shared, to varying degrees, by EMDE regions. These include undiversified economies, weak governance, widespread informality, poor learning outcomes, and low trade and financial openness.

A. Share of commodities in total exports, 2013-2018

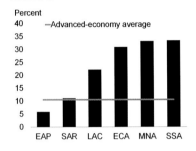

B. Government effectiveness, 2013-2018

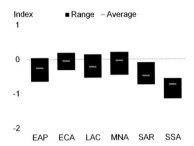

C. Informal economy, 2016

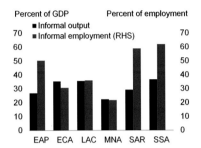

D. Educational attainment, 2017

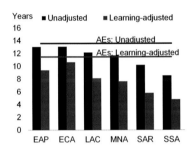

E. Trade and financial openness, 2013-2018

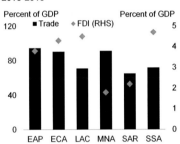

F. Business climates, 2020

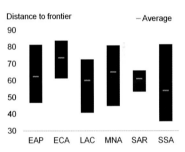

Source: United Nations; World Bank, Doing Business, Human Capital Project, World Development Indicators, Worldwide Governance Indicators.
A. Exports of metals, agricultural and energy products in percent of total exports. GDP-weighted average for each region. Average during 2013-2018.
B. WGI index defined as capturing perceptions of the quality of public services, the quality of the civil service and the degree of its independence from political pressures, the quality of policy formation and implementation, and the credibility of the government's commitment to such policies. Bars show interquartile range.
C. Average informal output (DGE-based estimates, percent of official GDP) and employment estimate (self-employment, percent of total employment) in each region. Based on World Bank (2019a).
D. Expected years of schooling and learning-adjusted years of schooling from the World Bank's Human Capital Project. Learning-adjusted years of schooling uses harmonized cross-country test scores to adjust the average years of schooling.
E. Unweighted average of trade (exports plus imports) in percent of GDP and net foreign direct investment inflows in percent of GDP.
F. Unweighted average distance to frontier measure of the ease of doing business score from the 2020 Doing Business Indicators. A higher value indicates a business climate that is closer to best practices. Bars show range.

- In **LAC**, productivity could be boosted by policies to improve innovation and competition. Greater trade integration and more welcoming environments for FDI could lift productivity growth through knowledge and technology transfers.

- In **SAR**, productivity has been held back by below-average international trade integration and FDI, which limits technology and knowledge spillovers, and restricted access to finance from a banking system that is heavily state-dominated.

- In **SSA**, low productivity reflects the presence of large agricultural sectors, including widespread subsistence agriculture. A policy priority is therefore to lift productivity in the agricultural sector. In addition, SSA economies tend to be involved in supply chains only at early stages of production, producing primary products, and have few exporting firms.

average pace ahead of the crisis (2003-2008). Losses relative to the exceptionally high rate of productivity growth in EMDEs ahead of the crisis are closer to 14 percent, and higher still at 19 percent for EMDE commodity exporters.

Labor productivity convergence

EMDE productivity levels are less than one-fifth of the advanced-economy average, falling to just 2 percent in LICs. In some large EMDEs, such as China and India, productivity is growing substantially faster than in advanced economies, resulting in productivity catch-up. However, average EMDE productivity growth is just half a percentage point faster than in advanced economies, requiring more than a century to halve productivity gaps.

Faster productivity growth occurs in countries with lower initial productivity levels when controlling for factors such as the level of human capital and institutional quality (Durlauf, Johnson, and Temple 2005; Johnson and Papageorgiou 2018). At 3.6 percent in 2018, productivity growth in EMDEs remained more than four times as high as in the average advanced economy (0.8 percent). However, this aggregate growth rate is dominated by China and India, the largest EMDEs by output and population, where productivity growth is above five percent. Many EMDEs are growing at a substantially slower pace than China and India: *on average*, EMDE productivity is growing by just 0.5 percentage point faster than in advanced economies.

Productivity gaps. Despite some narrowing of the productivity gap in 60 percent of EMDEs since the 1990s, output per worker in EMDEs remains less than one-fifth that of the average advanced economy (Figure 3.4).[10] This productivity differential accounts for a considerable proportion of global income inequality since global per capita income differences (reflecting mainly productivity

differences) drive two-thirds of global inequality (World Bank 2018c).

- *Commodity importers and exporters.* Relative productivity levels are slightly higher in commodity-importing EMDEs on average (19 percent of advanced-economy productivity) than in commodity-exporting EMDEs (17 percent) and, lower in non-oil exporters (10 percent) than in oil exporters (28 percent) (Chapter 2 boxes).

- *LICs.* In LICs, productivity is just 2 percent of the advanced-economy average, having made negligible progress in narrowing this gap since the 1990s (World Bank 2019b).

- *Regions.* Productivity is lowest on average in SSA and SAR (8 and 7 percent of the advanced-economy average respectively). Within SSA, which hosts most LICs and mostly non-oil commodity exporters, productivity is even lower in many economies, falling to just 2 percent of the advanced economy average in the bottom quartile of the region (Box 3.1). It is highest in MNA (36 percent of the advanced-economy average), which hosts several high-income oil exporters, and ECA (19 percent of the advanced-economy average), parts of which are closely integrated with EU supply chains and EU labor markets. Throughout the 2000s, pre- as well as post-crisis, the gap with advanced economies has closed fastest in EAP and SAR but continued to widen in parts of LAC, MNA, and SSA.

Pace of productivity convergence. Productivity convergence between low and high-productivity economies became broad-based in the late 1990s, with little evidence for convergence prior to this (Patel, Sandefur, and Subramanian 2018; Figure 3.4).[11] While the presence of convergence during the 2000s is reassuring, its pace is disappointing. At current productivity growth rates, productivity gaps to advanced-economy average productivity

---

[10] This productivity gap is measured using output per worker in 2010 U.S. dollars at market exchange rates. When measured at Purchasing Power Parity (PPP) adjusted U.S. dollars, the gap to advanced economies is smaller, with EMDE productivity around one-third of the advanced economy average (World Bank 2018a).

[11] The speed of productivity convergence can be formally assessed using a "β convergence" test, where productivity growth is regressed on the initial level of productivity (Barro 1991; Barro and Sala-i-Martin 1992).

are narrowing by 0.3 percent per year on average—requiring more than a century just to close half of the gap. But the pace of convergence differs across regions. At current rates of productivity growth, less than 20 percent of economies in LAC, MNA or SSA—but at least 50 percent of those in EAP and SAR—are on course to halve their productivity gap over the next 40 years.

Sources of post-crisis slowdown in labor productivity growth

Aggregate labor productivity growth can be decomposed into its sources: into factor inputs and the efficiency of their use, or into sectors. These decompositions suggest that the post-crisis productivity growth slowdown in EMDEs, in approximately equal measure, reflected weak investment and a slowdown in total factor productivity growth, as well as fading gains from factor reallocation towards more productive sectors.

Decomposition into factor inputs

Approach. In the first step, productivity growth is decomposed into contributions from individual factor inputs (capital and human capital) and the effectiveness of their use (total factor productivity, or TFP, growth), assuming a Cobb-Douglas production function (Annex 3.2). Capital deepening directly increases labor productivity, while human capital improvements (e.g. education and training) enhances the quality of labor input and therefore the resulting output produced. TFP measures the efficiency with which all factors are employed, and is often considered a proxy for the technology behind the production process.[12] TFP growth can also be affected by non-technology

---

[12] The decomposition above is an accounting framework that does not control for dynamic interactions between TFP and investment growth. However, there is evidence that weak underlying TFP and investment growth reinforce each other, which could have amplified the post-crisis productivity slowdown. Weaker rates of investment reduce TFP growth by reducing the incorporation of new technologies into the production process (Adler et al. 2017; Hulten 1992). Conversely, slower technological change reduces the expected return on capital and, hence, the incentives to invest.

FIGURE 3.4 **Distribution of productivity levels and convergence progress**

On average, productivity in EMDEs is less than one-fifth of the advanced-economy average, and in LICs it is just 2 percent. EMDE productivity gaps with the advanced-economy average widened during the 1970s-1990s but narrowed from 2000 onwards. However, the implied pace of convergence is low—even at the peak of EMDE growth, the productivity gap would have taken over a century to halve.

A. EMDE productivity levels, 2013-18 simple average

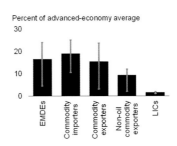

B. Simple average of productivity relative to advanced economies by region, 2013-18

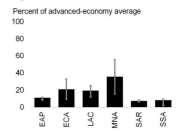

C. Share of EMDEs with narrowing productivity gap to advanced economies

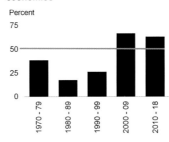

D. EMDE productivity levels since the 1990s, GDP-weighted average

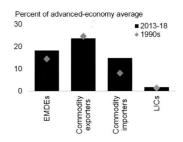

E. Estimated annual decline in productivity gap

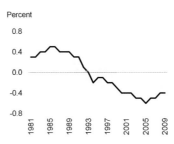

F. Share of economies, by years to halve the productivity gap with advanced economies

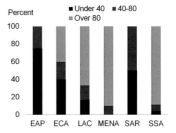

Source: Penn World Table; The Conference Board; World Bank, World Development Indicators.
Note: Productivity defined as output per worker in U.S. dollars (at 2010 prices and exchange rates). Based on 29 advanced economies and 74 EMDEs, which include 22 commodity-importing EMDEs and 52 commodity-exporting EMDEs.
A. Blue bars indicate unweighted average output per worker during 2013-18 relative to the advanced-economy average. Whiskers indicate interquartile range relative to the advanced-economy average.
B. Unweighted average productivity during 2013-18 relative to average advanced economy by region (2013-18). Includes 29 advanced economies and 74 EMDEs = 8 EMDEs in East Asia and the Pacific (EAP), 10 EMDEs in Eastern Europe and Central Asia (ECA), 18 EMDEs in Latin America and the Caribbean (LAC), 10 EMDEs in Middle East and North Africa (MNA), 2 EMDEs in South Asia (SAR), and 26 EMDEs in Sub-Saharan Africa (SSA).
C. Share of EMDEs with faster productivity growth than the advanced-economy average.
D. GDP-weighted (at 2010 prices and exchange rates) averages.
E. Line shows the implied annual rate of decline of the productivity gap based on a regression of labor productivity growth on initial productivity. Shaded area indicates 90 percent confidence intervals. Estimation performed over 10-year rolling windows in the specification

$\log\Delta y_t = c + \beta y_{t-10} + \varepsilon_t$ where y is output per worker. Coefficient converted to the average annual decline in the productivity gap following Sala-i-Martin (1992).
F. The proportion of EMDEs in each region that will close half of the productivity gap with the average advanced economy in each bracket of years based on average growth during 2013-18 relative to average advanced economy growth and the outstanding productivity gap over the same period.

factors, such as changing levels of capital and labor utilization—therefore estimates may over or understate the true change in the influence of technology on productivity. Efforts to control for utilization have found that while some of the pre-crisis surge in productivity in EMDEs was a demand-driven phenomenon of increased utilization, a large proportion of the subsequent slowdown was structural, reflecting factors other than fading demand after the global financial crisis (Dieppe, Kiliç Çelik, and Kindberg-Hanlon, Forthcoming).

Factors inputs versus the effectiveness of their use. Globally, the post-crisis (2013-18) slowdown in labor productivity growth from pre-crisis (2003-08) averages amounted to half of a percentage point, the majority of which was a result of a slowdown in capital accumulation (both public and private; World Bank 2019b). In advanced economies, the slowdown in TFP growth was a minor source of the post-crisis decline in labor productivity growth, due to a structural slowdown prior to the crisis.[13] In EMDEs, however, it accounted for about one-half of the slowdown in labor productivity growth.

- *Advanced economies.* Investment weakness accounted for virtually all of the post-crisis slowdown in productivity growth from pre-crisis averages in advanced economies (Figure 3.5). From 2008, investment growth slowed sharply in response to weak and highly uncertain growth prospects, heightened policy uncertainty, and credit constraints in the aftermath of the global financial crisis.[14] Investment contracted by an average of 6 percent per year between 2008-09. While the investment share of GDP has recovered close to pre-crisis levels, it has been accompanied by strong rates of employment growth, such that the growth of capital per worker has remained subdued (ECB 2017). TFP growth had already declined in the pre-crisis period

(2003-08) relative to the 1980s and 1990s and has now recovered modestly.[15]

- *EMDEs.* The post-crisis slowdown in EMDE productivity growth from pre-crisis averages reflected, in approximately equal measure, investment weakness and slowing TFP growth. In *commodity-exporters*, the contribution of capital accumulation faded almost entirely, after having accounted for about half of productivity growth pre-crisis. This was compounded by contracting TFP growth, which had accounted for most of the remainder of pre-crisis productivity growth. Investment stalled or contracted in commodity exporters during the commodity prices collapse of 2011-16 (Aslam et al. 2016; World Bank 2017). TFP growth has also been weak historically, contributing little to catch-up growth (De Gregorio 2018). In *commodity-importers*, especially China, capital deepening accounted for much of the productivity gains over the past four decades. This momentum has slowed since the global financial crisis reflecting diminishing growth prospects, heightened uncertainty, and weak FDI inflows. In the early 2000s, TFP was boosted by earlier reforms that allowed greater FDI inflows in the 1990s and WTO accession in 2001 which unleashed a productivity boom in China and its trading partners, while a decade of service-sector oriented reforms boosted productivity in India (Bosworth and Collins 2008; He and Zhang 2010; Tuan, Ng, and Zhao 2009).

- *LICs.* In LICs, heavy public infrastructure investment and business climate improvements have supported post-crisis output and productivity growth (World Bank 2019c). This followed on the heels of a decade of heavy investment into mines and oil fields

---

[13] This finding is in line with previous studies of the United States and other advanced economies (Adler et al. 2017; Fernald et al. 2017).

[14] See for details Duval, Hong, and Timmer (2017) and Ollivaud, Guillemette, and Turner (2016).

---

[15] Much of the recent discussion of advanced economy TFP growth has focused on the slowdown in the United States, where TFP has weakened further since the crisis following a surge from the mid-1990 to 2000s (Fernald et al. 2017; Cowen 2011; Gordon 2018). In contrast, average TFP growth was low in the pre-crisis period in major European economies such as Germany and France (0.1-0.4), and even negative in Italy and Spain, such that the post-crisis TFP slowdown is much less pronounced for advanced economies in aggregate.

amid surging pre-crisis commodity prices. As a result, continued post-crisis strength in productivity growth reflected increased capital accumulation. Modest improvements in human capital partly offset increasingly negative TFP growth in these economies. A continued concentration in the agricultural and extractives sectors has led to low technological progress, with additional negative shocks from conflict and from high levels of debt in the 1980s and 1990s also contributing to frequently negative TFP growth (Claessens et al. 1997; IMF 2014).

- *EMDE regions.* Capital accumulation accounted for virtually all of the post-crisis slowdown in productivity growth in MNA, where oil-exporting EMDEs suffered stalled or contracting investment amid the oil price collapse of 2014-16 (Stocker et al. 2018). It also accounted for most of the slowdown in ECA, whose banking systems were hard-hit by the Euro Area crisis and the subsequent retreat from the region of EU-headquartered banks (Arteta and Kasyanenko 2019). In EAP, a deliberate policy-guided public investment slowdown in China is underway and slower capital accumulation accounted for about two-fifths of the slowdown in post-crisis productivity growth. In SSA, which hosts most LICs, and in LAC, the slowdown was entirely driven by declining TFP growth. In contrast to other EMDE regions, TFP growth strengthened in MNA, from negative pre-crisis rates amid heavy resource investment, and in SAR, which was little-affected by the disruptions of the global financial crisis.

Decomposition into sectors

Approach. Higher aggregate productivity growth in EMDEs in the pre-crisis period was associated with a reallocation of resources towards more productive sectors in addition to productivity growth within sectors (Diao, McMillan, and Rodrik 2017). More recently, pre-crisis gains from such reallocation appear to have faded. This is illustrated in a decomposition of economy-wide labor productivity growth into within- and between-sector productivity growth for 80 economies, including 38 EMDEs, of which 7

FIGURE 3.5 **Decomposition of productivity growth**

Almost three-quarters of the post-crisis slowdown in global productivity growth from pre-crisis averages—and virtually all in advanced economies—reflected a slowdown in capital accumulation. The post-crisis slowdown in EMDE productivity growth from pre-crisis averages reflected, in approximately equal measure, investment weakness and slowing TFP growth. In LICs, strong investment has supported post-crisis output and productivity growth.

A. Contributions to productivity growth in advanced economies

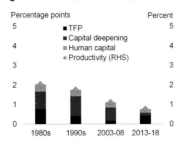

B. Contributions to productivity growth in EMDEs

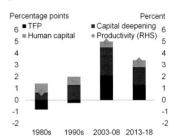

C. EMDE commodity exporter and importer productivity contributions

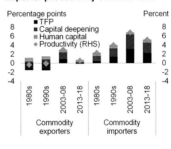

D. Contributions to productivity growth in LICs

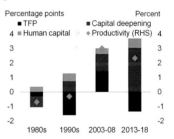

E. Contributions to regional productivity growth: EAP, ECA, LAC

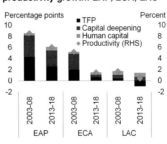

F. Contributions to regional productivity growth: MNA, SAR, SSA

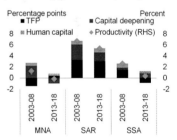

Source: Barro and Lee (2015); International Monetary Fund; Penn World Tables; The Conference Board; United Nations; Wittgenstein Centre for Demography and Global Human Capital; World Bank, World Development Indicators.
Note: Productivity defined as output per worker. Aggregate growth rates calculated using constant 2010 US dollar weights. 52 commodity exporters, 22 EMDE commodity importers, 8 East Asia and Pacific, 10 Europe and Central Asia, 18 Latin America and the Caribbean, 10 Middle East and North Africa, 2 South Asia, and 26 Sub - Saharan Africa economies. GDP weights. The sample includes 29 advanced economies, and 74 emerging market and developing economies including 11 low-income countries.

are LICs, for nine sectors during 1995-2015 (Box 3.2).

Wide differentials in sectoral productivity. Labor productivity varies widely across sectors, being lowest by far in agriculture and highest in mining, financial and business services, and utilities. In EMDEs, labor productivity in mining and financial and business services, which are often foreign-owned, is thirty to forty times the level of productivity in the agriculture sector, which is often characterized by smallholder farms (Figure 3.6; Lowder, Skoet, and Raney 2016). In advanced economies, this differential is considerably narrower (three times). As a result, agricultural productivity in EMDEs lags far behind that in advanced economies—in the average EMDE, agricultural productivity is less than one-fifth that in the average advanced-economy. In contrast, services sectors such as transport or financial and business services are small in EMDEs, accounting for 22 percent of value-added in total, but feature productivity that is two-fifths to one-half of advanced-economy productivity on average.

Fading gains from factor reallocation in EMDEs. In EMDEs, about one-half of the post-crisis (2013-15) slowdown in productivity growth from pre-crisis (2003-08) averages reflected fading gains from resource reallocation towards more productive sectors. In the 1990s and pre-crisis, such resource reallocation had accounted for more than one-third of average labor productivity growth, in line with earlier findings (Diao, McMillan, and Rodrik 2017). Productivity gains from such a reallocation were particularly large in Sub-Saharan Africa, where they accounted for over half of productivity growth during 2003-2008, amid a large fall in the share of agricultural employment.

Post-crisis, the contribution of reallocation to productivity growth fell to less than one-quarter on average in EMDEs. To some degree as countries reach middle-to high income, sectoral reallocation tends to become a less important driver of productivity growth (de Nicola, Kehayova, and Nguyen 2018; Mason and Shetty 2019). In addition, technology and knowledge

spillovers between sectors may also be diminishing (Foerster et al. 2019). However, productivity gaps between sectors in EMDEs remain sizeable. In contrast to other regions, productivity gains from reallocation continue to be sizable in SAR, accounting for one-half of post-crisis productivity growth, as agricultural employment moves into industrial sectors.

Challenges for within-sector productivity growth. Within-sector productivity gains also decelerated post-crisis, in EMDEs as well as advanced economies. The post-crisis slowdown may reflect the challenges faced by the most productive firms (large, export-oriented ones) amid post-crisis trade and investment weakness (Box 3.3). In many EMDEs, an additional challenge may arise from the sheer size of the informal sector (World Bank 2019a). The labor productivity of informal firms is, on average, only one-quarter of the productivity of formal firms. Informal firms are less able than formal firms to reap the productivity gains from economies of scale (size), accumulated experience (age), agglomeration benefits (location), and best managerial practices (Fajnzylber, Maloney, and Montes-Rojas 2011). Moreover, aggressive competition from informal firms can erode the productivity of exposed formal firms by about 24 percent relative to those formal firms that do not face informal competition (Loayza 2016; World Bank 2019a). A more conducive business climate, and economic development more broadly, can alleviate some of the corrosive productivity effects of informal competition on formal firms.

Fading gains from reallocation away from agriculture in LICs. In LICs, agriculture accounts for 31 percent of GDP, on average, but agricultural productivity is low (Cusolito and Maloney 2018). As a result, a reallocation of employment, especially from agriculture, to higher-productivity sectors accounted for almost two-thirds of LIC productivity growth prior to the global financial crisis (Box 3.2). Since then, however, this engine of LIC productivity growth appears to have stalled. In part, this is due to a collapse in global industrial commodity prices, which have discouraged further growth in employment in the mining and extraction sector,

BOX 3.2 Sectoral sources of productivity growth

Labor reallocation towards higher-productivity sectors has historically accounted for about one-third of aggregate productivity growth in EMDEs. This mechanism has, however, weakened since the global financial crisis. Fading productivity gains from labor reallocation have accounted for about one-half of the post-crisis productivity slowdown in EMDEs. In commodity-exporting EMDE regions, deindustrialization contributed to the slowdown.

Introduction

Factor reallocation towards higher-productivity sectors has long been recognized as one of the most powerful drivers of aggregate productivity growth (Baumol 1967).[1] It has been identified as an important driver of productivity growth in economies as diverse as Sub-Saharan Africa, China and Vietnam (Cusolito and Maloney 2018; de Vries, de Vries and Timmer 2015; Fuglie et al. 2019). Especially in East Asia, the move out of agriculture into higher-productivity industry and services has been credited with rapid productivity growth (Helble, Long, and Le 2019).

In part as a result of several decades of sectoral reallocation away from agriculture, agriculture now accounts for only 10 percent of EMDE value-added—one-quarter less than two decades earlier and less than one-third the share of industrial production (Figure 3.2.1). LICs are an exception where agriculture still accounts for one-third of value-added, more than industry, and accounts for over 60 of employment.

Meanwhile, services sectors have grown rapidly over the past two decades. They now account for about one-half of value-added in EMDEs as well as LICs, compared with three-quarters of value-added in advanced economies. Services sectors have also been the main source of post-crisis productivity growth, accounting for almost two-thirds of productivity growth in the average EMDE (compared with one-fifth accounted for by industry) and more than three-quarters in the average LIC.

Services describe a highly heterogeneous set of activities. Whereas industry mostly consists of manufacturing (64 percent in the average EMDE), services include in almost equal measure trade services, transport services, financial and business services, and government and personal services. These service subsectors vary widely in their skill- and capital-intensity as well as their productivity.

Against this backdrop, this box examines the sources of the post-crisis slowdown in productivity growth from a sectoral angle. Specifically, it addresses the following questions.

- What are the main features of sectoral productivity?

- What was the role of sectoral reallocation in the post-crisis productivity growth slowdown?

Much of the earlier literature on sectoral productivity has focused on three sectors (agriculture, manufacturing, and services) with only a limited number of cross-country studies including more sectors.[2] There is evidence that the findings of reallocation are sensitive to the level of aggregation (de Vries et al. 2012; Üngör 2017). To explore these issues, this box draws on a comprehensive dataset for 80 countries and 9 sectors over 1995-2015.

Features of sectoral productivity

Wide productivity differentials across sectors. Productivity differs widely across sectors, offering large potential for productivity gains by factor reallocation across sectors (Figure 3.2.3). In the average EMDE, productivity in the most productive sector—mining, which accounts for 4 percent of value-added—is twelve times that in the least productive sector—agriculture, which accounts for 10 percent of value-added.[3] In the average LIC, the range is even larger: productivity in the most productive sector—financial and business services, accounting for 13 percent of value-added—is twenty-two times that in the least productive sector—agriculture, which accounts for almost one-third of value-added

---

Note: This box was prepared by Alistair Dieppe and Hideaki Matsuoka.

[1] Throughout this box, productivity refers to labor productivity, defined as value added per employed worker.

[2] Diao, McMillan, and Rodrik (2017) and McMillan, Rodrik, and Verduzco-Gallo (2014) employ 38 and 39 countries; Martins (2019) use 7 sectors and 169 countries, and International Monetary Fund (2018) use 10 sectors and 62 countries. Further disaggregation using micro panel data (such as by Hicks et al. 2017) would help to ensure differences in marginal product are accounted for.

[3] The high productivity extractive sectors offer few opportunities for sectoral reallocation and are intrinsically limited by the size of the resource, and market power. It should be noted that refining and processing of extractives can sometimes be classified as manufacturing in resource rich countries.

BOX 3.2 Sectoral sources of productivity growth (*continued*)

FIGURE 3.2.1 Agriculture, industry and services

In part as a result of a several decades of sectoral reallocation away from agriculture, agriculture now accounts for only 10 percent of EMDE value-added—one-quarter less than two decades earlier and less than one-third the share of industrial production. LICs are an exception; agriculture still accounts for one-third of value-added in these economies, more than industry. Meanwhile, services sectors—which include a highly heterogeneous set of activities—have grown rapidly over the past two decades, accounting for about half of post-crisis productivity growth.

A. Composition of value-added

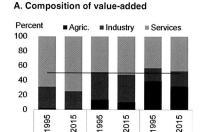

B. Composition of employment

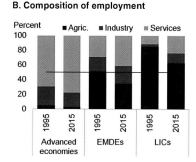

C. Contributions to productivity growth

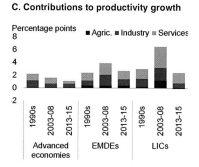

Source: APO productivity database, Expanded African Sector Database, Groningen Growth Development Center Database, Haver Analytics, ILOSTAT, OECD STAN, United Nations, World KLEMS.
Note: Based on sample of 80 countries.
A.B. Share of agricultural, industry and services in value added. Industry includes mining, manufacturing, utilities, and construction. Services include trade services, transport services, financial and business services, government and personal services. Black horizontal line indicates 50 percent.

(Figure 3.2.2).[4] Since the 1990s, the productivity dispersion within the manufacturing and service sectors, has narrowed. Similar differentials, between the most productive sector (financial and business services) and the least productive sector (agriculture), in advanced economies are considerably narrower.

Wide sectoral productivity differentials across countries. Productivity in all sectors is lower in EMDEs than in advanced economies, and lower again in LICs. The gap between EMDE and advanced-economy productivity is particularly wide (almost 80 percent) in agriculture, which tends to be characterized by smallholder ownership and family farms in EMDEs (Lowder, Skoet, and Raney 2016). This reflects in part slow technology adoption in the agriculture sector in some of the poorest EMDEs. In mining, which tends to be dominated globally by a few large companies, the productivity gap is considerably narrower (just over 20 percent).

Sectoral productivity growth. Productivity growth in the various subsectors of services varied widely, from negative

(pre-crisis) or near zero (post-crisis) in mining to the highest sectoral growth rates (4.8 percent) in transport services in EMDEs in 2003-08 (Duernecker, Herrendorf, and Valentinyi 2017).[5] The post-crisis (2013-15) slowdown in manufacturing productivity growth was the largest among all nine sectors, nearly 2 percentage points below the pre-crisis average (2003-08).

In advanced economies, the post-crisis productivity growth slowdown was broad-based across almost all sectors (except construction). More than one-half of the post-crisis (2013-15) slowdown in productivity growth from pre-crisis rates (2003-08) in the average EMDE originated in the manufacturing sector. The slowdown in agricultural productivity growth had only a limited aggregate effect in EMDEs due to its relatively small share in the economy. In contrast, EMDE productivity growth picked up after

---

[4] As agricultural workers often do not work full time in agriculture, the sectoral gap is diminished if productivity is measured per hours instead of per worker (McCullough 2017). However, even after accounting for hours and human capital per worker, a large sectoral gap remains for many of countries (Gollin, Lagakos, and Waugh 2014).

[5] Two waves of service sector growth have been identified in the literature: a first wave in countries with relatively lower income levels and a second wave in countries with higher income levels. The first wave appears to be made up primarily of traditional (personal) services, the second wave of modern (financial, communication, computer, technical, legal, advertising and business) services that are receptive to the application of information technologies and tradable across borders (Eichengreen and Gupta 2013). Moreover, there is evidence of the second wave also occurring in lower income countries after 1990 which are democracies, and have high trade and financial openness.

BOX 3.2 Sectoral sources of productivity growth (*continued*)

FIGURE 3.2.2 Sectoral labor productivity

Productivity differs widely across sectors and subsectors, especially in EMDEs and even more so in LICs. Productivity in all sectors is lower in EMDEs than in advanced economies, and lower again in LICs. The gap to advanced-economy productivity is particularly wide in agriculture, and narrow in mining. Industry was the main source of pre-crisis productivity growth; its slowdown accounted for more than half the post-crisis slowdown in aggregate productivity in EMDEs.

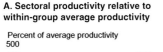

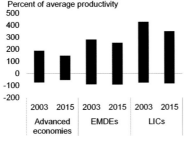

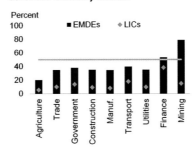

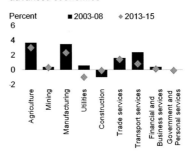

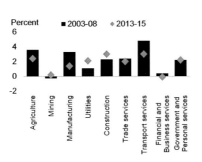

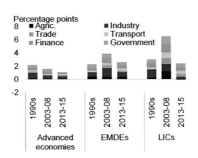

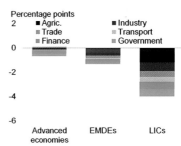

Source: APO productivity database, Expanded African Sector Database, Groningen Growth Development Center Database, Haver Analytics, ILOSTAT, OECD STAN, United Nations, World KLEMS.
Note: Based on samples of 80 countries. Median of the county-specific productivity level, or growth rate.
A. Bar charts range from the minimum to the maximum sector productivity gap.
B. Sectoral productivities compared at PPP exchange rates.
E.F. "Industry" includes mining, manufacturing, utilities, and construction; "Finance" includes business services; "Government" includes personal services.

the global financial crisis in construction, utilities and mining.

Role of sectoral reallocation

Framework. The productivity differentials between sectors offer the potential for productivity gains from labor reallocation towards higher-productivity sectors, in addition to within-sector productivity gains (Figure 3.2.3).[6] This is captured in a shift-share analysis that

───────────

[6] However, Fuglie et al. (2019) point out that different factor shares in value added would result in a gap of average labor productivity even if the factor allocation is efficient. A gap in average productivity is not sufficient evidence of misallocation because labor productivity can be equalized at the margin.

decompose aggregate labor productivity into within-sector and between-sector components (Wong 2006, Padilla-Pérez and Villarreal 2017). *Within-sector productivity growth* captures changes in aggregate labor productivity growth due to productivity improvements within sectors. This may reflect improvements in human capital, investments in physical capital, or the reallocation of resources from the least to the most productive firms within each sector. *Between-sector productivity growth* is driven by the change in employment share and the productivity differential. It reflects both the reallocation of resources to sectors with higher productivity *levels* (static sectoral effect), and the reallocation of employment towards sectors with higher productivity *growth* (dynamic

BOX 3.2 Sectoral sources of productivity growth (*continued*)

FIGURE 3.2.3 **Between- and within-sector sources to productivity growth**

While productivity growth in advanced economies has predominantly originated within sectors, between-sector gains have accounted for a sizable portion of EMDE productivity growth, and its post-crisis slowdown. In EMDEs, the between-sector productivity gains have involved shifts out of agriculture into higher-productivity sectors that have differed over time.

A. Sectoral productivity relative to country productivity

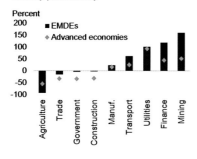

B. Contributions to productivity growth

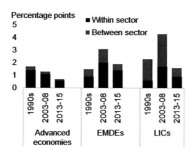

C. Contributions to within-sector productivity growth

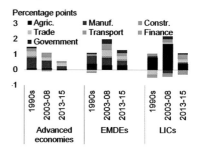

D. Contributions to between-sector productivity growth

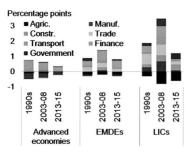

E. ECA, LAC, MNA: Composition of employment

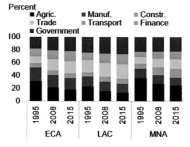

F. ECA, LAC, MNA: Contributions to productivity growth

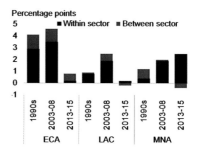

Source: APO productivity database, Expanded African Sector Database, Groningen Growth Development Center Database, Haver Analytics, ILOSTAT, OECD STAN, United Nations, World KLEMS.
B-D. Growth within sector shows the contribution of initial real value-added weighted productivity growth rate and structural change effect give the contribution arising from changes in the change in employment share. Median of the county-specific contributions. Based on samples of 80 countries. "Manuf." includes mining and utilities; "Finance" includes business services; "Government" includes personal services.

sectoral effect). Underlying drivers of such between-sector productivity growth include changes in household's preferences and changes in relative sectoral productivity, in part as a result of diverging evolutions of labor quality (Lagakos and Waugh 2013).[7]

Decomposition of aggregate productivity growth. While productivity growth in advanced-economies has predominantly originated within sectors, between-sector gains have accounted for one-third of EMDE productivity growth since the 1990s. In part as a result of narrowing cross-sector productivity differentials and, in some regions, labor movements into lower-productivity sectors, fading sectoral reallocation has accounted for about one-half of the post-crisis slowdown in EMDE productivity growth. The between-sector EMDE productivity gains have involved shifts out of agriculture into higher-productivity sectors that have differed over time.

---

[7] Improvements in agricultural productivity can significantly reduce agriculture's share of employment, contributing to between-sector productivity growth (Gollin, Parente, and Rogerson 2007). The role of agriculture in structural change depends on economic integration within the domestic economy and with global markets (Barrett et al. 2017).

BOX 3.2 Sectoral sources of productivity growth (*continued*)

- *Advanced economies.* Productivity growth in advanced economies, where sectoral productivity differentials tend to be narrower than in EMDEs, has been almost entirely driven by within-sector productivity growth since the 1990s. Within-sector productivity growth has dwindled to 0.6 percent during 2013-15—less than half its 1990s average (Figure 3.2.3). The predominant structural change has been the reallocation of resources from manufacturing to the financial and business services sector, two sectors with comparable levels of productivity.

- *EMDEs.* In contrast, between-sector productivity gains in EMDEs boosted productivity growth pre-crisis (2003-08) by 1.1 percentage points. Post-crisis, this contribution fell to 0.5 percentage points, accounting for about one-half of the slowdown in EMDE productivity growth. Between-sector productivity gains have mainly reflected a move out of agriculture and manufacturing into services. In LICs, between-sector gains accounted for almost half of post-crisis productivity growth, down from almost three-quarters of pre-crisis productivity growth.[8] Whereas pre-crisis between-sector productivity gains in LICs mainly reflected a shift out of agriculture into manufacturing, their main post-crisis source was a shift out of agriculture into services such as trade services and finance and business services that have benefited from information and computing technologies (Eichengreen and Gupta 2013).

Leapfrogging. Over the two decades until the global financial crisis, one-third of the EMDE employment that left agriculture moved into industrial sectors (predominantly manufacturing and construction) and another one-third into trade services. The share of agricultural employment in EMDEs declined by 9.4 percentage points between 1995 and 2008 while the shares of industry and trade services rose by 2.5 and 3.0 percentage points, respectively. Although trade services and construction typically have below-average productivity and manufacturing productivity is near the EMDE average, the employment shift out of extremely low-

productivity agriculture generate aggregate productivity gains. In LICs, a somewhat larger portion (almost half) of the 10 percentage point decline in the share of agricultural employment was absorbed by trade services and only just over one-third by industry. The phenomenon of employment shifting out of agriculture into services has been dubbed "leapfrogging" in the context of concerns about premature deindustrialization (Rodrik 2016). Looking ahead, productivity gains arising from low-skilled labor shifting out of agriculture into manufacturing or services may diminish if robotization and artificial intelligence discourage this movement.

Deindustrialization. In three regions—Europe and Central Asia (ECA), Latin America and the Caribbean (LAC), the Middle East and North Africa (MNA)—the manufacturing sector's (as well as agriculture's) share of employment has shrunk since the crisis, continuing a pre-crisis trend.[9] Employment has largely shifted into construction (MNA), finance (ECA, LAC) and trade services (ECA, MNA). Since some of these sectors, especially construction and trade services, have lower productivity than manufacturing, this has resulted in a sharply lower contribution (ECA) or even negative contribution (LAC, MNA) of between-sector sources of productivity growth (Rodrik 2016). In LAC, for example, trade liberalization in the 1990s led to cheaper manufacturing imports and a contraction in employment in the uncompetitive manufacturing sector. Much of this labor was absorbed in construction and trade services that were buoyed by pre-crisis commodity boom (Gollin, Jedwab, and Vollrath 2015).

Conclusion

Large sectoral productivity differentials in EMDEs and LICs offer the potential of additional productivity gains when labor moves towards higher-productivity sectors. Such between-sector productivity gains have contributed importantly to productivity growth in EMDEs and LICs since the 1990s. However, since the global financial crisis, these gains appear to have faded.

---

[8] This is consistent with Diao, McMillan, and Rodrik (2017) and, for Sub-Saharan Africa, McMillan, Rodrik, and Verduzco-Gallo (2014).

[9] To some degree this could reflect an outsourcing of parts of the manufacturing sector to the service sector.

FIGURE 3.6 Sectoral productivity developments

Productivity varies widely across sectors, with agricultural productivity in EMDEs lagging both advanced economies and other sectors in EMDEs. Fading gains from resource reallocation towards more productive sectors have accounted for about half of the post-crisis slowdown in productivity growth. Within-sector productivity growth has also slowed.

A. Sectoral productivity relative to country average

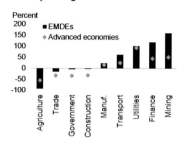

B. Sectoral productivity in EMDEs relative to advanced-economy levels

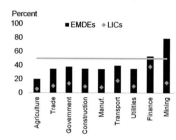

C. Composition of value-added

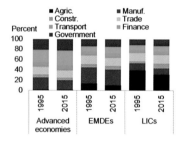

D. Contribution to aggregate productivity growth

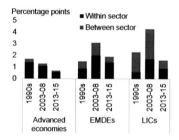

Source: APO productivity database, Expanded African Sector Database, Groningen Growth Development Center Database, Haver Analytics, ILOSTAT, OECD STAN, United Nations, World KLEMS.
Note: Sample includes 80 economies (including 46 EMDEs, of which 8 are LICs). "Manuf." includes mining and utilities; "Finance" includes business services; "Government" includes personal services.
A. Deviation of sectoral productivity level from country-specific average productivity.
B. Grey horizontal line indicates 50 percent.
C. Share of total value added.
D. Growth "within sector" shows the contribution to aggregate productivity growth of each sector holding employment shares fixed. The 'between sector' effect shows the contribution arising from changes in sectoral employment shares. Median of the country-specific contributions.

which have above-average productivity levels in LICs. Despite having high productivity levels, the mining and extraction sectors often offer limited scope for expanding employment outside of commodity booms, and therefore few opportunities for sustainable sectoral reallocation.

Long-run drivers of productivity growth

During the pre-crisis productivity surge in EMDEs, growth was highest in those economies with more favorable institutional environments, more developed product and factor markets, and higher or higher-quality factor inputs. Subsequently, improvements in

many of these and some other correlates of productivity growth have slowed or gone into reverse. These include investment weakness; a slower pace of urbanization; maturing gains from macroeconomic stability and global integration; and diminishing improvements or stagnation in educational attainment, gender equality, and governance.

A large number of variables have been proposed as possible drivers of productivity (Annex 3.3).[16] These drivers can be grouped into three categories: the quality and quantity of factors of production and the effectiveness of their use, such as capital, education, and innovation; the supporting economic environment, such as institutions and social conditions; and the degree of market development, such as trade integration and financial market development. This section presents the correlations of productivity growth with initial conditions for these drivers and, in a second step, discusses the evolution of these drivers.

Correlation between productivity growth and its drivers

Methodology. The contributions of potential drivers of productivity growth are estimated in a cross-section regression to identify the main initial country features associated with subsequently higher long-term productivity growth (1960-2018 and 1995-2018) for 59 countries, including 38 EMDEs. Key correlates of productivity growth are selected from a pool of 29 variables by Bayesian techniques to systematically exclude variables that have poor explanatory power for productivity growth and overlapping variables which reflect the same underlying driver (Annex 3.3).

Key initial conditions for higher productivity growth. Productivity in economies with favorable starting conditions in the 1960s grew significantly faster than other economies annually. A better educated workforce (proxied by years of schooling) and stronger institutions (proxied by improvements in the rule of law), greater

---

[16] See Durlauf, Johnson, and Temple (2005) and Kim and Loayza (2019).

BOX 3.3 Patterns of total factor productivity: A firm perspective

There is substantial variation in firm-level total factor productivity (TFP) across industries and across regions. Weak firm productivity in emerging market and developing economies (EMDEs) partly reflects the divergence between a few highly productive firms and a large number of firms that operate far from the productivity frontier. The difference between frontier and laggard firms is, on average, larger in EMDEs than in advanced economies. Among EMDE firms, large firms tend to be more productive than small firms. Firms in technology-intensive industries, mainly located in East Asia and Pacific (EAP), Europe and Central Asia (ECA), and South Asia (SAR), tend to be more productive than firms in more traditional sectors. Measures to promote exports and improve business climates can help close the observed TFP gap.

Introduction

Firm-level productivity in emerging markets and developing economies (EMDEs) has been low relative to advanced economies, and growth has lost momentum over the past decade. This has diminished prospects among many EMDEs to catch up with the advanced economies (Andrews, Criscuolo, and Gal 2016; Cusolito and Maloney 2018).

Numerous factors have been identified as underlying the low firm-level productivity observed in EMDEs: weak institutions and pervasive informality, slow technology innovation and adoption, subdued investment and poor quality infrastructure, low human capital and poor firm management practices, protectionist trade policies and weak economic integration (Cusolito and Maloney 2018; World Bank 2019d, 2019e).[1] Moreover, outdated technologies, lagging innovation, misallocation of labor to inefficient sectors, and market rigidities weigh on productivity and contribute to dispersion in total factor productivity (TFP) across countries (Araujo, Vostroknutova, and Wacker 2017; Bahar 2018; Syverson 2011). In some EMDEs, low participation in global value chains, or lack of openness to foreign direct investment and migration, has resulted in missed opportunities for a productivity boost through the transfer of innovative processes and managerial capabilities (Goldberg et al. 2010; World Bank 2019d).

This box undertakes a cross-sectional study to analyze firm-level TFP patterns, and maps these to firm

characteristics in EMDEs to address the following questions:

- How does firm-level TFP vary across EMDE sectors and regions?

- What firm characteristics account for the dispersion in TFP?

TFP variation across sectors and regions

Productivity varies across firms, within sectors, and across regions (Goñi and Maloney 2017). By focusing on TFP, differences due to capital deepening or other factor inputs can be abstracted from. This allows to identify where TFP dispersion and gaps are the largest, and where steps are needed to improve productivity. Firm-level TFP data are obtained from surveys conducted by the World Bank from 2007 to 2017 (Cusolito et al. 2018). The database of survey results contains TFP for 15,181 manufacturing firms in 108 EMDEs, including 20 low-income countries (LICs). A cross-sectional analysis of the firm-level TFP database is undertaken, which complements longitudinal studies that use micro-level panel data, but with a smaller country coverage.[2] Two measures of TFP are constructed: output and value-added revenue TFP measures. The latter is obtained by subtracting the value of intermediate inputs (materials, electricity, etc.) from output before computing TFP. TFP measurement challenges are discussed in Annex 3.5.

TFP across sectors. Differences in firm-level TFP across sectors have been frequently emphasized in the literature.[3] On average, firms in technology-intensive industries have higher TFP than those in other sectors (Figure 3.3.1.A). Technology-intensive industries, denoted by TINT, include computing and electrical machinery, precision equipment, electronics, information, and communication sectors (as in Fernald 2015). One explanation for this observation is that firms operating in a technology-intensive industry rely more on research and development (R&D) and network linkages than physical assets, and as

---

Note: This box was prepared by Cedric Okou.
[1] Many studies focus on labor productivity, which depends on both TFP and capital per worker–also known as capital deepening.

[2] This analysis does not explore the time series dimension because World Bank's firm output and input data used to construct TFP estimates were collected at different time in different countries. For example, these firm surveys were conducted in 2007 in South Africa and in 2017 in Ecuador. Moreover, the number of surveyed firms in many countries is small, which does not allow to conduct robust within and cross-country comparisons.
[3] See for example, Bartelsman and Doms (2000) and Levchenko and Zhang (2016).

BOX 3.3 Patterns of total factor productivity: A firm perspective *(continued)*

FIGURE 3.3.1 Firm TFP and distance-to-frontier in EMDEs by industry

Firms in technology-intensive industry (TINT) have higher average TFP. These technology-intensive firms are also more tightly clustered around their industry-specific frontier than firms in other sectors.

A. TFP estimates, by industry

B. Distance-to-frontier and average output TFP, by industry

C. Distance-to-frontier and average value-added TFP, by industry

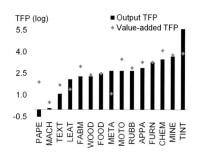
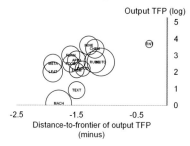
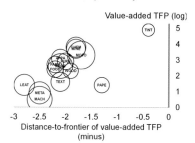

Source: World Bank Enterprise Surveys, World Bank.
Note: Firm-level TFP is computed using a Cobb-Douglas production function for each industry, assuming that elasticities of output with respect to inputs are the same across countries in a given income group. The distance-to-frontier of TFP is computed within each industry, excluding the top 2.5 percent of firms. For each sector, the location shows the average and the size of the marker (circle) is proportional to one standard deviation of distance to frontier of TFP. Averages and standard deviations are computed using survey weights. Sample includes 15,181 firms in 108 EMDEs, including 20 LICs, for the period 2007-17. Firms operate in 15 industries: APPA = apparel, CHEM = chemicals, FABM = fabricated metals, FOOD = food, FURN = furniture, LEAT = leather, MACH = non-electrical machinery, META = metals, MINE = non-metallic minerals, MOTO = motor vehicles, PAPE = paper, RUBB = rubber, TEXT = textiles, TINT=technology-intensive, WOOD = wood. The technology-intensive industry (TINT) includes firms in computing and electrical machinery, precision equipment, electronics, information, and communication sectors.
A. In the manufacture of paper (PAPE) industry, the value-added TFP is positive and much higher than the corresponding (negative) output TFP due to a relatively high elasticity of output with respect to intermediate inputs.
B. C. Distance-to-frontier of firm-level TFP (minus) and TFP (log), by industry. The right-hand-side y-axis represent the frontier.

---

such can reap the benefits of technology to boost productivity (Chevalier, Lecat, and Oulton 2012).

Distance to TFP frontier across sectors. TFP dispersion may signal rigidities in the generation, transfer and acquisition of technology across firms in a sector. To assess within-sector productivity dispersion, a firm's distance to an industry-specific TFP frontier is computed.[4] Firms in basic manufacturing industries, such as non-electrical machinery (MACH), textiles (TEXT), leather (LEAT), and basic metals (META), are not only on average less productive than firms in other sectors, but also relatively far from their industry-specific frontiers (Figure 3.3.1.B and 3.3.1.C). By contrast, firms in technology-intensive industries (TINT) are more tightly clustered around their industry-specific frontiers and are more productive.[5]

TFP across regions. Across regions, firms in East Asia and Pacific (EAP) are, on average, more productive than those

in other regions (Figure 3.3.2.A). EAP also has the highest proportion of large size firms and firms exporting more than half of their sales (Figure 3.3.2.C and Figure 3.3.2.D). Most firms in technology-intensive industries are located in EAP, Europe and Central Asia (ECA), and South Asia (SAR) (Figure 3.3.2.B; regional boxes in Chapter 2). Perceptions of corruption and licensing as obstacles for firm operation seem to correlate negatively with total factor productivity (Figure 3.3.2.E-F).

Robustness of TFP dispersion. Substantial TFP dispersion may signal misallocation of factor inputs or rigidities in the generation, transfer, and acquisition of technology across firms (Hsieh and Klenow 2009). However, commonly used dispersion metrics can also reflect mismeasurements, quality differences, adjustment costs, markups, and investment risks, among other factors. Recent evidence shows that half of the dispersion is unrelated to misallocation, and driven rather by markups and technology wedges (Cusolito and Maloney 2018). Thus, dispersion results should be interpreted with caution. Nonetheless, the variation in distance to frontier in technology-intensive industries is less than one-fifth of that in basic manufacturing industries (leather, metals, machinery), suggesting that firms in technology-intensive industries are much closer to their sector-specific frontier.

---

[4] For a given firm i, the distance to an industry-specific TFP frontier (97.5th quantile) is computed as $DTF_i = TFP_{0.975} - TFP_{is0.975}$. The top 2.5 percent firm-level TFP values are dropped to minimize the impact of extreme values. Results are robust to alternative 1 and 5 percent cutoffs of top firm TFP values.

[5] This finding is broadly in line with the evidence in Hallward-Driemeier and Nayyar (2017).

BOX 3.3 Patterns of total factor productivity: A firm perspective (*continued*)

FIGURE 3.3.2 **Firm TFP by regions**

Firms in EAP are more productive than those located in other EMDE regions. EAP also has the highest share of large-size firms and those exporting more than half of their sales. Most firms in technology-intensive industry (TINT) are located in EAP, ECA, and SAR. Perceptions of corruption and licensing as obstacles for firm operation correlate negatively with total factor productivity (TFP).

A. Firm-level TFP, by region

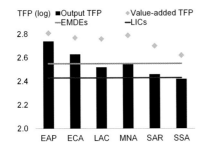

B. Percentage of firms in each region, by industry

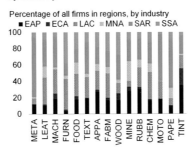

C. Firm size, by region

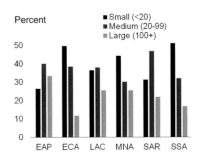

D. Exporting firms, by region

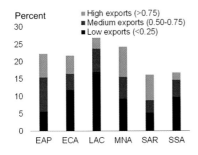

E. Perception of corruption, by region

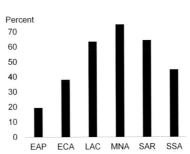

F. Perception of licensing obstacles, by region

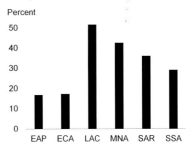

Source: World Bank Enterprise Surveys, World Bank.
Note: Firm-level TFP is computed using a Cobb-Douglas production function for each industry, assuming elasticities of output with respect to inputs are the same across countries in a given income group. Unweighted regional averages are computed. Sample includes 15,181 firms in 108 EMDEs, including 20 LICs, for the period 2007-17.
EAP = East Asia and Pacific, ECA = Europe and Central Asia, LAC = Latin America and the Caribbean, MNA = Middle East and North Africa, SAR = South Asia, and SSA = Sub-Saharan Africa.
A. Solid lines are averages of output TFP (log) for EMDEs (orange) and LICs (red). EMDEs = emerging markets and developing economies, LICs = low-income countries.
B. Bars show in each industry the percentage of firms in each region, by industry. Firms operate in 15 industries: APPA = apparel, CHEM = chemicals, FABM = fabricated metals, FOOD = food, FURN = furniture, LEAT = leather, MACH = non-electrical machinery, META = metals, MINE = non-metallic minerals, MOTO = motor vehicles, PAPE = paper, RUBB = rubber, TEXT = textiles, TINT = technology-intensive, WOOD = wood. The technology-intensive industry (TINT) includes firms in computing and electrical machinery, precision equipment, electronics, information, and communication sectors.
C. Firm size in terms of number of employees.
D. Share of exporting firms. High, medium, and low exports firms export more than 75 percent, between 50 and 75, and up to 25 percent of their sales, respectively.
E. Share of firms that perceive corruption as an obstacle for their operations.
F. Share of firms that perceive licensing and permits as an obstacle for their operations.

Firm characteristics associated with higher TFP growth

Heterogeneous characteristics related to entering, incumbent, and exiting firms can explain the observed patterns of TFP dispersion (Bartelsman and Doms 2000). A large and expanding literature points to three broad categories of correlates of sectoral TFP dispersion in EMDEs: within-firm upgrading and spillovers, regulatory environment, and managerial ability.

Within-firm upgrading and technology spillovers. Controlling for both size and exports, firms in the technology-intensive industry are on average much closer to the TFP frontier than firms in traditional industries such as non-electric machinery, food, and non-metallic

BOX 3.3 Patterns of total factor productivity: A firm perspective (*continued*)

FIGURE 3.3.3 Distance-to-frontier of TFP, firm characteristics, and regulations

The average firm in the technology-intensive industry (TINT) is significantly closer to the frontier than the average firm in non-electric machinery (MACH), food (FOOD), and non-metallic minerals (MINE) industries, after controlling for firms' size and exports. As firms grow by number of employees and increase their ratios of exports to total sales, they move closer to the TFP frontier. A conducive business environment can enhance firm-level TFP. Improvements in business freedom and control of corruption are correlated with a reduction in the distance-to-frontier of TFP.

A. Distance to TFP frontier differential between traditional industries and the technology-intensive industry

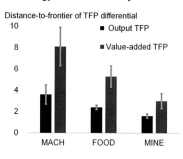

B. Distance to TFP frontier differential between firms in lowest and highest quartile of firm size and exports

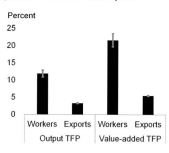

C. Distance to TFP frontier differential between firms in lowest and highest quartile of business environment

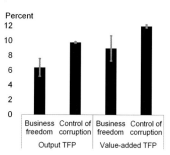

Source: World Bank Enterprise Surveys, World Bank.
Note: Firm-level TFP is computed using a Cobb-Douglas production function for each industry, assuming that elasticities of output with respect to inputs are the same across countries in a given income group. The distance-to-frontier (DTF) of TFP is computed within each sector, excluding the top 2.5 percent of firms. Sample includes 15,181 firms in 108 EMDEs, including 20 LICs, for the period 2007-17.
A. Distance-to-frontier of TFP differential between traditional industries, such as manufacturing of non-electric machinery (MACH), food (FOOD), and non-metallic minerals (MINE), and the technology-intensive (TINT) industry, controlling for firm characteristics (firm size and exports). Based on OLS regressions of the DTF of TFP (dependent variable) on industry dummies, controlling for firm characteristics and using the technology-intensive industry (TINT) as the base category as per Annex 3.5.
B. Distance to TFP frontier differential between the median firm in the lowest quartile and highest quartile of firms in terms of firm size (number of workers) and exports (share of exports in total sales). Based on OLS regressions of the DTF of TFP (dependent variable) on industry dummies, controlling for firm characteristics and using the technology-intensive industry (TINT) as the base category (Annex 3.5). A positive DTF differential implies that firms in the lowest quartile in terms of size and exports are far from the frontier relative to firms in the highest quartile. The lowest quartile of exports is zero, as more than half of firms have no exports.
C. Distance to TFP frontier differential between the median firm in the lowest quartile and highest quartile of firms in terms of business freedom and control of corruption index, controlling for firm characteristics. Based on OLS regressions of the DTF of TFP (dependent variable) on industry dummies and business environment quality, controlling for firm characteristics and using a technology-intensive industry (TINT) as the base category as per equation 3. A positive DTF differential implies that firms in the lowest quartile in terms of business freedom and control of corruption are far from the frontier relative to firms in the highest quartile.

minerals industries (Figure 3.3.3.A). Knowledge, experience, R&D, and information technology can raise TFP through improvements in product quality and production process upgrading within firms.[6] Firms with a large number of employees are significantly closer to the TFP frontier, as larger firms can invest more in R&D and bring together a richer set of ideas. On average, the productivity of a firm in the highest quartile of size is about 12 and 22 percent closer to output and value-added TFP frontiers relative to a firm in the lowest quartile of size (Figure 3.3.3.B). Moreover, technology in frontier firms can have positive spillovers for productivity in other firms through agglomeration linkages and cross-border flows of goods, capital and people. Firms can reap agglomeration benefits by emulating the best production

practices and organization structures of "nearby" highly productive firms (Dercon et al. 2004; Syverson 2011). Knowledge is also transferred through contacts with other firms, courtesy of trade, foreign direct investment and migration (De Loecker 2007). Firms with a high share of exports are significantly closer to the TFP frontier. A firm in the top quartile of exports, measured as a share of exports in total sales, is about 4 and 6 percent closer to output and value-added TFP frontiers relative to a firm in the lowest quartile of exports (Figure 3.3.3.B). Enabling effective innovation policies appears critical to boosting innovation gains (Cirera and Maloney 2017).

Regulatory environment. Institutions reflect political and legal forces that shape social and economic environments. Regulations and policies affect firms' productivity through incentives to acquire human capital, physical capital, and technology (Bartelsman and Doms 2000). Firm productivity tends to drop in poorly-regulated markets,

---

[6] See Brynjolfsson and Hitt (1995) and Goldberg et al. (2010).

BOX 3.3 Patterns of total factor productivity: A firm perspective (*continued*)

due to adverse incentives and the lack of creative destruction (Goldberg et al. 2010). In contrast, improvements in the business environment are associated with lower distance to TFP frontier, even after controlling for firm characteristics. Conducive regulatory practices—reflected in highest quartile values of business freedom index—may entail up to 9 percent reduction in the distance-to-frontier of TFP relative firms in the lowest quartile. Similarly, high quality governance—proxied by the top quartile estimates of control of corruption index—is associated with up to 12 percent drop in the distance to TFP frontier relative to firms in the bottom quartile (Figure 3.3.3.C).

Managerial ability. TFP also reflects how efficiently productive factors—labor, capital, and intermediate inputs—are assembled. Through their talents or the quality of their practices, managers coordinate the integration of factor inputs in the production process. Management and organizational styles may vary across firms due to competition, location, ownership, and trade ties. Intervention-led improvements in management

practices can raise productivity by more than 10 percent (Van Reenen 2011). A policy shift that is more focused on enhancing firm managerial capabilities can, therefore, strengthen production synergies and bolster TFP gains (Cusolito and Maloney 2018).

Conclusion

The dispersion of firm-level TFP within and across industries in emerging markets and developing economies (EMDEs) is associated with various firm characteristics. TFP dispersion correlates negatively with firm size, partly because large firms can invest more in R&D to innovate. Exports also facilitate the transfer and adoption of new technologies, and therefore, can help close the gap between laggards and frontier firms. Moreover, a conducive business climate characterized by a greater freedom in entrepreneurship and less corruption can support TFP improvements. Undertaking policies to support R&D and innovation, promote exports, combat corruption, increase the ease of doing business, and enhance firm managerial capabilities, appears critical to boosting productivity.

innovation (proxied by higher per capita patents), stronger investment (as a share of GDP), higher levels of urbanization (proxied by population density), price stability, and a diverse and sophisticated economic structure (proxied by the economic complexity index of Hidalgo and Hausmann 2009), are all significantly associated with higher productivity growth (Figure 3.7).[17]

Differences between EMDEs and advanced economies. The estimated impact of improved levels of each driver of productivity growth depends on the stage of development and therefore differs between EMDEs and advanced economies. The extent of urbanization has a larger impact on productivity growth in EMDEs than in advanced economies, reflecting higher returns to the reallocation of workers away from rural agricultural production to higher productivity

manufacturing and service sectors (Box 3.2). The level of education and investment also produces larger impacts on productivity in EMDEs in the long-run estimation, highlighting their importance at lower levels of productivity. Since 1995, the relationship between labor productivity and the economic complexity of tradable goods has strengthened in EMDEs.

Evolution of the drivers of productivity

Pre-crisis improvements. There were substantial gains in many of the underlying drivers of productivity growth in the pre-crisis period, growing faster in EMDEs than advanced economies (Figure 3.8). The selected drivers can be aggregated to an index based on the size of their estimated impacts on productivity—demographics, economic complexity, the number of patents filed, and price stability are all considered to be key determinants of productivity growth over this period by the econometric model. Cumulatively over 1995-2008, produc-tivity in the one-quarter of EMDEs with the most

---

[17] These are largely consistent with existing studies which tend to have shorter time spans and smaller cross-sections (Durlauf, Kourtellos, and Tan 2008; Kim and Loayza 2019).

FIGURE 3.7 Impact of drivers on productivity growth

Productivity in economies with favorable initial conditions grew by up to 0.8 percentage point per year faster than other economies. The scale of these effects varies over time and between EMDEs and advanced economies. In 1960, the importance of innovation and economic complexity was lower in EMDEs. Demography and economic complexity have become increasingly important determinants of EMDE productivity growth in recent decades.

A. Effects of initial level of drivers on productivity growth, 1960-2018

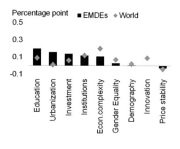

B. Effects of initial level of drivers for EMDEs on productivity growth, 1960-2018 vs. 1995-2018

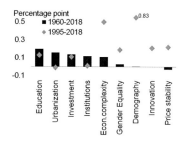

Source: World Bank.
A. B. Estimated marginal contribution to annual long-term productivity growth if the driver improves from the 25th to the 75th percentiles. Sample includes 59 economies, 36 of which are EMDEs. Groups which are not significant in both 1960-2018 and 1995-2018 (Finance, Income equality, and health) are excluded from the chart. Variables corresponding to each concept are: Institutions = ICRG rule of law index, Geography=share of non-tropical area, Innovation=patents per capita, Investment=investment to GDP ratio, Income equality=(-1)*Gini coefficient, Urbanization=urban population (% total), Econ. complexity = Economic Complexity Index of Hidalgo and Hausmann (2009), Education=years of schooling, Demography=share of working-age population, Gender equality= female average years of education minus male average years. See Annex 3.3 for details.
B. Marginal contribution of demography for 1995-2018 is 0.83.

favorable initial conditions grew by nearly 15 percent more than productivity in those with the least favorable initial conditions. Among LICs, the differential between the two groups was even larger (53 percent). LICs were better able to benefit from catch-up growth in the presence of favorable initial conditions.

Post-crisis slowdown in improvements. The pace of growth of the drivers most strongly associated with productivity growth has slowed in EMDEs since 2008, consistent with the slowdown in productivity growth over this period (Figure 3.9).

Investment growth in EMDEs slowed, reflecting weak activity and spillovers from advanced economies, weaker growth of commodity demand, and political uncertainty. In addition, earlier favorable demographic trends in many EMDEs have waned as the population ages. From 2018 to 2030 the working-age share of the population is expected to decline by 3 percentage points in advanced economies and 2.5 percentage points in

EMDEs. For educational attainment, growth has been three times higher than in advanced economies. Nonetheless, as countries catch up (as measured by average years of schooling), the potential for further growth has slowed.[18]

Other factors that had helped spur EMDE productivity growth also have deteriorated since the crisis. For example, the trend toward broadening production to a more diverse range of products at more upstream stages of the value chain slowed partly because the expansion of global value chains stagnated after 2008 (World Bank 2019d). In addition, improvements in inequality and measures of institutional quality have also stagnated or declined in many countries. Finally, gains in price stability, which had significantly improved operating environments for firms in the 1990s, slowed (Ha, Kose, and Ohnsorge 2019).

Prospects for productivity growth

The post-crisis weakness in several fundamental drivers of productivity growth is expected to persist or deepen. The weak outlook for the drivers can be improved though a concerted reform effort.

Weakening investment. The post-crisis period has been characterized by pronounced investment weakness reflecting adverse terms-of-trade shocks for commodity exporters, slowing foreign direct investment inflows for commodity importers, spillovers from advanced-economy growth weakness, heightened policy uncertainty, and private debt burdens (World Bank 2017). The legacy of weak investment since the crisis and diminishing long-term outlook for investment growth raises concerns about future productivity growth (World Bank 2019b). Moreover, subdued investment growth, especially in R&D-dependent sectors, can hinder technological progress and TFP growth through weaker capital-embodied technological change (Adler et al. 2017).

---

[18] While the gap in average years of education with advanced economies has declined, substantial gaps in the quality of education remain (World Bank 2018b).

Slower growth at the technology frontier. There has been a broad-based slowdown in both labor productivity and TFP growth in advanced economies since the early 2000s with limited signs of an impending upturn. To the extent that this reflects slowing productivity growth in multinationals and the origins of foreign direct investment—two major channels for knowledge and technology spillovers to EMDEs—this is likely to weigh on EMDE productivity, too (Wooster and Diebel 2010). However, there are mixed views on the prospects of groundbreaking technological progress that could return growth to historical norms, and also spillovers to EMDEs. On the one hand, the impact on productivity growth of new innovations compared to 20th-century innovations seems to be reduced (Fernald 2015; Gordon 2016). On the other hand, recently introduced new digital technologies and those on the horizon such as artificial intelligence and innovations in IT sectors may begin to feed through to measured productivity (Cusolito and Maloney 2018).

Fewer opportunities for technology transfer. Substantial productivity gaps to the frontier are still present in EMDEs, providing opportunities for rapid productivity growth. However, routes to technology transfer are narrowing. The expansion of global value chains has come to a halt in the post-crisis period after rapid expansion in the pre-crisis period (World Bank 2019d). Rising implementation of protectionist measures risks further compounding the weakness in global value chains and trade. Moreover, firms in EMDEs may lack the necessary capabilities to adopt new technologies without sustained improvements in human capital such as enhancements in educational quality and management abilities despite the progress in education attainments (Cirera and Maloney 2017).

A more challenging environment for structural transformation. As highlighted in Box 3.2, the contribution to productivity growth from the manufacturing sector has been in decline and presents fewer opportunities for EMDE productivity growth. Secular trends, such as a declining employment share in the manufacturing sector in some economies and risks from automation will make manufacturing-led

FIGURE 3.8 Pre-crisis developments in productivity drivers and productivity growth

All drivers of productivity growth in EMDEs, except for innovation, gender equality and institutions, improved more than in advanced economies during the pre-crisis period, helping to narrow the productivity gap with advanced economies. There was a strong link between drivers and productivity growth—those economies with better initial conditions in the 1990s grew at faster rates subsequently. The benefits of improving drivers are larger for LICs.

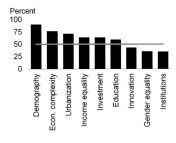

A. Share of EMDEs with faster improvements in drivers relative to advanced economies, 1995-2008

B. Quartiles of productivity drivers and average EMDE productivity growth, 1995-2008

Source: Barro and Lee (2015); International Monetary Fund; Observatory of Economic Complexity; United Nations; World Bank, World Development Indicators.
A. Share of EMDE countries whose improvement in drivers are larger than average changes for advanced economies. Variables corresponding to each concept are (sample in parentheses): Institutions (74) = WGI Rule of Law Index, Innovation (30) = patents per capita, Investment (72)= investment to GDP ratio, Income equality (72) = (-1)*Gini coefficient, Urbanization (74) = Urban population (% total), Econ complexity (56) defined as Economic Complexity Index of Hidalgo and Hausmann (2009), Education (69) = years of schooling, Demography (74) = share of working age population, Gender equality (28) = Ratio of female to male labor market participation.
B. Average level of productivity growth and "index of drivers" in each quartile over 1995-2008. "Index of drivers" created by weighting normalized levels of each potential driver in chart A by its estimated impact on productivity growth (Figure 3.7; Annex 3.3).

development increasingly challenging in the future (Hallward-Driemeier and Nayyar 2017; Sinha 2016). Furthermore, gains from faster productivity growth in the agricultural sector, freeing up workers to transition to other sectors, have declined.

Rising debt risk in EMDEs. Amid record-high EMDE debt, a wide range of adverse shocks could precipitate a financial crisis in EMDEs, which could do severe damage to productivity (Box 3.4). Since 2010, total debt in EMDEs has risen markedly by 54 percentage points, to 168 percent of GDP in 2018, with private debt growing faster than public debt, reaching 120 percent of GDP in 2018 (Chapter 4). Low productivity growth and rising sovereign debt burdens may even reinforce one another (Posen and Zettelmeyer 2019).

Climate change. Over the longer-term, climate change will likely increase the challenges to improving productivity in the agricultural sector,

FIGURE 3.9 Post-crisis slowdown of the drivers of productivity growth

In EMDEs, improvements in a broad range of productivity drivers slowed after 2008. Investment growth slowed to one-third of its pre-crisis rate in EMDEs. Working-age population shares are expected to contract in the coming years. And the growth of educational attainment has also slowed as EMDEs reduce the gap with advanced economies.

A. Share of EMDEs with a post-crisis slowdown in the growth of underlying drivers of productivity

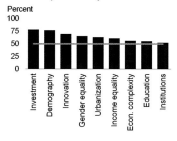

B. Average investment growth

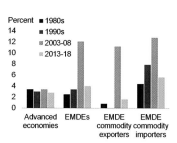

C. Average annual growth in educational attainment

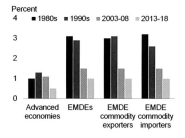

D. Change in working-age share of the population

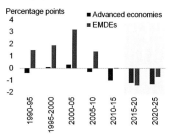

Source: Barro and Lee (2015); International Monetary Fund; Observatory of Economic Complexity; Penn World Table; IMF World Economic Outlook; United Nations; World Bank, World Development Indicators; Wittgenstein Centre for Demography and Global Human Capital.

A Post-crisis slowdown defined as the share of economies where improvements in each underlying driver of productivity during 2008-2017 was less than zero or the pace of improvement during the pre-crisis period 1998-2007. Variables corresponding to each concept are (sample in parentheses): Investment (69)=investment to GDP ratio, Demography (74)=share of working-age population, Innovation (33)=patents per capita, Gender equality(32)= Share of female labor market participation rate to male, Urbanization (74)=Urban population (% total), Institutions (74)= WGI Rule of Law Index, Income equality (72)=(-1)*Gini coefficient, Education (72)=years of schooling, ECI (55) defined as Economic Complexity Index of Hidalgo and Hausmann (2009). Price stability excluded due to demand-side influences on inflation following the global financial crisis.

B. GDP-weighted average annual investment (gross fixed capital formation) growth.

C. GDP-weighted change (at 2010 prices and exchange rates) in average years of education.

D. Changes in the working-age share of the population (aged 15-64).

with large falls in crop yields expected as global temperatures rise (Fuglie et al. 2019). Agriculture currently accounts for 30 percent of GDP in LICs, compared to just 9 percent in non-LIC EMDEs. In addition, EMDEs in several regions are heavily reliant on agriculture: around half of employment is in the agricultural sector in SAR and SSA.

Less favorable demographics. Younger populations and larger working-age population tend to adopt new technologies, skills, and organizational

structures more readily (Maestas, Mullen, and Powell 2016). The working-age share of the population rose by 13 percentage points of the population during 1995-2008 in MENA, the fastest-growing region, and 8 percentage points in EAP, the second-fastest growing. In the coming years, EMDE populations are set to age. In EAP and ECA, the working-age share of the population is expected to decline by 3-4 percentage points of the population by 2030, while, in LAC, MENA, SAR, and SSA it will stagnate.

Policy implications

Concerns about prospects for productivity growth in EMDEs call for a renewed emphasis on structural policies that can unlock productivity gains, but undertaking the right structural policies is challenging. Drawing on the findings in this chapter, four strands of policy options emerge.

The results suggest that a four-pronged policy approach can lift productivity. First, policies can raise labor productivity economy-wide by stimulating private and public investment and improving human capital. Second, policies can foster firm productivity by exposing firms to trade and foreign investment and strengthening human capital, and upgrading workforce skills including that of firm managers. Third, policies can facilitate the reallocation of resources towards more productive sectors and a more diversified set of sectors. Finally, to be effective, these policies need to be set in the context of a growth-friendly macroeconomic and institutional environment (Cirera and Maloney 2017).

Within these four broad strands, specific priorities depend on country characteristics. For example, countries with large unmet investment needs may want to prioritize expanding fiscal resources to achieve more and better public investment. Countries with anemic private investment may want to prioritize business climate and institutional reforms, reduce support for state-owned enterprises, and broadening access to finance to allow private sector investment to flourish. Countries with predominantly low-skilled workers may want to improve health and education for workers and managers alike. Countries with lethargic innovation may want to

BOX 3.4 Debt, financial crises, and productivity

High debt levels increase the probability of financial crises and weigh heavily on productivity growth through a wide range of channels. During debt accumulation episodes associated with financial crises, cumulative productivity gains three years into the episode are 2 percentage points lower than in episodes without crises. Financial crises are accompanied by large and protracted declines in productivity: five years after the financial crisis, productivity is 6.5 percent lower than it would have been without a crisis.

Introduction

Productivity growth is vulnerable to a range of adverse shocks including those associated with financial crises, especially in the context of rapid debt accumulation (Chapter 4). Following the global financial crisis and subsequent global recession of 2007-09, a broad range of countries experienced a rapid accumulation of debt together with a significant slowdown of productivity growth. Debt accumulation raises both long-term and short-term risks to productivity growth. In the long-term, it can lead to misallocation of resources towards low productivity projects, worsen investment prospects, weigh on competitiveness, and curb technological transfers embodied in investment.[1] In the short-term, debt accumulation also increases the probability of financial crises that sharply raise borrowing cost, worsen balance sheets and depress productivity growth, which can last over an extended period.[2]

Against this backdrop, this box discusses the linkages between productivity and financial crises as well as rapid debt accumulation. Specifically, it addresses the following two questions:

- Through which channels does debt affect productivity?

- What is the empirical link between financial crises and productivity?

Channels of transmission

Elevated debt levels can affect productivity growth via several channels. These include misallocation of resources, policy uncertainty and debt overhangs that weigh on productivity-enhancing investment, and a higher probability of financial crises.

Misallocation of resources. If used to fund productive investments with high rates of return, debt can have

positive effects on productivity and growth (Reinhart and Rogoff 2010; Poirson, Pattillo, and Ricci 2004). However, debt accumulation can impede productivity by encouraging a misallocation of resources towards projects that yield short-term returns at the expense of long-term returns or offer low risk at the expense of high returns (Poirson, Pattillo, and Ricci 2002; Checherita-Westphal and Rother 2012). These short-term projects can include those that rely heavily on returns from asset price appreciation on expectations of rapid future growth (Claessens and Kose 2017, 2018).

Debt overhangs. Rapid debt accumulation can lead to debt overhangs whose debt service crowds out productive investment.[3] At the firm level, a large outstanding debt stock can weigh on investment and, hence, the productivity growth that technology embedded in this investment can generate. At the government level, debt service on high debt may crowd out other productivity-enhancing spending, including for education, health or infrastructure.

Policy uncertainty. Especially high government debt increases uncertainty about growth prospects. For investors, large projected government debt service cost creates policy uncertainty because they may eventually compel governments to introduce distortionary taxation (including on future investment returns), curtail growth-enhancing spending, or delay reforms that may support innovation and productivity (IMF 2018). Such uncertainty lowers incentives to invest in productivity-enhancing technologies (Krugman 1988).

Higher probability of financial crises. Higher debt increases the probability of financial crises. These tend to be associated with severe short-run productivity losses and lasting productivity weaknesses. Financial crises include debt, banking, and currency crises.

- *Sovereign debt crises.* Higher government debt may encourage governments to shift towards lower-cost

---

Note: This box was prepared by Alistair Dieppe, Sinem Kilic Celik, and Cedric Okou.

[1] Blanchard and Wolfers (2000); Bulow and Rogoff (1989).

[2] See Aguiar and Gopinath (2006), Arteta and Hale (2008), Blanchard, Cerutti, and Summers (2015), Cerra and Saxena (2008, 2017), Furceri and Mourougane (2012a), Jordà, Schularick, and Taylor (2013), and Reinhart and Rogoff (2009, 2010).

[3] Debt overhang can occur in the presence of high levels of debt, as potential investors hold back new investments because they face heightened uncertainty about tax rates on future investment returns, given the government's large projected revenue needs to service the outstanding debt.

BOX 3.4 Debt, financial crises, and productivity (*continued*)

FIGURE 3.4.1 Productivity in debt accumulation episodes and financial crises

About 40 percent of all episodes of debt accumulation are associated with financial crises. During those episodes, productivity gains are significantly lower than during other episodes. Specifically, a financial (banking, currency and debt) crisis is accompanied on average by a 6.5 percent cumulative decline in the level of labor productivity after 5 years, and the negative effect is protracted, exceeding 7 percent at an 8 year-horizon.

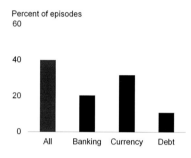

A. Total debt accumulation episodes around crises

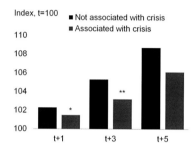

B. Cumulative productivity gains during episodes of rapid debt accumulation

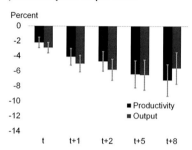

C. Impact of financial crises on EMDE productivity and output levels

Source: World Bank.

A. Share of total (government and private) debt accumulation episodes that were associated with financial (banking, currency, debt) crises.

B. * and ** indicates 10 and 5 percent significance level for the difference between productivity growth during the median total debt accumulation associated with crises and the median total debt accumulation episode not associated with crises.

C. Bars show the average loss in labor productivity and output levels in EMDEs, expressed in percent, at impact, 1, 2, … and 8 years after a financial crisis (Laeven and Valencia 2018). Financial crises include banking, currency and debt crises. Whiskers represent 90 percent confidence intervals. The estimation is based on local projection method (Jordà 2005), which includes control variables (country fixed effects, lagged shocks, forward bias correction terms, and lagged TFP growth) and bias correction (Teulings and Zubanov 2014) for forward values of the crisis dummy between time t and t+h-1.

but higher-risk debt issuance such as at shorter maturities or in foreign currency (Kalemli-Özcan, Laeven, and Moreno 2018). This heightens the probability that financial market stress precipitates a sovereign debt crisis that sharply raises investor risk premia and borrowing cost.[4] These tend to coincide with severe economic disruption just as sovereign debt distress prevents governments from supporting activity with counter-cyclical fiscal policy (Reinhart and Rogoff 2010). This depresses public and private investment and restricts other productivity-enhancing public spending.

- *Banking and currency crises.* Other types of financial crises, including systemic banking crises and currency crises, can also do lasting damage to productivity (Cerra and Saxena 2017; Oulton and Sebastiá-Barriel 2017). The disruptions in financial intermediation during banking crises curb the funding of productivity-enhancing technologies and typically trigger recessions (De Ridder 2017). In the subsequent protracted weakness, elevated long-term

unemployment erodes human capital.[5] Because of their shorter duration, currency crises are typically less harmful to productivity. However, combined banking and currency crises can be particularly damaging for economic activity and productivity.

Empirical link between financial crises and productivity

Productivity gains during rapid debt accumulation episodes. Long-term productivity gains during rapid debt accumulation episodes have been considerably lower when these debt accumulation episodes were associated with financial crises. As in Chapter 4, rapid debt accumulation episodes are defined as an expansion from trough to peak of total debt-to-GDP ratios by more than one standard deviation, with troughs and peaks identified using the Harding and Pagan (2002) algorithm. This yields 190 episodes, of which almost half were associated with financial crises—identified as in (Laeven and Valencia 2018) —at some point during the episode.

---

[4] Aguiar and Gopinath (2006); Arellano (2008); Sandri (2015).

[5] See Blanchard and Wolfers (2000) and Furceri and Mourougane (2012b).

BOX 3.4 Debt, financial crises, and productivity (*continued*)

In a debt accumulation episode accompanied by a crisis, median productivity three years into the episode was 3 percent higher than at the beginning of the episode. This is statistically significantly less than during a debt accumulation episode that was not associated with a crisis (5 percent). The difference may reflect the severe short-term damage to productivity driven by financial crises. Two years later (five years into the episode), productivity differences between the two types of episodes were no longer statistically significant.

Impact of financial crises on productivity. The productivity losses associated with financial crises are estimated in a local projections model of productivity levels in financial crises episodes. These episodes are identified as in (Laeven and Valencia 2018). There are 299 financial crisis episodes for which labor productivity estimates are available. 72 percent of these episodes occurred in 71 middle- or high-income EMDEs and 10 percent in 13 low-income countries.

Financial crises are accompanied by large and lasting productivity losses. Immediately after the onset of a debt crisis, labor productivity declines on average by about 2.2 percent and then falls by a cumulative 6.5

percent at the end of five years (Figure 3.4.1). The effect persists into the eighth year. This is consistent with earlier studies that document protracted effects of financial crises on productivity growth (Obstfeld 1996; Morris and Shin 1998; Barro 2001).[6]

Conclusion

Financial crises weigh heavily on productivity growth through a wide range of channels. During debt accumulation episodes associated with financial crises, cumulative productivity gains three years into the episode are 2 percentage points lower than in episodes without crises. Financial crises are accompanied by large and protracted productivity losses—following an initial drop of 2.2 percent, productivity falls by a cumulative 6.5 percent five years after the onset of the crisis. In this context, the rapid post-crisis build-up of debt in EMDEs increases vulnerability to financial crises and represents an important downside risk to productivity growth (Chapter 4).

---

[6] The damage to output and productivity does not differ statistically significantly over the first eight years following the crisis.

---

expose their private sectors to foreign knowledge and technologies through greater trade and foreign direct investment (Boxes 2.1-2.6).

Policy interactions can lead to unintended consequences. For instance, trade liberalization reforms can increase the exposure of private sector firms to foreign knowledge and frontier technologies, and boost productivity. However, trade liberalization can also be associated with greater informality in the short-run if labor markets are not flexible, thus counteracting policies that aim at facilitating the reallocation of resources towards more productive sectors (Bosch, Goni, and Maloney 2007; World Bank 2019a). Therefore, these potential interactions should be accounted for when designing a policy mix for a country.

Improving factors of production

Meet infrastructure investment needs. In several regions (ECA, MNA, SAR), weaker rates of capital deepening accounted for most of the post-crisis

slowdown in labor productivity growth. Elsewhere (SSA, SAR), sizable infrastructure deficits restrict firms' ability to improve productivity. Better physical capital and infrastructure—transport, power, telecommunications—can reinforce a country's competitiveness and boost its productivity (Calderón, Moral-Benito, and Servén 2015). A key challenge is to prioritize investments to reconcile large development needs with funding constraints and to improve public investment management. Low- and middle-income countries will need to spend between 4.5 to 8.2 percent of GDP on new infrastructure annually to 2030 in order to meet infrastructure-related Sustainable Development Goals (Rozenberg and Fay 2019).[19] Where fiscal space exists, governments should fund infrastructure spending in areas likely to generate high-returns. SSA is estimated to have the

---

[19] SDG targets for universal access to safely managed water, sanitation, and hygiene services, improved irrigation infrastructure to improve food supplies, universal access to electricity and improved transport infrastructure.

FIGURE 3.10 EMDE infrastructure and education gaps

Infrastructure needs to meet the Sustainable Development Goals are highest in SSA. While education gaps, measured as years of schooling, are closing in many regions, they remain large in SAR and SSA. The gaps to advanced economy levels are even larger after adjusting for educational quality.

A. Infrastructure gaps

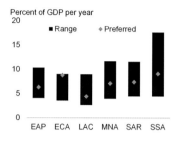

B. Years of education and learning-adjusted years of education (2017)

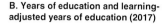
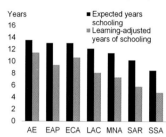

Source: Rozenberg and Fay (2019); World Bank, Human Capital Project.
A. Investment and maintenance needs based on the Sustainable Development Goals as set out in Rozenberg and Fay (2019) including both new investment and maintenance of existing capital stock. Infrastructure investment includes investment in electricity, transport, water supply and sanitation, flood protection, and irrigation. Preferred is defined as the infrastructure "pathway [that] limits stranded assets, has a relatively high per capita consumption due to electric mobility, and invests mostly in renewable energy and storage."
B. GDP-weighted expected years schooling and learning-adjusted years of schooling from the World Bank's Human Capital Project. Leaning-adjusted years of schooling use harmonized cross-country test scores to adjust average years of schooling.

FIGURE 3.11 Developments in Fintech and Govtech

Economies with the largest "unbanked" populations have also seen the biggest increases in fintech innovations to payment systems and other financial services. The rise of fintech has been largest in SSA. These systems are critical to improving access to finance to make productivity-enhancing investments. EMDE government transparency still lags advanced economies. New ICT can facilitate the rapid dissemination of information within and outside of government to monitor performance and service shortfalls.

A. Access to banking services and mobile money accounts

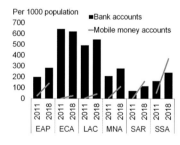

B. Information openness: national government data availability

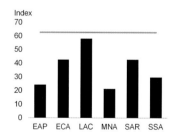

Source: GSM Association (GSMA), Open Knowledge Foundation, World Bank.
A. Mobile money accounts based on a sample of 16 EMDEs, excluding China, in East Asia and the Pacific (EAP), 7 EMDEs in Eastern Europe and Central Asia (ECA), 18 EMDES in Latin America and the Caribbean (LAC), 32 EMDEs in Middle East and North Africa (MNA), 7 EMDEs in South Asia (SAR), and 40 EMDEs in Sub-Saharan Africa (SSA).
Bank accounts, defined as depositors at commercial banks, based on a sample of 22 EMDEs, excluding China, in East Asia and the Pacific (EAP), 24 EMDEs in Eastern Europe and Central Asia (ECA), 32 EMDES in Latin America and the Caribbean (LAC), 19 EMDEs in Middle East and North Africa (MNA), 8 EMDEs in South Asia (SAR), and 48 EMDEs in Sub-Saharan Africa (SSA).
B. Global Open Data Index is a proxy for the availability of open national government data at large. GDP weighted average. 2016/7 data. It based on a sample of 27 Advanced economies, 14 EMDEs in Eastern Europe and Central Asia (ECA), 6 EMDEs in East Asia and the Pacific (EAP), 25 EMDES in Latin America and the Caribbean (LAC), 2 EMDEs in Middle East and North Africa (MNA), 6 EMDEs in South Asia (SAR), and 12 EMDEs in Sub-Saharan Africa (SSA).

highest infrastructure deficit required to meet the SDGs (Figure 3.10). Poor infrastructure, such as power supply problems, have been found to lower manufacturing TFP in Bangladesh and reduce export diversification in lower-income EMDEs (Osakwe and Kilolo 2018). A range of infrastructure investments in the road and telecommunications networks in South Africa were found to have positive effects on manufacturing TFP (Bogetic and Fedderke 2009).

Remove private sector investment constraints. Removing business environment constraints, labor and product market inefficiencies, and improving corporate governance should be prioritized (World Bank 2019a). In addition, credit constraints can also hold back investment, with many EMDEs lacking developed capital markets and financial products for much of the population (Sahay et al. 2015). Weak access to finance is a key constraint to small and medium firms in SAR–especially for women-owned businesses—and holds back firm-level productivity gains in India (Box 2.5). Efforts are needed to encourage the use of fintech products in regions where access to traditional banking products and sources of finance is low, while addressing associated risks of these technologies, such as financial crime and cybersecurity risks (Figure 3.11; IMF and World Bank 2019). Investing an additional 4.5 percent of GDP annually in infrastructure in EMDEs would lift long-run productivity growth by 0.3 percentage point (Figure 3.12).

Raise human capital. Better-educated and healthier workers hold better-paying jobs, have more stable careers, and are more productive. Moreover, a better educated and healthier workforce is more capable of advanced technology adoption (Bils and Klenow 2000). Educational gaps with advanced economies are largest in SAR and SSA, where expected years of schooling is 3 and 5 years lower than in advanced economies, respectively. This gap increases to 6 and 7 years when adjusting for quality, suggesting that educational reforms should be a priority in these regions (Figure 3.10). In addition, tailored interventions at early ages are important. These can include measures to expand school attendance, provide student grants, support nutrition programs for early childhood development, upgrade teachers' training, foster teacher accountability and incentivize performance, which can boost educational outcomes. Conditional cash transfer programs can have persistent effects on educational attainment and the quality of employment (Kugler and Rojas 2018). Transitioning to lower fertility rates can reduce dependency rates and free up resources to invest in education and health—Botswana and Ethiopia have experienced rapid declines in fertility rates in recent decades, alongside large falls in poverty rates (World Bank 2019f). By increasing educational attainment at the same rate as its fastest 10-year cumulative increase ending between 2000-2008, EMDEs could raise long-run productivity growth by about 0.1 percentage point (Figure 3.12).

Another key component of human capital is health. Although life expectancy at birth in EMDEs has increased to 70 years on average as of 2017, this is still about 10 years below average advanced-economy levels (81 years). Improvements in access to clean water, the provision of adequate sanitation, health care, training, and performance-based payments to health service providers can yield substantial rewards on the well-being of the population and lift productivity (World Bank 2012, 2018b).

Boosting firm productivity

Foster firm capabilities. The structural slowdown in TFP growth in EMDEs suggests a need to reinvigorate technology adoption and innovation. Interventions to ease international and domestic knowledge diffusion and boost firm absorptive capacities will buttress innovative activities (De Visscher, Eberhardt, and Everaert 2018). On-the-job training and targeted educational reforms can update skills to complement current and newly introduced technologies, many of which require higher cognitive skills and tertiary education levels compared to previous technologies. Firm management capabilities have been shown to be key in generating high-quality R&D and technology adoption. In India, firms provided with training on management practices saw productivity rise by 17 percent—a key factor for improving management quality has been

FIGURE 3.12 **Productivity growth: reform scenario**

A reform package that combines filling investment needs, boosting human capital, and improving the adoption of new technologies could lift productivity by just over half of a percentage point over 10 years. Replicating the success of China and Vietnam in shifting out of agriculture towards manufacturing and trade services could provide a significant boost to productivity growth in low-income economies.

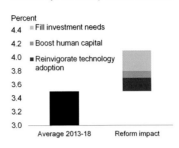

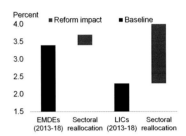

Source: World Bank
Note: GDP-weighted average. EMDEs = emerging markets and developing economies.
A. The reform scenario assumes: (1) Fill investment needs: the investment share of GDP increases by 4.5 percentage points as in the Rozenberg and Fay (2019) "preferred" infrastructure scenario. The increase is phased in over 10 years (2) Boost human capital: average years of education increases in each EMDE at its fastest cumulative 10-year pace ending during 2000-08; (3) Reinvigorate technology adoption: economic complexity (Hidalgo & Hausmann 2009) increases at the same pace as its fastest 10-year rate of increase ending during 2000-08.
B. The sectoral reallocation scenario assumes the sectoral reallocation reform replicates the successful transformation of China and Vietnam during 2003-2008. The share of employment in the agriculture sector falls by 15 percent and is reallocated to the manufacturing and trade services sectors over a 5 year period.

participation in global value chains to boost knowledge diffusion on management practices (Bloom et. al. 2013; Cirera and Maloney 2017). However, private firms may be reluctant to undertake costly investments in R&D to open foreign markets if competitors can free-ride. Policies that ensure property rights and promote public-private partnerships to create technology extension centers in sectoral clusters can increase firm participation in global value chains, and lift productivity (Cirera and Maloney 2017).[20]

Firm-level analysis suggests that to benefit from technology spillovers EMDEs need to foster trade and financial integration (Box 3.3). Reducing trade restrictions, alongside increasing levels of human capital, increase export diversification and reduce reliance on commodity exports (Giri, Quayyum, and Yin 2019). Efforts to improve trade openness can include regional trade agreements, such as the African Continental Free

---

[20] Technology extension centers generate and transfer new foreign and domestic technologies, tailored to a country's specific needs, to local users.

Trade Area which includes economies in MENA and SSA. In India, reforms in the 1990s to boost foreign (and domestic) competition in the service sector also had large positive spillovers to manufacturing productivity (Arnold et al. 2016). Bangladeshi garment exporters increased productivity after gaining tariff-free access to EU markets in 2001, which also boosted productivity in domestically-focused firms (World Bank 2019d). In China, firms' participation in foreign supply chains and FDI complemented domestically-led research and development, spurring homegrown innovation (Hu, Jefferson, and Jinchang 2005). Enhancing technology adoption in EMDEs—returning economic complexity growth to its fastest pace during the EMDE growth and trade surge during 2000-2008—could increase productivity growth by 0.2 percentage point annually (Figure 3.12).

Address informality. The informal sector is associated with lower average productivity levels and accounts for around 70 percent of employment in EMDEs, with particularly high concentrations in SSA and SAR (World Bank 2019a). In Paraguay, informal firms have been found to be not only less productive than formal firms, but to have negative spillovers on formal firms' productivity (Vargas 2015). Reducing the scope for rent-seeking bureaucratic processes that obstruct formalization, improving the fairness of regulation, and enhancing the even-handedness of regulatory and tax enforcement have been associated with a more efficient reallocation of input factors from less productive informal activities to more productive formal ones (Amin and Islam 2015; Amin, Ohnsorge, and Okou 2019). Beyond formalization, pro-productivity and skill-upgrading interventions could be more focused on informal small-scale firms and unskilled workers (Nguimkeu and Okou 2019).

Encouraging sectoral reallocation

Support sectoral reallocation and diversification. Sectoral reallocation is an important engine of productivity growth (Box 3.2). The largest gains in productivity occur at low levels of income as workers shift away from the agricultural sector, with lower benefits in middle-income EMDEs.

Furthermore, middle-income countries tend to be highly diversified across a broad range of both manufacturing and service sectors, although at high levels of development diversification tends to slow and there is a re-specialization (Imbs and Wacziarg 2003).

Sectoral diversification is of vital importance to economies with a high reliance on commodity extraction, who have usually experienced the lowest levels of productivity growth globally (Bahar and Santos 2018).[21] Commodity exporting economies in LAC, MENA, and SSA have had highly procyclical investment and low average TFP growth during the past three decades. The benefits of diversification include greater macroeconomic stability as well as higher average rates of productivity growth. Economies that have successfully reduced their reliance on oil exports, such as Malaysia, Mexico, and Indonesia, initially expanded to complementary industries, such as natural-resource processing and manufacturing, or expanded to labor-intensive manufacturing, before expanding to more complex manufacturing or services sectors. In addition, these economies established free trade zones, used tax incentives, and established industrial clusters to promote FDI (Cherif and Hasanov 2016).

Seek opportunities in services, boost lagging sectors. Many high value-added service sectors provide opportunities for rapid productivity catch-up growth (Box 3.2; Hallward-Driemeier and Nayyar 2017). High-productivity service sectors such as finance, ICT, accounting and legal services are likely to become increasingly tradable due to technological advances, but require an enhanced education, including at the tertiary level due to their skill-intensive nature. In LICs, notwithstanding rapid pre-crisis productivity gains, productivity levels in the agricultural sector remain less than 10 percent of the average advanced economy. SSA hosts the largest number of LICs and may stand to benefit most from reallocation away from agriculture. Yet, LICs in SSA have so

---

[21] EMDE commodity-exporters have historically experienced a "crowding-out" effect on other faster growth industries during periods of high commodity prices, which has hindered them from closing the productivity gap with advanced economies.

far shifted away from agriculture towards industrial sectors at a slower pace than LICs in Asia (Box 2.6).

Agricultural productivity can be improved through targeted measures to increase infrastructure in these regions, ensure secure land tenures, and promote access to finance. Productivity led growth in agriculture could free-up input factors. In Vietnam, successful reforms included strengthening of land property rights and relaxed restrictions on external and internal trade of agriculture goods. This could facilitate the reallocation of resources from agriculture to more productive sectors such as manufacturing and services, and boost overall productivity (Fuglie et al. 2019). If EMDEs replicated the successful 2003-08 sectoral reallocation of China and Vietnam from the agriculture sector to manufacturing and trade services, this would lift productivity growth by 0.3 percentage points. Given sizeable differences in sectoral productivity, LICs would particularly benefit, with a boost of over 1.5 percentage points (Figure 3.12).

Address market failures. Government efforts to promote specific sectors should first identify market failures that have prevented sectoral reallocation. In addition, the complexity and scale of interventions to foster new industries need to be balanced against government and institutional capacity to manage risks such as political capture by special interests (Maloney and Nayyar 2018). In addition, distortions that prevent the efficient allocation of resources to productive sectors and firms should be removed. Productivity in firms in India and China may be 30-60 percent lower due to misallocation of capital and labor across sectors which may be driven by market distortions (Hsieh and Klenow 2009). Where firm entry is costly—whether due to high levels of regulation or regulations that favor state-owned firms—regulations can be streamlined, access to finance expanded, implicit subsidies reduced, and corporate governance standard improved. In regions with high energy subsidies (LAC, MNA), lowering these subsidies can also reduce the misallocation of resources into low-productivity and inefficient energy-intensive sectors.

Creating a growth-friendly environment

Strengthen institutions and government efficiency. Over the long term, institutional quality is one of the most important determinants of productivity growth (Figure 3.7). Productivity gains have been shown to stem from fair competition, even-handed contract enforcement, simplified and transparent legal processes, and contained political risk (Acemoglu et al. 2019). Governments can promote productivity growth by lowering transaction costs, increasing trust in institutions and facilitating long-term contracts (Leipziger and Thomas 1993). Major governance reform spurts are associated with faster TFP and investment growth (Figure 3.13).[22] Other measures to improve the business environment, such as product market and trade reforms or cutting red tape, may boost productivity by more in the presence of good governance (IMF 2019). New information and communications technologies ("Govtech") can provide one channel through which governments can facilitate the rapid dissemination of information within and outside of government to monitor performance and service shortfalls and improve transparency (Figure 3.11; World Bank 2018d).

Safeguard macroeconomic stability. As highlighted in Box 3.4, episodes of rapid debt accumulation and other triggers for financial crises have historically had scarring effects on productivity. Total EMDE debt has risen by 54 percentage points since 2010 and currently stands at 168 percent of GDP, exposing many EMDEs to the risk of financial instability (Chapter 4). Even excluding China, where corporate debt has soared post-crisis, total EMDE debt has risen to a near-record 107 percent of GDP in 2018. Private sector debt vulnerabilities can be contained with macroprudential policies and supervisory monitoring of risks. Where sovereign debt vulnerabilities exist, including those from contingent private-sector liabilities, establishing fiscal rules can increase confidence in the sustainability of debt, lengthening the maturity of

---

[22] These spurts are defined as those that improve at least one of four Worldwide Governance Indicators (government effectiveness, control of corruption, rule of law, and regulatory quality) by at least 2 standard deviations over two years.

FIGURE 3.13 **Effect of governance reform spurts**

Governance reform spurts have been associated with increased potential TFP and investment growth. Setbacks, where perceptions of the quality of governance decline sharply, are associated with slowing investment and TFP growth.

A. Average change in potential TFP growth around World Governance Indicators reforms

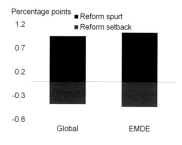

B. Average change in investment growth around World Governance Indicators reforms

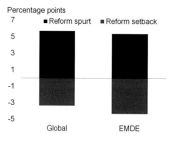

Source: World Bank.
Note: TFP growth refers to potential TFP growth, as estimated in World Bank 2018e
A.B. Simple averages of potential TFP (A) and investment (B) growth during reform spurts and setbacks (minus simple average potential TFP and investment growth outside such episodes) for all countries ("Global") or for EMDEs only ("EMDE") using World Governance Indicators. Based on an event study of 305 statistically significant reform events—defined as two-standard-error changes in one of four World Governance Indicators—for 136 EMDEs and 36 advanced economies. Data are from 1996-2018.

existing debt can ease near-term financing hurdles, and improving the quality of spending towards high-return infrastructure investment can yield growth improvements.

Improve gender equality. Improvements in gender equality, in particular by narrowing differentials in education and labor force participation, can drive sustained improvements in productivity growth by enhancing the human capital available for production. Women currently comprise only about one-fifth of the labor force in MNA and one-quarter of the labor force in SAR. In SSA, where female employment rates are high, female entrepreneurs tend to have lower profits and access to capital. Gender inequality can be addressed by ensuring equal legal rights, targeted training programs, relieving capital and financing constraints for women, and addressing social norms that constrain women's economic opportunities. Policies to empower women and boost their productivity include building skills beyond those taught in traditional training programs, such as a greater focus on developing an entrepreneurial mindset—this approach has been found to lift sales and profits in Togo (World Bank 2019f). In the analysis of the underlying drivers of productivity, economies with the lowest gap between female and male educational attainment grew by an average of 0.2 percentage point faster each year than those with the highest differential when controlling for other characteristics of the economy (Figure 3.7).

ANNEX 3.1 Challenges of Productivity Measurement

There are two primary ways of measuring productivity: labor productivity and total factor productivity (TFP). The former is defined by the total output produced by a unit of labor, the latter measures the efficiency with which factor inputs are combined. TFP can also be interpreted as the technology embedded in the production process, but may also incorporate wider factors such as organizational characteristics. This annex reviews the different techniques and challenges of these different productivity measures and explains how they are tackled in this study.

Labor productivity. One of the common approaches is measuring labor productivity as output per worker by taking the number of employees as the unit of labor input. Its advantage is in its wide availability across countries. Its disadvantage rests in the failure to account for the quality and intensity of labor input.

- *Comprehensiveness.* Having high ratios of informality in EMDEs makes it challenging to appropriately measure productivity. While both output and employment might be mismeasured due to non-registration, many national statistics offices estimate the size of the informal sector and adjust their GDP estimates accordingly (SNA 1993, 2008; UNECE 2008; Charmes 2012). The difficulty in estimating the scale of informal output and lack of consistency in approach allows scope for productivity misme-asurement. Labor input is intended to capture all of those involved in the production process. Thus, total employment figures include self-employment, which accounts for a large proportion of informal employment in EMDEs (World Bank 2019a). However, some self-employment does not involve the informal sector, while the scale of additional employment in the informal sector is also subject to uncertainty—therefore, difficulties in both the measurement of informal output and employment contribute to uncertainty around the productivity level, particularly in

EMDE economies (Fajnzylber, Maloney, and Montes-Rojas 2011).[1]

- *Intensity of labor input.* The number of people involved in the production process does not take into account various work-arrangements that vary the intensity of labor input (Katz and Krueger 2016; Brandolini and Viviano 2018). The intensity of labor input is, for example, better captured by hours worked but these data are not available for many countries.

- *Quality of labor input.* The effectiveness of labor input may be affected by the level of education, training, and health of workers. These aspects of human capital can be addressed by estimating the years of schooling for education and the number of expected years of life for health. However, the quality of formal education and health, and the amount of on-the-job training is difficult to measure consistently in a panel setting.

Total factor productivity. One of the most commonly used measures of technological enhancement is total factor productivity growth. The standard growth accounting approach is one of the most common methodologies in the literature to estimate TFP. It is appealing due to its simple nature and its ease of interpretation. Being estimated as residual, it depends on the assumed functional form and any measurement error for factor inputs. In the context of the United States, this has triggered a debate about the extent to which TFP growth adequately reflects new technologies.

- *Functional form.* TFP is defined as "a shift in the production function", in contrast to biased technological change. Its calculation assumes the existence of a well-behaved and stable production function which also accurately describes the technology in use (Baqaee and Farhi 2018). One of the

---

[1] The direction of the bias depends on how national statistics offices adjust their employment and official GDP to cover the informal sector, which may vary across countries (UNECE 2008).

commonly used functional forms is Cobb-Douglas with constant returns to scale and unitary elasticities of substitution between capital and labor. If the assumption of constant returns to scale is not valid, TFP estimations may be biased by market power in final goods (Dribe et al. 2017).

- *Capital measurement.* Physical capital is difficult to value accurately. Its value depends on the longevity of assets (*short-lived assets* such as computers versus *long-lived assets* such as roads) and the nature of capital (*intangible* capital such as research and development or marketing expenditures). A common way of measuring the capital stock is to apply the perpetual inventory methodology to the flow of expenditure on assets and their depreciation rates. Since data for the initial capital stock is usually not available, assumptions are made on capital to output ratio of the initial year but this ratio can be highly country-specific (Feenstra, Inklaar, and Timmer 2015).

- *Factor utilization.* Since TFP is measured as a residual, it estimates not only technological change but also any mismeasurement of capital and labor input (Basu, Fernald, and Kimball 2006). The capital stock measures the total physical capital available for production without necessarily considering how much of the existing capital is actually used in the production process. Similarly, labor input, even if it is finely measured as total working hours, does not include labor effort. This may lead to an overly cyclical measure of productivity.

New technologies and output measurement. There have been concerns that quality improvements in information technology have not been accurately captured because price deflators for information and communications technology understate the true price declines in these assets (Hatzius et al. 2016). Mismeasurement of new IT technologies could, therefore, explain some of the slowdown in measured productivity growth. Some studies find evidence of mismeasurement in both the pre and post-crisis period, such that mismeasurement explains little of the slowdown in

measured productivity (Byrne, Fernald, and Reinsdorf 2016). Others find evidence of sizable mismeasurement and attribute part of the United States productivity slowdown to measurement biases, particularly due to the increasing share of the services sector in output (Brynjolfsson and McAfee 2014; Feldstein 2017). Overall, while there is some evidence for mismeasurement, it is unlikely that a significant part of the slowdown can be explained by it alone (Cerra and Saxena 2017; Syverson 2016).

ANNEX 3.2 Data and Growth Accounting Approach

Data. The data on capital services and human capital are taken from the Penn World Table 9.1, while data on other macroeconomic aggregates such as GDP are primarily drawn from the World Bank's World Development Indicators (WDI) database, complemented by the ILO and Conference Board estimates of employment. This results in annual labor productivity, TFP and capital services data for 103 economies, of which 73 are EMDEs (including 11 low-income economies) and 29 are advanced economies, for 1981-2018. All aggregates are GDP-weighted averages at 2010 prices and exchange rates. These economies account for 96 percent of global GDP.

Growth accounting. Following Caselli (2005), productivity is decomposed into contributions from several factor inputs:

$$Labor\ productivity = Y_t/L_t = A_t(K_t/L_t)^{(1-\alpha)}H_t^{\alpha}$$

Following Solow (1957), a Cobb-Douglas production function with constant returns to scale is assumed. By taking log differences, labor productivity growth can be decomposed into the following factor inputs.

$$\Delta LP_t = (1 - \alpha)\Delta k_t + \alpha\Delta h_t + \Delta a_t$$

Where $k_t = log(\frac{K_t}{L_t})$ and $h_t = log(H_t)$, and a_t is the log of TFP, calculated here as a residual of labor productivity growth after subtracting the change in capital deepening and human capital indices, weighted by their respective shares in the production function (($1 - \alpha$) and α).

Capital services (K_t). Data on capital services are from the Penn World Table 9.1 (PWT) (Feenstra, Inklaar, and Timmer 2015). In contrast to previous versions of PWT, this edition utilizes capital *services* as a measure of capital inputs instead of capital *stocks* (Inklaar, Woltjer, and Gallardo 2019).

Human capital (H_t). The human capital index from the Penn World Table 9.1 is used throughout the sample. This measure uses average years of schooling of the working-age population in combination with an estimate of the global returns to education.

Labor share estimates. The output-labor elasticity (α), proxied by the labor income share, is also derived from the PWT 9.1 database. It is estimated using the labor compensation to output ratio, including adjustments to take account of mixed-income and wages from self-employment. Labor shares are allowed to vary across countries in this chapter's decompositions. This analysis uses constant labor shares over time, defined as the long-term average of labor share data from PWT 9.1, although it varies across countries.

ANNEX 3.3 Drivers of productivity[1]

Productivity improvements are key for spurring sustained economic growth and social progress in the presence of limited quantity and quality of factor inputs—labor inputs, physical capital, and natural resources (Easterly and Levine 2001; Caselli 2005). Drawing from growth theories, the empirical literature has identified many potential drivers of productivity growth.[2] These can be classified into three broad categories: inputs of production, such as innovation, physical capital and labor;

- supporting environments, such as institutions, policies and social conditions; and

- market development, such as trade integration and financial deepening.

This annex reviews the theoretical and empirical literature that establishes linkages between each of the most commonly identified drivers and productivity growth and assesses differences across EMDE regions as well as over time.

Inputs of production

Innovation. Technical innovations create better ways to produce goods, deliver services, and improve within-sector productivity of firms. Despite large productivity gaps in EMDEs relative to advanced economies, most EMDEs invest much less in formal research and development (R&D) than advanced economies (Goñi and Maloney 2017). The number of patents per capita—one indicator of the pace of innovation—is particularly low in Latin America and the Caribbean (LAC), South Asia (SAR), and Sub-Saharan Africa (SSA; Annex Figure 3.3.1). Nonetheless, gradual improvements in process or product quality have been reported across all income levels (Goñi and Maloney 2017). New patents tend to be more productivity-enhancing in countries with ample supply of highly educated and skilled labor force, while gradual improvements in productivity can be achieved even with low human capital levels (World Bank 2018e).

Physical capital. Labor productivity can be boosted by capital accumulation, underpinned by investment and matched with adequate absorptive capacity (Eberhardt and Presbitero 2015). In particular, investments in infrastructure, including transport, water and sanitation, power, and telecommunications can complement technological progress and lift productivity.[3] Infrastructure needs in EMDEs remain large. Achieving infrastructure-related SDGs in low- and middle-income countries will require an average

---

[1] This annex was prepared by Alistair Dieppe, Atsushi Kawamoto, Yoki Okawa, and Cedric Okou.

[2] As some concepts overlap there could be alternative classifications which focus on other concepts such as competition, geography, and social fragmentation.

[3] See, for example, Aschauer (1989); Servén (2015); and Martins (2019).

ANNEX FIGURE 3.3.1 Productivity drivers in 2017, by region

All EMDE regions fall short of advanced-economy conditions in important productivity drivers, including innovation, human capital, institutions, macroeconomic stability, and trade openness. There is considerable variation across regions: SSA and LAC tend to rank low in many of these dimensions whereas EAP and ECA tend to rank highly.

A. Patents per capita

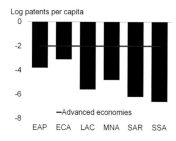

B. Years of schooling

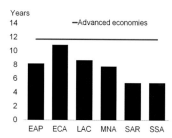

C. Rule of Law

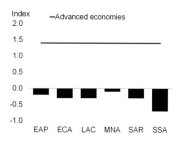

D. Inflation

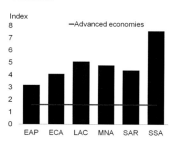

E. Trade openness

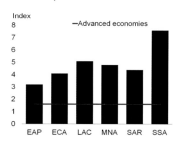

F. Economic complexity

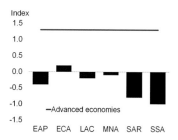

Source: Observatory of Economic Complexity; United Nations; World Bank, Worldwide Governance Indicators.
Note: Data for 2017. Unweighted averages. Trade openness is the sum of exports and imports in percent of GDP. Samples include 22-33 countries in advanced economies, 6-23 countries in EAP, 4-24 countries in ECA, 17-31 countries in LAC, 7-16 countries in MNA, 3-8 countries in SAR, and 10-48 countries in SSA,

yearly investment of 4 to 8 percent of GDP during 2015-30 (Rozenberg and Fay 2019; Vorisek and Yu, forthcoming).

Labor. The productivity of labor can be improved in several ways. A better-educated or healthier work-force can adjust more easily to productivity-enhancing changes.

- *Education.* As a labor force becomes better trained and more highly skilled, it has a greater propensity to contribute to technological advancements and to benefit from positive innovation. Countries with better-educated working-age populations tend to have higher productivity (Barro and Lee 2015). This could reflect workforces in EMDEs moving jobs from sectors requiring limited skills, such as agriculture, to sectors requiring greater skill levels, such as manufacturing and services (Box 3.2). Despite significant catch-up over the past five decades, the gap in average years of schooling between EMDEs (8.6 years) and advanced economies (12.3 years) remains sizeable. There is a substantial dispersion among EMDE regions. For instance, Europe and Central Asia (ECA) has the highest years of schooling among EMDEs, just one year short of the advanced-economy average. By contrast, SSA and SAR has low years of schooling, less than half of the advanced-economy average (Annex Figure 3.3.1).

- *Health.* Healthy workers can work more efficiently and learn faster; they are also more committed to improving their skills and are better equipped to innovate (World Bank 2018e). Better health complements education in reinforcing the supply of good-quality labor, in turn raising human capital, attracting investment, and improving productivity.

- *Demographic trends.* Workforce aging is often negatively associated with productivity growth (Aiyar, Ebeke and Shao 2016; Aksoy et al. 2019).[4] New technologies can disrupt the value of existing human capital, as senior and unskilled workers may need retraining. The strength of this mechanism may depend on the economic structure of the country, as productivity benefits more from experience in some occupations and from innovation in others. This effect is particularly pronounced in advanced economies, where the working-age share of the population shrank

---

[4] The Solow model suggests a decline of the working age population could increase the capital per worker and positively affect labor productivity.

by 3 percentage points between 2008 to 2018. In the decades ahead, EMDEs are projected to follow the same path. Between 2018 and 2030, the working-age population share is expected to decline by 3 percentage points for advanced economies and 2.5 percentage points for EMDEs. In East Asia and Pacific (EAP) and ECA, the working-age population share has already begun to decline, whereas SSA continues to benefit from rising working-age population shares. Realizing the potential of a youthful population requires investing in education and accelerating job creation.

Supporting environment

Institutions. Institutions are the entities that shape human interactions within a society (North 1990). Institutions come in many forms—rule of law, barriers to firm creation and operation, and system of government, to name a few. Better quality institutions are associated with fairer competition and higher productivity (Easterly and Levine 2003; Levchenko 2007). Increased competition is found to support innovation and raise productivity through improvements in management and product quality (Van Reenen 2011). Acemoglu et al. (2019) find that the transition to democracy raises productivity by 20 percent in the subsequent 25 years, but the results vary across studies and some have not uncovered an effect (Ruiz Pozuelo, Slipowitz, and Vuletin 2016). Productivity improvements depend on a country's distance to the technology frontier (Prati, Onorato, and Papageorgiou 2013). There remains a large gap between the quality of institutions, proxied by the government effectiveness index, between all EMDE regions and advanced economies, and the gap has remained almost unchanged over the past twenty years (Annex Figure 3.3.1).

Price stability. Price stability in part reflects the absence of major distortions and uncertainty in the macroeconomic environment (Rodrik, Subramanian, and Trebbi 2004b). Price instability, which can be reflected by high inflation or a large difference between the black market and official exchange rates, may hinder investment, lead to sizeable capital outflows, and are negatively correlate with productivity and

economic growth (Gramacy, Malone, and Horst 2014). Price stability in EMDEs, proxied by inflation, has substantially improved over time, and currently stands at about 4 percent (except in SSA), down from 18 percent in 1990 (Annex Figure 3.3.1). Nevertheless, in many EMDEs, monetary and fiscal policy frameworks still lag behind best practices (Koh and Yu 2019).

Income equality. Income inequality has been explored as a potential underlying driver of low productivity growth. However, the literature is agnostic about the impact of inequality on productivity and economic growth (Herzer and Vollmer 2012; Alvaredo et al. 2018). The elusive empirical link may be due to the u-shaped relationship between income equality and the stage of development: the adverse effects of income inequality tends to be high for low-income and high-income countries, but not high in middle-income countries (Banerjee and Duflo 2003). Income inequality has fallen in some EMDE regions, such as LAC. Yet, it remains much higher in EMDEs than in advanced economies. As of 2017, inequality measured by the Gini index, was 41 for EMDEs, compared to 33 for advanced economies.[5]

Gender equality. Large gaps between women and men in measures of education, health, and access to economic opportunities can lower productivity. Better income-earning opportunities for women can increase human and physical capital investment through higher household income and higher returns for building women's human capital (Klasen and Santos Silva 2018). It may also lower fertility and, hence, help provide each child with better education and health care. An increasing share of women in the labor force, with fair pay and equal job opportunity, can also be beneficial for productivity growth, as it brings a richer collection of perspectives to the decision-making and production process (Gallen 2018). By contrast, the exclusion of all women from managerial positions can reduce income per capita by 12 percent (Cuberes and Teignier 2012, 2014). The gap between EMDEs and advanced

---

[5] The Gini index is a measure of the distribution of income across income percentiles, presented on a scale of 0 to 100, where 100 is the most unequal.

economies for the latter of these indicators has declined during the last five decades.

Market development

Trade. Trade can significantly improve productivity growth (World Bank 2019d) although some studies find only a weak relationship between trade and productivity (Rodrik, Subramanian, and Trebbi 2004). Imports of machinery or high-technology goods can directly improve productivity at the firm, sector, and country level. Lower tariffs can increase imports, facilitate knowledge transfers, and strengthen firm-level productivity (Kraay, Soloaga, and Tybout 2002). Exporting firms tend to have higher productivity than non-exporting ones. The high productivity of exporting firms can be explained by self-selection in some cases (Clerides, Lach, and Tybout 1998). However, evidence from Kenya and the Republic of Korea suggests that exports can increase productivity after controlling for self-selection (Graner and Isaksson 2009). Learning-by-exporting effects on productivity depend on the income level of importers or exporters. The learning effect is large when the exporter and importer have similar productivity levels or importer's human capital is high (Graner and Isaksson 2009; Keller 2004; Blalock and Gertler 2004; Aw, Chung, and Roberts 1998). ECA and EAP are the EMDE regions that are most open to trade whereas SAR is the least open (Annex Figure 3.3.1).

Foreign direct investment. Investment from abroad can bring advanced technology, improved organizational structure, and good management practices from frontier technology economies, boosting productivity in host economies where it is lagging (Griffith, Redding, and Simpson 2003). Cross-border capital flows have a positive effect on productivity, especially those with a high level of development and high-quality institutions. However, this positive relationship is weaker for EMDEs (Keller and Yeaple 2009). In developing countries, the cost of subsidies offered to firms to attract foreign investments can exceed the positive effect of FDI on productivity (Haskel, Pereira, and Slaughter 2007).

Economic complexity. Economic complexity is

measured as a composite indicator that compares each country's sectoral export shares with the sector's share in world trade. The economic complexity is higher if the country exports more "complex" goods such as X-ray appliances, which can be exported from only a few other economies (Hausmann et al. 2014). Greater export complexity has been associated with higher labor productivity through its association with the diversification and sophistication of a country's economic structure (Hausmann and Hidalgo 2010). EMDEs largely lag behind advanced economies in terms of economic complexity (Annex Figure A3.3.1)

Urbanization. Urbanization can facilitate agglomeration benefits such as knowledge spillovers, and improved skills matching within the labor force. Densely populated areas bring people and firms closer together, making it easier to share ideas, exchange information, invent new technologies, design new projects, engage in new partnerships, and start new businesses (Abel, Dey, and Gabe 2012). These agglomeration benefits can in turn lift productivity.

Finance. Well-developed financial markets can improve the efficiency of capital allocation, facilitate technology spillovers and help firms take advantage of productivity-enhancing investments (Fisman and Love 2003; Levine 1997). Financial development and integration are associated with productivity growth (Aghion, Howitt, and Mayer-Foulkes 2005). Financial markets allow firms to diversify investment risk, increase liquidity, and stimulate entrepreneurship and productivity.

Estimating impacts of drivers on productivity growth

Methodology. A cross-section analysis is undertaken where the dependent variable is the long-run growth of productivity during 1960-2018 and separately over 1995-2018. In addition to the initial level of log productivity (y_0), other regressors (X_0)—discussed in the literature and measured at the beginning of the period—are included:

$$y_{T,j} - y_{o,j} = \beta y_{o,j} + X_{o,j}\gamma + \varepsilon_j,$$

where ε_j is a disturbance term, and j denotes a specific economy.[6] The set of coefficients γ capture how each covariate $(X_{0,j})$ drive productivity dynamics over the long-run. The wide range of potential drivers associated with productivity growth leads to a large range of potential model specifications (Fernández, Ley, and Steel 2001; Durlauf, Kourtellos, and Tan 2008, Durlauf, Johnson, and Temple 2005). In order to reduce the bias stemming from an ad-hoc selection and omission of variables, a Bayesian Model Averaging (BMA) approach is applied, which considers different subsets of potential variables and evaluates their inclusion probabilistically. Nonetheless, the estimation results can be unstable in the presence of strong collinearity, as many variables can essentially represent the same concepts (Ghosh and Ghattas 2015). Therefore, based on existing literature and growth theories, variables that represent common concepts are grouped together. The posterior distributions of the coefficients obtained from the BMA procedure are then aggregated to the group level.[7]

Impacts. The estimation is undertaken for 59 countries, including 36 EMDEs.[8] It shows that better educated workforce, stronger institutions, greater innovation, stronger investment, higher levels of urbanization, price stability and a diverse and sophisticated economic structure are all significantly associated with higher productivity growth (Figure 3.7). Furthermore, the estimated impact depends on the stage of development and has changed over the more recent period. The estimated coefficients can be interpreted as the hypothetical coefficient of each theoretical driver of productivity growth. Using these coefficients an

---

[6] Most candidate variables can be viewed as outcomes of productivity, in addition to drivers of productivity, which constrains the interpretation of causal claims from the regressions. To counter the reverse causality issue, the variables used in the analysis are levels in 1960 (or 1995), based on the assumption that serial correlation in 1960 and average growth for the next 58 years is small.

[7] Parametric estimations cannot exclude the possibility of omitted variable bias. Panel estimation focusing on more recent periods can reduce this issue by the inclusion of country fixed effects and a wider range of potential variables, but usually rely on the constant country effects assumption and can suffer from serial correlation and other types of biases.

[8] Variables related to theories in the existing literature are chosen where data exists before 1970 for a large sample of economies. Observations which are not available in the particular year was substituted by the observations in the closest year available.

ANNEX FIGURE 3.3.2 Productivity changes in productivity drivers, by region

Productivity drivers—here captured in a composite index—have improved considerably in EMDEs since the 1980s. However, in several regions, including EAP, ECA, LAC and SAR, the pace of improvement appears to have stalled since the global financial crisis.

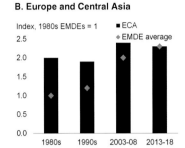

A. East Asia and Pacific

B. Europe and Central Asia

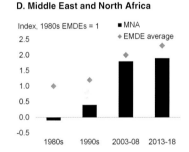

C. Latin America and the Caribbean

D. Middle East and North Africa

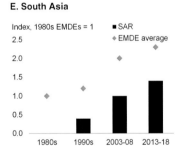

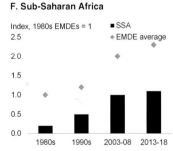

E. South Asia

F. Sub-Saharan Africa

Source: World Bank

Note: For each country, index is a weighted average—weighted by the normalized coefficients shown in Figure 3.7—of the normalized value of each driver of productivity. Drivers include the ICRG rule of law index, patents per capita, share of non-tropical area, investment in percent of GDP, ratio of female average years of education to male average years, share of population in urban areas, Economic Complexity Index, years of schooling, and share of working-age population. Regional and EMDE indices are GDP-weighted averages. Samples include 7 economies in EAP, 8 economies in ECA, 18 economies in LAC, 6 economies in MNA, 4 economies in SAR, and 11 economies in SSA.

aggregate index of drivers of productivity growth is formed. It shows it grew rapidly on average in EMDEs in the pre-crisis period supporting productivity growth (Annex Figure 3.3.2). However, since the global financial crisis, improvements in the drivers have begun to level off as the pace of improvement has slowed, particularly in several EMDE regions (EAP, ECA, LAC, and SAR) amid a productivity growth slowdown.

ANNEX TABLE 3.3.1 Variables included in the regressions and sources

Group	Variable	Source
Financial development	**Ratio of domestic credit to GDP**	**World Development Indicators (WDI)**
Investment	**Ratio of gross fixed capital formation to GDP**	**WDI**
Education	**Years of schooling**	**Barro & Lee, UN**
	Human capital	UNDP
	Years of tertiary schooling	Barro & Lee, UN
	Years of primary and secondary schooling	Barro & Lee, UN
Economic Complexity	**Economic Complexity Index plus**	**Economic observatory**
	(Exports + Imports)/GDP	WDI
Innovation	**Patents per capita**	**WDI**
	Patents per capita * years of tertiary schooling	WDI
Equality	**100 - Gini coefficient**	**UNU wider database**
Institutions	Political Rights Index	Freedom House
	Civil Rights Index	Freedom House
	Rule of Law Index	**International Country Risk Guide, PRS**
	Ratio of government consumption to GDP	WDI and various other sources
Urban	**Share of population in urban areas**	**WDI**
	Population density	WDI
Health	**Survival rate after 5 years per 1000 births = 1000-Infant mortality rate**	**WDI**
	Life expectancy at birth	WDI
Demography	**Share of population aged 15-64**	**WDI**
	Share of population aged below 15	WDI
Gender	**Ratio of years of schooling of female to male**	**Barro & Lee, UN**
	Ratio of years of primary schooling of female to male	Barro & Lee, UN
	Ratio of labor participation rate of female to male	WDI
Geography	Dummy for landlocked countries	WDI
	Share of land which is in tropical regions	**WDI**
	EMDE energy exporter dummy	World Bank
Stability	**(-1) * CPI Inflation Rate**	**WDI**
	Black market exchange rate relative to the official rate	WDI

Note: Sources and list of variables included in the Bayesian selection model. Variables selected with the highest probability of inclusion for each category are in bold.

ANNEX 3.4 Data and methodology for sectoral productivity

Data. The database consists of sectoral and aggregate labor productivity statistics for 80 countries, and nine sectors covering the period up to 2015. Compared with the literature using nine-sector data, it employs a large and diverse sample of countries. The database combine data from the OECD STAN database, World KLEMS (EU, LAC and Russia), the Groningen Growth Development Center (GGDC) database (de Vries, de Vries and Timmer 2015), and the Expanded Africa Sector Database (EASD, Mensah and Szirmai 2018) for value added data and employment. The APO Productivity Database, UN data, ILOSTAT and National sources are used for supplementary purposes. Following McMillan, Rodrik, and Verduzco-Gallo (2014), local currency value added is converted to U.S. dollars using 2011 PPP exchange rate obtained from Penn World Table for the international comparison of productivity levels.[1]

---

[1] Van Biesebroeck (2009) builds an expenditure-based sector-specific PPP in OECD countries, using detailed price data.

Shift-share analysis. Following (Wong 2006) and (Padilla-Pérez and Villarreal 2017), this chapter employs a shift-share-analysis which decomposes aggregate labor productivity into the growth within a sector and shifts between sectors:

$$\frac{\Delta y}{y} = \underbrace{\sum_{j=1}^{k} \frac{Y_j}{Y}\left(\frac{\Delta y_j}{y_j}\right)}_{\substack{\text{Intra-Sectoral} \\ \text{Effect}}} + \underbrace{\underbrace{\sum_{j=1}^{k} \frac{y_j}{y}\left(\frac{\Delta y_j}{y_j}\right)\Delta s_j}_{\substack{\text{Static Sectoral} \\ \text{Effect}}} + \underbrace{\sum_{j=1}^{k} \left(\frac{y_j}{y}\right)\frac{\Delta y_j}{y_j}\Delta s_j}_{\substack{\text{Dynamic Sectoral} \\ \text{Effect Shift}}}}_{\text{Structural Change Effect}}$$

where y is aggregate labor productivity, y_j is labor productivity of sector j, Y_j is initial value added of sector j, s_j is employment share of sector j. Structural changes are driven by the change in employment share. They are further decomposed into those which are due to the reallocation of sources to sectors which higher productivity levels (static sectoral effect), and those due to reallocation toward sectors with higher productivity growth (dynamic sectoral effect).

ANNEX TABLE 3.4.1 Sectoral classifications

Sector name	Description
1. Agriculture	Agriculture, forestry and fishing
2. Mining	Mining and quarrying
3. Manufacturing	Manufacturing
4. Utilities	Electricity, gas, steam and air conditioning supply
5. Construction	Construction
6. Trade services	Wholesale and retail trade; repair of motor vehicles and motorcycles; Accommodation and food service activities
7. Transport services	Transportation and storage; Information and communication
8. Financial and Business services	Financial and insurance activities; Real estate activities; Professional, scientific and technical activities; Administrative and support service activities
9. Government and Personal services	Public administration and defence; compulsory social security; Education; Human helath and social work activities; Arts, entertainment and recreation; Other service activities; Activities of households as employers; undifferentiated goods-and services-producing activities of households for own use; Activities of extraterritorial organizations and bodies.

ANNEX 3.5 Methodology for Box 3.3

Measurement challenges. Revenue-based TFP (TFPR) measures conflate physical productivity and price effects (Foster et al. 2008; Andrews, Criscuolo, and Gal 2016). These price effects can substantially distort TFPR estimates in non-competitive markets or when output prices and inputs choice are correlated. For instance, a high-productivity firm with market power can lower output prices to increase its market share. In this case, TPFR estimates can be low even though the firm is highly productive. Producer prices, if available, can be used to deflate firm-level sales and obtain physical TFP (TFPQ) estimates (Cusolito and Maloney 2018; Van Beveren 2012). Moreover, specifying a single production function for a firm using multiple production technologies is restrictive and can bias TFP estimates (Bernard, Redding, and Schott 2010; Goldberg et al. 2010). Disaggregated product-level data, if available, can be used to construct product-level TFP and help account for the richness in production mix.

Methodology. The fitted specification is

$$DTF_i^g = \theta_0 + \sum_g \rho_g I\left(g \in G \setminus \{\text{ref}\}\right) + \sum_j \gamma_j X_{ij} + v_i$$

where DTF_i^g is the distance-to-frontier of TFP for firm i in industry g, θ_0 stands for the constant term, $\text{ref} = TINT$ is the reference industry, and coefficients ρ_g are interpreted relatively to the reference group. X_{ij} is firm i's jth characteristic such as GDP per capita (in 2009 U.S. dollars per worker), size (number of employees), exports (as a proportion of total sales), and business climate (control of corruption, business freedom). The error term is denoted by v_i.

ANNEX 3.6 Local projection methodology for Box 3.4

The computation of crises impacts follows the local projection (LP) method (Jordà 2005). The dependent variable is the cumulative change in output or productivity levels between horizons *t-1* and *t+1*, measured as the natural logarithms ($y_{t,j}$). The baseline model is given by

$$y_{t+h,j} - y_{t-1,j} = \alpha_{(h),j} + \tau_{(h),t} + \beta_{(h)} E_{t,j} + \sum_{s=1}^{P} \gamma_{l(h)t,s} E_{t-s,j} + \sum_{s=1}^{h-1} \gamma_{f(h),s} E_{t+h-s,j} + \sum_{s=1}^{P} \delta_{(h),s} \Delta y_{t-s,j} + u_{(h)t,j}. \quad (1)$$

Where $h = 0,1,2,\ldots, 8$ is the horizon, $\alpha_{(h),j}$ and $\tau_{(h),t}$ are country j and time fixed effects, and $u_{(h)t,j}$ is an error term. The coefficient of interest $\beta_{(h)}$ captures the dynamic multiplier effect (impulse response) of the dependent variable with respect to the event dummy variable $E_{t,j}$. The number of lags for each variable is denoted by p and set to 1 for the estimation. The specification controls for (i) country and time specific trends, (ii) lagged event dates, (iii) future values of the event dummy between time t and *t+h-1* to correct for possible forward bias (Teulings and Zubanov 2014), and (iv) past changes $\Delta y_{t-s,j}$. Additional controls for country-specific interactions and non-linear effects may also be included.

References

Abel, J. R., I. Dey, and T. M. Gabe. 2012. "Productivity and the Density of Human Capital." *Journal of Regional Science* 52 (4): 562–86.

Acemoglu, D., S. Naidu, P. Restrepo, and J. A. Robinson. 2019. "Democracy Does Cause Growth." *Journal of Political Economy* 127 (1): 47–100.

ADB (Asian Development Bank). 2017. *Asian Development Outlook: Transcending the Middle-Income Challenge*. Manila: Asian Development Bank.

Adler, G., R. Duval, D. Furceri, S. Kilic Celik, K. Koloskova, and M. Poplawski-Ribeiro. 2017. "Gone with the Headwinds: Global Productivity." IMF Staff Discussion Note 17/04, International Monetary Fund, Washington, DC.

Ağca, Ş., and O. Celasun. 2012. "Sovereign Debt and Corporate Borrowing Costs in Emerging Markets." *Journal of International Economics* 88 (1): 198–208.

Aghion, P., P. Bacchetta, R. Rancière, and K. Rogoff. 2009. "Exchange Rate Volatility and Productivity Growth: The Role of Financial Development." *Journal of Monetary Economics* 56 (4): 494–513.

Aghion, P., P. Howitt, and D. Mayer-Foulkes. 2005. "The Effect of Financial Development on Convergence: Theory and Evidence." *Quarterly Journal of Economics* 120 (1): 173–222.

Aguiar, M., and G. Gopinath. 2006. "The Elephant Curve of Global Inequality and Growth." *Journal of International Economics* 69: 64–83.

Aiyar, S., C. Ebeke, and X. Shao. 2016. "The Impact of Workforce Aging on European Productivity." IMF Working Paper 16/238. International Monetary Fund, Washington, DC.

Aksoy, Y., H. S. Basso, R. P. Smith, and T. Grasl. 2019. "Demographic Structure and Macro-economic Trends." *American Economic Journal: Macroeconomics* 11 (1): 193–222.

Alvaredo, F., L. Chancel, T. Piketty, E. Saez, and G. Zucman. 2018. "The Elephant Curve of Global Inequality and Growth." *AEA Papers and Proceedings* 108 (May):103–08.

Amin, M., and A. Islam. 2015. "Are Large Informal Firms More Productive than the Small Informal Firms? Evidence from Firm-Level Surveys in Africa." *World Development* 74 (October): 374–85.

Amin, M., F. Ohnsorge, and C. Okou. 2019. "Casting a Shadow Productivity of Formal Firms and Informality." Policy Research Working Paper 8945. World Bank, Washington, DC.

Andrews, D., C. Criscuolo, and P. Gal. 2016. "The Best versus the Rest: The Global Productivity Slowdown, Divergence across Firms and the Role of Public Policy." OECD Productivity Working Paper 05, Organization for Economic Co-operation and Development, Paris, France.

Araujo, J. T., E. Vostroknutova, and K. Wacker. 2017. "Productivity Growth in Latin America and the Caribbean: Exploring the Macro-Micro Linkages." Discussion Paper 19, World Bank, Washington, DC.

Arellano, C. 2008. "Default Risk and Income Fluctuations in Emerging Economies." *American Economic Review* 98 (3): 690–712.

Arnold, J. M., B. Javorcik, M. Lipscomb, and A. Mattoo. 2016. "Services Reform and Manufacturing Performance: Evidence from India." *Economic Journal* 126 (590): 1–39.

Arteta, C., and G. Hale. 2008. "Sovereign Debt Crises and Credit to the Private Sector." *Journal of International Economics* 74 (1): 53–69.

Arteta, C., and S. Kasyanenko. 2019. "Financial Market Developments." In *A Decade after the Global Recession: Lessons and Challenges for Emerging and Developing Economies*, edited by M. A. Kose and F. Ohnsorge. Washington, DC: World Bank.

Aschauer, D. A. 1989. "Is Public Expenditure Productive?" *Journal of Monetary Economics* 23 (2): 177–200.

Aslam, A., S. Beidas-Strom, R. Bems, O. Celasun, S. Kiliç Çelik, and Z. Koczan. 2016. "Trading on Their Terms? Commodity Exporters in the Aftermath of the Commodity Boom." IMF Working Paper 16/27. International Monetary Fund, Washington, DC.

Atkin, D., A. K. Khandelwal, and A. Osman. 2017. "Exporting and Firm Performance: Evidence from a Randomized Experiment." *The Quarterly Journal of Economics* 132 (2): 551–615.

Bahar, D. 2018. "The Middle Productivity Trap: Dynamics of Productivity Dispersion." *Economics Letters* 167: 60–66.

Bahar, D., and M. A. Santos. 2018. "One More Resource Curse: Dutch Disease and Export Concentration." *Journal of Development Economics* 132 (1): 102–14.

Ball, L. 2009. "Hysteresis in Unemployment: Old and New Evidence." NBER Working Paper 14818, National Bureau of Economic Research, Cambridge, MA.

Banerjee, A. V., and E. Duflo. 2003. "Inequality and Growth: What Can the Data Say?" *Journal of Economic Growth* 8 (3): 267–99.

Baqaee, D., and E. Farhi. 2018. "The Microeconomic Foundations of Aggregate Production Functions." NBER Working Paper 2593, National Bureau of Economic Research, Cambridge, MA.

Barrett, C. B., L. Christiaensen, M. Sheahan, and A. Shimeles. 2017. "On the Structural Transformation of Rural Africa." *Journal of African Economies* 26 (1): 11–35.

Barro, R. J. 1991. "Economic Growth in a Cross Section of Countries." *The Quarterly Journal of Economics* 106 (2): 407–43.

———. 2000. "Inequality and Growth in a Panel of Countries." *Journal of Economic Growth* 5 (1): 5–32.

———. 2001. "Economic Growth in East Asia Before and After the Financial Crisis." NBER Working Paper 8330, National Bureau of Economic Research, Cambridge, MA.

Barro, R. J., and J.-W. Lee. 2015. *Education Matters: Global Schooling Gains from the 19th to the 21st Century.* New York: Oxford University Press.

Barro, R. J., and X. Sala-i-Martin. 1992. "Convergence." *Journal of Political Economy* 100 (2): 223–51.

Bartelsman, E. J., and M. Doms. 2000. "Understanding Productivity: Lessons from Longitudinal Microdata." *Journal of Economic Literature* 38 (3): 569–94.

Basu, S., J. G. Fernald, and M. S. Kimball. 2006. "Are Technology Improvements Contractionary?" *American Economic Review* 96 (5): 1418–48.

Baumol, W. J. 1967. "Macroeconomics of Unbalanced Growth: The Anatomy of Urban Crisis." *American Economic Review* 57 (3): 415–26.

Bils, M. J., and P. Klenow. 2000. "Does Schooling Cause Growth?" *American Economic Review* 90 (5): 1160–83.

Blanchard, O., E. Cerutti, and L. Summers. 2015. "Inflation and Activity - Two Explorations and Their Monetary Policy Implications." NBER Working Paper 21726, National Bureau of Economic Research, Cambridge, MA.

Blanchard, O., and J. Wolfers. 2000. "The Role of Shocks and Institutions in the Rise of European Unemployment: The Aggregate Evidence." *Economic Journal* 110: C1–33.

Bloom, N., B. Eifert, A. Mahajan, D. McKenzie, and J. Roberts. 2013. "Does Management Matter? Evidence from India." *Quarterly Journal of Economics* 128 (1): 1–51.

Bogetic, Z., and J. W. Fedderke. 2009. "Infrastructure and Growth in South Africa: Direct and Indirect Productivity Impacts of 19 Infrastructure Measures." *World Development* 37 (9): 1522–39.

Bosch, M., E. Goni, and W. Maloney. 2007. "The Determinants of Rising Informality in Brazil: Evidence from Gross Worker Flows." Policy Research Working Paper 4375, World Bank, Washington, DC.

Bosworth, B., and S. M. Collins. 2008. "Accounting for Growth: Comparing China and India." *Journal of Economic Perspectives* 22 (1): 45–66.

Brynjolfsson, E., and L. Hitt. 1995. "Information Technology as a Factor of Production: The Role of Differences among Firms." *Economics of Innovation and New Technology* 3 (3–4): 183–99.

Brynjolfsson, E., and A. McAfee. 2014. *The Second Machine Age: Work, Progress, and Prosperity in a Time of Brilliant Technologies.* New York: W W Norton & Co.

Bulow, B. J., and K. Rogoff. 1989. "Sovereign Debt: Is to Forgive to Forget?" *American Economic Review* 79 (1): 43–50.

Bustos, P., B. Caprettini, J. Ponticelli, D. Atkin, F. Buera, V. Carvalho, G. Gancia, et al. 2016. "Agricultural Productivity and Structural Transformation: Evidence from Brazil." *American Economic Review* 106 (6): 1320–65.

Byrne, D. M., J. G. Fernald, and M. B. Reinsdorf. 2016. "Does the United States Have a Productivity Slowdown or a Measurement Problem." *Finance and Economics Discussion Series* 2016 (17): 1–74.

Calderón, C., E. Moral-Benito, and L. Servén. 2015. "Is Infrastructure Capital Productive? A Dynamic Heterogeneous Approach." *Journal of Applied Econometrics* 30 (2): 177–98.

Caselli, F. 2005. "Accounting for Cross-Country Income Differences." In *Handbook of Economic Growth*, edited by Philippe Aghion and Steven N. Durlauf, 1:679–741. Amsterdam: Elsevier.

Cerra, V., and S. C. Saxena. 2008. "Growth Dynamics: The Myth of Economic Recovery." *American Economic Review* 98 (1): 439–57.

Cerra, V., and S. C. Saxena. 2017. "Booms, Crises, and Recoveries: A New Paradigm of the Business Cycle and Its Policy Implications." IMF Working Paper 17/250, International Monetary Fund, Washington, DC.

Charmes, J. 2012. "The Informal Economy World-wide: Trends and Characteristics." *The Journal of Applied Economic Research* 6 (2): 103–32.

Checherita-Westphal, C., and P. Rother. 2012. "The Impact of High Government Debt on Economic Growth and Its Channels: An Empirical Investigation for the Euro Area." *European Economic Review* 56 (7): 1392–1405.

Cherif, R., and F. Hasanov. 2016. "Breaking the Oil Spell: The Gulf Falcons' Path to Diversification." IMF Working Paper 14/177, International Monetary Fund, Washington, DC.

Chevalier, P. A., R. Lecat, and N. Oulton. 2012. "Convergence of Firm-Level Productivity, Globalisation and Information Technology: Evidence from France." *Economics Letters* 116 (2): 244–46.

Cirera, X., R. Fattal-Jaef, and H. Maemir. 2019. "Taxing the Good? Distortions, Misallocation, and Productivity in Sub-Saharan Africa." *The World Bank Economic Review* 00 (0): 1–26.

Cirera, X., and W. F. Maloney. 2017. *The Innovation Paradox: Developing-Country Capabilities and the Unrealized Promise of Technological Catch-Up.* Washington, DC: World Bank.

Claessens, S., E. Detragiache, R. Kanbur, and P. Wickham. 1997. "HIPCs' Debt Review of the Issues World Bank and International Monetary Fund." *Journal of African Economies* 6 (2): 231–54.

Claessens, S., and M. A. Kose. 2017. "Asset Prices and Macroeconomic Outcomes: A Survey." BIS Papers 676, Bank for International Settlements, Basel.

———. 2018. "Frontiers of Macrofinancial Linkages." BIS Papers 95, Bank for International Settlements, Basel.

Clerides, S. K., S. Lach, and J. R. Tybout. 1998. "Is Learning by Exporting Important? Micro-Dynamic Evidence from Colombia, Mexico, and Morocco." *The Quarterly Journal of Economics* 113 (3): 903–47.

Cuberes, D., and M. Teignier. 2012. "Gender Gaps in the Labor Market and Aggregate Productivity." *Sheffield Economic Research Paper Series* Sheffield, U.K.

———. 2014. "Gender Inequality and Economic Growth: A Critical Review." *Journal of International Development* 26 (2): 260-276.

Cusolito, A. P., D. C. Francis, N. Karalashvili, and J. R. Meza. 2018. "Firm Level Productivity Estimates." Methodological Note. World Bank, Washington, DC.

Cusolito, A. P., and W. F. Maloney. 2018. *Productivity Revisited - Shifting Paradigms in Analysis and Policy.* World Bank, Washington, DC.

Dabla-Norris, E., S. Guo, V. Haksar, M. Kim, K. Kochhar, K. Wiseman, and A. Zdzienicka. 2015. "The New Normal: A Sector-Level Perspective on Productivity Trends in Advanced Economies." IMF Staff Discussion Note 15/03, International Monetary Fund, Washington, DC.

De Gregorio, J. 2018. "Productivity in Emerging-Market Economies: Slowdown or Stagnation?" PIIE Working Paper 18-12, Peterson Institute for International Economics, Washington, DC.

De Loecker, J. 2007. "Do Exports Generate Higher Productivity? Evidence from Slovenia." *Journal of International Economics* 73 (1): 69–98.

de Nicola, F., V. Kehayova, and H. Nguyen. 2018. "On the Allocation of Resources in Developing East Asia and Pacific." Policy Research Working Paper 8634, World Bank, Washington, DC.

De Ridder, M. 2017. "Investment in Productivity and the Long-Run Effect of Financial Crises on Output." CESifo Working Paper 6243, Center for Economic Studies and Ifo Institute, Cambridge, U.K.

De Visscher, S., M. Eberhardt, and G. Everaert. 2018. "Estimating and Testing the Multicountry Endogenous Growth Model." Working Paper, 1–41.

de Vries, G., K. de Vries, and M. Timmer. 2015. "Structural Transformation in Africa: Static Gains, Dynamic Losses." *Journal of Development Studies* 51 (6): 674–88.

de Vries, G. J., A. A. Erumban, M. P. Timmer, I. Voskoboynikov, and H. X. Wu. 2012. "Deconstructing the BRICs: Structural Transformation and Aggregate Productivity Growth." *Journal of Comparative Economics* 40 (2): 211–27.

Dercon, S., M. Fafchamps, C. Pattillo, R. Oostendorp, J. Willem Gunning, P. Collier, A. Zeufack, et al. 2004. "Do African Manufacturing Firms Learn from Exporting?" *Journal of Development Studies* 40 (3): 115–41.

Diao, X., M. McMillan, and D. Rodrik. 2017. "The Recent Growth Boom in Developing Economies: A Structural Change Perspective." NBER Working Paper 23132, National Bureau of Economic Research, Cambridge, MA.

Dieppe, A., S. Kiliç Çelik, and G. Kindberg-Hanlon.

Forthcoming. "Global Productivity Trends: Looking Through the Turbulence." In *Productivity in Emerging and Developing Economies.* Washington, DC: World Bank.

Dribe, M., M. Breschi, A. Gagnon, D. Gauvreau, H. A. Hanson, T. N. Maloney, S. Mazzoni, et al. 2017. "Socio-Economic Status and Fertility Decline: Insights from Historical Transitions in Europe and North America." *Population Studies* 71 (1): 3–21.

Duernecker, G., B. Herrendorf, and A. Valentinyi. 2017. "Structural Change within the Service Sector and the Future of Baumol's Disease." CEPR Discussion Paper 12467, Center for Economic Policy Research, London, U.K.

Durlauf, S. N., P. A. Johnson, and J. R. W. Temple. 2005. "Growth Econometrics." In *Handbook of Economic Growth, Volume 1A,* edited by P. Aghion and S. N. Durlauf, 555–677. Amsterdam: North Holland.

Durlauf, S. N., A. Kourtellos, and C. M. Tan. 2008. "Are Any Growth Theories Robust?" *The Economic Journal* 118 (527): 329–46.

Duval, R., G. H. Hong, and Y. Timmer. 2017. "Financial Frictions and the Great Productivity Slowdown." IMF Working Papers 17/129, International Monetary Fund, Washington, DC.

Easterly, W., and S. Fischer. 1994. "The Soviet Economic Decline Revisited." Policy Research Working Paper 1284, World Bank, Washington, DC.

Easterly, W., and R. Levine. 2001. "What Have We Learned From a Decade of Empirical Research on Growth? It's Not Factor Accumulation: Stylized Facts and Growth Models." *World Bank Economic Review* 15 (2): 177-219.

————. 2003. "Tropics, Germs, and Crops: How Endowments Influence Economic Development." *Journal of Monetary Economics* 50 (1): 3–39.

Eberhardt, M., and A. F. Presbitero. 2015. "Public Debt and Growth: Heterogeneity and Non-Linearity." *Journal of International Economics* 97 (1): 45–58.

ECB (European Central Bank). 2017. "The Slowdown in Euro Area Productivity in a Global Context." ECB Economic Bulletin 3/2017. European Central Bank, Frankfurt.

Eichengreen, B., and P. Gupta. 2013. "The Two Waves of Service-Sector Growth." *Oxford Economic Papers* 65 (1): 96–123.

Enache, M., E. Ghani, and S. O'Connell. 2016. "Structural Transformation in Africa: A Historical View." Policy Research Working Paper 7743, World Bank, Washington, DC.

Fajnzylber, P., W. F. Maloney, and G. V. Montes-Rojas. 2011. "Does Formality Improve Micro-Firm Performance? Evidence from the Brazilian SIMPLES Program." *Journal of Development Economics* 94 (2): 262–76.

Feenstra, R. C., R. Inklaar, and M. P. Timmer. 2015. "The Next Generation of the Penn World Table." *American Economic Review* 105 (10): 3150–82.

Feldstein, M. 2017. "Underestimating the Real Growth of GDP, Personal Income, and Productivity." *Journal of Economic Perspectives* 31(2): 145–64.

Fernald, J. 2012. "A Quarterly, Utilization-Adjusted Series on Total Factor Productivity." Fed Working Paper Series 2012–19. Federal Reserve Bank of San Francisco, San Francisco, CA.

————. 2015. "Productivity and Potential Output Before, During, and After the Great Recession." Working Paper Series 01-51, Federal Reserve Bank of San Francisco.

Fernald, J., R. E. Hall, J. H. Stock, and M. W. Watson. 2017. "The Disappointing Recovery Of Output After 2009." NBER Working Paper 23543, National Bureau of Economic Research, Cambridge, MA.

Fernández, C., E. Ley, and M. F. J. Steel. 2001. "Model Uncertainty in Cross-Country Growth Regressions." *Journal of Applied Econometrics* 16 (5): 563–76.

Feyrer, J. 2008. "Aggregate Evidence on the Link between Age Structure and Productivity." *Population and Development Review* 34 (2008): 78–99.

Fisman, R., and I. Love. 2003. "Financial Development and the Composition of Industrial Growth." NBER Working Paper 9583, National Bureau of Economic Research, Cambridge, MA.

Foerster, A., A. Hornstein, P.-D. Sarte, and M. Watson. 2019. "Aggregate Implications of Changing Sectoral Trends." Federal Reserve Bank of San Francisco.

Foster-McGregor, N., A. Isaksson, and F. Kaulich. 2016. "Importing, Productivity and Absorptive Capacity in Sub-Saharan African Manufacturing and Services Firms." *Open Economies Review* 27 (1): 87–117.

Frankel, J. 2010. "The Natural Resource Curse: A Survey." NBER Working Paper 15836, National Bureau of Economic Research, Cambridge, MA.

Fuglie, K., M. Gautam, A. Goyal, and W. Maloney. 2019a. *Harvesting Prosperity: Technology and Productivity Growth in Agriculture.* World Bank, Washington, DC.

Furceri, D., and A. Mourougane. 2012a. "The Effect of Financial Crises on Potential Output: New Empirical Evidence from OECD Countries." *Journal of Macroeconomics* 34 (3): 822–32.

———. 2012b. "How Do Institutions Affect Structural Unemployment in Times of Crises?" *Panoeconomicus* 59 (4): 393–419.

Gallen, Y. 2018. "Motherhood and the Gender Productivity Gap." HCEO Working Paper 91, Human Capital and Economic Opportunity Global Working Group, Chicago, IL.

Galor, O., and D. N. Weil. 1996. "The Gender Gap , Fertility , and Growth." *American Economic Review* 86 (3): 374–87.

Georgiev, Y., P. Nagy-Mohacsi, and A. Plekhanov. 2018. "Structural Reform and Productivity Growth in Emerging Europe and Central Asia." ADB Economics Working Paper Series. Asian Development Bank, Manila, Philippines.

Giri, R., S. N. Quayyum, and R. J. Yin. 2019. "Understanding Export Diversification: Key Drivers and Policy Implications." IMF Working Paper. International Monetary Fund, Washington, DC.

Goldberg, P. K., A. K. Khandelwal, N. Pavcnik, and P. Topalova. 2010. "Multi-Product Firms and Product Turnover in the Developing World: Evidence from India." *Review of Economic Statistics* 92 (4): 1042–49.

Gollin, D., R. Jedwab, and D. Vollrath. 2015. "Urbanization with and without Industriali-zation." *Journal of Economic Growth* 21 (1): 35–70.

Gollin, D., D. Lagakos, and M. E. Waugh. 2014. "The Agricultural Productivity Gap." *Quarterly Journal of Economics* 129 (2): 939–93.

Gollin, D., S. L. Parente, and R. Rogerson. 2007. "The Food Problem and the Evolution of International Income Levels." *Journal of Monetary Economics* 54 (4): 1230–55.

Goñi, E., and W. F. Maloney. 2017. "Why Don't Poor Countries Do R&D? Varying Rates of Factor Returns across the Development Process." *European Economic Review* 94 (May): 126–47.

Gopinath, G., Ş. Kalemli-Özcan, L. Karabarbounis,

and C. Villegas-Sanchez. 2017. "Capital Allocation and Productivity in South Europe*." *The Quarterly Journal of Economics* 132 (4): 1915–67.

Gordon, R. J. 2016. *The Rise and Fall of American Growth: The U.S. Standard of Living since the Civil War.* New Jersey: Princeton University Press.

———. 2018. "Why Has Economic Growth Slowed When Innovation Appears to Be Accelerating?" NBER Working Paper 24554, National Bureau of Economic Research, Cambridge, MA.

Graner, M., and A. Isaksson. 2009. "Firm Efficiency and the Destination of Exports: Evidence from Kenyan Plant-Level Data." *The Developing Economies* 47 (3): 279–306.

Griffith, R., S. Redding, and H. Simpson. 2003. "Productivity Convergence and Foreign Ownership At the Establishment Level."

Ha, J., M. A. Kose, and F. Ohnsorge, eds. 2019. *Inflation in Emerging and Developing Economies: Evolution, Drivers, and Policies.* Washington, DC: World Bank.

Hall, R. E. 2014. "Quantifying the Lasting Harm to the U.S. Economy from the Financial Crisis." NBER Working Paper 20183, National Bureau of Economic Research, Cambridge, MA.

Hall, R. E., and C. I. Jones. 1999. "Why Do Some Countries Produce So Much More Output Per Worker than Others?" *The Quarterly Journal of Economics* 114 (1): 83–116.

Hallward-Driemeier, M., and G. Nayyar. 2017. *Trouble in the Making? The Future of Manufacturing-Led Development.* Washington, DC: World Bank.

Haltiwanger, J., S. Scarpetta, and H. Schweiger. 2014. "Cross Country Differences in Job Reallocation: The Role of Industry, Firm Size and Regulations." *Labour Economics* 26 (January): 11–25.

Harding, D., and A. Pagan. 2002. "Dissecting the Cycle: A Methodological Investigation." *Journal of Monetary Economics* 49 (2): 365–81.

Haskel, J. E., S. C. Pereira, and M. J. Slaughter. 2007. "Does Inward Foreign Direct Investment Boost the Productivity of Domestic Firms?" *Review of Economics and Statistics* 89 (3): 482–96.

Hatzius, J., Z. Pandl, A. Phillips, D. Mericle, E. Pashtan, D. Struyven, K. Reichgott, and A. Thakkar. 2016. "Productivity Paradox v2.0 Revisited." *US Economics Analyst.* Goldman Sachs.

Hausmann, R., and C. Hidalgo. 2010. "Country Diversification, Product Ubiquity, and Economic Divergence." HKS Working Paper 10-045, Kennedy School of Government, Harvard University, Cambridge, MA.

Hausmann, R., C. A. Hidalgo, S. Bustos, M. Coscia, S. Chung, J. Jimenez, A. Simoes, et al. 2014. *The Atlas of Economic Complexity: Mapping Paths to Prosperity. Mapping Paths to Prosperity.* Harvard Center for International Development, Cambridge, MA.

He, D., and W. Zhang. 2010. "How Dependent Is the Chinese Economy on Exports and in What Sense Has Its Growth Been Export-Led?" *Journal of Asian Economics* 21 (1): 87–104.

Helble, M., T. Long, and T. Le. 2019. "Sectoral and Skill Contributions to Labor Productivity in Asia." *ADBI Working Papers*, March.

Hicks, J. H., M. Kleemans, N. Y. Li, E. Miguel, D. Albouy, J. Alvarez, L. Beaman, et al. 2017. "Reevaluating Agricultural Productivity Gaps with Longitudinal Microdata." 23253. NBER Working Paper Series.

Hidalgo, C., and R. Hausmann. 2009. "The Building Blocks of Economic Complexity." *Proceedings of the National Academy of Sciences of the United States of America* 106 (26): 10570-10575.

Hsieh, C.-T., and P. J. Klenow. 2009. "Misallocation and Manufactring TFP in China and India." *Quarterly Journal of Economics* 124 (4): 1403–48.

Hu, A. G. Z., G. H. Jefferson, and Q. Jinchang. 2005. "R&D and Technology Transfer: Firm-Level Evidence from Chinese Industry." *Review of Economics and Statistics* 87 (4): 780–86.

Imbs, J., and R. Wacziarg. 2003. "Stages of Diversification." *American Economic Review* 93 (1): 63–86.

IMF (International Monetary Fund). 2018. "Macroeconomic Developments and Prospects in Low-Income Developing Countries - 2018." IMF Policy Paper, International Monetary Fund, Washington, DC.

———. 2014. "Sustaining Long-Run Growth and Macroeconomic Stability in Low-Income Countries - the Role of Structural Transformation and Diversification - Background Notes." IMF Policy paper. International Monetary Fund, Washington, DC.

———. 2018. "World Economic Outlook: Cyclical Upswing, Structural Change." International Monetary Fund, Washington, DC.

———. 2019. "Reigniting Growth in Low-Income and Emerging Market Economies: What Role Can

Structural Reforms Play?" In *World Economic Outlook: Global Manufacturing Downturn, Rising Trade Barriers.* Washington, DC: International Monetary Fund.

IMF and World Bank. 2019. "Fintech: The Experience so Far - Executive Summary." International Monetary Fund, Washington, DC.

Inklaar, R., P. Woltjer, and D. Gallardo. 2019. "The Composition of Capital and Cross-Country Productivity Comparisons." The Fifth World KLEMS Conference 36. University of Groningen, Netherlands.

Johnson, P., and C. Papageorgiou. 2018. "What Remains of Cross-Country Convergence?" MPRA Paper 89355, Munich Personal RePEc Archive, Munich, Germany.

Jordà, Ò. 2005. "Estimation and Inference of Impulse Responses by Local Projections." *American Economic Review* 95 (1): 161–82.

Jordà, Ò., M. Schularick, and A. M. Taylor. 2013. "When Credit Bites Back." *Journal of Money, Credit and Banking* 45 (2).

Jorgenson, D. W., M. S. Ho, and K. J. Stiroh. 2008. "A Retrospective Look at the U.S. Productivity Growth Resurgence." *Journal of Economic Perspetives* 22 (1): 3–24.

Kalemli-Özcan, S., L. Laeven, and D. Moreno. 2018. "Debt Overhang, Rollover Risk, and Corporate Investment: Evidence from the European Crisis." NBER Working Paper 24555, National Bureau of Economic Research, Cambridge, MA.

Keller, W. 2004. "International Technology Diffusion." *Journal of Economic Literature* 42 (3): 752–782.

Keller, W., and S. R. Yeaple. 2009. "Multinational Enterprises, International Trade, and Productivity Growth: Firm-Level Evidence from the United States." *Review of Economics and Statistics* 91 (4): 821–31.

Kim, Y. E., and N. V. Loayza. 2019. "Productivity Growth: Patterns and Determinants across the World." Policy Research Working Paper 8852, World Bank, Washington, DC.

Koh, W. C., and S. Yu. 2019. "Macroeconomic and Financial Sector Policies." In *A Decade after the Global Recession: Lessons and Challenges for Emerging and Developing Economies*, edited by A. Kose and F. Ohnsorge. Washington, DC: World Bank.

Kraay, A., I. Soloaga, and J. Tybout. 2002. "Product Quality, Productive Efficiency, and International Technology Diffusion: Evidence from Plant-Level Panel Data." Policy Research Working Paper 2759, World Bank, Washington, DC.

Krugman, P. 1988. "Financing vs. Forgiving a Debt Overhang." *Journal of Development Economics* 29 (3): 253–68.

Kugler, A., and I. Rojas. 2018. "Do CCTs Improve Employment and Earnings in the Very Long-Term? Evidence from Mexico." NBER Working Paper 24248, National Bureau of Economic Research, Cambridge, MA.

Laeven, L., and F. Valencia. 2018. "Systemic Banking Crises Revisited." IMF Working Paper 18/206, International Monetary Fund, Washington, DC.

Lagakos, D., and M. E. Waugh. 2013. "Selection, Agriculture, and Cross-Country Productivity Differences." *American Economic Review* 103 (2): 948–80.

Leipziger, D. M., and V. Thomas. 1993. "The Lessons of East Asia: An Overview of Country Experience." World Bank, Washington, DC.

Levchenko, A. A. 2007. "Institutional Quality and International Trade." *The Review of Economic Studies* 74 (3): 791–819.

Levchenko, A., and J. Zhang. 2016. "The Evolution of Comparative Advantage: Measurement and Welfare Implications." *Journal of Monetary Economics* 78 (April): 96–111.

Levine, R. 1997. "Financial Development and Economic Growth: Views and Agenda." *Journal of Economic Literature* 35 (2): 688–726.

Loayza, N. V. 2016. "Informality in the Process of Development and Growth." *World Economy* 39 (12): 1856–1916.

Lowder, S. K., J. Skoet, and T. Raney. 2016. "The Number, Size, and Distribution of Farms, Smallholder Farms, and Family Farms Worldwide." *World Development* 87 (November): 16–29.

Maestas, N., K. Mullen, and D. Powell. 2016. "The Effect of Population Aging on Economic Growth, the Labor Force and Productivity." Working Paper 1063. RAND Labor & Population, Santa Monica, CA.

Maloney, W. F., and G. Nayyar. 2018. "Industrial Policy, Information, and Government Capacity." *The World Bank Research Observer* 33 (2): 189–217.

Martins, P. M. G. 2019. "Structural Change: Pace, Patterns and Determinants." *Review of Development Economics* 23 (1): 1–32.

Mason, A. D., and S. Shetty. 2019. *A Resurgent East Asia: Navigating a Changing World*. Washington, DC: World Bank.

McCullough, E. B. 2017. "Labor Productivity and Employment Gaps in Sub-Saharan Africa." *Food Policy* 67 (February): 133–52.

Mcmillan, M., D. Rodrik, and C. Sepulveda. 2017. "Structural Change, Fundamentals and Growth: A Framework and Case Studies." NBER Working Paper 23378, National Bureau of Economic Research, Cambridge, MA.

Mcmillan, M., D. Rodrik, and Í. Verduzco-Gallo. 2014. "Globalization, Structural Change, and Productivity Growth, with an Update on Africa." *World Development* 63 (November): 11–32.

Melo, P. C., D. J. Graham, and R. Brage-Ardao. 2013. "The Productivity of Transport Infrastructure Investment: A Meta-Analysis of Empirical Evidence." *Regional Science and Urban Economics* 43 (5): 695–706.

Mensah, E. B., and A. Szirmai. 2018. "Africa Sector Database (ASD): Expansion and Update." UNU-MERIT Working Paper Series 2018-020,UNU-MERIT, Maastricht, Netherland.

Moretti, E. 2004. "Workers' Education, Spillovers, and Productivity: Evidence from Plant-Level Production Functions." *American Economic Review* 94 (3): 656–90.

Morris, S., and H. S. Shin. 1998. "Unique Equilibrium in a Model of Self-Fulfilling Currency Attacks." *American Economic Review* 88 (3): 587–97.

Nakamura, L. 2001. "What Is the U.S. Gross Investment in Intangibles? (At Least) One Trillion Dollars a Year!" Working Papers 01-15, Federal Reserve Bank of Philadelphia.

Nguimkeu, P., and C. Okou. 2019. "Informality." In *The Future of Work In Africa: Harnessing the Potential of Digital Technologies for All*, edited by J. Choi, M. Dutz, and Z. Usman, 107–39. Washington, DC: World Bank.

North, D. C. 1990. *Institutions, Institutional Change and Economic Performance*. Cambridge: Cambridge University Press.

Obstfeld, M. 1996. "Models of Currency Crises with Self-Fulfilling Features." *European Economic Review* 40 (95): 1037–47.

OECD (Organisation for Economic Co-operation and Development). 2015. *The Future of Productivity*. Paris: Organisation for Economic Co-operation and Development.

Ollivaud, P., Y. Guillemette, and D. Turner. 2016. "The Links Between Weak Investment and the Slowdown in OECD Productivity and Potential Output

Growth." Working Papers No. 1304, OECD Economics Department 1304. Organisation for Economic Co-operation and Development, Paris.

Osakwe, P. N., and J.-M. Kilolo. 2018. "What Drives Export Diversification? New Evidence from a Panel of Developing Countries." UNCTAD Research Paper 3, United Nations Conference on Trade and Development, New York.

Oulton, N., and M. Sebastiá-Barriel. 2017. "Effects of Financial Crises on Productivity, Capital and Employment." *Review of Income and Wealth* 63 (February): S90 –112.

Patel, D., J. Sandefur, and A. Subramanian. 2018. "Everything You Know about Cross-Country Convergence Is (Now) Wrong." Center for Global Development. Accessed October 15. https://www.cgdev.org/blog/everything-you-know-about-cross-country-convergence-now-wrong.

Pereira, A. M., and J. M. Andraz. 2013. "On the Economic Effects of Public Infrastructure Investment: A Survey of the International Evidence." College of William and Mary Department of Economics Working Paper 108, College of William and Mary, Williamsburg, VA.

Poirson, H., C. Pattillo, and L. Ricci. 2002. "External Debt and Growth." IMF Working Papers 02/69, International Monetary Fund, Washington, DC.

———. 2004. "What Are the Channels Through Which External Debt Affects Growth?" IMF Working Paper 04/15, International Monetary Fund, Washington, DC.

Posen, A., and J. Zettelmeyer. 2019. *Facing Up to Low Productivity Growth*. Washington, DC: Peterson Institute for International Economics.

Reinhart, C. M., and K. S. Rogoff. 2009. "The Aftermath of Financial Crises." *American Economic Review* 99 (2): 466–472.

———. 2010. "Growth in a Time of Debt." *American Economic Review: Papers & Proceedings* 100 (May): 573 –78.

Rodrik, D. 2011. "The Future of Economic Convergence." NBER Working Paper 17400, National Bureau of Economic Research, Cambridge, MA.

———. 2016. "Premature Deindustrialization." *Journal of Economic Growth* 21 (1): 1–33.

Rodrik, D., A. Subramanian, and F. Trebbi. 2004. "Institutions Rule: The Primacy of Institutions Over Geography and Integration in Economic Development." *Journal of Economic Growth* 9 (2): 131–65.

Roy, S., M. Kessler, and A. Subramanian. 2016. "Glimpsing the End of Economic History? Unconditional Convergence and the Missing Middle Income Trap." Center for Global Development Working Paper 438, Center for Global Development, Washington, DC.

Rozenberg, J., and M. Fay. 2019. *Beyond the Gap: How Countries Can Afford the Infrastructure They Need While Protecting the Planet*. Washington, DC: World Bank.

Ruiz Pozuelo, J., A. Slipowitz, and G. Vuletin. 2016. "Democracy Does Not Cause Growth: The Importance of Endogeneity Arguments." IDB Working Paper 694, Inter-American Development Bank, Washington, D.C.

Sahay, R., M. Cihak, P. N'Diaye, R. B. Barajas, D. Ayala, Y. Gao, A. Kyobe, et al. 2015. "Rethinking Financial Deepening: Stability and Growth in Emerging Markets." Staff Discussion Note 15/08, International Monetary Fund, Washington, DC.

Sandri, D. 2015. "Dealing with Systemic Sovereign Debt Crises: Fiscal Consolidation, Bail-Ins or Official Transfers?" IMF Working Paper 17/223, International Monetary Fund, Washington, DC.

Schnitzer, M. 2002. "Debt v. Foreign Direct Investment: The Impact of Sovereign Risk on the Structure of International Capital Flows." *Economica* 69: 41–67.

Sinha, R. 2016. "Sectoral Productivity Gaps and Aggregate Productivity." Policy Research Working Paper 7737. World Bank, Washington, DC.

SNA (System of National Accounts). 2008. *System of National Accounts*. New York: United National Statistical Commission. https://unstats.un.org/unsd/nationalaccount/sna2008.asp.

Solow, R. M. 1957. "Technical Change and the Aggregate Production Function." *The Review of Economics and Statistics* 39 (3): 312–20.

Stocker, M., J. Baffes, Y. M. Some, D. Vorisek, and C. M. Wheeler. 2018. "The 2014–16 Oil Price Collapse in Retrospect: Sources and Implications." Policy Research Working Paper. 8419 World Bank, Washington, DC.

Syverson, C. 2011. "What Determines Productivity?" *Journal of Economic Literature* 49 (2): 326–365.

———. 2016. "Challenges to Mismeasurement Explanations for the U.S. Productivity Slowdown." NBER Working Paper 21974, National Bureau of Economic Research, Cambridge, MA.

Teulings, C. N., and N. Zubanov. 2014. "Is Economic Recovery a Myth? Robust Estimation of Impulse Responses." *Journal of Applied Econometrics* 29 (3): 497–514.

Tuan, C., L. F. Y. Ng, and B. Zhao. 2009. "China's Post-Economic Reform Growth: The Role of FDI and Productivity Progress." *Journal of Asian Economics* 20 (3): 280–93.

UNECE (United Nations Economic Commission for Europe). 2008. *Non-Observed Economy in National Accounts.* Geneva: United Nations Economic Commission for Europe.

Üngör, M. 2013. "De-Agriculturalization as a Result of Productivity Growth in Agriculture." *Economics Letters* 119 (2): 141–45.

———. 2017. "Productivity Growth and Labor Reallocation: Latin America versus East Asia." *Review of Economic Dynamics* 24 (March): 25–42.

van Ark, B., M. O'Mahony, and M. P. Timmer. 2008. "The Productivity Gap between Europe and the United States: Trends and Causes." *Journal of Economic Perspectives* 22 (1): 25–44.

van Biesebroeck, J. 2009. "Disaggregate Productivity Comparisons: Sectoral Convergence in OECD Countries." *Journal of Productivity Analysis* 32 (2): 63-79.

Van Reenen, J. 2011. "Does Competition Raise Productivity through Improving Management Quality?" *International Journal of Industrial Organization* 29 (3): 306–16.

Vargas, M. 2015. "Informality in Paraguay; Macro-Micro Evidence and Policy Implications." IMF Working Papers 15/245, International Monetary Fund, Washington, DC.

Vorisek, D., and S. Yu. forthcoming. "Understanding the Cost of Achieving the Sustainable Development Goals." Policy Research Working Paper, World Bank, Washington, DC.

Wei, Y., and X. Liu. 2006. "Productivity Spillovers from R and D, Exports and FDI in China's Manufacturing Sector." *Journal of International Business Studies* 37 (4): 544–57.

Wooster, R. B., and D. S. Diebel. 2010. "Productivity Spillovers from Foreign Direct Investment in Developing Countries: A Meta-Regression Analysis." *Review of Development Economics* 14 (3): 640–55.

World Bank. 2012. *World Development Report: Gender Equality and Development.* Washington, DC: World Bank.

———. 2017. *Global Economic Prospects: Weak Investment in Uncertain Times.* January. Washington, DC: World Bank.

———. 2018a. *Africa's Pulse: An Analysis of Issues Shaping Africa's Economic Future.* October. Washington, DC: World Bank.

———. 2018b. *World Development Report 2018: Learning to Realize Education's Promise.* Washington, DC: World Bank.

———. 2018c. *Global Economic Prospects: Broad-Based Upturn, but for How Long?* January. Washington, DC: World Bank.

———. 2018d. *Improving Public Sector Performance: Through Innovation and Inter-Agency Coordination.* Washington, DC: World Bank.

———. 2018e. *The Human Capital Project.* Washington, DC: World Bank.

———. 2019a. *Global Economic Prospects: Darkening Skies.* January. Washington, DC: World Bank.

———. 2019b. *Global Economic Prospects: Heightened Tensions, Subdued Investment.* June. Washington, DC: World Bank.

———. 2019c. "Growth in Low-Income Countries: Evolution, Prospects, and Policies." In *Global Economic Prospects, Heightened Tensions, Subdued Investment.* Washington, DC: World Bank.

———. 2019d. *World Development Report 2020: Trading for Development in the Age of Global Value Chains.* Washington, DC: World Bank.

———. 2019e. *World Development Report: The Changing Nature of Work.* Washington, DC: World Bank.

———. 2019f. *Africa's Pulse: An Analysis of Issues Shaping Africa's Economic Future.* October. Washington, DC: World Bank.

World Bank and DRCSC (Development Research Center of the State Council, the People's Republic of China). 2019. *Innovative China: New Drivers of Growth.* Washington, DC: World Bank.

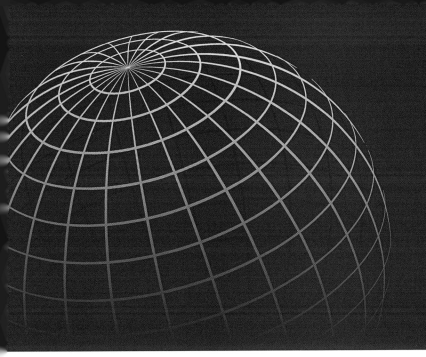

CHAPTER 4

THE FOURTH WAVE

Rapid Debt Buildup

The global economy has experienced four waves of debt accumulation over the past fifty years. The first three ended with financial crises in many emerging market and developing economies. During the current wave, which started in 2010, the increase in debt in these economies has already been larger, faster, and more broad-based than in any of the previous three waves. Current low interest rates —which markets expect to be sustained into the medium term—appear to mitigate some of the risks associated with high debt. However, emerging market and developing economies are also confronted by weak growth prospects, mounting vulnerabilities, and elevated global risks. A menu of policy options is available to reduce the likelihood of the current debt wave ending in crises and, if crises were to take place, to alleviate their impact.

Introduction

Waves of rapid debt accumulation have been a recurrent feature of the global economy over the past fifty years, in both advanced economies and emerging market and developing economies (EMDEs). Since the 2008-09 global financial crisis, another wave has been building, with global debt reaching an all-time high of about 230 percent of global GDP in 2018 (Figure 4.1).

Total EMDE debt reached almost 170 percent of GDP in 2018 ($55 trillion), an increase of 54 percentage points of GDP since 2010. Although China accounted for the bulk of this increase—in part due to its sheer size—the debt-buildup was broad-based: In about 80 percent of EMDEs total debt was higher in 2018 than in 2010. Following a steep fall during 2000-10, debt has also risen in low-income countries (LICs), reaching 67 percent of GDP (around $270 billion) in 2018, up from 48 percent of GDP (around $140 billion) in 2010.

In contrast, in advanced economies, total (public and private) debt has remained steady near the record levels reached in the early aftermath of the global financial crisis, at 264 percent of GDP in 2018 ($130 trillion). While government debt has risen to a high of 104 percent of GDP ($50 trillion), private sector debt has fallen slightly amid deleveraging in some sectors.

The current environment of low interest rates, combined with subpar global growth, has

triggered a lively debate about the benefits and risks of further government debt accumulation to finance increased spending. It is generally agreed that public borrowing can be beneficial, particularly in EMDEs with large development challenges, if it is used to finance growth-enhancing investments, such as infrastructure, health care, and education. Debt accumulation can also be appropriate temporarily as part of counter-cyclical fiscal policy, to boost demand and activity in economic downturns.

However, high debt carries significant risks for EMDEs, as it makes them more vulnerable to external shocks. The rollover of existing debt can become increasingly difficult during periods of financial stress, potentially leading to a crisis. High government debt levels can also limit the size and effectiveness of fiscal stimulus during downturns, and can dampen longer term growth by weighing on productivity-enhancing private investment.

EMDEs have been navigating dangerous waters as the current debt wave has coincided with a decade of repeated growth disappointments, and they are now confronted by weaker growth prospects in a fragile global economy (Kose and Ohnsorge 2019). In addition to their rapid debt buildup during the current wave, these economies have accumulated other vulnerabilities, such as growing fiscal and current account deficits, and a compositional shift toward short-term external debt, which could amplify the impact of shocks.

Thus, despite current exceptionally low real interest rates, including at long maturities, the latest wave of debt accumulation could follow the historical pattern and eventually culminate in financial crises in EMDEs. A sudden global shock, such as a sharp rise in interest rates or a spike in risk premia, could lead to financial stress in more

---

Note: This chapter was prepared by a team led by M. Ayhan Kose, Peter Nagle, Franziska Ohnsorge, and Naotaka Sugawara, with contributions from Jongrim Ha, Alain Kabundi, Sergiy Kasyanenko, Wee Chian Koh, Franz Ulrich Ruch, Lei (Sandy) Ye, and Shu Yu. It is based on Kose et al. 2019. Vanessa Banoni, Julia Norfleet, Jankeesh Sandhu, Shijie Shi, and Jinxin Wu provided research assistance.

FIGURE 4.1 Evolution of debt

Global debt has trended up since 1970, reaching around 230 percent of GDP in 2018. Debt has risen particularly rapidly in EMDEs, reaching a peak of about 170 percent of GDP in 2018. Much of the increase since 2010 has occurred in the private sector, particularly in China. Debt in low-income countries has started to rise after a prolonged period of decline following debt relief measures in the late 1990s and 2000s. Advanced-economy debt has been broadly flat since the global financial crisis, with increased government debt more than offsetting a mild deleveraging in the private sector.

A. Global debt

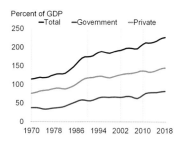

B. Debt in EMDEs

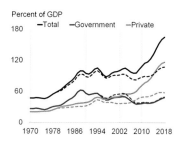

C. Debt in LICs

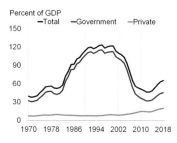

D. Debt in advanced economies

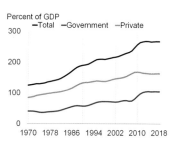

Source: International Monetary Fund; World Bank.
Note: Averages computed with current U.S. dollar GDP as weight and shown as a 3-year moving average. Vertical lines in gray are for years 1970, 1990, 2002, and 2010.
B. Dashed lines refer to EMDEs excluding China.

vulnerable economies. Indeed, these risks were illustrated by the recent experiences of Argentina and Turkey, which witnessed sudden episodes of sharply rising borrowing costs and severe growth slowdowns in 2018.

Among LICs, the rapid increase in debt and the shift from concessional toward financial market and non-Paris Club creditors have raised concerns about debt transparency and debt collateralization. Elevated debt in major EMDEs, including China, could amplify the impact of adverse events and trigger a growth slowdown, posing risks to global and EMDE growth.

Against this backdrop, this chapter compares the current wave of debt buildup to previous episodes and considers the policy implications. The chapter

employs a wide range of approaches, including event studies, econometric models, country case studies, and a detailed review of historical episodes. Specifically, it examines the following questions.

- How have previous waves of debt in EMDEs evolved?

- How does the current wave of debt accumulation compare to earlier waves?

- What are the macroeconomic implications of rapid debt accumulation?

- What are the lessons and policy implications for EMDEs?

Contributions. An extensive literature has studied various aspects of debt accumulation, especially in the context of government and private debt crises. This chapter adds to this literature in five dimensions. *First*, the chapter provides the first in-depth analysis of the similarities and differences among four distinct waves of broad-based debt accumulation in EMDEs since 1970.[1] Each wave contains episodes that have been widely examined in the literature but they have rarely been put into a common framework. Examining debt buildups as waves allows a richer analysis by considering the interaction of global drivers with country-specific conditions. Earlier work has taken on a longer historical perspective and focused mainly on debt developments in advanced economies, typically based on case studies. *Second*, in contrast to earlier studies, the chapter puts the ongoing (fourth) wave of broad-based debt accumulation in EMDEs into historical perspective.[2] *Third*, the

---

[1] Previous studies have examined the impact of mounting government debt in advanced economies (BIS 2015; Cecchetti, Mohanty, and Zampolli 2011; Erhardt and Presbitero 2015; Eichengreen et al. 2019; Mbaye, Moreno-Badia, and Chae 2018a; OECD 2017; Panizza and Presbitero 2014; Reinhart, Reinhart, and Rogoff 2012). For EMDEs, previous studies have often analyzed certain periods of debt distress, or crises in individual countries. For example, contagion from the Asian crisis has been examined by Baig and Goldfajn (1999); Chiodo and Owyang (2002); Claessens and Forbes (2013); Glick and Rose (1999); Kaminsky and Reinhart (2000, 2001); Kawai, Newfarmer, and Schmukler (2005); Moreno, Pasadilla, and Remolona (1998); and Sachs, Cooper, and Bosworth (1998).

[2] The recent debt accumulation, without the historical context, have been discussed in IMF (2019a, 2016a) and World Bank (2015, 2016a, 2017a).

chapter undertakes the first comprehensive empirical analysis of a large number of individual episodes of rapid government and private debt accumulation in 100 EMDEs since 1970. The separate analysis of individual episodes offers key insights into the macroeconomic consequences, at the country level, of debt accumulation. Earlier work has examined developments in government and private debt markets separately, or focused on a smaller group of (mostly advanced) economies or regions.[3] *Fourth,* the chapter identifies the most frequent triggers of crises and the country-level vulnerabilities that contribute to or exacerbate crises. *Fifth,* armed with insights from an extensive analysis of the global and national waves of debt accumulation and the empirical linkages between elevated debt and financial crises, as well as the earlier literature, the study distills lessons and presents a rich menu of policy options that can help EMDEs boost resilience to future crises.

The chapter documents the following findings.

Three previous waves. Prior to the current wave, EMDEs experienced three waves of broad-based and rapid debt buildup. The first (1970-89) was focused in Latin America and the Caribbean (LAC) and Sub-Saharan Africa (SSA), the second (1990-2001) in East Asia and Pacific (EAP) and some other EMDEs in Europe and Central Asia (ECA) and LAC, and the third (2002-09) was chiefly in ECA. The fourth wave (2010 onwards), in contrast, has covered all EMDE regions.

Similarities and differences among previous waves. All debt waves began during prolonged periods of very low real interest rates, and were often facilitated by changes in financial markets that contributed to rapid borrowing. The three earlier waves all ended with widespread financial crises and coincided with global recessions (1982, 1991, and 2009) or downturns (1998, 2001). Crises were usually followed by reforms designed

to lower external vulnerabilities and strengthen policy frameworks. These similarities notwithstanding, the financial instruments used for borrowing have shifted over time as new instruments or financial actors emerged. The nature of EMDE borrowers in international financial markets has also changed, with the private sector accounting for a growing share of borrowing through the first three waves.

Another global wave of debt underway. The debt buildup in EMDEs in the fourth wave, which started in 2010, has already been larger, faster and broader-based than in any of the previous waves. The annual increase in EMDE debt since 2010 has been larger, by some margin, than during the first three waves. Whereas previous waves were largely regional in nature, the fourth wave was global, with total debt rising in more than 70 percent of EMDEs in all regions and rising by at least 20 percentage points of GDP in more than one-third of EMDEs. In the fourth wave, most national episodes of debt accumulation combined government and private debt accumulation, in contrast to the previous three waves which had a greater focus a single sector.

Debt buildups often associated with crises. Since 1970, there have been about 520 national episodes of rapid debt accumulation in 100 EMDEs. Around half of these episodes were accompanied by a financial crisis, with sizeable economic costs. Crises during rapid *government* debt buildups featured larger output losses than crises during rapid *private* debt buildups.

Debt accumulation as shock amplifier. While financial crises during rapid debt accumulation episodes were often triggered by external shocks, such as sudden increases in global interest rates, domestic vulnerabilities often increased the likelihood of crises and amplified their adverse impact. Most countries where crises erupted suffered from unsustainable combinations of inadequate fiscal, monetary, or regulatory frameworks. Crises were more likely, or the economic distress they caused was more severe, in countries with higher external debt—especially short-term—and lower levels of international reserves.

---

[3] Government debt crises have been discussed in Kindleberger and Aliber (2011); Reinhart, Reinhart, and Rogoff (2012); Reinhart and Rogoff (2010, 2011); and World Bank (2019a). Credit booms have been examined in Dell'Arricia et al. (2014, 2016); Elekdag and Wu (2013); Jordà, Schularick, and Taylor (2011); Mendoza and Terrones (2008, 2012); Ohnsorge and Yu (2016); and Tornell and Westermann (2005).

Policy implications. While there is no magic bullet of a policy prescription to ensure that the current debt wave proceeds smoothly, the experience of past waves of debt points to the critical role of policy choices in determining the outcomes of these episodes. Sound debt management and debt transparency can help reduce borrowing costs, enhance debt sustainability, and dampen fiscal risks. Strong monetary, exchange rate, and fiscal policy frameworks can safeguard EMDEs' resilience in a fragile global economic environment. Robust regulatory and supervisory regimes, which are also well coordinated between home and host supervisors of foreign banks, can help contain financial market risks and encourage prudent lending to the private sector. Good corporate governance can help ensure that debt is used for the most productive purposes.

Evolution of past waves of debt

The buildup of EMDE debt since 1970 has not been linear. At different points in time, different countries, and regions, have undergone periods of rapid debt accumulation (Figure 4.2). These have often been followed by crises, and periods of deleveraging. This section examines "waves" of broad-based debt accumulation in EMDEs, and considers their similarities and differences. It identifies four waves of debt since 1970, of which the fourth is still ongoing.

Identification of the four waves

The dating of the four waves meets some basic criteria.

- The first wave begins in 1970.[4] Data limitations prevent more detailed analysis of the period prior to 1970.

- The end of a wave is broadly defined as the year in which the total debt-to-GDP ratio in the affected region or country group peaks

---

[4] 1970 is also used as the starting year by Laeven and Valencia (2018) in their database of financial crises.

and is followed by two consecutive years of decline.

- The dating of the end of waves is consistent with the approximate timing of policies to resolve the financial crises that they engendered. In 1989, for example, Mexico issued the first Brady bonds, marking the beginning of resolution of the Latin American debt crisis. In 1998-2001, a series of IMF programs led to debt resolution after the East Asian and Russian financial crises. In 2009, governments implemented a large-scale, internationally coordinated policy stimulus to combat the adverse effects of the global financial crisis.

Features of the first three waves

This identification yields three historical waves of global debt accumulation and one ongoing. The first wave runs from 1970 to 1989, the second from 1990 to 2001, the third from 2002-09, and the fourth since 2010.

First wave

The *first wave* spanned the 1970s-80s, with borrowing primarily accounted for by governments in LAC and low-income countries in SSA (Kose et al. 2019). The combination of low interest rates and a rapidly growing syndicated loan market encouraged EMDE governments to borrow heavily (Gadanecz 2004).

LAC. The debt buildup was greatest in LAC, which accounted for over half of all debt flows to EMDEs in 1973-81 (Bertola and Ocampo 2012; Devlin 1990). As part of a strategy of import substitution industrialization, countries relied on external debt to finance infrastructure and investment in heavy industries (Baer 1972; Bruton 1998; Diaz-Alejandro, Krugman, and Sachs 1984). Many LAC economies borrowed from international banks via new syndicated loan markets, which provided a way to recycle dollar-denominated oil revenues from oil-exporters to importers (Altunbaş, Gadanecz, and Kara 2006).

Vulnerabilities mounted, as widening current account and fiscal deficits were financed by external debt, and inflation rose, while pegged exchange rate regimes were backed by low levels of reserves. The late 1970s and early 1980s saw a series of global shocks, including an oil price spike and U.S. monetary policy tightening that accompanied a global recession. The crisis began in 1982 with Mexico announcing that it would not be able to service its debt, and spread rapidly to other LAC and SSA countries. The U.S. administration's Brady plan eventually provided comprehensive debt relief in 1989 (Cline 1995; Unal, Demirgüç-Kunt, and Leung 1993). The debt crisis resulted in a "lost decade" in LAC, with GDP per capita not recovering its pre-crisis level until 1993, after having grown by 50 percent during 1970-1980 (Loayza, Fajnzylber, and Calderón 2005).

SSA. Many low-income countries (LICs), especially in SSA, borrowed heavily in the 1970s and 1980s from official creditors (Daseking and Powell 1999). Debt was typically used to finance domestic-focused industry (Greene 1989). Amid rising global interest rates and deteriorating terms of trade, several countries suffered debt crises in the 1980s (Dornbusch, Branson, and Cline 1985). In response, the World Bank and IMF provided financial support for adjustment programs, while the Paris Club creditors agreed to "flow rescheduling," under which debt principal and interest payments were delayed. While these policies helped with liquidity issues, they led to a steady increase in debt (Dicks 1991).

While growth in LICs was robust in the 1970s, it was persistently weak in the subsequent two decades with income per capita falling during 1980-99 amid rapid population growth. Eventually, the World Bank and IMF, along with other multilaterals and bilateral creditors, announced the "Heavily Indebted Poor Countries" (HIPC) initiative in 1996, which was followed by the Multilateral Debt Relief Initiative (MDRI) in 2005 (IMF 2006; World Bank and IMF 2017a).

Second wave

The **second wave** ran from 1990 until the early 2000s as financial and capital market liberalization enabled banks and corporates in EAP and

FIGURE 4.2 Debt in EMDEs

The region and sector of debt accumulation has varied substantially over the four EMDE waves (1970-1989, 1990-2001, 2002-09, and since 2010).

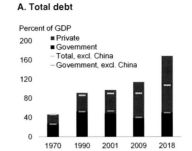

A. Total debt

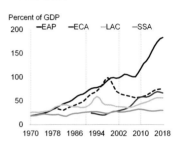

B. External debt

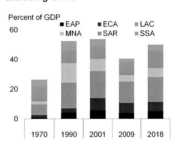

C. Government debt

D. Private debt

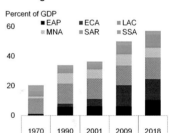

E. Government debt in EMDE regions, excluding China

F. Private debt in EMDE regions, excluding China

Source: International Monetary Fund; World Bank.
A. B. Light blue and yellow lines exclude China.
C.D. Averages computed with current U.S. dollar GDP as weight and shown as a 3-year moving average. Dashed lines for EAP refer to EAP excluding China. Lines for ECA start in 1995 due to smaller sample size prior to that year. Vertical lines in gray are for years 1970, 1990, 2002, and 2010.
E.F. GDP-weighted averages. EAP = East Asia and Pacific, ECA = Europe and Central Asia; LAC = Latin America and Caribbean; MNA = Middle East and North Africa; SAR = South Asia; SSA = Sub-Saharan Africa.

governments in ECA to borrow heavily; it ended with crises in these regions in 1997-2001.

EAP. The EAP region registered one of the fastest increases in private debt in the 1990s. Poor bank regulation and supervision, together with implicit government guarantees for banks and corporates, encouraged risk taking by the domestic financial sector and allowed already highly leveraged corporates to borrow heavily (Kose et al. 2019). Countries also suffered from poor corporate governance, a prominent presence of state-owned enterprises (e.g., Thailand), weak business climates (e.g., Indonesia), and heavy investment in non-tradeable sectors such as commercial real estate (e.g., Thailand; Krugman 2000). Rising private debt, particularly short-term debt, left several EAP countries (Indonesia, Malaysia, Philippines, and Thailand) vulnerable to a reversal in capital flows.

In early 1997, capital inflows to Thailand began to taper off amid investor concerns about external debt sustainability. Despite government intervention in early 1997, Thailand was forced to abandon its currency peg in July 1997. Financial markets quickly turned on countries with similar vulnerabilities, and Indonesia, Korea, Malaysia, and the Philippines experienced large capital outflows which resulted in substantial pressure on their currencies (Corsetti, Pesenti, and Roubini 1998; Kawai, Newfarmer, and Schmukler 2005).

Corporates were unable to service their debt, resulting in large loan losses for banks and triggering banking crises. Governments created "bad banks" to absorb non-performing loans of commercial lenders, recapitalized banks, and improved corporate debt restructuring regimes (Mishkin 1999). Prior to the crisis, the sharp rise in borrowing among EAP countries was accompanied by rapid GDP growth but, during the crisis, GDP and investment growth plummeted.

LAC and ECA. The late 1990s saw crises occur in some other major EMDEs, notably Russia, Argentina, and Turkey. These countries experienced sovereign debt crises when a broad-based loss of investor confidence triggered capital outflows and forced governments to abandon currency pegs. A notable exception was Brazil, which suffered a currency crisis in 1999, but avoided a banking and sovereign debt crisis. The authorities dampened exchange rate depreciation, but at considerable fiscal cost. The earlier "Tequila crisis" in 1995 also falls into the second wave, when Mexico accepted assistance from the IMF and others to stem a currency crisis but avoided a full sovereign debt crisis (Laeven and Valencia 2018; Kose et al. 2019).

Third wave

The ***third wave*** was a runup in private sector borrowing in ECA from U.S. and EU-headquartered "mega-banks" after regulatory easing and amid initially accommodative monetary policy in advanced economies (Cetorelli and Goldberg 2011). While the buildup of debt in the third wave primarily occurred in advanced economies, the emerging mega-banks fueled a steep increase in direct cross-border lending on the interbank market, lending through subsidiaries, and investment in EMDE debt markets (Balakrishnan et al. 2011).

This wave ended when the global financial crisis disrupted bank financing in 2008-09 and tipped several ECA economies into deep recessions (Aslund 2010). The crisis in ECA was short-lived, in part due to IMF and EU support (Berglof et al. 2009). In contrast to the ECA region (and advanced economies), most EMDEs proved resilient to the global financial crisis, in part because they had limited exposures to the actual global shocks at the time (Kose and Prasad 2010). Many EMDEs also improved debt management, supporting a reduction in currency, interest and maturity risks (Anderson, Silva, and Velandia-Rubiano 2010).

Similarities and differences between waves

The first three waves of broad-based debt accumulation featured several similarities (Box 4.1). At the beginning of each wave, the initial debt buildup was associated with low or falling global interest rates and major changes in financial markets, often in response to deregulation. The first three waves eventually witnessed severe and widespread financial crises in EMDEs with severe macroeconomic consequences, usually triggered by external shocks and amplified by domestic vulnerabilities. Financial crises were typically followed by reforms in affected countries to lower external vulnerabilities and strengthen policy frameworks.

There were also noticeable differences between the three waves. The sectors and regions that were the most active borrowers, and the financial instruments involved changed over the course of the three waves: borrowing shifted from the government sector to the private sector, while the type of debt moved from syndicated loan markets in the first wave, to government bond markets and international private sector borrowing in the second wave, to cross-border and foreign-owned bank lending in the third wave. In all three waves, financial crises resulted in substantial economic damage, but their severity varied between waves and across regions. The waves also varied in terms of the speed of resolution, with sovereign debt crises typically taking longer to resolve, and having much larger negative macroeconomic impacts than private debt crises.

The current wave of debt in historical context

Since 2010, another wave of debt accumulation has been building. The buildup has been global, but especially fast in EMDEs (Box 4.2, Figure 4.3). As a result, total debt in EMDEs has risen to almost 170 percent of GDP, on average, in 2018—a record high—from 114 percent of GDP in 2010 (Kose et al. 2019). China, where corporate debt has soared post-crisis, accounted for the bulk of this buildup—partly due to its sheer size—but the buildup was broad-based. Excluding China, total EMDE debt has risen to a near-record 107 percent of GDP in 2018. The debt-to-GDP ratio has risen in all EMDE regions with the exception of SAR, where it has been broadly flat, and in almost 80 percent of EMDEs, with more than one-third seeing increases of at least 20 percentage points of GDP.

The current, fourth, wave of debt accumulation bears many similarities to the previous waves. But there are also important differences. Among these is its sheer magnitude: it is the largest, fastest and most broad-based wave of debt accumulation yet.

Similarities with the previous three waves

The fourth wave shares a number of features with earlier waves: a changing global financial landscape, mounting vulnerabilities, and concerns about inefficient use of borrowed funds.

Financial landscape. As in the previous three waves, the current wave has seen changes in

FIGURE 4.3 The fourth wave: Debt accumulation

Since the global financial crisis, another wave of debt accumulation has been underway. The fourth wave has been especially rapid in EMDEs, and has seen government debt increasing in tandem with mounting private sector debt. The share of debt accounted for by bonds has continued to rise, and large EMDEs have seen a sharp increase in domestically issued bonds.

A. Total debt

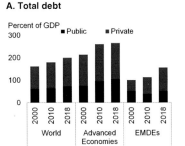

B. Government debt

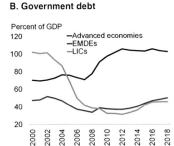

C. EMDE external debt, by borrower and type of instrument

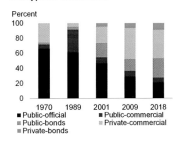

D. Change in EMDE bond issuance, 2010-16, by sector and domicile

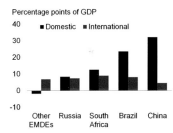

Source: International Monetary Fund; World Bank.
C. "Public-official" includes "private other" which is chiefly accounted for by export guarantee agencies.
D. Chart shows the change in debt securities (in percentage points of GDP) between 2010 and 2016 (last observation). Other EMDEs includes 8 countries. Data for India are unavailable.

financial markets, and very low interest rates (as a result of accommodative monetary policy following the global financial crisis). Financial systems in EMDEs have deepened and become more complex (Didier and Schmukler 2014). Both corporate and sovereign borrowers have increasingly accessed capital markets, in some regions following the retrenchment of large international banks. Over the past decade, more than 20 EMDEs have accessed international capital markets for the first time. In SSA, Eurobond issuance has grown, with several countries tapping the Eurobond market for the first time.

Domestic debt has also become increasingly important, with a rising share of local currency-denominated bonds (Essl et al. 2019; Kose and

BOX 4.1 Similarities and differences between the previous three waves

In each of the first three waves of broad-based debt accumulation, the initial runup in debt was facilitated by changes in financial markets, and low real interest rates in major advanced economies. These waves witnessed severe financial crises in EMDEs, usually triggered by external shocks and amplified by domestic vulnerabilities. They typically led to policy reforms in affected countries to lower external vulnerabilities and strengthen monetary and fiscal policy frameworks. The three waves differed in the composition of borrowers; the financial instruments involved; the speed of crisis resolution; and their macroeconomic impact.

Introduction

Since 1970, there have been four waves of EMDE debt accumulation, of which the fourth one is still underway (see Kose et al. 2019 for a detailed discussion of each of these waves). The first wave spanned the 1970-80s, with a rapid accumulation of debt by governments in LAC and SSA which led to a series of defaults in the early 1980s, and ended with debt relief and restructuring occurring in the late 1980s-90s (LAC), and 1990s-2000s (SSA). The second wave ran from 1990 until the early 2000s as financial and capital market liberalization enabled banks and corporates in East Asia and the Pacific (EAP) and governments in Europe and Central Asia (ECA) to borrow heavily; it ended with a series of crises in these regions in 1997-2001. The third wave was a runup in private sector borrowing in ECA from U.S. and EU-headquartered "mega-banks" after regulatory easing; this wave ended when the global financial crisis disrupted bank financing in 2008-09 and tipped especially ECA countries into deep (albeit short-lived) recessions.

This box synthesizes the main features of the three waves that have by now concluded. In particular, it addresses the following questions in detail.

- What were their similarities?

- What were their differences?

Similarities

The first three waves of broad-based debt accumulation featured several similarities. All of the waves had common drivers, including changes in financial markets and low interest rates. The waves also typically ended in crises with substantial macroeconomic impacts, which led to policy changes. In part as a result of these policy changes, countries weathered subsequent crises better.

Beginning of the waves: Low global interest rates, changes in financial landscape

The initial debt buildup in each wave was associated with

low or falling global interest rates, and major changes in financial markets, often in response to deregulation. These enabled previously credit constrained borrowers to access international financial markets and accumulate debt. Shortcomings in domestic policy frameworks often contributed to rapid debt buildups, and exacerbated the severity of crises.

Low or falling global interest rates. The beginning of each of the three waves was associated with low, or falling, global real interest rates, which encouraged borrowing (Figure 4.1.1). In the first wave, the U.S. real policy rate averaged around 0.6 percent over 1970-79, with several years of negative real interest rates. During the second wave, the U.S. real policy rate declined from a high of 5 percent in 1989 to a low of 0.5 percent in 1993, as the Federal Reserve cut policy rates in response to the global recession in 1991. Similarly, the U.S. real policy rate fell into negative territory at the beginning of the third wave following the 2001 recession in the United States.

New financial instruments. The emergence of the syndicated loan market in the 1970s set the stage for the first wave. The introduction of Brady bonds in the 1990s spurred the development of sovereign bond markets that underpinned sovereign borrowing in the second wave, while capital account liberalization in many EMDEs in the 1990s, especially in EAP, facilitated private sector borrowing. The third wave in the 2000s largely consisted of cross-border flows via international banks in advanced economies after deregulation in the United States and the EU.

Economic upturns. The beginnings of the first and second waves coincided with recoveries from global recessions (1975, 1991, 2009) and the beginning of the third wave with the recovery from the global slowdown of 2001 (Kose and Terrones 2015).

During the waves: Borrower country policies

Borrower country policies often encouraged rapid debt accumulation, or exacerbated the risks associated with it. Fixed exchange rate regimes and weak prudential frameworks encouraged risk taking; weak fiscal frameworks encouraged unfunded government spending; and

---

Note: This box was prepared by Peter Nagle.

BOX 4.1 Similarities and differences between the previous three waves *(continued)*

FIGURE 4.1.1 Comparison of previous waves

The start of each wave generally coincided with a period of low, or falling, interest rates. The end of waves was also associated with a sharp slowdown in capital inflows, which restarted as new waves got underway. Debt episodes that ended in banking crises typically resulted in large increases in government debt.

A. U.S. interest rates

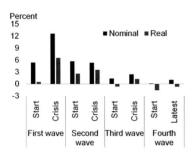

B. Capital flows to EMDEs

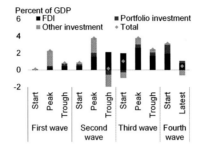

C. Government debt during past banking crises

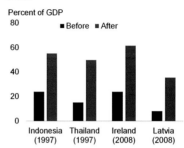

Source: Bloomberg; International Monetary Fund; World Bank.

A. Start of a wave defined as the first three years of the wave. Crisis defined as the year before, and year of, widespread crises. For the first wave, these are 1970-72, and 1981-82. For the second wave, these are 1990-92, and 1996-97. For the third wave, these are 2002-04, and 2008-09. For the final wave, the start is 2010-12, and the "latest" is the final two years of the sample, 2017-18. Real interest rates are calculated as the difference of nominal interest rates and the GDP deflator.

B. Net capital inflows to EMDEs, in percent of GDP. The start of each wave is the first year, the peak is the peak capital inflow before the start of crises in the wave, and the trough is the lowest point after the crisis year. For the first wave, these dates are 1970, 1978, and 1988 respectively. For the second wave, they are 1990, 1995, and 2000. For the third wave, they are 2002, 2007, and 2009. The fourth wave begins in 2010 and the latest data are for 2018.

C. "Before" and "after" denote, respectively, one year before and after the onset of banking crisis, as shown by numbers below the corresponding country names, taken from Laeven and Valencia (2018). Indonesia refers to central government debt only.

government spending priorities or weak prudential supervision directed funding to inefficient uses.

Fixed exchange rate regimes. During the first and second waves, especially, fixed or managed exchange rates in LAC, EAP and ECA encouraged capital inflows by leading lenders and borrowers to underestimate exchange rate risks. With interest rates on foreign currency loans below those for domestic currency loans and the fixed exchange rate interpreted as an implicit guarantee of foreign exchange claims, borrowers readily took on foreign currency-debt and domestic banks offered dollarized or euro-ized accounts on a large scale to local clients (Impavido, Rudolph, and Ruggerone 2013; Magud, Reinhart, and Rogoff 2011).

Weak prudential frameworks. Structural changes in financial markets were typically not accompanied by appropriate reforms to prudential or supervisory frameworks, allowing excessive risk-taking. In the second wave, for example, rapid liberalization of capital markets encouraged EAP banks to borrow heavily from international markets (Furman et al. 1998). In the third wave, the risks posed by growing cross-border lending and macro-financial linkages were underappreciated by financial supervisors (Briault et al. 2018; Claessens and Kose 2018).

Weak fiscal frameworks. In episodes of rapid government debt accumulation, in LAC and SSA in the first wave and in ECA in the second wave, many countries ran persistent fiscal deficits financed with external debt.

Inefficient use of debt. While debt flows were often used to finance productive investment, in some cases debt was used for domestic-facing investments, such as import substitution industrialization that eroded competitiveness in LAC in the first wave or construction and property booms that did not raise export revenues in EAP and ECA in the second and third waves. Weak corporate governance, including inadequate oversight of projects and investment decisions as well as declining profitability, also led to inefficient investment in several EAP countries (Capulong et al. 2000).

End of waves: Financial crises

Rapid debt accumulation initially supported growth but was often associated with financial crises.

Triggers. Financial crises have often been triggered by shocks that raised investor risk aversion, risk premiums and borrowing costs, followed by a sudden stop of capital flows, or by growth slowdowns that eroded debt sustainability (Frankel and Rose 1996; Easterly 2002; Kaminsky and Reinhart 2000; Summers 2001). In the first

BOX 4.1 Similarities and differences between the previous three waves *(continued)*

wave, around the global recession of 1982, deteriorating risk sentiment restricted access to new borrowing in LAC and SSA. In the second wave, capital flows to EMDEs stalled or reversed in the global slowdown of 1998, amid a loss of investor confidence following the East Asian and Russian crises (Kaminsky 2008; Kaminsky and Reinhart 2001). In the third wave, banking system liquidity dried up in the 2008 global financial crisis, interrupting cross-border lending in ECA. Domestic political events also contributed to some crises, for example in Turkey and Argentina in the third wave (Ozatay and Sak 2002).

Types of financial crises. Many crises began with sharp depreciations and capital outflows, which were occasionally the precursor to sovereign debt crises. Large depreciations increased debt service on dollar-denominated debt and led to surges in inflation. Sudden stops or reversals in capital flows complicated debt rollover. In all three waves, countries that slid into crises had sizable vulnerabilities, such as large external, short-term foreign currency-denominated or variable-rate debt; low reserves; pegged exchange rates; and weak monetary, fiscal, and prudential frameworks.

Macroeconomic impact. Debt buildup in the first three waves was often followed by crises or stagnation, especially when the debt buildup was predominantly driven by sovereign debt. Currency depreciations were often large, especially during the first and second wave, and triggered sharp spikes in inflation and deteriorating debt-to-GDP ratios when debt was denominated in dollars. That said, there were considerable differences in the severity of macroeconomic outcomes between the waves, as discussed below.

Fiscal impact. Financial crises were often fiscally costly. In the first wave, defaulting governments in LAC lost capital market access for many years. In the second and third waves, governments had to support ailing banks in recognition of implicit guarantees for financial systems.[1] 90 percent of banking crises have required bank restructuring, and roughly 60 percent have led to the nationalization of one or more banks.

Policy responses. In all waves, the countries suffering crises

implemented policies that helped build resilience to future financial stress. In the first and second waves, LAC and EAP governments took measures to increase reserves and limit future buildups of external debt. Many moved towards inflation targeting and flexible exchange rates. In the second and third waves, EAP and ECA governments eventually strengthened bank supervision, corporate bankruptcy laws and fiscal frameworks. However, progress has varied across countries, with some remaining more vulnerable to shocks than others.

Differences across the waves

The three waves differed in the most active borrowing sector and their regional focus; the financial instruments involved; the speed of resolution of crises; and their macroeconomic impact.

Borrowing sector and region

In the first wave, borrowing was primarily accounted for by the public sector in LAC and SSA (Figure 4.1.2).[2] In these two regions, governments ran persistent fiscal deficits which were used to fund current expenditure in some countries, as well as investment. In the second wave, both the private sector (EAP) and the public sector (ECA, LAC) played a role. In the third wave—with fewer countries with large debt runups than in the previous two waves—the private sector in ECA was the primary source of borrowing. Sovereign debt levels in most EMDEs were either muted or falling in the third wave. Governments in EAP (second wave) and ECA (third wave) typically had sound fiscal positions in the run-up to crises. As a result of these shifts, the share of the public sector in external borrowing fell from a high of 95 percent in 1989 to 53 percent in 2018.

Financial instruments and debt resolution

Financial instruments. The source of credit in each wave also evolved. In the first wave, sovereigns borrowed from the official sector through bilateral lending and multilateral loans, as well as from commercial banks via the syndicated loan market (lending from commercial banks accounted for around one-third of total external

---

[1] For a global sample, the average cost of government intervention in the financial sector during crises in 1990-2014 amounted to 9.7 percent of GDP, with a maximum of 55 percent of GDP (IMF 2016a). The average cost of government intervention in public sector enterprises during 1990–2014 amounted to about 3 percent of GDP and the average cost of the realization of contingent liabilities from public-private partnerships was 1.2 percent of GDP (Bova et al. 2016).

[2] The first and third waves were global in the sense of total EMDE debt rising whereas the second wave had a narrower regional focus. During the first wave, EMDE government debt rose sharply; similarly, during the third wave, EMDE private debt rose sharply, driving up EMDE total debt (Figure 4.1). In contrast, during the second wave, EMDE government debt declined while EMDE private debt, resulting in a limited overall increase in total EMDE debt over the course of the second wave.

BOX 4.1 Similarities and differences between the previous three waves *(continued)*

FIGURE 4.1.2 **Changes in debt by sector and region**

Whereas earlier waves were concentrated in a few regions, the debt buildup in the fourth wave has been broad-based. Like the third wave, private and government sectors accounted almost equally for external borrowing.

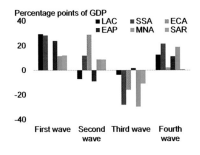

A. Change in government EMDE debt, by region

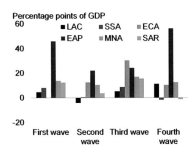

B. Change in private EMDE debt, by region

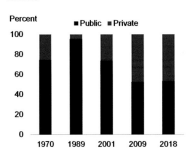

C. Composition of external debt in EMDEs

Source: World Bank.

A.B. EAP = East Asia and Pacific; ECA = Europe and Central Asia; LAC = Latin America and Caribbean; MNA = Middle East and North Africa; SAR = South Asia; SSA = Sub-Saharan Africa.

C. Long-term external debt only.

public debt in EMDEs by 1980-81). The introduction of Brady bonds in the 1990s spurred the development of sovereign bond markets, and in the 2000s, local bond markets deepened, allowing governments to obtain long-term finance, including from foreign investors. In the ECA region, the private sector accessed cross-border lending by European banks, whose subsidiaries and branches were based in ECA countries but headquartered in advanced economies. As a result, there has been a shift from international debt to domestic debt, and a move toward debt securities, including local currency bonds.

Debt resolution: speed, scope, and mechanisms. The speed of resolution largely depended on whether the debtors were in the public or private sector. The difficulty of debt restructuring led to gradual progress in debt resolution and restructuring mechanisms.

- *Slow government debt restructuring.* In the first wave, the resolution of widespread sovereign debt defaults in LAC and SSA was slow, given Paris Club countries' concerns about advanced economy bank solvency and the lack of a well-defined restructuring mechanism (Callaghy 2002).[3] In the second wave, debt resolution was again prolonged for sovereign debt crises in

Turkey and Argentina, which required IMF assistance. Restructuring after Argentina's 2001 debt default was not completed until many years later.[4]

- *Faster private debt resolution.* In the second wave, private sector debt in EAP was resolved quite quickly, with speedy support from the public sector through bank recapitalization and other support schemes, often with IMF assistance. Non-financial corporate debt resolution, particularly among larger conglomerates, was much slower than for the financial sector, and non-performing loans remained elevated for several years after the crisis (Kawai 2002). In the third wave, globally accommodative policies; IMF assistance; the European Bank Coordination ("Vienna") Initiative in 2009; and other banking system support together helped stem currency and banking crises.

- *New resolution mechanisms.* At the start of the first wave, there was little consideration for borrowers' ability to service their debt. Over time, creditors moved toward acceptance of some debt reduction. This paved the way for the conversion of syndicated

---

[3] Borensztein and Panizza (2009) find that the reputational and economic cost of sovereign debt defaults is significant although short-lived, in part because crises precede defaults and defaults tend to happen at the trough of the recession.

[4] Argentina arranged a first restructuring of its debt in 2005, which was accepted by about three-quarters of bond holders (Hornbeck 2013). A second restructuring was agreed in 2010, which two-thirds of the remaining bondholders accepted. 7 percent of bondholders were "holdout" creditors, who eventually reached a settlement in 2016.

BOX 4.1 Similarities and differences between the previous three waves *(continued)*

FIGURE 4.1.3 GDP per capita in EMDEs during the four waves

In the first wave of debt, countries in LAC and SSA saw prolonged stagnation in per capita growth after debt crises erupted. In the second wave, rapid growth in EAP was interrupted by the Asian financial crisis in 1998 but growth soon recovered. In the third wave, growth in ECA was robust throughout the period but fell in the final year when the crisis hit.

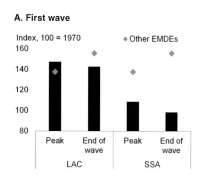

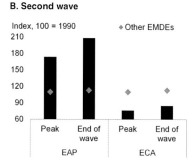

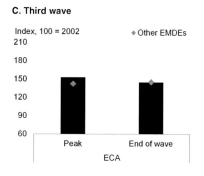

Source: World Bank.

Note: Data are per capita GDP level (at 2010 prices and exchange rates) in each region at the pre-crisis peak and the end of the wave in each region, indexed to the start of the wave. For LAC and SSA in the first wave, the peak was in 1980; in EAP and ECA in the second wave it was in 1997; and in ECA in the third wave it was in 2008. The orange diamonds in Figures A-C show the average for all EMDEs excluding the highlighted regions in each chart, for the corresponding years. EAP = East Asia and Pacific, ECA = Europe and Central Asia; LAC = Latin America and the Caribbean; SSA = Sub-Saharan Africa.

loans to Brady bonds, and later the HIPC and MDRI debt relief initiatives for official debt in low-income countries. Collective action clauses (CACs) were later introduced to facilitate sovereign debt restructuring with multiple bondholders (Eichengreen, Kletzer, and Mody 2003). For private debt, the Insolvency and Creditor Rights Standard developed best practices for national insolvency systems (Leroy and Grandolini 2016). There has been a substantial improvement in insolvency protections over the course of the three waves (World Bank 2019a).

Macroeconomic impact

During the first three waves, financial crises did substantial economic damage, but the severity varied between the waves, and across regions.

Output cost. In the first wave, LAC suffered a lost decade of stagnant per-capita incomes following the 1982 crisis (Figure 4.1.3). Per capita incomes in SSA fared even worse, with GDP per capita declining for many years. Sovereign debt crises in Turkey and Russia during the

second wave also generated severe output losses. In contrast, in the second wave, EAP countries with predominantly private debt buildups experienced only a temporary slowdown from the East Asia crisis. In the third wave, ECA countries with predominantly private debt buildups saw large but short-lived declines in output.

Currency depreciations. Depreciations were substantially larger and more common in the first and second waves, when exchange rates were mostly fixed or crawling pegs, and often had to be abandoned in the face of speculative attacks. By the third wave, more countries had flexible exchange rates, reducing the likelihood of substantial overvaluations to begin with.

Inflation. Inflation following crises rose more in the first wave, and to a lesser extent, in the second. In part, this was due to larger depreciations in these waves. It also reflected subsequent improvements in monetary frameworks—a move toward inflation-targeting and independent central banks that helped anchor inflation expectations (Ha, Kose, and Ohnsorge 2019).

Ohnsorge 2019; Turner 2002).[5] Especially in the largest EMDEs, domestic bond issuance has risen rapidly. Foreign portfolio investors are also becoming more active in local bond markets, accounting for a growing share of local currency-denominated sovereign bonds.

The current wave has also seen a significant increase in nonbank financial intermediation in EMDEs. These nonbank financial institutions have expanded rapidly in a number of EMDEs, particularly large economies.

Vulnerabilities. Over the course of the fourth wave, vulnerabilities have once again grown (Ruch 2019). Since 2010, EMDE total external debt has risen to 26 percent of GDP on average in 2018, reflecting sizable and persistent current account deficits. In 2018, 55 percent of EMDEs had weaker current account balances than in 2010; 76 percent ran current account deficits (compared with 69 percent in 2010); and 44 percent had current account deficits in excess of 5 percent of GDP (Figure 4.4). The number of countries with fiscal deficits has also risen.

In addition, both government and private debt have shifted toward riskier forms in many EMDEs, with a rise in the share of debt that is held by non-residents (for governments), is denominated in foreign currency (for corporates) and is on non-concessional terms. A greater share of corporate debt than before the global financial crisis is held by firms with riskier financial profiles, as supportive financing conditions have allowed firms to issue more debt with weaker credit quality (Beltran and Collins 2018; Feyen et al. 2017; IMF 2015a). EMDE financial markets are now more tightly integrated into the global financial system, which could in some circumstances facilitate the contagion of global financial shocks both to foreign currency and, to a lesser extent, local currency debt markets.

---

[5] However, such a switch may bring other risks, as countries switching from external to domestic debt could be trading a currency mismatch for a maturity mismatch (Panizza 2008; Broner, Lorenzoni and Schmukler 2013). Nominal interest rates on domestic debt tend to be higher than on external debt (IMF 2015a).

FIGURE 4.4 The fourth wave: Vulnerabilities and use of borrowed funds

The fourth wave has seen growing vulnerabilities in EMDEs, with a rise in both domestic and external debt as countries have run persistent current account and fiscal deficits. The composition of debt has shifted, with a greater share held by non-residents and a rise in non-concessional debt. Public investment has fallen sharply in EMDEs, suggesting that rising debt is being used for current spending, rather than growth-enhancing investment, despite a fall in interest payments.

A. EMDEs with current account deficits

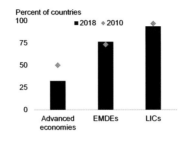

B. EMDEs with fiscal deficits

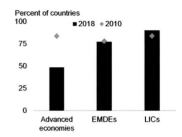

C. Average maturity and non-concessional debt in EMDEs

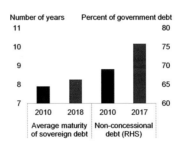

D. Non-resident share of government debt, foreign currency share of corporate debt

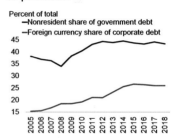

E. Public expenditures in EMDEs

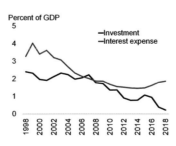

F. Cumulative change in house prices, selected country groups

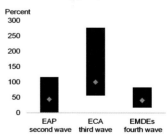

Source: Bank for International Settlements; International Monetary Fund; OECD; World Bank.
C. Median of 65 EMDEs for maturity and 122 EMDEs for non-concessional debt
D. Non-resident share of government debt is average for 45 EMDEs, with a smaller sample size for earlier years. Foreign currency share of corporate debt of average for 21 EMDEs.
F. Chart shows the cumulative percentage increase in house prices over the course of a wave, prior to the crisis. The range covers 1990-97 for EAP, 2001-2008 for ECA, and 2010-18 for EMDEs. EAP contains three countries, ECA contains 5, and EMDEs contains 31 countries. Orange diamonds denoted the median, and blue bars the interquartile range of country groups.

BOX 4.2 The fourth wave

Since 2010, another wave of debt accumulation has been building and total debt in EMDEs has reached almost 170 percent of GDP, on average, in 2018—a record high—from 114 percent of GDP in 2010. This increase was accompanied by shifts toward borrowing from non-traditional creditors and financial institutions, as well as capital markets. As with previous waves, the fourth wave has seen mounting vulnerabilities for EMDEs.

The fourth wave of debt buildup among EMDEs began in 2010. It was broad-based across EMDE regions and borrowing sectors. The debt buildup has been accompanied by a decade of anemic growth in EMDEs (Kose and Ohnsorge 2019). Changes in advanced-economy financial sectors also propelled shifts in creditors to EMDE governments and corporates. This box examines the fourth wave by addressing the following questions.

- How did debt evolve in the fourth wave?

- Which factors have contributed to debt accumulation during the fourth wave?

Evolution of debt

Broad-based public and private debt buildup. Since 2010, another wave of debt accumulation has been underway. The buildup has been especially fast in EMDEs, with government debt increasing in tandem with mounting private sector debt. As a result, total debt in EMDEs has risen to almost 170 percent of GDP, on average, in 2018—a record high—from 114 percent of GDP in 2010 (Kose et al. 2019). The debt-to-GDP ratio has risen in all EMDE regions with the exception of SAR, where it has been broadly flat, and in 80 percent of EMDEs, with more than one-third seeing an increase of at least 20 percentage points of GDP.[1] Excluding China, where corporate debt has soared post-crisis, total EMDE debt has risen to a near-record 107 percent of GDP in 2018. The pace of increase in EMDE debt excluding China has slowed since 2016, with a modest decrease in private sector debt offsetting a small increase in government debt. However, this masks substantial variation between regions, with large increases in debt-to-GDP ratios in SSA and LAC and declines in MNA and ECA.

- *Government debt*. Since 2010, EMDE government debt has risen, on average, by 12 percentage points of GDP to 50 percent of GDP at end-2018. Over this

period government debt-to-GDP has risen in three-quarters of EMDEs and by at least 10 percentage points in almost 60 percent of them. Government debt saw a marked increase among commodity-exporting countries in the aftermath of the commodity price plunge in 2014 (particularly oil prices), as fiscal deficits surged amid declining revenue and large fiscal stimulus (World Bank 2018c).

- *Private debt*. The private sector has also rapidly accumulated debt since the global financial crisis, particularly in China. About two-fifths of EMDEs witnessed private sector credit booms in at least one year during 2011-18 (Ohnsorge and Yu 2016; World Bank 2016a).[2] The rise in debt in China has been focused in a few sectors, notably the real estate, mining, and construction sectors, and among state-owned enterprises.

Shifts to riskier debt. Both government and private debt have shifted toward riskier funding sources in many EMDEs, making these countries more vulnerable to a deterioration in global investor sentiment (Figure 4.2.1).

- *Government debt*. The increase in government debt has been accompanied by a growing share of non-resident investors (to 43 percent in 2018) and an increasing reliance on non-concessional terms. Sovereign ratings have also been downgraded for many EMDEs since 2010. This also increases the fragility of EMDE banks where there is some evidence that exposures to sovereigns have increased (Feyen and Zuccardi 2019).

- *Private debt*. On average, across EMDEs with available data, foreign currency-denominated corporate debt has risen from 19 percent of GDP in 2010 to 26 percent of GDP in 2018, although its share of total corporate debt remained around 40 percent over this period (IIF 2019b). By end-2018, one third of these EMDEs had foreign currency denominated corporate debt above 20 percent of GDP. In addition, a greater share of corporate debt

---

Note: This box was prepared by Peter Nagle.

[1] Total debt has risen particularly rapidly in Argentina, Cambodia, Chile, and China. Turkey stands out as having the third fastest increase in private sector debt after Cambodia and China. Among low-income countries, Mozambique, The Gambia, and Togo and have seen the largest increases in debt.

[2] About half of all credit booms are followed by at least a mild deleveraging within three years (Ohnsorge and Shu 2016).

BOX 4.2 The fourth wave (*continued*)

FIGURE 4.2.1 The fourth wave: Debt developments

Low-income countries have seen a sharp increase in borrowing from non-Paris club bilateral sovereign lending and non-concessional lending. As EU- and U.S.-headquartered banks have downsized their EMDE operations, cross-border bank lending to EMDEs shifted to EMDE-headquartered banks. EMDE corporate and sovereign borrowers have increasingly turned to capital markets to raise new debt.

A. Share of non-concessional debt in LICS

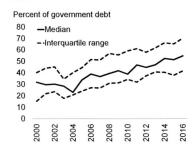

B. Creditor composition of LIC external public debt

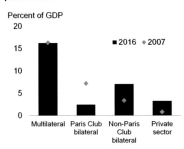

C. Pan-regional banks

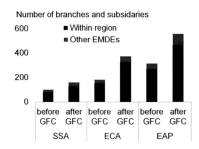

D. Global assets of 10 largest G-SIBs by bank domicile

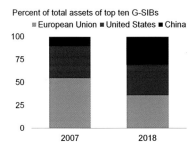

E. Debt securities outstanding

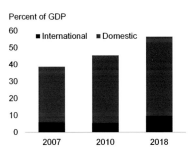

F. Claims on the official sector

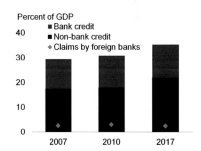

Source: Bank for International Settlements; Claessens and van Horen 2014; International Monetary Fund; World Bank.
A. Dashed blue lines denote the interquartile range, while solid blue line is the median. Includes 30 low-income countries and excludes Somalia, South Sudan, and Syria due to data restrictions.
B. GDP-weighted average across 32 low-income countries. Bilateral includes public and publicly guaranteed (PPG) loans from governments and their agencies (including central banks), loans from autonomous bodies, and direct loans from official export credit agencies. Multilateral includes PPG loans and credits from the World Bank, regional development banks, and other multilateral and intergovernmental agencies. It excludes loans from funds administered by an international organization on behalf of a single donor government. Private include PPG bonds that are either publicly issued or privately placed; PPG debt from commercial bank loans from private banks and other private financial institutions; as well as export and supplier credits.
C. GFC = global financial crisis. Based on annual bank statements; before the GFC = 2008 or 2009 depending on data availability; after GFC = 2018 or latest data available.
D. Based on the Financial Stability Board 2018 list of global systemically important banks (G-SIBs).
E. Sample includes Argentina, Brazil, Colombia, India, Indonesia, Malaysia, Mexico, Philippines, Russia, South Africa, Thailand and Turkey.
F. BIS estimates of the claims by foreign banks on official sector: sample includes Argentina, Brazil, Chile, Colombia, Hungary, India, Indonesia, Israel, Malaysia, Mexico, Poland, Russia, Thailand, Turkey, Republic of Korea, and South Africa

than before the global financial crisis has been owed by firms with riskier financial profiles, as supportive financing conditions have allowed firms to issue more debt with weaker credit quality (Beltran and Collins 2018; Feyen et al. 2017).

LIC government debt. In LICs, debt has also shifted toward non-concessional, non-Paris Club bilateral creditors, notably China, as well as commercial creditors over the past decade (World Bank 2018b; World Bank and IMF 2018a). In 2016, non-Paris Club debt accounted for more than a fifth of the median LIC's external debt, and about 13 percent of their public debt, raising concerns about debt transparency as well as debt collateralization (Essl et al. 2019).

BOX 4.2 The fourth wave (*continued*)

Estimates of current public debt levels in LICs also suffer from limited debt transparency, including issues related to contingent liabilities, state-owned enterprise debt and PPP transactions, and the assets held by LIC governments. These data limitations are especially acute for debt owed to commercial and non-Paris Club creditors. Poor data coverage can give rise to unexpected sudden increases in debt, for example when the debt of loss-making SOEs migrates onto the books of the central government. For example, in Mozambique and the Republic of Congo, the revelation of unreported debt led to large upward revisions to official debt figures, which resulted in debt distress (IMF 2018a). Only a third of the 59 countries eligible for International Development Association borrowing report private sector external debt statistics (World Bank and IMF 2018b).

Changes in the composition of creditors. Since the global financial crisis, borrowing by EMDEs has shifted toward capital markets and regional banks, and away from global banks. Bond issuance has allowed firms to access finance when bank credit supply tightened or at different terms from bank loans (Cortina, Didier, and Schmukler 2016). The role of regional EMDE banks has also grown as large international banks have retrenched from EMDEs in the aftermath of the global financial crisis (BIS 2018; Feyen and Gonzalez de Mazo 2013). As large international banks retrenched, cross-border bank lending to EMDEs shifted to EMDE-headquartered banks, which greatly expanded their regional presence, most notably in SSA (Cerutti and Zhou 2017, 2018; IMF 2015b; World Bank 2018c).

Chinese banks accounted for two-thirds of EMDE-to-EMDE lending between 2013 and 2017 and for most of the doubling in cross-border claims on SSA economies in the same period, to over 10 percent of GDP on average (Cerutti, Koch, and Pradham 2018; Dollar 2016). Other EMDE banks have also increased their presence in EMDEs within their respective regions. A notable exception has been the Middle East and North Africa region, where declining current account surpluses resulting from weaker oil revenues have reduced the region's ability to recirculate savings from high-income oil exporters to lower-income EMDEs with persistent current account deficits (World Bank 2019b).

In SSA, banks headquartered in Togo, Nigeria and South Africa have expanded rapidly to other EMDEs in the region (Arizala et al. 2018). In ECA, Russian banks initially expanded post-crisis within the region, as Western

European banks withdrew.[3] LAC was an exception, with a growing role of domestic banks, rather than of banks based in other countries in the region, as domestic banks acquired assets from exiting foreign lenders. The regional expansion of EMDE banks has yet to reach the scale of pre-crisis cross-border activity of lenders from the advanced economies.

Finally, the domestic institutional investor base has continued to grow in EMDEs, offering the prospect of a potentially stabilizing pool of domestic savings. Assets of pension funds and insurance companies had risen to 46 percent of GDP by end-2016, on average, in EMDEs. Such assets remain equivalent to only about half of the assets of the bank and non-bank financial system (World Bank 2019c).[4]

Contributing factors to debt accumulation

Evolving financial instruments. The latest wave has been associated with a growing importance of domestic debt, while external debt grew more slowly than in the most affected regions during previous waves. The fourth wave has seen rising demand for EMDE bonds from international investors such as asset managers (Shin 2014). Domestic bond issuance has risen sharply, particularly in large EMDEs, while exceptionally long-term (50- and 100-year) international bonds have been issued by some EMDEs, including Mexico in 2010, and Argentina in 2017. Over the past decade, more than 20 EMDEs accessed international capital markets for the first time. New frontier market bond indices, such as J.P. Morgan's NEXGEM launched in 2011 or MSCI's Frontier Market Index launched in 2007, have facilitated international capital market access and broadened the investor base for countries which thus far only had intermittent capital market access.

---

[3] For example, example, Russia's largest lender, Sberbank, acquired Volksbanken's VBI Eastern European operations in 2012.

[4] Data on assets of pension funds and insurance companies are only available for 22 EMDEs. Foreign institutional investors' role in EMDE financial markets has also grown but in some sectors remains small. For example, in just under 1000 infrastructure projects since 2011, the share of institutional investors has more than tripled but still accounts for only 0.7 percent of the average project value (World Bank 2018a). Some institutional investors in EMDEs have been shown to behave procyclically, leaving EMDE financial markets during times of stress rather than acting as stabilizing investors with deep pockets (Raddatz and Schmukler 2012).

BOX 4.2 The fourth wave (*continued*)

The share of corporate debt financed by debt securities on average rose from 16 percent to 25 percent of total lending between end-2007 and end-2018. This included issuance on both international and domestic debt markets. The volume of international debt securities issued by EMDEs increased more than three times between 2007 and 2018. Domestic debt issuance excluding China increased from 33 percent of GDP in 2007 to 47 percent of GDP in 2018.

EMDE sovereign borrowers are also relying more heavily on capital markets. From 2007 to 2017, debt securities issued by EMDE governments increased by 4.4 percentage points of GDP on average, to 22 percent of GDP. In SSA Eurobond issuance has grown, with several countries tapping this market for the first time. Sovereign debt issuance has grown particularly rapidly in domestic bond markets, especially in EAP (G20 IFAWG 2018). In some EMDEs, the share of nonresident investors in local currency sovereign bond holdings exceeds 30 percent, which makes these economies more vulnerable to sudden shifts in investor confidence (G20 IFAWG 2018).

New financing vehicles such as infrastructure bonds and green finance bonds have stimulated lending to specific EMDE sectors where banks used to be the primary source of funding (FSB 2018a; McKinsey Global Institute 2018).[5] However, infrastructure financing, in general, has declined in EMDEs following the sharp reduction in cross-border lending and stricter post-crisis regulations in the financial sector (G20 2013; Kose and Ohnsorge 2019).[6]

Very low interest rates, weak growth. Interest rates have been at very low levels throughout the fourth wave as a result of unconventional monetary policy among central banks, including negative policy rates and quantitative easing. This has encouraged an aggressive search for yield, large capital flows to EMDEs, and a sharp fall in bond spreads. Around one quarter of sovereign and corporate bonds in advanced economies—and some foreign-

currency bonds issued by Poland, and Hungary—currently trade at negative yields.[7] Spreads on emerging market debt both for corporate and sovereign bonds reached all-time lows in 2017, boosting borrowing. Average spreads on corporate bond issuance have fallen for all EMDEs, including LICs. Spreads have also fallen for lower rated corporate bonds.

An additional reason for rapid debt accumulation has been a sharp slowdown in growth over the course of the fourth wave that eroded EMDE fiscal positions and resulted in additional borrowing to maintain current spending levels. Government debt levels in commodity exporters surged following the collapse in commodity prices, particularly after the oil price plunge in 2014, driving much of the increase in EMDE debt (excluding China) in the second half of the current wave (World Bank 2018a).

Growing non-bank financial intermediation. The current wave has also seen a significant increase in shadow banking activities in EMDEs. Shadow banking refers to non-bank financial intermediation that takes place outside of the regulated financial system and may provide credit to riskier borrowers who often lack access to bank credit. Shadow banking systems, which were small before the global recession, have expanded rapidly in a number of EMDEs, particularly in large economies such as China and India (IMF 2014). In these two countries, assets of non-bank financial institutions now represent over a third of total financial system assets. In China alone, this share has more than doubled over the last decade, and the size and complexity of its non-bank financial sector is becoming comparable to those of advanced economies (Ehlers et al. 2018).

A decade of lighter regulation of non-banks than banks, combined with rapid growth, has increased maturity mismatches and credit risks in non-banks (IMF 2018c). Financial stress in non-banks may quickly propagate to the rest of the financial system, owing to its interconnectedness with banks (FSB 2017, 2018b, 2019; Pozsar et al. 2013). This has been illustrated by a recent shift toward stricter regulations and supervision of non-banks in China and a default of one of the largest non-bank lenders in India, which have already created tighter financial conditions for the private sector in those economies (IMF 2019b).

---

[5] In advanced economies, financial instruments that were widely used before the crisis have regained popularity. Especially in the United States, leveraged loan issuances—the majority of which are now covenant-lite with lesser protections for creditors, and which are predominantly held in Collateralized Loan Obligations (CLOs) and loan funds—have risen again above elevated pre-crisis levels. Concerns have been raised whether CLO prices are fully aligned with risks (Domanski 2018; FSB 2019).

[6] Grants and concessional loans are the primary source of infrastructure finance in LICs, with bank lending providing a complementary source of funding only in a small number of countries (Gurara et al. 2017).

[7] In the two EMDEs with negative yielding sovereign bond issuances, government, household and corporate debt have risen only marginally (at most 7 percentage points of GDP) over the past decade.

FIGURE 4.5 Comparison of features of fourth wave and earlier waves: Debt

The fourth wave has seen the largest and fastest increase in debt-to-GDP ratios among EMDEs. It has also been the most broad-based increase in debt across regions and borrowing sectors.

A. Change in total debt

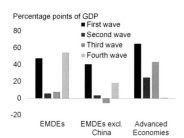

B. Annual average change in total debt

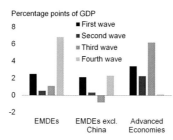

C. Share of economies with increase in government debt, by region

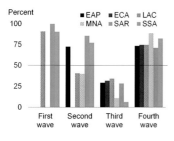

D. Share of economies with increase in private debt, by region

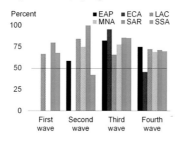

Source: . International Monetary Fund; World Bank.
Note: First wave: 1970-89; second wave: 1990-2001; third wave: 2002-09; fourth wave: 2010 onwards.
A. Change in total debt-to-GDP ratio over the source of each wave.
B. Average annual change calculated as total increase in debt-to-GDP ratio over the duration of the wave, divided by the number of years in a wave.
C.D. Sample includes 142 EMDEs. Data show the share of economies where the debt-to-GDP ratio increased over the duration of the wave. Regions are excluded if country-level data are available for less than one-third of the full region.

Use of debt. In the current wave of debt, there have been signs that government debt is being used for "less efficient" spending rather than on productive investment in physical or human capital that could boost potential growth in EMDEs. Public investment in EMDEs fell from an average of 2.1 percent of GDP in 2002-09, to 0.9 percent in 2010-18 (IMF 2019c). Among commodity exporters, declining tax revenues following the commodity price plunge in 2014-16 widened fiscal deficits and raised debt despite lower investment (World Bank 2018a). Meanwhile, house prices have risen sharply in some EMDEs, suggesting that some of the rise in

private debt has financed residential construction, which does not yield export earnings.

Differences from the previous three waves

The fourth wave has featured the largest, fastest and most broad-based debt accumulation in EMDEs yet. In contrast to earlier waves, government debt has risen in tandem with mounting private sector debt. Compared to the first and third waves—when advanced-economy debt accumulation outpaced EMDE debt accumulation—the fourth wave has been accompanied by near-stable advanced-economy debt-to-GDP ratios. However, some other developments have been more reassuring. During the latest wave, there have been reforms that have made the international financial system more resilient and enlarged the global financial safety net. Many EMDEs have improved their macroeconomic and prudential policy frameworks over the past two decades.

Largest, fastest, and most broad-based wave yet. Including or excluding China, the annual increase in EMDE debt since 2010 (almost 7 percentage points of GDP, on average) has been larger, by some margin, than during the first three waves (Figure 4.5). In contrast to previous waves, which were largely regional in nature, the fourth wave was global. Total debt has risen in more than 70 percent of EMDEs in all regions—previous waves saw higher rates of increase within specific regions, but not across all regions simultaneously. More than one-third of EMDEs have seen an increase in debt of at least 20 percentage points of GDP. Finally, the majority of debt accumulation episodes have featured combined government and private debt buildups—in contrast to the previous three waves when the majority of debt accumulation episodes were either predominantly government or predominantly private episodes.

Stronger policy frameworks. Many EMDEs learnt the lessons from crises in the previous waves and adopted reforms designed to improve resilience. These include greater exchange rate flexibility, and more robust monetary policy frameworks and central bank transparency—since 1999, the number of EMDEs who have adopted inflation targeting has increased from 3 to 24 (Figure 4.6). EMDEs have also made reforms to fiscal frameworks, with the number of countries with fiscal rules rising from 12 in 1999 to 62 in 2018, and substantial improvements in debt management policies and tools (World Bank 2013). Foreign exchange reserves to debt have risen markedly across EMDE regions, although they have fallen from the highs of 2009-10. More EMDEs are using macroprudential tools, particularly placing stricter limits on foreign exchange positions. Bankruptcy rights have also been strengthened, but there is still considerable room for improvement (Kose and Ohnsorge 2019).

Financial regulatory reforms. Financial sector reforms implemented since the global financial crisis are also increasing resilience (BIS 2018). The G20 global financial regulatory reform agenda has implemented major financial reforms since the global financial crisis, including the international adoption of the Basel III capital and liquidity standards (FSB 2018c).

Global financial safety nets have been significantly expanded, with resources available in country-specific, regional and multilateral financial safety nets tripling between 2007 and 2016, including through the creation of regional financing arrangements (RFAs), expanded IMF resources, and increased international reserve holdings (IMF 2018c).[6]

Stable debt in advanced economies. In contrast to the first and third waves—when advanced-economy debt accumulation outpaced EMDE debt accumulation—the fourth wave of EMDE debt accumulation was accompanied by near-stable advanced-economy debt-to-GDP ratios. Advanced economies have also seen pronounced private-sector deleveraging which reduced the share of private debt in total debt during the fourth wave.

---

[6] The global financial safety net consists of 1) self-insurance against external shocks using foreign reserves or fiscal space at national level, 2) bilateral are swap lines among countries, 3) regional financing arrangements, and 4) the global financial backstop provided by the IMF (Brueggemann et al. 2018).

FIGURE 4.6 Comparison of fourth wave and earlier waves: Policies and institutions

Many EMDEs learned lessons from crises in the previous waves and adopted policies to improve resilience. These include more robust monetary and exchange rate policy frameworks, fiscal rules, macroprudential tools, higher foreign exchange reserves relative to external debt, and improved bankruptcy processes.

A. EMDEs with inflation targeting central banks

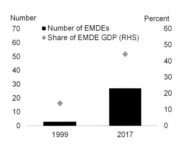

B. EMDEs with fiscal rules

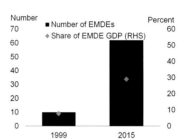

C. Foreign reserves in EMDE regions

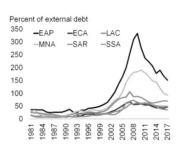

D. EMDEs with flexible exchange rates

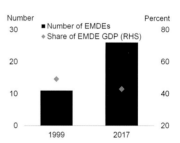

E. Macroprudential policy in EMDEs

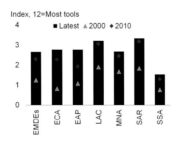

F. Bankruptcy rights protection in EMDEs

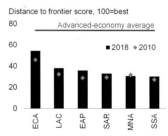

Source: Cerutti, Claessens, and Laeven (2017); Dincer and Eichengreen (2014); Ha, Kose, and Ohnsorge (2019); Huidrom et al. (2019); International Monetary Fund; Kose et al. (2017); World Bank.
A. Inflation targeting as classified in the International Monetary Fund's Annual Report of Exchange Arrangements and Exchange Restrictions.
B. An economy is considered to be implementing a fiscal rule if it has one or more fiscal rules on expenditure, revenue, budget balance, or debt.
D. An economy is considered to have a flexible exchange rate if it is classified as "Floating" or "Free Floating" in the International Monetary Fund's Annual Report of Exchange Arrangements and Exchange Restrictions.
E. Sample includes 123 EMDEs. Unweighted average of the Macroprudential Policy Index of Cerutti, Claessens, and Laeven (2017). The Macroprudential Policy Index measures the number of tools used by authorities and is based on a simple sum of up to 12 including, but not limited to, countercyclical capital buffers and loan-to-value ratios.
F. Distance to frontier score for strength of insolvency resolution. A higher index indicates reforms that improve the business climate. EAP, ECA, LAC, MNA, SAR, and SSA include 22, 22, 32, 19, 8, and 46 economies, respectively. Advanced economies include 36 economies. Based on World Bank Doing Business reports for 2010, and 2019.

BOX 4.3 Debt and crises

This box conducts an econometric exercise to illustrate the extent to which debt accumulation can increase the likelihood of a crisis. A substantial rise in either government or private debt is associated with a significantly higher probability of a crisis occurring in the following year. A combined increase in government and private debt had a particularly strong association with the probability of a currency crisis in the next year. A high share of short-term debt, or large debt servicing costs, similarly raised the likelihood of a crisis. Countries that experienced crises typically had major institutional shortcomings, including debt and fiscal mismanagement, inadequate banking regulation, poor corporate governance, and political uncertainty.

The event study suggests that episodes of debt accumulation that were accompanied by crises often featured larger debt buildups than episodes without crises. This box quantifies the effect of debt accumulation on the likelihood of financial crises using an econometric analysis. Specifically, it answers the following questions.

- What factors have been found to correlate with financial crises?

- What factors are associated with an increased likelihood of crises?

- What were the common features of crisis episodes?

Empirical literature

The econometric exercise here builds on an extensive literature on early warning models.[1] The first generation of early warning models, in the 1980s and 1990s, aimed at predicting currency crises and largely focused on macroeconomic and financial imbalances. Measures of balance sheet health became more prominent in such models after the Asian financial crisis, especially in predicting banking crises. A combination of government solvency and liquidity indicators have also been used in studies of sovereign debt crises.

Debt accumulation and financial crises: An econometric analysis

Econometric specification. In the baseline regression specification, the probability of a financial crisis is estimated as a function of the pace of debt accumulation

and several control variables in a panel logit model with random effects for a sample of 139 EMDEs over 1970-2018 (Annex 4.2). All explanatory variables are lagged because the focus is on pre-conditions that make crises more likely. In addition, the use of lagged variables attenuates potential endogeneity bias caused by contemporaneous interactions between economic fundamentals and crises. Regressions are estimated separately for sovereign debt crises, currency crises and banking crises since these are likely to be associated with different sectoral vulnerabilities.

The correlates of crises are drawn from a rich empirical literature on the determinants of financial crises, or of the vulnerabilities that worsen the impact of crises. This literature has identified the following correlates of higher crisis probabilities:

- *Factors that increase rollover risk.* These are particularly relevant during periods of financial stress; the include high short-term external debt and high or rapidly growing total, government, or private debt; current account deficits;

- *Factors that restrict policy room to respond.* These include low international reserves; large fiscal and current account deficits; and weak institutions.

- *Factors that suggest overvaluation of assets.* These indicate potential for large asset price corrections; the include exchange rate misalignment and credit or asset price booms.

Of these potential correlates, the regression model identifies several that are statistically significant and robust correlates of the probability of financial crises.[2] These include external vulnerabilities (higher short-term debt,

Note: This box was prepared by Wee Chian Koh and Peter Nagle, with contributions from Jongrim Ha, Alain Kabundi, Sergiy Kasyanenko, Wee Chian Koh, Franz Ulrich Ruch, Lei (Sandy) Ye, and Shu Yu.

[1] See Berg, Borensztein, and Patillo (2005); Chamon and Crowe (2012); Frankel and Saravelos (2012); Kaminsky, Lizondo, and Reinhart (1998) for extensive reviews of the literature on early warning models. For models involving currency crises, see Eichengreen, Rose, and Wyplosz (1995); Frankel and Rose (1996); and Kaminsky and Reinhart (2000). For models involving banking crises, see Borio and Lowe (2002); Demirgüç-Kunt and Detragiache (1998); and Rose and Spiegel (2012). For models involving debt crises, see Dawood, Horsewood, and Strobel (2017) and Manasse, Roubini, and Schimmelpfenning (2003).

[2] Annex 4.1 lists the variables used in the baseline model and presents a number of robustness tests; for example, for alternative model specifications (random effects probit model) and twin crises. Twin crises are defined as the simultaneous occurrence of any two types of financial crises (sovereign debt, banking, or currency). Such episodes are usually associated with much larger changes in typical leading indicators. The correlates in the baseline model indeed have higher statistical significance in predicting twin crises than individual crises.

BOX 4.3 Debt and crises (*continued*)

higher debt service, lower international reserves), adverse shocks (higher U.S. interest rates, lower domestic output growth), and faster debt accumulation—especially if true of both government and private debt.[3] These findings are broadly consistent with the existing literature on leading indicators of financial crises, particularly with regard to the important role of the composition of debt and pace of debt accumulation.[4] In addition, the regressions here suggest that combined private and government debt buildups significantly increase the probability of a currency crisis.

Debt accumulation. An increase in debt, either government or private, was associated with significantly higher probabilities of crises in the following year. For example, an increase of 30 percentage points of GDP in *government* debt over the previous year (equivalent to the median buildup during a government debt accumulation episode) increased the probability of entering a debt crisis to 2.0 percent (from 1.4 percent) and that of entering a currency crisis to 6.6 percent (from 4.1 percent). For *private* debt, a 15 percentage points of GDP increase in debt (equivalent to the median increase during a private debt accumulation episode) doubled the probability of entering a banking crisis, to 4.8 percent, or a currency crisis, to 7.5 percent, in the following year—probabilities that are considerably larger than those for a similarly-sized buildup in government debt.

Combined government and private debt increase. Simultaneous increases in both government and private debt amplified the probability of a currency crisis. Thus, a 15 percentage points of GDP increase together with a 30 percentage point of GDP increase in government debt resulted in a 24 percent probability of entering a currency crisis the next year—more than six times the probability had debt remained stable (3.9 percent) and about one-third more than similarly-sized government or private debt buildup separately.

Adverse shocks. Compared to average growth outside crises (4 percent), growth in EMDE crisis episodes

averaged -1 percent. Contractions of this magnitude increased the probability of entering a sovereign debt crisis in the subsequent year to 1.9 percent from 1.2 percent outside crisis episodes. A 2-percentage point increase in U.S. real interest rates—half the cumulative increase during a typical tightening phase of U.S. monetary policy—increased the probability of entering a currency crisis by one-half to 6.0 percent from 4.1 percent.

External vulnerabilities. A larger share of short-term debt in external debt, greater debt service cost and lower reserve cover were associated with significantly higher probabilities of financial crises.

- *Short-term debt.* Compared to the probability of a sovereign debt crisis of 1.2 percent associated with a share of short-term debt of 10 percent of external debt (the average during non-crisis episodes), a 30 percent share of short-term debt in external debt (Mexico's share before it plunged into a twin currency and debt crisis in 1982) raised the probability of entering a sovereign debt crisis in the following year to 2.0 percent.

- *Debt service.* A 50 percent ratio of debt service to exports—Mexico's average debt service burden in the early 1980s—was associated with probabilities of entering a sovereign debt crisis of 2.8 percent and a banking crisis of 5.5 percent. This was more than double the probabilities associated with a 15 percent debt service-to-export ratio in the average non-crisis episode.

- *Reserve coverage.* The probability of a debt or banking crisis exceeded 3 percent, and that of a currency crisis 5 percent, for a reserve coverage of 1 month of imports (which was the case in Mexico in the early 1980s) compared to probabilities of 0.6-2.0 percent for banking and debt crises, and 3.8 percent for currency crises, when the reserve coverage amounted to 4 months of imports (the average for non-crisis episodes).

Other vulnerabilities. Other vulnerabilities identified tended to be more specific to certain types of crises or borrowing sectors.

- *Wholesale funding.* Higher wholesale funding, proxied by the ratio of credit to deposits, was associated with a greater probability of a banking crisis but appears to have been largely unrelated to the probabilities of sovereign debt and currency crises.

---

[3] The same variables remain statistically significant in a regression that combines sovereign debt and banking crises, but the change in government debt becomes insignificant. This may reflect the fact that banking crises have been more than twice as common as sovereign debt crises since 1970. Since almost all crises in the sample are associated with debt accumulation episodes, dummy variables indicating the presence of a private or government or combined (private and government) debt accumulation episode are not statistically significant.

[4] Relevant empirical regularities are discussed in, for example, Manasse, Roubini, and Schimmelpfenning (2003) on sovereign debt crises; Kauko (2014) on banking crises; and Kaminsky, Lizondo, and Reinhart (1998) on currency crises.

BOX 4.3 Debt and crises (*continued*)

- *Real exchange rate overvaluation.* Real exchange rate overvaluation was associated with a higher probability of a currency crisis but tended to be largely unrelated to banking and sovereign debt crises (Dornbusch et al. 1995).

- *Concessional debt and FDI flows.* A higher share of concessional debt, which consists of loans extended on more generous terms than commercial ones, was associated with a lower probability of a sovereign debt crisis but tended to be largely unrelated to banking and currency crises. Larger FDI inflows, a more stable form of finance than portfolio inflows, were associated with a lower probability of a currency crisis.

Crisis probabilities: Small or large? In isolation, some of these probabilities may appear small. This is expected since they are associated with individual indicators. However, the probabilities could cumulate rapidly when multiple indicators deteriorate at the same time as has frequently happened prior to financial crises. Indeed, as documented in the previous chapters, in a typical financial crisis, an adverse shock is often compounded by elevated debt and multiple other vulnerabilities.

Lessons from financial crisis episodes

The preceding section quantified how shocks and vulnerabilities have affected the likelihood of crises. In addition, beyond measures that can be easily quantified, countries with financial crises during or after a debt accumulation episode shared some structural and institutional weaknesses that made their economies more prone to crises once an adverse shock hit. These structural and institutional weaknesses are explored in this section in a set of selected country case studies of financial crises.

These case studies look into 43 crisis episodes in 34 EMDEs that have witnessed rapid government or private debt accumulation episodes since 1970 (Annex 4.3). Most of these cases (65 percent) involved overlapping private and government debt accumulation episodes. Almost all cases (90 percent) involved twin crises, and 40 percent involved triplet crises.[5]

---

[5] The main references for these country case studies are provided in Kose et al.(2019). For a discussion of some of these macroeconomic, structural and institutional shortcomings see Balassa (1982); Kaufmann (1989); and Sachs (1985, 1989) on growth strategies and uses of debt; Roubini and Wachtel (1999) on current account sustainability; Daumont, Le Gall, and Leroux (2004) and Kawai, Newfarmer, and Schmukler (2005) on inadequate banking regulation; Brownbridge and Kirkpatrick (2000) on balance sheet mismatch; and Capulong et. al. (2000) for poor corporate governance.

Macroeconomic policies

Inefficient use of debt. In addition to financing import substitution policies, public debt was used in some countries in the first wave to finance current government spending and policies that led to overly expansionary macroeconomic policies (Argentina, Brazil, Chile, Peru). In other countries, rapid private-sector borrowing resulted in debt-fueled domestic demand booms, including property booms (Thailand, Ukraine) or inefficient manufacturing investment (Korea).

Inadequate fiscal management. Many countries had severe fiscal weaknesses. This included weak revenue collection (Argentina, Brazil, Indonesia, Russia), widespread tax evasion (Argentina, Russia), public wage and pension indexing (Argentina, Brazil, Mexico, Uruguay), monetary financing of fiscal deficits (Argentina, Brazil), and substantial use of energy and food subsidies (Egypt, Venezuela).

Risky composition of debt. Many of the crisis countries borrowed in foreign currency. They struggled to meet debt service obligations and faced steep jumps in debt ratios following currency depreciations (Indonesia, Mexico, Thailand). In Uruguay, for example, almost all public debt was denominated in U.S. dollars in the mid-1990s. Several countries relied on short-term borrowing and faced rollover difficulties when investor sentiment deteriorated (Indonesia, Korea, Philippines, Russia in the late 1990s). In Europe and Central Asia (ECA) in the 2000s, countries borrowed cross-border from nonresident lenders and faced a credit crunch once liquidity conditions tightened for global banks that were the source of this lending (Hungary, Kazakhstan in the late 2000s).

Balance sheet mismatches. A substantial number of currency and banking crises, and the majority of concurrent currency and banking crises, were associated with balance sheet mismatches (Indonesia, Malaysia, Mexico, and Russia in the late 1990s). Sovereign debt crises less frequently involved balance sheet mismatches, except when banking supervision was weak (Indonesia, Turkey in the 1990s).

Structural and institutional features

Poorly designed growth strategies. Many of the case studies of crises in the 1970s and early 1980s showed heavy state intervention through state-led industrialization, state-owned companies, and state-owned banks (Balassa 1982). Industrial policy in countries such as Argentina,

BOX 4.3 Debt and crises (*continued*)

Brazil, and Venezuela focused on import substitution industrialization, typically financed by external borrowing.

Lack of economic diversification. A number of the crisis countries had undiversified economies, which increased their vulnerability to terms of trade shocks. Several countries in Latin America and the Caribbean (LAC) and Sub-Saharan Africa (SSA), in particular, were heavily dependent on both oil and non-oil commodity exports (Bolivia, Niger, Nigeria, Paraguay, Uruguay in the 1970s and 1980s). When commodity prices fell in the 1980s, the profitability of (often state-owned) corporates in the resource sector, fiscal revenues, and export proceeds collapsed, which triggered financial crises.

Inadequate banking regulation. Poor banking regulation was a common feature in many case studies. Several SSA countries experienced banking crises in the 1980s primarily because of the failure of banks that were typically state-owned and subject to little oversight (Cameroon, Kenya, Niger, and Tanzania). In EAP, financial deregulation contributed to insufficient regulation and oversight of the financial sector in the second wave (Indonesia, Korea, Malaysia, Philippines, and Thailand). This resulted in growing weaknesses, including balance sheet mismatches, and excessive risk taking by corporates (see below). In several countries in ECA during the 2000s, cross-border lending was inadequately regulated by domestic regulators (Hungary and Kazakhstan).

Poor corporate governance. Among case studies of the 1980s and 1990s, poor corporate governance was a common shortcoming, notably in some East Asian countries (Indonesia, Korea, and Thailand). Along with poor bank regulation, this led to inefficient corporate investment, as banks lent to firms without rigorously evaluating their creditworthiness.

Political uncertainty. Many sovereign debt crises were associated with severe political uncertainty (Indonesia, Philippines, Turkey, Venezuela).

Triggers and resolution of crises

Triggers. The case studies suggest that crises were usually triggered by external shocks, although in a small number of countries domestic factors also played a role.

- *External macroeconomic shocks.* The most common trigger of crises was an external shock to the real economy. These included a sudden rise in global interest rates (LAC in the 1980s), a slowdown in global growth (ECA in the 2000s), a fall in

commodity prices for commodity exporting economies (LAC and SSA in the 1980s, Russia in the 1990s), and contagion from both global crises (2007-09 global financial crisis) and regional crises (East Asian financial and Russian crises in the 1990s), which generated sudden withdrawals of capital inflows.

- *Natural disasters and domestic shocks.* Natural disasters such as droughts were a major contributing factor to crises in some countries, typically smaller, less diversified economies (e.g. Bangladesh in the 1970s, Nepal in the 1980s, Zimbabwe in the 2000s).

- *Other domestic shocks.* In a small number of countries, crises were triggered, or exacerbated, by other domestic shocks. Typically, these were episodes of political turmoil (Turkey, Zimbabwe).

Crisis resolution. Many, though not all, crises were resolved by policy programs of adjustment and structural reform supported by financing from the IMF, World Bank, and other multilateral bodies and partner countries.

- *IMF support.* The vast majority of countries in these case studies adopted IMF-supported policy programs to overcome their crises. The countries that did not use IMF support typically had stronger fundamentals, including lower public debt and larger international reserves (e.g. Colombia, Kazakhstan, Malaysia).

- *Debt restructuring.* Among the case studies of sovereign debt crises, many ended with default and restructuring of debt (e.g. Argentina, Mexico, Nigeria). These cases were more common in the 1980s, 1990s, and early 2000s. Debt restructuring was often prolonged and occurred well after the initial sovereign debt crisis.

- *Reforms.* IMF support was conditional on the implementation of macroeconomic and structural reforms. For many EMDEs in LAC in the 1980s and in EAP in the late 1990s, crises were the trigger for policy changes to allow greater exchange rate flexibility and strengthen monetary policy regimes.

Conclusion

Crises are typically sparked by an adverse shock, such as an increase in global interest rates or a growth slowdown, whose impact is amplified and propagated via country vulnerabilities such as high levels of debt, especially short-term debt, and low international reserves. In line with the literature, the econometric exercise conducted here

BOX 4.3 Debt and crises (*continued*)

documents that a rapid rise in government or private debt increases the probability of crises. A combined runup in government and private debt—as has been the case during the fourth global wave—increases the probability of a currency crisis.

In several cases, crises revealed shortcomings that were mainly recognized *ex post* but had rarely been flagged before these crises. Following these crises, research (described in academic studies and policy reports) shifted its focus to these issues. For example, the Asian financial crisis propelled the challenges of balance sheet mismatches and weak corporate governance as well as the need for

robust bank supervision to the forefront of policy discussions (Brownbridge and Kirkpatrick 2000; IMF 1999). The launch of the Financial System Assessment Program in 1999 started systematic assessments of financial sectors (IMF 2000). The 2007-09 global financial crisis shifted an earlier consensus on the use of capital controls. Before 2008, capital controls were largely considered ineffective and detrimental (Forbes 2004, 2007). After the global financial crisis, the literature shifted to a guarded endorsement of capital controls is appropriately designed and implemented in the "right" circumstances (Forbes, Fratzscher, and Straub 2015; IMF 2012, 2015b).

Rapid debt accumulation episodes

Spurts in debt buildups are common in EMDEs. When they coincide in many EMDEs, they form the global waves of debt discussed above. This section examines the implications of national rapid debt accumulation episodes at the country level. It uses an event study approach that compares rapid debt accumulation episodes that coincided with a financial crisis (which might be a currency, banking, or sovereign debt crisis) with those that escaped a crisis. Box 4.3 analyses the factors which increase the likelihood of a financial crisis occurring, including quantifying the impact of a rise in debt.

Features of national rapid debt accumulation episodes

Definition of episodes. An episode of rapid debt accumulation is defined as a period during which the government debt-to-GDP ratio or the private sector debt-to-GDP ratio rises by more than one standard deviation from a trough to its next peak. This approach closely follows the dating of turning points of business cycles but the key results are robust to using a definition more closely aligned with the literature on credit booms (Claessens, Kose, and Terrones 2012; Mendoza and Terrones 2012; Annex 4.1). This approach results in 256

episodes of rapid *government* debt accumulation in 99 EMDEs since 1970, among a sample of 100 EMDEs with available data for 1970-2018. It also yields 263 episodes of rapid *private* debt accumulation in 100 EMDEs, out of a sample of 100 EMDEs with available data for 1970-2018.

Frequency of episodes. Debt accumulation episodes have been common (Figure 4.7). EMDEs in SAR, SSA, and LAC—the regions with the largest number of episodes per country—had, on average, about 3 government and 3 private debt accumulation episodes since 1970. Most episodes occurred in SSA (34 percent of all government and 33 percent of all private debt accumulation episodes), in part reflecting the large number of countries in the region.

Duration. The average duration—the time between trough and peak debt-to-GDP ratios—for both private and public episodes varied widely but amounted to 7 years for the median government episodes and 8 years for the median private episode. Most episodes had run their course in less than a decade. However, 21 percent of government episodes and 29 percent of private debt episodes lasted for more than a decade. The long duration of some of these episodes suggests that the debt buildup in part reflected financial development.

Amplitude. Although again with wide

heterogeneity among the episodes, the government debt buildup in the median government debt accumulation episode (30 percentage points of GDP from trough to peak) was double the private debt buildup in the median private debt accumulation episode (15 percentage points of GDP). Variation in the amplitude of debt accumulation episodes across countries was particularly wide for government debt accumulation episodes. In one-quarter of such episodes, the government debt buildup amounted to more than 50 percentage points of GDP. Debt accumulation on such a scale was rare for the private sector: in three-quarters of private debt accumulation episodes, private debt rose by less than 30 percentage points of GDP.

Combined government and private debt accumulation episodes. About 70 percent of government and private debt accumulation episodes overlap. These overlapping, combined government and private episodes, are statistically significantly shorter and more pronounced than solely-private or solely-government debt accumulation episodes (Annex Table 4.1.1).

Episodes coinciding with crises. Financial crises—defined as in Laeven and Valencia (2018)—can occur at any point during a debt accumulation episode, and more than one type of crisis can occur during an episode. Since 1970, based on all episodes that have concluded, more than half of government debt accumulation episodes and 40 percent of private debt accumulation episodes have been associated with crises (Figure 4.8). Crises were particularly common during the first and second waves. Most crises occurred well before the end of the debt accumulation episode (Annex 4.1). Crises were equally common in longer-lasting (such as those lasting a decade or more) and shorter episodes (lasting less than a decade).

Macroeconomic outcomes during national rapid debt accumulation episodes

The one-half of debt accumulation episodes that were associated with financial crises had considerably weaker macroeconomic outcomes than those that subsided without crises. The

FIGURE 4.7 Episodes of rapid debt accumulation in EMDEs

Episodes of rapid debt accumulation have been common among EMDEs, in both the government and private sectors. In the average year between 1970 and 2018, three-quarters of EMDEs were in either a government or a private debt accumulation episode or both. Since the early 2000s, the number of combined government and private debt accumulation episodes has increased. During 1970-2018, the median debt accumulation episode lasted 7-8 years. During rapid debt accumulation episodes, government debt typically rose (trough to peak) by 30 percentage points of GDP, and private debt by 15 percentage points of GDP.

A. EMDEs in rapid debt accumulation episodes

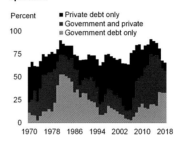

B. EMDEs in rapid debt accumulation episodes

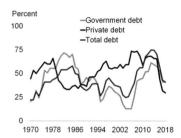

C. Rapid government debt accumulation episodes by region

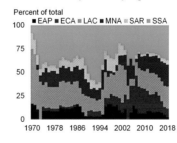

D. Rapid private debt accumulation episodes by region

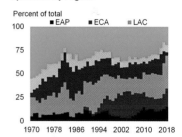

E. Duration of rapid debt accumulation episodes

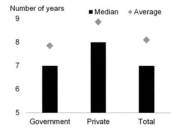

F. Change in debt during rapid accumulation episodes

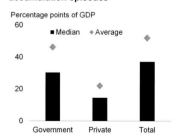

Source: International Monetary Fund; World Bank.
A.-D. Share of EMDEs in the sample that are in rapid debt accumulation episodes.

FIGURE 4.8 Crises during rapid debt accumulation episodes in EMDEs

About half of all episodes of government and private debt accumulation during 1970-2018 were associated with financial crises. Different types of crises often occurred at the same time. The number of crises has fallen since the first two waves of debt.

A. Government debt accumulation episodes associated with crises

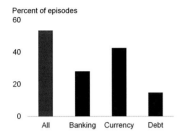

B. Private debt accumulation episodes associated with crises

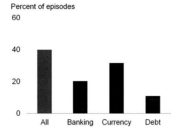

C. Crises in EMDEs

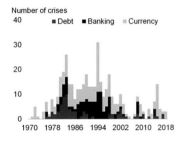

D. Crises during debt waves

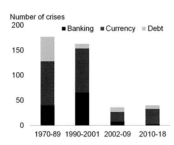

Source: International Monetary Fund; World Bank.
Note: Episodes associated with crises are those which experienced financial crises (banking, currency, and debt crises, as in Laeven and Valencia 2018) during or within two years after the end of episodes. For definition of episodes and sample, see Annex 4.1.

macroeconomic implications have tended to be worse when rapid debt growth stemmed from both the government and the private sector.[7]

Government debt accumulation episodes. Government debt accumulation episodes that involved crises were typically associated with greater debt buildups, weaker economic outcomes, and higher vulnerabilities than non-crisis episodes (Figure 4.9). In the episodes associated with financial crises, the government debt buildup was about 14 percentage points of GDP larger after eight years than in non-crisis episodes. After eight years, output and output per capita in episodes

---

[7] Combined government and private debt accumulation episodes were accompanied by significantly weaker investment and consumption growth than solely-private episodes. Excluding episodes associated with crises, combined episodes also featured slower overall growth than solely private debt accumulation episodes.

with crises were around 10 percent lower than in episodes without a crisis; investment was 22 percent lower; and consumption was 6 percent lower. External indicators—international reserves, external debt—deteriorated more in episodes associated with crisis than in non-crisis episodes as governments drew down reserves in an effort to stem depreciation.

Private debt accumulation episodes. After eight years, private debt accumulation episodes associated with crises featured weaker output and per capita income (by about 6 percent); consumption (by 8 percent); and investment (by 15 percent). Private debt accumulation episodes with crises also saw significantly more pronounced deteriorations in external positions—international reserves, external debt—than non-crisis episodes.

Similarities. Regardless of the borrowing sector, rapid debt accumulation episodes with crises featured considerably worse macroeconomic outcomes and vulnerabilities than those not associated with crises. Both types of debt accumulation episodes associated with crises saw larger falls in reserves and greater increases in external debt than non-crisis episodes. Fiscal and current account deficits widened in both types of episodes but more in government debt accumulation episodes than in private debt accumulation episodes.

Differences. *Government* debt accumulation episodes associated with crises tended to be more costly than *private* debt accumulation episodes associated with crises, with much larger shortfalls in output growth, especially in the early years after a crisis. Conversely, government debt accumulation episodes associated with crises featured much larger drops in investment than similar private debt accumulation episodes, possibly reflecting greater disruptions to financing conditions in crises during government debt accumulation episodes.

What comes next?

The current wave, not yet a decade old, has already included the euro area debt crisis and several EMDE currency crises. Although EMDEs have gone through periods of volatility during the current wave of debt, they have not yet experienced widespread financial crises. The key question is whether the current wave of debt accumulation will at some point end in financial crises in many EMDEs, as all its predecessors eventually did, or whether such crises will be avoided perhaps because EMDEs have learned and applied their lessons from the past.

Prolonged period of low interest rates. The current environment of low interest rates and persistently low inflation in advanced economies alleviates some risks associated with the latest wave of debt. Policy interest rates in many advanced economies are near historical lows after major central banks recently reverted to an easing stance after winding down tightening cycles in 2018 (Figure 4.10). Monetary policy in advanced economies is likely to be accommodative for the foreseeable future as growth prospects and inflation expectations remain subdued. Interest payments on government debt in EMDEs have fallen from an average of 2.6 percent of GDP in 2000-07, to 1.6 percent of GDP in 2010-18, despite the increase in debt over that period. At current nominal GDP growth and long-term interest rates, debt appears to be on stable or falling trajectories in almost half of EMDEs.

An easing of U.S. financial conditions, a bellwether for global financial conditions, has typically accompanied an increase in capital flows to EMDEs (Feyen et al. 2015). But increased borrowing can also raise vulnerability to a future rebound in interest rates. Historically, rising global interest rates have been a key trigger for financial crises (Bulow et al. 1992; Bulow and Rogoff 1989; Reinhart and Rogoff 2010, 2011). Hence, low or falling global interest rates provide no sure protection against financial crises for EMDEs. Half of all crises during episodes of rapid debt accumulation occurred in years when U.S. long-term (10-year) interest rates were falling and one-eighth of episodes occurred in years when U.S. long-term real interest rates were below 1 percent (as they have been since 2016).

Weak growth prospects. In addition to interest rates and fiscal positions, growth is another major determinant of debt sustainability. An important

FIGURE 4.9 Macroeconomic developments during debt accumulation episodes

Rapid debt accumulation episodes associated with financial crises show slower output, investment and consumption growth. Private debt accumulation episodes associated with crises also had lower international reserves and higher external debt than episodes without any crisis events.

A. Government episodes: Government debt

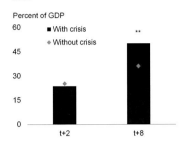

B. Private episodes: Private debt

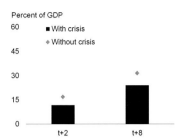

C. Government episodes: Output, investment and consumption

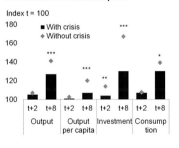

D. Private episodes: Output, investment and consumption

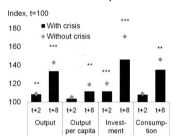

E. Government episodes: International reserves and external debt

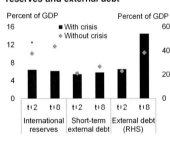

F. Private episodes: International reserves and external debt

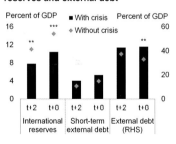

Source: Bruegel; International Monetary Fund; Laeven and Valencia (2018); World Bank.
Note: Median for episodes with data available for at least 8 years from the beginning of the episode. Year "t" refers to the beginning of rapid government debt accumulation episodes. Episodes associated with crises are those that experienced financial crises (banking, currency, and debt crises, as in Laeven and Valencia (2018)) during or within two years after the end of episodes. "*", "**", and "***" denote that medians between episodes associated with crises and those with no crises are statistically different at 10 percent, 5 percent, and 1 percent levels, respectively, based on Wilcoxon rank-sum tests.
A.B. Government (A) or private (B) debt in percent of GDP two and eight years after the beginning of the government debt accumulation episode (t).
C.D. Cumulative percent increase from t, based on real growth rates for output (GDP), output (GDP) per capita, investment, and consumption.
E.F. Series shown as percent of GDP.

FIGURE 4.10 **Fourth wave: Opportunities and risks**

The current environment of very low interest rates has alleviated immediate risks associated with the latest accumulation of debt since long-term interest rates are below growth in about half of EMDEs. However, while debt levels in advanced economies are on a sustainable path, debt levels in almost half of EMDEs are on a rising path. Although current levels of EMDE government or private debt are, on average, still below or near those in the median rapid debt accumulation episode, increases in government or private debt since 2010 have already exceeded those of the typical historical episode in about one-quarter of EMDEs.

A. Long-term interest rates

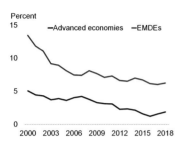

B. Share of economies with interest rates below growth

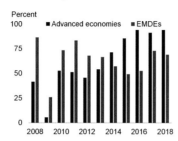

C. Sustainability gaps

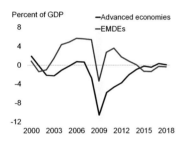

D. Countries with negative sustainability gaps

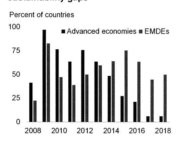

E. Current levels of government debt vs. previous rapid debt accumulation episodes

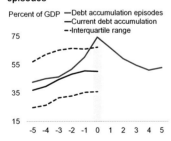

F. Current levels of private debt vs. previous rapid debt accumulation episodes

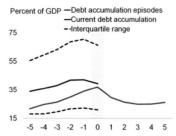

Source: Bloomberg; Kose et al. (2017); World Bank.
A. Average long-term nominal government bond yields (with maturity of 10 years) computed with current U.S. dollar GDP as a weight, based on up to 36 advanced economies and 84 EMDEs.
B. Share of countries where long-term nominal interest rates (represented by 10-year local currency government bond yields) are below nominal GDP growth for 1990-2018 in up to 34 advanced economies and 83 EMDEs.
C.D. A sustainability gap is defined as the difference between the actual primary balance and the debt-stabilizing balance. Averages computed with current U.S. dollar GDP as weights, based on at most 34 advanced economies and 83 EMDEs.
D. Share of economies in which sustainability gaps are negative (for example, debt is on a rising trajectory, or fiscal positions are debt-increasing). Sample includes 34 advanced economies and 83 EMDEs.
E.F. Median levels of debt during debt accumulation episodes, as defined in Annex 4.1. t=0 indicates the peak of debt accumulation episodes that were completed before 2018. For current debt accumulation, t=0 indicates 2018.

reason for rapid debt accumulation has been the sharp growth slowdown over the course of the fourth wave. EMDE growth slowed after 2020 to a trough of 4.1 percent in 2016 before a modest recovery took hold (Kose and Ohnsorge 2019). Current trends in fundamental drivers of growth suggest that it is likely to slow further over the next decade, to a pace about 0.5 percentage point lower than in 2013-17 (Ruch 2019; World Bank 2018a). For commodity-exporting EMDEs— almost two-thirds of EMDEs—prospects will be further dimmed by the expected slowdown in commodity demand growth as major commodity-consuming EMDEs slow and mature (World Bank 2018b). The past decade has been marked by repeated growth disappointments. If these persist into the next decade, they could lead to growing concerns about debt sustainability, even in a world of low interest rates.

Vulnerability to external shocks. The previous three waves highlight the risks associated with a sharp buildup of debt. Financial crises typically occurred when external shocks hit EMDEs with domestic vulnerabilities. Many EMDEs have improved their monetary and fiscal policy frameworks over the past two decades. However, elevated debt levels in the current wave of debt accumulation have been accompanied by rising fiscal, corporate and external vulnerabilities. These include lower international reserves and larger shares of EMDEs with current account and fiscal deficits.

There has been a significant change in the composition of debt in EMDEs. This shift could generate new vulnerabilities. Increasing issuance of foreign-currency-denominated corporate debt in EMDEs has contributed to rising currency exposures and heightened the risks of financial distress in the corporate sector and the banking system in the event of U.S. dollar appreciation.[8] In some EMDEs, the share of nonresident-held bonds in local currency bond markets has grown to more than 30 percent. In LICs, debt has been increasingly financed by non-concessional sources.

_____

[8] This appreciation could be triggered, for example, by reversals of capital flows to EMDEs on heightened global risk aversion.

Shocks could have several sources:

- Although it seems unlikely in the foreseeable future, a return to monetary policy normalization in advanced economies could raise borrowing cost. It would be likely to trigger U.S. dollar appreciation and a turn in investor sentiment that would, especially, affected those EMDEs with large foreign participation in local bond markets (Cerutti, Claessens, and Ratnovski 2017; Ruch 2019).

- A decade of tightening banking regulation has been accompanied by the emergence of credit risk and maturity mismatches in the non-bank financial system in advanced economies (Kose and Ohnsorge 2019). Financial stress in non-bank financial institutions could quickly propagate to the rest of the financial system, owing to the interconnectedness between nonbanks and banks. Growing linkages between non-bank financial systems in advanced economies and EMDEs have increased both the likelihood and the potential magnitude of spillovers from distress in advanced-economy nonbanks to EMDE bond markets and broader financial systems.

- Many commodity-exporting EMDEs rely heavily on revenues from the resource sector to find government expenditures and service sovereign debt (Correa and Sapriza 2014). As a result, commodity price shocks have periodically disrupted government finances and been a source of financial instability in EMDEs, culminating in some cases in sovereign debt default or other financial crises.

- The large corporate debt buildup in China has been primarily to domestic creditors. Its counterpart in the financial system could eventually reveal non-performing loans and result in a growth slowdown in China. Concerns remain that the rapid pace of investment growth may have contributed to overcapacity in some industries (Yu and Shen 2019; Wang, Wan and Song 2018; Maliszewski et al. 2016). Although it has recently declined, high corporate leverage in China, particularly that of state-owned enterprises, has been associated with a

deterioration of corporate financial performance, and many corporates are facing deteriorating profitability (Molnar and Lu 2019; World Bank 2018b, 2019a). In view of the size of China's economy, adverse spillovers to other EMDEs would be likely (Ahmed et al. 2019; World Bank 2016b).

- LICs have accumulated debt rapidly and increasingly from non-concessional and less transparent sources (Essl et al. 2019). This increases their vulnerability to financing shocks and to the revelation of previously undisclosed debt obligations (Bova et al. 2016; Horn, Reinhart, and Trebesch 2019; Lee and Bachmair 2019).

- For some EMDEs, risks related to climate change are substantial. The experience of several economies in LAC shows that debt crises can be triggered by natural disasters (Rasmussen 2004). To the extent that natural disasters are becoming more frequent and persistent as a result of climate change, they pose a growing risk to debt sustainability in vulnerable EMDEs. Furthermore, the move to a low-carbon economy could have a material effect for energy-exporting EMDEs. A shift away from the use of carbon-intensive fuels could leave the assets of fossil fuel companies, including state-owned companies, stranded by rules to curb climate change (Carney 2015). This could have critical implications for debt sustainability both at the firm and the country level.

Vulnerability to domestic shocks. Elevated debt increases an economy's vulnerability to domestic financing and political shocks even in an environment of benign global financing conditions. Domestic financing shocks can trigger sharp increases in borrowing cost. These may include the sudden emergence of contingent government liabilities, including in state-owned enterprises or public-private partnerships. Policy surprises or sudden bouts of policy uncertainty can also fuel investor concerns about debt repayment, causing a jump in borrowing cost.

Broader costs of debt accumulation. In addition to restricting economies' ability to weather shocks, high debt may also act as a constraint on growth of its own accord through three effects (Kose et al. 2019). First, high debt constrains governments' ability to respond to downturns. For example, fiscal stimulus during the 2008-09 global financial crisis was considerably smaller in countries with high government debt than in those with low government debt (World Bank 2015).

As well as limiting the use of fiscal policy, high government debt tends to render fiscal policy less effective (Huidrom et al. 2019). Second, high debt service costs may crowd out growth-enhancing public investment or social safety nets (Obstfeld 2013; Reinhart and Rogoff 2010; Romer and Romer 2018). Third, high debt could also create uncertainty about macroeconomic and policy prospects (IMF 2018a; Kumar and Woo 2010). This can crowd out productivity-enhancing private investment and weigh on output growth.

Seven lessons

The analysis of waves of global and national debt accumulation episodes yields several important lessons for EMDEs. Box 4.3 complements the lessons learned by considering 43 episodes of debt accumulation followed by financial crises in 34 EMDEs, and examining the similarities and differences between these case studies.

Accumulate debt with care. Borrowing, when well spent and sustainable, could support growth. Waves of broad-based debt accumulation have typically coincided with global upturns amid accommodative monetary policy and financial market development. However, about half of rapid debt accumulation episodes at the country level were associated with financial crises. Episodes of rapid government debt accumulation were more likely than episodes of rapid private debt accumulation to be associated with crisis, and were costlier than rapid buildups of private debt.

Use debt efficiently. The present combination of weak global growth and low interest rates makes government debt accumulation an appealing option for EMDEs to boost growth-friendly spending (World Bank 2019d). However, it is critical that the debt be used for productive

purposes to boost potential growth and exports, as painfully learned from the experience of the first wave. Crises were common in countries that borrowed heavily to finance state-led industrialization or real estate markets (e.g. Argentina and Brazil in the first wave, Thailand in the second wave).

Maintain a resilient debt composition. A debt composition tilted toward foreign currency-denominated, short-term, or nonresident-held debt makes countries more vulnerable to shifts in market sentiment, currency depreciation, or spikes in global interest rates and risk premia. Crises have been more likely when the share of short-term debt was higher. The first and second waves showed how a high share of foreign currency-denominated debt meant that currency depreciations led to an increase in both debt servicing costs and debt ratios.

Regulation and supervision matter. Inadequate regulatory and supervisory regimes, including gaps in coordination between home and host supervisors, can encourage excessively risky lending and debt buildup. This was the case in the Asian financial crisis during the second wave and in ECA countries during the third wave. Conversely, a robust regulatory system, that is also well coordinated between home and host supervisors of foreign banks, can temper the incentive to take excessive risks resulting from the public safety net for the financial system (moral hazard; Briault et al. 2018).

Beware of external shocks (especially when there are domestic vulnerabilities). Crises typically occurred when external shocks hit countries that had substantial domestic vulnerabilities, including a reliance on external and short-term debt in conjunction with a fixed exchange rate and low levels of international reserves (Bordo, Meissner, and Stuckler 2010; Mishkin 1999). In contrast, countries with higher international reserves were significantly more resilient to these types of shocks (Gourinchas and Obstfeld 2012). In addition to external shocks, domestic political shocks contributed to crises by increasing policy uncertainty and weakening investor sentiment.

Private debt can rapidly turn into government debt. Large private sector losses, including losses threatening bank solvency, and the materialization of contingent liabilities, including those of state-owned enterprises, can lead governments to provide substantial financial support (Mbaye, Moreno-Badia, and Chae 2018b). This occurred in the EAP region in the second wave, and in ECA in the third wave, with governments providing substantial support to banks. While the provision of government support can save the banking system from collapse, it can also lead to a steep jump in public debt which, in turn, can heighten the fragility of banks with large sovereign exposures (Bova et al. 2016; Claessens et al. 2014; Feyen and Zuccardi 2019; World Bank 2015). Fiscal space can shrink rapidly as a result even though fiscal deficits may have been moderate.

Develop effective mechanisms to recognize losses and restructure debt. Having mechanisms in place to promptly recognize and restructure debt can improve the prospects for recovery from crisis, particularly public debt crises (Kroszner 2003) or banking crises (Rutledge et al. 2012). The protracted resolution after the Latin American crises of the 1970s and the SSA debt distress in the 1980s and 1990s were associated with a period of very low, or even negative, per capita income growth. Growth only rebounded after the Brady plan and the HIPC and MDRI debt initiatives resolved debt distress and reduced debt overhangs.

Policy implications

Policy frameworks have improved in many EMDEs since the first two waves of debt. These improvements played a critical role in mitigating the adverse impact of the global financial crisis on these economies at the end of the third wave of debt accumulation. However, there is still considerable scope for further improvement. Specific policy priorities ultimately depend on country circumstances but there are four broad strands of policies that can help contain the risks associated with the recent debt accumulation.

Policies for managing debt

Governments need to put in place mechanisms and institutions that help them strike the proper balance between the benefits and costs of additional debt. These include sound debt management, high debt transparency, and thorough monitoring of contingent liabilities. While these policies mostly apply to borrowers, creditors also need to implement measures to mitigate risks associated with excessive debt accumulation.

Sound debt management can help reduce borrowing costs, enhance debt sustainability, and dampen fiscal risks.[9] Debt managers are increasingly adopting pro-active policies to build buffers and make the composition of debt more resilient, but further progress is needed (World Bank 2013). Prudent debt management favors debt contracted on terms that preserve macroeconomic and financial resilience—preferably at longer maturities, at fixed (and favorable) interest rates, and in local currency. A debt composition that is less vulnerable to market disruptions reduces the likelihood that a decline in market sentiment, sharp depreciations, or interest rate spikes erode debt sustainability. A well-developed and liquid domestic bond market can reduce the need for foreign currency-denominated lending and help ensure stability in government financing (Arvai and Heenan 2008; World Bank and IMF 2001).

Transparency about balance sheets is a pre-requisite for sound debt management. History shows that public debt spikes can reflect the revelation of previously undisclosed liabilities such as those revealed in Mozambique during the fourth wave (Jaramillo, Mulas-Granados, and Jalles 2017; Weber 2012). Greater fiscal transparency is associated with lower borrowing costs, improvements in government effectiveness and lower government debt (Kemoe and Zhan 2018; Montes, Bastos, and de Oliveira 2019). Improvements in data collection practices for LIC debt would help policymakers undertake better-informed borrowing decisions, and have been associated with lower borrowing costs (Cady and Pellechio 2006; World Bank and IMF 2018c).

---

[9] Recognizing the need for better debt management, the World Bank and IMF have developed guidelines, best practices, and frameworks to assist countries in implementing debt management strategies (World Bank and IMF 2014).

Principles and guidelines for debt transparency have been created, both by international financial institutions, including the IMF's fiscal transparency code, and by the private sector (IIF 2019a; IMF 2019d).

Monitoring and mitigation of contingent liabilities are integral for sound public debt management. Recent survey evidence suggests that a majority of public debt managers are *monitoring* risks of contingent liabilities; only a minority, however, use risk *mitigation* tools, such as reserve accounts (40 percent of respondents) or risk exposure limits on contingent liabilities (30 percent of respondents; Lee and Bachmair 2019).

Creditors, including international financial institutions, play an important role in mitigating the risks associated with debt accumulation. For example, while country authorities have the primary responsibility to transparently report their debt data, international financial institutions support transparency and sustainable lending practices through several measures. The IMF and the World Bank collect and disseminate debt statistics that are used by a wide range of stakeholders; produce published analyses of public debt data via debt sustainability analyses (DSAs); support countries' efforts to produce medium-term debt management strategies (MTDSs); publish information on countries' borrowing capacity; and directly liaise with multilateral, bilateral, and private creditors. All of these efforts provide important support to borrowers and lenders in their decision making.

Macroeconomic policies

Notwithstanding substantial improvements since the 1990s, macroeconomic policy frameworks can be strengthened further in many EMDEs (Kose and Ohnsorge 2019). Monetary policy frameworks and exchange rate regimes can be strengthened to increase central bank credibility. Fiscal frameworks can ensure that borrowing remains within sustainable limits and borrowed funds are used well.

Macroeconomic and exchange rate policy frameworks. The benefits of stability-oriented and resilient monetary policy frameworks cannot be overstated. During episodes of financial stress, when EMDE currencies tend to depreciate sharply, strong monetary policy frameworks will be helpful not least because the exchange rate pass-through to inflation tends to be smaller in countries with more credible, transparent and independent central banks; inflation-targeting monetary policy regimes; and better-anchored inflation expectations (Kose et al. 2019). With less pass-through from depreciation to inflation, central banks in EMDEs will have more scope to support activity. Flexible exchange rates can provide an effective mechanism for macroeconomic adjustment and can help avoid currency overvaluations and the buildup of large currency mismatches on balance sheets—a common precursor of crises. A flexible exchange rate regime requires, however, that monetary policy pursue a credible policy of inflation control to provide an effective nominal anchor to the economy. Such a policy framework needs to be complemented by strong macroeconomic and institutional arrangements.

Fiscal rules can help avoid fiscal slippages, ensure that revenue windfalls during times of strong growth are prudently managed, and manage and contain risks from contingent liabilities (Cebotari 2008; Currie and Velandia 2002; Romer and Romer 2019; Ulgenturk 2017). Strong fiscal frameworks have also been associated with lower inflation and inflation volatility, supporting the central bank in delivering its mandate (Ha, Kose, and Ohnsorge 2019). EMDEs have made important strides in the adoption and design of fiscal rules (Schaechter et al. 2012).[10] However, fiscal rules may only be effective once a certain degree of broader government effectiveness is achieved and sound budgetary institutions are in place.[11]

---

[10] Schaechter et al. (2012) create an overall fiscal rule index that captures both the number and characteristics of fiscal rules in operation in advanced economies and EMDEs and show how EMDEs have played catch-up to advanced economies since 2000. Ardanaz et al. (2019) find that well-designed fiscal rules can help safeguard public investment during downturns.

[11] Calderón and Nguyen (2016) estimate that fiscal and monetary policy procyclicality is greater in countries with weak institutions. Bergman and Hutchison (2015, 2018) show that fiscal rules are effective only when government effectiveness exceeds a minimum threshold. World Bank (2015) discusses the circumstances and features that can make fiscal rules more effective.

Alternatives to debt accumulation are available to expand fiscal resources for priority spending. Public spending can be reallocated to uses that are more likely to boost future growth, including education and health spending as well as climate-smart infrastructure investment to strengthen economic resilience. Government revenue bases can be broadened by removing special exemptions and strengthening tax administration (Gaspar, Ralyea, and Ture 2019; IMF 2019c; World Bank 2017b). Government can also take action to foster private sector-led growth. Reform agendas to improve business climates and institutions have resulted in significant gains in investment and productivity EMDEs (World Bank 2018a). In turn, increased private sector growth expands the revenue base and, ultimately, strengthens government revenues.

Financial sector policies

Robust financial sector regulation and supervision can help prevent risks from building up. Financial market deepening can help mobilize domestic savings that may provide more stable sources of financing than capital inflows.

Improved financial system regulation and supervision, by acting on systemic exposures and ensuring adequate capital buffers, can help prevent risks from building up. Robust prudential regulation and supervision can help pre-empt the buildup of systemic financial weaknesses. Macroprudential policies can help moderate lending to households and corporates. The use of living wills for banks and robust bank bankruptcy regimes can also help with the orderly winding down of insolvent institutions, including through the bail-in of creditors. Credibility and predictability of bank resolution can help prevent spillovers from the failure of one financial institution to others by reassuring creditors about the continued functioning of the financial system as a whole (Hoshi 2011).

Financial market deepening can help expand the pool of stable long-term domestic savings available for domestic investment. This requires an enabling environment of robust institutions, protection of creditor rights, sound regulatory quality and macroeconomic stability (Laeven 2014; Sahay et al. 2008). At the same time, however, excessively rapid growth in financial markets can generate financial stability risks. A careful balance between measures to promote financial market deepening and supervision and regulation is critical.

Strengthening institutions

Well-enforced frameworks for sound corporate governance can help ensure that funds borrowed by private corporates are well used. Sound bankruptcy frameworks can help prevent debt overhangs from weighing on investment for prolonged periods.

The promotion of good corporate governance can mitigate risks arising from the corporate sector. Stronger corporate governance can tilt firms' financing towards equity rather than debt (Mande, Park, and Son 2011); increase hedging of foreign currency positions to protect against external shocks (Lel 2012); and encourage more efficient firm operation (Henry 2010). Other measures can also help contain risks from corporate credit growth, such as increased stress testing of listed corporates' balance sheets.

Effective bankruptcy and insolvency regimes can help in the resolution of private debt crises and have benefits outside of crises (Leroy and Grandolini 2016). Several EMDEs have recently reformed bankruptcy procedures, but in general, EMDE bankruptcy protection laws lag international best practices.[12] Strengthening bankruptcy protection can boost investment and facilitate responsible corporate risk-taking, helping to relieve the costs of debt overhang (World Bank 2014b). Well-functioning legal, regulatory, and institutional frameworks are crucial for commercial banks and companies to resolve non-performing loans and facilitate business exit and reorganization (Menezes 2014). A robust insolvency regime can improve financial inclusion and increase access to credit, by reducing the cost of lending.

---

[12] These include the introduction of a new bankruptcy law in Egypt and strengthening of secured creditors' rights in India.

ANNEX FIGURE 4.1.1 Country examples of debt accumulation episodes

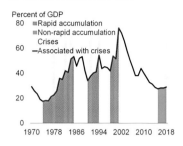

A. Turkey: Government debt

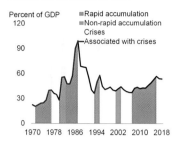

B. Mexico: Government debt

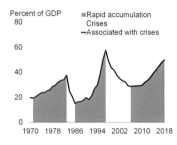

C. Philippines: Private debt

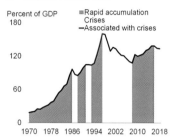

D. Malaysia: Private debt

Source: International Monetary Fund; World Bank.
Note: Blue line indicates debt outside debt accumulation episodes. A period of debt accumulation is identified with the algorithm in Harding and Pagan (2002). When a change in debt-to-GDP ratios over an accumulation period is above the maximum of 10-year moving standard deviation of the ratios during the period, it is considered as a rapid debt accumulation (shown as an orange area). When it is below the threshold, it is treated as a non-rapid accumulation (shown as a light blue area). If a crisis (i.e., banking, currency, or debt crisis) occurs during a rapid debt accumulation period or within two years since the end of the period, it is regarded as an episode of rapid debt accumulation associated with a crisis (shown as a red line). An ongoing episode (e.g., the third orange area in Panel C) is also classified as either rapid or non-rapid accumulation, based on the same methodology.

ANNEX 4.1 Event study methodology

Identifying episodes of rapid debt accumulation. The identification of episodes of rapid accumulation of government and private debt proceeds in two steps. First, the Harding and Pagan's (2002) algorithm is used to identify the cyclical turning points in the debt-to-GDP ratios. In particular, a debt cycle (from one peak debt-to-GDP ratio to the next peak debt-to-GDP ratio) is assumed to last at least five years with a minimum two-year duration of the contraction phase (from peak to trough) and the expansion (or accumulation) phase (from trough to peak).[1]

Second, an expansion phase is labeled as a rapid accumulation episode if an increase in debt-to-GDP ratio (from trough to peak) exceeds the maximum ten-year moving standard deviation (over the period t-9 to t) of the debt-to-GDP ratio during the phase (Figure A4.1.1).

In scaling debt by GDP, this approach implicitly focuses on the concept of debt burden, which captures the ability of borrowers to repay their debt.[2] An increase in the debt burden, as measured by the debt-to-GDP ratio used here, could reflect an output collapse, an exchange rate depreciation, or outright borrowing. Regardless of these underlying reasons, an increase in the debt burden makes it more challenging to service debt and makes the debt burden more likely to become a source of financial or economic stress.

In practice, output contractions are the source of increases in debt-to-GDP ratios only in a minority of episodes identified here (one-third of government debt episodes and two-fifths of private debt episodes). Currency crises are indeed associated with larger debt buildups during the debt accumulation episodes identified here, but these currency crises typically happen well before (two years before) debt peaks and the increase in debt during the year of the currency crisis only accounts for one-tenth (private debt episodes) to one-quarter (government debt episodes) of the total debt buildup during these debt accumulation episodes associated with currency crises.

Phases at the beginning and end of data series are also classified as either rapid or non-rapid accumulation, if they are on the expansion trajectory. While they are identified in the same way as in the other cases, the beginning and end of episodes are set when data availability of government and private debt begins and ends.

An episode of rapid debt accumulation is associated with a financial crisis if a crisis—banking, currency, or debt crisis—occurs during the period of rapid debt accumulation or at least within two years since the end of the episode. The

---

[1] This dating method is documented in Kose, Nagle, Ohnsorge, and Sugawara (2019).

[2] Debt buildup results from both demand and supply factors. Regardless of which of these predominates, a high debt-to-GDP ratio presents a vulnerability in the event of adverse shocks.

ANNEX TABLE 4.1.1 Comparison of combined government and private debt accumulation episodes with solely government or private debt accumulation episodes.

	Rapid accumulation with crises			Rapid accumulation without crises		
	Government debt	Private debt	Both (combined)	Government debt	Private debt	Both (combined)
Duration (years)	7	8	3	7	8	4
Amplitude (percentage points)	**42.6**	**13.1**	35.3	**21.6**	**14.8**	26.0
Growth (percent)	2.2	3.7	2.7	4.1	**4.6**	4.2
Per capita growth (percent)	**0.1**	1.9	0.9	2.0	**2.5**	2.0
Investment growth (percent)	1.9	**5.7**	2.2	6.3	**7.2**	6.1
Private consumption growth (percent)	2.5	**4.0**	2.9	4.1	**4.8**	4.2
Reserves (percent of GDP)	7.2	7.2	6.6	12.9	13.2	12.9
Short-term external debt (percent of GDP)	4.4	4.8	4.3	3.9	3.7	3.8

Note: Amplitude for "Both (combined)" is measured as an average of amplitudes of government debt and private debt during a combined part. Bold numbers indicate statistically significant difference from combined episodes.

information on crisis years is obtained from Laeven and Valencia (2018). The year coverage for currency crises is extended to 2018, by following the methodology in Laeven and Valencia (2018) using data on end-of-year exchange rates vis-à-vis U.S. dollars from the IMF. This association only describes the timing or coincidence between rapid accumulation of debt and financial crisis, and therefore does not imply any causal link between the two.

Sample. The sample includes data for 100 EMDEs for 1970-2018, while the identification of debt accumulation uses data prior to 1970 (see Kose et al. 2019 for details). Small states, as defined by the World Bank, are excluded. This results in 256 episodes of rapid *government debt* accumulation and 263 episodes of rapid *private debt* accumulation in a sample of 100 EMDEs with available data for 1970-2018.

ANNEX 4.2 Regression methodology

Discrete choice modelling. The most common estimation methods used in the empirical literature on predicting crises are logit and probit models. The baseline specification used in this study is a panel logit model with random effects, but for robustness purposes, a random effects probit model and a fixed effects logit model are

also used. The Hausman test suggests that the random effects model is appropriate for debt and banking crises but not for currency crises. However, even for currency crises, the coefficient estimates and their statistical significance remain similar in fixed effects and random effects models. To exploit the time and cross-sectional dimensions, a panel dataset of 139 EMDEs with annual data over the period 1970–2018 is constructed. The details of the methodology are described in Kose et al. (2019).

Selection of explanatory variables. The variables are chosen from a close examination of the empirical findings from the early warning crisis literature (see Chamon and Crowe 2012; Frankel and Saravelos 2012; and Kaminsky, Lizondo, and Reinhart 1998 for an extensive review). A large number of variables is included (with various data transformations, such as levels, growth rate, percentage point change, deviation from trend) that can be grouped into several categories:

- Debt profile: public and private debt (percent of GDP); short-term debt and concessional debt (in percent of total debt); debt service on external debt (in percent of exports).

- Capital account: international reserves (in months of imports), currency mismatch (foreign liabilities to foreign assets), net FDI inflows (in percent of GDP).

- Current account: exchange rate overvaluation (percent deviation from Hodrick Prescott-filtered trend).

- Foreign environment: U.S. interest rate (deflated by GDP deflator, in percent).

- Domestic environment: GDP growth (in percent).

- Banking sector: funding ratio (banking system credit to deposits);

To attenuate potential endogeneity bias caused by contemporaneous interaction between economic fundamentals and crises, lagged values of the explanatory variables are used, except for U.S. interest rate. Robustness checks using alternative model specifications as well as results for probabilities of twin and triplet crises are provided in Kose et al. (2019).

Probability of crises. The probability of crises occurring are evaluated at specific points of interest for illustration (while keeping all other variables at their average values). For details, see Kose et al. (2019).

ANNEX 4.3 Case studies

The in-depth literature review of Box 4.3 covered 43 crisis case studies for 30 EMDEs since 1970. While non-exhaustive, the case studies were chosen to: (i) be representative of debt accumulation episodes over the past fifty years; (ii) include the large EMDEs in major regional debt crises episodes; (iii) represent crises in low-income countries; and (iv) a sufficiently comprehensive literature to base an assessment on.

In the case of the in-depth literature review, the search covered all publicly available country reports and flagship publications of international financial institutions (Asian Development Bank, African Development Bank, European Bank for Reconstruction and Development, Inter-American Development Bank, International Monetary Fund, World Bank) and academic publications published during 1970-2018. Publications were found on the institutions' websites and, especially before 1997, in the EconLit database. The main sources are detailed in Kose et al. (2019).

References

Ahmed, S., R. Correa, D. A. Dias, N. Gornemann, J. Hoek, A. Jain, E. Liu, and A. Wong. 2019. "Global Spillovers of a China Hard Landing." International Finance Discussion Papers 1260, Federal Reserve Board of Governors, Washington, DC.

Altunbaş, Y., B. Gadanecz, and A. Kara. 2006. "The Evolution of Syndicated Loan Markets." *The Service Industries Journal* 26 (6): 689-707.

Anderson, P. R. D., A. C. Silva; A. Velandia-Rubiano. 2010. "Public Debt Management in Emerging Market Economies: Has This Time Been Different?" Policy Research Working Paper 5399, World Bank, Washington, DC.

Ardanaz, M., E. Cavallo, A., Izquierdo, and J. Puig. 2019. "Growth-Friendly Fiscal Rules? Protecting Public Investment from Budget Cuts Through Fiscal Rule Design." IDB Discussion Paper 698, Inter-American Development Bank, Washington, DC.

Arizala, F., M. Bellon, M. MacDonald, M. Mlachila, and M. Yenice. 2018. "Regional Spillovers in Sub-Saharan Africa: Exploring Different Channels." *Spillover Notes 18/01*, International Monetary Fund, Washington, DC.

Árvai, Z., and G. Heenan. 2008. "A Framework for Developing Secondary Markets for Government Securities." IMF Working Paper 8/174, International Monetary Fund, Washington, DC.

Aslund, A. 2010. *The Last Shall Be the First: The East European Financial Crisis.* Washington, DC: Peterson Institute for International Economics.

Baig, T., and I. Goldfajn. 1999. "Financial Market Contagion in the Asian Crisis." *IMF Staff Papers* 46 (2): 167-195.

Balakrishnan, R., S. Danninger, S. Elekdag, and I. Tytell. 2011. "The Transmission of Financial Stress from Advanced to Emerging Economies." *Emerging Markets Finance and Trade* 47 (2): 40-68.

Balassa, B. 1982. *Development Strategies in Semi-Industrial Economies.* Washington, DC: World Bank.

Beltran, D.O., and C. G. Collins. 2018. "How Culnerable are EME Corporates?" IFDP Notes K.7, Board of Governors of the Federal Reserve System, Washington, DC.

Berg, A., E. Borensztein, and C. Pattillo. 2005.

"Assessing Early Warning Systems: How Have They Worked in Practice?" *IMF Staff Papers* 52 (3): 462-502.

Berglöf, E., Y. Korniyenko, A. Plekhanov, and J. Zettelmeyer. 2009. "Understanding the Crisis in Emerging Europe." EBRD Working Paper 109, European Bank for Reconstruction and Development, London.

Bergman, U. M., and M. Hutchison. 2015. "Economic Stabilization in the Post-Crisis World: Are Fiscal Rules the Answer?" *Journal of International Money and Finance* 52 (April): 82-101.

———. 2018. "Fiscal Procyclicality in Developing Economies: The Role of Fiscal Rules, Institutions and Economic Conditions." Unpublished paper available at https://www.researchgate.net/ publication/325820923_Fiscal_Procyclicality_in_Dev eloping_Economics_The_Role_of_Fiscal_Rules_Institu tions_and_Economic_Conditions.

Bertola, L., and J. A. Ocampo. 2012. *The Economic Development of Latin America Since Independence.* Oxford: Oxford University Press.

BIS (Bank for International Settlements). 2015. "Debt." *BIS Papers* 80, Bank for International Settlements, Basel.

———. 2018. "Structural Changes in Banking After the Crisis." CGFS Papers 60, Committee on the Global Financial System, Bank for International Settlements, Basel.

Bordo, M., C. Meissner, and D. Stuckler. 2010. "Foreign Currency Debt, Financial Crises and Economic Growth: A Long-run View." *Journal of International Money and Finance* 29 (4): 642-665.

Borio, C. and P. Lowe. 2002. "Assessing the Risk of Banking Crises." *BIS Quarterly Review* 7 (1): 43-54.

Bova, E., M. Ruiz-Arranz, F. Toscani, and H. E. Ture. 2016. "The Fiscal Costs of Contingent Liabilities; A New Dataset." IMF Working Paper 16/14, International Monetary Fund, Washington, DC.

Briault, C., E. Feyen, I. Del Mazo, B. Yee, J. , Rademacher, and I. Skamnelos. 2018. *"Cross-border Spillover Effects of the G20 Financial Regulatory Reforms: Results from a Pilot Survey.* Washington, DC: World Bank.

Broner, F., G. Lorenzoni, and S. Schmukler. 2013. "Why Do Emerging Economies Borrow Short Term?" *Journal of the European Economic Association* 11 (1): 67–100.

Brownbridge, M., and C. Kirkpatrick. 2000. "Financial Regulation in Developing Countries." *The Journal of Development Studies* 31 (1): 1-24.

Brueggemann, A., M. Bussière, L. Chitu, J. Estefanía, S. Gallego Herrero, I. Garrido, C. Janssens, et al. 2018. "Strengthening the Global Financial Safety Net." Occasional Paper 207, European Central Bank, Frankfurt.

Brunnermeier, M., and L. Pedersen. 2009. "Market Liquidity and Funding Liquidity." *The Review of Financial Studies,* 22(6): 2201-38.

Bulow, J., and K. Rogoff. 1989. "A Constant Recontracting Model of Sovereign Debt." *Journal of Political Economy* 97 (1): 155-178.

Bulow, J., K. Rogoff, A. Bevilaqua, S. Collins, and M. Bruno. 1992. "Official Creditor Seniority and Burden-Sharing in the Former Soviet Bloc." *Brookings Papers on Economic Activity,* 1992(1): 195-234.

Cady, J., and A. Pellechio. 2006. "Sovereign Borrowing Cost and the IMF's Data Standards Initiatives." IMF Working Paper 06/78, International Monetary Fund, Washington, DC.

Calderón, C., R. Duncan, and K. Schmidt-Hebbel. 2016. "Do Good Institutions Promote Countercyclical Macroeconomic Policies?" *Oxford Bulletin of Economics and Statistics* 78 (5): 650-670.

Calderón, C., and H. Nguyen. 2016. "The Cyclical Nature of Fiscal Policy in Sub-Saharan Africa." *Journal of African Economies*, 25(4): 548-579.

Callaghy, T. 2002. "Innovation in the Sovereign Debt Regime: From the Paris Club to Enhanced HIPC and Beyond." Operations Evaluation Department, World Bank, Washington, DC.

Capulong, M.V., D. Edwards, D. Webb, and J. Zhuang. 2000. *An Analytic Framework of Corporate Governance and Finance. Corporate Governance and Finance in East Asia: A Study of Indonesia, Republic of Korea, Malaysia, Philippines, and Thailand.* Manila: Asian Development Bank.

Carney, M. 2015. "Breaking the Tragedy on the Horizon—Climate Change and Financial Stability." Speech at Lloyd's of London, September 29, London .

Cebotari, A. 2008. "Contingent Liabilities: Issues and Practice." IMF Working Paper 245, International Monetary Fund, Washington, DC.

Cecchetti, S., Mohanty, M., and Zampolli, F. 2011.

"The Real Effects of Debt." BIS Working Paper 352, Bank for International Settlements, Basel.

Cerutti, E., S. Claessens, and L. Laeven. 2017. "The Use and Effectiveness of Macroprudential Policies: New Evidence." *Journal of Financial Stability* 28 (February): 203–224.

Cerutti, E., S. Claessens, and L. Ratnovski. 2017. "Global Liquidity and Cross-border Bank Flows." *Economic Policy* 32 (89): 81–125.

Cerutti, E., and H. Zhou. 2017. "The Global Banking Network in the Aftermath of the Crisis: Is There Evidence of De-globalization?" IMF Working Paper 17/232, International Monetary Fund, Washington, DC.

———. 2018. "The Global Banking Network: What is Behind the Increasing Regionalization Trend?" IMF Working Paper 18/46, International Monetary Fund, Washington, DC.

Cetorelli, N., and L. S. Goldberg. 2011. "Global Banks and International Shock Transmission: Evidence from the Crisis." *IMF Economic Review* 59 (1): 41-76.

Chamon M., and C. Crowe. 2012. "Predictive Indicators of Crises." In *Handbook in Financial Globalization: The Evidence and Impact of Financial Globalization,* edited by G. Caprio, 499–505. London: Elsevier.

Claessens, S., and K. Forbes, eds. 2013. *International Financial Contagion.* Berlin: Springer.

Claessens, S., and M. A. Kose. 2018. "Frontiers of Macrofinancial Linkages." BIS Papers 95, Switzerland, Bank for International Settlements, Basel.

Claessens, S., M. A. Kose, L. Laeven, and F. Valencia. 2014. *Financial Crises: Causes, Consequences, and Policy Responses.* Washington, DC: International Monetary Fund.

Claessens, S., M. A. Kose, and M. Terrones. 2012. "How do Business and Financial Cycles Interact?" *Journal of International Economics* 87 (1): 178-90.

Claessens, S., C. Pazarbasioglu, L. Laeven, M. Dobbler, F. Valencia, O. Nedelescu, and K. Seal. 2014. "Crisis Management and Resolution: Early Lessons from the 2007-09 Financial Crisis." In *Financial Crises: Causes, Consequences, and Policy Responses*, edited by S. Claessens, M. A. Kose, L. Laeven, and F. Valencia. Washington, DC: International Monetary Fund.

Claessens, S., and N. van Horen. 2014. "Foreign

Banks: Trends and Impact." *Journal of Money, Credit and Banking* 46 (1): 295-326.

Cline, W. 1995. *International Debt Reexamined.* Washington, DC: Institute for International Economics.

Correa, R., and H. Sapriza. 2014. "Sovereign Debt Crises." International Finance Discussion Paper 1104, May, Board of Governors of the Federal Reserve System, Washington, DC.

Corsetti, G., P. Pesenti, and N. Roubini. 1998. "What Caused the Asian Financial Crisis? Part I: A Macroeconomic Overview." NBER Working Paper 6833, National Bureau of Economic Research, Cambridge, MA.

Cortina-Lorente, J. J., T. Didier, and S. L. Schmukler. 2016. "How Long is the Maturity of Corporate Borrowing? Evidence from Bond and Loan Issuances Across Markets." Policy Research Working Paper 7815, World Bank, Washington, DC.

Currie, E., and A. Velandia. 2002. "Risk Management of Contingent Liabilities Within a Sovereign Asset-Liability Framework." World Bank, Washington, DC.

Daseking C., and R. Powell. 1999. "From Toronto Terms to the HIPC Initiative: A Brief History of Debt Relief for Low-Income Countries." IMF Working Paper 99/142, International Monetary Fund, Washington, DC.

Daumont, R., F. Le Gall, and F. Leroux. 2004. "Banking in Sub-Saharan Africa: What Went Wrong?" IMF Working Paper 04/55, International Monetary Fund, Washington, DC.

Dawood, M., N. Horsewood, and F. Strobel. 2017. "Predicting Sovereign Debt Crises: An Early Warning System Approach." *Journal of Financial Stability* 28: 16-28.

Dell'Ariccia, G, D. Igan, L. Laeven, and H. Tong. 2014. "Policies for Macrofinancial Stability: Dealing with Credit Booms and Busts." In *Financial Crises: Causes, Consequences, and Policy Responses*, edited by S. Claessens, M.A. Kose, L. Laeven, and F. Valencia. Washington, DC: International Monetary Fund.

————. 2016. "Credit Booms and Macrofinancial Stability." *Economic Policy* 31 (86): 299–355.

Demirgüç-Kunt, A., and E. Detragiache. 1998. "The Determinants of Banking Crises in Developing and Developed Countries." *Staff Papers* 45 (1): 81-109.

Devlin, R. 1990. *Debt and Crisis in Latin America: The Supply Side of the Story.* Princeton, NJ: Princeton University Press.

Dicks, M. 1991. "The LDC Debt Crisis." *Bank of England Quarterly Bulletin* (Q4): 498-508.

Didier, T., C. Hevia, and S. Schmukler. 2012. "How Resilient and Countercyclical were Emerging Economies to the Global Crisis?" *Journal of International Money and Finance* 31 (8): 2052–2077.

Didier, T., M. A. Kose, F. Ohnsorge, and L. Ye. 2015. "Slowdown in Emerging Markets: Rough Patch or Prolonged Weakness?" Policy Research Note 4, World Bank, Washington, DC.

Dincer, N., and B. Eichengreen. 2014. "Central Bank Transparency and Independence: Updates and New Measures." *International Journal of Central Banking* 10 (1): 189-259.

Dollar, D. 2016. *China's Engagement with Africa: From Natural Resources to Human Resources.* Washington, DC: Brookings Institution.

Dornbusch, R., W. Branson, and W. Cline. 1985. "Policy and Performance Links between LDC Debtors and Industrial Nations." *Brookings Papers on Economic Activity* 1985 (2): 303–368.

Dornbusch, R., I. Goldfajn, R. Valdés, S. Edwards, and M. Bruno. 1995. "Currency Crises and Collapses." *Brookings Papers on Economic Activity* 1995 (2): 219-293.

Easterly, W. 2002. "How Did the Heavily Indebted Poor Countries Become Heavily Indebted? Reviewing Two Decades of Debt Relief." *World Development* 30 (10): 1677-1696.

Eberhardt, M., and A. F. Presbitero. 2015. "Public Debt and Growth: Heterogeneity and Non-linearity." *Journal of International Economics* 97 (1): 45-58.

Ehlers, T., S. Kong, and F. Zhu. 2018. "Mapping Shadow Banking in China: Structure and Dynamics." Working Paper 701, Bank for International Settlements, Basel.

Eichengreen, B., A. El-Ganainy, R. Esteves, and K. J. Mitchener. 2019. "Public Debt through the Ages." NBER Working Paper 25494, National Bureau of Economic Research, Cambridge, MA.

Eichengreen, B., K. Kletzer, and A. Mody. 2003. "Crisis Resolution: Next Steps." In *Brookings Trade*

Forum 2003, edited by S. M. Collins and D. Rodrik. Washington, DC: Brookings Institution.

Eichengreen, B., A. K. Rose, and C. Wyplosz. 1995. "Exchange Market Mayhem: The Antecedents and Aftermath of Speculative Attacks." *Economic Policy* 10 (21): 249-312.

Elekdag, S., and Y. Wu. 2013. "Rapid Credit Growth in Emerging Markets: Boon or Boom-Bust?" *Emerging Markets Finance and Trade* 49 (5): 45-62.

Essl, S., S. Kilic Celik, P. Kirby, and A. Proite. 2019. "Debt in Low-Income Countries: Evolution, Implications, Remedies." Policy Research Working Paper 8794, World Bank, Washington, DC.

Feyen, E., N. Fiess, I. Z. Huertas, and L. Lambert. 2017. "Which Emerging Markets and Developing Economies Face Corporate Balance Sheet Vulnerabilities? A Novel Monitoring Framework." Policy Research Working Paper 8198, World Bank, Washington, DC.

Feyen, E., S. Ghosh, K. Kibuuka, and S. Farazi. 2015. "Global Liquidity and External Bond Issuance in Emerging Markets and Developing Economies." Policy Research Working Paper 7373, World Bank, Washington, DC.

Feyen, E., and I. Gonzalez de Mazo. 2013. "European Bank Deleveraging and Global Credit Conditions: Implications of a Multi-Year Process on Long-Term Finance and Beyond." Policy Research Working Paper 6388, World Bank, Washington, DC.

Feyen, E., and I. Zuccardi. 2019. "The Sovereign-Bank Nexus in EMDEs: What Is It, Is It Rising, and What Are the Policy Implications?" Policy Research Working Paper 8950, World Bank, Washington, DC.

Forbes, K. J. 2004. "Capital Controls: Mud in the Wheels of Market Discipline." NBER Working Paper 10284, National Bureau of Economic Research, Cambridge, MA.

———. 2007. "The Microeconomic Evidence on Capital Controls: No Free Lunch." In *Capital Controls and Capital Flows in Emerging Economies: Policies, Practices and Consequences*, edited by S. Edwards, 171-202. Chicago: University of Chicago Press.

Forbes, K., M. Fratzscher, and R. Straub. 2015. "Capital-Flow Management Measures: What Are They Good For?" *Journal of International Economics* 96 (July): S76-S97.

Frankel, J. A., and A. K. Rose. 1996. "Currency Crashes in Emerging Markets: An Empirical Treatment." *Journal of International Economics* 41 (3-4): 351-366.

Frankel, J. A., and G. Saravelos. 2012. "Can Leading Indicators Assess Country Vulnerability? Evidence from the 2008-09 Global Financial Crisis." *Journal of International Economics* 87 (2): 216-231.

FSB (Financial Stability Board). 2017. *Assessment of Shadow Banking Activities, Risks and the Adequacy of Post-Crisis Policy Tools to Address Financial Stability Concerns.* Basel: Financial Stability Board.

———. 2018a. *Evaluation of the Effects of Financial Regulatory Reforms on Infrastructure Finance.* Basel: Financial Stability Board.

———. 2018b. *Global Shadow Banking Monitoring Report 2017.* Basel: Financial Stability Board.

———. 2018c. *Implementation and Effects of the G20 Financial Regulatory Reforms.* Basel: Financial Stability Board.

———. 2019. "Implementation of G20/FSB financial reforms in other areas: Summary of Key Findings Based on the 2018 FSB Implementation Monitoring Network (IMN) Survey." Financial Stability Board, Basel, Switzerland.

Furman, J., J. Stiglitz, B. Bosworth, and S. Radelet. 1998. "Economic Crises: Evidence and Insights from East Asia." *Brookings Papers on Economic Activity* 1998 (2): 1-135.

G-20 (Group of 20). 2013. "Long-Term Investment Financing for Growth and Development: Umbrella Paper."

G20 IFAWG. 2018. "Recent Development of Local Currency Bond Markets in Emerging Economies." Staff note, International Financial Architecture Working Group.

Gadanecz, B. 2004. "The Syndicated Loan Market: Structure, Development and Implications." *BIS Quarterly Review*, December, Bank for International Settlements, Basel.

Gaspar, V., J. Ralyea, and E. Ture. 2019. "High Debt Hampers Countries' Response to a Fast-Changing Global Economy." *IMFBlog; Insights & Analysis on Economics & Finance* (blog), April 10.

Glick, R., and A. K. Rose. 1999. "Contagion and Trade: Why are Currency Crises Regional?" *Journal of International Money and Finance* 18 (4): 603-617.

Gourinchas, P.-O., and M. Obstfeld. 2012. "Stories of the Twentieth Century for the Twenty-first," *American Economic Journal: Macroeconomics* 4 (1): 226-65.

Greene, J. 1989. "The External Debt Problem of Sub-Saharan Africa." *IMF Staff Papers* 36 (4): 836-874.

Ha, J., M. A. Kose, and F. Ohnsorge. 2019. *Inflation in Emerging and Developing Economies: Evolution, Drivers and Policies*. Washington, DC: World Bank.

Henry, D. 2010. Agency Costs, Ownership Structure and Corporate Governance Compliance: A Private Contracting Perspective. *Pacific-Basin Finance Journal* 18 (1): 24-46.

Horn, S., C. M. Reinhart, and C. Trebesch. 2019. "China's Overseas Lending." NBER Working Paper 26050, National Bureau of Economic Research, Cambridge, MA.

Hoshi, T. 2011. "Financial Regulation: Lessons from the Recent Financial Crises." *Journal of Economic Literature* 49 (1): 120-28.

Huidrom, R., M. A. Kose, J. J. Lim, and F. Ohnsorge. 2019. "Why Do Fiscal Multipliers Depend on Fiscal Positions?" *Journal of Monetary Economics*. Advance online publication. https://doi.org/10.1016/.

IMF (International Monetary Fund). 1999. *Report of the Managing Director to the Interim Committee on Progress in Strengthening the Architecture of the International Financial System*. Washington, DC: International Monetary Fund.

————. 2000. *Financial Sector Assessment Program (FSAP) A Review: Lessons from the Pilot and Issues Going Forward*. Washington, DC: International Monetary Fund.

————. 2006. "The Multilateral Debt Relief Initiative." Factsheet. International Monetary Fund, Washington, DC.

————. 2012. *The Liberalization and Management of Capital Flows—An Institutional View*. Washington, DC: International Monetary Fund.

————. 2014. *Global Financial Stability Report: Risk Taking, Liquidity, and Shadow Banking*. International Monetary Fund, Washington, DC.

————. 2015a. *Global Financial Stability Report:, Vulnerabilities, Legacies, and Policy Challenges - Risks Rotating to Emerging Markets*. International Monetary Fund, Washington, DC.

————. 2015b. *Pan-African Banks: Opportunities and Challenges for Cross-Border Oversight*. Washington, DC: International Monetary Fund.

————. 2016. *Analyzing and Managing Fiscal Risks—Best Practices*. Washington, DC: International Monetary Fund.

————. 2018a. *Fiscal Monitor: Capitalizing on Good Times*. April Washington, DC: International Monetary Fund.

————. 2018b. *Macroeconomic Developments and Prospects in Low-Income Developing Countries*. Washington, DC: International Monetary Fund.

————. 2018c. *Global Financial Stability Report. A Decade After the Global Financial Crisis: Are We Safer?* Washington, DC: International Monetary Fund.

————. 2019a. *Global Financial Stability Report. Lower for Longer*. October. Washington, DC: International Monetary Fund.

————. 2019b. *Global Financial Stability Report. Vulnerabilities in a Maturing Credit Cycle*. Washington, DC: International Monetary Fund.

————. 2019c. *Fiscal Monitor: Curbing Corruption*. April. Washington, DC: International Monetary Fund.

————. 2019d. "Fiscal Transparency Initiative: Integration of Natural Resource Management Issues." IMF Policy Paper, International Monetary Fund, Washington DC.

Impavido, G., H. Rudolph, and L. Ruggerone. 2013. "Bank Funding in Central, Eastern and South Eastern Europe Post Lehman: A 'New Normal'?" IMF Working Paper 13/148, International Monetary Fund, Washington, DC.

Jaramillo, L., C. Mulas-Granados, and J. T. Jalles. 2017. "Debt Spikes, Blind Spots, and Financial Stress." *International Journal of Finance & Economics* 22 (4): 421-437.

Jordà, Ò., M. Schularick, and A. M. Taylor. 2011. "Financial Crises, Credit Booms, and External Imbalances: 140 Years of Lessons." *IMF Economic Review* 59 (2): 340-378.

Kaminsky, G. L. 2008. "Crises and Sudden Stops: Evidence from International Bond and Syndicated-Loan Markets." *Monetary and Economic Studies* 26: 107-129.

Kaminsky, G. L., S. Lizondo, and C. M. Reinhart. 1998. "Leading Indicators of Currency Crises." *IMF Staff Papers* 45 (1): 1-48.

Kaminsky, G. L., and C. M. Reinhart. 1999. "The Twin Crises: The Causes of Banking and Balance-of-Payments Problems." *American Economic Review* 89 (3): 473-500.

Kaminsky, G. L., and C. M. Reinhart. 2000. "On Crises, Contagion, and Confusion." *Journal of International Economics* 51 (1): 145-168.

————. 2001. "Bank Lending and Contagion: Evidence from the Asian Crisis." In *Regional and Global Capital Flows: Macroeconomic Causes and Consequences*, edited by T. Ito and A. O. Krueger, 73-99. Chicago: University of Chicago Press.

Kaufman, R. R. 1989. "The Politics of Economic Adjustment Policy in Argentina, Brazil, and Mexico: Experiences in the 1980s and Challenges for the Future." *Policy Sciences* 22 (3): 395-413.

Kawai, M. 2002. "Exchange Rate Arrangements in East Asia: Lessons from the 1997-98 Currency Crisis." *Monetary and Economic Studies* 20 (S1): 167-204.

Kawai, M., R. Newfarmer, and S. Schmukler. 2005. "Crisis and Contagion in East Asia: Nine Lessons." *Eastern Economic Journal* 31 (2): 185-207.

Kemoe, L., and Z. Zhan. 2018. "Fiscal Transparency, Borrowing Costs, and Foreign Holdings of Sovereign Debt." IMF Working Paper 18/189, International Monetary Fund, Washington, DC.

Kindleberger, C. P., and R. Z. Aliber. 2011. *Manias, Panics and Crashes: A History of Financial Crises.* London: Palgrave Macmillan.

Kose, M. A., S. Kurlat, F. Ohnsorge, and N. Sugawara. 2017. "A Cross-Country Database of Fiscal Space." Policy Research Working Paper 8157, World Bank, Washington, DC.

Kose, M. A., H. Matsuoka, U. Panizza, and D. Vorisek. 2019. "Inflation Expectations: Review and Evidence." Policy Research Working Paper 8785, World Bank, Washington, DC.

Kose, M. A., P. Nagle, F. Ohnsorge, and N. Sugawara. 2019. *Global Waves of Debt: Causes and Consequences.* Washington, DC: World Bank.

Kose, M. A., and F. Ohnsorge, eds. 2019. *A Decade Since the Global Recession: Lessons and Challenges for Emerging and Developing Economies.* Washington, DC: World Bank.

Kose, M. A., and E. Prasad. 2010. *Emerging Markets: Resilience and Growth Amid Global Turmoil.* Washington, DC: Brookings Institution Press.

Kose, M. A., and M. E. Terrones. 2015. *Collapse and Revival: Understanding Global Recessions and Recoveries.* Washington, DC: International Monetary Fund.

Kroszner, R. S. 2003. "Sovereign Debt Restructuring." *American Economic Review* 93 (2): 75-79.

Krugman, P. 2000. *Currency Crises.* Chicago: University of Chicago Press.

Kumar, M., and J. Woo. 2010. "Public Debt and Growth." IMF Working Paper 174, International Monetary Fund, Washington, DC.

Laeven, L. 2014. "The Development of Local Capital Markets: Rationale and Challenges." IMF Working Paper 14/234, International Monetary Fund, Washington, DC.

Laeven, L., and F. Valencia. 2018. "Systemic Banking Crises Revisited." IMF Working Paper 18/206, International Monetary Fund, Washington, DC.

Lee, A., and F. Bachmair. 2019. "A Look Inside the Mind of Debt Managers: A Survey on Contingent Liabilities Risk Management." World Bank Treasury Public Debt Management, World Bank, Washington, DC.

Lel, U. 2012. "Currency Hedging and Corporate Governance: A Cross-country Analysis." *Journal of Corporate Finance* 18 (2): 221-237.

Leroy, A., and G. Grandolini. 2016. *Principles for Effective Insolvency and Creditor and Debtor Regimes.* Washington, DC: World Bank.

Loayza, N., P. Fajnzylber, and C. Calderón. 2005. "Economic Growth in Latin America and the Caribbean: Stylized Facts, Explanations, and Forecasts." Working Papers of the Central Bank of Chile 265, Central Bank of Chile.

Magud, N. E., C. M. Reinhart, and K. S. Rogoff. 2011. "Capital Controls: Myth and Reality—A Portfolio Balance Approach." NBER Working Paper 16805, National Bureau of Economic Research, Cambridge, MA.

Maliszewski, W., S. Arslanalp, J. Caparusso, J. Garrido, S. Guo, J. Kang, W. Lam, et al. 2016. "Resolving China's Corporate Debt Problem." IMF Working Paper 16/203, International Monetary Fund, Washington, DC.

Manasse, P., N. Roubini, and A. Schimmelpfennig. 2003. "Predicting Sovereign Debt Crises." IMF Working Paper 221, International Monetary Fund, Washington, DC.

Mande, V., Y. K. Park, and M. Son. 2012. Equity or Debt Financing: Does Good Corporate Governance Matter? *Corporate Governance: An International Review* 20 (2): 195-211.

Mbaye, S., M. Moreno-Badia, and K. Chae. 2018a. "Bailing Out the People? When Private Debt Becomes Public." IMF Working Paper 18/141, International Monetary Fund, Washington, DC.

————. 2018b. "Global Debt Database: Methodology and Sources." IMF Working Paper 18/111, International Monetary Fund, Washington, DC.

Mendoza, E. G., and M. E. Terrones. 2008. "An Anatomy of Credit Booms: Evidence from Macro Aggregates and Micro Data." NBER Working Paper 14049, National Bureau of Economic Research, Cambridge, MA.

————. 2012. "An Anatomy of Credit Booms and their Demise" NBER Working Paper 18379, National Bureau of Economic Research, Cambridge, MA.

Menezes, A. 2014. "Debt Resolution and Business Exit: Insolvency Reform for Credit, Entrepreneurship, and Growth." *Viewpoint; Public Policy for the Private Sector* series, No. 343, World Bank, Washington, DC.

Mishkin, F. 1999. "Global Financial Instability: Framework, Events, Issues." *Journal of Economic Perspectives* 13 (4): 3-20.

Molnar, M., and J. Lu. 2019. "State-owned Firms Behind China's Corporate Debt." OECD Economics Department Working Paper 1536, Organisation for Economic Co-operation and Development, Paris.

Montes, G. C., J. C. A. Bastos, and A. J. de Oliveira. 2019. "Fiscal Transparency, Government Effectiveness and Government Spending Efficiency: Some International Evidence Based on Panel Data Approach." *Economic Modelling* 79 (June): 211-225.

Moreno, R., G. Pasadilla, and E. Remolona. 1998. "Asia's Financial Crisis: Lessons and Policy Responses." Pacific Basin Working Paper Series 98-02, Federal Reserve Bank of San Francisco.

Obstfeld, M. 2013. "On Keeping Your Powder Dry: Fiscal Foundations of Financial and Price Stability." *Monetary and Economic Studies* 31 (November): 25–37.

Obstfeld, M., and Rogoff, K. 1986. "Ruling Out Divergent Speculative Bubbles." *Journal of Monetary Economics* 17 (3): 349-362.

OECD (Organisation for Economic Co-operation and Development). 2017. *OECD Economic Outlook.* November. Paris: Organisation for Economic Co-operation and Development.

Ohnsorge, F., and S. Yu. 2016. "Recent Credit Surge in Historical Context." Policy Research Working Paper 7704, World Bank, Washington, DC.

Ozatay, F., and G. Sak. 2002. "Banking Sector Fragility and Turkey's 2000-01 Financial Crisis." In *Brookings Trade Forum 2002*, edited by S. M. Collins and D. Rodrik. Washington, DC: Brookings Institution.

Panizza, U. 2008. "Domestic and External Public Debt in Developing Countries." United Nations Conference on Trade and Development Discussion Paper 188, New York.

Panizza, U., and A. F. Presbitero. 2014. "Public Debt and Economic Growth: Is There a Causal Effect?" *Journal of Macroeconomics* 41 (September): 21–41.

Pozsar, Z., T. Adrian, A. Ashcraft, and H. Boesky. 2010. "Shadow Banking." *FRBNY Economic Policy Review* 458: 3-9.

Rasmussen, M. 2004. *Macroeconomic implications of natural disasters in the Caribbean* (No. 4-224). International Monetary Fund.

Reinhart, C., V. Reinhart, and K. Rogoff. 2012. "Public Debt Overhangs: Advanced-Economy Episodes Since 1800." *Journal of Economic Perspectives* 26 (3): 69-86.

Reinhart, C. M., and K. S. Rogoff. 2010. "Growth in a Time of Debt." *American Economic Review* 100 (2): 573–578.

————. 2011. "From Financial Crash to Debt Crisis." *American Economic Review* 101 (5): 1676-1706.

Romer, C. D., and D. H. Romer. 2018. "Phillips Lecture—Why Some Times are Different: Macroeconomic Policy and the Aftermath of Financial Crises." *Economica* 85 (337): 1–40.

————. 2019. "Fiscal Space and the Aftermath of Financial Crises: How it Matters and Why." NBER Working Paper 25768, National Bureau of Economic Research, Cambridge, MA.

Rose, A. K., and M. M. Spiegel. 2012. "Dollar Illiquidity and Central Bank Swap Arrangements During the Global Financial Crisis." *Journal of International Economics* 88 (2): 326-340.

Roubini, N., and P. Wachtel. 1999. "Current-Account Sustainability in Transition Economies." In *Balance of Payments, Exchange Rates, and Competitiveness in Transition Economies*, edited by M. I. Blejer and M. Škreb. Boston: Kluwer Academic Publishers.

Ruch, F. U. 2019. "Prospects, Risks and Vulnerabilities." In *A Decade After the Global Recession: Lessons and Challenges for Emerging and Developing Economies,* edited by M. A. Kose and F. Ohnsorge. Washington, DC: World Bank.

Rutledge, V., M. Moore, M. Dobler, W. Bossu, N. Jassaud, and J. Zhou. 2012. "From Bail-Out to Bail-In: Mandatory Debt Restructuring of Systemic Financial Institutions." Staff Discussion Note 2012/03, International Monetary Fund, Washington, DC.

Sachs, J. 1985. "External Debt and Macroeconomic Performance in Latin America and East Asia." *Brookings Papers on Economic Activity* 1985 (2): 523-573.

———. 1989. "New Approaches to the Latin American Debt Crisis." In *Essays in International Finance* 174, Princeton University Press, Princeton, NJ.

Sachs, J., R. Cooper, and B. Bosworth. 1998. "The East Asian Financial Crisis: Diagnosis, Remedies, Prospects." *Brookings Papers on Economic Activity* 1998 (1): 1-90.

Sahay, R., M. Čihák, P. N'Diaye, A. Barajas, R. Bi, D. Ayala, Y. Gao, et al. 2008. "Rethinking Financial Deepening: Stability and Growth in Emerging Markets." Staff Discussion Note 5/08, International Monetary Fund, Washington, DC.

Schaechter, A., T. Kinda, N. T. Budina, and A. Weber. 2012. "Fiscal Rules in Response to the Crisis-Toward the 'Next-Generation' Rules: A New Dataset." IMF Working Paper 12/187, International Monetary Fund, Washington, DC.

Shin, H. 2014. "The Second Phase of Global Liquidity and Its Impact on Emerging Economies." In *Volatile Capital Flows in Korea: Current Policies and Future Responses,* edited by K. Chung, S. Kim, H. Park, C. Choi, and H. S. Shin, 247-257. London: Palgrave Macmillan.

Tornell, A., A. Velasco, and J. Sachs. 1996. "Financial Crises in Emerging Markets: The Lessons from 1995." *Brookings Papers on Economic Activity* 1996 (1): 147–215.

Tornell, A., and F. Westermann. 2005. *Boom-Bust Cycles and Financial Liberalization.* Cambridge, MA: MIT Press Books.

Turner, P. 2002. "Bond Markets in Emerging Economies: An Overview of Policy Issues." BIS Papers 11, Bank for International Settlements, Basel.

Ülgentürk, L. 2017. "The Role of Public Debt Managers in Contingent Liability Management." OECD Working Paper on Sovereign Borrowing and Public Debt Management 8, Organisation for Economic Co-operation and Development, Paris.

Unal, H., A. Demirgüç-Kunt, and K. Leung. 1993. "The Brady Plan, 1989 Mexican Debt-Reduction Agreement, and Bank Stock Returns in United States and Japan." *Journal of Money, Credit and Banking* 25 (3): 410-429.

Wang, D., K. Wan, and X. Song. 2018. "Quota Allocation of Coal Overcapacity Reduction Among Provinces in China." *Energy Policy* 116: 170-181.

Weber, A. 2012. "Stock-Flow Adjustments and Fiscal Transparency: A Cross-Country Comparison." IMF Working Paper 12/39, International Monetary Fund, Washington, DC.

World Bank. 2013. *Europe and Central Asia: Sovereign Debt Management in Crisis: A Toolkit for Policymakers.* Washington, DC: World Bank.

———. 2015. *Global Economic Prospects Report: Having Fiscal Space and Using It.* January. Washington, DC: World Bank.

———. 2016a. *Global Economic Prospects: Divergences and Risks.* June. Washington, DC: World Bank.

———. 2016b. *Global Economic Prospects: Spillovers Amid Weak Growth.* January. Washington, DC: World Bank.

———. 2017a. "Heavily Indebted Poor Countries (HIPC) Initiative and Multilateral Debt Relief Initiative (MDRI) - Statistical Update." World Bank, Washington, DC.

———. 2017b. *Tax Revenue Mobilization: Lessons from World Bank Group Support for Tax Reform.* Washington, DC: World Bank.

————. 2018a. *Global Economic Prospects: Broad-Based Upturn, but for How Long?* January. Washington, DC: World Bank.

————. 2018b. *Global Economic Prospects: The Turning of the Tide.* June. Washington, DC: World Bank.

————. 2019a. *Doing Business 2019: Training for Reform.* Washington, DC: World Bank.

————. 2019b. *MENA Economic Update: Reforms and External Imbalances: The Labor-Productivity Connection in the Middle East and North Africa.* Washington, DC: World Bank.

————. 2019c. *Global Financial Development Report 2019/2020: Bank Regulation and Supervision a Decade after the Global Financial Crisis.* Washington, DC: World Bank.

————. 2019d. *Global Economic Prospects: Heightened Tensions, Subdued Investment.* June. Washington, DC: World Bank.

World Bank and IMF (International Monetary Fund). 2001. *Developing Government Bond Markets: A Handbook.* Washington, DC: World Bank.

————. 2014. "Revised Guidelines for Public Debt Management." World Bank, Washington, DC.

————. 2018a. Debt Vulnerabilities in Emerging and Low-Income Economies. October 2018 Meeting of the Development Committee. Washington DC: World Bank.

————. 2018b. "G-20 Note: Improving Public Debt Recording, Monitoring and Reporting Capacity in Low and Lower Middle-Income Countries: Proposed Reforms." World Bank, Washington, DC.

Yu, B. and C. Shen. 2019. "Environmental Regulation and Industrial Capacity Utilization: An Empirical Study of China." *Journal of Cleaner Production.* Advance online publication. https://www.science direct.com/science/article/pii/S0959652619338569.

STATISTICAL
APPENDIX

Real GDP growth

	Annual estimates and forecasts[1] (Percent change)						Quarterly estimates[2] (Percent change, year-on-year)					
	2017	2018	2019e	2020f	2021f	2022f	18Q2	18Q3	18Q4	19Q1	19Q2	19Q3e
World	3.2	3.0	2.4	2.5	2.6	2.7	3.1	2.8	2.5	2.4	2.3	..
Advanced economies	2.4	2.2	1.6	1.4	1.5	1.5	2.4	2.0	1.7	1.8	1.6	1.7
United States	2.4	2.9	2.3	1.8	1.7	1.7	3.2	3.1	2.5	2.7	2.3	2.1
Euro Area	2.5	1.9	1.1	1.0	1.3	1.3	2.2	1.6	1.2	1.4	1.2	1.2
Japan	1.9	0.8	1.1	0.7	0.6	0.4	1.0	-0.3	-0.3	0.8	0.8	1.9
Emerging market and developing economies	4.5	4.3	3.5	4.1	4.3	4.4	4.5	4.3	4.0	3.6	3.6	..
East Asia and Pacific	6.5	6.3	5.8	5.7	5.6	5.6	6.4	6.2	6.1	6.1	5.9	5.7
Cambodia	7.0	7.5	7.0	6.8	6.8	6.8	..	..	..	..	..	..
China	6.8	6.6	6.1	5.9	5.8	5.7	6.7	6.5	6.4	6.4	6.2	6.0
Fiji	5.2	4.2	1.0	1.7	2.9	3.0	..	..	..	..	..	..
Indonesia	5.1	5.2	5.0	5.1	5.2	5.2	5.3	5.2	5.2	5.1	5.1	5.0
Lao PDR	6.9	6.3	5.2	5.8	5.7	5.6	..	..	..	..	..	..
Malaysia	5.7	4.7	4.6	4.5	4.5	4.5	4.5	4.4	4.7	4.5	4.9	4.4
Mongolia	5.3	7.2	5.7	5.5	5.2	5.5	5.3	4.5	9.1	8.6	6.2	4.2
Myanmar	6.8	6.5	6.6	6.7	6.8	6.8	..	..	..	..	..	..
Papua New Guinea	3.5	-0.8	5.6	2.9	2.9	3.0	..	..	..	..	..	..
Philippines	6.7	6.2	5.8	6.1	6.2	6.2	6.2	6.0	6.3	5.6	5.5	6.2
Solomon Islands	3.0	3.5	2.9	2.8	2.8	2.7	..	..	..	..	..	..
Thailand	4.0	4.1	2.5	2.7	2.8	2.9	4.7	3.2	3.6	2.8	2.3	2.4
Timor-Leste	-3.5	-1.1	4.2	4.6	4.9	5.0	..	..	..	..	..	..
Vietnam	6.8	7.1	6.8	6.5	6.5	6.4	6.7	6.8	7.3	6.8	6.7	7.3
Europe and Central Asia	4.1	3.2	2.0	2.6	2.9	2.9	3.9	3.0	1.8	1.1	1.3	..
Albania	3.8	4.1	2.9	3.4	3.6	3.5	4.3	4.7	3.3	2.4	2.3	..
Armenia	7.5	5.2	6.9	5.1	5.2	5.2	..	..	..	..	..	..
Azerbaijan	-0.3	1.4	2.5	2.3	2.1	2.1	..	..	..	..	..	..
Belarus	2.5	3.0	1.0	0.9	0.5	0.5	3.9	2.2	1.3	1.3	0.5	..
Bosnia and Herzegovina	3.2	3.6	3.1	3.4	3.9	3.9	3.9	3.1	3.9	2.8	2.6	..
Bulgaria	3.5	3.1	3.6	3.0	3.1	3.1	3.0	3.3	3.0	4.5	3.8	3.1
Croatia	3.1	2.7	2.9	2.6	2.4	2.4	3.2	3.0	2.2	4.1	2.4	2.9
Georgia	4.8	4.8	5.2	4.3	4.5	4.5	5.4	3.6	5.1	5.0	4.6	5.8
Hungary	4.3	5.1	4.9	3.0	2.6	2.6	5.0	5.3	5.3	5.3	4.9	5.0
Kazakhstan	4.1	4.1	4.0	3.7	3.9	3.7	4.3	3.9	4.1	3.8	4.4	..
Kosovo	4.2	3.8	4.0	4.2	4.1	4.0	..	..	..	..	..	..
Kyrgyz Republic	4.7	3.5	4.2	4.0	4.0	4.2	..	..	..	..	..	..
Moldova	4.7	4.0	3.6	3.6	3.8	3.8	5.3	3.3	3.8	4.4	5.8	4.3
Montenegro[5]	4.7	5.1	3.0	3.1	2.8	3.2	..	..	..	..	..	..
North Macedonia	0.2	2.9	3.1	3.2	3.3	3.1	1.7	2.4	6.2	3.9	3.4	3.6
Poland	4.9	5.1	4.3	3.6	3.3	3.1	5.4	5.5	4.4	4.6	4.1	4.1
Romania	7.1	4.0	3.9	3.4	3.1	3.1	3.8	4.0	4.2	5.0	4.4	3.0
Russia	1.6	2.3	1.2	1.6	1.8	1.8	2.2	2.2	2.7	0.5	0.9	1.7
Serbia	2.0	4.4	3.3	3.9	4.0	4.0	5.0	4.2	3.5	2.7	2.9	4.8
Tajikistan	7.1	7.3	6.2	5.5	5.0	5.0	..	..	..	..	..	..
Turkey	7.5	2.8	0.0	3.0	4.0	4.0	5.6	2.3	-2.8	-2.3	-1.6	0.9
Turkmenistan	6.5	6.2	5.0	5.2	5.5	5.5	..	..	..	..	..	..
Ukraine	2.5	3.3	3.6	3.7	4.2	4.2	3.8	2.8	3.5	2.5	4.6	4.1
Uzbekistan	4.5	5.1	5.5	5.7	6.0	6.0	..	..	..	..	..	..

Real GDP growth *(continued)*

	Annual estimates and forecasts[1] (Percent change)						Quarterly estimates[2] (Percent change, year-on-year)					
	2017	2018	2019e	2020f	2021f	2022f	18Q2	18Q3	18Q4	19Q1	19Q2	19Q3e
Latin America and the Caribbean	1.9	1.7	0.8	1.8	2.4	2.6	1.8	1.6	1.1	0.6	0.7	..
Argentina	2.7	-2.5	-3.1	-1.3	1.4	2.3	-3.8	-3.6	-6.1	-5.8	0.0	-1.7
Belize	1.9	2.1	2.7	2.1	1.8	1.8	..	..	..	..	..	..
Bolivia	4.2	4.2	2.2	3.0	3.2	3.4	4.8	4.0	3.3	3.4	2.8	..
Brazil	1.3	1.3	1.1	2.0	2.5	2.4	1.1	1.5	1.2	0.6	1.1	1.2
Chile	1.3	4.0	1.3	2.5	3.0	3.0	5.3	2.6	3.6	1.5	1.9	3.3
Colombia	1.4	2.6	3.3	3.6	3.9	3.9	2.9	2.6	2.7	3.2	3.0	3.3
Costa Rica	3.4	2.6	2.0	2.5	3.0	3.2	3.8	2.6	1.3	2.2	0.6	..
Dominican Republic	4.7	7.0	5.3	5.0	5.0	5.0	7.3	7.6	6.3	5.6	3.7	..
Ecuador	2.4	1.4	-0.3	0.2	0.8	1.2	1.4	1.5	0.8	0.6	0.3	..
El Salvador	2.3	2.5	2.4	2.5	2.5	2.5	2.9	2.2	2.2	2.5	1.8	..
Grenada	4.4	4.2	3.5	2.9	2.9	3.2	..	..	..	..	..	..
Guatemala	2.8	3.1	3.4	3.0	3.2	3.2	3.6	3.6	3.5	3.1	3.5	..
Guyana	2.1	4.1	4.5	86.7	10.5	14.6	..	..	..	..	..	..
Haiti[3]	1.2	1.5	-0.9	-1.4	-0.5	1.4	..	..	..	..	..	..
Honduras	4.8	3.7	3.3	3.5	3.5	3.5	4.0	3.3	4.5	2.8	1.7	2.6
Jamaica[2]	1.0	1.9	1.0	1.1	1.2	2.0	2.2	1.9	2.0	1.8	1.3	..
Mexico	2.1	2.1	0.0	1.2	1.8	2.3	3.0	2.5	1.4	1.2	-0.9	-0.3
Nicaragua	4.7	-3.8	-5.0	-0.5	0.6	1.0	-5.2	-4.4	-7.7	..	..	..
Panama	5.6	3.7	3.5	4.2	4.6	4.8	3.0	3.3	4.2	3.1	2.9	2.7
Paraguay	5.0	3.7	0.7	3.1	3.9	3.8	6.9	1.6	1.0	-2.1	-3.0	..
Peru	2.5	4.0	2.6	3.2	3.5	3.6	5.4	2.5	4.8	2.4	1.2	3.0
St. Lucia	2.6	0.9	1.8	3.2	3.0	2.4	..	..	..	..	..	..
St. Vincent and the Grenadines	1.0	2.2	2.3	2.3	2.3	2.3	..	..	..	..	..	..
Suriname	1.8	2.6	2.2	2.5	2.1	2.1	..	..	..	..	..	..
Uruguay	2.6	1.6	0.5	2.5	3.5	3.2	2.2	1.8	0.6	-0.5	0.0	0.9
Middle East and North Africa	1.1	0.8	0.1	2.4	2.7	2.8	2.4	2.8	3.5	2.4	1.7	..
Algeria	1.3	1.4	1.3	1.9	2.2	2.2	..	..	..	..	..	..
Bahrain	3.8	2.2	2.0	2.1	2.4	2.4	2.1	1.9	5.3	2.6	0.8	..
Djibouti	5.1	5.5	7.2	7.5	8.0	8.4	..	..	..	..	..	..
Egypt[3]	4.2	5.3	5.6	5.8	6.0	6.0	5.4	5.3	5.5	5.6	5.7	5.6
Iran	3.8	-4.9	-8.7	0.0	1.0	1.0	2.5	..	..	..	..	..
Iraq	-2.5	-0.6	4.8	5.1	2.7	2.5	..	..	..	..	..	..
Jordan	2.1	1.9	2.0	2.2	2.4	2.5	..	..	..	..	..	..
Kuwait	-3.5	1.2	0.4	2.2	2.0	2.0	0.6	2.7	2.0	0.9	0.4	..
Lebanon	0.6	0.2	-0.2	0.3	0.4	0.5	..	..	..	..	..	..
Morocco	4.2	3.0	2.7	3.5	3.6	3.8	..	..	..	..	..	..
Oman	0.3	1.8	0.0	3.7	4.3	4.3	..	..	..	..	..	..
Qatar	1.6	1.5	0.5	1.5	3.2	3.2	1.9	1.5	0.5	0.8	-1.4	..
Saudi Arabia	-0.7	2.4	0.4	1.9	2.2	2.4	1.6	2.4	4.3	1.7	0.5	..
Tunisia	1.8	2.5	1.6	2.2	2.6	2.6	..	..	..	..	..	..
United Arab Emirates	0.5	1.7	1.8	2.6	3.0	3.0	..	..	..	..	..	..
West Bank and Gaza	3.1	0.9	0.5	2.5	2.6	2.7	..	..	..	..	..	..

Real GDP growth *(continued)*

	Annual estimates and forecasts[1] *(Percent change)*						Quarterly estimates[2] *(Percent change, year-on-year)*					
	2017	2018	2019e	2020f	2021f	2022f	18Q2	18Q3	18Q4	19Q1	19Q2	19Q3e
South Asia	6.7	7.1	4.9	5.5	5.9	6.0	7.8	6.9	6.4	5.8	4.9	4.5
Afghanistan	2.7	1.8	2.5	3.0	3.5	3.5	..	..	..	..	..	..
Bangladesh[3,4]	7.3	7.9	8.1	7.2	7.3	7.3	..	..	..	..	..	..
Bhutan[3,4]	6.3	3.8	3.9	5.6	7.6	6.2	..	..	..	..	..	..
India[3,4]	7.2	6.8	5.0	5.8	6.1	6.1	8.0	7.0	6.6	5.8	5.0	4.5
Maldives	6.9	6.7	5.2	5.5	5.6	5.6	..	..	..	..	..	..
Nepal[3,4]	8.2	6.7	7.1	6.4	6.5	6.6	..	..	..	..	..	..
Pakistan[3,4]	5.2	5.5	3.3	2.4	3.0	3.9	..	..	..	..	..	..
Sri Lanka	3.4	3.2	2.7	3.3	3.7	3.7	3.9	3.5	1.8	3.7	1.5	2.7
Sub-Saharan Africa	2.7	2.6	2.4	2.9	3.1	3.3	2.0	2.7	2.8	2.2	2.5	..
Angola	-0.1	-1.2	-0.7	1.5	2.4	3.0	..	..	..	..	..	..
Benin	5.8	6.7	6.4	6.7	6.7	6.7	..	..	..	..	..	..
Botswana	2.9	4.5	4.0	4.1	4.2	4.2	5.3	4.1	4.2	4.3	3.1	3.1
Burkina Faso	6.3	6.8	6.0	6.0	6.0	6.0	..	..	..	..	..	..
Burundi	0.5	1.6	1.8	2.0	2.1	2.2	..	..	..	..	..	..
Cabo Verde	3.7	5.1	5.0	5.0	5.0	5.0	..	..	..	..	..	..
Cameroon	3.5	4.1	4.0	4.2	4.3	4.5	..	..	..	..	..	..
Chad	-3.0	2.6	3.0	5.5	4.8	4.8	..	..	..	..	..	..
Comoros	3.8	3.4	1.7	4.8	3.7	3.6	..	..	..	..	..	..
Congo, Dem. Rep.	3.7	5.8	4.3	3.9	3.4	3.6	..	..	..	..	..	..
Congo, Rep.	-1.8	1.6	2.2	4.6	1.9	2.4	..	..	..	..	..	..
Côte d'Ivoire	7.7	7.4	7.3	7.0	7.1	7.1	..	..	..	..	..	..
Equatorial Guinea	-4.7	-6.1	-4.3	-2.3	1.0	-4.8	..	..	..	..	..	..
Eswatini	2.0	2.4	1.3	2.6	2.5	2.5	..	..	..	..	..	..
Ethiopia[3]	10.0	7.9	9.0	6.3	6.4	7.1	..	..	..	..	..	..
Gabon	0.5	0.8	2.9	3.0	3.2	3.3	..	..	..	..	..	..
Gambia, The	4.8	6.6	6.0	6.3	5.8	5.5	..	..	..	..	..	..
Ghana	8.1	6.3	7.0	6.8	5.2	4.6	5.4	7.4	6.8	6.7	5.7	5.6
Guinea	10.0	5.8	5.9	6.0	6.0	6.0	..	..	..	..	..	..
Guinea-Bissau	5.9	3.8	4.6	4.9	5.0	5.0	..	..	..	..	..	..
Kenya	4.9	6.3	5.8	6.0	5.8	5.8	6.4	6.4	5.9	5.6	5.6	..
Lesotho	-0.4	1.5	2.6	0.7	2.1	2.8	0.2	-3.1	3.0	-1.4	1.2	..
Liberia	2.5	1.2	-1.4	1.4	3.4	4.2	..	..	..	..	..	..
Madagascar	4.3	5.1	4.7	5.3	4.4	5.0	..	..	..	..	..	..
Malawi	4.0	3.5	4.4	4.8	5.2	5.3	..	..	..	..	..	..
Mali	5.3	4.7	5.0	5.0	4.9	4.9	..	..	..	..	..	..
Mauritania	3.0	3.6	6.4	5.7	5.8	8.7	..	..	..	..	..	..
Mauritius	3.8	3.8	3.9	3.9	4.0	4.0	..	..	..	..	..	..
Mozambique	3.7	3.4	2.0	3.7	4.2	4.4	..	..	..	..	..	..
Namibia	-0.9	-0.1	-0.5	0.9	1.7	1.9	..	..	..	..	..	..
Niger	4.9	6.5	6.3	6.0	5.6	11.9	..	..	..	..	..	..
Nigeria	0.8	1.9	2.0	2.1	2.1	2.1	1.5	1.8	2.4	2.1	2.1	2.1
Rwanda	6.1	8.6	8.5	8.1	8.0	8.0	..	..	..	..	..	..
Senegal	7.1	6.8	6.3	6.8	7.0	7.0	..	..	..	..	..	..
Seychelles	4.3	4.1	3.5	3.3	3.3	3.4	..	..	..	..	..	..
Sierra Leone	3.8	3.5	4.8	4.9	4.9	5.0	..	..	..	..	..	..

Real GDP growth *(continued)*

	Annual estimates and forecasts[1] (Percent change)						Quarterly estimates[2] (Percent change, year-on-year)					
	2017	2018	2019e	2020f	2021f	2022f	18Q2	18Q3	18Q4	19Q1	19Q2	19Q3e
Sub-Saharan Africa (continued)												
South Africa	1.4	0.8	0.4	0.9	1.3	1.5	0.1	1.3	1.1	0.0	0.9	0.1
Sudan	4.3	-2.3	-2.6	-1.4	-0.6	0.2	..	..	..	..	..	..
Tanzania	6.8	5.4	5.6	5.8	6.1	6.2	6.1	7.1	7.1	6.5	7.2	..
Togo	4.4	4.9	5.3	5.5	5.5	5.5	..	..	..	..	..	..
Uganda[3]	3.9	5.9	6.1	6.5	5.9	6.0	5.0	6.5	6.8	5.6	5.4	..
Zambia	4.1	3.1	1.8	2.6	2.6	4.0	4.7	6.0	2.5	2.3	2.2	..
Zimbabwe	4.7	3.5	-7.5	2.7	2.5	2.8	..	..	..	..	..	..

World Bank and Haver Analytics.

Note: e = estimate; f = forecast.

1. Aggregate growth rates calculated using GDP weights at 2010 prices and market exchange rates.

2. Quarterly estimates are based on non-seasonally-adjusted real GDP, except for advanced economies, as well as Ecuador and Poland. Data for Bosnia and Herzegovina are from the production approach. Quarterly data for Jamaica are gross value added.

Regional averages are calculated based on data from following countries.

East Asia and Pacific: China, Indonesia, Malaysia, Mongolia, Philippines, Thailand, and Vietnam.

Europe and Central Asia: Albania, Belarus, Bosnia and Herzegovina, Bulgaria, Croatia, Georgia, Hungary, Kazakhstan, North Macedonia, Poland, Romania, Russia, Serbia, Turkey, and Ukraine.

Latin America and the Caribbean: Argentina, Bolivia, Brazil, Chile, Colombia, Costa Rica, Dominican Republic, Ecuador, El Salvador, Guatemala, Honduras, Jamaica, Mexico, Nicaragua, Panama, Paraguay, Peru, and Uruguay.

Middle East and North Africa: Bahrain, Egypt, Iran, Kuwait, Qatar, and Saudi Arabia.

South Asia: India and Sri Lanka.

Sub-Saharan Africa: Botswana, Ghana, Kenya, Nigeria, South Africa, Tanzania, Uganda, and Zambia.

3. Annual GDP is on fiscal year basis, as per reporting practice in the country.

4. GDP data for Pakistan are based on factor cost. For Bangladesh, Bhutan, Nepal, and Pakistan, the column labeled 2019 refers to FY2018/19. For India, the column labeled 2018 refers to FY2018/19.

5. Quarterly data are preliminary.

To download the data in this table, please visit www.worldbank.org/gep.

Data and Forecast Conventions

The macroeconomic forecasts presented in this report are prepared by staff of the Prospects Group of the Development Economics Vice-Presidency, in coordination with staff from the Macroeconomics, Trade, and Investment Global Practice and from regional and country offices, and with input from regional Chief Economist offices. They are the result of an iterative process that incorporates data, macroeconometric models, and judgment.

Data. Data used to prepare country forecasts come from a variety of sources. National Income Accounts (NIA), Balance of Payments (BOP), and fiscal data are from Haver Analytics; the World Development Indicators by the World Bank; the World Economic Outlook, Balance of Payments Statistics, and International Financial Statistics by the International Monetary Fund. Population data and forecasts are from the United Nations World Population Prospects. Country- and lending-group classifications are from the World Bank. DECPG databases include commodity prices, data on previous forecast vintages, and in-house country classifications. Other internal databases include high-frequency indicators such as industrial production, consumer price indexes, house prices, exchange rates, exports, imports, and stock market indexes, based on data from Bloomberg, Haver Analytics, OECD Analytical House Prices Indicators, IMF Balance of Pay-

ments Statistics, and IMF International Financial Statistics.

Aggregations. Aggregate growth for the world and all sub-groups of countries (such as regions and income groups) is calculated as GDP-weighted average (at 2010 prices) of country-specific growth rates. Income groups are defined as in the World Bank's classification of country groups.

Forecast Process. The process starts with initial assumptions about advanced-economy growth and commodity price forecasts. These are used as conditioning assumptions for the first set of growth forecasts for EMDEs, which are produced using macroeconometric models, accounting frameworks to ensure national account identities and global consistency, estimates of spillovers from major economies, and high-frequency indicators. These forecasts are then evaluated to ensure consistency of treatment across similar EMDEs. This is followed by extensive discussions with World Bank country teams, who conduct continuous macroeconomic monitoring and dialogue with country authorities and finalize growth forecasts for EMDEs. The Prospects Group prepares advanced-economy and commodity price forecasts. Throughout the forecasting process, staff use macro-econometric models that allow the combination of judgement and consistency with model-based insights.

Global Economic Prospects: Selected Topics, 2015-20

Global Economic Prospects: Selected Topics, 2015-20

Global Economic Prospects: Selected Topics, 2015-20

Prospects Group:
Selected Other Publications on the Global Economy, 2015-20

Commodity Markets Outlook	
Food price shocks: Channels and implications	April 2019, Special Focus
The implications of tariffs for commodity markets	October 2018, Box
The changing of the guard: Shifts in industrial commodity demand	October 2018, Special Focus
Oil exporters: Policies and challenges	April 2018, Special Focus
Investment weakness in commodity exporters	January 2017, Special Focus
OPEC in historical context: Commodity agreements and market fundamentals	October 2016, Special Focus
Energy and food prices: Moving in tandem?	July 2016, Special Focus
Resource development in an era of cheap commodities	April 2016, Special Focus
Weak growth in emerging market economies: What does it imply for commodity markets?	January 2016, Special Focus
Understanding El Niño: What does it mean for commodity markets?	October 2015, Special Focus
How important are China and India in global commodity consumption?	July 2015, Special Focus
Anatomy of the last four oil price crashes	April 2015, Special Focus
Putting the recent plunge in oil prices in perspective	January 2015, Special Focus

Inflation in Emerging and Developing Economies	
Inflation: Concepts, evolution, and correlates	Chapter 1
Understanding global inflation synchronization	Chapter 2
Sources of inflation: Global and domestic drivers	Chapter 3
Inflation expectations: Review and evidence	Chapter 4
Inflation and exchange rate pass-through	Chapter 5
Inflation in low-income countries	Chapter 6
Poverty impact of food price shocks and policies	Chapter 7

A Decade After the Global Recession: Lessons and Challenges for Emerging and Developing Economies	
A Decade After the Global Recession: Lessons and Challenges	Chapter 1
What Happens During Global Recessions?	Chapter 2
Macroeconomic Developments	Chapter 3
Financial Market Developments	Chapter 4
Macroeconomic and Financial Sector Policies	Chapter 5
Prospects, Risks, and Vulnerabilities	Chapter 6
Policy Challenges	Chapter 7
The Role of the World Bank Group	Chapter 8

Global Waves of Debt: Causes and Consequences	
Debt: Evolution, Causes, and Consequences	Chapter 1
Benefits and Costs of Debt: The Dose Makes the Poison	Chapter 2
Global Waves of Debt: What Goes up Must Come Down?	Chapter 3
The Fourth Wave: Ripple or Tsunami?	Chapter 4
Debt and Financial Crises: From Euphoria to Distress	Chapter 5
Policies: Turning Mistakes into Experience	Chapter 6

High-Frequency Monitoring	
Global Monthly newsletter	

ECO-AUDIT

Environmental Benefits Statement

The World Bank Group is committed to reducing its environmental footprint. In support of this commitment, we leverage electronic publishing options and print-on-demand technology, which is located in regional hubs worldwide. Together, these initiatives enable print runs to be lowered and shipping distances decreased, resulting in reduced paper consumption, chemical use, greenhouse gas emissions, and waste.

We follow the recommended standards for paper use set by the Green Press Initiative. The majority of our books are printed on Forest Stewardship Council (FSC)-certified paper, with nearly all containing 50-100 percent recycled content. The recycled fiber in our book paper is either unbleached or bleached using totally chlorine-free (TCF), processed chlorine-free (PCF), or enhanced elemental chlorine-free (EECF) processes.

More information about the Bank's environmental philosophy can be found at http://www.worldbank.org/corporateresponsibility.